JIST's *Best Jobs* Series

200 Best Jobs

for College

Graduates

Second Edition

Developed by Michael Farr and LaVerne L. Ludden, Ed.D.

With database work by Laurence Shatkin, Ph.D.

Also in JIST's *Best Jobs* Series

▲ **Award-winning *Best Jobs for the 21ˢᵗ Century***

▲ ***300 Best Jobs Without a Four-Year Degree***

jist
Works

200 Best Jobs for College Graduates, Second Edition

Previous edition was titled *Best Jobs for the 21ˢᵗ Century for College Graduates*

© 2003 by JIST Publishing, Inc.

Published by JIST Works, an imprint of JIST Publishing, Inc.
8902 Otis Avenue
Indianapolis, IN 46216-1033

Phone: 1-800-648-JIST   Fax: 1-800-JIST-FAX   E-mail: info@jist.com

Visit our Web site at www.jist.com for information on JIST, free job search information, book excerpts, and ordering information on our many products. For free information on 14,000 job titles, visit www.careeroink.com.

Some Other Books by the Authors

Michael Farr and LaVerne L. Ludden

Best Jobs for the 21st Century
300 Best Jobs Without a Four-Year Degree
Enhanced Occupational Outlook Handbook
Guide for Occupational Exploration

Michael Farr

The Quick Resume & Cover Letter Book
America's Top Resumes for America's Top Jobs
Getting the Job You Really Want
The Very Quick Job Search

Quantity discounts are available for JIST books. Please call our sales department at 1-800-648-JIST for a free catalog and more information.

Editors: Stephanie Koutek, Susan Pines
Cover and Interior Designer: Aleata Howard
Page Layout Coordinator: Carolyn J. Newland
Proofreader: Jeanne Clark

Printed in Canada
06 05 04 03 02   9 8 7 6 5 4 3 2 1

Library of Congress Cataloging-in-Publication Data is on file with the Library of Congress.

ISBN 1-56370-855-8

This Is a Big Book, But It Is Very Easy to Use

This book is designed to help you explore career options in a variety of interesting ways. The nice thing about it is that you don't have to read it all. Instead, we designed it to allow you to browse and find information that most interests you.

The Table of Contents will give you a good idea of what's inside and how to use the book, so we suggest you start there. Part I of the book is made up of interesting lists that will help you explore jobs based on pay, interests, education level, personality type, and many other criteria. Part II provides descriptions for all major jobs that require a two-year associate's degree, a bachelor's degree, or higher. Just find a job that interests you in one of the lists in Part I and look up its description in Part II. Simple.

How We Selected the 200 Best Jobs for College Graduates

Deciding on the "best" job is a choice that only you can make, but objective criteria can help you identify jobs that are, for example, better paying than other jobs with similar duties. We have sorted through the data for *all* major jobs and selected only those jobs that meet the following criteria:

1. **They require a college degree.** The U.S. Department of Labor assigns a minimum level of training or education for entry into each job they track. This book includes all jobs that require at least a two-year associate's degree. We included jobs requiring an associate's degree; bachelor's degree; work experience, plus degree; master's degree; doctoral degree; or first professional degree. There were 294 jobs that met this criteria.

2. **They have the highest combined scores for high pay, fast growth, and large number of openings.** Of the 294 jobs that require a college degree or above, more than 30 were for specialized postsecondary teaching jobs. We collapsed these jobs into one title, Postsecondary Teachers. (A list of these specialized job titles is provided in Part I's Introduction.) For the 258 job titles that remained, we collected data from a variety of government sources and created three lists that organized the jobs from highest to lowest on three measures: annual earnings, percentage growth rate, and number of job openings per year.

(continued)

(continued)

We then sorted the 258 jobs from highest to lowest for each of the three measures and assigned a number to their relative position on each list. The job position numbers on the three lists were then combined, and jobs with the highest total scores were put on top, followed by jobs with lower total scores, on down the list. The first list in Part I is called "The 200 Best Jobs for College Graduates," and the 200 jobs with the highest scores are presented in this list in bold type, followed by the remaining 58 jobs in order of their combined score on all three measures. You can find descriptions for all 258 of these jobs in Part II, along with descriptions or the various specialized postsecondary teaching jobs, for a total of 294 descriptions in all.

We are not suggesting that the 200 jobs with the highest overall scores for earnings, growth, and number of openings are all good ones for you to consider—some will not be. But the 200 jobs that met our criteria present such a wide range of jobs that you are likely to find one or more that will interest you. The jobs that met our "best jobs" criteria are also more likely than average to have higher pay, faster projected growth, and a larger number of openings than other jobs at similar levels of education and training.

Some Things You Can Do with This Book

▲ Identify more-interesting or better-paying jobs that don't require additional training or education.

▲ Develop long-term plans that may require additional training, education, or experience.

▲ Explore and select a college major or a training or educational program that relates to a career objective.

▲ Find reliable earnings information to negotiate pay.

▲ Prepare for interviews.

These are a few of the many ways you can use this book. We hope you find it as interesting to browse as we did to put together. We have tried to make it easy to use and as interesting as occupational information can be.

When you are done with this book, pass it along or tell someone else about it. We wish you well in your career and in your life.

Credits and Acknowledgments: While the authors created this book, it is based on the work of many others. The occupational information is based on data obtained from the U.S. Department of Labor and the U.S. Census Bureau. These sources provide the most authoritative occupational information available. The job titles and their related descriptions are from the O*NET database, which was developed by researchers and developers under the direction of the U.S. Department of Labor. They, in turn, were assisted by thousands of employers who provided details on the nature of work in the many thousands of job samplings used in the database's development. We used the most recent version of the O*NET database, release 4.0, that was first available in 2002. We appreciate and thank the staff of the U.S. Department of Labor for their efforts and expertise in providing such a rich source of data.

Table of Contents

Summary of Major Sections

Introduction. A short overview to help you better understand and use the book. *Starts on Page 1.*

Part I—The Best Jobs Lists: Jobs That Require a Two- or Four-Year College Degree or More. Very useful for exploring career options! Lists are arranged into easy-to-use groups. The first group of lists presents the best overall jobs that require a college degree—jobs with the highest earnings, projected growth, and number of openings. More specialized lists follow, presenting the best jobs for graduates age 20–29, graduates 55 and older, part-time graduates, self-employed graduates, women graduates, and men graduates. Other lists present the best jobs at various levels of education, by interest, and by personality type. The column starting at right presents all the list titles within the groups. *Starts on Page 13.*

Part II—The Job Descriptions. Provides complete descriptions of all major jobs that require a college degree. *Starts on Page 135.*

Part II—The Job Descriptions........... 135

Descriptions for all the jobs in this book are included in this part. They are presented in alphabetical order here, along with the page numbers where you can find them, and they also appear in alphabetical order in this part. We suggest that you use the lists in Part I to identify job titles that interest you and then locate their descriptions in Part II.

⊞ Table of Contents

Introduction

We kept this introduction short to encourage you to scan it. For this reason, we won't provide many details on the technical issues involved in creating the job lists or descriptions. Instead, we give you short explanations to help you understand and use the information the book provides for career exploration or planning.

Why We Created This Book

This book is for the many people who have or are considering getting a two- or four-year college degree or more and want to change or move ahead in their careers. It covers all the jobs in the U.S. Department of Labor's O*NET (Occupational Information Network) database that require a two-year associate's degree, a four-year bachelor's degree, or higher.

We decided to create this book after the success of another book we did called *Best Jobs for the 21st Century.* That book covered all major jobs at all levels of education and training that met our criteria for earnings, projected growth rate, and number of job openings. It had information on about 500 jobs. But covering that many jobs required a whopping 702 pages, and the book included many jobs that would not be of interest to people having or considering a college education.

So this book, *200 Best Jobs for College Graduates,* covers only those jobs that require a college degree. Our database has about 300 jobs that require a two- or four-year college degree or higher, so this approach allowed us to create a book that is less expensive, includes more-targeted lists, and has more useful information in the descriptions.

1

Where the Information Comes From

The information we used in creating this book comes from three major government sources:

▲ **The U.S. Department of Labor:** We used a variety of data sources to construct the information we used in this book. Most comes from various databases of information provided by the U.S. Department of Labor. We started with the jobs included in the O*NET database. The O*NET includes information on about 1,000 occupations and is now the primary source of detailed information on occupations. The Labor Department updates the O*NET on a regular basis, and we used the most recent one available—version 4.

▲ **The U.S. Census Bureau:** Because we wanted to include earnings, growth, number of openings, and other data not included in the O*NET, we used information on earnings from the U.S. Bureau of Labor Statistics (BLS). Some of this data came from the Current Population Survey, conducted by the U.S. Census Bureau, and other data came from the BLS's own Occupational Employment Statistics survey. The information on earnings is the most reliable information we could obtain. The BLS uses a slightly different system of job titles than the O*NET does, but we were able to link the BLS data to most of the O*NET job titles we used to develop this book. The Current Population Survey also provided information about the proportion of workers in each job who are self employed or work part time.

▲ **The U.S. Department of Education:** We used the Classification of Instructional Programs, a system developed by the U.S. Department of Education, to cross-reference the education or training programs related to each job.

The Data Complexities

For those of you who like details, we present some of the complexities inherent in our sources of information and what we did to make sense of them here. You don't need to know this to use the book, so jump to the next section of the Introduction if you are bored with details.

Earnings, Growth, and Number of Openings

We include information on earnings, projected growth, and number of job openings for each job throughout this book.

Earnings

The employment security agency of each state gathers information on earnings for various jobs and forwards this to the U.S. Bureau of Labor Statistics. This information is organized in standardized ways by a BLS program called the Occupational Employment Statistics, or OES. To keep the earnings for the various jobs and regions comparable, the OES screens out certain types of earnings and includes others, so the OES earnings we use in this book represent straight-time, gross pay exclusive of premium pay. More specifically, the OES earnings include the job's base rate; cost-of-living allowances; guaranteed pay; hazardous-duty pay; incentive pay, including commissions and production bonuses; on-call pay; and tips—but do not include back pay, jury duty pay, overtime pay, severance pay, shift differentials, non-production bonuses, or tuition reimbursements. Also, self-employed workers are not included in the estimates, and they can be a significant segment in certain occupations.

The OES earnings data uses a system of job titles called the Standard Occupational Classification system, or SOC. Most of these jobs can be cross-referenced to the O*NET job titles we use in this book, so we can attach earnings information to most job titles and descriptions. But some of the O*NET jobs simply do not have earnings data available for them from the sources we used, so some jobs in the book have no earnings data presented for them.

Projected Growth and Number of Job Openings

This information comes from the Office of Occupational Statistics and Employment Projections, a program within the Bureau of Labor Statistics that develops information about projected trends in the nation's labor market for the next ten years. The most recent projections available cover the years from 2000 to 2010. The projections are based on information about people moving into and out of occupations. The BLS uses data from various sources in projecting the growth and number of openings for each job title—some data comes from the Census Bureau's Current Population Survey, and some comes from an OES survey. The projections assume that there will be no major war, depression, or other economic upheaval. Like the earnings figures, the figures on projected growth and job openings are reported according to the SOC classification, so again you will find that a few jobs in this book do not include this information.

Information in the Job Descriptions

▲ **Job title:** We use the job titles as presented in the O*NET database as maintained by the U.S. Department of Labor.

▲ **Earnings, Percent Growth, Annual Job Openings, Percent Self-Employed, Percent Part-Time:** The source of the earnings, growth, and number of openings information is the same as described in this section and as used in the lists in Part I. The data on percentage of self-employed and part-time workers comes from the U.S. Census Bureau's Current Population Survey. The SOC and O*NET classification schemes did not exist at that time, so some of the job-to-job matches are not exact, and for several jobs no figures are available.

▲ **Job description text:** This information comes from the O*NET database.

▲ **Skills:** This information is also from the O*NET database. Data is provided on many skills for each job, and we used a formula to list only those skills with the highest ratings for each job.

▲ **GOE Information:** We used the newest interest areas and work groups as presented in the *Guide for Occupational Exploration,* Third Edition (JIST Publishing, 2001). The GOE groupings allow you to explore all major jobs in the O*NET database based on your interests. The process we used to cross-reference the O*NET jobs to the GOE interest groupings is explained in the *GOE* book itself, should you want to know more about how this was done. Looking at jobs based on your interests is a very useful approach because it introduces you to a variety of related jobs you may not consider otherwise.

▲ **Personality Type:** We used a field in the O*NET database that assigns each job to its most closely related personality type.

▲ **Education/Training Programs:** We linked the O*NET job titles we use in this book to related educational and training programs listed in another database called the Classification of Instructional Programs, or CIP. To do this, we used a "cross-walk" (a type of cross-reference system) created by the National Crosswalk Service Center, part of the Iowa Department of Education. Because this crosswalk was based on SOC rather than O*NET job titles, we made various changes to connect the O*NET job titles to the education or training programs related to them. We also modified the names of some education and training programs so they would be more easily understood.

▲ **Related Knowledge/Courses:** The information we used for this section of each job description comes from the O*NET database. We extracted information we thought would be most helpful to understand the areas of knowledge required for success in each job. In many cases, these knowledge areas will help you identify specific courses or learning programs to take to best prepare for entry into the jobs that interest you.

Getting all the data to connect in a useful way was not a simple process, and it is not always perfect. Even so, we used the best and most recent sources of data we could find and think that our efforts will be helpful to many people.

How the 200 Best Jobs for College Graduates Were Selected

The "This Is a Big Book..." statement at the beginning of this book gives a brief description of how we selected the jobs we include in this book. Here are a few more details:

1. We began by creating our own database of information from the O*NET, Census Bureau, and other sources to include the information we wanted. This database covered about 1,000 job titles at all levels of education and training.

2. We cut our initial list to include only those jobs requiring a two-year associate's degree or a four-year bachelor's degree or higher. A total of 294 jobs met this criteria at education/experience levels of two-year associate's degree; four-year bachelor's degree; work experience, plus degree; master's degree; doctoral degree; or first professional degree. Among these 294 jobs are 36 specialized postsecondary education jobs that we combined into one job titled Postsecondary Teachers. We use this one job title throughout the lists but provide descriptions for all 36 of these specialized postsecondary jobs in Part II. This means that we used 258 job titles to construct the lists but have a total of 294 job descriptions in Part II.

3. We created three lists that ranked all 258 of these jobs based on three major criteria: median annual earnings, projected growth through 2010, and number of job openings projected per year. Each of these lists was then sorted from highest to lowest and assigned a number score of from 258 (highest pay, for example) to 1 (lowest pay, for example).

4. We then created a new list that added the number scores for all three lists and presented all 258 jobs in order from highest to lowest total score. For example, the job of Accountants has the highest total combined score for earnings, growth, and number of job openings, so Accountants is listed first in our 200 Best Jobs for College Graduates list, even though this job is not the highest-paying job (which is Internists, General), the fastest-growing job (which is Computer Software Engineers, Applications), or the job with the most openings (which is General and Operations Managers).

Why This Book Has More Than 200 Jobs

We didn't think you would mind that this book actually provides information on more than 200 jobs. The reason for this is that we wanted to emphasize jobs with the best combined total scores for pay, growth, and number of openings, but doing this would have left out jobs that we think will interest many people. So we compromised: We gave the book a more memorable title that can stay the same over time *(200 Best Jobs for College Graduates)* and included descriptions of all the 294 jobs that require a college education.

Our first list in Section I does present the 200 jobs with the highest total scores for earnings, growth, and number of openings in bold type. We figured that no one would complain about getting even more than they thought they were getting, based on the book's title. So there it is, truth in advertising. And for those who only want information on the 200 jobs with the highest total scores, we suggest that you simply go through the book and use a marker to cross out the jobs that are lower on the list. Just kidding on that last part.

The Data in This Book Can Be Misleading

We use the most reliable data we can obtain for the earnings, projected growth, number of openings, and other information to create this book, but keep in mind that this information may or may not be accurate for your situation.

As you look at the data, it is important to remember that they are averages that may or may not relate to your situation. They give you a general idea about the number of workers employed, annual earnings, rate of job growth, and annual job openings. Understand, however, that this information is true on the average. But just as there is no precisely average person, there is no such thing as a statistically average example of a particular job. We say this because data, while helpful, can also be misleading.

Take, for example, the yearly earnings information in this book. This is highly reliable data obtained from a very large U.S. working population sample by the Bureau of Labor Statistics. It tells us the median annual pay received by people in various job titles. This sounds great, except that half of all people in that occupation earned less than that amount, and half earn more. (We often use "average" instead of "median" elsewhere in this book for ease of explanation).

For example, people just entering the occupation or with a few years of work experience will often earn much less than the average. People who live in rural areas or who work for smaller employers typically earn less than those who do similar work in cities, where the cost of living is higher, or for larger employers.

So, in reviewing the information in this book, please understand the limitations of the data it presents. You need to use common sense in career decision-making as in most other things in life. Even so, we hope that you find the information helpful and interesting.

Part I—The Best Jobs Lists: Jobs That Require a Two- or Four-Year College Degree or More

There are 60 separate lists in Part I of this book—look in the Table of Contents for a complete list of them. The lists are not difficult to understand because they have clear titles and are organized into groupings of related lists.

Depending on your situation, some of the jobs lists in Part I will interest you more than others. For example, if you are young, you may be interested to learn the highest-paying jobs that employ high percentages of college graduates age 20–29. Other lists show jobs within interest groupings, personality types, levels of education, or other ways that you might find helpful in exploring your career options.

Whatever your situation, we suggest you use the lists that make sense for you to help explore career options. Following are the names of each group of lists along with short comments on each group. You will find additional information in a brief introduction provided at the beginning of each group of lists in Part I.

Here is an overview of each major group of lists you will find in Part I.

Best Jobs Overall: Lists of Jobs for College Graduates with the Highest Pay, Fastest Growth, and Most Openings

Four lists are in this group, and they are the ones that most people want to see first. The first list presents all 258 job titles in order of their combined scores for earnings, growth, and number of job openings. The 200 of these jobs with the highest total scores are presented in bold type. Three more lists in this group present the 100 jobs with the highest earnings, the 100 jobs projected to grow most rapidly, and the 100 jobs with the most openings.

Best Jobs Lists with High Percentages of Workers Age 20–29, Workers Age 55 and Over, Part-Time Workers, Self-Employed Workers, Women, and Men

This group of lists presents interesting information for a variety of types of people based on data from the U.S. Census Bureau. The lists are arranged into groups for workers age 20–29, workers 55 and older, part-time workers, self-employed workers, women, and men. We created five lists for each group, basing the last four on the information in the first list:

▲ The 100 jobs having the highest percentage of people of each type

▲ The 25 jobs with the highest combined scores for earnings, growth, and number of openings

▲ The 25 jobs with the highest earnings

▲ The 25 jobs with the highest growth rates

▲ The 25 jobs with the largest number of openings

Best Jobs Lists Based on Levels of Education and Experience

We created separate lists for each level of college education and training as defined by the U.S. Department of Labor. We put each of the 258 job titles into one of the lists based on the education and training required for entry. Jobs within these lists are presented in order of their total combined scores for earnings, growth, and number of openings. The lists include jobs in these groupings:

▲ Associate's degree

▲ Bachelor's degree

▲ Work experience, plus degree

▲ Master's degree

▲ Doctoral degree

▲ First professional degree

Best Jobs Lists for College Graduates Based on Interests

These lists organize the 258 jobs into groups based on interests. Within each list, jobs are presented in order of their total scores for earnings, growth, and number of openings. Here are the 14 interest areas used in these lists: Arts, Entertainment, and Media; Science, Math, and Engineering; Plants and Animals; Law, Law Enforcement, and Public Safety; Mechanics, Installers, and Repairers; Construction, Mining, and Drilling; Transportation; Industrial Production; Business Detail; Sales and Marketing; Recreation, Travel, and Other Personal Services; Education and Social Service; General Management and Support; and Medical and Health Services.

Best Jobs Lists for College Graduates Based on Personality Types

These lists organize the 258 jobs into one of six personality types described in the introduction to the lists, including Realistic, Investigative, Artistic, Social, Enterprising, and Conventional. The jobs within each list are presented in order of their total scores for earnings, growth, and number of openings.

Part II—The Job Descriptions

This part of the book provides a brief but information-packed description for each of the 294 jobs that met our criteria for this book. The descriptions are presented in alphabetical order, which makes it easy to look up a job you've identified in a list from Part I that you want to learn more about.

We used the most current information from a variety of government sources to create the descriptions. We designed the descriptions to be easy to understand, but the sample that follows, with an explanation of each of its component parts, may help you better understand and use the descriptions.

Here are details for each of the major parts of the job descriptions in Part II:

▲ **Job Title:** This is the job title for the job as defined by the U.S. Department of Labor and used in its O*NET database.

▲ **Data Elements:** The information on earnings, growth, annual openings, percent self-employed workers, and percent part-time workers comes from various government databases for this occupation, as we explain earlier in this Introduction.

▲ **Summary Description and Tasks:** The first sentence provides a summary description of the occupation. It is followed by a listing of tasks that are generally performed by people who work in the job. This information comes from the O*NET database.

▲ **Skills:** The O*NET database provides data on 46 skills, so we decided to list only those that were most important for each job rather than list pages of unhelpful details. For each job, we identified any skill with a rating that was higher than the average rating for this skill for all jobs. If there are more than five such skills, we include only those five with the highest ratings and present them from highest to lowest score. We include up to seven skills if scores were tied for fifth place. Finally, at least one skill is listed for each job, even if the rating for that skill is lower than the average for all jobs. Each listed skill is followed by a brief description of that skill.

Data Elements

Job Title

Copy Writers

▲ Education/Training Required: Bachelor's degree
▲ Annual Earnings: $42,270
▲ Growth: 28%
▲ Annual Job Openings: 18,000
▲ Self-Employed: 31.2%
▲ Part-Time: 18.5%

Summary Description and Tasks

Write advertising copy for use by publication or broadcast media to promote sale of goods and services. Writes advertising copy for use by publication or broadcast media and revises copy according to supervisor's instructions. Writes articles, bulletins, sales letters, speeches, and other related informative and promotional material. Prepares advertising copy, using computer. Consults with sales media and marketing representatives to obtain information on product or service and discuss style and length of advertising copy. Reviews advertising trends, consumer surveys, and other data regarding marketing of goods and services to formulate approach. Obtains additional background and current development information through research and interview. **SKILLS**—Writing: Communicating effectively in writing as appropriate for the needs of the audience. Reading Comprehension: Understanding written sentences and paragraphs in work-related documents. Active Learning: Understanding the implications of new information for both current and future problem-solving and decision-making. Critical Thinking: Using logic and reasoning to identify the strengths and weaknesses of alternative solutions, conclusions, or approaches to problems. Active Listening: Giving full attention to what other people are saying, taking time to understand the points being made, asking questions as appropriate, and not interrupting at inappropriate times.

Skills

GOE INFORMATION—**Interest Area:** 01. Arts, Entertainment, and Media. **Work Group:** 01.02. Writing and Editing. **Other Job Titles in This Work Group:** Creative Writers; Editors; Poets and Lyricists;

GOE Information

Technical Writers; Writers and Authors. **PERSONALITY TYPE**—Artistic. Artistic occupations frequently involve working with forms, designs, and patterns. They often require self-expression, and the work can be done without following a clear set of rules.

Personality Type

EDUCATION/TRAINING PROGRAM(S)—Broadcast Journalism; Business Communications; Communications, Other; English Creative Writing; Journalism; Mass Communications; Playwriting and Screenwriting; Technical and Business Writing. **RELATED KNOWLEDGE/COURSES**—**Sales and Marketing:** Knowledge of principles and methods for showing, promoting, and selling products or services. This includes marketing strategy and tactics, product demonstration, sales techniques, and sales control systems. **English Language:** Knowledge of the structure and content of the English language, including the meaning and spelling of words, rules of composition, and grammar. **Computers and Electronics:** Knowledge of circuit boards, processors, chips, electronic equipment, and computer hardware and software, including applications and programming. **Communications and Media:** Knowledge of media production, communication, and dissemination techniques and methods. This includes alternative ways to inform and entertain via written, oral, and visual media. **Clerical Studies:** Knowledge of administrative and clerical procedures and systems such as word processing, managing files and records, stenography and transcription, designing forms, and other office procedures and terminology.

Education/ Training Programs

Related Knowledge/ Courses

▲ **GOE Information:** This information cross-references the *Guide for Occupational Information* (or the *GOE*), a system developed by the U.S. Department of Labor that organizes jobs based on interests. The GOE system is used in a variety of career information systems, and we use the groups from the new third edition of the *GOE,* as published by JIST. The description includes the major Interest Area the job fits into, its more-specific Work Group, and a list of related O*NET job titles that are in this same GOE Work Group. This information will help you identify other job titles that have similar interests or require similar skills. You can find more information on the GOE and its Interest Areas in the introduction to the lists of jobs based on interests in Part I.

▲ **Personality Type:** This part gives the name of the personality type that most closely matches each job, as well as a brief definition of this personality type. You can find more information on the personality types in the introduction to the lists of jobs based on personality types in Part I.

▲ **Education/Training Programs:** This entry provides the name of the educational or training program or programs listed for the job in a related government data source called the Classification of Instruction Programs (CIP). This information will help you identify sources of formal or informal training for a job that interests you.

▲ **Related Knowledge/Courses:** This entry will help you understand the most important knowledge areas that are required for the job and the types of courses or programs you will likely need to take to prepare for it. We used information in the Department of Labor's O*NET database for this entry. We went through a process similar to the one described for the skills noted above to end up with entries that are most important for each job.

Sources of Additional Information

Hundreds of sources of career information exist, so here are a few we consider most helpful in getting additional information on the jobs listed in this book.

Print References

▲ *O*NET Dictionary of Occupational Titles:* Revised on a regular basis, this book provides good descriptions for all jobs listed in the U.S. Department of Labor's O*NET database. There are about 1,000 job descriptions at all levels of education and training, plus lists of related job titles in other major career information sources, educational programs, and other information. Published by JIST.

(continued)

(continued)

▲ *Guide for Occupational Exploration,* Third Edition: The new edition of the *GOE* is cross-referenced in the descriptions in Part II. The *GOE* provides helpful information to consider on each of the interest areas and work groups, descriptions of all O*NET jobs within each GOE group, and many other features useful for exploring career options. Published by JIST in 2001.

▲ *Enhanced Occupational Outlook Handbook:* Updated regularly, this book provides thorough descriptions for 260 major jobs in the *Occupational Outlook Handbook,* brief descriptions for the O*NET jobs that are related to each, brief descriptions of thousands of more specialized jobs from the *Dictionary of Occupational Titles,* and other information. Published by JIST.

Internet Resources

▲ **The U.S. Department of Labor Web site:** The Department of Labor Web site (http://www.bls.gov) provides a lot of career information, including links to other pages that provide information on the jobs covered in this book. Their Web site is a bit formal and, well, confusing, but it will take you to the major sources of government career information if you explore its options.

▲ **O*NET site:** Go to http://www.onetcenter.org for a variety of information on the O*NET database, including links to sites that provide detailed information on the O*NET job titles presented in Part II of this book.

▲ **CareerOINK.com:** This site (at http://www.careeroink.com) is operated by JIST and includes free information on thousands of jobs, easy-to-use crosswalks between major career information systems, links from military to civilian jobs, sample resumes, and many other features. A link at http://www.jist.com will also take you to the CareerOINK Web site.

Thanks

Thanks for reading this introduction. You are surely a more thorough person than those who jumped into the book without reading it, and you will probably get more out of the book as a result.

We wish you a satisfying career and, more importantly, a good life.

Part I

The Best Jobs Lists: Jobs That Require a Two- or Four-Year College Degree or More

Tips on Using These Lists

We've tried to make the Best Jobs lists in this section both fun to use and informative. You can use the Table of Contents at the front of the book to find a complete listing of all the list titles in this section. You can then review the lists that most interest you or simply browse the lists in this section. Most, such as the list of jobs with the highest pay, are easy to understand and require little explanation. We provide comments on each group of related lists to inform you of the selection criteria or other details we think you may want to know.

As you review the lists, mark job titles that appeal to you (or, if someone else will be using this book, write them on a separate sheet of paper) so that you can look up their descriptions later in Part II.

Understand the Limitations of the Information

Most of the lists emphasize jobs with high pay, high growth, or large numbers of openings. Many people consider these factors important in selecting a desirable job, and they are also easily quantifiable. While these measures are important, we think you

(continued)

(continued)

should also think about other factors in considering your career options. For example, location, liking the people you work with, having an opportunity to serve others, and enjoying your work are just a few of the many factors that may define the ideal job for you. These measures are difficult or impossible to objectively quantify based on the data we have available and are not, therefore, presented in this book. For this reason, we suggest that you consider the importance of these issues yourself and that you thoroughly research any job before making a firm decision.

For example, of the 258 jobs that require a college degree in our Best Jobs Overall list, the job with the lowest combined score for earnings, growth, and number of openings is Recreational Therapist. It has annual earnings of $28,650, a 9 percent growth rate, and 1,000 job openings per year. Is this a bad job, one you should avoid? No, of course not. It all depends on what you like or want to do. Another example is the job that had the very best overall score for earnings, growth, and number of openings, Computer and Information Systems Manager. Is this job a great job to consider? Many people (the authors included) would not want to work in this job or may not have the skills or interest needed to do it well. It would be a great job for someone who was good at it and who would enjoy doing it, but it would simply not be right for someone else. On the other hand, the perfect job for some people would be Recreational Therapist because they enjoy it and are good at it.

So, as you look at the lists that follow, keep in mind that earnings, growth, and number of openings are just some things to consider. Also consider that half of all people in a given job earn more than the earnings you will see in this book—and half earn less. If a job really appeals to you, you should consider it even if it is not among the highest paying. And you should also consider jobs not among the fastest growing and jobs with few openings for similar reasons, because openings are always available, even for jobs with slow or negative growth projections or with small numbers of openings.

Some Details on the Lists

The sources of the information we used in constructing these lists are presented in this book's Introduction. Here are some additional details on how we created the lists.

▲ **We collapsed a number of specialized postsecondary education jobs into one title.** The government database we used for the job titles and descriptions included more than 30 job titles for postsecondary educators, yet the data source we used for growth and number of openings provided data only for the more general job of Postsecondary Teacher. To make our lists more useful, we included only one listing, Postsecondary Teacher, rather than separate listings for each specialized job. We did, however, include descriptions for all the specific postsecondary teaching jobs in Part II. Should you wonder, here are the more specialized titles: Agricultural Sciences Teachers, Postsecondary; Anthropology and Archeology Teachers, Postsecondary; Architecture Teachers, Postsecondary; Area, Ethnic, and Cultural Studies Teachers, Postsecondary; Art, Drama, and Music Teachers, Postsecondary; Atmospheric, Earth, Marine, and Space Sciences Teachers, Postsecondary; Biological Science Teachers, Postsecondary; Business Teachers, Postsecondary; Chemistry Teachers, Postsecondary; Communications Teachers, Postsecondary; Computer Science Teachers, Postsecondary; Criminal Justice and Law Enforcement Teachers, Postsecondary; Economics Teachers, Postsecondary; Education Administrators, Postsecondary; Education Teachers, Postsecondary; Engineering Teachers, Postsecondary; English Language and Literature Teachers, Post-secondary; Environmental Science Teachers, Postsecondary; Foreign Language and Literature Teachers, Postsecondary; Forestry and Conservation Science Teachers, Postsecondary; Geography Teachers, Postsecondary; Graduate Teaching Assistants; Health Specialties Teachers, Postsecondary; History Teachers, Postsecondary; Home Economics Teachers, Postsecondary; Law Teachers, Postsecondary; Library Science Teachers, Postsecondary; Mathematical Science Teachers, Postsecondary; Nursing Instructors and Teachers, Postsecondary; Philosophy and Religion Teachers, Postsecondary; Physics Teachers, Post-secondary; Political Science Teachers, Postsecondary; Psychology Teachers, Postsecondary; Recreation and Fitness Studies Teachers, Postsecondary; Social Work Teachers, Postsecondary; Sociology Teachers, Postsecondary.

▲ **We excluded some jobs from some lists due to a lack of available data.** There were 13 jobs that did not have data available for us to use in the Best Jobs with High Percentages of Workers Age 20–29, Workers Age 55 and Over, Part-Time Workers, Self-Employed Workers, Women, and Men section. The reason was that the government information source we used did not collect this data for these jobs. As a result, we had to exclude these jobs from those lists, even though many would likely be included in those lists if we could get accurate data for them. The excluded jobs are Cartographers and Photogrammetrists; Computer Support Specialists; Health and Safety Engineers, Except Mining Safety Engineers and Inspectors; Marine Architects; Marine Engineers and Naval Architects; Marriage and Family Therapists; Medical Transcriptionists; Mental Health Counselors; Network Systems and Data Communications Analysts; Nuclear Technicians; Rehabilitation Counselors; Securities, Commodities, and Financial Services Sales Agents; and Survey Researchers.

(continued)

(continued)

▲ **Many jobs have tied scores.** Many jobs have the same scores for one or more data elements. For example, in the category of jobs with the highest percentage of workers age 20 to 29, there are 23 jobs in which 20.4 percent of the workers are between the ages of 20 and 29. Yet, because these jobs were at the lower end of the list, only eight of them could be listed among the 100 with the highest percentage of workers age 20 to 29. In other cases, jobs with the same numbers are listed one after another, making it appear that those listed first have a higher rating when that is not the case. There was no way to avoid these issues, so simply understand that the difference of several positions on a list may not mean as much as it seems.

▲ **Some jobs have similar titles.** We merged two databases of information, and some titles are similar. For example, the job title "Accountants and Auditors" cross-references to two separate job titles in another database, "Accountants" and "Auditors." These entries are not errors; they just reflect the imperfect cross-referencing we had to use to attach data from one source to the job description data in another.

Best Jobs Overall: Lists of Jobs for College Graduates with the Highest Pay, Fastest Growth, and Most Openings

We consider the four lists that follow to be our premier lists. They are the lists that are most often mentioned in the media and the ones that most readers want to see. To create these lists, we first identified 258 major jobs that typically require a two- or four-year college degree or more for entry. The first list presents these jobs according to their combined rankings for pay, growth, and number of openings. This is a very popular list because it represents jobs from the labor market according to quantifiable measures. Three additional lists present jobs with the highest measures in each of three measures: annual earnings, projected percentage growth through 2010, and number of annual openings. As you review these lists, keep in mind that the lists include jobs with the highest measures from a database that included all major jobs in our economy. Descriptions for all the jobs in these lists are included in Part II.

The 200 Best Jobs Overall for College Graduates—Jobs with the Best Combination of Pay, Growth, and Openings

This list arranges all 258 jobs that require a two- or four-year college degree or more in order of their overall scores for pay, growth, and number of openings. To obtain this list, we sorted the 258 jobs into three lists based on pay, growth, and number of openings. We sorted each of these lists from highest to lowest and then assigned a number to each entry. For example, the job with the highest pay was given a score of 1, the one with the next highest pay was given a score of 2, and so on. This scoring process was continued for each job on each of the three lists, and we combined the three scores for each job to create a new list ranked by the total score for all three measures.

This list presents all 258 jobs in order of their total scores. The job with the best overall score was Computer and Information Systems Managers. Other jobs follow in order of their total scores for pay, growth, and openings.

We included the data on all 258 major jobs requiring a college degree; the 200 jobs with the best overall total scores are presented in bold type. These 200 jobs are the ones that are referred to in the title of this book as being among the best based on earnings, growth, and number of openings criteria. You can find descriptions for all 258 of these jobs in Part II of this book.

The 200 Best Jobs for College Graduates

Job	Annual Earnings	Percent Growth	Annual Openings
1. Computer and Information Systems Managers	$78,830	48%	28,000
2. Computer Software Engineers, Applications	$67,670	100%	28,000
3. Computer Software Engineers, Systems Software	$69,530	90%	23,000
4. Computer Systems Analysts	$59,330	60%	34,000
5. Sales Managers	$68,520	33%	21,000
6. Medical and Health Services Managers	$56,370	32%	27,000
7. Management Analysts	$55,040	29%	50,000
8. Pharmacists	$70,950	24%	20,000
9. Lawyers	$88,280	18%	35,000
10. Marketing Managers	$71,240	29%	12,000
11. Internists, General	$142,400	18%	27,000
12. Pediatricians, General	$125,970	18%	27,000
13. Psychiatrists	$118,640	18%	27,000
14. Family and General Practitioners	$114,170	18%	27,000
15. Computer Security Specialists	$51,280	82%	18,000
16. Financial Managers	$67,020	18%	53,000
17. Financial Managers, Branch or Department	$67,020	18%	53,000
18. Network and Computer Systems Administrators	$51,280	82%	18,000
19. Treasurers, Controllers, and Chief Financial Officers	$67,020	18%	53,000
20. Chief Executives	$113,810	17%	48,000
21. Government Service Executives	$113,810	17%	48,000
22. Private Sector Executives	$113,810	17%	48,000
23. Sales Agents, Financial Services	$56,080	22%	55,000
24. Sales Agents, Securities and Commodities	$56,080	22%	55,000
25. Securities, Commodities, and Financial Services Sales Agents	$56,080	22%	55,000
26. Personal Financial Advisors	$55,320	34%	13,000
27. Physician Assistants	$61,910	54%	5,000
28. Registered Nurses	$44,840	26%	140,000
29. Network Systems and Data Communications Analysts	$54,510	78%	9,000
30. Postsecondary Teachers	$46,330	24%	184,000
31. Financial Analysts	$52,420	26%	20,000

The 200 Best Jobs for College Graduates

Job	Annual Earnings	Percent Growth	Annual Openings
32. General and Operations Managers	$61,160	15%	235,000
33. Database Administrators	$51,990	66%	8,000
34. Industrial-Organizational Psychologists	$66,880	18%	18,000
35. Computer Support Specialists	$36,460	97%	40,000
36. Public Relations Managers	$54,540	36%	7,000
37. Computer and Information Scientists, Research	$70,590	40%	2,000
38. Advertising and Promotions Managers	$53,360	34%	7,000
39. Physical Therapists	$54,810	33%	6,000
40. Education Administrators, Elementary and Secondary School	$66,930	13%	35,000
41. Computer Programmers	$57,590	16%	36,000
42. Copy Writers	$42,270	28%	18,000
43. Creative Writers	$42,270	28%	18,000
44. Poets and Lyricists	$42,270	28%	18,000
45. Writers and Authors	$42,270	28%	18,000
46. Public Relations Specialists	$39,580	36%	19,000
47. Dental Hygienists	$51,330	37%	5,000
48. Market Research Analysts	$51,190	24%	13,000
49. Special Education Teachers, Preschool, Kindergarten, and Elementary School	$40,880	37%	15,000
50. Construction Managers	$58,250	16%	26,000
51. Administrative Services Managers	$47,080	20%	31,000
52. Accountants	$43,500	18%	100,000
53. Accountants and Auditors	$43,500	18%	100,000
54. Auditors	$43,500	18%	100,000
55. Veterinarians	$60,910	32%	2,000
56. Computer Hardware Engineers	$67,300	25%	3,000
57. Educational, Vocational, and School Counselors	$42,110	25%	22,000
58. Engineering Managers	$84,070	8%	24,000
59. Instructional Coordinators	$44,230	25%	15,000
60. Occupational Therapists	$49,450	34%	4,000
61. Paralegals and Legal Assistants	$35,360	33%	23,000
62. Secondary School Teachers, Except Special and Vocational Education	$40,870	19%	60,000

(continued)

(continued)

The 200 Best Jobs for College Graduates

Job	Annual Earnings	Percent Growth	Annual Openings
63. Environmental Engineers	$57,780	26%	3,000
64. Technical Writers	$47,790	30%	5,000
65. Speech-Language Pathologists	$46,640	39%	4,000
66. Agents and Business Managers of Artists, Performers, and Athletes	$57,040	28%	2,000
67. Clinical Psychologists	$48,320	18%	18,000
68. Clinical, Counseling, and School Psychologists	$48,320	18%	18,000
69. Counseling Psychologists	$48,320	18%	18,000
70. Educational Psychologists	$48,320	18%	18,000
71. Art Directors	$56,880	21%	6,000
72. Commercial and Industrial Designers	$48,780	24%	7,000
73. Graphic Designers	$34,570	27%	28,000
74. Directors—Stage, Motion Pictures, Television, and Radio	$41,030	27%	11,000
75. Producers	$41,030	27%	11,000
76. Producers and Directors	$41,030	27%	11,000
77. Program Directors	$41,030	27%	11,000
78. Medical Scientists, Except Epidemiologists	$57,810	26%	2,000
79. Child, Family, and School Social Workers	$31,470	27%	35,000
80. Cost Estimators	$45,800	16%	28,000
81. Industrial Production Managers	$61,660	6%	22,000
82. Human Resources Managers	$59,000	13%	14,000
83. Biochemists	$54,230	21%	5,000
84. Biochemists and Biophysicists	$54,230	21%	5,000
85. Biophysicists	$54,230	21%	5,000
86. Economists	$64,830	18%	3,000
87. Property, Real Estate, and Community Association Managers	$36,020	23%	24,000
88. Medical and Public Health Social Workers	$34,790	32%	13,000
89. Social and Community Service Managers	$39,130	25%	13,000
90. Training and Development Specialists	$40,830	19%	20,000
91. Physical Therapist Assistants	$33,870	45%	9,000
92. Special Education Teachers, Secondary School	$41,290	25%	8,000

The 200 Best Jobs for College Graduates

Job	Annual Earnings	Percent Growth	Annual Openings
93. Probation Officers and Correctional Treatment Specialists	$38,150	24%	14,000
94. Biologists	$49,033	21%	5,000
95. Editors	$39,370	23%	14,000
96. Medical Records and Health Information Technicians	$22,750	49%	14,000
97. Sales Engineers	$56,520	18%	4,000
98. Biomedical Engineers	$57,480	31%	fewer than 500
99. Microbiologists	$48,890	21%	5,000
100. Chemists	$50,080	19%	6,000
101. Electrical Engineers	$64,910	11%	8,000
102. Political Scientists	$81,040	17%	2,000
103. Optometrists	$82,860	19%	1,000
104. Epidemiologists	$48,390	26%	2,000
105. Hydrologists	$55,410	26%	1,000
106. Mental Health and Substance Abuse Social Workers	$30,170	39%	10,000
107. Diagnostic Medical Sonographers	$44,820	26%	3,000
108. Mechanical Engineers	$58,710	13%	7,000
109. Multi-Media Artists and Animators	$41,130	22%	8,000
110. Audiologists	$44,830	45%	1,000
111. Elementary School Teachers, Except Special Education	$39,700	13%	144,000
112. Respiratory Therapists	$37,680	35%	4,000
113. Medical Transcriptionists	$25,270	30%	15,000
114. Architects, Except Landscape and Naval	$52,510	18%	4,000
115. Gaming Managers	$53,380	30%	fewer than 500
116. Medical and Clinical Laboratory Technologists	$40,510	17%	19,000
117. Zoologists and Wildlife Biologists	$43,980	21%	5,000
118. Radiologic Technicians	$36,000	23%	13,000
119. Radiologic Technologists	$36,000	23%	13,000
120. Radiologic Technologists and Technicians	$36,000	23%	13,000
121. Airline Pilots, Copilots, and Flight Engineers	$110,940	6%	5,000
122. Geologists	$56,230	18%	2,000

(continued)

(continued)

The 200 Best Jobs for College Graduates

Job	Annual Earnings	Percent Growth	Annual Openings
123. Geoscientists, Except Hydrologists and Geographers	$56,230	18%	2,000
124. Preschool Teachers, Except Special Education	$17,810	20%	55,000
125. Employment Interviewers, Private or Public Employment Service	$36,480	18%	19,000
126. Employment, Recruitment, and Placement Specialists	$36,480	18%	19,000
127. Personnel Recruiters	$36,480	18%	19,000
128. Electronics Engineers, Except Computer	$64,830	10%	6,000
129. Environmental Scientists and Specialists, Including Health	$44,180	22%	4,000
130. Materials Scientists	$60,620	20%	1,000
131. Substance Abuse and Behavioral Disorder Counselors	$28,510	35%	7,000
132. Physical Therapist Aides	$19,670	46%	7,000
133. Budget Analysts	$48,370	15%	8,000
134. Special Education Teachers, Middle School	$38,600	24%	6,000
135. Natural Sciences Managers	$75,880	8%	4,000
136. Aerospace Engineers	$67,930	14%	2,000
137. Landscape Architects	$43,540	31%	1,000
138. Middle School Teachers, Except Special and Vocational Education	$39,750	10%	54,000
139. Nuclear Equipment Operation Technicians	$59,160	21%	fewer than 500
140. Nuclear Monitoring Technicians	$59,160	21%	fewer than 500
141. Nuclear Technicians	$59,160	21%	fewer than 500
142. Purchasing Agents, Except Wholesale, Retail, and Farm Products	$41,370	12%	23,000
143. Industrial Engineers	$58,580	4%	10,000
144. Recreation Workers	$17,130	20%	32,000
145. Occupational Therapist Assistants	$34,340	40%	3,000
146. Semiconductor Processors	$25,430	32%	7,000
147. Veterinary Technologists and Technicians	$21,640	39%	6,000
148. Fashion Designers	$48,530	20%	2,000
149. Architectural Drafters	$35,220	21%	12,000

The 200 Best Jobs for College Graduates

Job	Annual Earnings	Percent Growth	Annual Openings
150. Biological Technicians	$31,540	26%	7,000
151. Electrical and Electronics Drafters	$38,210	23%	5,000
152. Electrical Drafters	$38,210	23%	5,000
153. Podiatrists	$107,560	14%	1,000
154. Kindergarten Teachers, Except Special Education	$37,610	14%	23,000
155. Cardiovascular Technologists and Technicians	$33,350	35%	3,000
156. Health Educators	$33,860	24%	7,000
157. Calibration and Instrumentation Technicians	$40,020	11%	22,000
158. Electrical and Electronic Engineering Technicians	$40,020	11%	22,000
159. Electrical Engineering Technicians	$40,020	11%	22,000
160. Electronics Engineering Technicians	$40,020	11%	22,000
161. Loan Officers	$41,420	5%	28,000
162. Medical and Clinical Laboratory Technicians	$27,540	19%	19,000
163. Rehabilitation Counselors	$24,450	24%	12,000
164. Radiation Therapists	$47,470	23%	1,000
165. Purchasing Managers	$53,030	–6%	17,000
166. Compensation, Benefits, and Job Analysis Specialists	$41,660	16%	8,000
167. Adult Literacy, Remedial Education, and GED Teachers and Instructors	$33,540	19%	12,000
168. Arbitrators, Mediators, and Conciliators	$43,060	27%	fewer than 500
169. Civil Engineers	$55,740	10%	4,000
170. Marriage and Family Therapists	$34,660	30%	2,000
171. Insurance Sales Agents	$38,750	3%	43,000
172. Physicists	$83,310	10%	1,000
173. Survey Researchers	$26,200	34%	3,000
174. Credit Analysts	$40,180	16%	7,000
175. Education Administrators, Preschool and Child Care Center/Program	$30,420	13%	35,000
176. Fire-Prevention and Protection Engineers	$54,630	11%	3,000
177. Health and Safety Engineers, Except Mining Safety Engineers and Inspectors	$54,630	11%	3,000

(continued)

(continued)

The 200 Best Jobs for College Graduates

Job	Annual Earnings	Percent Growth	Annual Openings
178. Industrial Safety and Health Engineers	$54,630	11%	3,000
179. Product Safety Engineers	$54,630	11%	3,000
180. Nuclear Medicine Technologists	$44,130	22%	1,000
181. Judges, Magistrate Judges, and Magistrates	$86,760	1%	2,000
182. Environmental Engineering Technicians	$34,000	29%	2,000
183. Astronomers	$74,510	10%	1,000
184. Atmospheric and Space Scientists	$58,510	17%	fewer than 500
185. Urban and Regional Planners	$46,500	16%	3,000
186. Vocational Education Teachers, Secondary School	$42,080	13%	7,000
187. Directors, Religious Activities and Education	$27,000	16%	23,000
188. Geographers	$46,690	17%	2,000
189. Mental Health Counselors	$27,570	22%	7,000
190. Interior Designers	$36,540	17%	7,000
191. Chemical Engineers	$65,960	4%	2,000
192. Operations Research Analysts	$53,420	8%	4,000
193. Meeting and Convention Planners	$35,540	23%	3,000
194. Chemical Technicians	$35,450	15%	13,000
195. Environmental Science and Protection Technicians, Including Health	$33,830	24%	3,000
196. Film and Video Editors	$34,160	26%	2,000
197. Occupational Health and Safety Specialists	$42,750	15%	4,000
198. Occupational Health and Safety Technicians	$42,750	15%	4,000
199. Exhibit Designers	$31,440	27%	2,000
200. Set and Exhibit Designers	$31,440	27%	2,000
201. Set Designers	$31,440	27%	2,000
202. Materials Engineers	$59,100	5%	2,000
203. Insurance Underwriters	$43,150	2%	11,000
204. Nuclear Engineers	$79,360	2%	1,000
205. Agricultural Engineers	$55,850	15%	fewer than 500
206. Financial Examiners	$53,060	10%	2,000
207. Clergy	$31,760	15%	12,000
208. Actuaries	$66,590	5%	1,000
209. Dietitians and Nutritionists	$38,450	15%	5,000

The 200 Best Jobs for College Graduates

Job	Annual Earnings	Percent Growth	Annual Openings
210. Orthotists and Prosthetists	$45,740	17%	1,000
211. Mechanical Engineering Technicians	$39,570	14%	5,000
212. Historians	$39,860	17%	2,000
213. Librarians	$41,700	7%	6,000
214. Industrial Engineering Technicians	$40,910	10%	5,000
215. Civil Engineering Technicians	$35,990	12%	9,000
216. Wholesale and Retail Buyers, Except Farm Products	$37,200	–9%	18,000
217. Administrative Law Judges, Adjudicators, and Hearing Officers	$61,240	1%	1,000
218. Tax Examiners, Collectors, and Revenue Agents	$40,180	8%	6,000
219. Petroleum Engineers	$78,910	–7%	fewer than 500
220. Composers	$31,510	13%	9,000
221. Music Arrangers and Orchestrators	$31,510	13%	9,000
222. Music Directors	$31,510	13%	9,000
223. Music Directors and Composers	$31,510	13%	9,000
224. Aerospace Engineering and Operations Technicians	$48,600	6%	2,000
225. Cartographers and Photogrammetrists	$39,410	18%	1,000
226. Mathematicians	$68,640	–2%	fewer than 500
227. Statisticians	$51,990	2%	2,000
228. Surveyors	$36,700	8%	7,000
229. Marine Architects	$60,890	2%	fewer than 500
230. Marine Engineers	$60,890	2%	fewer than 500
231. Marine Engineers and Naval Architects	$60,890	2%	fewer than 500
232. Athletic Trainers	$32,080	18%	2,000
233. Anthropologists	$36,040	17%	2,000
234. Anthropologists and Archeologists	$36,040	17%	2,000
235. Archeologists	$36,040	17%	2,000
236. Electro-Mechanical Technicians	$36,150	14%	4,000
237. Pilots, Ship	$47,510	3%	2,000
238. Fire Investigators	$41,630	15%	1,000
239. Mining and Geological Engineers, Including Mining Safety Engineers	$60,820	–1%	fewer than 500
240. Vocational Education Teachers, Middle School	$39,330	13%	2,000

(continued)

(continued)

The 200 Best Jobs for College Graduates

Job	Annual Earnings	Percent Growth	Annual Openings
241. Loan Counselors	$32,160	16%	3,000
242. Conservation Scientists	$47,140	8%	1,000
243. Park Naturalists	$47,140	8%	1,000
244. Range Managers	$47,140	8%	1,000
245. Soil Conservationists	$47,140	8%	1,000
246. Funeral Directors	$41,110	3%	3,000
247. Foresters	$43,640	7%	1,000
248. Agricultural Technicians	$27,080	15%	3,000
249. Food Science Technicians	$27,080	15%	3,000
250. Broadcast News Analysts	$29,110	3%	9,000
251. Law Clerks	$28,510	13%	3,000
252. Forensic Science Technicians	$37,520	13%	1,000
253. Geological and Petroleum Technicians	$36,490	6%	2,000
254. Geological Data Technicians	$36,490	6%	2,000
255. Geological Sample Test Technicians	$36,490	6%	2,000
256. Farm and Home Management Advisors	$36,290	6%	2,000
257. Forest and Conservation Technicians	$29,580	3%	2,000
258. Recreational Therapists	$28,650	9%	1,000

The 100 Best-Paying Jobs for College Graduates

We sorted all 258 jobs that require a college degree based on their annual median earnings from highest to lowest. *Median earnings* means that half of all workers in these jobs earn more than that amount and half earn less. We then selected the 100 jobs with the highest earnings to create the list that follows.

It shouldn't be a big surprise to learn that most of the highest-paying jobs require advanced levels of education, training, and experience. For example, most of the 20 jobs with the highest earnings require a doctoral or professional degree, and others, such as Chief Executives and Airline Pilots, Copilots, and Flight Engineers, require extensive training and experience. Although the top 20 jobs may not appeal to you for a variety of reasons, you are likely to find others that will among the top 100 jobs with the highest earnings. Keep in mind that the earnings reflect the national average for all workers in the occupation. This is an important consideration because starting pay in the job is usually a lot less than the pay that workers can earn with several years of experience. Earnings also vary significantly by region of the country, so actual pay in your area could be substantially different.

The 100 Best-Paying Jobs for College Graduates

Job	Annual Earnings
1. Internists, General	$142,400
2. Pediatricians, General	$125,970
3. Psychiatrists	$118,640
4. Family and General Practitioners	$114,170
5. Chief Executives	$113,810
6. Government Service Executives	$113,810
7. Private Sector Executives	$113,810
8. Airline Pilots, Copilots, and Flight Engineers	$110,940
9. Podiatrists	$107,560
10. Lawyers	$88,280
11. Judges, Magistrate Judges, and Magistrates	$86,760
12. Engineering Managers	$84,070
13. Physicists	$83,310
14. Optometrists	$82,860
15. Political Scientists	$81,040
16. Nuclear Engineers	$79,360

(continued)

(continued)

The 100 Best-Paying Jobs for College Graduates

Job	Annual Earnings
17. Petroleum Engineers	$78,910
18. Computer and Information Systems Managers	$78,830
19. Natural Sciences Managers	$75,880
20. Astronomers	$74,510
21. Marketing Managers	$71,240
22. Pharmacists	$70,950
23. Computer and Information Scientists, Research	$70,590
24. Computer Software Engineers, Systems Software	$69,530
25. Mathematicians	$68,640
26. Sales Managers	$68,520
27. Aerospace Engineers	$67,930
28. Computer Software Engineers, Applications	$67,670
29. Computer Hardware Engineers	$67,300
30. Financial Managers	$67,020
31. Financial Managers, Branch or Department	$67,020
32. Treasurers, Controllers, and Chief Financial Officers	$67,020
33. Education Administrators, Elementary and Secondary School	$66,930
34. Industrial-Organizational Psychologists	$66,880
35. Actuaries	$66,590
36. Chemical Engineers	$65,960
37. Electrical Engineers	$64,910
38. Economists	$64,830
39. Electronics Engineers, Except Computer	$64,830
40. Physician Assistants	$61,910
41. Industrial Production Managers	$61,660
42. Administrative Law Judges, Adjudicators, and Hearing Officers	$61,240
43. General and Operations Managers	$61,160
44. Veterinarians	$60,910
45. Marine Architects	$60,890
46. Marine Engineers	$60,890
47. Marine Engineers and Naval Architects	$60,890
48. Mining and Geological Engineers, Including Mining Safety Engineers	$60,820
49. Materials Scientists	$60,620
50. Computer Systems Analysts	$59,330

The 100 Best-Paying Jobs for College Graduates

Job	Annual Earnings
51. Nuclear Equipment Operation Technicians	$59,160
52. Nuclear Monitoring Technicians	$59,160
53. Nuclear Technicians	$59,160
54. Materials Engineers	$59,100
55. Human Resources Managers	$59,000
56. Mechanical Engineers	$58,710
57. Industrial Engineers	$58,580
58. Atmospheric and Space Scientists	$58,510
59. Construction Managers	$58,250
60. Medical Scientists, Except Epidemiologists	$57,810
61. Environmental Engineers	$57,780
62. Computer Programmers	$57,590
63. Biomedical Engineers	$57,480
64. Agents and Business Managers of Artists, Performers, and Athletes	$57,040
65. Art Directors	$56,880
66. Sales Engineers	$56,520
67. Medical and Health Services Managers	$56,370
68. Geologists	$56,230
69. Geoscientists, Except Hydrologists and Geographers	$56,230
70. Sales Agents, Financial Services	$56,080
71. Sales Agents, Securities and Commodities	$56,080
72. Securities, Commodities, and Financial Services Sales Agents	$56,080
73. Agricultural Engineers	$55,850
74. Civil Engineers	$55,740
75. Hydrologists	$55,410
76. Personal Financial Advisors	$55,320
77. Management Analysts	$55,040
78. Physical Therapists	$54,810
79. Fire-Prevention and Protection Engineers	$54,630
80. Health and Safety Engineers, Except Mining Safety Engineers and Inspectors	$54,630
81. Industrial Safety and Health Engineers	$54,630
82. Product Safety Engineers	$54,630
83. Public Relations Managers	$54,540
84. Network Systems and Data Communications Analysts	$54,510

(continued)

(continued)

The 100 Best-Paying Jobs for College Graduates

Job	Annual Earnings
85. Biochemists	$54,230
86. Biochemists and Biophysicists	$54,230
87. Biophysicists	$54,230
88. Operations Research Analysts	$53,420
89. Gaming Managers	$53,380
90. Advertising and Promotions Managers	$53,360
91. Financial Examiners	$53,060
92. Purchasing Managers	$53,030
93. Architects, Except Landscape and Naval	$52,510
94. Financial Analysts	$52,420
95. Database Administrators	$51,990
96. Statisticians	$51,990
97. Dental Hygienists	$51,330
98. Computer Security Specialists	$51,280
99. Network and Computer Systems Administrators	$51,280
100. Market Research Analysts	$51,190

The 100 Fastest-Growing Jobs for College Graduates

We created this list by sorting all 258 jobs that require a college degree by their projected growth over a ten-year period. Growth rates are one measure to consider in exploring career options, as jobs with higher growth rates tend to provide more job opportunities.

Jobs in the computer and medical fields dominate the 20 fastest-growing jobs. Computer Software Engineers, Applications is the job with the highest growth rate—the number employed is projected to double during this time. You can find a wide range of rapidly growing jobs in a variety of fields and at different levels of training and education among the list of the 100 fastest-growing jobs.

The 100 Fastest-Growing Jobs for College Graduates

Job	Percent Growth
1. Computer Software Engineers, Applications	100%
2. Computer Support Specialists	97%
3. Computer Software Engineers, Systems Software	90%
4. Computer Security Specialists	82%
5. Network and Computer Systems Administrators	82%
6. Network Systems and Data Communications Analysts	78%
7. Database Administrators	66%
8. Computer Systems Analysts	60%
9. Physician Assistants	54%
10. Medical Records and Health Information Technicians	49%
11. Computer and Information Systems Managers	48%
12. Physical Therapist Aides	46%
13. Audiologists	45%
14. Physical Therapist Assistants	45%
15. Computer and Information Scientists, Research	40%
16. Occupational Therapist Assistants	40%
17. Speech-Language Pathologists	39%
18. Mental Health and Substance Abuse Social Workers	39%
19. Veterinary Technologists and Technicians	39%
20. Dental Hygienists	37%

(continued)

(continued)

The 100 Fastest-Growing Jobs
for College Graduates

Job	Percent Growth
21. Special Education Teachers, Preschool, Kindergarten, and Elementary School	37%
22. Public Relations Managers	36%
23. Public Relations Specialists	36%
24. Respiratory Therapists	35%
25. Cardiovascular Technologists and Technicians	35%
26. Substance Abuse and Behavioral Disorder Counselors	35%
27. Personal Financial Advisors	34%
28. Advertising and Promotions Managers	34%
29. Occupational Therapists	34%
30. Survey Researchers	34%
31. Sales Managers	33%
32. Physical Therapists	33%
33. Paralegals and Legal Assistants	33%
34. Veterinarians	32%
35. Medical and Health Services Managers	32%
36. Medical and Public Health Social Workers	32%
37. Semiconductor Processors	32%
38. Biomedical Engineers	31%
39. Landscape Architects	31%
40. Gaming Managers	30%
41. Technical Writers	30%
42. Marriage and Family Therapists	30%
43. Medical Transcriptionists	30%
44. Marketing Managers	29%
45. Management Analysts	29%
46. Environmental Engineering Technicians	29%
47. Agents and Business Managers of Artists, Performers, and Athletes	28%
48. Copy Writers	28%
49. Creative Writers	28%
50. Poets and Lyricists	28%
51. Writers and Authors	28%
52. Arbitrators, Mediators, and Conciliators	27%

The 100 Fastest-Growing Jobs for College Graduates

Job	Percent Growth
53. Directors—Stage, Motion Pictures, Television, and Radio	27%
54. Producers	27%
55. Producers and Directors	27%
56. Program Directors	27%
57. Graphic Designers	27%
58. Child, Family, and School Social Workers	27%
59. Exhibit Designers	27%
60. Set and Exhibit Designers	27%
61. Set Designers	27%
62. Medical Scientists, Except Epidemiologists	26%
63. Environmental Engineers	26%
64. Hydrologists	26%
65. Financial Analysts	26%
66. Epidemiologists	26%
67. Registered Nurses	26%
68. Diagnostic Medical Sonographers	26%
69. Film and Video Editors	26%
70. Biological Technicians	26%
71. Computer Hardware Engineers	25%
72. Instructional Coordinators	25%
73. Educational, Vocational, and School Counselors	25%
74. Special Education Teachers, Secondary School	25%
75. Social and Community Service Managers	25%
76. Pharmacists	24%
77. Market Research Analysts	24%
78. Commercial and Industrial Designers	24%
79. Special Education Teachers, Middle School	24%
80. Probation Officers and Correctional Treatment Specialists	24%
81. Health Educators	24%
82. Environmental Science and Protection Technicians, Including Health	24%
83. Rehabilitation Counselors	24%
84. Postsecondary Teachers	24%
85. Radiation Therapists	23%

(continued)

(continued)

The 100 Fastest-Growing Jobs for College Graduates

Job	Percent Growth
86. Editors	23%
87. Electrical and Electronics Drafters	23%
88. Electrical Drafters	23%
89. Property, Real Estate, and Community Association Managers	23%
90. Radiologic Technicians	23%
91. Radiologic Technologists	23%
92. Radiologic Technologists and Technicians	23%
93. Meeting and Convention Planners	23%
94. Sales Agents, Financial Services	22%
95. Sales Agents, Securities and Commodities	22%
96. Securities, Commodities, and Financial Services Sales Agents	22%
97. Environmental Scientists and Specialists, Including Health	22%
98. Nuclear Medicine Technologists	22%
99. Multi-Media Artists and Animators	22%
100. Mental Health Counselors	22%

The 100 Jobs with the Most Openings for College Graduates

We created this list by sorting all 258 jobs that require a college degree by number of job openings that each is expected to have per year. It makes sense that jobs that employ large numbers of people are likely to have more job openings in a given year. Jobs with the most annual openings often provide easier entry for new workers or make it easier to move from one position to another. Some of these jobs may also be attractive to people re-entering the labor market, part-time workers, and workers who want to move from one employer to another.

The 100 Jobs with the Most Openings for College Graduates

Job	Annual Openings
1. General and Operations Managers	235,000
2. Postsecondary Teachers	184,000
3. Elementary School Teachers, Except Special Education	144,000
4. Registered Nurses	140,000
5. Accountants	100,000
6. Accountants and Auditors	100,000
7. Auditors	100,000
8. Secondary School Teachers, Except Special and Vocational Education	60,000
9. Sales Agents, Financial Services	55,000
10. Sales Agents, Securities and Commodities	55,000
11. Securities, Commodities, and Financial Services Sales Agents	55,000
12. Preschool Teachers, Except Special Education	55,000
13. Middle School Teachers, Except Special and Vocational Education	54,000
14. Financial Managers	53,000
15. Financial Managers, Branch or Department	53,000
16. Treasurers, Controllers, and Chief Financial Officers	53,000
17. Management Analysts	50,000
18. Chief Executives	48,000
19. Government Service Executives	48,000
20. Private Sector Executives	48,000
21. Insurance Sales Agents	43,000
22. Computer Support Specialists	40,000
23. Computer Programmers	36,000

(continued)

(continued)

The 100 Jobs with the Most Openings for College Graduates

Job	Annual Openings
24. Child, Family, and School Social Workers	35,000
25. Lawyers	35,000
26. Education Administrators, Elementary and Secondary School	35,000
27. Education Administrators, Preschool and Child Care Center/Program	35,000
28. Computer Systems Analysts	34,000
29. Recreation Workers	32,000
30. Administrative Services Managers	31,000
31. Computer Software Engineers, Applications	28,000
32. Computer and Information Systems Managers	28,000
33. Graphic Designers	28,000
34. Cost Estimators	28,000
35. Loan Officers	28,000
36. Medical and Health Services Managers	27,000
37. Internists, General	27,000
38. Pediatricians, General	27,000
39. Psychiatrists	27,000
40. Family and General Practitioners	27,000
41. Construction Managers	26,000
42. Property, Real Estate, and Community Association Managers	24,000
43. Engineering Managers	24,000
44. Computer Software Engineers, Systems Software	23,000
45. Paralegals and Legal Assistants	23,000
46. Directors, Religious Activities and Education	23,000
47. Kindergarten Teachers, Except Special Education	23,000
48. Purchasing Agents, Except Wholesale, Retail, and Farm Products	23,000
49. Educational, Vocational, and School Counselors	22,000
50. Calibration and Instrumentation Technicians	22,000
51. Electrical and Electronic Engineering Technicians	22,000
52. Electrical Engineering Technicians	22,000
53. Electronics Engineering Technicians	22,000
54. Industrial Production Managers	22,000
55. Sales Managers	21,000
56. Financial Analysts	20,000

The 100 Jobs with the Most Openings for College Graduates

Job	Annual Openings
57. Pharmacists	20,000
58. Training and Development Specialists	20,000
59. Public Relations Specialists	19,000
60. Medical and Clinical Laboratory Technicians	19,000
61. Employment Interviewers, Private or Public Employment Service	19,000
62. Employment, Recruitment, and Placement Specialists	19,000
63. Personnel Recruiters	19,000
64. Medical and Clinical Laboratory Technologists	19,000
65. Computer Security Specialists	18,000
66. Network and Computer Systems Administrators	18,000
67. Copy Writers	18,000
68. Creative Writers	18,000
69. Poets and Lyricists	18,000
70. Writers and Authors	18,000
71. Industrial-Organizational Psychologists	18,000
72. Clinical Psychologists	18,000
73. Clinical, Counseling, and School Psychologists	18,000
74. Counseling Psychologists	18,000
75. Educational Psychologists	18,000
76. Wholesale and Retail Buyers, Except Farm Products	18,000
77. Purchasing Managers	17,000
78. Special Education Teachers, Preschool, Kindergarten, and Elementary School	15,000
79. Medical Transcriptionists	15,000
80. Instructional Coordinators	15,000
81. Medical Records and Health Information Technicians	14,000
82. Probation Officers and Correctional Treatment Specialists	14,000
83. Editors	14,000
84. Human Resources Managers	14,000
85. Personal Financial Advisors	13,000
86. Medical and Public Health Social Workers	13,000
87. Social and Community Service Managers	13,000
88. Market Research Analysts	13,000
89. Radiologic Technicians	13,000

(continued)

(continued)

The 100 Jobs with the Most Openings for College Graduates

Job	Annual Openings
90. Radiologic Technologists	13,000
91. Radiologic Technologists and Technicians	13,000
92. Chemical Technicians	13,000
93. Marketing Managers	12,000
94. Rehabilitation Counselors	12,000
95. Architectural Drafters	12,000
96. Adult Literacy, Remedial Education, and GED Teachers and Instructors	12,000
97. Clergy	12,000
98. Directors—Stage, Motion Pictures, Television, and Radio	11,000
99. Producers	11,000
100. Producers and Directors	11,000

Best Jobs Lists with High Percentages of Workers Age 20–29, Workers Age 55 and Over, Part-Time Workers, Self-Employed Workers, Women, and Men

We decided it would be interesting to include lists in this section that show what sorts of jobs different types of people are most likely to have. For example, what jobs have the highest percentage of men college graduates or recent college graduates? We're not saying that men or recent grads should consider these jobs over others, but it is interesting information to know.

In some cases, the lists can give you ideas for jobs to consider that you might otherwise overlook. For example, perhaps women should consider some jobs that traditionally have high percentages of men in them. Or older workers might consider some jobs typically held by recent graduates. Although these are not obvious ways of using these lists, the lists may give you some good ideas on jobs to consider. The lists may also help you identify jobs that work well for others in your situation (for example, jobs with plentiful opportunities for part-time work, if that is something you want to do).

All of the lists in this section were created using a similar process. We began with all 258 jobs in the database that require a two- or four-year college degree. Next, we sorted those jobs in order of the primary criteria for each set of lists. For example, we sorted all 258 jobs based on the percentage of workers age 20 to 29 from highest to lowest percentage. We then selected the 100 jobs with the highest percentage of workers age 20 to 29 and listed them along with their earnings, growth, and number of openings data. From the list of 100 jobs for each type of worker, we created four more-specialized lists:

- ▲ 25 Best Jobs Overall (jobs with the highest combined score for earnings, growth rate, and number of openings)
- ▲ 25 Best-Paying Jobs
- ▲ 25 Fastest-Growing Jobs
- ▲ 25 Jobs with the Most Openings

Again, each of these four lists only includes jobs from among those with the 100 highest percentages of different types of workers. The same basic process was used to create all the lists in this section. The lists are very interesting, and we hope you find them helpful.

Best Jobs with a High Percentage of College Graduates Age 20–29

These jobs have higher percentages of recent college graduates. Recent grads are found in all jobs, but those with higher percentages of recent grads may present more opportunities for initial entry or upward mobility. Many jobs with the highest percentages of recent grads are those requiring technical training lasting two years, though there is a wide variety of jobs in different fields among the top 100.

The 100 Jobs with the Highest Percentage of College Graduates Age 20–29

Job	Percent Age 20–29	Annual Earnings	Percent Growth	Annual Openings
1. Paralegals and Legal Assistants	33.9%	$35,360	33%	23,000
2. Nuclear Equipment Operation Technicians	32.1%	$59,160	21%	fewer than 500
3. Nuclear Monitoring Technicians	32.1%	$59,160	21%	fewer than 500
4. Veterinary Technologists and Technicians	32.1%	$21,640	39%	6,000
5. Biological Technicians	32.1%	$31,540	26%	7,000
6. Chemical Technicians	32.1%	$35,450	15%	13,000
7. Environmental Science and Protection Technicians, Including Health	32.1%	$33,830	24%	3,000
8. Agricultural Technicians	32.1%	$27,080	15%	3,000
9. Food Science Technicians	32.1%	$27,080	15%	3,000
10. Forensic Science Technicians	32.1%	$37,520	13%	1,000
11. Geological Data Technicians	32.1%	$36,490	6%	2,000
12. Geological Sample Test Technicians	32.1%	$36,490	6%	2,000
13. Forest and Conservation Technicians	31.2%	$29,580	3%	2,000
14. Preschool Teachers, Except Special Education	28.9%	$17,810	20%	55,000
15. Kindergarten Teachers, Except Special Education	28.9%	$37,610	14%	23,000
16. Wholesale and Retail Buyers, Except Farm Products	28.4%	$37,200	–9%	18,000
17. Surveyors	28.0%	$36,700	8%	7,000
18. Physical Therapist Assistants	27.9%	$33,870	45%	9,000
19. Physical Therapist Aides	27.9%	$19,670	46%	7,000

The 100 Jobs with the Highest Percentage of College Graduates Age 20–29

Job	Percent Age 20–29	Annual Earnings	Percent Growth	Annual Openings
20. Architectural Drafters	26.5%	$35,220	21%	12,000
21. Electrical and Electronics Drafters	26.5%	$38,210	23%	5,000
22. Electrical Drafters	26.5%	$38,210	23%	5,000
23. Physical Therapists	26.3%	$54,810	33%	6,000
24. Occupational Therapists	26.3%	$49,450	34%	4,000
25. Speech-Language Pathologists	26.3%	$46,640	39%	4,000
26. Audiologists	26.3%	$44,830	45%	1,000
27. Respiratory Therapists	26.3%	$37,680	35%	4,000
28. Substance Abuse and Behavioral Disorder Counselors	26.3%	$28,510	35%	7,000
29. Recreational Therapists	26.3%	$28,650	9%	1,000
30. Accountants	25.9%	$43,500	18%	100,000
31. Accountants and Auditors	25.9%	$43,500	18%	100,000
32. Auditors	25.9%	$43,500	18%	100,000
33. Occupational Therapist Assistants	25.8%	$34,340	40%	3,000
34. Dental Hygienists	25.4%	$51,330	37%	5,000
35. Medical Records and Health Information Technicians	25.4%	$22,750	49%	14,000
36. Cardiovascular Technologists and Technicians	25.4%	$33,350	35%	3,000
37. Semiconductor Processors	24.7%	$25,430	32%	7,000
38. Sales Agents, Financial Services	24.3%	$56,080	22%	55,000
39. Sales Agents, Securities and Commodities	24.3%	$56,080	22%	55,000
40. Child, Family, and School Social Workers	23.9%	$31,470	27%	35,000
41. Medical and Public Health Social Workers	23.9%	$34,790	32%	13,000
42. Probation Officers and Correctional Treatment Specialists	23.9%	$38,150	24%	14,000
43. Mental Health and Substance Abuse Social Workers	23.9%	$30,170	39%	10,000
44. Radiologic Technicians	23.9%	$36,000	23%	13,000
45. Radiologic Technologists	23.9%	$36,000	23%	13,000
46. Radiologic Technologists and Technicians	23.9%	$36,000	23%	13,000

(continued)

(continued)

The 100 Jobs with the Highest Percentage of College Graduates Age 20–29

Job	Percent Age 20–29	Annual Earnings	Percent Growth	Annual Openings
47. Radiation Therapists	23.9%	$47,470	23%	1,000
48. Nuclear Medicine Technologists	23.9%	$44,130	22%	1,000
49. Public Relations Specialists	23.6%	$39,580	36%	19,000
50. Directors—Stage, Motion Pictures, Television, and Radio	23.6%	$41,030	27%	11,000
51. Producers	23.6%	$41,030	27%	11,000
52. Producers and Directors	23.6%	$41,030	27%	11,000
53. Program Directors	23.6%	$41,030	27%	11,000
54. Diagnostic Medical Sonographers	23.6%	$44,820	26%	3,000
55. Film and Video Editors	23.6%	$34,160	26%	2,000
56. Occupational Health and Safety Specialists	23.6%	$42,750	15%	4,000
57. Occupational Health and Safety Technicians	23.6%	$42,750	15%	4,000
58. Orthotists and Prosthetists	23.6%	$45,740	17%	1,000
59. Athletic Trainers	23.6%	$32,080	18%	2,000
60. Broadcast News Analysts	23.6%	$29,110	3%	9,000
61. Computer Programmers	23.3%	$57,590	16%	36,000
62. Adult Literacy, Remedial Education, and GED Teachers and Instructors	23.0%	$33,540	19%	12,000
63. Vocational Education Teachers, Secondary School	23.0%	$42,080	13%	7,000
64. Vocational Education Teachers, Middle School	23.0%	$39,330	13%	2,000
65. Farm and Home Management Advisors	23.0%	$36,290	6%	2,000
66. Medical and Clinical Laboratory Technologists	22.9%	$40,510	17%	19,000
67. Medical and Clinical Laboratory Technicians	22.9%	$27,540	19%	19,000
68. Graphic Designers	22.5%	$34,570	27%	28,000
69. Multi-Media Artists and Animators	22.5%	$41,130	22%	8,000
70. Law Clerks	22.5%	$28,510	13%	3,000
71. Electrical and Electronic Engineering Technicians	22.1%	$40,020	11%	22,000

The 100 Jobs with the Highest Percentage of College Graduates Age 20–29

Job	Percent Age 20–29	Annual Earnings	Percent Growth	Annual Openings
72. Environmental Engineering Technicians	22.1%	$34,000	29%	2,000
73. Mechanical Engineering Technicians	22.1%	$39,570	14%	5,000
74. Industrial Engineering Technicians	22.1%	$40,910	10%	5,000
75. Civil Engineering Technicians	22.1%	$35,990	12%	9,000
76. Aerospace Engineering and Operations Technicians	22.1%	$48,600	6%	2,000
77. Geological and Petroleum Technicians	22.1%	$36,490	6%	2,000
78. Environmental Engineers	21.7%	$57,780	26%	3,000
79. Sales Engineers	21.7%	$56,520	18%	4,000
80. Biomedical Engineers	21.7%	$57,480	31%	fewer than 500
81. Health Educators	21.7%	$33,860	24%	7,000
82. Fire-Prevention and Protection Engineers	21.7%	$54,630	11%	3,000
83. Industrial Safety and Health Engineers	21.7%	$54,630	11%	3,000
84. Product Safety Engineers	21.7%	$54,630	11%	3,000
85. Agricultural Engineers	21.7%	$55,850	15%	fewer than 500
86. Marine Engineers	21.7%	$60,890	2%	fewer than 500
87. Electro-Mechanical Technicians	21.6%	$36,150	14%	4,000
88. Insurance Underwriters	20.7%	$43,150	2%	11,000
89. Composers	20.5%	$31,510	13%	9,000
90. Music Arrangers and Orchestrators	20.5%	$31,510	13%	9,000
91. Music Directors	20.5%	$31,510	13%	9,000
92. Music Directors and Composers	20.5%	$31,510	13%	9,000
93. Medical Scientists, Except Epidemiologists	20.4%	$57,810	26%	2,000
94. Biochemists	20.4%	$54,230	21%	5,000
95. Biochemists and Biophysicists	20.4%	$54,230	21%	5,000
96. Biophysicists	20.4%	$54,230	21%	5,000
97. Biologists	20.4%	$49,033	21%	5,000
98. Microbiologists	20.4%	$48,890	21%	5,000
99. Chemists	20.4%	$50,080	19%	6,000
100. Epidemiologists	20.4%	$48,390	26%	2,000

Best Jobs Overall for College Graduates Age 20–29

Job	Percent Age 20–29	Annual Earnings	Percent Growth	Annual Openings
1. Sales Agents, Financial Services	24.3%	$56,080	22%	55,000
2. Sales Agents, Securities and Commodities	24.3%	$56,080	22%	55,000
3. Physical Therapists	26.3%	$54,810	33%	6,000
4. Paralegals and Legal Assistants	33.9%	$35,360	33%	23,000
5. Dental Hygienists	25.4%	$51,330	37%	5,000
6. Accountants	25.9%	$43,500	18%	100,000
7. Accountants and Auditors	25.9%	$43,500	18%	100,000
8. Auditors	25.9%	$43,500	18%	100,000
9. Public Relations Specialists	23.6%	$39,580	36%	19,000
10. Occupational Therapists	26.3%	$49,450	34%	4,000
11. Computer Programmers	23.3%	$57,590	16%	36,000
12. Speech-Language Pathologists	26.3%	$46,640	39%	4,000
13. Child, Family, and School Social Workers	23.9%	$31,470	27%	35,000
14. Physical Therapist Assistants	27.9%	$33,870	45%	9,000
15. Directors—Stage, Motion Pictures, Television, and Radio	23.6%	$41,030	27%	11,000
16. Producers	23.6%	$41,030	27%	11,000
17. Producers and Directors	23.6%	$41,030	27%	11,000
18. Program Directors	23.6%	$41,030	27%	11,000
19. Graphic Designers	22.5%	$34,570	27%	28,000
20. Environmental Engineers	21.7%	$57,780	26%	3,000
21. Medical and Public Health Social Workers	23.9%	$34,790	32%	13,000
22. Medical Records and Health Information Technicians	25.4%	$22,750	49%	14,000
23. Probation Officers and Correctional Treatment Specialists	23.9%	$38,150	24%	14,000
24. Audiologists	26.3%	$44,830	45%	1,000
25. Respiratory Therapists	26.3%	$37,680	35%	4,000

Best-Paying Jobs for College Graduates Age 20–29

Job	Percent Age 20–29	Annual Earnings
1. Marine Engineers	21.7%	$60,890
2. Nuclear Equipment Operation Technicians	32.1%	$59,160
3. Nuclear Monitoring Technicians	32.1%	$59,160
4. Medical Scientists, Except Epidemiologists	20.4%	$57,810
5. Environmental Engineers	21.7%	$57,780
6. Computer Programmers	23.3%	$57,590
7. Biomedical Engineers	21.7%	$57,480
8. Sales Engineers	21.7%	$56,520
9. Sales Agents, Financial Services	24.3%	$56,080
10. Sales Agents, Securities and Commodities	24.3%	$56,080
11. Agricultural Engineers	21.7%	$55,850
12. Physical Therapists	26.3%	$54,810
13. Fire-Prevention and Protection Engineers	21.7%	$54,630
14. Industrial Safety and Health Engineers	21.7%	$54,630
15. Product Safety Engineers	21.7%	$54,630
16. Biochemists	20.4%	$54,230
17. Biochemists and Biophysicists	20.4%	$54,230
18. Biophysicists	20.4%	$54,230
19. Dental Hygienists	25.4%	$51,330
20. Chemists	20.4%	$50,080
21. Occupational Therapists	26.3%	$49,450
22. Biologists	20.4%	$49,033
23. Microbiologists	20.4%	$48,890
24. Aerospace Engineering and Operations Technicians	22.1%	$48,600
25. Epidemiologists	20.4%	$48,390

Fastest-Growing Jobs for College Graduates Age 20–29

Job	Percent Age 20–29	Percent Growth
1. Medical Records and Health Information Technicians	25.4%	49%
2. Physical Therapist Aides	27.9%	46%
3. Audiologists	26.3%	45%
4. Physical Therapist Assistants	27.9%	45%
5. Occupational Therapist Assistants	25.8%	40%
6. Speech-Language Pathologists	26.3%	39%
7. Mental Health and Substance Abuse Social Workers	23.9%	39%
8. Veterinary Technologists and Technicians	32.1%	39%
9. Dental Hygienists	25.4%	37%
10. Public Relations Specialists	23.6%	36%
11. Respiratory Therapists	26.3%	35%
12. Cardiovascular Technologists and Technicians	25.4%	35%
13. Substance Abuse and Behavioral Disorder Counselors	26.3%	35%
14. Occupational Therapists	26.3%	34%
15. Physical Therapists	26.3%	33%
16. Paralegals and Legal Assistants	33.9%	33%
17. Medical and Public Health Social Workers	23.9%	32%
18. Semiconductor Processors	24.7%	32%
19. Biomedical Engineers	21.7%	31%
20. Environmental Engineering Technicians	22.1%	29%
21. Directors—Stage, Motion Pictures, Television, and Radio	23.6%	27%
22. Producers	23.6%	27%
23. Producers and Directors	23.6%	27%
24. Program Directors	23.6%	27%
25. Graphic Designers	22.5%	27%

Jobs with the Most Openings for College Graduates Age 20–29

Job	Percent Age 20–29	Annual Openings
1. Accountants	25.9%	100,000
2. Accountants and Auditors	25.9%	100,000
3. Auditors	25.9%	100,000
4. Sales Agents, Financial Services	24.3%	55,000
5. Sales Agents, Securities and Commodities	24.3%	55,000
6. Preschool Teachers, Except Special Education	28.9%	55,000
7. Computer Programmers	23.3%	36,000
8. Child, Family, and School Social Workers	23.9%	35,000
9. Graphic Designers	22.5%	28,000
10. Paralegals and Legal Assistants	33.9%	23,000
11. Kindergarten Teachers, Except Special Education	28.9%	23,000
12. Electrical and Electronic Engineering Technicians	22.1%	22,000
13. Public Relations Specialists	23.6%	19,000
14. Medical and Clinical Laboratory Technicians	22.9%	19,000
15. Medical and Clinical Laboratory Technologists	22.9%	19,000
16. Wholesale and Retail Buyers, Except Farm Products	28.4%	18,000
17. Medical Records and Health Information Technicians	25.4%	14,000
18. Probation Officers and Correctional Treatment Specialists	23.9%	14,000
19. Medical and Public Health Social Workers	23.9%	13,000
20. Radiologic Technicians	23.9%	13,000
21. Radiologic Technologists	23.9%	13,000
22. Radiologic Technologists and Technicians	23.9%	13,000
23. Chemical Technicians	32.1%	13,000
24. Architectural Drafters	26.5%	12,000
25. Adult Literacy, Remedial Education, and GED Teachers and Instructors	23.0%	12,000

Best Jobs with a High Percentage of College Graduates Age 55 and Over

Older workers don't change careers as often as younger ones do and, on the average, they tend to have been in their jobs for quite some time. Many of the jobs with the highest percentages of college graduates age 55 and over—and those with the highest earnings—require considerable preparation, either through experience or through education and training. These are not the sort of jobs most young graduates could easily get just out of college. That should not come as a big surprise, as many of these folks would have been in the workforce for a long time and would therefore have lots of experience.

But go down the list of the 100 jobs with the highest percentage of older workers and you will find a variety of jobs that many older workers could more easily enter if they were changing careers. Some would make good "retirement" jobs, particularly if they allowed for part-time work or self-employment.

The 100 Jobs with the Highest Percentage of College Graduates Age 55 and Over

Job	Percent Age 55 and Over	Annual Earnings	Percent Growth	Annual Openings
1. Clergy	31.2%	$31,760	15%	12,000
2. Property, Real Estate, and Community Association Managers	27.0%	$36,020	23%	24,000
3. Management Analysts	22.3%	$55,040	29%	50,000
4. Librarians	20.7%	$41,700	7%	6,000
5. Composers	19.4%	$31,510	13%	9,000
6. Music Arrangers and Orchestrators	19.4%	$31,510	13%	9,000
7. Music Directors	19.4%	$31,510	13%	9,000
8. Music Directors and Composers	19.4%	$31,510	13%	9,000
9. Postsecondary Teachers	19.0%	$46,330	24%	184,000
10. Insurance Sales Agents	18.7%	$38,750	3%	43,000
11. Government Service Executives	18.5%	$113,810	17%	48,000
12. Family and General Practitioners	18.0%	$114,170	18%	27,000
13. Internists, General	18.0%	$142,400	18%	27,000
14. Pediatricians, General	18.0%	$125,970	18%	27,000
15. Psychiatrists	18.0%	$118,640	18%	27,000
16. Civil Engineers	17.3%	$55,740	10%	4,000

▲▲▲▲▲▲▲▲▲▲▲▲▲▲▲▲▲▲▲▲ *200 Best Jobs for College Graduates, Second Edition* © *JIST Works*

The 100 Jobs with the Highest Percentage of College Graduates Age 55 and Over

Job	Percent Age 55 and Over	Annual Earnings	Percent Growth	Annual Openings
17. Directors, Religious Activities and Education	17.3%	$27,000	16%	23,000
18. Optometrists	17.3%	$82,860	19%	1,000
19. Podiatrists	17.3%	$107,560	14%	1,000
20. Recreation Workers	17.3%	$17,130	20%	32,000
21. Veterinarians	17.3%	$60,910	32%	2,000
22. Tax Examiners, Collectors, and Revenue Agents	16.8%	$40,180	8%	6,000
23. Dietitians and Nutritionists	15.3%	$38,450	15%	5,000
24. Education Administrators, Elementary and Secondary School	15.3%	$66,930	13%	35,000
25. Education Administrators, Preschool and Child Care Center/Program	15.3%	$30,420	13%	35,000
26. Instructional Coordinators	15.3%	$44,230	25%	15,000
27. Financial Examiners	15.2%	$53,060	10%	2,000
28. Health Educators	15.0%	$33,860	24%	7,000
29. Pilots, Ship	14.9%	$47,510	3%	2,000
30. Administrative Services Managers	14.7%	$47,080	20%	31,000
31. Chief Executives	14.7%	$113,810	17%	48,000
32. Computer and Information Systems Managers	14.7%	$78,830	48%	28,000
33. Construction Managers	14.7%	$58,250	16%	26,000
34. Engineering Managers	14.7%	$84,070	8%	24,000
35. Industrial Production Managers	14.7%	$61,660	6%	22,000
36. Natural Sciences Managers	14.7%	$75,880	8%	4,000
37. Private Sector Executives	14.7%	$113,810	17%	48,000
38. Gaming Managers	14.6%	$53,380	30%	fewer than 500
39. General and Operations Managers	14.6%	$61,160	15%	235,000
40. Medical and Health Services Managers	14.6%	$56,370	32%	27,000
41. Network and Computer Systems Administrators	14.6%	$51,280	82%	18,000
42. Social and Community Service Managers	14.6%	$39,130	25%	13,000

(continued)

(continued)

The 100 Jobs with the Highest Percentage of College Graduates Age 55 and Over

Job	Percent Age 55 and Over	Annual Earnings	Percent Growth	Annual Openings
43. Funeral Directors	14.4%	$41,110	3%	3,000
44. Mechanical Engineers	14.4%	$58,710	13%	7,000
45. Administrative Law Judges, Adjudicators, and Hearing Officers	13.8%	$61,240	1%	1,000
46. Judges, Magistrate Judges, and Magistrates	13.8%	$86,760	1%	2,000
47. Adult Literacy, Remedial Education, and GED Teachers and Instructors	13.7%	$33,540	19%	12,000
48. Farm and Home Management Advisors	13.7%	$36,290	6%	2,000
49. Vocational Education Teachers, Middle School	13.7%	$39,330	13%	2,000
50. Vocational Education Teachers, Secondary School	13.7%	$42,080	13%	7,000
51. Airline Pilots, Copilots, and Flight Engineers	13.6%	$110,940	6%	5,000
52. Copy Writers	13.6%	$42,270	28%	18,000
53. Creative Writers	13.6%	$42,270	28%	18,000
54. Editors	13.6%	$39,370	23%	14,000
55. Poets and Lyricists	13.6%	$42,270	28%	18,000
56. Technical Writers	13.6%	$47,790	30%	5,000
57. Writers and Authors	13.6%	$42,270	28%	18,000
58. Art Directors	13.2%	$56,880	21%	6,000
59. Commercial and Industrial Designers	13.2%	$48,780	24%	7,000
60. Exhibit Designers	13.2%	$31,440	27%	2,000
61. Fashion Designers	13.2%	$48,530	20%	2,000
62. Interior Designers	13.2%	$36,540	17%	7,000
63. Set and Exhibit Designers	13.2%	$31,440	27%	2,000
64. Set Designers	13.2%	$31,440	27%	2,000
65. Graphic Designers	13.1%	$34,570	27%	28,000
66. Multi-Media Artists and Animators	13.1%	$41,130	22%	8,000
67. Athletic Trainers	12.9%	$32,080	18%	2,000
68. Broadcast News Analysts	12.9%	$29,110	3%	9,000

The 100 Jobs with the Highest Percentage of College Graduates Age 55 and Over

Job	Percent Age 55 and Over	Annual Earnings	Percent Growth	Annual Openings
69. Directors—Stage, Motion Pictures, Television, and Radio	12.9%	$41,030	27%	11,000
70. Film and Video Editors	12.9%	$34,160	26%	2,000
71. Producers	12.9%	$41,030	27%	11,000
72. Producers and Directors	12.9%	$41,030	27%	11,000
73. Program Directors	12.9%	$41,030	27%	11,000
74. Public Relations Specialists	12.9%	$39,580	36%	19,000
75. Educational, Vocational, and School Counselors	12.8%	$42,110	25%	22,000
76. Lawyers	12.6%	$88,280	18%	35,000
77. Industrial Engineers	12.5%	$58,580	4%	10,000
78. Surveyors	12.4%	$36,700	8%	7,000
79. Electro-Mechanical Technicians	12.2%	$36,150	14%	4,000
80. Physical Therapist Aides	12.2%	$19,670	46%	7,000
81. Physical Therapist Assistants	12.2%	$33,870	45%	9,000
82. Aerospace Engineers	12.1%	$67,930	14%	2,000
83. Chemical Engineers	12.1%	$65,960	4%	2,000
84. Materials Engineers	12.1%	$59,100	5%	2,000
85. Meeting and Convention Planners	12.1%	$35,540	23%	3,000
86. Mining and Geological Engineers, Including Mining Safety Engineers	12.1%	$60,820	−1%	fewer than 500
87. Nuclear Engineers	12.1%	$79,360	2%	1,000
88. Personal Financial Advisors	12.1%	$55,320	34%	13,000
89. Petroleum Engineers	12.1%	$78,910	−7%	fewer than 500
90. Arbitrators, Mediators, and Conciliators	12.0%	$43,060	27%	fewer than 500
91. Human Resources Managers	12.0%	$59,000	13%	14,000
92. Insurance Underwriters	12.0%	$43,150	2%	11,000
93. Purchasing Agents, Except Wholesale, Retail, and Farm Products	12.0%	$41,370	12%	23,000
94. Budget Analysts	11.9%	$48,370	15%	8,000
95. Credit Analysts	11.9%	$40,180	16%	7,000

(continued)

(continued)

The 100 Jobs with the Highest Percentage of College Graduates Age 55 and Over

Job	Percent Age 55 and Over	Annual Earnings	Percent Growth	Annual Openings
96. Loan Counselors	11.9%	$32,160	16%	3,000
97. Loan Officers	11.9%	$41,420	5%	28,000
98. Sales Agents, Financial Services	11.2%	$56,080	22%	55,000
99. Sales Agents, Securities and Commodities	11.2%	$56,080	22%	55,000
100. Compensation, Benefits, and Job Analysis Specialists	10.9%	$41,660	16%	8,000

Best Jobs Overall for College Graduates Age 55 and Over

Job	Percent Age 55 and Over	Annual Earnings	Percent Growth	Annual Openings
1. Computer and Information Systems Managers	14.7%	$78,830	48%	28,000
2. Medical and Health Services Managers	14.6%	$56,370	32%	27,000
3. Management Analysts	22.3%	$55,040	29%	50,000
4. Lawyers	12.6%	$88,280	18%	35,000
5. Internists, General	18.0%	$142,400	18%	27,000
6. Pediatricians, General	18.0%	$125,970	18%	27,000
7. Psychiatrists	18.0%	$118,640	18%	27,000
8. Family and General Practitioners	18.0%	$114,170	18%	27,000
9. Network and Computer Systems Administrators	14.6%	$51,280	82%	18,000
10. Chief Executives	14.7%	$113,810	17%	48,000
11. Government Service Executives	18.5%	$113,810	17%	48,000
12. Private Sector Executives	14.7%	$113,810	17%	48,000
13. Sales Agents, Financial Services	11.2%	$56,080	22%	55,000
14. Sales Agents, Securities and Commodities	11.2%	$56,080	22%	55,000
15. Personal Financial Advisors	12.1%	$55,320	34%	13,000
16. Postsecondary Teachers	19.0%	$46,330	24%	184,000
17. General and Operations Managers	14.6%	$61,160	15%	235,000
18. Education Administrators, Elementary and Secondary School	15.3%	$66,930	13%	35,000
19. Copy Writers	13.6%	$42,270	28%	18,000
20. Creative Writers	13.6%	$42,270	28%	18,000
21. Poets and Lyricists	13.6%	$42,270	28%	18,000
22. Writers and Authors	13.6%	$42,270	28%	18,000
23. Public Relations Specialists	12.9%	$39,580	36%	19,000
24. Construction Managers	14.7%	$58,250	16%	26,000
25. Administrative Services Managers	14.7%	$47,080	20%	31,000

Best-Paying Jobs for College Graduates Age 55 and Over

Job	Percent Age 55 and Over	Annual Earnings
1. Internists, General	18.0%	$142,400
2. Pediatricians, General	18.0%	$125,970
3. Psychiatrists	18.0%	$118,640
4. Family and General Practitioners	18.0%	$114,170
5. Chief Executives	14.7%	$113,810
6. Government Service Executives	18.5%	$113,810
7. Private Sector Executives	14.7%	$113,810
8. Airline Pilots, Copilots, and Flight Engineers	13.6%	$110,940
9. Podiatrists	17.3%	$107,560
10. Lawyers	12.6%	$88,280
11. Judges, Magistrate Judges, and Magistrates	13.8%	$86,760
12. Engineering Managers	14.7%	$84,070
13. Optometrists	17.3%	$82,860
14. Nuclear Engineers	12.1%	$79,360
15. Petroleum Engineers	12.1%	$78,910
16. Computer and Information Systems Managers	14.7%	$78,830
17. Natural Sciences Managers	14.7%	$75,880
18. Aerospace Engineers	12.1%	$67,930
19. Education Administrators, Elementary and Secondary School	15.3%	$66,930
20. Chemical Engineers	12.1%	$65,960
21. Industrial Production Managers	14.7%	$61,660
22. Administrative Law Judges, Adjudicators, and Hearing Officers	13.8%	$61,240
23. General and Operations Managers	14.6%	$61,160
24. Veterinarians	17.3%	$60,910
25. Mining and Geological Engineers, Including Mining Safety Engineers	12.1%	$60,820

Fastest-Growing Jobs for College Graduates Age 55 and Over

Job	Percent Age 55 and Over	Percent Growth
1. Network and Computer Systems Administrators	14.6%	82%
2. Computer and Information Systems Managers	14.7%	48%
3. Physical Therapist Aides	12.2%	46%
4. Physical Therapist Assistants	12.2%	45%
5. Public Relations Specialists	12.9%	36%
6. Personal Financial Advisors	12.1%	34%
7. Medical and Health Services Managers	14.6%	32%
8. Veterinarians	17.3%	32%
9. Gaming Managers	14.6%	30%
10. Technical Writers	13.6%	30%
11. Management Analysts	22.3%	29%
12. Copy Writers	13.6%	28%
13. Creative Writers	13.6%	28%
14. Poets and Lyricists	13.6%	28%
15. Writers and Authors	13.6%	28%
16. Arbitrators, Mediators, and Conciliators	12.0%	27%
17. Directors—Stage, Motion Pictures, Television, and Radio	12.9%	27%
18. Exhibit Designers	13.2%	27%
19. Graphic Designers	13.1%	27%
20. Producers	12.9%	27%
21. Producers and Directors	12.9%	27%
22. Program Directors	12.9%	27%
23. Set and Exhibit Designers	13.2%	27%
24. Set Designers	13.2%	27%
25. Film and Video Editors	12.9%	26%

Jobs with the Most Openings for College Graduates Age 55 and Over

Job	Percent Age 55 and Over	Annual Openings
1. General and Operations Managers	14.6%	235,000
2. Postsecondary Teachers	19.0%	184,000
3. Sales Agents, Financial Services	11.2%	55,000
4. Sales Agents, Securities and Commodities	11.2%	55,000
5. Management Analysts	22.3%	50,000
6. Chief Executives	14.7%	48,000
7. Government Service Executives	18.5%	48,000
8. Private Sector Executives	14.7%	48,000
9. Insurance Sales Agents	18.7%	43,000
10. Education Administrators, Elementary and Secondary School	15.3%	35,000
11. Education Administrators, Preschool and Child Care Center/Program	15.3%	35,000
12. Lawyers	12.6%	35,000
13. Recreation Workers	17.3%	32,000
14. Administrative Services Managers	14.7%	31,000
15. Computer and Information Systems Managers	14.7%	28,000
16. Graphic Designers	13.1%	28,000
17. Loan Officers	11.9%	28,000
18. Family and General Practitioners	18.0%	27,000
19. Internists, General	18.0%	27,000
20. Medical and Health Services Managers	14.6%	27,000
21. Pediatricians, General	18.0%	27,000
22. Psychiatrists	18.0%	27,000
23. Construction Managers	14.7%	26,000
24. Engineering Managers	14.7%	24,000
25. Property, Real Estate, and Community Association Managers	27.0%	24,000

Best Jobs for College Graduates with a High Percentage of Part-Time Workers

Technically, these lists don't show jobs with a high percentage of part-time workers who are college graduates. The data could only show us jobs typically requiring a college degree that had a higher percentage of part-time workers.

Look over the list of 100 jobs with high percentages of part-time college grads and you will find some interesting things. For example, the top four all involve music, which leads one to think that many people working in the music business do so less than full time. In some cases, people work part time in these jobs because they want the freedom of time this arrangement can provide, but others may do so because they can't find full-time employment in these areas. These folks may work in other full- or part-time jobs to make ends meet. If you want to work part time now or in the future, these lists will help you identify jobs that are more likely to provide that opportunity. If you want full-time work, the lists may also help you identify jobs that may make such opportunities more difficult to find. In either case, it's good information to know in advance.

The 100 Jobs for College Graduates with the Highest Percentage of Part-Time Workers

Job	Percent Part-Time Workers	Annual Earnings	Percent Growth	Annual Openings
1. Composers	53.5%	$31,510	13%	9,000
2. Music Arrangers and Orchestrators	53.5%	$31,510	13%	9,000
3. Music Directors	53.5%	$31,510	13%	9,000
4. Music Directors and Composers	53.5%	$31,510	13%	9,000
5. Adult Literacy, Remedial Education, and GED Teachers and Instructors	42.5%	$33,540	19%	12,000
6. Vocational Education Teachers, Secondary School	42.5%	$42,080	13%	7,000
7. Vocational Education Teachers, Middle School	42.5%	$39,330	13%	2,000
8. Farm and Home Management Advisors	42.5%	$36,290	6%	2,000
9. Health Educators	39.7%	$33,860	24%	7,000
10. Physical Therapist Assistants	34.5%	$33,870	45%	9,000
11. Physical Therapist Aides	34.5%	$19,670	46%	7,000

(continued)

(continued)

The 100 Jobs for College Graduates with the Highest Percentage of Part-Time Workers

Job	Percent Part-Time Workers	Annual Earnings	Percent Growth	Annual Openings
12. Preschool Teachers, Except Special Education	32.4%	$17,810	20%	55,000
13. Kindergarten Teachers, Except Special Education	32.4%	$37,610	14%	23,000
14. Postsecondary Teachers	32.3%	$46,330	24%	184,000
15. Dietitians and Nutritionists	29.1%	$38,450	15%	5,000
16. Registered Nurses	26.3%	$44,840	26%	140,000
17. Public Relations Specialists	25.3%	$39,580	36%	19,000
18. Directors—Stage, Motion Pictures, Television, and Radio	25.3%	$41,030	27%	11,000
19. Producers	25.3%	$41,030	27%	11,000
20. Producers and Directors	25.3%	$41,030	27%	11,000
21. Program Directors	25.3%	$41,030	27%	11,000
22. Film and Video Editors	25.3%	$34,160	26%	2,000
23. Athletic Trainers	25.3%	$32,080	18%	2,000
24. Broadcast News Analysts	25.3%	$29,110	3%	9,000
25. Occupational Therapist Assistants	24.9%	$34,340	40%	3,000
26. Pharmacists	24.6%	$70,950	24%	20,000
27. Physician Assistants	24.6%	$61,910	54%	5,000
28. Graphic Designers	24.0%	$34,570	27%	28,000
29. Multi-Media Artists and Animators	24.0%	$41,130	22%	8,000
30. Industrial-Organizational Psychologists	23.4%	$66,880	18%	18,000
31. Clinical Psychologists	23.4%	$48,320	18%	18,000
32. Clinical, Counseling, and School Psychologists	23.4%	$48,320	18%	18,000
33. Counseling Psychologists	23.4%	$48,320	18%	18,000
34. Educational Psychologists	23.4%	$48,320	18%	18,000
35. Airline Pilots, Copilots, and Flight Engineers	23.3%	$110,940	6%	5,000
36. Dental Hygienists	22.9%	$51,330	37%	5,000
37. Medical Records and Health Information Technicians	22.9%	$22,750	49%	14,000

The 100 Jobs for College Graduates with the Highest Percentage of Part-Time Workers

Job	Percent Part-Time Workers	Annual Earnings	Percent Growth	Annual Openings
38. Cardiovascular Technologists and Technicians	22.9%	$33,350	35%	3,000
39. Librarians	22.4%	$41,700	7%	6,000
40. Diagnostic Medical Sonographers	22.3%	$44,820	26%	3,000
41. Occupational Health and Safety Specialists	22.3%	$42,750	15%	4,000
42. Occupational Health and Safety Technicians	22.3%	$42,750	15%	4,000
43. Orthotists and Prosthetists	22.3%	$45,740	17%	1,000
44. Property, Real Estate, and Community Association Managers	21.9%	$36,020	23%	24,000
45. Physical Therapists	20.8%	$54,810	33%	6,000
46. Occupational Therapists	20.8%	$49,450	34%	4,000
47. Speech-Language Pathologists	20.8%	$46,640	39%	4,000
48. Audiologists	20.8%	$44,830	45%	1,000
49. Respiratory Therapists	20.8%	$37,680	35%	4,000
50. Substance Abuse and Behavioral Disorder Counselors	20.8%	$28,510	35%	7,000
51. Recreational Therapists	20.8%	$28,650	9%	1,000
52. Art Directors	20.0%	$56,880	21%	6,000
53. Commercial and Industrial Designers	20.0%	$48,780	24%	7,000
54. Fashion Designers	20.0%	$48,530	20%	2,000
55. Interior Designers	20.0%	$36,540	17%	7,000
56. Exhibit Designers	20.0%	$31,440	27%	2,000
57. Set and Exhibit Designers	20.0%	$31,440	27%	2,000
58. Set Designers	20.0%	$31,440	27%	2,000
59. Management Analysts	19.5%	$55,040	29%	50,000
60. Medical and Clinical Laboratory Technologists	19.5%	$40,510	17%	19,000
61. Medical and Clinical Laboratory Technicians	19.5%	$27,540	19%	19,000
62. Copy Writers	18.5%	$42,270	28%	18,000
63. Creative Writers	18.5%	$42,270	28%	18,000
64. Poets and Lyricists	18.5%	$42,270	28%	18,000

(continued)

(continued)

The 100 Jobs for College Graduates with the Highest Percentage of Part-Time Workers

Job	Percent Part-Time Workers	Annual Earnings	Percent Growth	Annual Openings
65. Writers and Authors	18.5%	$42,270	28%	18,000
66. Technical Writers	18.5%	$47,790	30%	5,000
67. Editors	18.5%	$39,370	23%	14,000
68. Political Scientists	18.1%	$81,040	17%	2,000
69. Urban and Regional Planners	18.1%	$46,500	16%	3,000
70. Historians	18.1%	$39,860	17%	2,000
71. Anthropologists	18.1%	$36,040	17%	2,000
72. Anthropologists and Archeologists	18.1%	$36,040	17%	2,000
73. Archeologists	18.1%	$36,040	17%	2,000
74. Educational, Vocational, and School Counselors	18.0%	$42,110	25%	22,000
75. Radiologic Technicians	17.5%	$36,000	23%	13,000
76. Radiologic Technologists	17.5%	$36,000	23%	13,000
77. Radiologic Technologists and Technicians	17.5%	$36,000	23%	13,000
78. Radiation Therapists	17.5%	$47,470	23%	1,000
79. Nuclear Medicine Technologists	17.5%	$44,130	22%	1,000
80. Forest and Conservation Technicians	17.5%	$29,580	3%	2,000
81. Wholesale and Retail Buyers, Except Farm Products	16.5%	$37,200	−9%	18,000
82. Recreation Workers	14.0%	$17,130	20%	32,000
83. Directors, Religious Activities and Education	14.0%	$27,000	16%	23,000
84. Special Education Teachers, Preschool, Kindergarten, and Elementary School	12.9%	$40,880	37%	15,000
85. Special Education Teachers, Secondary School	12.9%	$41,290	25%	8,000
86. Special Education Teachers, Middle School	12.9%	$38,600	24%	6,000
87. Paralegals and Legal Assistants	12.5%	$35,360	33%	23,000
88. Child, Family, and School Social Workers	11.9%	$31,470	27%	35,000

The 100 Jobs for College Graduates with the Highest Percentage of Part-Time Workers

Job	Percent Part-Time Workers	Annual Earnings	Percent Growth	Annual Openings
89. Medical and Public Health Social Workers	11.9%	$34,790	32%	13,000
90. Probation Officers and Correctional Treatment Specialists	11.9%	$38,150	24%	14,000
91. Mental Health and Substance Abuse Social Workers	11.9%	$30,170	39%	10,000
92. Elementary School Teachers, Except Special Education	11.7%	$39,700	13%	144,000
93. Nuclear Equipment Operation Technicians	11.7%	$59,160	21% fewer than 500	
94. Nuclear Monitoring Technicians	11.7%	$59,160	21% fewer than 500	
95. Veterinary Technologists and Technicians	11.7%	$21,640	39%	6,000
96. Biological Technicians	11.7%	$31,540	26%	7,000
97. Chemical Technicians	11.7%	$35,450	15%	13,000
98. Environmental Science and Protection Technicians, Including Health	11.7%	$33,830	24%	3,000
99. Agricultural Technicians	11.7%	$27,080	15%	3,000
100. Food Science Technicians	11.7%	$27,080	15%	3,000

Best Overall Part-Time Jobs for College Graduates

Job	Percent Part-Time Workers	Annual Earnings	Percent Growth	Annual Openings
1. Pharmacists	24.6%	$70,950	24%	20,000
2. Management Analysts	19.5%	$55,040	29%	50,000
3. Registered Nurses	26.3%	$44,840	26%	140,000
4. Physician Assistants	24.6%	$61,910	54%	5,000
5. Postsecondary Teachers	32.3%	$46,330	24%	184,000
6. Industrial-Organizational Psychologists	23.4%	$66,880	18%	18,000
7. Public Relations Specialists	25.3%	$39,580	36%	19,000
8. Physical Therapists	20.8%	$54,810	33%	6,000
9. Dental Hygienists	22.9%	$51,330	37%	5,000
10. Copy Writers	18.5%	$42,270	28%	18,000
11. Creative Writers	18.5%	$42,270	28%	18,000
12. Poets and Lyricists	18.5%	$42,270	28%	18,000
13. Writers and Authors	18.5%	$42,270	28%	18,000
14. Directors—Stage, Motion Pictures, Television, and Radio	25.3%	$41,030	27%	11,000
15. Producers	25.3%	$41,030	27%	11,000
16. Producers and Directors	25.3%	$41,030	27%	11,000
17. Program Directors	25.3%	$41,030	27%	11,000
18. Graphic Designers	24.0%	$34,570	27%	28,000
19. Clinical Psychologists	23.4%	$48,320	18%	18,000
20. Clinical, Counseling, and School Psychologists	23.4%	$48,320	18%	18,000
21. Counseling Psychologists	23.4%	$48,320	18%	18,000
22. Educational Psychologists	23.4%	$48,320	18%	18,000
23. Occupational Therapists	20.8%	$49,450	34%	4,000
24. Speech-Language Pathologists	20.8%	$46,640	39%	4,000
25. Educational, Vocational, and School Counselors	18.0%	$42,110	25%	22,000

Best-Paying Part-Time Jobs for College Graduates

Job	Percent Part-Time Workers	Annual Earnings
1. Airline Pilots, Copilots, and Flight Engineers	23.3%	$110,940
2. Political Scientists	18.1%	$81,040
3. Pharmacists	24.6%	$70,950
4. Industrial-Organizational Psychologists	23.4%	$66,880
5. Physician Assistants	24.6%	$61,910
6. Nuclear Equipment Operation Technicians	11.7%	$59,160
7. Nuclear Monitoring Technicians	11.7%	$59,160
8. Art Directors	20.0%	$56,880
9. Management Analysts	19.5%	$55,040
10. Physical Therapists	20.8%	$54,810
11. Dental Hygienists	22.9%	$51,330
12. Occupational Therapists	20.8%	$49,450
13. Commercial and Industrial Designers	20.0%	$48,780
14. Fashion Designers	20.0%	$48,530
15. Clinical Psychologists	23.4%	$48,320
16. Clinical, Counseling, and School Psychologists	23.4%	$48,320
17. Counseling Psychologists	23.4%	$48,320
18. Educational Psychologists	23.4%	$48,320
19. Technical Writers	18.5%	$47,790
20. Radiation Therapists	17.5%	$47,470
21. Speech-Language Pathologists	20.8%	$46,640
22. Urban and Regional Planners	18.1%	$46,500
23. Postsecondary Teachers	32.3%	$46,330
24. Orthotists and Prosthetists	22.3%	$45,740
25. Registered Nurses	26.3%	$44,840

Fastest-Growing Part-Time Jobs for College Graduates

Job	Percent Part-Time Workers	Percent Growth
1. Physician Assistants	24.6%	54%
2. Medical Records and Health Information Technicians	22.9%	49%
3. Physical Therapist Aides	34.5%	46%
4. Audiologists	20.8%	45%
5. Physical Therapist Assistants	34.5%	45%
6. Occupational Therapist Assistants	24.9%	40%
7. Speech-Language Pathologists	20.8%	39%
8. Mental Health and Substance Abuse Social Workers	11.9%	39%
9. Veterinary Technologists and Technicians	11.7%	39%
10. Dental Hygienists	22.9%	37%
11. Special Education Teachers, Preschool, Kindergarten, and Elementary School	12.9%	37%
12. Public Relations Specialists	25.3%	36%
13. Respiratory Therapists	20.8%	35%
14. Cardiovascular Technologists and Technicians	22.9%	35%
15. Substance Abuse and Behavioral Disorder Counselors	20.8%	35%
16. Occupational Therapists	20.8%	34%
17. Physical Therapists	20.8%	33%
18. Paralegals and Legal Assistants	12.5%	33%
19. Medical and Public Health Social Workers	11.9%	32%
20. Technical Writers	18.5%	30%
21. Management Analysts	19.5%	29%
22. Copy Writers	18.5%	28%
23. Creative Writers	18.5%	28%
24. Poets and Lyricists	18.5%	28%
25. Writers and Authors	18.5%	28%

Part-Time Jobs with the Most Openings for College Graduates

Job	Percent Part-Time Workers	Annual Openings
1. Postsecondary Teachers	32.3%	184,000
2. Elementary School Teachers, Except Special Education	11.7%	144,000
3. Registered Nurses	26.3%	140,000
4. Preschool Teachers, Except Special Education	32.4%	55,000
5. Management Analysts	19.5%	50,000
6. Child, Family, and School Social Workers	11.9%	35,000
7. Recreation Workers	14.0%	32,000
8. Graphic Designers	24.0%	28,000
9. Property, Real Estate, and Community Association Managers	21.9%	24,000
10. Paralegals and Legal Assistants	12.5%	23,000
11. Directors, Religious Activities and Education	14.0%	23,000
12. Kindergarten Teachers, Except Special Education	32.4%	23,000
13. Educational, Vocational, and School Counselors	18.0%	22,000
14. Pharmacists	24.6%	20,000
15. Public Relations Specialists	25.3%	19,000
16. Medical and Clinical Laboratory Technicians	19.5%	19,000
17. Medical and Clinical Laboratory Technologists	19.5%	19,000
18. Copy Writers	18.5%	18,000
19. Creative Writers	18.5%	18,000
20. Poets and Lyricists	18.5%	18,000
21. Writers and Authors	18.5%	18,000
22. Industrial-Organizational Psychologists	23.4%	18,000
23. Clinical Psychologists	23.4%	18,000
24. Clinical, Counseling, and School Psychologists	23.4%	18,000
25. Counseling Psychologists	23.4%	18,000

Best Jobs with a High Percentage of Self-Employed College Graduates

More than 10 percent of the workforce is self-employed. Although you may think of the self-employed as having similar jobs, they actually work in an enormous range of situations, fields, and work environments that you may not have considered.

Among the self-employed are people who own small or large businesses; professionals such as lawyers, psychologists, and medical doctors; part-time workers; people working on a contract basis for one or more employers; people running home consulting or other businesses; and people in other situations. They may go to the same office every day, like an attorney might; visit multiple employers during the course of a week; or do most of their work from home. Some work part time, others full time, some as a way to have fun, some so they can spend time with their kids or go to school.

The point is that there is an enormous range of situations, and one of them could make sense for you now or in the future. Although people work part time in almost all jobs, these lists focus on the ones with the highest percentage of college grads working in them part time. So browse these lists if they interest you, and think creatively about the opportunities they might offer.

The 100 Jobs with the Highest Percentage of Self-Employed College Graduates

Job	Percent Self-Employed Workers	Annual Earnings	Percent Growth	Annual Openings
1. Graphic Designers	60.9%	$34,570	27%	28,000
2. Multi-Media Artists and Animators	60.9%	$41,130	22%	8,000
3. Medical and Health Services Managers	49.4%	$56,370	32%	27,000
4. Network and Computer Systems Administrators	49.4%	$51,280	82%	18,000
5. General and Operations Managers	49.4%	$61,160	15%	235,000
6. Social and Community Service Managers	49.4%	$39,130	25%	13,000
7. Gaming Managers	49.4%	$53,380	30%	fewer than 500
8. Adult Literacy, Remedial Education, and GED Teachers and Instructors	48.9%	$33,540	19%	12,000
9. Podiatrists	46.6%	$107,560	14%	1,000
10. Management Analysts	46.4%	$55,040	29%	50,000
11. Interior Designers	46.3%	$36,540	17%	7,000

The 100 Jobs with the Highest Percentage of Self-Employed College Graduates

Job	Percent Self-Employed Workers	Annual Earnings	Percent Growth	Annual Openings
12. Industrial-Organizational Psychologists	43.7%	$66,880	18%	18,000
13. Clinical Psychologists	43.7%	$48,320	18%	18,000
14. Clinical, Counseling, and School Psychologists	43.7%	$48,320	18%	18,000
15. Counseling Psychologists	43.7%	$48,320	18%	18,000
16. Educational Psychologists	43.7%	$48,320	18%	18,000
17. Property, Real Estate, and Community Association Managers	40.2%	$36,020	23%	24,000
18. Veterinarians	39.6%	$60,910	32%	2,000
19. Optometrists	37.5%	$82,860	19%	1,000
20. Lawyers	36.0%	$88,280	18%	35,000
21. Art Directors	31.9%	$56,880	21%	6,000
22. Commercial and Industrial Designers	31.9%	$48,780	24%	7,000
23. Fashion Designers	31.9%	$48,530	20%	2,000
24. Exhibit Designers	31.9%	$31,440	27%	2,000
25. Set and Exhibit Designers	31.9%	$31,440	27%	2,000
26. Set Designers	31.9%	$31,440	27%	2,000
27. Athletic Trainers	31.4%	$32,080	18%	2,000
28. Copy Writers	31.2%	$42,270	28%	18,000
29. Creative Writers	31.2%	$42,270	28%	18,000
30. Poets and Lyricists	31.2%	$42,270	28%	18,000
31. Writers and Authors	31.2%	$42,270	28%	18,000
32. Technical Writers	31.2%	$47,790	30%	5,000
33. Editors	31.2%	$39,370	23%	14,000
34. Architects, Except Landscape and Naval	30.8%	$52,510	18%	4,000
35. Insurance Sales Agents	30.1%	$38,750	3%	43,000
36. Composers	25.8%	$31,510	13%	9,000
37. Music Arrangers and Orchestrators	25.8%	$31,510	13%	9,000
38. Music Directors	25.8%	$31,510	13%	9,000
39. Music Directors and Composers	25.8%	$31,510	13%	9,000

(continued)

The 100 Jobs with the Highest Percentage of Self-Employed College Graduates

Job	Percent Self-Employed Workers	Annual Earnings	Percent Growth	Annual Openings
40. Directors—Stage, Motion Pictures, Television, and Radio	23.7%	$41,030	27%	11,000
41. Producers	23.7%	$41,030	27%	11,000
42. Producers and Directors	23.7%	$41,030	27%	11,000
43. Program Directors	23.7%	$41,030	27%	11,000
44. Film and Video Editors	23.7%	$34,160	26%	2,000
45. Sales Agents, Financial Services	22.4%	$56,080	22%	55,000
46. Sales Agents, Securities and Commodities	22.4%	$56,080	22%	55,000
47. Landscape Architects	21.6%	$43,540	31%	1,000
48. Internists, General	20.4%	$142,400	18%	27,000
49. Pediatricians, General	20.4%	$125,970	18%	27,000
50. Psychiatrists	20.4%	$118,640	18%	27,000
51. Family and General Practitioners	20.4%	$114,170	18%	27,000
52. Market Research Analysts	18.9%	$51,190	24%	13,000
53. Economists	18.9%	$64,830	18%	3,000
54. Hydrologists	15.1%	$55,410	26%	1,000
55. Geologists	15.1%	$56,230	18%	2,000
56. Geoscientists, Except Hydrologists and Geographers	15.1%	$56,230	18%	2,000
57. Education Administrators, Elementary and Secondary School	13.8%	$66,930	13%	35,000
58. Instructional Coordinators	13.8%	$44,230	25%	15,000
59. Education Administrators, Preschool and Child Care Center/Program	13.8%	$30,420	13%	35,000
60. Dietitians and Nutritionists	13.2%	$38,450	15%	5,000
61. Forest and Conservation Technicians	12.0%	$29,580	3%	2,000
62. Actuaries	11.6%	$66,590	5%	1,000
63. Funeral Directors	11.6%	$41,110	3%	3,000
64. Accountants	10.6%	$43,500	18%	100,000
65. Accountants and Auditors	10.6%	$43,500	18%	100,000
66. Auditors	10.6%	$43,500	18%	100,000
67. Speech-Language Pathologists	10.5%	$46,640	39%	4,000
68. Audiologists	10.5%	$44,830	45%	1,000
69. Wholesale and Retail Buyers, Except Farm Products	10.5%	$37,200	−9%	18,000

The 100 Jobs with the Highest Percentage of Self-Employed College Graduates

Job	Percent Self-Employed Workers	Annual Earnings	Percent Growth	Annual Openings
70. Recreational Therapists	9.8%	$28,650	9%	1,000
71. Substance Abuse and Behavioral Disorder Counselors	8.4%	$28,510	35%	7,000
72. Pilots, Ship	7.9%	$47,510	3%	2,000
73. Computer Systems Analysts	7.7%	$59,330	60%	34,000
74. Environmental Scientists and Specialists, Including Health	7.6%	$44,180	22%	4,000
75. Materials Scientists	7.6%	$60,620	20%	1,000
76. Geographers	7.6%	$46,690	17%	2,000
77. Surveyors	7.3%	$36,700	8%	7,000
78. Physical Therapists	5.9%	$54,810	33%	6,000
79. Public Relations Specialists	5.6%	$39,580	36%	19,000
80. Occupational Therapists	5.6%	$49,450	34%	4,000
81. Personal Financial Advisors	5.4%	$55,320	34%	13,000
82. Meeting and Convention Planners	5.4%	$35,540	23%	3,000
83. Materials Engineers	5.4%	$59,100	5%	2,000
84. Political Scientists	5.2%	$81,040	17%	2,000
85. Historians	5.2%	$39,860	17%	2,000
86. Anthropologists	5.2%	$36,040	17%	2,000
87. Anthropologists and Archeologists	5.2%	$36,040	17%	2,000
88. Archeologists	5.2%	$36,040	17%	2,000
89. Physicists	5.0%	$83,310	10%	1,000
90. Astronomers	5.0%	$74,510	10%	1,000
91. Biochemists	4.9%	$54,230	21%	5,000
92. Biochemists and Biophysicists	4.9%	$54,230	21%	5,000
93. Biophysicists	4.9%	$54,230	21%	5,000
94. Biologists	4.9%	$49,033	21%	5,000
95. Microbiologists	4.9%	$48,890	21%	5,000
96. Zoologists and Wildlife Biologists	4.9%	$43,980	21%	5,000
97. Civil Engineers	4.9%	$55,740	10%	4,000
98. Computer Programmers	4.8%	$57,590	16%	36,000
99. Pharmacists	4.2%	$70,950	24%	20,000
100. Computer Software Engineers, Applications	4.1%	$67,670	100%	28,000

Best Jobs Overall for Self-Employed College Graduates

Job	Percent Self-Employed Workers	Annual Earnings	Percent Growth	Annual Openings
1. Medical and Health Services Managers	49.4%	$56,370	32%	27,000
2. Management Analysts	46.4%	$55,040	29%	50,000
3. Computer Systems Analysts	7.7%	$59,330	60%	34,000
4. Computer Software Engineers, Applications	4.1%	$67,670	100%	28,000
5. Network and Computer Systems Administrators	49.4%	$51,280	82%	18,000
6. Lawyers	36.0%	$88,280	18%	35,000
7. Internists, General	20.4%	$142,400	18%	27,000
8. Pediatricians, General	20.4%	$125,970	18%	27,000
9. Psychiatrists	20.4%	$118,640	18%	27,000
10. Family and General Practitioners	20.4%	$114,170	18%	27,000
11. General and Operations Managers	49.4%	$61,160	15%	235,000
12. Sales Agents, Financial Services	22.4%	$56,080	22%	55,000
13. Sales Agents, Securities and Commodities	22.4%	$56,080	22%	55,000
14. Industrial-Organizational Psychologists	43.7%	$66,880	18%	18,000
15. Pharmacists	4.2%	$70,950	24%	20,000
16. Personal Financial Advisors	5.4%	$55,320	34%	13,000
17. Veterinarians	39.6%	$60,910	32%	2,000
18. Copy Writers	31.2%	$42,270	28%	18,000
19. Creative Writers	31.2%	$42,270	28%	18,000
20. Poets and Lyricists	31.2%	$42,270	28%	18,000
21. Writers and Authors	31.2%	$42,270	28%	18,000
22. Education Administrators, Elementary and Secondary School	13.8%	$66,930	13%	35,000
23. Graphic Designers	60.9%	$34,570	27%	28,000
24. Clinical Psychologists	43.7%	$48,320	18%	18,000
25. Clinical, Counseling, and School Psychologists	43.7%	$48,320	18%	18,000

Best-Paying Jobs for Self-Employed College Graduates

Job	Percent Self-Employed Workers	Annual Earnings
1. Internists, General	20.4%	$142,400
2. Pediatricians, General	20.4%	$125,970
3. Psychiatrists	20.4%	$118,640
4. Family and General Practitioners	20.4%	$114,170
5. Podiatrists	46.6%	$107,560
6. Lawyers	36.0%	$88,280
7. Physicists	5.0%	$83,310
8. Optometrists	37.5%	$82,860
9. Political Scientists	5.2%	$81,040
10. Astronomers	5.0%	$74,510
11. Pharmacists	4.2%	$70,950
12. Computer Software Engineers, Applications	4.1%	$67,670
13. Education Administrators, Elementary and Secondary School	13.8%	$66,930
14. Industrial-Organizational Psychologists	43.7%	$66,880
15. Actuaries	11.6%	$66,590
16. Economists	18.9%	$64,830
17. General and Operations Managers	49.4%	$61,160
18. Veterinarians	39.6%	$60,910
19. Materials Scientists	7.6%	$60,620
20. Computer Systems Analysts	7.7%	$59,330
21. Materials Engineers	5.4%	$59,100
22. Computer Programmers	4.8%	$57,590
23. Art Directors	31.9%	$56,880
24. Medical and Health Services Managers	49.4%	$56,370
25. Geologists	15.1%	$56,230

Fastest-Growing Jobs for Self-Employed College Graduates

Job	Percent Self-Employed Workers	Percent Growth
1. Computer Software Engineers, Applications	4.1%	100%
2. Network and Computer Systems Administrators	49.4%	82%
3. Computer Systems Analysts	7.7%	60%
4. Audiologists	10.5%	45%
5. Speech-Language Pathologists	10.5%	39%
6. Public Relations Specialists	5.6%	36%
7. Substance Abuse and Behavioral Disorder Counselors	8.4%	35%
8. Personal Financial Advisors	5.4%	34%
9. Occupational Therapists	5.6%	34%
10. Physical Therapists	5.9%	33%
11. Veterinarians	39.6%	32%
12. Medical and Health Services Managers	49.4%	32%
13. Landscape Architects	21.6%	31%
14. Gaming Managers	49.4%	30%
15. Technical Writers	31.2%	30%
16. Management Analysts	46.4%	29%
17. Copy Writers	31.2%	28%
18. Creative Writers	31.2%	28%
19. Poets and Lyricists	31.2%	28%
20. Writers and Authors	31.2%	28%
21. Directors—Stage, Motion Pictures, Television, and Radio	23.7%	27%
22. Producers	23.7%	27%
23. Producers and Directors	23.7%	27%
24. Program Directors	23.7%	27%
25. Graphic Designers	60.9%	27%

Jobs with the Most Openings for Self-Employed College Graduates

Job	Percent Self-Employed Workers	Annual Openings
1. General and Operations Managers	49.4%	235,000
2. Accountants	10.6%	100,000
3. Accountants and Auditors	10.6%	100,000
4. Auditors	10.6%	100,000
5. Sales Agents, Financial Services	22.4%	55,000
6. Sales Agents, Securities and Commodities	22.4%	55,000
7. Management Analysts	46.4%	50,000
8. Insurance Sales Agents	30.1%	43,000
9. Computer Programmers	4.8%	36,000
10. Lawyers	36.0%	35,000
11. Education Administrators, Elementary and Secondary School	13.8%	35,000
12. Education Administrators, Preschool and Child Care Center/Program	13.8%	35,000
13. Computer Systems Analysts	7.7%	34,000
14. Computer Software Engineers, Applications	4.1%	28,000
15. Graphic Designers	60.9%	28,000
16. Medical and Health Services Managers	49.4%	27,000
17. Internists, General	20.4%	27,000
18. Pediatricians, General	20.4%	27,000
19. Psychiatrists	20.4%	27,000
20. Family and General Practitioners	20.4%	27,000
21. Property, Real Estate, and Community Association Managers	40.2%	24,000
22. Pharmacists	4.2%	20,000
23. Public Relations Specialists	5.6%	19,000
24. Network and Computer Systems Administrators	49.4%	18,000
25. Copy Writers	31.2%	18,000

Best Jobs with a High Percentage of Women College Graduates

These are our most controversial lists, and we knew we would create some controversy when we first included the best jobs lists with high percentages of men and women. But these lists are not meant to restrict women or men from considering job options— our reason for including these lists is exactly the opposite. We hope the lists help people see possibilities that they might not otherwise have considered.

The fact is that jobs with high percentages of women or high percentages of men offer good opportunities for both men and women if they want to do one of these jobs. So we suggest that women browse the lists of jobs that employ high percentages of men and that men browse the lists of jobs with high percentages of women. There are jobs among both lists that pay well, and women or men who are interested in them and who have or can obtain the necessary education and training should consider them.

An interesting and unfortunate tidbit to bring up at your next party is that the average earnings for the 100 jobs with the highest percentage of women college grads is $41,627, compared to average earnings of $59,193 for the 100 jobs with the highest percentage of men college grads.

The 100 Jobs with the Highest Percentage of Women College Graduates

Job	Percent Women	Annual Earnings	Percent Growth	Annual Openings
1. Kindergarten Teachers, Except Special Education	98.0%	$37,610	14%	23,000
2. Preschool Teachers, Except Special Education	98.0%	$17,810	20%	55,000
3. Registered Nurses	93.8%	$44,840	26%	140,000
4. Dietitians and Nutritionists	91.9%	$38,450	15%	5,000
5. Cost Estimators	86.5%	$45,800	16%	28,000
6. Pharmacists	86.1%	$70,950	24%	20,000
7. Physician Assistants	86.1%	$61,910	54%	5,000
8. Elementary School Teachers, Except Special Education	85.5%	$39,700	13%	144,000
9. Librarians	83.7%	$41,700	7%	6,000
10. Special Education Teachers, Middle School	83.7%	$38,600	24%	6,000

The 100 Jobs with the Highest Percentage of Women College Graduates

Job	Percent Women	Annual Earnings	Percent Growth	Annual Openings
11. Special Education Teachers, Preschool, Kindergarten, and Elementary School	83.7%	$40,880	37%	15,000
12. Special Education Teachers, Secondary School	83.7%	$41,290	25%	8,000
13. Cardiovascular Technologists and Technicians	81.5%	$33,350	35%	3,000
14. Dental Hygienists	81.5%	$51,330	37%	5,000
15. Medical Records and Health Information Technicians	81.5%	$22,750	49%	14,000
16. Occupational Therapist Assistants	81.0%	$34,340	40%	3,000
17. Paralegals and Legal Assistants	79.8%	$35,360	33%	23,000
18. Physical Therapist Aides	78.5%	$19,670	46%	7,000
19. Physical Therapist Assistants	78.5%	$33,870	45%	9,000
20. Diagnostic Medical Sonographers	77.7%	$44,820	26%	3,000
21. Occupational Health and Safety Technicians	77.7%	$42,750	15%	4,000
22. Occupational Health and Safety Specialists	77.7%	$42,750	15%	4,000
23. Orthotists and Prosthetists	77.7%	$45,740	17%	1,000
24. Medical and Clinical Laboratory Technicians	76.8%	$27,540	19%	19,000
25. Medical and Clinical Laboratory Technologists	76.8%	$40,510	17%	19,000
26. Audiologists	74.2%	$44,830	45%	1,000
27. Occupational Therapists	74.2%	$49,450	34%	4,000
28. Physical Therapists	74.2%	$54,810	33%	6,000
29. Recreational Therapists	74.2%	$28,650	9%	1,000
30. Respiratory Therapists	74.2%	$37,680	35%	4,000
31. Speech-Language Pathologists	74.2%	$46,640	39%	4,000
32. Substance Abuse and Behavioral Disorder Counselors	74.2%	$28,510	35%	7,000
33. Nuclear Medicine Technologists	74.0%	$44,130	22%	1,000
34. Radiation Therapists	74.0%	$47,470	23%	1,000
35. Radiologic Technicians	74.0%	$36,000	23%	13,000

(continued)

(continued)

The 100 Jobs with the Highest Percentage of Women College Graduates

Job	Percent Women	Annual Earnings	Percent Growth	Annual Openings
36. Radiologic Technologists and Technicians	74.0%	$36,000	23%	13,000
37. Radiologic Technologists	74.0%	$36,000	23%	13,000
38. Child, Family, and School Social Workers	69.3%	$31,470	27%	35,000
39. Medical and Public Health Social Workers	69.3%	$34,790	32%	13,000
40. Mental Health and Substance Abuse Social Workers	69.3%	$30,170	39%	10,000
41. Probation Officers and Correctional Treatment Specialists	69.3%	$38,150	24%	14,000
42. Educational, Vocational, and School Counselors	67.8%	$42,110	25%	22,000
43. Electro-Mechanical Technicians	65.1%	$36,150	14%	4,000
44. Compensation, Benefits, and Job Analysis Specialists	64.9%	$41,660	16%	8,000
45. Employment, Recruitment, and Placement Specialists	64.9%	$36,480	18%	19,000
46. Employment Interviewers, Private or Public Employment Service	64.9%	$36,480	18%	19,000
47. Personnel Recruiters	64.9%	$36,480	18%	19,000
48. Training and Development Specialists	64.9%	$40,830	19%	20,000
49. Adult Literacy, Remedial Education, and GED Teachers and Instructors	62.8%	$33,540	19%	12,000
50. Farm and Home Management Advisors	62.8%	$36,290	6%	2,000
51. Vocational Education Teachers, Middle School	62.8%	$39,330	13%	2,000
52. Vocational Education Teachers, Secondary School	62.8%	$42,080	13%	7,000
53. Education Administrators, Elementary and Secondary School	62.0%	$66,930	13%	35,000

The 100 Jobs with the Highest Percentage of Women College Graduates

Job	Percent Women	Annual Earnings	Percent Growth	Annual Openings
54. Education Administrators, Preschool and Child Care Center/Program	62.0%	$30,420	13%	35,000
55. Instructional Coordinators	62.0%	$44,230	25%	15,000
56. Arbitrators, Mediators, and Conciliators	61.9%	$43,060	27%	fewer than 500
57. Human Resources Managers	61.9%	$59,000	13%	14,000
58. Clinical Psychologists	58.8%	$48,320	18%	18,000
59. Clinical, Counseling, and School Psychologists	58.8%	$48,320	18%	18,000
60. Counseling Psychologists	58.8%	$48,320	18%	18,000
61. Educational Psychologists	58.8%	$48,320	18%	18,000
62. Industrial-Organizational Psychologists	58.8%	$66,880	18%	18,000
63. Health Educators	57.6%	$33,860	24%	7,000
64. Middle School Teachers, Except Special and Vocational Education	55.4%	$39,750	10%	54,000
65. Secondary School Teachers, Except Special and Vocational Education	55.4%	$40,870	19%	60,000
66. Art Directors	55.3%	$56,880	21%	6,000
67. Commercial and Industrial Designers	55.3%	$48,780	24%	7,000
68. Exhibit Designers	55.3%	$31,440	27%	2,000
69. Fashion Designers	55.3%	$48,530	20%	2,000
70. Interior Designers	55.3%	$36,540	17%	7,000
71. Set Designers	55.3%	$31,440	27%	2,000
72. Set and Exhibit Designers	55.3%	$31,440	27%	2,000
73. Wholesale and Retail Buyers, Except Farm Products	54.9%	$37,200	–9%	18,000
74. Insurance Underwriters	53.7%	$43,150	2%	11,000
75. Meeting and Convention Planners	53.7%	$35,540	23%	3,000
76. Personal Financial Advisors	53.7%	$55,320	34%	13,000
77. Anthropologists and Archeologists	53.5%	$36,040	17%	2,000

(continued)

The 100 Jobs with the Highest Percentage of Women College Graduates

Job	Percent Women	Annual Earnings	Percent Growth	Annual Openings
78. Anthropologists	53.5%	$36,040	17%	2,000
79. Archeologists	53.5%	$36,040	17%	2,000
80. Historians	53.5%	$39,860	17%	2,000
81. Political Scientists	53.5%	$81,040	17%	2,000
82. Urban and Regional Planners	53.5%	$46,500	16%	3,000
83. Accountants and Auditors	52.0%	$43,500	18%	100,000
84. Accountants	52.0%	$43,500	18%	100,000
85. Auditors	52.0%	$43,500	18%	100,000
86. Copy Writers	52.0%	$42,270	28%	18,000
87. Creative Writers	52.0%	$42,270	28%	18,000
88. Editors	52.0%	$39,370	23%	14,000
89. Poets and Lyricists	52.0%	$42,270	28%	18,000
90. Technical Writers	52.0%	$47,790	30%	5,000
91. Writers and Authors	52.0%	$42,270	28%	18,000
92. Directors, Religious Activities and Education	51.4%	$27,000	16%	23,000
93. Recreation Workers	51.4%	$17,130	20%	32,000
94. Law Clerks	50.9%	$28,510	13%	3,000
95. Property, Real Estate, and Community Association Managers	50.9%	$36,020	23%	24,000
96. Graphic Designers	49.4%	$34,570	27%	28,000
97. Multi-Media Artists and Animators	49.4%	$41,130	22%	8,000
98. Financial Managers, Branch or Department	48.9%	$67,020	18%	53,000
99. Financial Managers	48.9%	$67,020	18%	53,000
100. Treasurers, Controllers, and Chief Financial Officers	48.9%	$67,020	18%	53,000

Best Jobs Overall with High Percentages of Women College Graduates

Job	Percent Women	Annual Earnings	Percent Growth	Annual Openings
1. Pharmacists	86.1%	$70,950	24%	20,000
2. Financial Managers, Branch or Department	48.9%	$67,020	18%	53,000
3. Financial Managers	48.9%	$67,020	18%	53,000
4. Treasurers, Controllers, and Chief Financial Officers	48.9%	$67,020	18%	53,000
5. Personal Financial Advisors	53.7%	$55,320	34%	13,000
6. Physician Assistants	86.1%	$61,910	54%	5,000
7. Registered Nurses	93.8%	$44,840	26%	140,000
8. Industrial-Organizational Psychologists	58.8%	$66,880	18%	18,000
9. Physical Therapists	74.2%	$54,810	33%	6,000
10. Education Administrators, Elementary and Secondary School	62.0%	$66,930	13%	35,000
11. Copy Writers	52.0%	$42,270	28%	18,000
12. Creative Writers	52.0%	$42,270	28%	18,000
13. Poets and Lyricists	52.0%	$42,270	28%	18,000
14. Writers and Authors	52.0%	$42,270	28%	18,000
15. Dental Hygienists	81.5%	$51,330	37%	5,000
16. Special Education Teachers, Preschool, Kindergarten, and Elementary School	83.7%	$40,880	37%	15,000
17. Accountants and Auditors	52.0%	$43,500	18%	100,000
18. Accountants	52.0%	$43,500	18%	100,000
19. Auditors	52.0%	$43,500	18%	100,000
20. Educational, Vocational, and School Counselors	67.8%	$42,110	25%	22,000
21. Instructional Coordinators	62.0%	$44,230	25%	15,000
22. Occupational Therapists	74.2%	$49,450	34%	4,000
23. Paralegals and Legal Assistants	79.8%	$35,360	33%	23,000
24. Secondary School Teachers, Except Special and Vocational Education	55.4%	$40,870	19%	60,000
25. Technical Writers	52.0%	$47,790	30%	5,000

Best-Paying Jobs with High Percentages of Women College Graduates

Job	Percent Women	Annual Earnings
1. Political Scientists	53.5%	$81,040
2. Pharmacists	86.1%	$70,950
3. Financial Managers, Branch or Department	48.9%	$67,020
4. Financial Managers	48.9%	$67,020
5. Treasurers, Controllers, and Chief Financial Officers	48.9%	$67,020
6. Education Administrators, Elementary and Secondary School	62.0%	$66,930
7. Industrial-Organizational Psychologists	58.8%	$66,880
8. Physician Assistants	86.1%	$61,910
9. Human Resources Managers	61.9%	$59,000
10. Art Directors	55.3%	$56,880
11. Personal Financial Advisors	53.7%	$55,320
12. Physical Therapists	74.2%	$54,810
13. Dental Hygienists	81.5%	$51,330
14. Occupational Therapists	74.2%	$49,450
15. Commercial and Industrial Designers	55.3%	$48,780
16. Fashion Designers	55.3%	$48,530
17. Clinical Psychologists	58.8%	$48,320
18. Clinical, Counseling, and School Psychologists	58.8%	$48,320
19. Counseling Psychologists	58.8%	$48,320
20. Educational Psychologists	58.8%	$48,320
21. Technical Writers	52.0%	$47,790
22. Radiation Therapists	74.0%	$47,470
23. Speech-Language Pathologists	74.2%	$46,640
24. Urban and Regional Planners	53.5%	$46,500
25. Cost Estimators	86.5%	$45,800

Fastest-Growing Jobs with High Percentages of Women College Graduates

Job	Percent Women	Percent Growth
1. Physician Assistants	86.1%	54%
2. Medical Records and Health Information Technicians	81.5%	49%
3. Physical Therapist Aides	78.5%	46%
4. Audiologists	74.2%	45%
5. Physical Therapist Assistants	78.5%	45%
6. Occupational Therapist Assistants	81.0%	40%
7. Speech-Language Pathologists	74.2%	39%
8. Mental Health and Substance Abuse Social Workers	69.3%	39%
9. Dental Hygienists	81.5%	37%
10. Special Education Teachers, Preschool, Kindergarten, and Elementary School	83.7%	37%
11. Respiratory Therapists	74.2%	35%
12. Cardiovascular Technologists and Technicians	81.5%	35%
13. Substance Abuse and Behavioral Disorder Counselors	74.2%	35%
14. Personal Financial Advisors	53.7%	34%
15. Occupational Therapists	74.2%	34%
16. Physical Therapists	74.2%	33%
17. Paralegals and Legal Assistants	79.8%	33%
18. Medical and Public Health Social Workers	69.3%	32%
19. Technical Writers	52.0%	30%
20. Copy Writers	52.0%	28%
21. Creative Writers	52.0%	28%
22. Poets and Lyricists	52.0%	28%
23. Writers and Authors	52.0%	28%
24. Arbitrators, Mediators, and Conciliators	61.9%	27%
25. Graphic Designers	49.4%	27%

Jobs with the Most Openings Employing High Percentages of Women College Graduates

Job	Percent Women	Annual Openings
1. Elementary School Teachers, Except Special Education	85.5%	144,000
2. Registered Nurses	93.8%	140,000
3. Accountants and Auditors	52.0%	100,000
4. Accountants	52.0%	100,000
5. Auditors	52.0%	100,000
6. Secondary School Teachers, Except Special and Vocational Education	55.4%	60,000
7. Preschool Teachers, Except Special Education	98.0%	55,000
8. Middle School Teachers, Except Special and Vocational Education	55.4%	54,000
9. Financial Managers, Branch or Department	48.9%	53,000
10. Financial Managers	48.9%	53,000
11. Treasurers, Controllers, and Chief Financial Officers	48.9%	53,000
12. Child, Family, and School Social Workers	69.3%	35,000
13. Education Administrators, Elementary and Secondary School	62.0%	35,000
14. Education Administrators, Preschool and Child Care Center/Program	62.0%	35,000
15. Recreation Workers	51.4%	32,000
16. Graphic Designers	49.4%	28,000
17. Cost Estimators	86.5%	28,000
18. Property, Real Estate, and Community Association Managers	50.9%	24,000
19. Paralegals and Legal Assistants	79.8%	23,000
20. Directors, Religious Activities and Education	51.4%	23,000
21. Kindergarten Teachers, Except Special Education	98.0%	23,000
22. Educational, Vocational, and School Counselors	67.8%	22,000
23. Pharmacists	86.1%	20,000
24. Training and Development Specialists	64.9%	20,000
25. Medical and Clinical Laboratory Technicians	76.8%	19,000

Best Jobs with a High Percentage of Men College Graduates

If you have not already read the intro to the previous group of lists, jobs with high percentages of women college graduates, consider doing so. Much of the content there applies to these lists as well.

We did not include these groups of lists with the assumption that men college grads should consider jobs with high percentages of men college grads or that women should consider jobs with high percentages of women. Instead, these lists are here because we think they are interesting and perhaps helpful in considering nontraditional career options. For example, some men college graduates would do very well in and enjoy some of the jobs with high percentages of women college graduates but may not have considered them seriously. In a similar way, some women college graduates would very much enjoy and do well in some jobs that have traditionally been held by high percentages of men college graduates. We hope that these lists help you consider options that you simply did not seriously consider as a result of gender stereotypes.

The 100 Jobs with the Highest Percentage of Men College Graduates

Job	Percent Men	Annual Earnings	Percent Growth	Annual Openings
1. Fire Investigators	98.0%	$41,630	15%	1,000
2. Pilots, Ship	97.7%	$47,510	3%	2,000
3. Airline Pilots, Copilots, and Flight Engineers	96.8%	$110,940	6%	5,000
4. Mechanical Engineers	94.8%	$58,710	13%	7,000
5. Computer Hardware Engineers	93.5%	$67,300	25%	3,000
6. Electrical Engineers	93.5%	$64,910	11%	8,000
7. Electronics Engineers, Except Computer	93.5%	$64,830	10%	6,000
8. Forest and Conservation Technicians	92.8%	$29,580	3%	2,000
9. Civil Engineers	91.9%	$55,740	10%	4,000
10. Surveyors	91.8%	$36,700	8%	7,000
11. Aerospace Engineers	91.7%	$67,930	14%	2,000
12. Chemical Engineers	91.7%	$65,960	4%	2,000
13. Materials Engineers	91.7%	$59,100	5%	2,000
14. Nuclear Engineers	91.7%	$79,360	2%	1,000

(continued)

(continued)

The 100 Jobs with the Highest Percentage of Men College Graduates

Job	Percent Men	Annual Earnings	Percent Growth	Annual Openings
15. Petroleum Engineers	91.7%	$78,910	−7%	fewer than 500
16. Mining and Geological Engineers, Including Mining Safety Engineers	91.7%	$60,820	−1%	fewer than 500
17. Environmental Engineers	89.6%	$57,780	26%	3,000
18. Sales Engineers	89.6%	$56,520	18%	4,000
19. Biomedical Engineers	89.6%	$57,480	31%	fewer than 500
20. Fire-Prevention and Protection Engineers	89.6%	$54,630	11%	3,000
21. Industrial Safety and Health Engineers	89.6%	$54,630	11%	3,000
22. Product Safety Engineers	89.6%	$54,630	11%	3,000
23. Agricultural Engineers	89.6%	$55,850	15%	fewer than 500
24. Marine Engineers	89.6%	$60,890	2%	fewer than 500
25. Clergy	88.6%	$31,760	15%	12,000
26. Calibration and Instrumentation Technicians	85.0%	$40,020	11%	22,000
27. Electrical Engineering Technicians	85.0%	$40,020	11%	22,000
28. Electronics Engineering Technicians	85.0%	$40,020	11%	22,000
29. Industrial Engineers	84.8%	$58,580	4%	10,000
30. Architects, Except Landscape and Naval	83.5%	$52,510	18%	4,000
31. Landscape Architects	83.5%	$43,540	31%	1,000
32. Architectural Drafters	79.6%	$35,220	21%	12,000
33. Electrical and Electronics Drafters	79.6%	$38,210	23%	5,000
34. Electrical Drafters	79.6%	$38,210	23%	5,000
35. Veterinarians	78.5%	$60,910	32%	2,000
36. Optometrists	78.5%	$82,860	19%	1,000
37. Podiatrists	78.5%	$107,560	14%	1,000
38. Internists, General	77.8%	$142,400	18%	27,000
39. Pediatricians, General	77.8%	$125,970	18%	27,000
40. Psychiatrists	77.8%	$118,640	18%	27,000
41. Family and General Practitioners	77.8%	$114,170	18%	27,000
42. Electrical and Electronic Engineering Technicians	76.5%	$40,020	11%	22,000

The 100 Jobs with the Highest Percentage of Men College Graduates

Job	Percent Men	Annual Earnings	Percent Growth	Annual Openings
43. Environmental Engineering Technicians	76.5%	$34,000	29%	2,000
44. Mechanical Engineering Technicians	76.5%	$39,570	14%	5,000
45. Industrial Engineering Technicians	76.5%	$40,910	10%	5,000
46. Civil Engineering Technicians	76.5%	$35,990	12%	9,000
47. Aerospace Engineering and Operations Technicians	76.5%	$48,600	6%	2,000
48. Geological and Petroleum Technicians	76.5%	$36,490	6%	2,000
49. Lawyers	75.4%	$88,280	18%	35,000
50. Judges, Magistrate Judges, and Magistrates	75.3%	$86,760	1%	2,000
51. Administrative Law Judges, Adjudicators, and Hearing Officers	75.3%	$61,240	1%	1,000
52. Computer and Information Systems Managers	71.8%	$78,830	48%	28,000
53. Chief Executives	71.8%	$113,810	17%	48,000
54. Private Sector Executives	71.8%	$113,810	17%	48,000
55. Construction Managers	71.8%	$58,250	16%	26,000
56. Administrative Services Managers	71.8%	$47,080	20%	31,000
57. Engineering Managers	71.8%	$84,070	8%	24,000
58. Industrial Production Managers	71.8%	$61,660	6%	22,000
59. Natural Sciences Managers	71.8%	$75,880	8%	4,000
60. Financial Examiners	71.8%	$53,060	10%	2,000
61. Semiconductor Processors	71.5%	$25,430	32%	7,000
62. Computer Programmers	70.9%	$57,590	16%	36,000
63. Sales Agents, Financial Services	70.2%	$56,080	22%	55,000
64. Sales Agents, Securities and Commodities	70.2%	$56,080	22%	55,000
65. Computer Security Specialists	69.1%	$51,280	82%	18,000
66. Database Administrators	69.1%	$51,990	66%	8,000
67. Computer and Information Scientists, Research	69.1%	$70,590	40%	2,000
68. Medical Scientists, Except Epidemiologists	69.1%	$57,810	26%	2,000
69. Biochemists	69.1%	$54,230	21%	5,000

(continued)

(continued)

The 100 Jobs with the Highest Percentage of Men College Graduates

Job	Percent Men	Annual Earnings	Percent Growth	Annual Openings
70. Biochemists and Biophysicists	69.1%	$54,230	21%	5,000
71. Biophysicists	69.1%	$54,230	21%	5,000
72. Biologists	69.1%	$49,033	21%	5,000
73. Microbiologists	69.1%	$48,890	21%	5,000
74. Chemists	69.1%	$50,080	19%	6,000
75. Epidemiologists	69.1%	$48,390	26%	2,000
76. Hydrologists	69.1%	$55,410	26%	1,000
77. Zoologists and Wildlife Biologists	69.1%	$43,980	21%	5,000
78. Geologists	69.1%	$56,230	18%	2,000
79. Geoscientists, Except Hydrologists and Geographers	69.1%	$56,230	18%	2,000
80. Environmental Scientists and Specialists, Including Health	69.1%	$44,180	22%	4,000
81. Materials Scientists	69.1%	$60,620	20%	1,000
82. Physicists	69.1%	$83,310	10%	1,000
83. Astronomers	69.1%	$74,510	10%	1,000
84. Atmospheric and Space Scientists	69.1%	$58,510	17%	fewer than 500
85. Geographers	69.1%	$46,690	17%	2,000
86. Conservation Scientists	69.1%	$47,140	8%	1,000
87. Park Naturalists	69.1%	$47,140	8%	1,000
88. Range Managers	69.1%	$47,140	8%	1,000
89. Soil Conservationists	69.1%	$47,140	8%	1,000
90. Foresters	69.1%	$43,640	7%	1,000
91. Computer Software Engineers, Applications	68.7%	$67,670	100%	28,000
92. Computer Software Engineers, Systems Software	68.7%	$69,530	90%	23,000
93. Computer Systems Analysts	68.7%	$59,330	60%	34,000
94. Composers	68.0%	$31,510	13%	9,000
95. Music Arrangers and Orchestrators	68.0%	$31,510	13%	9,000
96. Music Directors	68.0%	$31,510	13%	9,000
97. Music Directors and Composers	68.0%	$31,510	13%	9,000
98. Financial Analysts	66.4%	$52,420	26%	20,000
99. Actuaries	66.4%	$66,590	5%	1,000
100. Mathematicians	66.4%	$68,640	−2%	fewer than 500

Best Jobs Overall with High Percentages of Men College Graduates

Job	Percent Men	Annual Earnings	Percent Growth	Annual Openings
1. Computer and Information Systems Managers	71.8%	$78,830	48%	28,000
2. Computer Software Engineers, Applications	68.7%	$67,670	100%	28,000
3. Computer Software Engineers, Systems Software	68.7%	$69,530	90%	23,000
4. Computer Systems Analysts	68.7%	$59,330	60%	34,000
5. Lawyers	75.4%	$88,280	18%	35,000
6. Internists, General	77.8%	$142,400	18%	27,000
7. Pediatricians, General	77.8%	$125,970	18%	27,000
8. Psychiatrists	77.8%	$118,640	18%	27,000
9. Family and General Practitioners	77.8%	$114,170	18%	27,000
10. Computer Security Specialists	69.1%	$51,280	82%	18,000
11. Chief Executives	71.8%	$113,810	17%	48,000
12. Private Sector Executives	71.8%	$113,810	17%	48,000
13. Sales Agents, Financial Services	70.2%	$56,080	22%	55,000
14. Sales Agents, Securities and Commodities	70.2%	$56,080	22%	55,000
15. Financial Analysts	66.4%	$52,420	26%	20,000
16. Database Administrators	69.1%	$51,990	66%	8,000
17. Computer and Information Scientists, Research	69.1%	$70,590	40%	2,000
18. Computer Programmers	70.9%	$57,590	16%	36,000
19. Construction Managers	71.8%	$58,250	16%	26,000
20. Administrative Services Managers	71.8%	$47,080	20%	31,000
21. Veterinarians	78.5%	$60,910	32%	2,000
22. Computer Hardware Engineers	93.5%	$67,300	25%	3,000
23. Engineering Managers	71.8%	$84,070	8%	24,000
24. Environmental Engineers	89.6%	$57,780	26%	3,000
25. Medical Scientists, Except Epidemiologists	69.1%	$57,810	26%	2,000

Best-Paying Jobs with High Percentages of Men College Graduates

Job	Percent Men	Annual Earnings
1. Internists, General	77.8%	$142,400
2. Pediatricians, General	77.8%	$125,970
3. Psychiatrists	77.8%	$118,640
4. Family and General Practitioners	77.8%	$114,170
5. Chief Executives	71.8%	$113,810
6. Private Sector Executives	71.8%	$113,810
7. Airline Pilots, Copilots, and Flight Engineers	96.8%	$110,940
8. Podiatrists	78.5%	$107,560
9. Lawyers	75.4%	$88,280
10. Judges, Magistrate Judges, and Magistrates	75.3%	$86,760
11. Engineering Managers	71.8%	$84,070
12. Physicists	69.1%	$83,310
13. Optometrists	78.5%	$82,860
14. Nuclear Engineers	91.7%	$79,360
15. Petroleum Engineers	91.7%	$78,910
16. Computer and Information Systems Managers	71.8%	$78,830
17. Natural Sciences Managers	71.8%	$75,880
18. Astronomers	69.1%	$74,510
19. Computer and Information Scientists, Research	69.1%	$70,590
20. Computer Software Engineers, Systems Software	68.7%	$69,530
21. Mathematicians	66.4%	$68,640
22. Aerospace Engineers	91.7%	$67,930
23. Computer Software Engineers, Applications	68.7%	$67,670
24. Computer Hardware Engineers	93.5%	$67,300
25. Actuaries	66.4%	$66,590

Fastest-Growing Jobs with High Percentages of Men College Graduates

Job	Percent Men	Percent Growth
1. Computer Software Engineers, Applications	68.7%	100%
2. Computer Software Engineers, Systems Software	68.7%	90%
3. Computer Security Specialists	69.1%	82%
4. Database Administrators	69.1%	66%
5. Computer Systems Analysts	68.7%	60%
6. Computer and Information Systems Managers	71.8%	48%
7. Computer and Information Scientists, Research	69.1%	40%
8. Veterinarians	78.5%	32%
9. Semiconductor Processors	71.5%	32%
10. Biomedical Engineers	89.6%	31%
11. Landscape Architects	83.5%	31%
12. Environmental Engineering Technicians	76.5%	29%
13. Medical Scientists, Except Epidemiologists	69.1%	26%
14. Environmental Engineers	89.6%	26%
15. Hydrologists	69.1%	26%
16. Financial Analysts	66.4%	26%
17. Epidemiologists	69.1%	26%
18. Computer Hardware Engineers	93.5%	25%
19. Electrical and Electronics Drafters	79.6%	23%
20. Electrical Drafters	79.6%	23%
21. Sales Agents, Financial Services	70.2%	22%
22. Sales Agents, Securities and Commodities	70.2%	22%
23. Environmental Scientists and Specialists, Including Health	69.1%	22%
24. Biochemists	69.1%	21%
25. Biochemists and Biophysicists	69.1%	21%

Jobs with the Most Openings Employing High Percentages of Men College Graduates

Job	Percent Men	Annual Openings
1. Sales Agents, Financial Services	70.2%	55,000
2. Sales Agents, Securities and Commodities	70.2%	55,000
3. Chief Executives	71.8%	48,000
4. Private Sector Executives	71.8%	48,000
5. Computer Programmers	70.9%	36,000
6. Lawyers	75.4%	35,000
7. Computer Systems Analysts	68.7%	34,000
8. Administrative Services Managers	71.8%	31,000
9. Computer Software Engineers, Applications	68.7%	28,000
10. Computer and Information Systems Managers	71.8%	28,000
11. Internists, General	77.8%	27,000
12. Pediatricians, General	77.8%	27,000
13. Psychiatrists	77.8%	27,000
14. Family and General Practitioners	77.8%	27,000
15. Construction Managers	71.8%	26,000
16. Engineering Managers	71.8%	24,000
17. Computer Software Engineers, Systems Software	68.7%	23,000
18. Calibration and Instrumentation Technicians	85.0%	22,000
19. Electrical Engineering Technicians	85.0%	22,000
20. Electronics Engineering Technicians	85.0%	22,000
21. Electrical and Electronic Engineering Technicians	76.5%	22,000
22. Industrial Production Managers	71.8%	22,000
23. Financial Analysts	66.4%	20,000
24. Computer Security Specialists	69.1%	18,000
25. Architectural Drafters	79.6%	12,000

Best Jobs Lists Based on Levels of Education and Experience

The lists in this section organize the 258 jobs requiring a two- or four-year college degree or more into groups based on the education or training typically required for entry. Unlike many of the previous sections, here we do not include separate lists for highest pay, growth, or number of openings. Instead, we provide one list that includes all the occupations in our database that fit into each of the education levels and ranks them by their total combined score for earnings, growth, and number of openings.

These lists can help you identify a job with higher earnings or upward mobility but with a similar level of education to the job you now hold. For example, you will find jobs within the same level of education that require similar skills, yet one pays significantly better than the other, is projected to grow more rapidly, or has significantly more job openings per year. This information can help you leverage your present skills and experience into jobs that might be better for you.

You can also use these lists to explore possible job options if you were to get additional training, education, or work experience. For example, students can use these lists to identify occupations that offer high potential, and graduates can use them to identify degrees that could improve their employment options.

The lists can also help you when you plan your education. For example, you might be thinking about a particular college major because the pay is very good, but the lists may help you identify a college major that interests you more and offers even better potential for the same general educational requirements.

The Education Levels

College degrees have no universal standards. Each college or university determines the number of credit hours and courses that are required for a specific degree. For example, the requirements for a major in anthropology varied at three universities from 27 to 36 semester hours, and the total hours required to get the bachelor's degree varied from 120 to 126 hours. Also, there can be a wide difference in degree requirements depending on the type of major. At one university, a Bachelor of Architecture degree requires 160 semester hours while a Bachelor of Arts in History requires 126 hours. Thus, when a job indicates that a bachelor's degree is required, additional research is needed to determine the investment in years and courses required for the specific degree necessary for that occupation.

There are, however, guidelines that can help you understand what is generally required to earn a specific degree. The following definitions are used by the federal government to classify jobs based on the minimum level of education typically required for entry and are the definitions we use for constructing the lists in this section.

▲ **Associate's degree:** The associate's degree usually requires 60 to 63 semester hours to complete. A normal course load for a full-time student each semester is 15 hours. This means that it typically takes two years to complete an associate's degree.

▲ **Bachelor's degree:** A bachelor's degree usually requires 120 to 130 semester hours to complete. A full-time student usually takes four to five years to complete a bachelor's degree, depending on the complexity of courses. Traditionally, people have thought of the bachelor's degree as a four-year degree. There are some bachelor's degrees—like the Bachelor of Architecture degree we previously mentioned—that are considered a first professional degree and take five or more years to complete.

▲ **Work experience, plus degree:** Some jobs require work experience in a related job in addition to a degree. For example, almost all managers have worked in a related job before being promoted into a management position. Most of the jobs in this group require a four-year bachelor's degree, although some require an associate's degree or a master's degree.

▲ **Master's degree:** This degree usually requires 33 to 60 semester hours beyond the bachelor's degree. The academic master's degrees—like a Master of Arts in Political Science—usually require 33 to 36 hours. A first professional degree at the master's level—like a Master of Social Work—requires almost two years of full-time work.

▲ **Doctoral degree:** The doctoral degree prepares students for careers that consist primarily of theory development, research, and/or college teaching. This type of degree is typically the Doctor of Philosophy (Ph.D.) or Doctor of Education (Ed.D.). Normally, a requirement for a doctoral degree is the completion of a master's degree plus an additional two to three years of full-time coursework and a one- to two-semester research project and paper called the dissertation. It usually takes four to five years beyond the bachelor's degree to complete a doctoral degree.

▲ **First professional degree:** Some professional degrees require three or more years of full-time academic study beyond the bachelor's degree. A professional degree prepares students for a specific profession. It uses theory and research to teach practical applications in a professional occupation. Examples of this type of degree are Doctor of Medicine (M.D.) for physicians, Doctor of Ministry (D.Min.) for clergy, and Juris Doctor (J.D.) for attorneys.

Another Warning About the Data

We warned you in the Introduction to this book to use caution in interpreting the data we use, and we want to do it again here. The occupational data we use is the most accurate available anywhere, but it has limitations. For example, a four-year degree in accounting, finance, or a related area is typically required for entry into the accounting profession. But some people working as accountants don't have such a degree, and others have much more education than the "minimum" required for entry.

In a similar way, people with a graduate degree will typically earn considerably more than someone with an associate's or bachelor's degree. However, some people with an associate's degree earn considerably more than the average for those with higher levels of education. In a similar way, new entrants to any job will typically earn less than the average, and some areas of the country have lower wages overall (but may also have lower costs of living).

So as you browse the lists that follow, please use them as a way to be encouraged rather than discouraged. Education and training are very important for success in the labor market of the future, but so are ability, drive, initiative, and, yes, luck.

Having said this, we encourage you to get as much education and training as you can. It used to be that you got your schooling and never went back, but this is not a good attitude to have now. You will probably need to continue learning new things throughout your working life. This can be done by going to school, which is a good thing for many people to do. But there are also many other ways to learn, such as workshops, adult education programs, certification programs, employer training, professional conferences, Internet training, reading related books and magazines, and many others. Upgrading your computer skills—and other technical skills—is particularly important in our rapidly changing workplace, and you avoid doing so at your peril.

Best Jobs Requiring an Associate's Degree

Job	Annual Earnings	Percent Growth	Annual Openings
1. Registered Nurses	$44,840	26%	140,000
2. Computer Support Specialists	$36,460	97%	40,000
3. Dental Hygienists	$51,330	37%	5,000
4. Paralegals and Legal Assistants	$35,360	33%	23,000
5. Physical Therapist Assistants	$33,870	45%	9,000
6. Medical Records and Health Information Technicians	$22,750	49%	14,000
7. Diagnostic Medical Sonographers	$44,820	26%	3,000
8. Respiratory Therapists	$37,680	35%	4,000
9. Medical Transcriptionists	$25,270	30%	15,000
10. Radiologic Technicians	$36,000	23%	13,000
11. Radiologic Technologists and Technicians	$36,000	23%	13,000
12. Radiologic Technologists	$36,000	23%	13,000
13. Physical Therapist Aides	$19,670	46%	7,000
14. Nuclear Monitoring Technicians	$59,160	21%	fewer than 500
15. Nuclear Equipment Operation Technicians	$59,160	21%	fewer than 500
16. Nuclear Technicians	$59,160	21%	fewer than 500
17. Occupational Therapist Assistants	$34,340	40%	3,000
18. Semiconductor Processors	$25,430	32%	7,000
19. Veterinary Technologists and Technicians	$21,640	39%	6,000
20. Architectural Drafters	$35,220	21%	12,000
21. Biological Technicians	$31,540	26%	7,000
22. Electrical Drafters	$38,210	23%	5,000
23. Electrical and Electronics Drafters	$38,210	23%	5,000
24. Cardiovascular Technologists and Technicians	$33,350	35%	3,000
25. Electrical and Electronic Engineering Technicians	$40,020	11%	22,000
26. Electronics Engineering Technicians	$40,020	11%	22,000
27. Calibration and Instrumentation Technicians	$40,020	11%	22,000
28. Electrical Engineering Technicians	$40,020	11%	22,000
29. Medical and Clinical Laboratory Technicians	$27,540	19%	19,000
30. Radiation Therapists	$47,470	23%	1,000
31. Nuclear Medicine Technologists	$44,130	22%	1,000

Best Jobs Requiring an Associate's Degree

Job	Annual Earnings	Percent Growth	Annual Openings
32. Environmental Engineering Technicians	$34,000	29%	2,000
33. Chemical Technicians	$35,450	15%	13,000
34. Environmental Science and Protection Technicians, Including Health	$33,830	24%	3,000
35. Occupational Health and Safety Technicians	$42,750	15%	4,000
36. Mechanical Engineering Technicians	$39,570	14%	5,000
37. Industrial Engineering Technicians	$40,910	10%	5,000
38. Civil Engineering Technicians	$35,990	12%	9,000
39. Aerospace Engineering and Operations Technicians	$48,600	6%	2,000
40. Electro-Mechanical Technicians	$36,150	14%	4,000
41. Funeral Directors	$41,110	3%	3,000
42. Agricultural Technicians	$27,080	15%	3,000
43. Food Science Technicians	$27,080	15%	3,000
44. Forensic Science Technicians	$37,520	13%	1,000
45. Geological Sample Test Technicians	$36,490	6%	2,000
46. Geological Data Technicians	$36,490	6%	2,000
47. Geological and Petroleum Technicians	$36,490	6%	2,000
48. Forest and Conservation Technicians	$29,580	3%	2,000

Best Jobs Requiring a Bachelor's Degree

Job	Annual Earnings	Percent Growth	Annual Openings
1. Computer Software Engineers, Applications	$67,670	100%	28,000
2. Computer Software Engineers, Systems Software	$69,530	90%	23,000
3. Computer Systems Analysts	$59,330	60%	34,000
4. Network and Computer Systems Administrators	$51,280	82%	18,000
5. Computer Security Specialists	$51,280	82%	18,000
6. Securities, Commodities, and Financial Services Sales Agents	$56,080	22%	55,000
7. Sales Agents, Securities and Commodities	$56,080	22%	55,000
8. Sales Agents, Financial Services	$56,080	22%	55,000
9. Personal Financial Advisors	$55,320	34%	13,000
10. Physician Assistants	$61,910	54%	5,000
11. Network Systems and Data Communications Analysts	$54,510	78%	9,000
12. Financial Analysts	$52,420	26%	20,000
13. Database Administrators	$51,990	66%	8,000
14. Computer Programmers	$57,590	16%	36,000
15. Poets and Lyricists	$42,270	28%	18,000
16. Copy Writers	$42,270	28%	18,000
17. Public Relations Specialists	$39,580	36%	19,000
18. Writers and Authors	$42,270	28%	18,000
19. Creative Writers	$42,270	28%	18,000
20. Market Research Analysts	$51,190	24%	13,000
21. Special Education Teachers, Preschool, Kindergarten, and Elementary School	$40,880	37%	15,000
22. Construction Managers	$58,250	16%	26,000
23. Accountants and Auditors	$43,500	18%	100,000
24. Accountants	$43,500	18%	100,000
25. Auditors	$43,500	18%	100,000
26. Computer Hardware Engineers	$67,300	25%	3,000
27. Occupational Therapists	$49,450	34%	4,000
28. Secondary School Teachers, Except Special and Vocational Education	$40,870	19%	60,000
29. Environmental Engineers	$57,780	26%	3,000

Best Jobs Requiring a Bachelor's Degree

Job	Annual Earnings	Percent Growth	Annual Openings
30. Technical Writers	$47,790	30%	5,000
31. Commercial and Industrial Designers	$48,780	24%	7,000
32. Graphic Designers	$34,570	27%	28,000
33. Child, Family, and School Social Workers	$31,470	27%	35,000
34. Cost Estimators	$45,800	16%	28,000
35. Industrial Production Managers	$61,660	6%	22,000
36. Economists	$64,830	18%	3,000
37. Property, Real Estate, and Community Association Managers	$36,020	23%	24,000
38. Medical and Public Health Social Workers	$34,790	32%	13,000
39. Social and Community Service Managers	$39,130	25%	13,000
40. Training and Development Specialists	$40,830	19%	20,000
41. Special Education Teachers, Secondary School	$41,290	25%	8,000
42. Probation Officers and Correctional Treatment Specialists	$38,150	24%	14,000
43. Editors	$39,370	23%	14,000
44. Sales Engineers	$56,520	18%	4,000
45. Biomedical Engineers	$57,480	31%	fewer than 500
46. Chemists	$50,080	19%	6,000
47. Electrical Engineers	$64,910	11%	8,000
48. Hydrologists	$55,410	26%	1,000
49. Mechanical Engineers	$58,710	13%	7,000
50. Multi-Media Artists and Animators	$41,130	22%	8,000
51. Elementary School Teachers, Except Special Education	$39,700	13%	144,000
52. Architects, Except Landscape and Naval	$52,510	18%	4,000
53. Medical and Clinical Laboratory Technologists	$40,510	17%	19,000
54. Airline Pilots, Copilots, and Flight Engineers	$110,940	6%	5,000
55. Geologists	$56,230	18%	2,000
56. Preschool Teachers, Except Special Education	$17,810	20%	55,000
57. Employment, Recruitment, and Placement Specialists	$36,480	18%	19,000
58. Geoscientists, Except Hydrologists and Geographers	$56,230	18%	2,000
59. Employment Interviewers, Private or Public Employment Service	$36,480	18%	19,000

(continued)

(continued)

Best Jobs Requiring a Bachelor's Degree

Job	Annual Earnings	Percent Growth	Annual Openings
60. Personnel Recruiters	$36,480	18%	19,000
61. Electronics Engineers, Except Computer	$64,830	10%	6,000
62. Environmental Scientists and Specialists, Including Health	$44,180	22%	4,000
63. Materials Scientists	$60,620	20%	1,000
64. Budget Analysts	$48,370	15%	8,000
65. Special Education Teachers, Middle School	$38,600	24%	6,000
66. Aerospace Engineers	$67,930	14%	2,000
67. Landscape Architects	$43,540	31%	1,000
68. Middle School Teachers, Except Special and Vocational Education	$39,750	10%	54,000
69. Purchasing Agents, Except Wholesale, Retail, and Farm Products	$41,370	12%	23,000
70. Industrial Engineers	$58,580	4%	10,000
71. Recreation Workers	$17,130	20%	32,000
72. Fashion Designers	$48,530	20%	2,000
73. Kindergarten Teachers, Except Special Education	$37,610	14%	23,000
74. Loan Officers	$41,420	5%	28,000
75. Rehabilitation Counselors	$24,450	24%	12,000
76. Compensation, Benefits, and Job Analysis Specialists	$41,660	16%	8,000
77. Adult Literacy, Remedial Education, and GED Teachers and Instructors	$33,540	19%	12,000
78. Civil Engineers	$55,740	10%	4,000
79. Insurance Sales Agents	$38,750	3%	43,000
80. Survey Researchers	$26,200	34%	3,000
81. Credit Analysts	$40,180	16%	7,000
82. Health and Safety Engineers, Except Mining Safety Engineers and Inspectors	$54,630	11%	3,000
83. Product Safety Engineers	$54,630	11%	3,000
84. Fire-Prevention and Protection Engineers	$54,630	11%	3,000
85. Industrial Safety and Health Engineers	$54,630	11%	3,000
86. Atmospheric and Space Scientists	$58,510	17%	fewer than 500

(continued)

Best Jobs Requiring a Bachelor's Degree

Job	Annual Earnings	Percent Growth	Annual Openings
87. Vocational Education Teachers, Secondary School	$42,080	13%	7,000
88. Directors, Religious Activities and Education	$27,000	16%	23,000
89. Geographers	$46,690	17%	2,000
90. Interior Designers	$36,540	17%	7,000
91. Chemical Engineers	$65,960	4%	2,000
92. Meeting and Convention Planners	$35,540	23%	3,000
93. Film and Video Editors	$34,160	26%	2,000
94. Exhibit Designers	$31,440	27%	2,000
95. Set Designers	$31,440	27%	2,000
96. Set and Exhibit Designers	$31,440	27%	2,000
97. Materials Engineers	$59,100	5%	2,000
98. Insurance Underwriters	$43,150	2%	11,000
98. Nuclear Engineers	$79,360	2%	1,000
100. Agricultural Engineers	$55,850	15%	fewer than 500
101. Financial Examiners	$53,060	10%	2,000
102. Dietitians and Nutritionists	$38,450	15%	5,000
103. Orthotists and Prosthetists	$45,740	17%	1,000
104. Historians	$39,860	17%	2,000
105. Wholesale and Retail Buyers, Except Farm Products	$37,200	–9%	18,000
106. Petroleum Engineers	$78,910	–7%	fewer than 500
107. Tax Examiners, Collectors, and Revenue Agents	$40,180	8%	6,000
108. Music Arrangers and Orchestrators	$31,510	13%	9,000
109. Cartographers and Photogrammetrists	$39,410	18%	1,000
110. Surveyors	$36,700	8%	7,000
111. Marine Engineers and Naval Architects	$60,890	2%	fewer than 500
112. Athletic Trainers	$32,080	18%	2,000
113. Marine Engineers	$60,890	2%	fewer than 500
114. Marine Architects	$60,890	2%	fewer than 500
115. Anthropologists and Archeologists	$36,040	17%	2,000
116. Anthropologists	$36,040	17%	2,000
117. Archeologists	$36,040	17%	2,000
118. Fire Investigators	$41,630	15%	1,000

(continued)

(continued)

Best Jobs Requiring a Bachelor's Degree

Job	Annual Earnings	Percent Growth	Annual Openings
119. Mining and Geological Engineers, Including Mining Safety Engineers	$60,820	−1%	fewer than 500
120. Vocational Education Teachers, Middle School	$39,330	13%	2,000
121. Loan Counselors	$32,160	16%	3,000
122. Range Managers	$47,140	8%	1,000
123. Conservation Scientists	$47,140	8%	1,000
124. Soil Conservationists	$47,140	8%	1,000
125. Park Naturalists	$47,140	8%	1,000
126. Foresters	$43,640	7%	1,000
127. Broadcast News Analysts	$29,110	3%	9,000
128. Law Clerks	$28,510	13%	3,000
129. Farm and Home Management Advisors	$36,290	6%	2,000
130. Recreational Therapists	$28,650	9%	1,000

Best Jobs Requiring Work Experience, Plus Degree

Job	Annual Earnings	Percent Growth	Annual Openings
1. Computer and Information Systems Managers	$78,830	48%	28,000
2. Sales Managers	$68,520	33%	21,000
3. Medical and Health Services Managers	$56,370	32%	27,000
4. Management Analysts	$55,040	29%	50,000
5. Marketing Managers	$71,240	29%	12,000
6. Treasurers, Controllers, and Chief Financial Officers	$67,020	18%	53,000
7. Financial Managers, Branch or Department	$67,020	18%	53,000
8. Financial Managers	$67,020	18%	53,000
9. Government Service Executives	$113,810	17%	48,000
10. Private Sector Executives	$113,810	17%	48,000
11. Chief Executives	$113,810	17%	48,000
12. General and Operations Managers	$61,160	15%	235,000
13. Public Relations Managers	$54,540	36%	7,000
14. Advertising and Promotions Managers	$53,360	34%	7,000
15. Education Administrators, Elementary and Secondary School	$66,930	13%	35,000
16. Administrative Services Managers	$47,080	20%	31,000
17. Engineering Managers	$84,070	8%	24,000
18. Agents and Business Managers of Artists, Performers, and Athletes	$57,040	28%	2,000
19. Art Directors	$56,880	21%	6,000
20. Producers	$41,030	27%	11,000
21. Directors—Stage, Motion Pictures, Television, and Radio	$41,030	27%	11,000
22. Program Directors	$41,030	27%	11,000
23. Producers and Directors	$41,030	27%	11,000
24. Human Resources Managers	$59,000	13%	14,000
25. Gaming Managers	$53,380	30%	fewer than 500
26. Natural Sciences Managers	$75,880	8%	4,000
27. Purchasing Managers	$53,030	−6%	17,000
28. Arbitrators, Mediators, and Conciliators	$43,060	27%	fewer than 500
29. Education Administrators, Preschool and Child Care Center/Program	$30,420	13%	35,000
30. Judges, Magistrate Judges, and Magistrates	$86,760	1%	2,000
31. Actuaries	$66,590	5%	1,000
32. Administrative Law Judges, Adjudicators, and Hearing Officers	$61,240	1%	1,000
33. Pilots, Ship	$47,510	3%	2,000

Best Jobs Requiring a Master's Degree

Job	Annual Earnings	Percent Growth	Annual Openings
1. Postsecondary Teachers	$46,330	23.5%	184,000
2. Industrial-Organizational Psychologists	$66,880	18%	18,000
3. Physical Therapists	$54,810	33%	6,000
4. Educational, Vocational, and School Counselors	$42,110	25%	22,000
5. Instructional Coordinators	$44,230	25%	15,000
6. Speech-Language Pathologists	$46,640	39%	4,000
7. Counseling Psychologists	$48,320	18%	18,000
8. Clinical Psychologists	$48,320	18%	18,000
9. Clinical, Counseling, and School Psychologists	$48,320	18%	18,000
10. Educational Psychologists	$48,320	18%	18,000
11. Political Scientists	$81,040	17%	2,000
12. Mental Health and Substance Abuse Social Workers	$30,170	39%	10,000
13. Audiologists	$44,830	45%	1,000
14. Substance Abuse and Behavioral Disorder Counselors	$28,510	35%	7,000
15. Health Educators	$33,860	24%	7,000
16. Marriage and Family Therapists	$34,660	30%	2,000
17. Urban and Regional Planners	$46,500	16%	3,000
18. Mental Health Counselors	$27,570	22%	7,000
19. Operations Research Analysts	$53,420	8%	4,000
20. Occupational Health and Safety Specialists	$42,750	15%	4,000
21. Librarians	$41,700	7%	6,000
22. Composers	$31,510	13%	9,000
23. Music Directors	$31,510	13%	9,000
24. Music Directors and Composers	$31,510	13%	9,000
25. Mathematicians	$68,640	-2%	fewer than 500
26. Statisticians	$51,990	2%	2,000

Best Jobs Requiring a Doctoral Degree

Job	Annual Earnings	Percent Growth	Annual Openings
1. Computer and Information Scientists, Research	$70,590	40%	2,000
2. Medical Scientists, Except Epidemiologists	$57,810	26%	2,000
3. Biophysicists	$54,230	21%	5,000
4. Biochemists	$54,230	21%	5,000
5. Biochemists and Biophysicists	$54,230	21%	5,000
6. Biologists	$49,033	21%	5,000
7. Microbiologists	$48,890	21%	5,000
8. Epidemiologists	$48,390	26%	2,000
9. Zoologists and Wildlife Biologists	$43,980	21%	5,000
10. Physicists	$83,310	10%	1,000
11. Astronomers	$74,510	10%	1,000

Best Jobs Requiring a First Professional Degree

Job	Annual Earnings	Percent Growth	Annual Openings
1. Pharmacists	$70,950	24%	20,000
2. Lawyers	$88,280	18%	35,000
3. Internists, General	$142,400	18%	27,000
4. Pediatricians, General	$125,970	18%	27,000
5. Psychiatrists	$118,640	18%	27,000
6. Family and General Practitioners	$114,170	18%	27,000
7. Veterinarians	$60,910	32%	2,000
8. Optometrists	$82,860	19%	1,000
9. Podiatrists	$107,560	14%	1,000
10. Clergy	$31,760	15%	12,000

Best Jobs Lists for College Graduates Based on Interests

This group of lists organizes the 258 jobs that typically require a college degree or more into 14 interest areas. These interest areas are used in a variety of career exploration systems and can help you to quickly identify jobs based on your interests.

Simply find the area or areas that interest you most. Then review the jobs in those areas to identify jobs you want to explore in more detail and look up their descriptions in Part II. You can also review interest areas where you have had past experience, education, or training to see if other jobs in those areas would meet your current requirements.

Within each interest area, jobs are listed in order of their total combined scores based on earnings, growth, and number of openings.

Some of the interest areas will have just a few or even no jobs listed in them. This is because few jobs in those interest areas typically require a college degree. Even so, if one of those areas interests you most, you can often come up with a creative way to use your education and training in that interest area. For example, you might start or manage a business in an area that interests you or work in an industry that involves your interest area.

Note: The 14 interest areas used in these lists are those used in the Guide for Occupational Exploration. The GOE system was developed by the U.S. Department of Labor as an intuitive way to assist in career exploration. Our lists use the revised GOE interest areas from the *Guide for Occupational Exploration*, Third Edition, published by JIST.

Descriptions for the 14 Interest Areas

Brief descriptions for the 14 interest areas we use in the lists follow. Note that the descriptions are as they appear in the *Guide for Occupational Exploration* and include some job titles that differ from those used in our lists.

Also note that we put each job into only one interest area list, the one it fit into best. However, many jobs could be included in more than one list, so consider reviewing a variety of these interest areas to find jobs that you might otherwise overlook.

▲ **Arts, Entertainment, and Media:** *An interest in creatively expressing feelings or ideas, in communicating news or information, or in performing.* You can satisfy this interest in several creative, verbal, or performing activities. For example, if you enjoy literature, perhaps writing or editing would appeal to you. Do you prefer to work in the performing arts? If so, you could direct or perform in drama, music, or dance. If you especially enjoy the visual arts, you could become a critic in painting, sculpture, or ceramics. You may want to use your hands to create or decorate products. You may prefer to model clothes or develop sets for entertainment. Or you may want to participate in sports professionally as an athlete or coach.

▲ **Science, Math, and Engineering:** *An interest in discovering, collecting, and analyzing information about the natural world; in applying scientific research findings to problems in medicine, the life sciences, and the natural sciences; in imagining and manipulating quantitative data; and in applying technology to manufacturing, transportation, mining, and other economic activities.* You can satisfy this interest by working with the knowledge and processes of the sciences. You may enjoy researching and developing new knowledge in mathematics, or perhaps solving problems in the physical or life sciences would appeal to you. You may wish to study engineering and help create new machines, processes, and structures. If you want to work with scientific equipment and procedures, you could seek a job in a research or testing laboratory.

▲ **Plants and Animals:** *An interest in working with plants and animals, usually outdoors.* You can satisfy this interest by working in farming, forestry, fishing, and related fields. You may like doing physical work outdoors, such as on a farm. You may enjoy animals; perhaps training or taking care of animals would appeal to you. If you have management ability, you could own, operate, or manage a farm or related business.

▲ **Law, Law Enforcement, and Public Safety:** *An interest in upholding people's rights or in protecting people and property by using authority, inspecting, or monitoring.* You can satisfy this interest by working in law, law enforcement, firefighting, and related fields. For example, if you enjoy mental challenge and intrigue, you could investigate crimes or fires for a living. If you enjoy working with verbal skills, you may want to defend citizens in court or research deeds, wills, and other legal documents. You may prefer to fight fires and respond to other emergencies. Or, if you want more routine work, perhaps a job in guarding or patrolling would appeal to you; if you have management ability, you could seek a leadership position in law enforcement and the protective services. Work in the military gives you the chance to use technical and/or leadership skills while serving your country.

▲ **Mechanics, Installers, and Repairers:** *An interest in applying mechanical and electrical/electronic principles to practical situations by use of machines or hand tools.* You can satisfy this interest working with a variety of tools, technologies, materials, and settings. If you enjoy making machines run efficiently or fixing them when they break down, you could seek a job installing or repairing such devices as copiers, aircraft engines, automobiles, or watches. You may instead prefer to deal directly with certain materials and find work cutting and shaping metal or wood. Or, if electricity and electronics interest you, you could install cables, troubleshoot telephone networks, or repair videocassette recorders. If you prefer routine or physical work in settings other than factories, perhaps work repairing tires or batteries would appeal to you.

▲ **Construction, Mining, and Drilling:** *An interest in assembling components of buildings and other structures or in using mechanical devices to drill or excavate.* If construction interests you, you can find fulfillment in the many building projects that are being undertaken at all times. If you like to organize and plan, you can find careers in management. On the other hand, you can play a more direct role in putting up and finishing buildings by doing jobs such as plumbing, carpentry, masonry, painting, or roofing. You may like working at a mine or oilfield, operating the powerful drilling or digging equipment. There are also several jobs that let you put your hands to the task.

▲ **Transportation:** *An interest in operations that move people or materials.* You can satisfy this interest by managing a transportation service, by helping vehicles keep on their assigned schedules and routes, or by driving or piloting a vehicle. If you enjoy taking responsibility, perhaps managing a rail line would appeal to you. If you work well with details and can take pressure on the job, you might consider being an air traffic controller. Or would you rather get out on the highway, on the water, or up in the air? If so, then you could drive a truck from state to state, sail down the Mississippi on a barge, or fly a crop duster over a cornfield. If you prefer to stay closer to home, you could drive a delivery van, taxi, or school bus. You can use your physical strength to load freight and arrange it so it gets to its destination in one piece.

▲ **Industrial Production:** *An interest in repetitive, concrete, organized activities most often done in a factory setting.* You can satisfy this interest by working in one of many industries that mass-produce goods or for a utility that distributes electric power, gas, telephone service, and related services. You may enjoy manual work, using your hands or hand tools. Perhaps you prefer to operate machines. You may like to inspect, sort, count, or weigh products. Using your training and experience to set up machines or supervise other workers may appeal to you.

▲ **Business Detail:** *An interest in organized, clearly defined activities requiring accuracy and attention to details, primarily in an office setting.* You can satisfy this interest in a variety of jobs in which you attend to the details of a business operation. You may enjoy using your math skills; if so, perhaps a job in billing, computing, or financial record-keeping would satisfy you. If you prefer to deal with people, you may want a job in which you meet the public, talk on the telephone, or supervise other workers. You may like to do word processing on a computer, turn out copies on a duplicating machine, or work out sums on a calculator. Perhaps a job in filing or recording would satisfy you. Or you may wish to use your training and experience to manage an office.

▲ **Sales and Marketing:** *An interest in bringing others to a particular point of view by personal persuasion, using sales and promotional techniques.* You can satisfy this interest in a variety of sales and marketing jobs. If you like using technical knowledge of science or agriculture, you may enjoy selling technical products or services. Or perhaps you are more interested in selling business-related services, such as insurance coverage, advertising space, or investment opportunities. Real estate offers several kinds of sales jobs. Perhaps you'd rather work with something you can pick up and show to people. You may work in stores, sales offices, or customers' homes.

▲ **Recreation, Travel, and Other Personal Services:** *An interest in catering to the personal wishes and needs of others so that they may enjoy cleanliness, good food and drink, comfortable lodging away from home, and enjoyable recreation.* You can satisfy this interest by providing services for the convenience, feeding, and pampering of others in hotels, restaurants, airplanes, and so on. If you enjoy improving the appearance of others, perhaps working in the hair and beauty care field would satisfy you. You may wish to provide personal services such as taking care of small children, tailoring garments, or ushering. Or you may use your knowledge of the field to manage workers who are providing these services.

▲ **Education and Social Service:** *An interest in teaching people or improving their social or spiritual well-being.* You can satisfy this interest by teaching students, who may be preschoolers, retirees, or any age in between. Or, if you are interested in helping people sort out their complicated lives, you may find fulfillment as a counselor, social worker, or religious worker. Working in a museum or library may give you opportunities to expand people's understanding of the world. If you also have an interest in business, you may find satisfaction in managerial work in this field.

▲ **General Management and Support:** *An interest in making an organization run smoothly.* You can satisfy this interest by working in a position of leadership or by specializing in a function that contributes to the overall effort. The organization may be a profit-making business, a non-profit, or a government agency. If you especially enjoy working with people, you may find fulfillment from working in human resources. An interest in numbers may cause you to consider accounting, finance, budgeting, or purchasing. Or perhaps you would enjoy managing the organization's physical resources (such as land, buildings, equipment, and utilities).

▲ **Medical and Health Services:** *An interest in helping people be healthy.* You can satisfy this interest by working in a health-care team as a doctor, therapist, or nurse. You might specialize in one of the many different parts of the body or types of care, or you might be a generalist who deals with the whole patient. If you like technology, you might find satisfaction working with X rays, one of the electronic means of diagnosis, or clinical laboratory testing. You might work with healthy people, helping them stay in condition through exercise and eating right. If you like to organize, analyze, and plan, a managerial role might be right for you.

Best Jobs for College Graduates Interested in Arts, Entertainment, and Media

Job	Annual Earnings	Percent Growth	Annual Openings
1. Poets and Lyricists	$42,270	28%	18,000
2. Copy Writers	$42,270	28%	18,000
3. Public Relations Specialists	$39,580	36%	19,000
4. Writers and Authors	$42,270	28%	18,000
5. Creative Writers	$42,270	28%	18,000
6. Technical Writers	$47,790	30%	5,000
7. Agents and Business Managers of Artists, Performers, and Athletes	$57,040	28%	2,000
8. Art Directors	$56,880	21%	6,000
9. Commercial and Industrial Designers	$48,780	24%	7,000
10. Graphic Designers	$34,570	27%	28,000
11. Producers	$41,030	27%	11,000
12. Directors—Stage, Motion Pictures, Television, and Radio	$41,030	27%	11,000
13. Program Directors	$41,030	27%	11,000
14. Producers and Directors	$41,030	27%	11,000
15. Editors	$39,370	23%	14,000
16. Multi-Media Artists and Animators	$41,130	22%	8,000
17. Fashion Designers	$48,530	20%	2,000
18. Interior Designers	$36,540	17%	7,000
19. Film and Video Editors	$34,160	26%	2,000
20. Exhibit Designers	$31,440	27%	2,000
21. Set Designers	$31,440	27%	2,000
22. Set and Exhibit Designers	$31,440	27%	2,000
23. Composers	$31,510	13%	9,000
24. Music Arrangers and Orchestrators	$31,510	13%	9,000
25. Music Directors	$31,510	13%	9,000
26. Music Directors and Composers	$31,510	13%	9,000
27. Broadcast News Analysts	$29,110	3%	9,000

Best Jobs for College Graduates Interested in Science, Math, and Engineering

Job	Annual Earnings	Percent Growth	Annual Openings
1. Computer and Information Systems Managers	$78,830	48%	28,000
2. Computer Software Engineers, Applications	$67,670	100%	28,000
3. Computer Software Engineers, Systems Software	$69,530	90%	23,000
4. Computer Systems Analysts	$59,330	60%	34,000
5. Network and Computer Systems Administrators	$51,280	82%	18,000
6. Computer Security Specialists	$51,280	82%	18,000
7. Network Systems and Data Communications Analysts	$54,510	78%	9,000
8. Database Administrators	$51,990	66%	8,000
9. Industrial-Organizational Psychologists	$66,880	18%	18,000
10. Computer Support Specialists	$36,460	97%	40,000
11. Computer and Information Scientists, Research	$70,590	40%	2,000
12. Computer Programmers	$57,590	16%	36,000
13. Computer Hardware Engineers	$67,300	25%	3,000
14. Engineering Managers	$84,070	8%	24,000
15. Environmental Engineers	$57,780	26%	3,000
16. Medical Scientists, Except Epidemiologists	$57,810	26%	2,000
17. Biophysicists	$54,230	21%	5,000
18. Biochemists	$54,230	21%	5,000
19. Biochemists and Biophysicists	$54,230	21%	5,000
20. Economists	$64,830	18%	3,000
21. Biologists	$49,033	21%	5,000
22. Sales Engineers	$56,520	18%	4,000
23. Biomedical Engineers	$57,480	31%	fewer than 500
24. Microbiologists	$48,890	21%	5,000
25. Chemists	$50,080	19%	6,000
26. Electrical Engineers	$64,910	11%	8,000
27. Political Scientists	$81,040	17%	2,000
28. Epidemiologists	$48,390	26%	2,000
29. Hydrologists	$55,410	26%	1,000
30. Mechanical Engineers	$58,710	13%	7,000
31. Architects, Except Landscape and Naval	$52,510	18%	4,000
32. Zoologists and Wildlife Biologists	$43,980	21%	5,000
33. Geologists	$56,230	18%	2,000

Best Jobs for College Graduates Interested in Science, Math, and Engineering

Job	Annual Earnings	Percent Growth	Annual Openings
34. Geoscientists, Except Hydrologists and Geographers	$56,230	18%	2,000
35. Electronics Engineers, Except Computer	$64,830	10%	6,000
36. Environmental Scientists and Specialists, Including Health	$44,180	22%	4,000
37. Materials Scientists	$60,620	20%	1,000
38. Natural Sciences Managers	$75,880	8%	4,000
39. Aerospace Engineers	$67,930	14%	2,000
40. Landscape Architects	$43,540	31%	1,000
41. Nuclear Equipment Operation Technicians	$59,160	21%	fewer than 500
42. Industrial Engineers	$58,580	4%	10,000
43. Nuclear Technicians	$59,160	21%	fewer than 500
44. Architectural Drafters	$35,220	21%	12,000
45. Biological Technicians	$31,540	26%	7,000
46. Electrical Drafters	$38,210	23%	5,000
47. Electrical and Electronics Drafters	$38,210	23%	5,000
48. Electrical and Electronic Engineering Technicians	$40,020	11%	22,000
49. Electronics Engineering Technicians	$40,020	11%	22,000
50. Calibration and Instrumentation Technicians	$40,020	11%	22,000
51. Electrical Engineering Technicians	$40,020	11%	22,000
52. Civil Engineers	$55,740	10%	4,000
53. Physicists	$83,310	10%	1,000
54. Survey Researchers	$26,200	34%	3,000
55. Health and Safety Engineers, Except Mining Safety Engineers and Inspectors	$54,630	11%	3,000
56. Product Safety Engineers	$54,630	11%	3,000
57. Fire-Prevention and Protection Engineers	$54,630	11%	3,000
58. Environmental Engineering Technicians	$34,000	29%	2,000
59. Industrial Safety and Health Engineers	$54,630	11%	3,000
60. Astronomers	$74,510	10%	1,000
61. Atmospheric and Space Scientists	$58,510	17%	fewer than 500
62. Urban and Regional Planners	$46,500	16%	3,000
63. Geographers	$46,690	17%	2,000

(continued)

Best Jobs for College Graduates Interested in Science, Math, and Engineering

Job	Annual Earnings	Percent Growth	Annual Openings
64. Chemical Engineers	$65,960	4%	2,000
65. Operations Research Analysts	$53,420	8%	4,000
66. Chemical Technicians	$35,450	15%	13,000
67. Environmental Science and Protection Technicians, Including Health	$33,830	24%	3,000
68. Materials Engineers	$59,100	5%	2,000
69. Nuclear Engineers	$79,360	2%	1,000
70. Agricultural Engineers	$55,850	15%	fewer than 500
71. Actuaries	$66,590	5%	1,000
72. Mechanical Engineering Technicians	$39,570	14%	5,000
73. Historians	$39,860	17%	2,000
74. Industrial Engineering Technicians	$40,910	10%	5,000
75. Civil Engineering Technicians	$35,990	12%	9,000
76. Petroleum Engineers	$78,910	−7%	fewer than 500
77. Aerospace Engineering and Operations Technicians	$48,600	6%	2,000
78. Cartographers and Photogrammetrists	$39,410	18%	1,000
79. Mathematicians	$68,640	−2%	fewer than 500
80. Statisticians	$51,990	2%	2,000
81. Surveyors	$36,700	8%	7,000
82. Marine Engineers and Naval Architects	$60,890	2%	fewer than 500
83. Marine Engineers	$60,890	2%	fewer than 500
84. Marine Architects	$60,890	2%	fewer than 500
85. Anthropologists and Archeologists	$36,040	17%	2,000
86. Electro-Mechanical Technicians	$36,150	14%	4,000
87. Anthropologists	$36,040	17%	2,000
88. Archeologists	$36,040	17%	2,000
89. Mining and Geological Engineers, Including Mining Safety Engineers	$60,820	−1%	fewer than 500
90. Range Managers	$47,140	8%	1,000
91. Conservation Scientists	$47,140	8%	1,000
92. Soil Conservationists	$47,140	8%	1,000
93. Foresters	$43,640	7%	1,000

Best Jobs for College Graduates Interested in Science, Math, and Engineering

Job	Annual Earnings	Percent Growth	Annual Openings
94. Agricultural Technicians	$27,080	15%	3,000
95. Food Science Technicians	$27,080	15%	3,000
96. Geological Sample Test Technicians	$36,490	6%	2,000
97. Geological Data Technicians	$36,490	6%	2,000
98. Geological and Petroleum Technicians	$36,490	6%	2,000

Best Jobs for College Graduates Interested in Plants and Animals

Job	Annual Earnings	Percent Growth	Annual Openings
1. Veterinarians	$60,910	32%	2,000
2. Veterinary Technologists and Technicians	$21,640	39%	6,000
3. Forest and Conservation Technicians	$29,580	3%	2,000

Only three jobs are listed here because most jobs in this interest area do not typically require college degrees to enter, although many people with college degrees do work in these jobs.

Best Jobs for College Graduates Interested in Law, Law Enforcement, and Public Safety

Job	Annual Earnings	Percent Growth	Annual Openings
1. Lawyers	$88,280	18%	35,000
2. Paralegals and Legal Assistants	$35,360	33%	23,000
3. Nuclear Monitoring Technicians	$59,160	21%	fewer than 500
4. Arbitrators, Mediators, and Conciliators	$43,060	27%	fewer than 500
5. Judges, Magistrate Judges, and Magistrates	$86,760	1%	2,000
6. Occupational Health and Safety Technicians	$42,750	15%	4,000
7. Occupational Health and Safety Specialists	$42,750	15%	4,000
8. Financial Examiners	$53,060	10%	2,000
9. Administrative Law Judges, Adjudicators, and Hearing Officers	$61,240	1%	1,000
10. Fire Investigators	$41,630	15%	1,000
11. Forensic Science Technicians	$37,520	13%	1,000
12. Law Clerks	$28,510	13%	3,000

Best Jobs for College Graduates Interested in Being Mechanics, Installers, and Repairers

No jobs are listed in this interest area. This is because these jobs do not typically require college degrees to enter, although many people with college degrees do work in these jobs.

Best Jobs for College Graduates Interested in Construction, Mining, and Drilling

Job	Annual Earnings	Percent Growth	Annual Openings
1. Construction Managers	$58,250	16%	26,000

Only one job is listed here because most jobs in this interest area do not typically require college degrees to enter, although many people with college degrees do work in these jobs.

Best Jobs for College Graduates Interested in Transportation

Job	Annual Earnings	Percent Growth	Annual Openings
1. Airline Pilots, Copilots, and Flight Engineers	$110,940	6%	5,000
2. Pilots, Ship	$47,510	3%	2,000

Only two jobs are listed here because most jobs in this interest area do not typically require college degrees to enter, although many people with college degrees do work in these jobs.

Best Jobs for College Graduates Interested in Industrial Production

Job	Annual Earnings	Percent Growth	Annual Openings
1. Industrial Production Managers	$61,660	6%	22,000
2. Semiconductor Processors	$25,430	32%	7,000

Only two jobs are listed here because most jobs in this interest area do not typically require college degrees to enter, although many people with college degrees do work in these jobs.

Best Jobs for College Graduates Interested in Business Detail

Job	Annual Earnings	Percent Growth	Annual Openings
1. Administrative Services Managers	$47,080	20%	31,000
2. Medical Records and Health Information Technicians	$22,750	49%	14,000
3. Medical Transcriptionists	$25,270	30%	15,000

Only three jobs are listed here because most jobs in this interest area do not typically require college degrees to enter, although many people with college degrees do work in these jobs.

Best Jobs for College Graduates Interested in Sales and Marketing

Job	Annual Earnings	Percent Growth	Annual Openings
1. Sales Managers	$68,520	33%	21,000
2. Marketing Managers	$71,240	29%	12,000
3. Securities, Commodities, and Financial Services Sales Agents	$56,080	22%	55,000
4. Sales Agents, Securities and Commodities	$56,080	22%	55,000
5. Sales Agents, Financial Services	$56,080	22%	55,000
6. Advertising and Promotions Managers	$53,360	34%	7,000
7. Insurance Sales Agents	$38,750	3%	43,000

Best Jobs for College Graduates Interested in Recreation, Travel, and Other Personal Services

Job	Annual Earnings	Percent Growth	Annual Openings
1. Gaming Managers	$53,380	30%	fewer than 500
2. Recreation Workers	$17,130	20%	32,000
3. Meeting and Convention Planners	$35,540	23%	3,000

Only three jobs are listed here because most jobs in this interest area do not typically require college degrees to enter, although many people with college degrees do work in these jobs.

Best Jobs for College Graduates Interested in Education and Social Service

Job	Annual Earnings	Percent Growth	Annual Openings
1. Personal Financial Advisors	$55,320	34%	13,000
2. Postsecondary Teachers	$46,330	23.5%	184,000
3. Education Administrators, Elementary and Secondary School	$66,930	13%	35,000
4. Special Education Teachers, Preschool, Kindergarten, and Elementary School	$40,880.	37%	15,000
5. Educational, Vocational, and School Counselors	$42,110	25%	22,000
6. Instructional Coordinators	$44,230	25%	15,000
7. Secondary School Teachers, Except Special and Vocational Education	$40,870	19%	60,000
8. Counseling Psychologists	$48,320	18%	18,000
9. Clinical Psychologists	$48,320	18%	18,000
10. Clinical, Counseling, and School Psychologists	$48,320	18%	18,000
11. Educational Psychologists	$48,320	18%	18,000
12. Child, Family, and School Social Workers	$31,470	27%	35,000
13. Medical and Public Health Social Workers	$34,790	32%	13,000
14. Social and Community Service Managers	$39,130	25%	13,000
15. Special Education Teachers, Secondary School	$41,290	25%	8,000
16. Probation Officers and Correctional Treatment Specialists	$38,150	24%	14,000
17. Mental Health and Substance Abuse Social Workers	$30,170	39%	10,000
18. Elementary School Teachers, Except Special Education	$39,700	13%	144,000
19. Preschool Teachers, Except Special Education	$17,810	20%	55,000
20. Substance Abuse and Behavioral Disorder Counselors	$28,510	35%	7,000
21. Special Education Teachers, Middle School	$38,600	24%	6,000
22. Middle School Teachers, Except Special and Vocational Education	$39,750	10%	54,000
23. Kindergarten Teachers, Except Special Education	$37,610	14%	23,000
24. Rehabilitation Counselors	$24,450	24%	12,000

(continued)

(continued)

Best Jobs for College Graduates Interested in Education and Social Service

Job	Annual Earnings	Percent Growth	Annual Openings
25. Adult Literacy, Remedial Education, and GED Teachers and Instructors	$33,540	19%	12,000
26. Marriage and Family Therapists	$34,660	30%	2,000
27. Education Administrators, Preschool and Child Care Center/Program	$30,420	13%	35,000
28. Vocational Education Teachers, Secondary School	$42,080	13%	7,000
29. Directors, Religious Activities and Education	$27,000	16%	23,000
30. Mental Health Counselors	$27,570	22%	7,000
31. Clergy	$31,760	15%	12,000
32. Librarians	$41,700	7%	6,000
33. Vocational Education Teachers, Middle School	$39,330	13%	2,000
34. Park Naturalists	$47,140	8%	1,000
35. Farm and Home Management Advisors	$36,290	6%	2,000

Best Jobs for College Graduates Interested in General Management and Support

Job	Annual Earnings	Percent Growth	Annual Openings
1. Management Analysts	$55,040	29%	50,000
2. Treasurers, Controllers, and Chief Financial Officers	$67,020	18%	53,000
3. Financial Managers, Branch or Department	$67,020	18%	53,000
4. Financial Managers	$67,020	18%	53,000
5. Government Service Executives	$113,810	17%	48,000
6. Private Sector Executives	$113,810	17%	48,000
7. Chief Executives	$113,810	17%	48,000
8. Financial Analysts	$52,420	26%	20,000
9. General and Operations Managers	$61,160	15%	235,000
10. Public Relations Managers	$54,540	36%	7,000
11. Market Research Analysts	$51,190	24%	13,000
12. Accountants and Auditors	$43,500	18%	100,000
13. Accountants	$43,500	18%	100,000
14. Auditors	$43,500	18%	100,000
15. Cost Estimators	$45,800	16%	28,000
16. Human Resources Managers	$59,000	13%	14,000
17. Property, Real Estate, and Community Association Managers	$36,020	23%	24,000
18. Training and Development Specialists	$40,830	19%	20,000
19. Employment, Recruitment, and Placement Specialists	$36,480	18%	19,000
20. Employment Interviewers, Private or Public Employment Service	$36,480	18%	19,000
21. Personnel Recruiters	$36,480	18%	19,000
22. Budget Analysts	$48,370	15%	8,000
23. Purchasing Agents, Except Wholesale, Retail, and Farm Products	$41,370	12%	23,000
24. Loan Officers	$41,420	5%	28,000
25. Purchasing Managers	$53,030	−6%	17,000
26. Compensation, Benefits, and Job Analysis Specialists	$41,660	16%	8,000
27. Credit Analysts	$40,180	16%	7,000
28. Insurance Underwriters	$43,150	2%	11,000

(continued)

Best Jobs for College Graduates Interested in General Management and Support

Job	Annual Earnings	Percent Growth	Annual Openings
29. Wholesale and Retail Buyers, Except Farm Products	$37,200	−9%	18,000
30. Tax Examiners, Collectors, and Revenue Agents	$40,180	8%	6,000
31. Loan Counselors	$32,160	16%	3,000
32. Funeral Directors	$41,110	3%	3,000

Best Jobs for College Graduates Interested in Medical and Health Services

Job	Annual Earnings	Percent Growth	Annual Openings
1. Medical and Health Services Managers	$56,370	32%	27,000
2. Pharmacists	$70,950	24%	20,000
3. Internists, General	$142,400	18%	27,000
4. Pediatricians, General	$125,970	18%	27,000
5. Psychiatrists	$118,640	18%	27,000
6. Family and General Practitioners	$114,170	18%	27,000
7. Physician Assistants	$61,910	54%	5,000
8. Registered Nurses	$44,840	26%	140,000
9. Physical Therapists	$54,810	33%	6,000
10. Dental Hygienists	$51,330	37%	5,000
11. Occupational Therapists	$49,450	34%	4,000
12. Speech-Language Pathologists	$46,640	39%	4,000
13. Physical Therapist Assistants	$33,870	45%	9,000
14. Optometrists	$82,860	19%	1,000
15. Diagnostic Medical Sonographers	$44,820	26%	3,000
16. Audiologists	$44,830	45%	1,000
17. Respiratory Therapists	$37,680	35%	4,000
18. Medical and Clinical Laboratory Technologists	$40,510	17%	19,000
19. Radiologic Technicians	$36,000	23%	13,000
20. Radiologic Technologists and Technicians	$36,000	23%	13,000
21. Radiologic Technologists	$36,000	23%	13,000
22. Physical Therapist Aides	$19,670	46%	7,000
23. Occupational Therapist Assistants	$34,340	40%	3,000
24. Podiatrists	$107,560	14%	1,000
25. Cardiovascular Technologists and Technicians	$33,350	35%	3,000
26. Health Educators	$33,860	24%	7,000
27. Medical and Clinical Laboratory Technicians	$27,540	19%	19,000
28. Radiation Therapists	$47,470	23%	1,000
29. Nuclear Medicine Technologists	$44,130	22%	1,000
30. Dietitians and Nutritionists	$38,450	15%	5,000
31. Orthotists and Prosthetists	$45,740	17%	1,000
32. Athletic Trainers	$32,080	18%	2,000
33. Recreational Therapists	$28,650	9%	1,000

Best Jobs Lists for College Graduates Based on Personality Types

These lists organize the 258 jobs requiring a college degree into groups matching six personality types. The personality types are Realistic, Investigative, Artistic, Social, Enterprising, and Conventional. This system was developed by John Holland and is used in the Self Directed Search (SDS) and other career assessment inventories and information systems.

If you have used one of these career inventories or systems, the lists will help you identify jobs that most closely match these personality types. Even if you have not used one of these systems, the concept of personality types and the jobs that are related to them can help you identify jobs that most closely match the type of person you are.

We've ranked the jobs within each personality type based on their total combined scores for earnings, growth, and annual job openings. Like the job lists for education levels, there is only one list for each personality type. Note that each of the 258 jobs is listed in the one personality type it most closely matches, even though it might also fit into others. Consider reviewing the jobs for more than one personality type so you don't overlook possible jobs that would interest you.

Following are brief descriptions for each of the six personality types used in the lists. Select the two or three descriptions that most closely describe you and then use the lists to identify jobs that best fit these personality types.

Descriptions of the Six Personality Types

▲ **Realistic:** These occupations frequently involve work activities that include practical, hands-on problems and solutions. They often deal with plants, animals, and real-world materials like wood, tools, and machinery. Many of the occupations require working outside and do not involve a lot of paperwork or working closely with others.

▲ **Investigative:** These occupations frequently involve working with ideas and require an extensive amount of thinking. These occupations can involve searching for facts and figuring out problems mentally.

▲ **Artistic:** These occupations frequently involve working with forms, designs, and patterns. They often require self-expression, and the work can be done without following a clear set of rules.

▲ **Social:** These occupations frequently involve working with, communicating with, and teaching people. These occupations often involve helping or providing service to others.

▲ **Enterprising:** These occupations frequently involve starting up and carrying out projects. These occupations can involve leading people and making many decisions. They sometimes require risk taking and often deal with business.

▲ **Conventional:** These occupations frequently involve following set procedures and routines. These occupations can include working with data and details more than with ideas. Usually there is a clear line of authority to follow.

Best Jobs for College Graduates with a Realistic Personality Type

Job	Annual Earnings	Percent Growth	Annual Openings
1. Financial Managers	$67,020	18%	53,000
2. Network and Computer Systems Administrators	$51,280	82%	18,000
3. Chief Executives	$113,810	17%	48,000
4. Securities, Commodities, and Financial Services Sales Agents	$56,080	22%	55,000
5. General and Operations Managers	$61,160	15%	235,000
6. Mechanical Engineers	$58,710	13%	7,000
7. Radiologic Technologists and Technicians	$36,000	23%	13,000
8. Radiologic Technicians	$36,000	23%	13,000
9. Radiologic Technologists	$36,000	23%	13,000
10. Airline Pilots, Copilots, and Flight Engineers	$110,940	6%	5,000
11. Nuclear Technicians	$59,160	21%	fewer than 500
12. Nuclear Equipment Operation Technicians	$59,160	21%	fewer than 500
13. Nuclear Monitoring Technicians	$59,160	21%	fewer than 500
14. Semiconductor Processors	$25,430	32%	7,000
15. Veterinary Technologists and Technicians	$21,640	39%	6,000
16. Architectural Drafters	$35,220	21%	12,000
17. Biological Technicians	$31,540	26%	7,000
18. Calibration and Instrumentation Technicians	$40,020	11%	22,000
19. Electrical Engineering Technicians	$40,020	11%	22,000
20. Electronics Engineering Technicians	$40,020	11%	22,000
21. Medical and Clinical Laboratory Technicians	$27,540	19%	19,000
22. Civil Engineers	$55,740	10%	4,000
23. Chemical Technicians	$35,450	15%	13,000
24. Mechanical Engineering Technicians	$39,570	14%	5,000
25. Civil Engineering Technicians	$35,990	12%	9,000
26. Petroleum Engineers	$78,910	−7%	fewer than 500

(continued)

(continued)

Best Jobs for College Graduates with a Realistic Personality Type

Job	Annual Earnings	Percent Growth	Annual Openings
27. Marine Engineers and Naval Architects	$60,890	2%	fewer than 500
28. Marine Architects	$60,890	2%	fewer than 500
29. Marine Engineers	$60,890	2%	fewer than 500
30. Electro-Mechanical Technicians	$36,150	14%	4,000
31. Pilots, Ship	$47,510	3%	2,000
32. Foresters	$43,640	7%	1,000
33. Agricultural Technicians	$27,080	15%	3,000
34. Food Science Technicians	$27,080	15%	3,000
35. Geological and Petroleum Technicians	$36,490	6%	2,000
36. Geological Data Technicians	$36,490	6%	2,000
37. Geological Sample Test Technicians	$36,490	6%	2,000
38. Forest and Conservation Technicians	$29,580	3%	2,000

Best Jobs for College Graduates with an Investigative Personality Type

Job	Annual Earnings	Percent Growth	Annual Openings
1. Computer Software Engineers, Applications	$67,670	100%	28,000
2. Computer Software Engineers, Systems Software	$69,530	90%	23,000
3. Computer Systems Analysts	$59,330	60%	34,000
4. Pharmacists	$70,950	24%	20,000
5. Internists, General	$142,400	18%	27,000
6. Pediatricians, General	$125,970	18%	27,000
7. Psychiatrists	$118,640	18%	27,000
8. Family and General Practitioners	$114,170	18%	27,000
9. Computer Security Specialists	$51,280	82%	18,000
10. Physician Assistants	$61,910	54%	5,000
11. Network Systems and Data Communications Analysts	$54,510	78%	9,000
12. Financial Analysts	$52,420	26%	20,000
13. Database Administrators	$51,990	66%	8,000
14. Industrial-Organizational Psychologists	$66,880	18%	18,000
15. Computer Support Specialists	$36,460	97%	40,000
16. Computer and Information Scientists, Research	$70,590	40%	2,000
17. Computer Programmers	$57,590	16%	36,000
18. Market Research Analysts	$51,190	24%	13,000
19. Veterinarians	$60,910	32%	2,000
20. Computer Hardware Engineers	$67,300	25%	3,000
21. Environmental Engineers	$57,780	26%	3,000
22. Clinical Psychologists	$48,320	18%	18,000
23. Educational Psychologists	$48,320	18%	18,000
24. Medical Scientists, Except Epidemiologists	$57,810	26%	2,000
25. Biochemists	$54,230	21%	5,000
26. Biochemists and Biophysicists	$54,230	21%	5,000
27. Biophysicists	$54,230	21%	5,000
28. Economists	$64,830	18%	3,000
29. Biologists	$49,033	21%	5,000
30. Biomedical Engineers	$57,480	31%	fewer than 500
31. Microbiologists	$48,890	21%	5,000
32. Chemists	$50,080	19%	6,000

(continued)

(continued)

Best Jobs for College Graduates with an Investigative Personality Type

Job	Annual Earnings	Percent Growth	Annual Openings
33. Electrical Engineers	$64,910	11%	8,000
34. Political Scientists	$81,040	17%	2,000
35. Optometrists	$82,860	19%	1,000
36. Epidemiologists	$48,390	26%	2,000
37. Hydrologists	$55,410	26%	1,000
38. Diagnostic Medical Sonographers	$44,820	26%	3,000
39. Respiratory Therapists	$37,680	35%	4,000
40. Medical and Clinical Laboratory Technologists	$40,510	17%	19,000
41. Zoologists and Wildlife Biologists	$43,980	21%	5,000
42. Geologists	$56,230	18%	2,000
43. Geoscientists, Except Hydrologists and Geographers	$56,230	18%	2,000
44. Electronics Engineers, Except Computer	$64,830	10%	6,000
45. Environmental Scientists and Specialists, Including Health	$44,180	22%	4,000
46. Materials Scientists	$60,620	20%	1,000
47. Natural Sciences Managers	$75,880	8%	4,000
48. Aerospace Engineers	$67,930	14%	2,000
49. Cardiovascular Technologists and Technicians	$33,350	35%	3,000
50. Compensation, Benefits, and Job Analysis Specialists	$41,660	16%	8,000
51. Physicists	$83,310	10%	1,000
52. Survey Researchers	$26,200	34%	3,000
53. Fire-Prevention and Protection Engineers	$54,630	11%	3,000
54. Health and Safety Engineers, Except Mining Safety Engineers and Inspectors	$54,630	11%	3,000
55. Industrial Safety and Health Engineers	$54,630	11%	3,000
56. Product Safety Engineers	$54,630	11%	3,000
57. Nuclear Medicine Technologists	$44,130	22%	1,000
58. Environmental Engineering Technicians	$34,000	29%	2,000
59. Astronomers	$74,510	10%	1,000
60. Atmospheric and Space Scientists	$58,510	17%	fewer than 500
61. Urban and Regional Planners	$46,500	16%	3,000
62. Geographers	$46,690	17%	2,000

Best Jobs for College Graduates with an Investigative Personality Type

Job	Annual Earnings	Percent Growth	Annual Openings
63. Chemical Engineers	$65,960	4%	2,000
64. Operations Research Analysts	$53,420	8%	4,000
65. Environmental Science and Protection Technicians, Including Health	$33,830	24%	3,000
66. Occupational Health and Safety Technicians	$42,750	15%	4,000
67. Materials Engineers	$59,100	5%	2,000
68. Nuclear Engineers	$79,360	2%	1,000
69. Agricultural Engineers	$55,850	15%	fewer than 500
70. Dietitians and Nutritionists	$38,450	15%	5,000
71. Historians	$39,860	17%	2,000
72. Industrial Engineering Technicians	$40,910	10%	5,000
73. Aerospace Engineering and Operations Technicians	$48,600	6%	2,000
74. Mathematicians	$68,640	-2%	fewer than 500
75. Statisticians	$51,990	2%	2,000
76. Surveyors	$36,700	8%	7,000
77. Anthropologists	$36,040	17%	2,000
78. Anthropologists and Archeologists	$36,040	17%	2,000
79. Archeologists	$36,040	17%	2,000
80. Fire Investigators	$41,630	15%	1,000
81. Mining and Geological Engineers, Including Mining Safety Engineers	$60,820	-1%	fewer than 500
82. Conservation Scientists	$47,140	8%	1,000
83. Range Managers	$47,140	8%	1,000
84. Soil Conservationists	$47,140	8%	1,000
85. Forensic Science Technicians	$37,520	13%	1,000

Best Jobs for College Graduates with an Artistic Personality Type

Job	Annual Earnings	Percent Growth	Annual Openings
1. Advertising and Promotions Managers	$53,360	34%	7,000
2. Writers and Authors	$42,270	28%	18,000
3. Copy Writers	$42,270	28%	18,000
4. Creative Writers	$42,270	28%	18,000
5. Poets and Lyricists	$42,270	28%	18,000
6. Technical Writers	$47,790	30%	5,000
7. Art Directors	$56,880	21%	6,000
8. Commercial and Industrial Designers	$48,780	24%	7,000
9. Graphic Designers	$34,570	27%	28,000
10. Producers and Directors	$41,030	27%	11,000
11. Directors—Stage, Motion Pictures, Television, and Radio	$41,030	27%	11,000
12. Producers	$41,030	27%	11,000
13. Editors	$39,370	23%	14,000
14. Multi-Media Artists and Animators	$41,130	22%	8,000
15. Architects, Except Landscape and Naval	$52,510	18%	4,000
16. Landscape Architects	$43,540	31%	1,000
17. Fashion Designers	$48,530	20%	2,000
18. Interior Designers	$36,540	17%	7,000
19. Film and Video Editors	$34,160	26%	2,000
20. Set and Exhibit Designers	$31,440	27%	2,000
21. Exhibit Designers	$31,440	27%	2,000
22. Set Designers	$31,440	27%	2,000
23. Librarians	$41,700	7%	6,000
24. Music Directors and Composers	$31,510	13%	9,000
25. Composers	$31,510	13%	9,000
26. Music Arrangers and Orchestrators	$31,510	13%	9,000
27. Music Directors	$31,510	13%	9,000
28. Broadcast News Analysts	$29,110	3%	9,000

Best Jobs for College Graduates with a Social Personality Type

Job	Annual Earnings	Percent Growth	Annual Openings
1. Personal Financial Advisors	$55,320	34%	13,000
2. Registered Nurses	$44,840	26%	140,000
3. Postsecondary Teachers	$46,330	24%	184,000
4. Physical Therapists	$54,810	33%	6,000
5. Education Administrators, Elementary and Secondary School	$66,930	13%	35,000
6. Dental Hygienists	$51,330	37%	5,000
7. Special Education Teachers, Preschool, Kindergarten, and Elementary School	$40,880	37%	15,000
8. Educational, Vocational, and School Counselors	$42,110	25%	22,000
9. Instructional Coordinators	$44,230	25%	15,000
10. Occupational Therapists	$49,450	34%	4,000
11. Secondary School Teachers, Except Special and Vocational Education	$40,870	19%	60,000
12. Speech-Language Pathologists	$46,640	39%	4,000
13. Clinical, Counseling, and School Psychologists	$48,320	18%	18,000
14. Counseling Psychologists	$48,320	18%	18,000
15. Child, Family, and School Social Workers	$31,470	27%	35,000
16. Medical and Public Health Social Workers	$34,790	32%	13,000
17. Social and Community Service Managers	$39,130	25%	13,000
18. Training and Development Specialists	$40,830	19%	20,000
19. Physical Therapist Assistants	$33,870	45%	9,000
20. Special Education Teachers, Secondary School	$41,290	25%	8,000
21. Probation Officers and Correctional Treatment Specialists	$38,150	24%	14,000
22. Mental Health and Substance Abuse Social Workers	$30,170	39%	10,000
23. Elementary School Teachers, Except Special Education	$39,700	13%	144,000
24. Audiologists	$44,830	45%	1,000
25. Preschool Teachers, Except Special Education	$17,810	20%	55,000
26. Employment Interviewers, Private or Public Employment Service	$36,480	18%	19,000
27. Substance Abuse and Behavioral Disorder Counselors	$28,510	35%	7,000

(continued)

(continued)

Best Jobs for College Graduates with a Social Personality Type

Job	Annual Earnings	Percent Growth	Annual Openings
28. Physical Therapist Aides	$19,670	46%	7,000
29. Special Education Teachers, Middle School	$38,600	24%	6,000
30. Middle School Teachers, Except Special and Vocational Education	$39,750	10%	54,000
31. Recreation Workers	$17,130	20%	32,000
32. Occupational Therapist Assistants	$34,340	40%	3,000
33. Podiatrists	$107,560	14%	1,000
34. Kindergarten Teachers, Except Special Education	$37,610	14%	23,000
35. Health Educators	$33,860	24%	7,000
36. Radiation Therapists	$47,470	23%	1,000
37. Rehabilitation Counselors	$24,450	24%	12,000
38. Adult Literacy, Remedial Education, and GED Teachers and Instructors	$33,540	19%	12,000
39. Marriage and Family Therapists	$34,660	30%	2,000
40. Education Administrators, Preschool and Child Care Center/Program	$30,420	13%	35,000
41. Vocational Education Teachers, Secondary School	$42,080	13%	7,000
42. Directors, Religious Activities and Education	$27,000	16%	23,000
43. Mental Health Counselors	$27,570	22%	7,000
44. Occupational Health and Safety Specialists	$42,750	15%	4,000
45. Clergy	$31,760	15%	12,000
46. Orthotists and Prosthetists	$45,740	17%	1,000
47. Athletic Trainers	$32,080	18%	2,000
48. Vocational Education Teachers, Middle School	$39,330	13%	2,000
49. Park Naturalists	$47,140	8%	1,000
50. Farm and Home Management Advisors	$36,290	6%	2,000
51. Recreational Therapists	$28,650	9%	1,000

Best Jobs for College Graduates with an Enterprising Personality Type

Job	Annual Earnings	Percent Growth	Annual Openings
1. Computer and Information Systems Managers	$78,830	48%	28,000
2. Sales Managers	$68,520	33%	21,000
3. Management Analysts	$55,040	29%	50,000
4. Medical and Health Services Managers	$56,370	32%	27,000
5. Lawyers	$88,280	18%	35,000
6. Marketing Managers	$71,240	29%	12,000
7. Financial Managers, Branch or Department	$67,020	18%	53,000
8. Treasurers, Controllers, and Chief Financial Officers	$67,020	18%	53,000
9. Government Service Executives	$113,810	17%	48,000
10. Private Sector Executives	$113,810	17%	48,000
11. Sales Agents, Financial Services	$56,080	22%	55,000
12. Sales Agents, Securities and Commodities	$56,080	22%	55,000
13. Public Relations Managers	$54,540	36%	7,000
14. Public Relations Specialists	$39,580	36%	19,000
15. Construction Managers	$58,250	16%	26,000
16. Administrative Services Managers	$47,080	20%	31,000
17. Engineering Managers	$84,070	8%	24,000
18. Paralegals and Legal Assistants	$35,360	33%	23,000
19. Agents and Business Managers of Artists, Performers, and Athletes	$57,040	28%	2,000
20. Program Directors	$41,030	27%	11,000
21. Industrial Production Managers	$61,660	6%	22,000
22. Human Resources Managers	$59,000	13%	14,000
23. Property, Real Estate, and Community Association Managers	$36,020	23%	24,000
24. Sales Engineers	$56,520	18%	4,000
25. Gaming Managers	$53,380	30%	fewer than 500
26. Personnel Recruiters	$36,480	18%	19,000
27. Employment, Recruitment, and Placement Specialists	$36,480	18%	19,000
28. Purchasing Agents, Except Wholesale, Retail, and Farm Products	$41,370	12%	23,000
29. Industrial Engineers	$58,580	4%	10,000

(continued)

(continued)

Best Jobs for College Graduates with an Enterprising Personality Type

Job	Annual Earnings	Percent Growth	Annual Openings
30. Loan Officers	$41,420	5%	28,000
31. Purchasing Managers	$53,030	−6%	17,000
32. Arbitrators, Mediators, and Conciliators	$43,060	27%	fewer than 500
33. Insurance Sales Agents	$38,750	3%	43,000
34. Judges, Magistrate Judges, and Magistrates	$86,760	1%	2,000
35. Meeting and Convention Planners	$35,540	23%	3,000
36. Financial Examiners	$53,060	10%	2,000
37. Wholesale and Retail Buyers, Except Farm Products	$37,200	−9%	18,000
38. Administrative Law Judges, Adjudicators, and Hearing Officers	$61,240	1%	1,000
39. Loan Counselors	$32,160	16%	3,000
40. Funeral Directors	$41,110	3%	3,000
41. Law Clerks	$28,510	13%	3,000

Best Jobs for College Graduates with a Conventional Personality Type

Job	Annual Earnings	Percent Growth	Annual Openings
1. Accountants and Auditors	$43,500	18%	100,000
2. Accountants	$43,500	18%	100,000
3. Auditors	$43,500	18%	100,000
4. Cost Estimators	$45,800	16%	28,000
5. Medical Records and Health Information Technicians	$22,750	49%	14,000
6. Medical Transcriptionists	$25,270	30%	15,000
7. Budget Analysts	$48,370	15%	8,000
8. Electrical and Electronics Drafters	$38,210	23%	5,000
9. Electrical Drafters	$38,210	23%	5,000
10. Electrical and Electronic Engineering Technicians	$40,020	11%	22,000
11. Credit Analysts	$40,180	16%	7,000
12. Insurance Underwriters	$43,150	2%	11,000
13. Actuaries	$66,590	5%	1,000
14. Tax Examiners, Collectors, and Revenue Agents	$40,180	8%	6,000
15. Cartographers and Photogrammetrists	$39,410	18%	1,000

Part II

The Job Descriptions

This part provides descriptions for all the jobs included in one or more of the lists in Part I. The Introduction gives more details on how to use and interpret the job descriptions, but here is some additional information:

▲ Job descriptions are arranged in alphabetical order by job title. This approach allows you to quickly find a description if you know its correct title from one of the lists in Part I.

▲ If you are using this section to browse for interesting options, we suggest you begin with the Table of Contents. Part I features many interesting lists that will help you identify job titles to explore in more detail. If you have not browsed Part I's lists, consider spending some time there. The lists are interesting and will help you identify job titles you can find described in the material that follows. The job titles are also listed in the Table of Contents for Part II.

▲ We include descriptions for the many specific jobs that we included under the single job title of Postsecondary Teachers in the lists in Part I. These more-specific job titles are also cross-referenced under the Postsecondary Teachers job title in Part II and include Law Teachers, Postsecondary; Engineering Teachers, Postsecondary; Agricultural Sciences Teachers, Postsecondary; Economics Teachers, Postsecondary; Health Specialties Teachers, Postsecondary; Physics Teachers, Postsecondary; Forestry and Conservation Science Teachers, Postsecondary; Anthropology and Archeology Teachers, Postsecondary; Atmospheric, Earth, Marine, and Space Sciences Teachers, Postsecondary; Biological Science Teachers, Postsecondary; Graduate Teaching Assistants; Environmental Science Teachers, Postsecondary; Geography Teachers, Postsecondary; Business Teachers, Postsecondary; Political Science Teachers, Postsecondary; Chemistry Teachers, Postsecondary; Area, Ethnic, and Cultural Studies Teachers, Postsecondary; Psychology Teachers, Postsecondary;

(continued)

(continued)

Architecture Teachers, Postsecondary; Education Administrators, Postsecondary; Library Science Teachers, Postsecondary; History Teachers, Postsecondary; Social Work Teachers, Postsecondary; Sociology Teachers, Postsecondary; Nursing Instructors and Teachers, Postsecondary; Mathematical Science Teachers, Postsecondary; Computer Science Teachers, Postsecondary; Home Economics Teachers, Postsecondary; Philosophy and Religion Teachers, Postsecondary; Communications Teachers, Postsecondary; Art, Drama, and Music Teachers, Postsecondary; Education Teachers, Postsecondary; Foreign Language and Literature Teachers, Postsecondary; English Language and Literature Teachers, Postsecondary; Recreation and Fitness Studies Teachers, Postsecondary; and Criminal Justice and Law Enforcement Teachers, Postsecondary.

Accountants

- ▲ Education/Training Required: Bachelor's degree
- ▲ Annual Earnings: $43,500
- ▲ Growth: 18%
- ▲ Annual Job Openings: 100,000
- ▲ Self-Employed: 10.6%
- ▲ Part-Time: 7.8%

Analyze financial information and prepare financial reports to determine or maintain record of assets, liabilities, profit and loss, tax liability, or other financial activities within an organization. Analyzes operations, trends, costs, revenues, financial commitments, and obligations incurred to project future revenues and expenses, using computer. Computes taxes owed; ensures compliance with tax payment, reporting, and other tax requirements; and represents establishment before taxing authority. Directs activities of workers performing accounting and bookkeeping tasks. Adapts accounting and recordkeeping functions to current technology of computerized accounting systems. Appraises, evaluates, and inventories real property and equipment and records description, value, location, and other information. Prepares forms and manuals for workers performing accounting and bookkeeping tasks. Audits contracts and prepares reports to substantiate transactions prior to settlement. Establishes table of accounts and assigns entries to proper accounts. Surveys establishment operations to ascertain accounting needs. Predicts revenues and expenditures and submits reports to management. Develops, maintains, and analyzes budgets and prepares periodic reports comparing budgeted costs to actual costs. Prepares balance sheet, profit and loss statement, amortization and depreciation schedules, and other financial reports, using calculator or computer. Reports finances of establishment to management and advises management about resource utilization, tax strategies, and assumptions underlying budget forecasts. Develops, implements, modifies, and documents budgeting, cost, general, property, and tax accounting systems. Analyzes records of financial transactions to determine accuracy and completeness of entries, using computer. **SKILLS**—Management of Financial Resources: Determining how money will be spent to get the work done and accounting for these expenditures. Judgment and Decision Making: Considering the relative costs and benefits of potential actions to choose the most appropriate one. Mathematics: Using mathematics to solve problems. Systems Evaluation: Identifying measures or indicators of system performance and the actions needed to improve or correct performance relative to the goals of the system. Monitoring: Monitoring/Assessing your performance or that of other individuals or organizations to make improvements or take corrective action.

GOE INFORMATION—Interest Area: 13. General Management and Support. **Work Group:** 13.02. Management Support. **Other Job Titles in This Work Group:** Accountants and Auditors; Appraisers and Assessors of Real Estate; Appraisers, Real Estate; Assessors; Auditors; Budget Analysts; Claims Adjusters, Examiners, and Investigators; Claims Examiners, Property and Casualty Insurance; Compensation, Benefits, and Job Analysis Specialists; Cost Estimators; Credit Analysts; Employment Interviewers, Private or Public Employment Service; Employment, Recruitment, and Placement Specialists; Financial Analysts; Human Resources, Training, and Labor Relations Specialists, All Other; Insurance Adjusters, Examiners, and Investigators; Insurance Appraisers, Auto Damage; Insurance Underwriters; Loan Counselors; Loan Officers; Logisticians; Management Analysts; Market Research Analysts; Personnel Recruiters; Purchasing Agents and Buyers, Farm Products; Purchasing Agents, Except Wholesale, Retail, and Farm Products; Tax Examiners, Collectors, and Revenue Agents; Training and Development Specialists; Wholesale and Retail Buyers, Except Farm Products. **PERSONALITY TYPE**—Conventional. Conventional occupations frequently involve following set procedures and routines. These occupations can include working with data and details more than with ideas. Usually there is a clear line of authority to follow.

EDUCATION/TRAINING PROGRAM(S)—Accounting; Taxation. **RELATED KNOWLEDGE/COURSES—Economics and Accounting:** Knowledge of economic and accounting principles and practices, the financial markets, banking, and the analysis and reporting of financial data. **Mathematics:** Knowledge of arithmetic, algebra, geometry, calculus, and statistics and their applications. **Administration and Management:** Knowledge of business and management principles involved in strategic planning, resource allocation, human resources modeling, leadership technique, production methods, and coordination of people and resources. **English Language:** Knowledge of the structure and content of the English language, including the meaning and spelling of words, rules of composition, and grammar. **Clerical Studies:** Knowledge of administrative and clerical procedures and systems such as word processing, managing files and records, stenography and transcription, designing forms, and other office procedures and terminology.

Accountants and Auditors

- ▲ Education/Training Required: Bachelor's degree
- ▲ Annual Earnings: $43,500
- ▲ Growth: 18%
- ▲ Annual Job Openings: 100,000
- ▲ Self-Employed: 10.6%
- ▲ Part-Time: 7.8%

Examine, analyze, and interpret accounting records for the purpose of giving advice or preparing statements. Install or advise on systems of recording costs or other financial and budgetary data. SKILLS—No data available.

GOE INFORMATION—Interest Area: 13. General Management and Support. **Work Group:** 13.02. Management Support. **Other Job Titles in This Work Group:** Accountants; Appraisers and Assessors of Real Estate; Appraisers, Real Estate; Assessors; Auditors; Budget Analysts; Claims Adjusters, Examiners, and Investigators; Claims Examiners, Property and Casualty Insurance; Compensation, Benefits, and Job Analysis Specialists; Cost Estimators; Credit Analysts; Employment Interviewers, Private or Public Employment Service; Employment, Recruitment, and Placement Specialists; Financial Analysts; Human Resources, Training, and Labor Relations Specialists, All Other; Insurance Adjusters, Examiners, and Investigators; Insurance Appraisers, Auto Damage; Insurance Underwriters; Loan Counselors; Loan Officers; Logisticians; Management Analysts; Market Research Analysts; Personnel Recruiters; Purchasing Agents and Buyers, Farm Products; Purchasing Agents, Except Wholesale, Retail, and Farm Products; Tax Examiners, Collectors, and Revenue Agents; Training and Development Specialists; Wholesale and Retail Buyers, Except Farm Products. **PERSONALITY TYPE**—No data available.

EDUCATION/TRAINING PROGRAM(S)—Accounting; Taxation. **RELATED KNOWLEDGE/COURSES**—No data available.

Actuaries

- ▲ Education/Training Required: Work experience, plus degree
- ▲ Annual Earnings: $66,590
- ▲ Growth: 5%
- ▲ Annual Job Openings: 1,000
- ▲ Self-Employed: 11.6%
- ▲ Part-Time: 5.2%

Analyze statistical data, such as mortality, accident, sickness, disability, and retirement rates, and construct probability tables to forecast risk and liability for payment of future benefits. May ascertain premium rates required and cash reserves necessary to ensure payment of future benefits. Determines mortality, accident, sickness, disability, and retirement rates. Constructs probability tables regarding fire, natural disasters, and unemployment, based on analysis of statistical data and other pertinent information. Determines equitable basis for distributing surplus earnings under participating insurance and annuity contracts in mutual companies. Ascertains premium rates required and cash reserves and liabilities necessary to ensure payment of future benefits. Designs or reviews insurance and pension plans and calculates premiums. **SKILLS—Mathematics:** Using mathematics to solve problems. Reading Comprehension: Understanding written sentences and paragraphs in work-related documents. Critical Thinking: Using logic and reasoning to identify the strengths and weaknesses of alternative solutions, conclusions, or approaches to problems. Monitoring: Monitoring/Assessing your performance or that of other individuals or organizations to make improvements or take corrective action. Active Learning: Understanding the implications of new information for both current and future problem-solving and decision-making.

GOE INFORMATION—Interest Area: 02. Science, Math, and Engineering. **Work Group:** 02.06. Mathematics and Computers. **Other Job Titles in This Work Group:** Computer and Information Scientists, Research; Computer Programmers; Computer Security Specialists; Computer Specialists, All Other; Computer Support Specialists; Computer Systems Analysts; Database Administrators; Mathematical Science Occupations, All Other; Mathematical Technicians; Mathematicians; Network and Computer Systems Administrators; Network Systems and Data Communications Analysts; Operations Research Analysts; Statistical Assistants; Statisticians. **PERSONALITY TYPE—Conventional.** Conventional occupations frequently involve following set procedures and routines. These occupations can include working with data and details more than with ideas. Usually there is a clear line of authority to follow.

EDUCATION/TRAINING PROGRAM(S)— Actuarial Science. **RELATED KNOWLEDGE/ COURSES—Mathematics:** Knowledge of arithmetic, algebra, geometry, calculus, and statistics and their applications. **Economics and Accounting:** Knowledge of economic and accounting principles and practices, the financial markets, banking, and the analysis and reporting of financial data. **English Language:** Knowledge of the structure and content of the English language, including the meaning and spelling of words, rules of composition, and grammar. **Clerical Studies:** Knowledge of administrative and clerical procedures and systems such as word processing, managing files and records, stenography and transcription, designing forms, and other office procedures and terminology. **Computers and Electronics:** Knowledge of circuit boards, processors, chips, electronic equipment, and computer hardware and software, including applications and programming.

Administrative Law Judges, Adjudicators, and Hearing Officers

- ▲ Education/Training Required: Work experience, plus degree
- ▲ Annual Earnings: $61,240
- ▲ Growth: 1%
- ▲ Annual Job Openings: 1,000
- ▲ Self-Employed: 0%
- ▲ Part-Time: 7.8%

Conduct hearings to decide or recommend decisions on claims concerning government programs or other government-related matters and prepare decisions. Determine penalties or the existence and the amount of liability or recommend the acceptance or rejection of claims or compromise settlements. Arranges and conducts hearings to obtain information and evidence relative to disposition of claim. Determines existence and amount of liability, according to law, administrative and judicial precedents, and evidence. Analyzes evidence and applicable law, regulations, policy, and precedent decisions to determine conclusions. Questions witnesses to obtain information. Rules on exceptions, motions, and admissibility of evidence. Participates in court proceedings. Obtains additional information to clarify evidence. Conducts studies of appeals procedures in field agencies to ensure adherence to legal requirements and to facilitate determination of cases. Notifies claimant of denied claim and appeal rights. Authorizes payment of valid claims. Issues subpoenas and administers oaths to prepare for formal hearing. Researches laws, regulations, policies, and precedent decisions to prepare for hearings. Reviews and evaluates data on documents, such as claim applications, birth or death certificates, and physician or employer records. Interviews or corresponds with claimants or agents to elicit information. Prepares written opinions and decisions. Counsels parties and recommends acceptance or rejection of compromise settlement offers. **SKILLS**—Active Listening: Giving full attention to what other people are saying, taking time to understand the points being made, asking questions as appropriate, and not interrupting at inappropriate times. Judgment and Decision Making: Considering the relative costs and benefits of potential actions to choose the most appropriate one. Critical Thinking: Using logic and reasoning to iden-

tify the strengths and weaknesses of alternative solutions, conclusions, or approaches to problems. Reading Comprehension: Understanding written sentences and paragraphs in work-related documents. Writing: Communicating effectively in writing as appropriate for the needs of the audience.

GOE INFORMATION—Interest Area: 04. Law, Law Enforcement, and Public Safety. **Work Group:** 04.02. Law. **Other Job Titles in This Work Group:** Arbitrators, Mediators, and Conciliators; Judges, Magistrate Judges, and Magistrates; Law Clerks; Lawyers; Legal Support Workers, All Other; Paralegals and Legal Assistants; Title Examiners and Abstractors; Title Examiners, Abstractors, and Searchers; Title Searchers. **PERSONALITY TYPE**—Enterprising. Enterprising occupations frequently involve starting up and carrying out projects. These occupations can involve leading people and making many decisions. They sometimes require risk taking and often deal with business.

EDUCATION/TRAINING PROGRAM(S)—Law (LL.B., J.D.); Law and Legal Studies, Other. **RELATED KNOWLEDGE/COURSES—Law and Government:** Knowledge of laws, legal codes, court procedures, precedents, government regulations, executive orders, agency rules, and the democratic political process. **Administration and Management:** Knowledge of business and management principles involved in strategic planning, resource allocation, human resources modeling, leadership technique, production methods, and coordination of people and resources. **English Language:** Knowledge of the structure and content of the English language, including the meaning and spelling of words, rules of composition, and grammar. **Psychology:** Knowledge of human behavior and performance; individual differences in ability, personality, and interests; learning and motivation; psychological research methods; and the assessment and treatment of behavioral and affective disorders. **Computers and Electronics:** Knowledge of circuit boards, processors, chips, electronic equipment, and computer hardware and software, including applications and programming. **Education and Training:** Knowledge of principles and methods for curriculum and training design, teaching and instruction for individuals and groups, and the measurement of training effects. **Mathematics:** Knowledge of arithmetic, algebra, geometry, calculus, and statistics and their applications.

Administrative Services Managers

- ▲ Education/Training Required: Work experience, plus degree
- ▲ Annual Earnings: $47,080
- ▲ Growth: 20%
- ▲ Annual Job Openings: 31,000
- ▲ Self-Employed: 0%
- ▲ Part-Time: 6.1%

Plan, direct, or coordinate supportive services of an organization, such as recordkeeping, mail distribution, telephone operator/receptionist, and other office support services. May oversee facilities planning and maintenance and custodial operations. Coordinates activities of clerical and administrative personnel in establishment or organization. Prepares and reviews operational reports and schedules to ensure accuracy and efficiency. Formulates budgetary reports. Hires and terminates clerical and administrative personnel. Conducts classes to teach procedures to staff. Recommends cost-saving methods, such as supply changes and disposal of records, to improve efficiency of department. Analyzes internal processes and plans or implements procedural and policy changes to improve operations. **SKILLS**—Reading Comprehension: Understanding written sentences and paragraphs in work-related documents. Coordination: Adjusting actions in relation to others' actions. Writing: Communicating effectively in writing as appropriate for the needs of the audience. Monitoring: Monitoring/Assessing your performance or that of other individuals or organizations to make improvements or take corrective action. Speaking: Talking to others to convey information effectively. Management of Personnel Resources: Motivating, developing, and directing people as they work, identifying the best people for the job. Time Management: Managing one's own time and the time of others.

GOE INFORMATION—**Interest Area:** 09. Business Detail. **Work Group:** 09.01. Managerial Work in Business Detail. **Other Job Titles in This Work Group:** First-Line Supervisors, Administrative Support; First-Line Supervisors, Customer Service; First-Line Supervisors/Managers of Office and Administrative Support Workers. **PERSONALITY TYPE**—Enterprising. Enterprising occupations frequently involve starting up and carrying out projects. These occupations can involve leading people and making many decisions. They sometimes require risk taking and often deal with business.

EDUCATION/TRAINING PROGRAM(S)— Business Administration and Management, General; Public Administration; Purchasing, Procurement and Contracts Management. **RELATED KNOWLEDGE/ COURSES**—**Administration and Management:** Knowledge of business and management principles involved in strategic planning, resource allocation, human resources modeling, leadership technique, production methods, and coordination of people and resources. **Personnel and Human Resources:** Knowledge of principles and procedures for personnel recruitment, selection, training, compensation and benefits, labor relations and negotiation, and personnel information systems. **Economics and Accounting:** Knowledge of economic and accounting principles and practices, the financial markets, banking, and the analysis and reporting of financial data. **English Language:** Knowledge of the structure and content of the English language, including the meaning and spelling of words, rules of composition, and grammar. **Clerical Studies:** Knowledge of administrative and clerical procedures and systems such as word processing, managing files and records, stenography and transcription, designing forms, and other office procedures and terminology.

Adult Literacy, Remedial Education, and GED Teachers and Instructors

- ▲ Education/Training Required: Bachelor's degree
- ▲ Annual Earnings: $33,540
- ▲ Growth: 19%
- ▲ Annual Job Openings: 12,000
- ▲ Self-Employed: 48.9%
- ▲ Part-Time: 42.5%

Teach or instruct out-of-school youths and adults in remedial education classes, preparatory classes for the General Educational Development test, literacy, or English as a Second Language. Teaching may or may not take place in a traditional educational institution. Presents lectures and conducts discussions to increase students' knowledge and competence. Observes and evaluates students' work to determine progress and makes suggestions for improvement. Adapts course of study and training methods to meet students' needs and abilities. Conducts classes, workshops, and demonstrations to teach principles, techniques, procedures, or methods of designated subject. Prepares outline of instructional program and lesson plans and establishes course goals. Observes students to determine and evaluate qualifications, limitations, abilities, interests, aptitudes, temperament, and individual characteristics. Evaluates success of instruction, based on number and enthusiasm of participants, and recommends retaining or eliminating course in future. Confers with leaders of government and other groups to coordinate training or to assist students to fulfill required criteria. Writes instructional articles on designated subjects. Orders, stores, and inventories books, materials, and supplies. Maintains records, such as student grades, attendance, and supply inventory. Plans and conducts field trips to enrich instructional programs. Directs and supervises student project activities, performances, tournaments, exhibits, contests, or plays. Selects and assembles books, materials, and supplies for courses or projects. Administers oral, written, and performance tests and issues grades in accordance with performance. Plans course content and method of instruction. **SKILLS—** Writing: Communicating effectively in writing as appropriate for the needs of the audience. Speaking: Talking to others to convey information effectively. Reading Comprehension: Understanding written sentences and paragraphs in work-related documents. Instructing: Teaching others how to do something. Active Listening: Giving full attention to what other people are saying, taking time to understand the points being made, asking questions as appropriate, and not interrupting at inappropriate times.

GOE INFORMATION—Interest Area: 12. Education and Social Service. **Work Group:** 12.03. Educational Services. **Other Job Titles in This Work Group:** Agricultural Sciences Teachers, Postsecondary; Anthropology and Archeology Teachers, Postsecondary; Architecture Teachers, Postsecondary; Archivists; Area, Ethnic, and Cultural Studies Teachers, Postsecondary; Art, Drama, and Music Teachers, Postsecondary; Atmospheric, Earth, Marine, and Space Sciences Teachers, Postsecondary; Audio-Visual Collections Specialists; Biological Science Teachers, Postsecondary; Business Teachers, Postsecondary; Chemistry Teachers, Postsecondary; Child Care Workers; Communications Teachers, Postsecondary; Computer Science Teachers, Postsecondary; Criminal Justice and Law Enforcement Teachers, Postsecondary; Curators; Economics Teachers, Postsecondary; Education Teachers, Postsecondary; Educational Psychologists; Educational, Vocational, and School Counselors; Elementary School Teachers, Except Special Education; Engineering Teachers, Postsecondary; English Language and Literature Teachers, Postsecondary; Environmental Science Teachers, Postsecondary; Farm and Home Management Advisors;

Foreign Language and Literature Teachers, Postsecondary; Forestry and Conservation Science Teachers, Postsecondary; Geography Teachers, Postsecondary; Graduate Teaching Assistants; Health Specialties Teachers, Postsecondary; History Teachers, Postsecondary; Home Economics Teachers, Postsecondary; Kindergarten Teachers, Except Special Education; Law Teachers, Postsecondary; Librarians; Library Assistants, Clerical; Library Science Teachers, Postsecondary; Library Technicians; others. **PERSONALITY TYPE**—Social. Social occupations frequently involve working with, communicating with, and teaching people. These occupations often involve helping or providing service to others.

EDUCATION/TRAINING PROGRAM(S)—Adult and Continuing Teacher Education; Teaching English as a Second Language/Foreign Language. **RELATED KNOWLEDGE/COURSES—Education and Training:** Knowledge of principles and methods for curriculum and training design, teaching and instruction for individuals and groups, and the measurement of training effects. **English Language:** Knowledge of the structure and content of the English language, including the meaning and spelling of words, rules of composition, and grammar. **Administration and Management:** Knowledge of business and management principles involved in strategic planning, resource allocation, human resources modeling, leadership technique, production methods, and coordination of people and resources. **Mathematics:** Knowledge of arithmetic, algebra, geometry, calculus, and statistics and their applications. **Computers and Electronics:** Knowledge of circuit boards, processors, chips, electronic equipment, and computer hardware and software, including applications and programming. **Economics and Accounting:** Knowledge of economic and accounting principles and practices, the financial markets, banking, and the analysis and reporting of financial data. **Clerical Studies:** Knowledge of administrative and clerical procedures and systems such as word processing, managing files and records, stenography and transcription, designing forms, and other office procedures and terminology.

Advertising and Promotions Managers

- ▲ Education/Training Required: Work experience, plus degree
- ▲ Annual Earnings: $53,360
- ▲ Growth: 34%
- ▲ Annual Job Openings: 7,000
- ▲ Self-Employed: 2.4%
- ▲ Part-Time: 2.6%

Plan and direct advertising policies and programs or produce collateral materials, such as posters, contests, coupons, or giveaways, to create extra interest in the purchase of a product or service for a department or an entire organization or on an account basis. Directs activities of workers engaged in developing and producing advertisements. Plans and executes advertising policies of organization. Plans and prepares advertising and promotional material. Coordinates activities of departments, such as sales, graphic arts, media, finance, and research. Formulates plans to extend business with established accounts and transacts business as agent for advertising accounts. Confers with department heads and/or staff to discuss topics such as contracts, selection of advertising media, or product to be advertised. Confers with clients to provide marketing or technical advice. Inspects layouts and advertising copy and edits scripts, audio and video tapes, and other promotional material for adherence to specifications. Reads trade journals and professional literature to stay informed on trends, innovations, and changes that affect media planning. Inspects premises of assigned stores for adequate security and compliance with safety codes and ordinances. Directs conversion of products from USA to foreign standards. Adjusts broadcasting schedules due to program cancellation. Contacts organizations to explain services and facilities offered or to secure props, audiovisual materials, and sound effects. Directs product research and development. Represents company at trade association meetings to promote products. Consults publications to learn about conventions and social functions and organizes prospect files for promotional purposes. Supervises and trains service representatives. Monitors and analyzes sales promotion results to determine cost-effectiveness of promotion campaign. **SKILLS**—Coordination: Adjusting actions in relation to others' actions. Reading Comprehension: Understanding written sentences and paragraphs in work-related documents. Systems Evaluation: Identifying measures or indicators of system performance and the actions needed to improve or correct performance relative to the goals of the system. Judgment and Decision Making: Considering the relative costs and benefits of potential actions to choose the most appropriate one. Complex Problem Solving: Identifying complex problems and reviewing related information to develop and evaluate options and implement solutions.

GOE INFORMATION—**Interest Area:** 10. Sales and Marketing. **Work Group:** 10.01. Managerial Work in Sales and Marketing. **Other Job Titles in This Work Group:** First-Line Supervisors/Managers of Non-Retail Sales Workers; First-Line Supervisors/Managers of Retail Sales Workers; Marketing Managers; Sales Managers. **PERSONALITY TYPE**—Artistic. Artistic occupations frequently involve working with forms, designs,

and patterns. They often require self-expression, and the work can be done without following a clear set of rules.

EDUCATION/TRAINING PROGRAM(S)— Advertising; Business Marketing and Marketing Management; Public Relations and Organizational Communications. **RELATED KNOWLEDGE/ COURSES**—**Sales and Marketing:** Knowledge of principles and methods for showing, promoting, and selling products or services. This includes marketing strategy and tactics, product demonstration, sales techniques, and sales control systems. **Administration and Management:** Knowledge of business and management principles involved in strategic planning, resource allocation, human resources modeling, leadership technique, production methods, and coordination of people and resources. **Communications and Media:** Knowledge of media production, communication, and dissemination techniques and methods. This includes alternative ways to inform and entertain via written, oral, and visual media. **Customer and Personal Service:** Knowledge of principles and processes for providing customer and personal services. This includes customer needs assessment, meeting quality standards for services, and evaluation of customer satisfaction. **English Language:** Knowledge of the structure and content of the English language, including the meaning and spelling of words, rules of composition, and grammar.

Aerospace Engineering and Operations Technicians

- ▲ Education/Training Required: Associate's degree
- ▲ Annual Earnings: $48,600
- ▲ Growth: 6%
- ▲ Annual Job Openings: 2,000
- ▲ Self-Employed: 1.9%
- ▲ Part-Time: 7.4%

Operate, install, calibrate, and maintain integrated computer/communications systems consoles, simulators, and other data acquisition, test, and measurement instruments and equipment to launch, track, position, and evaluate air and space vehicles. May record and interpret test data. Determines data required, plans data acquisition operations, and sets up required data acquisition, test, and measure-

ment equipment. Sets up, operates, maintains, and monitors computer systems and devices for data acquisition and analysis to detect malfunctions. Discusses test data requirements and results with other personnel, determines data required, and calculates and modifies test parameters or equipment. Fabricates and installs parts and systems to be tested in test equipment, using hand tools, power tools, and test instruments. Inputs commands and data into computer systems to modify programs for specific test requirements or for equipment maintenance and calibration. Records and interprets test data on parts, assemblies, and mechanisms and confers with engineering personnel regarding test procedures and results. Constructs and maintains test facilities for aircraft parts and systems according to specifications, using hand tools, power tools, and test instruments. Inspects, diagnoses, maintains, and operates test setup and equipment to detect malfunctions and adjusts, repairs, or replaces faulty components. Tests aircraft systems under simulated operational conditions, using test instrumentation and equipment, to determine design or fabrication parameters. **SKILLS**—Science: Using scientific rules and methods to solve problems. Mathematics: Using mathematics to solve problems. Equipment Maintenance: Performing routine maintenance on equipment and determining when and what kind of maintenance is needed. Quality Control Analysis: Conducting tests and inspections of products, services, or processes to evaluate quality or performance. Operation and Control: Controlling operations of equipment or systems. Operation Monitoring: Watching gauges, dials, or other indicators to make sure a machine is working properly. Installation: Installing equipment, machines, wiring, or programs to meet specifications.

GOE INFORMATION—**Interest Area:** 02. Science, Math, and Engineering. **Work Group:** 02.08. Engineering Technology. **Other Job Titles in This Work Group:** Architectural and Civil Drafters; Architectural Drafters; Calibration and Instrumentation Technicians; Cartographers and Photogrammetrists; Civil Drafters; Civil Engineering Technicians; Construction and Building Inspectors; Drafters, All Other; Electrical and Electronic Engineering Technicians; Electrical and Electronics Draft-

ers; Electrical Drafters; Electrical Engineering Technicians; Electro-Mechanical Technicians; Electronic Drafters; Electronics Engineering Technicians; Engineering Technicians, Except Drafters, All Other; Environmental Engineering Technicians; Industrial Engineering Technicians; Mapping Technicians; Mechanical Drafters; Mechanical Engineering Technicians; Numerical Tool and Process Control Programmers; Pressure Vessel Inspectors; Surveying and Mapping Technicians; Surveying Technicians; Surveyors. **PERSONALITY TYPE**—Investigative. Investigative occupations frequently involve working with ideas and require an extensive amount of thinking. These occupations can involve searching for facts and figuring out problems mentally.

EDUCATION/TRAINING PROGRAM(S)— Aeronautical and Aerospace Engineering Technologist/ Technician; Solar Technologist/Technician. **RELATED KNOWLEDGE/COURSES**—**Engineering and Technology:** Knowledge of the practical application of engineering science and technology. This includes applying principles, techniques, procedures, and equipment to the design and production of various goods and services. **Computers and Electronics:** Knowledge of circuit boards, processors, chips, electronic equipment, and computer hardware and software, including applications and programming. **Mathematics:** Knowledge of arithmetic, algebra, geometry, calculus, and statistics and their applications. **Physics:** Knowledge and prediction of physical principles and laws and their interrelationships and applications to understanding fluid, material, and atmospheric dynamics and mechanical, electrical, atomic, and sub-atomic structures and processes. **Principles of Mechanical Devices:** Knowledge of machines and tools, including their designs, uses, repair, and maintenance.

Aerospace Engineers

▲ Education/Training Required: Bachelor's degree
▲ Annual Earnings: $67,930
▲ Growth: 14%
▲ Annual Job Openings: 2,000
▲ Self-Employed: 1.8%
▲ Part-Time: 1.6%

Perform a variety of engineering work in designing, constructing, and testing aircraft, missiles, and spacecraft. May conduct basic and applied research to evaluate adaptability of materials and equipment to aircraft design and manufacture. May recommend improvements in testing equipment and techniques. Develops design criteria for aeronautical or aerospace products or systems, including testing methods, production costs, quality standards, and completion dates. Directs and coordinates activities of engineering or technical personnel designing, fabricating, modifying, or testing aircraft or aerospace products. Reviews performance reports and documentation from customers and field engineers and inspects malfunctioning or damaged products to determine problem. Writes technical reports and other documentation, such as handbooks and bulletins, for use by engineering staff, management, and customers. Evaluates and approves selection of vendors by study of past performance and new advertisements. Maintains records of performance reports for future reference. Plans and coordinates activities concerned with investigating and resolving customers' reports of technical problems with aircraft or aerospace vehicles. Directs research and development programs to improve production methods, parts, and equipment technology and reduce costs. Evaluates product data and design from inspections and reports for conformance to engineering principles, customer requirements, and quality standards. Formulates conceptual design of aeronautical or aerospace products or systems to meet customer requirements. Formulates mathematical models or other methods of computer analysis to develop, evaluate, or modify design according to customer engineering requirements. Plans and conducts experimental, environmental, operational, and stress tests on models and prototypes of aircraft and aerospace systems and equipment. Analyzes project requests, proposals, and engineering data to determine feasibility, producibility, cost, and production time of aerospace or aeronautical product. **SKILLS**—Mathematics: Using mathematics to solve problems. Science: Using scientific rules and methods to solve problems. Active Learning: Understanding the implications of new information for both current and future problem-solving and decision-making. Writing: Communicating effectively in writing as appropriate for the needs of the audience. Technology Design: Generating or adapting equipment and technology to serve user needs.

GOE INFORMATION—Interest Area: 02. Science, Math, and Engineering. **Work Group:** 02.07. Engineering. **Other Job Titles in This Work Group:** Agricultural Engineers; Architects, Except Landscape and Naval; Biomedical Engineers; Chemical Engineers; Civil Engineers; Computer Hardware Engineers; Computer Software Engineers, Applications; Computer Software Engineers, Systems Software; Electrical Engineers; Electronics Engineers, Except Computer; Engineers, All Other; Environmental Engineers; Fire-Prevention and Protection Engineers; Health and Safety Engineers, Except Mining Safety Engineers and Inspectors; Industrial Engineers; Industrial Safety and Health Engineers; Landscape Architects; Marine Architects; Marine Engineers; Marine Engineers and Naval Architects; Materials Engineers; Mechanical Engineers; Mining and Geological Engineers, Including Mining Safety Engineers; Nuclear Engineers; Petroleum Engineers; Product Safety Engineers; Sales Engineers. **PERSONALITY TYPE**—Investigative. Investigative occupations frequently involve working with ideas and require an extensive amount of thinking. These occupations can involve searching for facts and figuring out problems mentally.

EDUCATION/TRAINING PROGRAM(S)—Aerospace, Aeronautical and Astronautical Engineering. **RELATED KNOWLEDGE/COURSES**—**Engineering and Technology:** Knowledge of the practical application of engineering science and technology. This includes applying principles, techniques, procedures, and equipment to the design and production of various goods and services. **Mathematics:** Knowledge of arithmetic, algebra, geometry, calculus, and statistics and their applications. **Physics:** Knowledge and prediction of physical principles and laws and their interrelationships and applications to understanding fluid, material, and atmospheric dynamics and mechanical, electrical, atomic, and sub-atomic structures and processes. **English Language:** Knowledge of the structure and content of the English language, including the meaning and spelling of words, rules of composition, and grammar. **Administration and Management:** Knowledge of business and management principles involved in strategic planning, resource allocation, human resources modeling, leadership technique, production methods, and coordination of people and resources.

Agents and Business Managers of Artists, Performers, and Athletes

- ▲ Education/Training Required: Work experience, plus degree
- ▲ Annual Earnings: $57,040
- ▲ Growth: 28%
- ▲ Annual Job Openings: 2,000
- ▲ Self-Employed: 2.4%
- ▲ Part-Time: 2.6%

Represent and promote artists, performers, and athletes to prospective employers. May handle contract negotiation and other business matters for clients. Negotiates with management, promoters, union officials, and other persons to obtain contracts for clients, such as entertainers, artists, and athletes. Obtains information and inspects facilities, equipment, and accommodations of potential performance venue. Prepares periodic accounting statements for clients concerning financial affairs. Conducts auditions or interviews new clients. Hires trainer or coach to advise client on performance matters, such as training techniques or presentation of act. Collects fees, commission, or other payment according to contract terms. Manages business affairs for clients, such as obtaining travel and lodging accommodations, selling tickets, marketing and advertising, and paying expenses. Schedules promotional or performance engagements for clients. Advises clients on financial and legal matters, such as investments and taxes. **SKILLS**—Negotiation: Bringing others together and trying to reconcile differences. Reading Comprehension: Understanding written sentences and paragraphs in work-related documents. Speaking: Talking to others to convey information effectively. Time Management: Managing one's own time and the time of others. Active Listening: Giving full attention to what other people are saying, taking time to understand the points being made, asking questions as appropriate, and not interrupting at inappropriate times. Coordination: Adjusting actions in relation to others' actions. Critical Thinking: Using logic and reasoning to identify the strengths and weaknesses of alternative solutions, conclusions, or approaches to problems.

GOE INFORMATION—**Interest Area:** 01. Arts, Entertainment, and Media. **Work Group:** 01.01. Mana-

gerial Work in Arts, Entertainment, and Media. **Other Job Titles in This Work Group:** Art Directors; Producers; Producers and Directors; Program Directors; Technical Directors/Managers. **PERSONALITY TYPE**—Enterprising. Enterprising occupations frequently involve starting up and carrying out projects. These occupations can involve leading people and making many decisions. They sometimes require risk taking and often deal with business.

EDUCATION/TRAINING PROGRAM(S)—Arts Management; Entrepreneurship; Human Resources Management; Labor/Personnel Relations and Studies; Personal and Miscellaneous Services, Other; Purchasing, Procurement and Contracts Management. **RELATED KNOWLEDGE/COURSES**—**Administration and Management:** Knowledge of business and management principles involved in strategic planning, resource allocation, human resources modeling, leadership technique, production methods, and coordination of people and resources. **Economics and Accounting:** Knowledge of economic and accounting principles and practices, the financial markets, banking, and the analysis and reporting of financial data. **Sales and Marketing:** Knowledge of principles and methods for showing, promoting, and selling products or services. This includes marketing strategy and tactics, product demonstration, sales techniques, and sales control systems. **Personnel and Human Resources:** Knowledge of principles and procedures for personnel recruitment, selection, training, compensation and benefits, labor relations and negotiation, and personnel information systems. **Mathematics:** Knowledge of arithmetic, algebra, geometry, calculus, and statistics and their applications.

Agricultural Engineers

- ▲ Education/Training Required: Bachelor's degree
- ▲ Annual Earnings: $55,850
- ▲ Growth: 15%
- ▲ Annual Job Openings: Fewer than 500
- ▲ Self-Employed: 2.7%
- ▲ Part-Time: 4.5%

Apply knowledge of engineering technology and biological science to agricultural problems concerned with power and machinery, electrification, structures, soil and water conservation, and processing of agricultural products. Designs and directs manufacture of equipment for land tillage and fertilization, plant and animal disease and insect control, and harvesting or moving commodities. Develops criteria for design, manufacture, or construction of equipment, structures, and facilities. Plans and directs construction of rural electric-power distribution systems and irrigation, drainage, and flood control systems for soil and water conservation. Designs and supervises installation of equipment and instruments used to evaluate and process farm products and to automate agricultural operations. Designs and supervises erection of crop storage, animal shelter, and residential structures and heating, lighting, cooling, plumbing, and waste disposal systems. Designs sensing, measuring, and recording devices and instrumentation used to study plant or animal life. Conducts research to develop agricultural machinery and equipment. Conducts tests on agricultural machinery and equipment. Designs agricultural machinery and equipment. Studies such problems as effect of temperature, humidity, and light on plants and animals and effectiveness of different insecticides. **SKILLS—** Mathematics: Using mathematics to solve problems. Operations Analysis: Analyzing needs and product requirements to create a design. Science: Using scientific rules and methods to solve problems. Active Learning: Understanding the implications of new information for both current and future problem-solving and decision-making. Technology Design: Generating or adapting equipment and technology to serve user needs.

GOE INFORMATION—Interest Area: 02. Science, Math, and Engineering. **Work Group:** 02.07. Engineering. **Other Job Titles in This Work Group:**
Aerospace Engineers; Architects, Except Landscape and Naval; Biomedical Engineers; Chemical Engineers; Civil Engineers; Computer Hardware Engineers; Computer Software Engineers, Applications; Computer Software Engineers, Systems Software; Electrical Engineers; Electronics Engineers, Except Computer; Engineers, All Other; Environmental Engineers; Fire-Prevention and Protection Engineers; Health and Safety Engineers, Except Mining Safety Engineers and Inspectors; Industrial Engineers; Industrial Safety and Health Engineers; Landscape Architects; Marine Architects; Marine Engineers; Marine Engineers and Naval Architects; Materials Engineers; Mechanical Engineers; Mining and Geological Engineers, Including Mining Safety Engineers; Nuclear Engineers; Petroleum Engineers; Product Safety Engineers; Sales Engineers. **PERSONALITY TYPE**—Investigative. Investigative occupations frequently involve working with ideas and require an extensive amount of thinking. These occupations can involve searching for facts and figuring out problems mentally.

EDUCATION/TRAINING PROGRAM(S)— Agricultural Engineering. **RELATED KNOWLEDGE/COURSES—Engineering and Technology:** Knowledge of the practical application of engineering science and technology. This includes applying principles, techniques, procedures, and equipment to the design and production of various goods and services. **Design:** Knowledge of design techniques, tools, and principles involved in production of precision technical plans, blueprints, drawings, and models. **Biology:** Knowledge of plant and animal organisms and their tissues, cells, functions, interdependencies, and interactions with each other and the environment. **Mathematics:** Knowledge of arithmetic, algebra, geometry, calculus, and statistics and their applications. **Principles of Mechanical Devices:** Knowledge of machines and tools, including their designs, uses, repair, and maintenance.

Agricultural Sciences Teachers, Postsecondary

- ▲ Education/Training Required: Master's degree
- ▲ Annual Earnings: $62,690
- ▲ Growth: 24% for all Postsecondary Teachers
- ▲ Annual Job Openings: 184,000 for all Postsecondary Teachers
- ▲ Self-Employed: 0%
- ▲ Part-Time: 32.3% for all Postsecondary Teachers

Teach courses in the agricultural sciences. Includes teachers of agronomy, dairy sciences, fisheries management, horticultural sciences, poultry sciences, range management, and agricultural soil conservation. Prepares and delivers lectures to students. Stimulates class discussions. Compiles bibliographies of specialized materials for outside reading assignments. Advises students on academic and vocational curricula. Conducts research in particular field of knowledge and publishes findings in professional journals. Serves on faculty committee providing professional consulting services to government and industry. Acts as adviser to student organizations. Directs research of other teachers or graduate students working for advanced academic degrees. Compiles, administers, and grades examinations or assigns this work to others. **SKILLS**—Reading Comprehension: Understanding written sentences and paragraphs in work-related documents. Instructing: Teaching others how to do something. Learning Strategies: Selecting and using training/instructional methods and procedures appropriate for the situation when learning or teaching new things. Writing: Communicating effectively in writing as appropriate for the needs of the audience. Critical Thinking: Using logic and reasoning to identify the strengths and weaknesses of alternative solutions, conclusions, or approaches to problems. Active Learning: Understanding the implications of new information for both current and future problem-solving and decision-making. Science: Using scientific rules and methods to solve problems.

GOE INFORMATION—Interest Area: 12. Education and Social Service. **Work Group:** 12.03. Educational Services. **Other Job Titles in This Work Group:** Adult Literacy, Remedial Education, and GED Teachers and Instructors; Anthropology and Archeology Teachers, Postsecondary; Architecture Teachers, Postsecondary; Archivists; Area, Ethnic, and Cultural Studies Teachers, Postsecondary; Art, Drama, and Music Teachers, Postsecondary; Atmospheric, Earth, Marine, and Space Sciences Teachers, Postsecondary; Audio-Visual Collections Specialists; Biological Science Teachers, Postsecondary; Business Teachers, Postsecondary; Chemistry Teachers, Postsecondary; Child Care Workers; Communications Teachers, Postsecondary; Computer Science Teachers, Postsecondary; Criminal Justice and Law Enforcement Teachers, Postsecondary; Curators; Economics Teachers, Postsecondary; Education Teachers, Postsecondary; Educational Psychologists; Educational, Vocational, and School Counselors; Elementary School Teachers, Except Special Education; Engineering Teachers, Postsecondary; English Language and Literature Teachers, Postsecondary; Environmental Science Teachers, Postsecondary; Farm and Home Management Advisors; Foreign Language and Literature Teachers, Postsecondary; Forestry and Conservation Science Teachers, Postsecondary; Geography Teachers, Postsecondary; Graduate Teaching Assistants; Health Specialties Teachers, Postsecondary; History Teachers, Postsecondary; Home Economics Teachers, Postsecondary; Kindergarten Teachers, Except Special Education; Law Teachers, Postsecondary; Librarians; Library Assistants, Clerical; Library Science Teachers, Postsecondary; others. **PERSONALITY TYPE**—Investigative. Investigative occupations frequently involve working with ideas and require an extensive amount of thinking. These occupations can involve searching for facts and figuring out problems mentally.

EDUCATION/TRAINING PROGRAM(S)—
Agricultural Animal Breeding and Genetics; Agricultural
Animal Health; Agricultural Animal Nutrition; Agricul-
tural Animal Physiology; Agricultural Plant Pathology;
Agricultural Plant Physiology; Agricultural Teacher Edu-
cation (Vocational); Agriculture/Agricultural Sciences,
General; Agronomy and Crop Science; Animal Sciences,
General; Animal Sciences, Other; Dairy Science; Food
Sciences and Technology; Horticulture Science; Plant
Breeding and Genetics; Plant Protection (Pest Manage-
ment); Plant Sciences, General; Plant Sciences, Other;
Poultry Science; Range Science and Management;
Soil Sciences. RELATED KNOWLEDGE/
COURSES—Education and Training: Knowledge
of principles and methods for curriculum and training design, teaching and instruction for individuals and groups,
and the measurement of training effects. Biology: Knowledge of plant and animal organisms and their tissues, cells,
functions, interdependencies, and interactions with each
other and the environment. Psychology: Knowledge of
human behavior and performance; individual differences in
ability, personality, and interests; learning and motivation;
psychological research methods; and the assessment and
treatment of behavioral and affective disorders. Chemistry: Knowledge of the chemical composition, structure,
and properties of substances and of the chemical processes
and transformations that they undergo. This includes uses
of chemicals and their interactions, danger signs, production techniques, and disposal methods. English Language: Knowledge of the structure and content of the
English language, including the meaning and spelling of
words, rules of composition, and grammar.

Agricultural Technicians

- ▲ Education/Training Required: Associate's degree
- ▲ Annual Earnings: $27,080
- ▲ Growth: 15%
- ▲ Annual Job Openings: 3,000
- ▲ Self-Employed: 0.9%
- ▲ Part-Time: 11.7%

**Set up and maintain laboratory and collect and
record data to assist scientist in biology or related agricultural science experiments.** Sets up laboratory and field equipment to assist research workers.
Adjusts testing equipment and prepares culture media, following standard procedures. Measures or weighs ingredients used in testing or as animal feed. Records production
and test data for evaluation by personnel. Cleans and maintains laboratory and field equipment and work areas. Examines animals and specimens to determine presence of
disease or other problems. Pricks animals and collects blood
samples for testing, using hand-held devices. Waters and
feeds rations to livestock and laboratory animals. Plants
seeds in specified area and counts plants that grow to determine germination rate of seeds. **SKILLS—Mathematics:** Using mathematics to solve problems. Reading
Comprehension: Understanding written sentences and paragraphs in work-related documents. Science: Using scientific rules and methods to solve problems. Writing:
Communicating effectively in writing as appropriate for
the needs of the audience.

GOE INFORMATION—Interest Area: 02. Sci-
ence, Math, and Engineering. **Work Group:** 02.03. Life
Sciences. **Other Job Titles in This Work Group:**
Agricultural and Food Science Technicians; Animal Scientists; Biochemists; Biochemists and Biophysicists; Biologi-
cal Scientists, All Other; Biologists; Biophysicists;
Conservation Scientists; Environmental Scientists and Specialists, Including Health; Epidemiologists; Food Science
Technicians; Food Scientists and Technologists; Foresters;
Life Scientists, All Other; Medical Scientists, Except Epidemiologists; Microbiologists; Plant Scientists; Range Managers; Soil and Plant Scientists; Soil Conservationists; Soil
Scientists; Zoologists and Wildlife Biologists. **PERSON-
ALITY TYPE—Realistic.** Realistic occupations frequently involve work activities that include practical,
hands-on problems and solutions. They often deal with

plants, animals, and real-world materials like wood, tools, and machinery. Many of the occupations require working outside and do not involve a lot of paperwork or working closely with others.

EDUCATION/TRAINING PROGRAM(S)— Agricultural Animal Breeding and Genetics; Agricultural Animal Husbandry and Production Management; Agricultural Animal Nutrition; Agronomy and Crop Science; Animal Sciences, General; Crop Production Operations and Management; Dairy Science; Food Sciences and Technology. RELATED KNOWLEDGE/COURSES— Biology: Knowledge of plant and animal organisms and their tissues, cells, functions, interdependencies, and interactions with each other and the environment. Mathemat-

ics: Knowledge of arithmetic, algebra, geometry, calculus, and statistics and their applications. Food Production: Knowledge of techniques and equipment for planting, growing, and harvesting food products (both plant and animal) for consumption, including storage/handling techniques. Clerical Studies: Knowledge of administrative and clerical procedures and systems such as word processing, managing files and records, stenography and transcription, designing forms, and other office procedures and terminology. Medicine and Dentistry: Knowledge of the information and techniques needed to diagnose and treat human injuries, diseases, and deformities. This includes symptoms, treatment alternatives, drug properties and interactions, and preventive health-care measures.

Airline Pilots, Copilots, and Flight Engineers

- ▲ Education/Training Required: Bachelor's degree
- ▲ Annual Earnings: $110,940
- ▲ Growth: 6%
- ▲ Annual Job Openings: 5,000
- ▲ Self-Employed: 2.2%
- ▲ Part-Time: 23.3%

Pilot and navigate the flight of multi-engine aircraft in regularly scheduled service for the transport of passengers and cargo. Requires Federal Air Transport rating and certification in specific aircraft type used. Starts engines, operates controls, and pilots airplane to transport passengers, mail, or freight, adhering to flight plan and regulations and procedures. Conducts in-flight tests and evaluations at specified altitudes in all types of weather to determine receptivity and other characteristics of equipment and systems. Gives training and instruction in aircraft operations for students and other pilots. Plans and formulates flight activities and test schedules and prepares flight evaluation reports. Logs information, such as flight time, altitude flown, and fuel consumption. Holds commercial pilot's license issued by Federal Aviation Administration. Plots flight pattern and files flight plan with appropriate officials. Conducts pre-flight checks and reads gauges to verify that fluids and pressure are at prescribed levels. Operates radio equipment and contacts control tower for takeoff, clearance,

arrival instructions, and other information. Coordinates flight activities with ground-crew and air-traffic control and informs crewmembers of flight and test procedures. Orders changes in fuel supply, load, route, or schedule to ensure safety of flight. Obtains and reviews data such as load weight, fuel supply, weather conditions, and flight schedule. SKILLS—Operation and Control: Controlling operations of equipment or systems. Operation Monitoring: Watching gauges, dials, or other indicators to make sure a machine is working properly. Instructing: Teaching others how to do something. Coordination: Adjusting actions in relation to others' actions. Judgment and Decision Making: Considering the relative costs and benefits of potential actions to choose the most appropriate one.

GOE INFORMATION—Interest Area: 07. Transportation. Work Group: 07.03. Air Vehicle Operation. Other Job Titles in This Work Group: Commercial Pilots. PERSONALITY TYPE—Realistic. Realistic occupations frequently involve work activities that include practical, hands-on problems and solutions. They often deal with plants, animals, and real-world materials like wood, tools, and machinery. Many of the occupations require working outside and do not involve a lot of paperwork or working closely with others.

EDUCATION/TRAINING PROGRAM(S)—Aircraft Pilot (Private); Aircraft Pilot and Navigator (Professional). **RELATED KNOWLEDGE/ COURSES—Transportation:** Knowledge of principles and methods for moving people or goods by air, rail, sea, or road, including the relative costs and benefits. **Physics:** Knowledge and prediction of physical principles and laws and their interrelationships and applications to understanding fluid, material, and atmospheric dynamics and me-

chanical, electrical, atomic, and sub-atomic structures and processes. **Public Safety and Security:** Knowledge of relevant equipment, policies, procedures, and strategies to promote effective local, state, or national security operations for the protection of people, data, property, and institutions. **Geography:** Knowledge of principles and methods for describing the features of land, sea, and air masses, including their physical characteristics, locations, interrelationships, and distribution of plant, animal, and human life. **Telecommunications:** Knowledge of transmission, broadcasting, switching, control, and operation of telecommunications systems. **Mathematics:** Knowledge of arithmetic, algebra, geometry, calculus, and statistics and their applications.

Anthropologists

- ▲ Education/Training Required: Bachelor's degree
- ▲ Annual Earnings: $36,040
- ▲ Growth: 17%
- ▲ Annual Job Openings: 2,000
- ▲ Self-Employed: 5.2%
- ▲ Part-Time: 18.1%

Research or study the origins and physical, social, and cultural development and behavior of humans and the cultures and organizations they have created. Gathers, analyzes, and reports data on human physique, social customs, and artifacts, such as weapons, tools, pottery, and clothing. Studies museum collections of skeletal remains and human fossils to determine their meaning in terms of long-range human evolution. Studies physical and physiological adaptations to differing environments and hereditary characteristics of living populations. Studies cultures, particularly preindustrial and non-Western societies, including religion, economics, mythology and traditions, and intellectual and artistic life. Studies relationships between language and culture and sociolinguistic studies, relationship between individual personality and culture, or complex industrialized societies. Applies anthropological concepts to current problems. Applies anthropological data and techniques to solution of problems in human relations. Formulates general laws of cultural development, general rules of social and cultural behavior, or general value orientations. Observes and mea-

sures bodily variations and physical attributes of existing human types. Studies growth patterns, sexual differences, and aging phenomena of human groups, current and past. **SKILLS—Writing:** Communicating effectively in writing as appropriate for the needs of the audience. Active Learning: Understanding the implications of new information for both current and future problem-solving and decision-making. Critical Thinking: Using logic and reasoning to identify the strengths and weaknesses of alternative solutions, conclusions, or approaches to problems. Reading Comprehension: Understanding written sentences and paragraphs in work-related documents. Complex Problem Solving: Identifying complex problems and reviewing related information to develop and evaluate options and implement solutions.

GOE INFORMATION—Interest Area: 02. Science, Math, and Engineering. **Work Group:** 02.04. Social Sciences. **Other Job Titles in This Work Group:** Anthropologists and Archeologists; Archeologists; City Planning Aides; Economists; Historians; Industrial-

Organizational Psychologists; Political Scientists; Psychologists, All Other; Social Science Research Assistants; Social Scientists and Related Workers, All Other; Sociologists; Survey Researchers; Urban and Regional Planners. **PERSONALITY TYPE**—Investigative. Investigative occupations frequently involve working with ideas and require an extensive amount of thinking. These occupations can involve searching for facts and figuring out problems mentally.

EDUCATION/TRAINING PROGRAM(S)—Anthropology; Archeology. **RELATED KNOWLEDGE/COURSES—Sociology and Anthropology:** Knowledge of group behavior and dynamics, societal trends and influences, human migrations, ethnicity, cultures, and their history and origins. **History and Archeology:** Knowledge of historical events and their causes, indicators, and effects on civilizations and cultures. **English Language:** Knowledge of the structure and content of the English language, including the meaning and spelling of words, rules of composition, and grammar. **Geography:** Knowledge of principles and methods for describing the features of land, sea, and air masses, including their physical characteristics, locations, interrelationships, and distribution of plant, animal, and human life. **Biology:** Knowledge of plant and animal organisms and their tissues, cells, functions, interdependencies, and interactions with each other and the environment.

Anthropologists and Archeologists

- ▲ Education/Training Required: Bachelor's degree
- ▲ Annual Earnings: $36,040
- ▲ Growth: 17%
- ▲ Annual Job Openings: 2,000
- ▲ Self-Employed: 5.2%
- ▲ Part-Time: 18.1%

Study the origin, development, and behavior of humans. May study the way of life, language, or physical characteristics of existing people in various parts of the world. May engage in systematic recovery and examination of material evidence, such as tools or pottery remaining from past human cultures, in order to determine the history, customs, and living habits of earlier civilizations. **SKILLS**—No data available.

GOE INFORMATION—**Interest Area:** 02. Science, Math, and Engineering. **Work Group:** 02.04. Social Sciences. **Other Job Titles in This Work Group:** Anthropologists; Archeologists; City Planning Aides; Economists; Historians; Industrial-Organizational Psychologists; Political Scientists; Psychologists, All Other; Social Science Research Assistants; Social Scientists and Related Workers, All Other; Sociologists; Survey Researchers; Urban and Regional Planners. **PERSONALITY TYPE**—No data available.

EDUCATION/TRAINING PROGRAM(S)—Anthropology; Archeology. **RELATED KNOWLEDGE/COURSES**—No data available.

Anthropology and Archeology Teachers, Postsecondary

- ▲ Education/Training Required: Master's degree
- ▲ Annual Earnings: $56,540
- ▲ Growth: 24% for all Postsecondary Teachers
- ▲ Annual Job Openings: 184,000 for all Postsecondary Teachers
- ▲ Self-Employed: 0%
- ▲ Part-Time: 32.3% for all Postsecondary Teachers

Teach courses in anthropology or archeology. Prepares and delivers lectures to students. Stimulates class discussions. Compiles bibliographies of specialized materials for outside reading assignments. Directs research of other teachers or graduate students working for advanced academic degrees. Serves on faculty committee providing professional consulting services to government and industry. Acts as adviser to student organizations. Conducts research in particular field of knowledge and publishes findings in professional journals. Advises students on academic and vocational curricula. Compiles, administers, and grades examinations or assigns this work to others. **SKILLS**—Reading Comprehension: Understanding written sentences and paragraphs in work-related documents. Instructing: Teaching others how to do something. Active Learning: Understanding the implications of new information for both current and future problem-solving and decision-making. Speaking: Talking to others to convey information effectively. Learning Strategies: Selecting and using training/instructional methods and procedures appropriate for the situation when learning or teaching new things. Writing: Communicating effectively in writing as appropriate for the needs of the audience. Active Listening: Giving full attention to what other people are saying, taking time to understand the points being made, asking questions as appropriate, and not interrupting at inappropriate times.

GOE INFORMATION—**Interest Area:** 12. Education and Social Service. **Work Group:** 12.03. Educational Services. **Other Job Titles in This Work Group:** Adult Literacy, Remedial Education, and GED Teachers and Instructors; Agricultural Sciences Teachers, Postsecondary; Architecture Teachers, Postsecondary;

Archivists; Area, Ethnic, and Cultural Studies Teachers, Postsecondary; Art, Drama, and Music Teachers, Postsecondary; Atmospheric, Earth, Marine, and Space Sciences Teachers, Postsecondary; Audio-Visual Collections Specialists; Biological Science Teachers, Postsecondary; Business Teachers, Postsecondary; Chemistry Teachers, Postsecondary; Child Care Workers; Communications Teachers, Postsecondary; Computer Science Teachers, Postsecondary; Criminal Justice and Law Enforcement Teachers, Postsecondary; Curators; Economics Teachers, Postsecondary; Education Teachers, Postsecondary; Educational Psychologists; Educational, Vocational, and School Counselors; Elementary School Teachers, Except Special Education; Engineering Teachers, Postsecondary; English Language and Literature Teachers, Postsecondary; Environmental Science Teachers, Postsecondary; Farm and Home Management Advisors; Foreign Language and Literature Teachers, Postsecondary; Forestry and Conservation Science Teachers, Postsecondary; Geography Teachers, Postsecondary; Graduate Teaching Assistants; Health Specialties Teachers, Postsecondary; History Teachers, Postsecondary; Home Economics Teachers, Postsecondary; Kindergarten Teachers, Except Special Education; Law Teachers, Postsecondary; Librarians; Library Assistants, Clerical; Library Science Teachers, Postsecondary; others. **PERSONALITY TYPE**—Social. Social occupations frequently involve working with, communicating with, and teaching people. These occupations often involve helping or providing service to others.

EDUCATION/TRAINING PROGRAM(S)—Anthropology; Archeology; Social Science Teacher Education. **RELATED KNOWLEDGE/COURSES**—**Education and Training:** Knowledge of principles and methods for curriculum and training design, teaching and instruction for individuals and groups, and the measurement of training effects. **Sociology and Anthropology:** Knowledge of group behavior and dynamics, societal trends and influences, human migrations, ethnicity, cultures, and their history and origins. **Psychology:** Knowledge of human behavior and performance; individual differences in ability, personality, and interests;

learning and motivation; psychological research methods; and the assessment and treatment of behavioral and affective disorders. **History and Archeology:** Knowledge of historical events and their causes, indicators, and effects on civilizations and cultures. **English Language:** Knowledge of the structure and content of the English language, including the meaning and spelling of words, rules of composition, and grammar.

Arbitrators, Mediators, and Conciliators

- ▲ Education/Training Required: Work experience, plus degree
- ▲ Annual Earnings: $43,060
- ▲ Growth: 27%
- ▲ Annual Job Openings: Fewer than 500
- ▲ Self-Employed: 0.5%
- ▲ Part-Time: 3.6%

Facilitate negotiation and conflict resolution through dialogue. Resolve conflicts outside of the court system by mutual consent of parties involved. Arranges and conducts hearings to obtain information and evidence relative to disposition of claim. Counsels parties and recommends acceptance or rejection of compromise settlement offers. Analyzes evidence and applicable law, regulations, policy, and precedent decisions to determine conclusions. Questions witnesses to obtain information. Rules on exceptions, motions, and admissibility of evidence. Participates in court proceedings. Obtains additional information to clarify evidence. Conducts studies of appeals procedures in field agencies to ensure adherence to legal requirements and to facilitate determination of cases. Notifies claimant of denied claim and appeal rights. Authorizes payment of valid claims. Issues subpoenas and administers oaths to prepare for formal hearing. Researches laws, regulations, policies, and precedent decisions to prepare for hearings. Reviews and evaluates data on documents, such as claim applications, birth or death certificates, and physician or employer records. Interviews or corresponds with claimants or agents to elicit information. Prepares written opinions and decisions. Determines existence and amount of liability, according to law, administrative and judicial precedents, and evidence. **SKILLS**—Active Listening: Giving full attention to what other people are saying, taking time to understand the

points being made, asking questions as appropriate, and not interrupting at inappropriate times. Critical Thinking: Using logic and reasoning to identify the strengths and weaknesses of alternative solutions, conclusions, or approaches to problems. Judgment and Decision Making: Considering the relative costs and benefits of potential actions to choose the most appropriate one. Reading Comprehension: Understanding written sentences and paragraphs in work-related documents. Writing: Communicating effectively in writing as appropriate for the needs of the audience.

GOE INFORMATION—Interest Area: 04. Law, Law Enforcement, and Public Safety. **Work Group:** 04.02. Law. **Other Job Titles in This Work Group:** Administrative Law Judges, Adjudicators, and Hearing Officers; Judges, Magistrate Judges, and Magistrates; Law Clerks; Lawyers; Legal Support Workers, All Other; Paralegals and Legal Assistants; Title Examiners and Abstractors; Title Examiners, Abstractors, and Searchers; Title Searchers. **PERSONALITY TYPE**—Enterprising. Enterprising occupations frequently involve starting up and carrying out projects. These occupations can involve leading people and making many decisions. They sometimes require risk taking and often deal with business.

EDUCATION/TRAINING PROGRAM(S)—Law (LL.B., J.D.); Law and Legal Studies, Other.

RELATED KNOWLEDGE/COURSES—**Law and Government:** Knowledge of laws, legal codes, court procedures, precedents, government regulations, executive orders, agency rules, and the democratic political process. **Administration and Management:** Knowledge of business and management principles involved in strategic planning, resource allocation, human resources modeling, leadership technique, production methods, and coordination of people and resources. **English Language:** Knowledge of the structure and content of the English language, including the meaning and spelling of words, rules of composition, and grammar. **Psychology:** Knowledge of human behavior and performance; individual differences in ability, personality, and interests; learning and motivation; psychological research methods; and the assessment and treatment of behavioral and affective disorders. **Education and Training:** Knowledge of principles and methods for curriculum and training design, teaching and instruction for individuals and groups, and the measurement of training effects. **Mathematics:** Knowledge of arithmetic, algebra, geometry, calculus, and statistics and their applications. **Computers and Electronics:** Knowledge of circuit boards, processors, chips, electronic equipment, and computer hardware and software, including applications and programming.

Archeologists

- ▲ Education/Training Required: Bachelor's degree
- ▲ Annual Earnings: $36,040
- ▲ Growth: 17%
- ▲ Annual Job Openings: 2,000
- ▲ Self-Employed: 5.2%
- ▲ Part-Time: 18.1%

Conduct research to reconstruct record of past human life and culture from human remains, artifacts, architectural features, and structures recovered through excavation, underwater recovery, or other means of discovery. Studies artifacts, architectural features, and types of structures recovered by excavation in order to determine age and cultural identity. Classifies and interprets artifacts, architectural features, and types of structures recovered by excavation to determine age and cultural identity. Establishes chronological sequence of development of each culture from simpler to more advanced levels. **SKILLS**—Reading Comprehension: Understanding written sentences and paragraphs in work-related documents. Writing: Communicating effectively in writing as appropriate for the needs of the audience. Active Learning: Understanding the implications of new information for both current and future problem-solving and decision-making. Critical Thinking: Using logic and reasoning to identify the strengths and weaknesses of alternative solutions, conclusions, or approaches to problems. Science: Using scientific rules and methods to solve problems.

GOE INFORMATION—**Interest Area:** 02. Science, Math, and Engineering. **Work Group:** 02.04. Social Sciences. **Other Job Titles in This Work Group:** Anthropologists; Anthropologists and Archeologists; City Planning Aides; Economists; Historians; Industrial-Organizational Psychologists; Political Scientists; Psychologists, All Other; Social Science Research Assistants; Social Scientists and Related Workers, All Other; Sociologists; Survey Researchers; Urban and Regional Planners. **PERSONALITY TYPE**—Investigative. Investigative occupations frequently involve working with ideas and require an extensive amount of thinking. These occupations can involve searching for facts and figuring out problems mentally.

EDUCATION/TRAINING PROGRAM(S)—Anthropology; Archeology. **RELATED KNOWLEDGE/COURSES**—**History and Archeology:** Knowledge of historical events and their causes, indicators, and effects on civilizations and cultures. **Sociology and Anthropology:** Knowledge of group behavior and dynamics, societal trends and influences, human migrations, ethnicity, cultures, and their history and origins. **Geography:** Knowledge of principles and methods for describing the features of land, sea, and air masses, including their physical characteristics, locations, interrelationships, and distribution of plant, animal, and human life. **English Language:** Knowledge of the structure and content of the English language, including the meaning and spelling of words, rules of composition, and grammar.

Clerical Studies: Knowledge of administrative and clerical procedures and systems such as word processing, managing files and records, stenography and transcription, designing forms, and other office procedures and terminology. **Philosophy and Theology:** Knowledge of different philosophical systems and religions. This includes their basic principles, values, ethics, ways of thinking, customs, and practices and their impact on human culture.

Architects, Except Landscape and Naval

- ▲ Education/Training Required: Bachelor's degree
- ▲ Annual Earnings: $52,510
- ▲ Growth: 18%
- ▲ Annual Job Openings: 4,000
- ▲ Self-Employed: 30.8%
- ▲ Part-Time: 8%

Plan and design structures, such as private residences, office buildings, theaters, factories, and other structural property. Prepares information regarding design, structure specifications, materials, color, equipment, estimated costs, and construction time. Plans layout of project. Integrates engineering element into unified design. Prepares scale drawings. Prepares contract documents for building contractors. Administers construction contracts. Prepares operating and maintenance manuals, studies, and reports. Represents client in obtaining bids and awarding construction contracts. Directs activities of workers engaged in preparing drawings and specification documents. Conducts periodic on-site observation of work during construction to monitor compliance with plans. Consults with client to determine functional and spatial requirements of structure. **SKILLS—Coordination:** Adjusting actions in relation to others' actions. Reading Comprehension: Understanding written sentences and paragraphs in work-related documents. Writing: Communicating effectively in writing as appropriate for the needs of the audience. Mathematics: Using mathematics to solve problems. Active Listening: Giving full attention to what other people are saying, taking time to understand the points being made, asking questions as appropriate, and not interrupting at inappropriate times.

GOE INFORMATION—Interest Area: 02. Science, Math, and Engineering. **Work Group:** 02.07. Engineering. **Other Job Titles in This Work Group:** Aerospace Engineers; Agricultural Engineers; Biomedical Engineers; Chemical Engineers; Civil Engineers; Computer Hardware Engineers; Computer Software Engineers, Applications; Computer Software Engineers, Systems Software; Electrical Engineers; Electronics Engineers, Except Computer; Engineers, All Other; Environmental Engineers; Fire-Prevention and Protection Engineers; Health and Safety Engineers, Except Mining Safety Engineers and Inspectors; Industrial Engineers; Industrial Safety and Health Engineers; Landscape Architects; Marine Architects; Marine Engineers; Marine Engineers and Naval Architects; Materials Engineers; Mechanical Engineers; Mining and Geological Engineers, Including Mining Safety Engineers; Nuclear Engineers; Petroleum Engineers; Product Safety Engineers; Sales Engineers. **PERSONALITY TYPE—** Artistic. Artistic occupations frequently involve working with forms, designs, and patterns. They often require self-expression, and the work can be done without following a clear set of rules.

EDUCATION/TRAINING PROGRAM(S)— Architectural Environmental Design; Architecture; Architecture and Related Programs, Other. **RELATED**

KNOWLEDGE/COURSES—**Design:** Knowledge of design techniques, tools, and principles involved in production of precision technical plans, blueprints, drawings, and models. **Building and Construction:** Knowledge of materials, methods, and tools involved in the construction or repair of houses, buildings, or other structures, such as highways and roads. **Administration and Management:** Knowledge of business and management principles involved in strategic planning, resource allocation, human resources modeling, leadership technique, production methods, and coordination of people and resources. **Mathematics:** Knowledge of arithmetic, algebra, geometry, calculus, and statistics and their applications. **English Language:** Knowledge of the structure and content of the English language, including the meaning and spelling of words, rules of composition, and grammar.

Architectural Drafters

- ▲ Education/Training Required: Associate's degree
- ▲ Annual Earnings: $35,220
- ▲ Growth: 21%
- ▲ Annual Job Openings: 12,000
- ▲ Self-Employed: 3%
- ▲ Part-Time: 7.9%

Prepare detailed drawings of architectural designs and plans for buildings and structures according to specifications provided by architect. Draws rough and detailed scale plans, to scale, for foundations, buildings, and structures, according to specifications. Prepares colored drawings of landscape and interior designs for presentation to client. Develops diagrams for construction, fabrication, and installation of equipment, structures, components, and systems, using field documents and specifications. Lays out and plans interior room arrangements for commercial buildings and draws charts, forms, and records, using computer-assisted equipment. Lays out schematics and wiring diagrams used to erect, install, and repair establishment cable and electrical systems, using computer equipment. Drafts and corrects topographical maps to represent geological stratigraphy, mineral deposits, and pipeline systems, using survey data and aerial photographs. Builds landscape models, using data provided by landscape architect. Calculates heat loss and gain of buildings and structures to determine required equipment specifications, following standard procedures. Traces copies of plans and drawings, using transparent paper or cloth, ink, pencil, and standard drafting instruments for reproduction purposes. SKILLS—**Mathematics:** Using mathematics to solve problems. **Programming:** Writing computer programs for various purposes. **Reading Comprehension:** Understanding written sentences and paragraphs in work-related documents. **Active Learning:** Understanding the implications of new information for both current and future problem-solving and decision-making. **Operations Analysis:** Analyzing needs and product requirements to create a design.

GOE INFORMATION—**Interest Area:** 02. Science, Math, and Engineering. **Work Group:** 02.08. Engineering Technology. **Other Job Titles in This Work Group:** Aerospace Engineering and Operations Technicians; Architectural and Civil Drafters; Calibration and Instrumentation Technicians; Cartographers and Photogrammetrists; Civil Drafters; Civil Engineering Technicians; Construction and Building Inspectors; Drafters, All Other; Electrical and Electronic Engineering Technicians; Electrical and Electronics Drafters; Electrical Drafters; Electrical Engineering Technicians; Electro-Mechanical Technicians; Electronic Drafters; Electronics Engineering Technicians; Engineering Technicians, Except Drafters, All Other; Environmental Engineering Technicians; Industrial Engineering Technicians; Mapping Technicians; Mechanical Drafters; Mechanical Engineering Technicians; Numerical Tool and Process Control Programmers; Pressure Vessel Inspectors; Surveying and Mapping Technicians; Surveying Technicians; Surveyors. **PERSONALITY TYPE**—Realistic. Realistic occupations frequently involve work activities that include practical, hands-on problems and solutions. They often deal with plants, animals, and real-world materials like wood, tools, and machinery. Many of the occupations require working outside and do not involve a lot of paperwork or working closely with others.

EDUCATION/TRAINING PROGRAM(S)— Architectural Drafting; Civil/Structural Drafting. RELATED KNOWLEDGE/COURSES—Design: Knowledge of design techniques, tools, and principles involved in production of precision technical plans, blueprints, drawings, and models. Mathematics: Knowledge of arithmetic, algebra, geometry, calculus, and statistics and their applications. Engineering and Technology: Knowledge of the practical application of engineering science and technology. This includes applying principles, techniques, procedures, and equipment to the design and production of various goods and services. Computers and Electronics: Knowledge of circuit boards, processors, chips, electronic equipment, and computer hardware and software, including applications and programming. Physics: Knowledge and prediction of physical principles and laws and their interrelationships and applications to understanding fluid, material, and atmospheric dynamics and mechanical, electrical, atomic, and sub-atomic structures and processes.

Architecture Teachers, Postsecondary

▲ Education/Training Required: Master's degree
▲ Annual Earnings: $50,800
▲ Growth: 24% for all Postsecondary Teachers
▲ Annual Job Openings: 184,000 for all Postsecondary Teachers
▲ Self-Employed: 0%
▲ Part-Time: 32.3% for all Postsecondary Teachers

Teach courses in architecture and architectural design, such as architectural environmental design, interior architecture/design, and landscape architecture. SKILLS—No data available.

GOE INFORMATION—Interest Area: 12. Education and Social Service. Work Group: 12.03. Educational Services. Other Job Titles in This Work Group: Adult Literacy, Remedial Education, and GED Teachers and Instructors; Agricultural Sciences Teachers, Postsecondary; Anthropology and Archeology Teachers, Postsecondary; Archivists; Area, Ethnic, and Cultural Studies Teachers, Postsecondary; Art, Drama, and Music Teachers, Postsecondary; Atmospheric, Earth, Marine, and Space Sciences Teachers, Postsecondary; Audio-Visual Collections Specialists; Biological Science Teachers, Postsecondary; Business Teachers, Postsecondary; Chemistry Teachers, Postsecondary; Child Care Workers; Communications Teachers, Postsecondary; Computer Science Teachers, Postsecondary; Criminal Justice and Law Enforcement Teachers, Postsecondary; Curators; Economics Teachers, Postsecondary; Education Teachers, Postsecondary; Educational Psychologists; Educational, Vocational, and School Counselors; Elementary School Teachers, Except Special Education; Engineering Teachers, Postsecondary; English Language and Literature Teachers, Postsecondary; Environmental Science Teachers, Postsecondary; Farm and Home Management Advisors; Foreign Language and Literature Teachers, Postsecondary; Forestry and Conservation Science Teachers, Postsecondary; Geography Teachers, Postsecondary; Graduate Teaching Assistants; Health Specialties Teachers, Postsecondary; History Teachers, Postsecondary; Home Economics Teachers, Postsecondary; Kindergarten Teachers, Except Special Education; Law Teachers, Postsecondary; Librarians; Library Assistants, Clerical; Library Science Teachers, Postsecondary; others. PERSONALITY TYPE—No data available.

EDUCATION/TRAINING PROGRAM(S)— Architectural Engineering; Architectural Environmental Design; Architectural Urban Design and Planning; Architecture; City/Urban, Community and Regional Planning; Interior Architecture; Landscape Architecture; Teacher Education, Specific Academic and Vocational Programs. **RELATED KNOWLEDGE/COURSES**—No data available.

Area, Ethnic, and Cultural Studies Teachers, Postsecondary

- ▲ Education/Training Required: Master's degree
- ▲ Annual Earnings: $52,290
- ▲ Growth: 24% for all Postsecondary Teachers
- ▲ Annual Job Openings: 184,000 for all Postsecondary Teachers
- ▲ Self-Employed: 0%
- ▲ Part-Time: 32.3% for all Postsecondary Teachers

Teach courses pertaining to the culture and development of an area (e.g., Latin America), an ethnic group, or any other group (e.g., women's studies, urban affairs). Prepares and delivers lectures to students. Compiles, administers, and grades examinations or assigns this work to others. Advises students on academic and vocational curricula. Conducts research in particular field of knowledge and publishes findings in professional journals. Acts as adviser to student organizations. Serves on faculty committee providing professional consulting services to government and industry. Directs research of other teachers or graduate students working for advanced academic degrees. Compiles bibliographies of specialized materials for outside reading assignments. Stimulates class discussions. **SKILLS**—Reading Comprehension: Understanding written sentences and paragraphs in work-related documents. Instructing: Teaching others how to do something. Speaking: Talking to others to convey information effectively. Active Learning: Understanding the implications of new information for both current and future problem-solving and decision-making. Learning Strategies: Selecting and using training/instructional methods and procedures appropriate for the situation when learning or teaching new things. Writing: Communicating effectively in writing as appropriate for the needs of the audience. Active Listening: Giving full attention to what other people are saying, taking time to understand the points being made, asking questions as appropriate, and not interrupting at inappropriate times.

GOE INFORMATION—Interest Area: 12. Education and Social Service. **Work Group:** 12.03. Educational Services. **Other Job Titles in This Work Group:** Adult Literacy, Remedial Education, and GED Teachers and Instructors; Agricultural Sciences Teachers, Postsecondary; Anthropology and Archeology Teachers, Postsecondary; Architecture Teachers, Postsecondary; Archivists; Art, Drama, and Music Teachers, Postsecondary; Atmospheric, Earth, Marine, and Space Sciences Teachers, Postsecondary; Audio-Visual Collections Specialists; Biological Science Teachers, Postsecondary; Business Teachers, Postsecondary; Chemistry Teachers, Postsecondary; Child Care Workers; Communications Teachers, Postsecondary; Computer Science Teachers, Postsecondary; Criminal Justice and Law Enforcement Teachers, Postsecondary; Curators; Economics Teachers, Postsecondary; Education Teachers, Postsecondary; Educational Psychologists; Educational, Vocational, and School Counselors; Elementary School Teachers, Except Special Education; Engineering Teachers, Postsecondary; English Language and Literature Teachers, Postsecondary; Environmental Science Teachers, Postsecondary; Farm and Home Management Advisors; Foreign Language and Literature Teachers, Postsecondary; Forestry and Conservation Science Teachers, Postsecondary; Geography Teachers, Postsecondary; Graduate Teaching Assistants; Health Specialties Teachers, Postsecondary; History Teachers, Postsecondary; Home Economics Teachers, Postsecondary;

Kindergarten Teachers, Except Special Education; Law Teachers, Postsecondary; Librarians; Library Assistants, Clerical; Library Science Teachers, Postsecondary; Library Technicians; others. **PERSONALITY TYPE**—Social. Social occupations frequently involve working with, communicating with, and teaching people. These occupations often involve helping or providing service to others.

EDUCATION/TRAINING PROGRAM(S)—African Studies; Afro-American (Black) Studies; American Indian/Native American Studies; American Studies/Civilization; Area Studies, Other; Area, Ethnic and Cultural Studies, Other; Asian Studies; Asian-American Studies; Canadian Studies; East Asian Studies; Eastern European Area Studies; Ethnic and Cultural Studies, Other; European Studies; Hispanic-American Studies; Islamic Studies; Jewish/Judaic Studies; Latin American Studies; Middle Eastern Studies; Pacific Area Studies; Russian and Slavic Area Studies; Scandinavian Area Studies; Social Studies Teacher Education; South Asian Studies; Southeast Asian Studies; Western European Studies; Women's Studies. **RELATED KNOWLEDGE/COURSES**—**Education and Training:** Knowledge of principles and methods for curriculum and training design, teaching and instruction for individuals and groups, and the measurement of training effects. **Sociology and Anthropology:** Knowledge of group behavior and dynamics, societal trends and influences, human migrations, ethnicity, cultures, and their history and origins. **English Language:** Knowledge of the structure and content of the English language, including the meaning and spelling of words, rules of composition, and grammar. **History and Archeology:** Knowledge of historical events and their causes, indicators, and effects on civilizations and cultures. **Psychology:** Knowledge of human behavior and performance; individual differences in ability, personality, and interests; learning and motivation; psychological research methods; and the assessment and treatment of behavioral and affective disorders.

Art Directors

- ▲ Education/Training Required: Work experience, plus degree
- ▲ Annual Earnings: $56,880
- ▲ Growth: 21%
- ▲ Annual Job Openings: 6,000
- ▲ Self-Employed: 31.9%
- ▲ Part-Time: 20%

Formulate design concepts and presentation approaches and direct workers engaged in art work, layout design, and copy writing for visual communications media, such as magazines, books, newspapers, and packaging. Assigns and directs staff members to develop design concepts into art layouts or prepare layouts for printing. Formulates basic layout design or presentation approach and conceives material details, such as style and size of type, photographs, graphics, and arrangement. Reviews and approves art and copy materials developed by staff and proofs of printed copy. Reviews illustrative material and confers with client concerning objectives, budget, background information, and presentation approaches, styles, and techniques. Writes typography instructions, such as margin widths and type sizes, and submits for typesetting or printing. Draws custom illustrations for project. Marks up, pastes, and completes layouts to prepare for printing. Prepares detailed storyboard showing sequence and timing of story development for television production. Presents final layouts to client for approval. Confers with creative, art, copy writing, or production department heads to discuss client requirements, outline presentation concepts, and coordinate creative activities. **SKILLS**—Coordination: Adjusting actions in relation to others' actions. Active Learning: Understanding the implications of new information for both current and future problem-solving and decision-making. Speaking: Talking to others to convey information effectively. Operations Analysis: Analyzing needs and product requirements to create a design. Persuasion: Persuading others to change their minds or behavior. Time Management: Managing one's own time and the time of others.

GOE INFORMATION—**Interest Area:** 01. Arts, Entertainment, and Media. **Work Group:** 01.01. Managerial Work in Arts, Entertainment, and Media. **Other Job Titles in This Work Group:** Agents and Business Managers of Artists, Performers, and Athletes; Producers; Producers and Directors; Program Directors; Technical Directors/Managers. **PERSONALITY TYPE**—Artistic. Artistic occupations frequently involve working with forms, designs, and patterns. They often require self-expression, and the work can be done without following a clear set of rules.

EDUCATION/TRAINING PROGRAM(S)—Art, General; Graphic Design, Commercial Art and Illustration; Intermedia. **RELATED KNOWLEDGE/ COURSES**—**Design:** Knowledge of design techniques, tools, and principles involved in production of precision technical plans, blueprints, drawings, and models. **Fine Arts:** Knowledge of the theory and techniques required to compose, produce, and perform works of music, dance, visual arts, drama, and sculpture. **Administration and Management:** Knowledge of business and management principles involved in strategic planning, resource allocation, human resources modeling, leadership technique, production methods, and coordination of people and resources. **Sales and Marketing:** Knowledge of principles and methods for showing, promoting, and selling products or services. This includes marketing strategy and tactics, product demonstration, sales techniques, and sales control systems. **Telecommunications:** Knowledge of transmission, broadcasting, switching, control, and operation of telecommunications systems. **English Language:** Knowledge of the structure and content of the English language, including the meaning and spelling of words, rules of composition, and grammar. **Communications and Media:** Knowledge of media production, communication, and dissemination techniques and methods. This includes alternative ways to inform and entertain via written, oral, and visual media.

Art, Drama, and Music Teachers, Postsecondary

- ▲ Education/Training Required: Master's degree
- ▲ Annual Earnings: $45,530
- ▲ Growth: 24% for all Postsecondary Teachers
- ▲ Annual Job Openings: 184,000 for all Postsecondary Teachers
- ▲ Self-Employed: 0%
- ▲ Part-Time: 32.3% for all Postsecondary Teachers

Teach courses in drama, music, and the arts, including fine and applied art, such as painting and sculpture or design and crafts. Prepares and delivers lectures to students. Stimulates class discussions. Compiles bibliographies of specialized materials for outside reading assignments. Compiles, administers, and grades examinations or assigns this work to others. Advises students on academic and vocational curricula. Directs research of other teachers or graduate students working for advanced academic degrees. Conducts research in particular field of knowledge and publishes findings in professional journals. Serves on faculty committee providing professional consulting services to government and industry. Acts as adviser to student organizations. **SKILLS**—Reading Comprehension: Understanding written sentences and paragraphs in work-related documents. Instructing: Teaching others how to do something. Learning Strategies: Selecting and using training/instructional methods and procedures appropriate for the situation when learning or teaching new things. Writing: Communicating effectively in writing as appropriate for the needs of the audience. Speaking: Talking to others to convey information effectively.

GOE INFORMATION—**Interest Area:** 12. Education and Social Service. **Work Group:** 12.03. Educational Services. **Other Job Titles in This Work Group:** Adult Literacy, Remedial Education, and GED Teachers and Instructors; Agricultural Sciences Teachers, Postsecondary; Anthropology and Archeology Teachers, Postsecondary; Architecture Teachers, Postsecondary; Archivists; Area, Ethnic, and Cultural Studies Teachers, Postsecondary; Atmospheric, Earth, Marine, and Space Sciences Teachers, Postsecondary; Audio-Visual Collections Specialists; Biological Science Teachers, Postsecondary; Business Teachers, Postsecondary; Chemistry Teachers, Postsecondary; Child Care Workers; Communications Teachers, Postsecondary; Computer Science Teachers, Postsecondary; Criminal Justice and Law Enforcement Teachers, Postsecondary; Curators; Economics Teachers, Postsecondary; Education Teachers, Postsecondary; Educational Psychologists; Educational, Vocational, and School Counselors; Elementary School Teachers, Except Special Education; Engineering Teachers, Postsecondary; English Language and Literature Teachers, Postsecondary; Environmental Science Teachers, Postsecondary; Farm and Home Management Advisors; Foreign Language and Literature Teachers, Postsecondary; Forestry and Conservation Science Teachers, Postsecondary; Geography Teachers, Postsecondary; Graduate Teaching Assistants; Health Specialties Teachers, Postsecondary; History Teachers, Postsecondary; Home Economics Teachers, Postsecondary; Kindergarten Teachers, Except Special Education; Law Teachers, Postsecondary; Librarians; Library Assistants, Clerical; Library Science Teachers, Postsecondary; others. **PERSONALITY TYPE**—Artistic. Artistic occupations frequently involve working with forms, designs, and patterns. They often require self-expression, and the work can be done without following a clear set of rules.

EDUCATION/TRAINING PROGRAM(S)—Drama/Theater Arts, General; Music, General; Visual and Performing Arts. **RELATED KNOWLEDGE/ COURSES—Fine Arts:** Knowledge of the theory and techniques required to compose, produce, and perform works of music, dance, visual arts, drama, and sculpture. **Education and Training:** Knowledge of principles and methods for curriculum and training design, teaching and instruction for individuals and groups, and the measurement of training effects. **English Language:** Knowledge of the structure and content of the English language, including the meaning and spelling of words, rules of composition, and grammar. **Administration and Management:** Knowledge of business and management principles involved in strategic planning, resource allocation, human resources modeling, leadership technique, production methods, and coordination of people and resources. **Communications and Media:** Knowledge of media production, communication, and dissemination techniques and methods. This includes alternative ways to inform and entertain via written, oral, and visual media.

Astronomers

- ▲ Education/Training Required: Doctoral degree
- ▲ Annual Earnings: $74,510
- ▲ Growth: 10%
- ▲ Annual Job Openings: 1,000
- ▲ Self-Employed: 5%
- ▲ Part-Time: 6.6%

Observe, research, and interpret celestial and astronomical phenomena to increase basic knowledge and apply such information to practical problems. Studies celestial phenomena from ground or above atmosphere, using various optical devices such as telescopes situated on ground or attached to satellites. Designs optical, mechanical, and electronic instruments for astronomical research. Develops mathematical tables giving positions of sun, moon, planets, and stars at given times for use by air and sea navigators. Analyzes wave lengths of radiation from celestial bodies as observed in all ranges of spectrum. Determines exact time by celestial observations and conducts research into relationships between time and space. Studies history, structure, extent, and evolution of stars, stellar systems, and universe. Computes positions of sun, moon, planets, stars, nebulae, and galaxies. Calculates orbits and determines sizes, shapes, brightness, and motions of different celestial bodies. **SKILLS**—Mathematics: Using mathematics to solve problems. Science: Using scientific rules and methods to solve problems. Critical Thinking: Using logic and reasoning to identify the strengths and weaknesses of alternative solutions, conclusions, or approaches to problems. Active Learning: Understanding the implications of new information for both current and future problem-solving and decision-making. Reading Comprehension: Understanding written sentences and paragraphs in work-related documents.

GOE INFORMATION—**Interest Area:** 02. Science, Math, and Engineering. **Work Group:** 02.02. Physical Sciences. **Other Job Titles in This Work Group:** Atmospheric and Space Scientists; Chemists; Geographers; Geologists; Geoscientists, Except Hydrologists and Geographers; Hydrologists; Materials Scientists; Physical Scientists, All Other; Physicists. **PERSONALITY TYPE**—Investigative. Investigative occupations frequently involve working with ideas and require an exten-

sive amount of thinking. These occupations can involve searching for facts and figuring out problems mentally.

EDUCATION/TRAINING PROGRAM(S)—Astronomy; Astrophysics. **RELATED KNOWLEDGE/COURSES**—**Physics:** Knowledge and prediction of physical principles and laws and their interrelationships and applications to understanding fluid, material, and atmospheric dynamics and mechanical, electrical, atomic, and sub-atomic structures and processes. **Mathematics:** Knowledge of arithmetic, algebra, geometry, calculus, and statistics and their applications. **Design:** Knowledge of design techniques, tools, and principles involved in production of precision technical plans, blueprints, drawings, and models. **Computers and Electronics:** Knowledge of circuit boards, processors, chips, electronic equipment, and computer hardware and software, including applications and programming. **English Language:** Knowledge of the structure and content of the English language, including the meaning and spelling of words, rules of composition, and grammar. **Engineering and Technology:** Knowledge of the practical application of engineering science and technology. This includes applying principles, techniques, procedures, and equipment to the design and production of various goods and services.

Athletic Trainers

- ▲ Education/Training Required: Bachelor's degree
- ▲ Annual Earnings: $32,080
- ▲ Growth: 18%
- ▲ Annual Job Openings: 2,000
- ▲ Self-Employed: 31.4%
- ▲ Part-Time: 25.3%

Evaluate, advise, and treat athletes to assist recovery from injury, avoid injury, or maintain peak physical fitness. Evaluates physical condition of athletes and advises or prescribes routine and corrective exercises to strengthen muscles. Recommends special diets to improve health, increase stamina, and reduce weight of athletes. Administers emergency first aid, treats minor chronic disabilities, or refers injured person to physician. Massages body parts to relieve soreness, strains, and bruises.

Wraps ankles, fingers, wrists, or other body parts with synthetic skin, gauze, or adhesive tape to support muscles and ligaments. **SKILLS**—Speaking: Talking to others to convey information effectively. Active Listening: Giving full attention to what other people are saying, taking time to understand the points being made, asking questions as appropriate, and not interrupting at inappropriate times. Service Orientation: Actively looking for ways to help people. Reading Comprehension: Understanding written sentences and paragraphs in work-related documents. Social Perceptiveness: Being aware of others' reactions and understanding why they react as they do. Judgment and Decision Making: Considering the relative costs and benefits of potential actions to choose the most appropriate one. Critical Thinking: Using logic and reasoning to identify the strengths and weaknesses of alternative solutions, conclusions, or approaches to problems.

GOE INFORMATION—Interest Area: 14. Medical and Health Services. Work Group: 14.08. Health Protection and Promotion. Other Job Titles in This Work Group: Dietetic Technicians; Dietitians and Nutritionists; Health Educators. PERSONALITY TYPE—Social. Social occupations frequently involve working with, communicating with, and teaching people. These occupations often involve helping or providing service to others.

EDUCATION/TRAINING PROGRAM(S)— Athletic Training and Sports Medicine; Health and Physical Education, General; Physical Education Teaching and Coaching. RELATED KNOWLEDGE/ COURSES—Biology: Knowledge of plant and ani-

mal organisms and their tissues, cells, functions, interdependencies, and interactions with each other and the environment. Therapy and Counseling: Knowledge of principles, methods, and procedures for diagnosis, treatment, and rehabilitation of physical and mental dysfunctions and for career counseling and guidance. Medicine and Dentistry: Knowledge of the information and techniques needed to diagnose and treat human injuries, diseases, and deformities. This includes symptoms, treatment alternatives, drug properties and interactions, and preventive health-care measures. Customer and Personal Service: Knowledge of principles and processes for providing customer and personal services. This includes customer needs assessment, meeting quality standards for services, and evaluation of customer satisfaction. Education and Training: Knowledge of principles and methods for curriculum and training design, teaching and instruction for individuals and groups, and the measurement of training effects. Psychology: Knowledge of human behavior and performance; individual differences in ability, personality, and interests; learning and motivation; psychological research methods; and the assessment and treatment of behavioral and affective disorders.

Atmospheric and Space Scientists

▲ Education/Training Required: Bachelor's degree

▲ Annual Earnings: $58,510

▲ Growth: 17%

▲ Annual Job Openings: Fewer than 500

▲ Self-Employed: 0%

▲ Part-Time: 6.6%

Investigate atmospheric phenomena and interpret meteorological data gathered by surface and air stations, satellites, and radar to prepare reports and forecasts for public and other uses. Analyzes and interprets meteorological data gathered by surface and upper air stations, satellites, and radar to prepare reports and forecasts. Directs forecasting services at weather station or at radio or television broadcasting facility. Broadcasts weather forecast over television or radio. Issues hurricane and other severe weather warnings. Conducts basic or applied research in meteorology. Studies and interprets synoptic reports, maps, photographs, and prog-

nostic charts to predict long- and short-range weather conditions. Operates computer graphic equipment to produce weather reports and maps for analysis, distribution, or use in televised weather broadcast. Prepares special forecasts and briefings for air and sea transportation, agriculture, fire prevention, air-pollution control, and school groups. SKILLS—Science: Using scientific rules and methods to solve problems. Active Learning: Understanding the implications of new information for both current and future problem-solving and decision-making. Critical Thinking: Using logic and reasoning to identify the strengths and weaknesses of alternative solutions, conclusions, or approaches to problems. Reading Comprehension: Understanding written sentences and paragraphs in work-related documents. Speaking: Talking to others to convey information effectively.

GOE INFORMATION—Interest Area: 02. Science, Math, and Engineering. Work Group: 02.02. Physical Sciences. Other Job Titles in This Work Group: Astronomers; Chemists; Geographers; Geologists; Geoscientists, Except Hydrologists and Geographers; Hydrologists; Materials Scientists; Physical Scientists, All Other; Physicists. PERSONALITY TYPE—Investigative. Investigative occupations frequently involve working with ideas and require an extensive amount of thinking. These occupations can involve searching for facts and figuring out problems mentally.

EDUCATION/TRAINING PROGRAM(S)—Atmospheric Sciences and Meteorology. RELATED KNOWLEDGE/COURSES—Physics: Knowledge and prediction of physical principles and laws and their interrelationships and applications to understanding fluid, material, and atmospheric dynamics and mechanical, electrical, atomic, and sub-atomic structures and processes. Communications and Media: Knowledge of media production, communication, and dissemination techniques and methods. This includes alternative ways to inform and entertain via written, oral, and visual media. Geography: Knowledge of principles and methods for describing the features of land, sea, and air masses, including their physical characteristics, locations, interrelationships, and distribution of plant, animal, and human life. Mathematics: Knowledge of arithmetic, algebra, geometry, calculus, and statistics and their applications. Computers and Electronics: Knowledge of circuit boards, processors, chips, electronic equipment, and computer hardware and software, including applications and programming. English Language: Knowledge of the structure and content of the English language, including the meaning and spelling of words, rules of composition, and grammar.

Atmospheric, Earth, Marine, and Space Sciences Teachers, Postsecondary

▲ Education/Training Required: Master's degree

▲ Annual Earnings: $56,090

▲ Growth: 24% for all Postsecondary Teachers

▲ Annual Job Openings: 184,000 for all Postsecondary Teachers

▲ Self-Employed: 0%

▲ Part-Time: 32.3% for all Postsecondary Teachers

Teach courses in the physical sciences, except chemistry and physics. SKILLS—No data available.

GOE INFORMATION—Interest Area: 12. Education and Social Service. Work Group: 12.03. Educational Services. Other Job Titles in This Work Group: Adult Literacy, Remedial Education, and GED Teachers and Instructors; Agricultural Sciences Teachers, Postsecondary; Anthropology and Archeology Teachers, Postsecondary; Architecture Teachers, Postsecondary; Archivists; Area, Ethnic, and Cultural Studies Teachers, Postsecondary; Art, Drama, and Music Teachers, Postsecondary; Audio-Visual Collections Specialists; Biological Science Teachers, Postsecondary; Business Teachers, Postsecondary; Chemistry Teachers, Postsecondary; Child Care Workers; Communications Teachers, Postsecondary; Computer Science Teachers, Postsecondary; Criminal Justice and Law Enforcement Teachers, Postsecondary; Curators; Economics Teachers, Postsecondary; Education Teachers, Postsecondary; Educational Psychologists; Educational, Vocational, and School Counselors; Elementary School Teachers, Except Special Education; Engineering Teachers, Postsecondary; English Language and Literature Teachers, Postsecondary; Environmental Science Teachers, Postsecondary; Farm and

Home Management Advisors; Foreign Language and Literature Teachers, Postsecondary; Forestry and Conservation Science Teachers, Postsecondary; Geography Teachers, Postsecondary; Graduate Teaching Assistants; Health Specialties Teachers, Postsecondary; History Teachers, Postsecondary; Home Economics Teachers, Postsecondary; Kindergarten Teachers, Except Special Education; Law Teachers, Postsecondary; Librarians; Library Assistants, Clerical; Library Science Teachers, Postsecondary; Library Technicians; others. **PERSONALITY TYPE**—No data available.

EDUCATION/TRAINING PROGRAM(S)— Astronomy; Astrophysics; Atmospheric Sciences and Meteorology; Earth and Planetary Sciences; Geochemistry; Geological and Related Sciences, Other; Geology; Geophysics and Seismology; Metallurgy; Miscellaneous Physical Sciences, Other; Oceanography; Paleontology; Physics Teacher Education; Science Teacher Education, General. **RELATED KNOWLEDGE/COURSES**—No data available.

Audiologists

- ▲ Education/Training Required: Master's degree
- ▲ Annual Earnings: $44,830
- ▲ Growth: 45%
- ▲ Annual Job Openings: 1,000
- ▲ Self-Employed: 10.5%
- ▲ Part-Time: 20.8%

Assess and treat persons with hearing and related disorders. May fit hearing aids and provide auditory training. May perform research related to hearing problems. Refers clients to additional medical or educational services if needed. Advises educators or other medical staff on speech or hearing topics. Counsels and instructs clients in techniques to improve speech or hearing impairment, including sign language or lip-reading. Evaluates hearing and speech/language test results and medical or background information to determine hearing or speech impairment and treatment. Conducts or directs research and reports findings on speech or hearing topics to develop procedures, technology, or treatments. Administers hearing or speech/language evaluations, tests, or examinations to patients to collect information on type and degree of impairment. Participates in conferences or training to update or share knowledge of new hearing or speech disorder treatment methods or technology. Records and maintains reports of speech or hearing research or treatments. Plans and conducts prevention and treatment programs for clients' hearing or speech problems. **SKILLS**—Reading Comprehension: Understanding written sentences and paragraphs in work-related documents. Writing: Communicating effectively in writing as appro-

priate for the needs of the audience. Instructing: Teaching others how to do something. Speaking: Talking to others to convey information effectively. Learning Strategies: Selecting and using training/instructional methods and procedures appropriate for the situation when learning or teaching new things. Active Learning: Understanding the implications of new information for both current and future problem-solving and decision-making. Critical Thinking: Using logic and reasoning to identify the strengths and weaknesses of alternative solutions, conclusions, or approaches to problems.

GOE INFORMATION—**Interest Area:** 14. Medical and Health Services. **Work Group:** 14.06. Medical Therapy. **Other Job Titles in This Work Group:** Massage Therapists; Occupational Therapist Aides; Occupational Therapist Assistants; Occupational Therapists; Physical Therapist Aides; Physical Therapist Assistants; Physical Therapists; Radiation Therapists; Recreational Therapists; Respiratory Therapists; Respiratory Therapy Technicians; Speech-Language Pathologists; Therapists, All Other. **PERSONALITY TYPE**—Social. Social occupations frequently involve working with, communicating with, and teaching people. These occupations often involve helping or providing service to others.

EDUCATION/TRAINING PROGRAM(S)—Audiology/Hearing Sciences; Communication Disorders Sciences and Services, Other; Communication Disorders, General; Speech-Language Pathology and Audiology. **RELATED KNOWLEDGE/COURSES—Therapy and Counseling:** Knowledge of principles, methods, and procedures for diagnosis, treatment, and rehabilitation of physical and mental dysfunctions and for career counseling and guidance. **English Language:** Knowledge of the structure and content of the English language, including the meaning and spelling of words, rules of composition, and grammar. **Medicine and Dentistry:** Knowledge of the information and techniques needed to diagnose and treat human injuries, diseases, and deformities. This includes symptoms, treatment alternatives, drug properties and interactions, and preventive health-care measures. **Education and Training:** Knowledge of principles and methods for curriculum and training design, teaching and instruction for individuals and groups, and the measurement of training effects. **Personnel and Human Resources:** Knowledge of principles and procedures for personnel recruitment, selection, training, compensation and benefits, labor relations and negotiation, and personnel information systems. **Administration and Management:** Knowledge of business and management principles involved in strategic planning, resource allocation, human resources modeling, leadership technique, production methods, and coordination of people and resources.

Auditors

- ▲ Education/Training Required: Bachelor's degree
- ▲ Annual Earnings: $43,500
- ▲ Growth: 18%
- ▲ Annual Job Openings: 100,000
- ▲ Self-Employed: 10.6%
- ▲ Part-Time: 7.8%

Examine and analyze accounting records to determine financial status of establishment and prepare financial reports concerning operating procedures. Reviews data about material assets, net worth, liabilities, capital stock, surplus, income, and expenditures. Reports to management about asset utilization and audit results and recommends changes in operations and financial activities. Analyzes data for deficient controls, duplicated effort, extravagance, fraud, or non-compliance with laws, regulations, and management policies. Examines payroll and personnel records to determine worker's compensation coverage. Verifies journal and ledger entries by examining inventory. Directs activities of personnel engaged in filing, recording, compiling and transmitting financial records. Supervises auditing of establishments and determines scope of investigation required. Examines records and interviews workers to ensure recording of transactions and compliance with laws and regulations. Evaluates taxpayer finances to determine tax liability, using knowledge of interest and discount, annu-ities, valuation of stocks and bonds, and amortization valuation of depletable assets. Confers with company officials about financial and regulatory matters. Examines records, tax returns, and related documents pertaining to settlement of decedent's estate. Audits records to determine unemployment insurance premiums, liabilities, and compliance with tax laws. Reviews taxpayer accounts and conducts audits on-site, by correspondence, or by summoning taxpayer to office. Inspects cash on hand, notes receivable and payable, negotiable securities, and canceled checks. Analyzes annual reports, financial statements, and other records, using accepted accounting and statistical procedures, to determine financial condition. Inspects account books and system for efficiency, effectiveness, and use of accepted accounting procedures to record transactions. **SKILLS—Systems Evaluation:** Identifying measures or indicators of system performance and the actions needed to improve or correct performance relative to the goals of the system. Critical Thinking: Using logic and reasoning to identify the strengths and weaknesses of alternative solutions, conclusions, or approaches to problems. Mathematics: Using mathematics to solve problems. Reading Comprehension: Understanding written sentences and paragraphs in work-related documents. Complex Problem Solving: Identifying complex problems and reviewing related information to develop and evaluate options and implement solutions.

GOE INFORMATION—Interest Area: 13. General Management and Support. Work Group: 13.02. Management Support. Other Job Titles in This Work Group: Accountants; Accountants and Auditors; Appraisers and Assessors of Real Estate; Appraisers, Real Estate; Assessors; Budget Analysts; Claims Adjusters, Examiners, and Investigators; Claims Examiners, Property and Casualty Insurance; Compensation, Benefits, and Job Analysis Specialists; Cost Estimators; Credit Analysts; Employment Interviewers, Private or Public Employment Service; Employment, Recruitment, and Placement Specialists; Financial Analysts; Human Resources, Training, and Labor Relations Specialists, All Other; Insurance Adjusters, Examiners, and Investigators; Insurance Appraisers, Auto Damage; Insurance Underwriters; Loan Counselors; Loan Officers; Logisticians; Management Analysts; Market Research Analysts; Personnel Recruiters; Purchasing Agents and Buyers, Farm Products; Purchasing Agents, Except Wholesale, Retail, and Farm Products; Tax Examiners, Collectors, and Revenue Agents; Training and Development Specialists; Wholesale and Retail Buyers, Except Farm Products. PERSONALITY TYPE— Conventional. Conventional occupations frequently involve following set procedures and routines. These occupations can include working with data and details more than with ideas. Usually there is a clear line of authority to follow.

EDUCATION/TRAINING PROGRAM(S)— Accounting; Taxation. RELATED KNOWLEDGE/ COURSES—Economics and Accounting: Knowledge of economic and accounting principles and practices, the financial markets, banking, and the analysis and reporting of financial data. Mathematics: Knowledge of arithmetic, algebra, geometry, calculus, and statistics and their applications. Administration and Management: Knowledge of business and management principles involved in strategic planning, resource allocation, human resources modeling, leadership technique, production methods, and coordination of people and resources. Law and Government: Knowledge of laws, legal codes, court procedures, precedents, government regulations, executive orders, agency rules, and the democratic political process. English Language: Knowledge of the structure and content of the English language, including the meaning and spelling of words, rules of composition, and grammar.

Biochemists

- ▲ Education/Training Required: Doctoral degree
- ▲ Annual Earnings: $54,230
- ▲ Growth: 21%
- ▲ Annual Job Openings: 5,000
- ▲ Self-Employed: 4.9%
- ▲ Part-Time: 6.6%

Research or study chemical composition and processes of living organisms that affect vital processes, such as growth and aging, to determine chemical actions and effects on organisms, such as the action of foods, drugs, or other substances on body functions and tissues. Studies chemistry of living processes, such as cell development, breathing and digestion, and living energy changes, such as growth, aging, and death. Researches methods of transferring characteristics, such as resistance to disease, from one organism to another. Examines chemical aspects of formation of antibodies and researches chemistry of cells and blood corpuscles. Develops and executes tests to detect disease, genetic disorders, or other abnormalities. Develops and tests new drugs and medications used for commercial distribution. Designs and builds laboratory equipment needed for special research projects. Analyzes foods to determine nutritional value and effects of cooking, canning, and processing on this value. Cleans, purifies, refines, and otherwise prepares pharmaceutical compounds for commercial distribution. Prepares reports and recommendations based upon research outcomes. Develops methods to process, store, and use food, drugs, and chemical compounds. Isolates, analyzes, and identifies hormones, vitamins, allergens, minerals, and enzymes and determines their effects on body functions. Researches and determines chemical action of substances such as drugs, serums, hormones, and food on tissues and vital processes. **SKILLS**—Science: Using scientific rules and methods to solve problems. Reading Comprehension: Understanding written sentences and paragraphs in work-related documents. Writing: Communicating effectively in writing as appropriate for the needs of the audience. Critical Thinking: Using logic and reasoning to identify the strengths and weaknesses of alternative solutions, conclusions, or approaches to problems. Active Learning: Understanding the implications of new information for both current and future problem-solving and decision-making.

GOE INFORMATION—**Interest Area:** 02. Science, Math, and Engineering. **Work Group:** 02.03. Life Sciences. **Other Job Titles in This Work Group:** Agricultural and Food Science Technicians; Agricultural Technicians; Animal Scientists; Biochemists and Biophysicists; Biological Scientists, All Other; Biologists; Biophysicists; Conservation Scientists; Environmental Scientists and Specialists, Including Health; Epidemiologists; Food Sci-

ence Technicians; Food Scientists and Technologists; Foresters; Life Scientists, All Other; Medical Scientists, Except Epidemiologists; Microbiologists; Plant Scientists; Range Managers; Soil and Plant Scientists; Soil Conservationists; Soil Scientists; Zoologists and Wildlife Biologists. **PERSONALITY TYPE**—Investigative. Investigative occupations frequently involve working with ideas and require an extensive amount of thinking. These occupations can involve searching for facts and figuring out problems mentally.

EDUCATION/TRAINING PROGRAM(S)— Biochemistry; Biophysics; Cell and Molecular Biology, Other. **RELATED KNOWLEDGE/COURSES**— **Chemistry:** Knowledge of the chemical composition, structure, and properties of substances and of the chemical processes and transformations that they undergo. This includes uses of chemicals and their interactions, danger signs, production techniques, and disposal methods. **Biology:** Knowledge of plant and animal organisms and their tissues, cells, functions, interdependencies, and interactions with each other and the environment. **Mathematics:** Knowledge of arithmetic, algebra, geometry, calculus, and statistics and their applications. **English Language:** Knowledge of the structure and content of the English language, including the meaning and spelling of words, rules of composition, and grammar. **Building and Construction:** Knowledge of materials, methods, and tools involved in the construction or repair of houses, buildings, or other structures, such as highways and roads.

Biochemists and Biophysicists

- ▲ Education/Training Required: Doctoral degree
- ▲ Annual Earnings: $54,230
- ▲ Growth: 21%
- ▲ Annual Job Openings: 5,000
- ▲ Self-Employed: 4.9%
- ▲ Part-Time: 6.6%

Study the chemical composition and physical principles of living cells and organisms, their electrical and mechanical energy, and related phenomena. May conduct research to further

understanding of the complex chemical combinations and reactions involved in metabolism, reproduction, growth, and heredity. May determine the effects of foods, drugs, serums, hormones, and other substances on tissues and vital processes of living organisms. **SKILLS**—No data available.

GOE INFORMATION—Interest Area: 02. Science, Math, and Engineering. **Work Group:** 02.03. Life Sciences. **Other Job Titles in This Work Group:** Agricultural and Food Science Technicians; Agricultural Technicians; Animal Scientists; Biochemists; Biological Scientists, All Other; Biologists; Biophysicists; Conservation Scientists; Environmental Scientists and Specialists, Including Health; Epidemiologists; Food Science Techni-

cians; Food Scientists and Technologists; Foresters; Life Scientists, All Other; Medical Scientists, Except Epidemiologists; Microbiologists; Plant Scientists; Range Managers; Soil and Plant Scientists; Soil Conservationists; Soil Scientists; Zoologists and Wildlife Biologists. **PERSONALITY TYPE**—No data available.

EDUCATION/TRAINING PROGRAM(S)—Biochemistry; Biophysics; Cell and Molecular Biology, Other. **RELATED KNOWLEDGE/COURSES**—No data available.

Biological Science Teachers, Postsecondary

- ▲ Education/Training Required: Master's degree
- ▲ Annual Earnings: $54,450
- ▲ Growth: 24% for all Postsecondary Teachers
- ▲ Annual Job Openings: 184,000 for all Postsecondary Teachers
- ▲ Self-Employed: 0%
- ▲ Part-Time: 32.3% for all Postsecondary Teachers

Teach courses in biological sciences. Prepares and delivers lectures to students. Stimulates class discussions. Compiles bibliographies of specialized materials for outside reading assignments. Compiles, administers, and grades examinations or assigns this work to others. Acts as adviser to student organizations. Serves on faculty committee providing professional consulting services to government and industry. Conducts research in particular field of knowledge and publishes findings in professional journals. Directs research of other teachers or graduate students working for advanced academic degrees. Advises students on academic and vocational curricula. **SKILLS**—Reading Comprehension: Understanding written sentences and paragraphs in work-related documents. Instructing: Teaching others how to do something. Learning Strategies: Selecting and using training/instructional methods and procedures appropriate for the situation when learning or teaching new things. Science: Using scientific rules and methods to solve problems. Writing: Communicating effectively in writing as appropriate for the needs of the audience. Active Learning: Understanding the implications

of new information for both current and future problem-solving and decision-making. Critical Thinking: Using logic and reasoning to identify the strengths and weaknesses of alternative solutions, conclusions, or approaches to problems.

GOE INFORMATION—Interest Area: 12. Education and Social Service. **Work Group:** 12.03. Educational Services. **Other Job Titles in This Work Group:** Adult Literacy, Remedial Education, and GED Teachers and Instructors; Agricultural Sciences Teachers, Postsecondary; Anthropology and Archeology Teachers, Postsecondary; Architecture Teachers, Postsecondary; Archivists; Area, Ethnic, and Cultural Studies Teachers, Postsecondary; Art, Drama, and Music Teachers, Postsecondary; Atmospheric, Earth, Marine, and Space Sciences Teachers, Postsecondary; Audio-Visual Collections Specialists; Business Teachers, Postsecondary; Chemistry Teachers, Postsecondary; Child Care Workers; Communications Teachers, Postsecondary; Computer Science Teachers, Postsecondary; Criminal Justice and Law

Enforcement Teachers, Postsecondary; Curators; Economics Teachers, Postsecondary; Education Teachers, Postsecondary; Educational Psychologists; Educational, Vocational, and School Counselors; Elementary School Teachers, Except Special Education; Engineering Teachers, Postsecondary; English Language and Literature Teachers, Postsecondary; Environmental Science Teachers, Postsecondary; Farm and Home Management Advisors; Foreign Language and Literature Teachers, Postsecondary; Forestry and Conservation Science Teachers, Postsecondary; Geography Teachers, Postsecondary; Graduate Teaching Assistants; Health Specialties Teachers, Postsecondary; History Teachers, Postsecondary; Home Economics Teachers, Postsecondary; Kindergarten Teachers, Except Special Education; Law Teachers, Postsecondary; Librarians; Library Assistants, Clerical; Library Science Teachers, Postsecondary; others. **PERSONALITY TYPE**—Investigative. Investigative occupations frequently involve working with ideas and require an extensive amount of thinking. These occupations can involve searching for facts and figuring out problems mentally.

EDUCATION/TRAINING PROGRAM(S)— Anatomy; Biochemistry; Biological Immunology; Biological Sciences/Life Sciences, Other; Biology, General; Biometrics; Biophysics; Biotechnology Research; Botany, General; Cell Biology; Ecology; Entomology; Evolution-ary Biology; Genetics, Plant and Animal; Marine/Aquatic Biology; Microbiology/Bacteriology; Miscellaneous Biological Specializations, Other; Molecular Biology; Neuroscience; Nutritional Sciences; Parasitology; Pathology, Human and Animal; Pharmacology, Human and Animal; Physiology, Human and Animal; Plant Pathology; Plant Physiology; Radiation Biology/Radiobiology; Toxicology; Virology; Zoology, General. **RELATED KNOWLEDGE/COURSES—Education and Training:** Knowledge of principles and methods for curriculum and training design, teaching and instruction for individuals and groups, and the measurement of training effects. **Biology:** Knowledge of plant and animal organisms and their tissues, cells, functions, interdependencies, and interactions with each other and the environment. **Psychology:** Knowledge of human behavior and performance; individual differences in ability, personality, and interests; learning and motivation; psychological research methods; and the assessment and treatment of behavioral and affective disorders. **Chemistry:** Knowledge of the chemical composition, structure, and properties of substances and of the chemical processes and transformations that they undergo. This includes uses of chemicals and their interactions, danger signs, production techniques, and disposal methods. **English Language:** Knowledge of the structure and content of the English language, including the meaning and spelling of words, rules of composition, and grammar.

Biological Technicians

- ▲ Education/Training Required: Associate's degree
- ▲ Annual Earnings: $31,540
- ▲ Growth: 26%
- ▲ Annual Job Openings: 7,000
- ▲ Self-Employed: 0.9%
- ▲ Part-Time: 11.7%

Assist biological and medical scientists in laboratories. Set up, operate, and maintain laboratory instruments and equipment, monitor experiments, make observations, and calculate and record results. May analyze organic substances, such as blood, food, and drugs. Sets up laboratory and field equipment to assist research workers. Cleans and maintains laboratory and field equipment and work areas. Examines animals and specimens to determine presence of disease or other problems. Pricks animals and collects blood samples for testing, using hand-held devices. Plants seeds in specified area and counts plants that grow to determine germination rate of seeds. Waters and feeds rations to livestock and laboratory animals. Adjusts testing equipment and prepares culture media, following standard procedures. Measures or weighs ingredients used in testing or as animal feed. Records production and test data for evaluation by personnel. **SKILLS**—Mathematics: Using mathematics to solve problems. Reading Comprehension: Understanding written sentences and paragraphs in work-related documents. Science: Using scientific rules and methods to solve problems. Equipment Selection: Determining the kind of tools and equipment needed to do a job.

GOE INFORMATION—**Interest Area:** 02. Science, Math, and Engineering. **Work Group:** 02.05. Laboratory Technology. **Other Job Titles in This Work Group:** Chemical Technicians; Environmental Science and Protection Technicians, Including Health; Geological and Petroleum Technicians; Geological Data Technicians; Geological Sample Test Technicians; Nuclear Equipment Operation Technicians; Nuclear Technicians; Photographers, Scientific. **PERSONALITY TYPE**—Realistic. Realistic occupations frequently involve work activities that include practical, hands-on problems and solutions. They often deal with plants, animals, and real-world materials like wood, tools, and machinery. Many of the occupations require working outside and do not involve a lot of paperwork or working closely with others.

EDUCATION/TRAINING PROGRAM(S)— Biological Technologist/Technician. **RELATED KNOWLEDGE/COURSES**—**Biology:** Knowledge of plant and animal organisms and their tissues, cells, functions, interdependencies, and interactions with each other and the environment. **Mathematics:** Knowledge of arithmetic, algebra, geometry, calculus, and statistics and their applications. **Food Production:** Knowledge of techniques and equipment for planting, growing, and harvesting food products (both plant and animal) for consumption, including storage/handling techniques. **Clerical Studies:** Knowledge of administrative and clerical procedures and systems such as word processing, managing files and records, stenography and transcription, designing forms, and other office procedures and terminology. **Medicine and Dentistry:** Knowledge of the information and techniques needed to diagnose and treat human injuries, diseases, and deformities. This includes symptoms, treatment alternatives, drug properties and interactions, and preventive health-care measures.

Biologists

▲ Education/Training Required: Doctoral degree

▲ Annual Earnings: $49,033

▲ Growth: 21%

▲ Annual Job Openings: 5,000

▲ Self-Employed: 4.9%

▲ Part-Time: 6.6%

Research or study basic principles of plant and animal life, such as origin, relationship, development, anatomy, and functions. Studies basic principles of plant and animal life, such as origin, relationship, development, anatomy, and functions. Studies aquatic plants and animals and environmental conditions affecting them, such as radioactivity or pollution. Collects and analyzes biological data about relationship among and between organisms and their environment. Identifies, classifies, and studies structure, behavior, ecology, physiology, nutrition, culture, and distribution of plant and animal species. Develops methods and apparatus for securing representa-

tive plant, animal, aquatic, or soil samples. Studies and manages wild animal populations. Measures salinity, acidity, light, oxygen content, and other physical conditions of water to determine their relationship to aquatic life. Studies reactions of plants, animals, and marine species to parasites. Investigates and develops pest management and control measures. Develops methods of extracting drugs from aquatic plants and animals. Researches environmental effects of present and potential uses of land and water areas and determines methods of improving environment or crop yields. Plans and administers biological research programs for government, research firms, medical industries, or manufacturing firms. Cultivates, breeds, and grows aquatic life, such as lobsters, clams, or fish farming. Prepares environmental impact reports for industry, government, or publication. Communicates test results to state and federal representatives and general public. **SKILLS—Science:** Using scientific rules and methods to solve problems. **Reading Comprehension:** Understanding written sentences and paragraphs in work-related documents. **Writing:** Communicating effectively in writing as appropriate for the needs of the audience. **Mathematics:** Using mathematics to solve problems. **Critical Thinking:** Using logic and reasoning to identify the strengths and weaknesses of alternative solutions, conclusions, or approaches to problems. **Active Learning:** Understanding the implications of new information for both current and future problem-solving and decision-making.

GOE INFORMATION—Interest Area: 02. Science, Math, and Engineering. **Work Group:** 02.03. Life Sciences. **Other Job Titles in This Work Group:** Agricultural and Food Science Technicians; Agricultural Technicians; Animal Scientists; Biochemists; Biochemists and Biophysicists; Biological Scientists, All Other; Biophysicists; Conservation Scientists; Environmental Scientists and Specialists, Including Health; Epidemiologists; Food Science Technicians; Food Scientists and Technologists; Foresters; Life Scientists, All Other; Medical Scientists, Except Epidemiologists; Microbiologists; Plant

Scientists; Range Managers; Soil and Plant Scientists; Soil Conservationists; Soil Scientists; Zoologists and Wildlife Biologists. **PERSONALITY TYPE—**Investigative. Investigative occupations frequently involve working with ideas and require an extensive amount of thinking. These occupations can involve searching for facts and figuring out problems mentally.

EDUCATION/TRAINING PROGRAM(S)— Biology, General. **RELATED KNOWLEDGE/ COURSES—Biology:** Knowledge of plant and animal organisms and their tissues, cells, functions, interdependencies, and interactions with each other and the environment. **Mathematics:** Knowledge of arithmetic, algebra, geometry, calculus, and statistics and their applications. **Chemistry:** Knowledge of the chemical composition, structure, and properties of substances and of the chemical processes and transformations that they undergo. This includes uses of chemicals and their interactions, danger signs, production techniques, and disposal methods. **English Language:** Knowledge of the structure and content of the English language, including the meaning and spelling of words, rules of composition, and grammar. **Physics:** Knowledge and prediction of physical principles and laws and their interrelationships and applications to understanding fluid, material, and atmospheric dynamics and mechanical, electrical, atomic, and sub-atomic structures and processes.

Biomedical Engineers

- ▲ Education/Training Required: Bachelor's degree
- ▲ Annual Earnings: $57,480
- ▲ Growth: 31%
- ▲ Annual Job Openings: Fewer than 500
- ▲ Self-Employed: 2.7%
- ▲ Part-Time: 4.5%

Apply knowledge of engineering, biology, and biomechanical principles to the design, development, and evaluation of biological and health systems and products, such as artificial organs, prostheses, instrumentation, medical information systems, and health management and care delivery systems. **SKILLS—**No data available.

GOE INFORMATION—Interest Area: 02. Science, Math, and Engineering. **Work Group:** 02.07. Engineering. **Other Job Titles in This Work Group:** Aerospace Engineers; Agricultural Engineers; Architects, Except Landscape and Naval; Chemical Engineers; Civil Engineers; Computer Hardware Engineers; Computer Software Engineers, Applications; Computer Software Engineers, Systems Software; Electrical Engineers; Electronics Engineers, Except Computer; Engineers, All Other; Environmental Engineers; Fire-Prevention and Protection Engineers; Health and Safety Engineers, Except Mining Safety Engineers and Inspectors; Industrial Engineers; Industrial Safety and Health Engineers; Landscape Architects; Marine Architects; Marine Engineers; Marine Engineers and Naval Architects; Materials Engineers; Mechanical Engi-

neers; Mining and Geological Engineers, Including Mining Safety Engineers; Nuclear Engineers; Petroleum Engineers; Product Safety Engineers; Sales Engineers. **PERSONALITY TYPE**—No data available.

EDUCATION/TRAINING PROGRAM(S)—Bioengineering and Biomedical Engineering; Engineering Design; Geophysical Engineering. **RELATED KNOWLEDGE/COURSES**—No data available.

Biophysicists

- ▲ Education/Training Required: Doctoral degree
- ▲ Annual Earnings: $54,230
- ▲ Growth: 21%
- ▲ Annual Job Openings: 5,000
- ▲ Self-Employed: 4.9%
- ▲ Part-Time: 6.6%

Research or study physical principles of living cells and organisms, their electrical and mechanical energy, and related phenomena. Studies physical principles of living cells and organisms and their electrical and mechanical energy. Investigates transmission of electrical impulses along nerves and muscles. Studies absorption of light by chlorophyll in photosynthesis or by pigments of eye involved in vision. Researches cancer treatment, using radiation and nuclear particles. Analyzes functions of electronic and human brains, such as learning, thinking, and memory. Investigates dynamics of seeing and hearing. Studies spatial configuration of submicroscopic molecules, such as proteins, using x-ray and electron microscope. Researches manner in which characteristics of plants and animals are carried through successive generations. Investigates damage to cells and tissues caused by x-rays and nuclear particles. Researches transformation of substances in cells, using atomic isotopes. **SKILLS**—Science: Using scientific rules and methods to solve problems. Reading Comprehension: Understanding written sentences and paragraphs in work-related documents. Writing: Communicating effectively in writing as appropriate for the needs of the audience. Active Learning: Understanding the implications of new information for both current and future problem-solving and decision-making. Mathematics: Using mathematics to solve problems.

GOE INFORMATION—Interest Area: 02. Science, Math, and Engineering. **Work Group:** 02.03. Life Sciences. **Other Job Titles in This Work Group:** Agricultural and Food Science Technicians; Agricultural Technicians; Animal Scientists; Biochemists; Biochemists and Biophysicists; Biological Scientists, All Other; Biologists; Conservation Scientists; Environmental Scientists and Specialists, Including Health; Epidemiologists; Food Science Technicians; Food Scientists and Technologists; Foresters; Life Scientists, All Other; Medical Scientists, Except Epidemiologists; Microbiologists; Plant Scientists; Range Managers; Soil and Plant Scientists; Soil Conservationists; Soil Scientists; Zoologists and Wildlife Biologists. **PERSONALITY TYPE**—Investigative. Investigative occupations frequently involve working with ideas and require an extensive amount of thinking. These occupations can involve searching for facts and figuring out problems mentally.

EDUCATION/TRAINING PROGRAM(S)—Biochemistry; Biophysics; Cell and Molecular Biology, Other. **RELATED KNOWLEDGE/COURSES**—**Biology:** Knowledge of plant and animal organisms and their tissues, cells, functions, interdependencies, and interactions with each other and the environment. **Physics:** Knowledge and prediction of physical principles and laws and their interrelationships and applications to understanding fluid, material, and atmospheric dynamics and mechanical, electrical, atomic, and sub-atomic structures and processes. **Mathematics:** Knowledge of arithmetic, algebra, geometry, calculus, and statistics and their applications. **Chemistry:** Knowledge of the chemical composition, structure, and properties of substances and of the chemical processes and transformations that they undergo. This includes uses of chemicals and their interactions, danger signs, production techniques, and disposal methods. **English Language:** Knowledge of the structure and content of the English language, including the meaning and spelling of words, rules of composition, and grammar.

Broadcast News Analysts

- ▲ Education/Training Required: Bachelor's degree
- ▲ Annual Earnings: $29,110
- ▲ Growth: 3%
- ▲ Annual Job Openings: 9,000
- ▲ Self-Employed: 0%
- ▲ Part-Time: 25.3%

Analyze, interpret, and broadcast news received from various sources. Gathers information and develops subject perspective through research, interview, observation, and experience. Analyzes and interprets information to formulate and outline story ideas. Records commentary or presents commentary or news live when working in broadcast medium. Writes commentary, column, or script, using computer. Selects material most pertinent to presentation and organizes material into acceptable media form and format. Examines news items of local, national, and international significance to determine selection or is assigned items for broadcast by editorial staff. Edits material for available time or space. **SKILLS—Writing:** Communicating effectively in writing as appropriate for the needs of the audience. **Speaking:** Talking to others to convey information effectively. **Reading Comprehension:** Understanding written sentences and paragraphs in work-related documents. **Active Listening:** Giving full attention to what other people are saying, taking time to understand the points being made, asking questions as appropriate, and not interrupting at inappropriate times. **Critical Thinking:** Using logic and reasoning to identify the strengths and weaknesses of alternative solutions, conclusions, or approaches to problems.

GOE INFORMATION—Interest Area: 01. Arts, Entertainment, and Media. **Work Group:** 01.03. News, Broadcasting and Public Relations. **Other Job Titles in** This Work Group: Caption Writers; Interpreters and Translators; Public Relations Specialists; Reporters and Correspondents. **PERSONALITY TYPE—**Artistic. Artistic occupations frequently involve working with forms, designs, and patterns. They often require self-expression, and the work can be done without following a clear set of rules.

EDUCATION/TRAINING PROGRAM(S)— Broadcast Journalism; Journalism; Radio and Television Broadcasting. **RELATED KNOWLEDGE/ COURSES—Communications and Media:** Knowledge of media production, communication, and dissemination techniques and methods. This includes alternative ways to inform and entertain via written, oral, and visual media. **English Language:** Knowledge of the structure and content of the English language, including the meaning and spelling of words, rules of composition, and grammar. **Computers and Electronics:** Knowledge of circuit boards, processors, chips, electronic equipment, and computer hardware and software, including applications and programming. **Telecommunications:** Knowledge of transmission, broadcasting, switching, control, and operation of telecommunications systems. **Clerical Studies:** Knowledge of administrative and clerical procedures and systems such as word processing, managing files and records, stenography and transcription, designing forms, and other office procedures and terminology. **Geogra-**

phy: Knowledge of principles and methods for describing the features of land, sea, and air masses, including their physical characteristics, locations, interrelationships, and distribution of plant, animal, and human life.

Budget Analysts

- ▲ Education/Training Required: Bachelor's degree
- ▲ Annual Earnings: $48,370
- ▲ Growth: 15%
- ▲ Annual Job Openings: 8,000
- ▲ Self-Employed: 0%
- ▲ Part-Time: 7.2%

Examine budget estimates for completeness, accuracy, and conformance with procedures and regulations. Analyze budgeting and accounting reports for the purpose of maintaining expenditure controls. Analyzes accounting records to determine financial resources required to implement program and submits recommendations for budget allocations. Consults with unit heads to ensure adjustments are made in accordance with program changes to facilitate long-term planning. Testifies regarding proposed budgets before examining and fund-granting authorities to clarify reports and gain support for estimated budget needs. Directs compilation of data based on statistical studies and analyses of past and current years to prepare budgets. Directs preparation of regular and special budget reports to interpret budget directives and to establish policies for carrying out directives. Reviews operating budgets periodically to analyze trends affecting budget needs. Recommends approval or disapproval of requests for funds. Advises staff on cost analysis and fiscal allocations. Correlates appropriations for specific programs with appropriations for divisional programs and includes items for emergency funds. Analyzes costs in relation to services performed during previous fiscal years to prepare comparative analyses of operating programs. **SKILLS**—Management of Financial Resources: Determining how money will be spent to get the work done and accounting for these expenditures. Judgment and Decision Making: Considering the relative costs and benefits of potential actions to choose the most appropriate one. Mathematics: Using mathematics to solve problems. Systems Analysis: Determining how a system should work and how changes in conditions, operations, and the environment will affect outcomes. Critical Thinking: Us-

ing logic and reasoning to identify the strengths and weaknesses of alternative solutions, conclusions, or approaches to problems. Systems Evaluation: Identifying measures or indicators of system performance and the actions needed to improve or correct performance relative to the goals of the system.

GOE INFORMATION—Interest Area: 13. General Management and Support. **Work Group:** 13.02. Management Support. **Other Job Titles in This Work Group:** Accountants; Accountants and Auditors; Appraisers and Assessors of Real Estate; Appraisers, Real Estate; Assessors; Auditors; Claims Adjusters, Examiners, and Investigators; Claims Examiners, Property and Casualty Insurance; Compensation, Benefits, and Job Analysis Specialists; Cost Estimators; Credit Analysts; Employment Interviewers, Private or Public Employment Service; Employment, Recruitment, and Placement Specialists; Financial Analysts; Human Resources, Training, and Labor Relations Specialists, All Other; Insurance Adjusters, Examiners, and Investigators; Insurance Appraisers, Auto Damage; Insurance Underwriters; Loan Counselors; Loan Officers; Logisticians; Management Analysts; Market Research Analysts; Personnel Recruiters; Purchasing Agents and Buyers, Farm Products; Purchasing Agents, Except Wholesale, Retail, and Farm Products; Tax Examiners, Collectors, and Revenue Agents; Training and Development Specialists; Wholesale and Retail Buyers, Except Farm Products. **PERSONALITY TYPE**—Conventional. Conventional occupations frequently involve following set procedures and routines. These occupations can include working with data and details more than with ideas. Usually there is a clear line of authority to follow.

EDUCATION/TRAINING PROGRAM(S)—Accounting; Finance, General. **RELATED KNOWL-EDGE/COURSES—Economics and Accounting:** Knowledge of economic and accounting principles and practices, the financial markets, banking, and the analysis and reporting of financial data. **Mathematics:** Knowledge of arithmetic, algebra, geometry, calculus, and statistics and their applications. **Administration and Management:** Knowledge of business and management principles involved in strategic planning, resource alloca-tion, human resources modeling, leadership technique, pro-duction methods, and coordination of people and re-sources. **Computers and Electronics:** Knowledge of circuit boards, processors, chips, electronic equipment, and computer hardware and software, including applica-tions and programming. **English Language:** Knowledge of the structure and content of the English language, in-cluding the meaning and spelling of words, rules of compo-sition, and grammar.

Business Teachers, Postsecondary

- ▲ Education/Training Required: Master's degree
- ▲ Annual Earnings: $53,840
- ▲ Growth: 24% for all Postsecondary Teachers
- ▲ Annual Job Openings: 184,000 for all Postsecondary Teachers
- ▲ Self-Employed: 0%
- ▲ Part-Time: 32.3% for all Postsecondary Teachers

Teach courses in business administration and management, such as accounting, finance, human resources, labor relations, marketing, and operations research. **SKILLS**—No data available.

GOE INFORMATION—Interest Area: 12. Education and Social Service. **Work Group:** 12.03. Educational Services. **Other Job Titles in This Work Group:** Adult Literacy, Remedial Education, and GED Teachers and Instructors; Agricultural Sciences Teachers, Postsecondary; Anthropology and Archeology Teachers, Postsecondary; Architecture Teachers, Postsecondary; Archivists; Area, Ethnic, and Cultural Studies Teachers, Postsecondary; Art, Drama, and Music Teachers, Postsecondary; Atmospheric, Earth, Marine, and Space Sciences Teachers, Postsecondary; Audio-Visual Collections Specialists; Biological Science Teachers, Postsecondary; Chemistry Teachers, Postsecondary; Child Care Workers; Communications Teachers, Postsecondary; Computer Science Teachers, Postsecondary; Criminal Justice and Law Enforcement Teachers, Postsecondary; Curators; Economics Teachers, Postsecondary; Education Teachers, Postsecondary; Educational Psychologists; Educational, Vocational, and School Counselors; Elementary School Teachers, Except Special Education; Engineering Teachers, Postsecondary; English Language and Literature Teachers, Postsecondary; Environmental Science Teachers, Postsecondary; Farm and Home Management Advisors; Foreign Language and Literature Teachers, Postsecondary; Forestry and Conservation Science Teachers, Postsecondary; Geography Teachers, Postsecondary; Graduate Teaching Assistants; Health Specialties Teachers, Postsecondary; History Teachers, Postsecondary; Home Economics Teachers, Postsecondary; Kindergarten Teachers, Except Special Education; Law Teachers, Postsecondary; Librarians; Library Assistants, Clerical; Library Science Teachers, Postsecondary; others. **PERSONALITY TYPE**—No data available.

EDUCATION/TRAINING PROGRAM(S)—Accounting; Actuarial Science; Business Administration and Management, General; Business Communications; Business Marketing and Marketing Management; Business Statistics; Business Teacher Education (Vocational); Business,

General; Enterprise Management and Operation, General; Finance, General; Financial Planning; Franchise Operation; Human Resources Management; Insurance and Risk Management; International Business; International Business Marketing; International Finance; Investments and Securities; Labor/Personnel Relations and Studies; Logistics and Materials Management; Management Science; Marketing Research; Operations Management and Supervision; Organizational Behavior Studies; Public Finance; Purchasing, Procurement and Contracts Management. **RELATED KNOWLEDGE/COURSES—** No data available.

Calibration and Instrumentation Technicians

- ▲ Education/Training Required: Associate's degree
- ▲ Annual Earnings: $40,020
- ▲ Growth: 11%
- ▲ Annual Job Openings: 22,000
- ▲ Self-Employed: 2.2%
- ▲ Part-Time: 3.1%

Develop, test, calibrate, operate, and repair electrical, mechanical, electromechanical, electrohydraulic, or electronic measuring and recording instruments, apparatus, and equipment. Plans sequence of testing and calibration program for instruments and equipment according to blueprints, schematics, technical manuals, and other specifications. Performs preventative and corrective maintenance of test apparatus and peripheral equipment. Confers with engineers, supervisor, and other technical workers to assist with equipment installation, maintenance, and repair techniques. Analyzes and converts test data, using mathematical formulas, and reports results and proposed modifications. Sets up test equipment and conducts tests on performance and reliability of mechanical, structural, or electromechanical equipment. Selects sensing, telemetering, and recording instrumentation and circuitry. Disassembles and reassembles instruments and equipment, using hand tools, and inspects instruments and equipment for defects. Sketches plans for developing jigs, fixtures, instruments, and related nonstandard apparatus. Modifies performance and operation of component parts and circuitry to specifications, using test equipment and precision instruments. **SKILLS—**Technology Design: Generating or adapting equipment and technology to serve user needs. Equipment Selection: Determining the kind of tools and equipment needed to do a job. Quality Control Analysis: Conducting tests and inspections of products, services, or processes to evaluate quality or performance. Equipment Maintenance: Performing routine maintenance on equipment and determining when and what kind of maintenance is needed. Active Listening: Giving full attention to what other people are saying, taking time to understand the points being made, asking questions as appropriate, and not interrupting at inappropriate times. Mathematics: Using mathematics to solve problems.

GOE INFORMATION—Interest Area: 02. Science, Math, and Engineering. **Work Group:** 02.08. Engineering Technology. **Other Job Titles in This Work Group:** Aerospace Engineering and Operations Technicians; Architectural and Civil Drafters; Architectural Drafters; Cartographers and Photogrammetrists; Civil Drafters; Civil Engineering Technicians; Construction and Building Inspectors; Drafters, All Other; Electrical and Electronic Engineering Technicians; Electrical and Electronics Drafters; Electrical Drafters; Electrical Engineering Technicians; Electro-Mechanical Technicians; Electronic Drafters; Electronics Engineering Technicians; Engineering Technicians, Except Drafters, All Other; Environmental Engineering Technicians; Industrial Engineering Technicians; Mapping Technicians; Mechanical Drafters; Mechanical Engineering Technicians; Numerical Tool and Process Control Programmers; Pressure Vessel Inspectors; Surveying and Mapping Technicians; Surveying Technicians; Surveyors. **PERSONALITY TYPE—**Realistic. Realistic occupations frequently involve work activities that include practical, hands-on problems and solutions. They often deal with plants, animals, and real-world materials like wood, tools, and machinery. Many of the occupations require working outside and do not involve a lot of paperwork or working closely with others.

EDUCATION/TRAINING PROGRAM(S)—Computer Engineering Technologist/Technician; Electrical and Electronic Engineering-Related Technologist/Technician; Electrical, Electronic and Communications Engineering Technologist/Technician. **RELATED KNOWLEDGE/COURSES—Design:** Knowledge of design techniques, tools, and principles involved in production of precision technical plans, blueprints, drawings, and models. **Mathematics:** Knowledge of arithmetic, algebra, geometry, calculus, and statistics and their applications. **Principles of Mechanical Devices:** Knowledge of machines and tools, including their designs, uses, repair, and maintenance. **Engineering and Technology:** Knowledge of the practical application of engineering science and technology. This includes applying principles, techniques, procedures, and equipment to the design and production of various goods and services. **Computers and Electronics:** Knowledge of circuit boards, processors, chips, electronic equipment, and computer hardware and software, including applications and programming.

Cardiovascular Technologists and Technicians

- ▲ Education/Training Required: Associate's degree
- ▲ Annual Earnings: $33,350
- ▲ Growth: 35%
- ▲ Annual Job Openings: 3,000
- ▲ Self-Employed: 0%
- ▲ Part-Time: 22.9%

Conduct tests on pulmonary or cardiovascular systems of patients for diagnostic purposes. May conduct or assist in electrocardiograms; cardiac catheterizations; and pulmonary-functions, lung capacity, and similar tests. Operates diagnostic imaging equipment to produce contrast-enhanced radiographs of heart and cardiovascular system. Injects contrast medium into blood vessels of patient. Conducts electrocardiogram, phonocardiogram, echocardiogram, stress testing, and other cardiovascular tests, using specialized electronic test equipment, recording devices, and laboratory instruments. Operates monitor to measure and record functions of cardiovascular and pulmonary systems as part of cardiac catheterization team. Observes gauges, recorder, and video screens of data analysis system during imaging of cardiovascular system. Conducts tests of pulmonary system, using spirometer and other respiratory testing equipment. Activates fluoroscope and camera to produce images used to guide catheter through cardiovascular system. Records variations in action of heart muscle, using electrocardiograph. Prepares and positions patients for testing. Records test results and other data into patient's record. Reviews test results with physician. Explains testing procedures to patient to obtain cooperation and reduce anxiety. Adjusts equipment and controls according to physicians' orders or established protocol. Alerts physician to abnormalities or changes in patient responses. Enters factors such as amount and quality of radiation beam and filming sequence into computer. Assesses cardiac physiology and calculates valve areas from blood flow velocity measurements. Compares measurements of heart wall thickness and chamber sizes to standard norms to identify abnormalities. Observes ultrasound display screen and listens to signals to acquire data for measurement of blood flow velocities. Records analyses of heart and related structures, using ultrasound equipment. **SKILLS—Reading Comprehension:** Understanding written sentences and paragraphs in work-related documents. Mathematics: Using mathematics to solve problems. Operation Monitoring: Watching gauges, dials, or other indicators to make sure a machine is working properly. Active Listening: Giving full attention to what other people are saying, taking time to understand the points being made, asking questions as appropriate, and not interrupting at inappropriate times. Operation and Control:

Controlling operations of equipment or systems. Writing: Communicating effectively in writing as appropriate for the needs of the audience. Science: Using scientific rules and methods to solve problems.

GOE INFORMATION—Interest Area: 14. Medical and Health Services. **Work Group:** 14.05. Medical Technology. **Other Job Titles in This Work Group:** Diagnostic Medical Sonographers; Health Technologists and Technicians, All Other; Medical and Clinical Laboratory Technicians; Medical and Clinical Laboratory Technologists; Medical Equipment Preparers; Nuclear Medicine Technologists; Orthotists and Prosthetists; Radiologic Technicians; Radiologic Technologists; Radiologic Technologists and Technicians. **PERSONALITY TYPE—** Investigative. Investigative occupations frequently involve working with ideas and require an extensive amount of thinking. These occupations can involve searching for facts and figuring out problems mentally.

Cartographers and Photogrammetrists

EDUCATION/TRAINING PROGRAM(S)— Cardiovascular Technologist/Technician; Electrocardiograph Technologist/Technician; Perfusion Technologist/Technician. **RELATED KNOWLEDGE/COURSES—Medicine and Dentistry:** Knowledge of the information and techniques needed to diagnose and treat human injuries, diseases, and deformities. This includes symptoms, treatment alternatives, drug properties and interactions, and preventive health-care measures. **Computers and Electronics:** Knowledge of circuit boards, processors, chips, electronic equipment, and computer hardware and software, including applications and programming. **Biology:** Knowledge of plant and animal organisms and their tissues, cells, functions, interdependencies, and interactions with each other and the environment. **Mathematics:** Knowledge of arithmetic, algebra, geometry, calculus, and statistics and their applications. **English Language:** Knowledge of the structure and content of the English language, including the meaning and spelling of words, rules of composition, and grammar.

- ▲ Education/Training Required: Bachelor's degree
- ▲ Annual Earnings: $39,410
- ▲ Growth: 18%
- ▲ Annual Job Openings: 1,000
- ▲ Self-Employed: No data available
- ▲ Part-Time: No data available

Collect, analyze, and interpret geographic information provided by geodetic surveys, aerial photographs, and satellite data. Research, study, and prepare maps and other spatial data in digital or graphic form for legal, social, political, educational, and design purposes. May work with Geographic Information Systems (GIS). May design and evaluate algorithms, data structures, and user interfaces for GIS and mapping systems. Prepares mosaic prints, contour maps, profile sheets, and related cartographic material, applying mastery of photogrammetric techniques and principles. Identifies, scales, and orients geodetic points, elevations, and other planimetric or topographic features, applying standard math formulas. Travels over photographed area to observe, iden-

tify, record, and verify all features shown and not shown in photograph. Determines guidelines for source material to be used, such as maps, automated mapping products, photographic survey data, and place names. Revises existing maps and charts and corrects maps in various stages of compilation. Studies legal records to establish boundaries of local, national, and international properties. Develops design concept of map product. Determines and defines production specifications, such as projection, scale, size, and colors of map product. Analyzes survey data, source maps and photos, computer or automated mapping products, and other records to determine location and name of features. **SKILLS—Mathematics:** Using mathematics to solve problems. Reading Comprehension: Understanding written sentences and paragraphs in work-related documents. Writing: Communicating effectively in writing as appropriate for the needs of the audience. Equipment Selection: Determining the kind of tools and equipment needed to do a job. Operations Analysis: Analyzing needs and product requirements to create a design. Active Learning: Understanding the implications of new information for both current and future problem-solving and decision-making.

GOE INFORMATION—**Interest Area:** 02. Science, Math, and Engineering. **Work Group:** 02.08. Engineering Technology. **Other Job Titles in This Work Group:** Aerospace Engineering and Operations Technicians; Architectural and Civil Drafters; Architectural Drafters; Calibration and Instrumentation Technicians; Civil Drafters; Civil Engineering Technicians; Construction and Building Inspectors; Drafters, All Other; Electrical and Electronic Engineering Technicians; Electrical and Electronics Drafters; Electrical Drafters; Electrical Engineering Technicians; Electro-Mechanical Technicians; Electronic Drafters; Electronics Engineering Technicians; Engineering Technicians, Except Drafters, All Other; Environmental Engineering Technicians; Industrial Engineering Technicians; Mapping Technicians; Mechanical Drafters; Mechanical Engineering Technicians; Numerical Tool and Process Control Programmers; Pressure Vessel Inspectors;

Surveying and Mapping Technicians; Surveying Technicians; Surveyors. **PERSONALITY TYPE**—Conventional. Conventional occupations frequently involve following set procedures and routines. These occupations can include working with data and details more than with ideas. Usually there is a clear line of authority to follow.

EDUCATION/TRAINING PROGRAM(S)— Cartography; Surveying. **RELATED KNOWLEDGE/COURSES**—**Geography:** Knowledge of principles and methods for describing the features of land, sea, and air masses, including their physical characteristics, locations, interrelationships, and distribution of plant, animal, and human life. **Mathematics:** Knowledge of arithmetic, algebra, geometry, calculus, and statistics and their applications. **Design:** Knowledge of design techniques, tools, and principles involved in production of precision technical plans, blueprints, drawings, and models. **Law and Government:** Knowledge of laws, legal codes, court procedures, precedents, government regulations, executive orders, agency rules, and the democratic political process. **Computers and Electronics:** Knowledge of circuit boards, processors, chips, electronic equipment, and computer hardware and software, including applications and programming.

Chemical Engineers

▲ Education/Training Required: Bachelor's degree

▲ Annual Earnings: $65,960

▲ Growth: 4%

▲ Annual Job Openings: 2,000

▲ Self-Employed: 2%

▲ Part-Time: 1.6%

Design chemical plant equipment and devise processes for manufacturing chemicals and products, such as gasoline, synthetic rubber, plastics, detergents, cement, paper, and pulp, by applying principles and technology of chemistry, physics, and engineering. Develops processes to separate components of liquids or gases or generate electrical currents, using controlled chemical processes. Designs measurement and control systems for chemical plants based on data

collected in laboratory experiments and in pilot plant operations. Determines most effective arrangement of operations, such as mixing, crushing, heat transfer, distillation, and drying. Designs and plans layout of equipment. Conducts research to develop new and improved chemical manufacturing processes. Performs laboratory studies of steps in manufacture of new product and tests proposed process in small-scale operation (pilot plant). Develops safety procedures to be employed by workers operating equipment or working in close proximity to on-going chemical reactions. Directs activities of workers who operate or who are engaged in constructing and improving absorption, evaporation, or electromagnetic equipment. Prepares estimate of production costs and production progress reports for management. Performs tests throughout stages of production to determine degree of control over variables, including temperature, density, specific gravity, and pressure. **SKILLS**—Science: Using scientific rules and methods to solve problems. Reading Comprehension: Understanding written sentences and paragraphs in work-related documents. Active Learning: Understanding the implications of new information for both current and future problem-solving and decision-making. Operations Analysis: Analyzing needs and product requirements to create a design. Operation Monitoring: Watching gauges, dials, or other indicators to make sure a machine is working properly.

GOE INFORMATION—**Interest Area:** 02. Science, Math, and Engineering. **Work Group:** 02.07. Engineering. **Other Job Titles in This Work Group:** Aerospace Engineers; Agricultural Engineers; Architects, Except Landscape and Naval; Biomedical Engineers; Civil Engineers; Computer Hardware Engineers; Computer Software Engineers, Applications; Computer Software Engineers, Systems Software; Electrical Engineers; Electronics Engineers, Except Computer; Engineers, All Other; Environmental Engineers; Fire-Prevention and Protection Engineers; Health and Safety Engineers, Except Mining Safety Engineers and Inspectors; Industrial Engineers; Industrial Safety and Health Engineers; Landscape Architects;

Marine Architects; Marine Engineers; Marine Engineers and Naval Architects; Materials Engineers; Mechanical Engineers; Mining and Geological Engineers, Including Mining Safety Engineers; Nuclear Engineers; Petroleum Engineers; Product Safety Engineers; Sales Engineers. **PERSONALITY TYPE**—Investigative. Investigative occupations frequently involve working with ideas and require an extensive amount of thinking. These occupations can involve searching for facts and figuring out problems mentally.

EDUCATION/TRAINING PROGRAM(S)— Chemical Engineering. **RELATED KNOWLEDGE/ COURSES**—**Chemistry:** Knowledge of the chemical composition, structure, and properties of substances and of the chemical processes and transformations that they undergo. This includes uses of chemicals and their interactions, danger signs, production techniques, and disposal methods. **Engineering and Technology:** Knowledge of the practical application of engineering science and technology. This includes applying principles, techniques, procedures, and equipment to the design and production of various goods and services. **Physics:** Knowledge and prediction of physical principles and laws and their interrelationships and applications to understanding fluid, material, and atmospheric dynamics and mechanical, electrical, atomic, and sub-atomic structures and processes. **Mathematics:** Knowledge of arithmetic, algebra, geometry, calculus, and statistics and their applications. **Design:** Knowledge of design techniques, tools, and principles involved in production of precision technical plans, blueprints, drawings, and models.

Chemical Technicians

- ▲ Education/Training Required: Associate's degree
- ▲ Annual Earnings: $35,450
- ▲ Growth: 15%
- ▲ Annual Job Openings: 13,000
- ▲ Self-Employed: 0.9%
- ▲ Part-Time: 11.7%

Conduct chemical and physical laboratory tests to assist scientists in making qualitative and quantitative analyses of solids, liquids, and gaseous materials for purposes such as research and development of new products or processes, quality control, maintenance of environmental standards, and other work involving experimental, theoretical, or practical application of chemistry and related sciences. Tests and analyzes chemical and physical properties of liquids, solids, gases, radioactive and biological materials, and products such as perfumes. Documents results of tests and analyses and writes technical reports or prepares graphs and charts. Directs other workers in compounding and distilling chemicals. Reviews process paperwork for products to ensure compliance to standards and specifications. Cleans and sterilizes laboratory equipment. Prepares chemical solutions for products and processes, following standardized formulas, or creates experimental formulas. Sets up and calibrates laboratory equipment and instruments used for testing, process control, product development, and research. **SKILLS**—Science: Using scientific rules and methods to solve problems. Reading Comprehension: Understanding written sentences and paragraphs in work-related documents. Mathematics: Using mathematics to solve problems. Critical Thinking: Using logic and reasoning to identify the strengths and weaknesses of alternative solutions, conclusions, or approaches to problems. Active Listening: Giving full attention to what other people are saying, taking time to understand the points being made, asking questions as appropriate, and not interrupting at inappropriate times. Writing: Communicating effectively in writing as appropriate for the needs of the audience.

GOE INFORMATION—**Interest Area:** 02. Science, Math, and Engineering. **Work Group:** 02.05. Laboratory Technology. **Other Job Titles in This Work Group:** Biological Technicians; Environmental Science and Protection Technicians, Including Health; Geological and Petroleum Technicians; Geological Data Technicians; Geological Sample Test Technicians; Nuclear Equipment Operation Technicians; Nuclear Technicians; Photographers, Scientific. **PERSONALITY TYPE**—Realistic. Realistic occupations frequently involve work activities that include practical, hands-on problems and solutions. They often deal with plants, animals, and real-world materials like wood, tools, and machinery. Many of the occupations require working outside and do not involve a lot of paperwork or working closely with others.

EDUCATION/TRAINING PROGRAM(S)—Chemical Technologist/Technician; Food Sciences and Technology. **RELATED KNOWLEDGE/COURSES**—**Chemistry:** Knowledge of the chemical composition, structure, and properties of substances and of the chemical processes and transformations that they undergo. This includes uses of chemicals and their interactions, danger signs, production techniques, and disposal methods. **Mathematics:** Knowledge of arithmetic, algebra, geometry, calculus, and statistics and their applications. **English Language:** Knowledge of the structure and content of the English language, including the meaning and spelling of words, rules of composition, and grammar. **Physics:** Knowledge and prediction of physical principles and laws and their interrelationships and applications to understanding fluid, material, and atmospheric dynamics and mechanical, electrical, atomic, and sub-atomic structures and processes. **Engineering and Technology:** Knowledge of the practical application of engineering science and technology. This includes applying principles, techniques, procedures, and equipment to the design and production of various goods and services.

Chemistry Teachers, Postsecondary

▲ Education/Training Required: Master's degree

▲ Annual Earnings: $52,530

▲ Growth: 24% for all Postsecondary Teachers

▲ Annual Job Openings: 184,000 for all Postsecondary Teachers

▲ Self-Employed: 0%

▲ Part-Time: 32.3% for all Postsecondary Teachers

Teach courses pertaining to the chemical and physical properties and compositional changes of substances. Work may include instruction in the methods of qualitative and quantitative chemical analysis. Includes both teachers primarily engaged in teaching and those who do a combination of both teaching and research. Prepares and delivers lectures to students. Compiles bibliographies of specialized materials for outside reading assignments. Directs research of other teachers or graduate students working for advanced academic degrees. Compiles, administers, and grades examinations or assigns this work to others. Stimulates class discussions. Advises students on academic and vocational curricula. Acts as adviser to student organizations. Serves on faculty committee providing professional consulting services to government and industry. Conducts research in particular field of knowledge and publishes findings in professional journals. **SKILLS**—Writing: Communicating effectively in writing as appropriate for the needs of the audience. Reading Comprehension: Understanding written sentences and paragraphs in work-related documents. Learning Strategies: Selecting and using training/instructional methods and procedures appropriate for the situation when learning or teaching new things. Instructing: Teaching others how to do something. Active Learning: Understanding the implications of new information for both current and future problem-solving and decision-making.

GOE INFORMATION—Interest Area: 12. Education and Social Service. **Work Group:** 12.03. Educational Services. **Other Job Titles in This Work Group:** Adult Literacy, Remedial Education, and GED Teachers and Instructors; Agricultural Sciences Teachers, Postsecondary; Anthropology and Archeology Teachers, Postsecondary; Architecture Teachers, Postsecondary; Archivists; Area, Ethnic, and Cultural Studies Teachers, Postsecondary; Art, Drama, and Music Teachers, Postsecondary; Atmospheric, Earth, Marine, and Space Sciences Teachers, Postsecondary; Audio-Visual Collections Specialists; Biological Science Teachers, Postsecondary; Business Teachers, Postsecondary; Child Care Workers; Communications Teachers, Postsecondary; Computer Science Teachers, Postsecondary; Criminal Justice and Law Enforcement Teachers, Postsecondary; Cura-

tors; Economics Teachers, Postsecondary; Education Teachers, Postsecondary; Educational Psychologists; Educational, Vocational, and School Counselors; Elementary School Teachers, Except Special Education; Engineering Teachers, Postsecondary; English Language and Literature Teachers, Postsecondary; Environmental Science Teachers, Postsecondary; Farm and Home Management Advisors; Foreign Language and Literature Teachers, Postsecondary; Forestry and Conservation Science Teachers, Postsecondary; Geography Teachers, Postsecondary; Graduate Teaching Assistants; Health Specialties Teachers, Postsecondary; History Teachers, Postsecondary; Home Economics Teachers, Postsecondary; Kindergarten Teachers, Except Special Education; Law Teachers, Postsecondary; Librarians; Library Assistants, Clerical; Library Science Teachers, Postsecondary; others. **PERSONALITY TYPE**—Investigative. Investigative occupations frequently involve working with ideas and require an extensive amount of thinking. These occupations can involve searching for facts and figuring out problems mentally.

EDUCATION/TRAINING PROGRAM(S)—Analytical Chemistry; Chemistry, General; Chemistry, Other; Inorganic Chemistry; Medicinal/Pharmaceutical Chemistry; Organic Chemistry; Physical and Theoretical Chemistry; Polymer Chemistry. **RELATED KNOWLEDGE/COURSES**—**Chemistry:** Knowledge of the chemical composition, structure, and properties of substances and of the chemical processes and transformations that they undergo. This includes uses of chemicals and their interactions, danger signs, production techniques, and disposal methods. **Mathematics:** Knowledge of arithmetic, algebra, geometry, calculus, and statistics and their applications. **Education and Training:** Knowledge of principles and methods for curriculum and training design, teaching and instruction for individuals and groups, and the measurement of training effects. **English Language:** Knowledge of the structure and content of the English language, including the meaning and spelling of words, rules of composition, and grammar. **Administration and Management:** Knowledge of business and management principles involved in strategic planning, resource allocation, human resources modeling, leadership technique, production methods, and coordination of people and resources.

Chemists

▲ Education/Training Required: Bachelor's degree
▲ Annual Earnings: $50,080
▲ Growth: 19%
▲ Annual Job Openings: 6,000
▲ Self-Employed: 1%
▲ Part-Time: 3.3%

Conduct qualitative and quantitative chemical analyses or chemical experiments in laboratories for quality or process control or to develop new products or knowledge. Analyzes organic and inorganic compounds to determine chemical and physical properties, composition, structure, relationships, and reactions, utilizing chromatography, spectroscopy, and spectrophotometry techniques. Develops, improves, and customizes products, equipment, formulas, processes, and analytical methods. Studies effects of various methods of processing, preserving, and packaging on composition and properties of foods. Confers with scientists and engineers to conduct analyses of research projects, interpret test results, or develop nonstandard tests. Directs, coordinates, and advises personnel in test procedures for analyzing components and physical properties of materials. Writes technical papers and reports and prepares standards and specifications for processes, facilities, products, and tests. Prepares test solutions, compounds, and reagents for laboratory personnel to conduct test. Compiles and analyzes test information to determine process or equipment operating efficiency and to diagnose malfunctions. Induces changes in composition of substances by introducing heat, light, energy, and chemical catalysts for quantitative and qualitative analysis. **SKILLS**—Science: Using scientific rules and methods to solve problems. Active Learning: Understanding the implications of new information for both current and future problem-solving and decision-making. Reading Comprehension: Understanding written sentences and paragraphs in work-related documents. Writing: Communicating effectively in writing as appropriate for the needs of the audience. Judgment and Decision Making: Considering the relative costs and benefits of potential actions to choose the most appropriate one. Mathematics: Using mathematics to solve problems. Critical Thinking: Using logic and reasoning to identify the strengths and weaknesses of alternative solutions, conclusions, or approaches to problems.

GOE INFORMATION—Interest Area: 02. Science, Math, and Engineering. **Work Group:** 02.02. Physical Sciences. **Other Job Titles in This Work Group:** Astronomers; Atmospheric and Space Scientists; Geographers; Geologists; Geoscientists, Except Hydrologists and Geographers; Hydrologists; Materials Scientists; Physical Scientists, All Other; Physicists. **PERSONALITY TYPE**—Investigative. Investigative occupations frequently involve working with ideas and require an extensive amount of thinking. These occupations can involve searching for facts and figuring out problems mentally.

EDUCATION/TRAINING PROGRAM(S)—Analytical Chemistry; Chemistry, General; Chemistry, Other; Inorganic Chemistry; Medicinal/Pharmaceutical Chemistry; Organic Chemistry; Physical and Theoretical Chemistry; Polymer Chemistry. **RELATED KNOWLEDGE/COURSES**—**Chemistry:** Knowledge of the chemical composition, structure, and properties of substances and of the chemical processes and transformations that they undergo. This includes uses of chemicals and their interactions, danger signs, production techniques, and disposal methods. **Mathematics:** Knowledge of arithmetic, algebra, geometry, calculus, and statistics and their applications. **English Language:** Knowledge of the structure and content of the English language, including the meaning and spelling of words, rules of composition, and grammar. **Computers and Electronics:** Knowledge of circuit boards, processors, chips, electronic equipment, and computer hardware and software, including applications and programming. **Physics:** Knowledge and prediction of physical principles and laws and their interrelationships and applications to understanding fluid, material, and atmospheric dynamics and mechanical, electrical, atomic, and sub-atomic structures and processes. **Engineering and Technology:** Knowledge of the practical application of engineering science and technology. This includes applying principles, techniques, procedures, and equipment to the design and production of various goods and services. **Administration and Management:** Knowledge of business and management principles involved in strategic planning, resource allocation, human resources modeling, leadership technique, production methods, and coordination of people and resources.

Chief Executives

▲ Education/Training Required: Work experience, plus degree

▲ Annual Earnings: $113,810

▲ Growth: 17%

▲ Annual Job Openings: 48,000

▲ Self-Employed: 0%

▲ Part-Time: 6.1%

Determine and formulate policies and provide the overall direction of companies or private and public sector organizations within the guidelines set up by a board of directors or similar governing body. Plan, direct, or coordinate operational activities at the highest level of management with the help of subordinate executives and staff managers. SKILLS—No data available.

GOE INFORMATION—**Interest Area:** 13. General Management and Support. **Work Group:** 13.01. General Management Work and Management of Support Functions. **Other Job Titles in This Work Group:** Compensation and Benefits Managers; Farm, Ranch, and Other Agricultural Managers; Financial Managers; Financial Managers, Branch or Department; Funeral Directors; General and Operations Managers; Government Service Executives; Human Resources Managers; Human Resources Managers, All Other; Legislators; Managers, All Other; Postmasters and Mail Superintendents; Private Sector Executives; Property, Real Estate, and Community Association Managers; Public Relations Managers; Purchasing Managers; Storage and Distribution Managers; Training and Development Managers; Transportation, Storage, and Distribution Managers; Treasurers, Controllers, and Chief Financial Officers. **PERSONALITY TYPE**—No data available.

EDUCATION/TRAINING PROGRAM(S)—Business Administration and Management, General; Enterprise Management and Operation, General; International Business; Public Administration; Public Administration and Services, Other; Public Policy Analysis. **RELATED KNOWLEDGE/COURSES**—No data available.

Child, Family, and School Social Workers

▲ Education/Training Required: Bachelor's degree

▲ Annual Earnings: $31,470

▲ Growth: 27%

▲ Annual Job Openings: 35,000

▲ Self-Employed: 3.1%

▲ Part-Time: 11.9%

Provide social services and assistance to improve the social and psychological functioning of children and their families and to maximize the family well-being and the academic functioning of children. May assist single parents, arrange adoptions, and find foster homes for abandoned or abused children. In schools, they address such problems as teenage pregnancy, misbehavior, and truancy. May also advise teachers on how to deal with problem children. Counsels individuals or family members regarding behavior modifications, rehabilitation, social adjustments, financial assistance, vocational training, child care, or medical care. Refers client to community resources for needed assistance. Leads group counseling sessions to provide support in such areas as grief, stress, or chemical dependency. Arranges for medical, psychiatric, and other tests that may disclose cause of difficulties and indicate remedial measures. Assists travelers, including runaways, migrants, transients, refugees, repatriated Americans, and problem families. Collects supplementary information, such as employment, medical records, or school reports. Maintains case history records and prepares reports. Evaluates personal characteristics of foster home or adoption applicants. Places children in foster or adoptive homes, institutions, or medical treatment centers. Reviews service plan and performs follow-up to determine quantity and quality of service provided to client. Determines client's eligibility for financial assistance. Develops program content and organizes and leads activities planned to enhance social development of individual members and accomplishment of group goals. Investigates home conditions to determine suitability of foster or adoptive home or to protect children from harmful environment. Serves as liaison between student, home, school, family service agencies, child guidance clinics, courts, protective services, doctors, and clergy members. Consults with parents, teachers, and other school personnel to determine causes of problems and effect solutions. Counsels students whose behavior, school progress, or mental or physical impairment indicates need for assistance. Arranges for day care, homemaker service, prenatal care, and child planning programs for clients in need of such services. Interviews individuals to assess social and emotional capabilities, physical and mental impairments, and financial needs. Counsels parents with child-rearing problems and children and youth with difficulties in social adjustments. **SKILLS**—Social

Perceptiveness: Being aware of others' reactions and understanding why they react as they do. Service Orientation: Actively looking for ways to help people. Active Listening: Giving full attention to what other people are saying, taking time to understand the points being made, asking questions as appropriate, and not interrupting at inappropriate times. Speaking: Talking to others to convey information effectively. Reading Comprehension: Understanding written sentences and paragraphs in work-related documents.

GOE INFORMATION—**Interest Area:** 12. Education and Social Service. **Work Group:** 12.02. Social Services. **Other Job Titles in This Work Group:** Clergy; Clinical Psychologists; Clinical, Counseling, and School Psychologists; Community and Social Service Specialists, All Other; Counseling Psychologists; Counselors, All Other; Directors, Religious Activities and Education; Marriage and Family Therapists; Medical and Public Health Social Workers; Mental Health and Substance Abuse Social Workers; Mental Health Counselors; Probation Officers and Correctional Treatment Specialists; Rehabilitation Counselors; Religious Workers, All Other; Residential Advisors; Social and Human Service Assistants; Social Workers, All Other; Substance Abuse and Behavioral Disorder Counselors. **PERSONALITY TYPE**—Social. Social occupations frequently involve working with, communicating with, and teaching people. These occupations often involve helping or providing service to others.

EDUCATION/TRAINING PROGRAM(S)— Social Work. **RELATED KNOWLEDGE/ COURSES**—**Therapy and Counseling:** Knowledge of principles, methods, and procedures for diagnosis, treatment, and rehabilitation of physical and mental dysfunctions and for career counseling and guidance. **Psychology:** Knowledge of human behavior and performance; individual differences in ability, personality, and interests; learning and motivation; psychological research methods; and the assessment and treatment of behavioral and affective disorders. **English Language:** Knowledge of the structure and content of the English language, including the meaning and spelling of words, rules of composition, and grammar. **Sociology and Anthropology:** Knowledge of group behavior and dynamics, societal trends and influences, human migrations, ethnicity, cultures, and their history and origins. **Administration and Man-**

agement: Knowledge of business and management principles involved in strategic planning, resource allocation, human resources modeling, leadership technique, production methods, and coordination of people and resources.

Civil Engineering Technicians

▲ Education/Training Required: Associate's degree

▲ Annual Earnings: $35,990

▲ Growth: 12%

▲ Annual Job Openings: 9,000

▲ Self-Employed: 1.9%

▲ Part-Time: 7.4%

Apply theory and principles of civil engineering in planning, designing, and overseeing construction and maintenance of structures and facilities under the direction of engineering staff or physical scientists. Evaluates facility to determine suitability for occupancy and square footage availability. Responds to public suggestions and complaints. Inspects project site and evaluates contractor work to detect design malfunctions and ensure conformance to design specifications and applicable codes. Analyzes proposed site factors and designs maps, graphs, tracings, and diagrams to illustrate findings. Drafts detailed dimensional drawings and designs layouts for projects and to ensure conformance to specifications. Reads and reviews project blueprints and structural specifications to determine dimensions of structure or system and material requirements. Prepares reports and documents project activities and data. Confers with supervisor to determine project details, such as plan preparation, acceptance testing, and evaluation of field conditions. Conducts materials test and analysis, using tools and equipment and applying engineering knowledge. Reports maintenance problems occurring at project site to supervisor and negotiates changes to resolve system conflicts. Calculates dimensions, square footage, profile and component specifications, and material quantities, using calculator or computer. Develops plans and estimates costs for installation of systems, utilization of facilities, or construction of structures. Plans and conducts field surveys to locate new sites and analyze details of project sites. **SKILLS**—Mathematics: Using mathematics to solve problems. Operations Analysis: Analyzing needs and product requirements to create a design. Reading Comprehension: Understanding written sentences and paragraphs in work-related documents. Critical Thinking: Using logic and reasoning to identify the strengths and weaknesses of alternative solutions, conclusions, or approaches to problems. Writing: Communicating effectively in writing as appropriate for the needs of the audience. Judgment and Decision Making: Considering the relative costs and benefits of potential actions to choose the most appropriate one. Active Listening: Giving full attention to what other people are saying, taking time to understand the points being made, asking questions as appropriate, and not interrupting at inappropriate times.

GOE INFORMATION—Interest Area: 02. Science, Math, and Engineering. **Work Group:** 02.08. Engineering Technology. **Other Job Titles in This Work Group:** Aerospace Engineering and Operations Technicians; Architectural and Civil Drafters; Architectural Drafters; Calibration and Instrumentation Technicians; Cartographers and Photogrammetrists; Civil Drafters; Construction and Building Inspectors; Drafters, All Other; Electrical and Electronic Engineering Technicians; Electrical and Electronics Drafters; Electrical Drafters; Electrical Engineering Technicians; Electro-Mechanical Technicians; Electronic Drafters; Electronics Engineering Technicians; Engineering Technicians, Except Drafters, All Other; Environmental Engineering Technicians; Industrial Engineering Technicians; Mapping Technicians; Mechanical Drafters; Mechanical Engineering Technicians; Numerical Tool and Process Control Programmers; Pressure Vessel Inspectors; Surveying and Mapping Technicians; Surveying Technicians; Surveyors. **PERSONALITY TYPE**—Realistic. Realistic occupations frequently involve work activities that include practical, hands-on problems and solutions.

They often deal with plants, animals, and real-world materials like wood, tools, and machinery. Many of the occupations require working outside and do not involve a lot of paperwork or working closely with others.

EDUCATION/TRAINING PROGRAM(S)—Civil Engineering/Civil Technologist/Technician; Construction/Building Technologist/Technician. **RELATED KNOWLEDGE/COURSES—Engineering and Technology:** Knowledge of the practical application of engineering science and technology. This includes applying principles, techniques, procedures, and equipment to the design and production of various goods and services.

Design: Knowledge of design techniques, tools, and principles involved in production of precision technical plans, blueprints, drawings, and models. **Mathematics:** Knowledge of arithmetic, algebra, geometry, calculus, and statistics and their applications. **Building and Construction:** Knowledge of materials, methods, and tools involved in the construction or repair of houses, buildings, or other structures, such as highways and roads. **English Language:** Knowledge of the structure and content of the English language, including the meaning and spelling of words, rules of composition, and grammar.

Civil Engineers

- ▲ Education/Training Required: Bachelor's degree
- ▲ Annual Earnings: $55,740
- ▲ Growth: 10%
- ▲ Annual Job Openings: 4,000
- ▲ Self-Employed: 4.9%
- ▲ Part-Time: 5.4%

Perform engineering duties in planning, designing, and overseeing construction and maintenance of building structures and facilities, such as roads, railroads, airports, bridges, harbors, channels, dams, irrigation projects, pipelines, power plants, water and sewage systems, and waste disposal units. Includes architectural, structural, traffic, ocean, and geo-technical engineers. Analyzes survey reports, maps, drawings, blueprints, aerial photography, and other topographical or geologic data to plan projects. Plans and designs transportation or hydraulic systems and structures, following construction and government standards and using design software and drawing tools. Directs construction, operations, and maintenance activities at project site. Directs or participates in surveying to lay out installations and establish reference points, grades, and elevations to guide construction. Conducts studies of traffic patterns or environmental conditions to identify engineering problems and assess the potential impact of projects. Prepares or presents public reports, such as bid proposals, deeds, environmental impact statements, and property and right-of-way descriptions. Provides tech-

nical advice regarding design, construction, or program modifications and structural repairs to industrial and managerial personnel. Tests soils and materials to determine the adequacy and strength of foundations, concrete, asphalt, or steel. Inspects project sites to monitor progress and ensure conformance to design specifications and safety or sanitation standards. Computes load and grade requirements, water flow rates, and material stress factors to determine design specifications. Estimates quantities and cost of materials, equipment, or labor to determine project feasibility. **SKILLS—Mathematics:** Using mathematics to solve problems. Operations Analysis: Analyzing needs and product requirements to create a design. Critical Thinking: Using logic and reasoning to identify the strengths and weaknesses of alternative solutions, conclusions, or approaches to problems. Reading Comprehension: Understanding written sentences and paragraphs in work-related documents. Writing: Communicating effectively in writing as appropriate for the needs of the audience. Speaking: Talking to others to convey information effectively.

GOE INFORMATION—Interest Area: 02. Science, Math, and Engineering. **Work Group:** 02.07.

Engineering. **Other Job Titles in This Work Group:**
Aerospace Engineers; Agricultural Engineers; Architects,
Except Landscape and Naval; Biomedical Engineers;
Chemical Engineers; Computer Hardware Engineers; Computer Software Engineers, Applications; Computer Software Engineers, Systems Software; Electrical Engineers;
Electronics Engineers, Except Computer; Engineers, All
Other; Environmental Engineers; Fire-Prevention and Protection Engineers; Health and Safety Engineers, Except
Mining Safety Engineers and Inspectors; Industrial Engineers; Industrial Safety and Health Engineers; Landscape
Architects; Marine Architects; Marine Engineers; Marine
Engineers and Naval Architects; Materials Engineers; Mechanical Engineers; Mining and Geological Engineers, Including Mining Safety Engineers; Nuclear Engineers;
Petroleum Engineers; Product Safety Engineers; Sales
Engineers. **PERSONALITY TYPE**—Realistic. Realistic occupations frequently involve work activities that
include practical, hands-on problems and solutions. They
often deal with plants, animals, and real-world materials
like wood, tools, and machinery. Many of the occupations
require working outside and do not involve a lot of paperwork or working closely with others.

EDUCATION/TRAINING PROGRAM(S)—
Civil Engineering, General; Civil Engineering, Other;
Geotechnical Engineering; Structural Engineering; Transportation and Highway Engineering; Water Resources
Engineering. **RELATED KNOWLEDGE/
COURSES—Engineering and Technology:** Knowledge of the practical application of engineering science and
technology. This includes applying principles, techniques,
procedures, and equipment to the design and production
of various goods and services. **Design:** Knowledge of design techniques, tools, and principles involved in production of precision technical plans, blueprints, drawings, and
models. **Administration and Management:** Knowledge of business and management principles involved in
strategic planning, resource allocation, human resources
modeling, leadership technique, production methods, and
coordination of people and resources. **Physics:** Knowledge and prediction of physical principles and laws and
their interrelationships and applications to understanding
fluid, material, and atmospheric dynamics and mechanical,
electrical, atomic, and sub-atomic structures and processes.
Building and Construction: Knowledge of materials,
methods, and tools involved in the construction or repair
of houses, buildings, or other structures, such as highways
and roads.

Clergy

- ▲ Education/Training Required: First professional degree
- ▲ Annual Earnings: $31,760
- ▲ Growth: 15%
- ▲ Annual Job Openings: 12,000
- ▲ Self-Employed: 0%
- ▲ Part-Time: 10.8%

**Conduct religious worship and perform other
spiritual functions associated with beliefs and
practices of religious faith or denomination. Provide spiritual and moral guidance and assistance
to members.** Leads congregation in worship services.
Conducts wedding and funeral services. Administers religious rites or ordinances. Counsels those in spiritual need.
Interprets doctrine of religion. Instructs people who seek
conversion to faith. Prepares and delivers sermons and
other talks. Visits sick and shut-ins and helps poor. Engages in interfaith, community, civic, educational, and recreational activities sponsored by or related to interest of
denomination. Writes articles for publication. **SKILLS—**
Service Orientation: Actively looking for ways to help
people. Speaking: Talking to others to convey information
effectively. Social Perceptiveness: Being aware of others'
reactions and understanding why they react as they do.
Reading Comprehension: Understanding written sentences
and paragraphs in work-related documents. Active Listening: Giving full attention to what other people are saying,

taking time to understand the points being made, asking questions as appropriate, and not interrupting at inappropriate times. Writing: Communicating effectively in writing as appropriate for the needs of the audience.

GOE INFORMATION—Interest Area: 12. Education and Social Service. Work Group: 12.02. Social Services. Other Job Titles in This Work Group: Child, Family, and School Social Workers; Clinical Psychologists; Clinical, Counseling, and School Psychologists; Community and Social Service Specialists, All Other; Counseling Psychologists; Counselors, All Other; Directors, Religious Activities and Education; Marriage and Family Therapists; Medical and Public Health Social Workers; Mental Health and Substance Abuse Social Workers; Mental Health Counselors; Probation Officers and Correctional Treatment Specialists; Rehabilitation Counselors; Religious Workers, All Other; Residential Advisors; Social and Human Service Assistants; Social Workers, All Other; Substance Abuse and Behavioral Disorder Counselors. PERSONALITY TYPE—Social. Social occupations frequently involve working with, communicating with, and teaching people. These occupations often involve helping or providing service to others.

EDUCATION/TRAINING PROGRAM(S)—Divinity/Ministry (B.D., M.Div.); Pastoral Counseling and Specialized Ministries; Pre-Theological/Pre-Ministerial Studies; Rabbinical and Talmudic Studies (M.H.L./Rav); Theological and Ministerial Studies, Other; Theological Studies and Religious Vocations, Other; Theology/Theological Studies. RELATED KNOWLEDGE/COURSES—Philosophy and Theology: Knowledge of different philosophical systems and religions. This includes their basic principles, values, ethics, ways of thinking, customs, and practices and their impact on human culture. Education and Training: Knowledge of principles and methods for curriculum and training design, teaching and instruction for individuals and groups, and the measurement of training effects. Psychology: Knowledge of human behavior and performance; individual differences in ability, personality, and interests; learning and motivation; psychological research methods; and the assessment and treatment of behavioral and affective disorders. Therapy and Counseling: Knowledge of principles, methods, and procedures for diagnosis, treatment, and rehabilitation of physical and mental dysfunctions and for career counseling and guidance. English Language: Knowledge of the structure and content of the English language, including the meaning and spelling of words, rules of composition, and grammar.

Clinical Psychologists

- ▲ Education/Training Required: Master's degree
- ▲ Annual Earnings: $48,320
- ▲ Growth: 18%
- ▲ Annual Job Openings: 18,000
- ▲ Self-Employed: 43.7%
- ▲ Part-Time: 23.4%

Diagnose or evaluate mental and emotional disorders of individuals through observation, interview, and psychological tests and formulate and administer programs of treatment. Observes individual at play, in group interactions, or in other situations to detect indications of mental deficiency, abnormal behavior, or maladjustment. Utilizes treatment methods, such as psychotherapy, hypnosis, behavior modification, stress reduction therapy, psychodrama, and play therapy. Devel-

ops, directs, and participates in staff training programs. Provides psychological services and advice to private firms and community agencies on individual cases or mental health programs. Directs, coordinates, and evaluates activities of psychological staff and student interns engaged in patient evaluation and treatment in psychiatric facility. Plans, supervises, and conducts psychological research in fields such as personality development and diagnosis, treatment, and prevention of mental disorders. Provides occupational, educational, and other information to enable individual to formulate realistic educational and vocational plans. Assists clients to gain insight, define goals, and plan action to achieve effective personal, social, educational, and vocational development and adjustment. Consults reference material, such as textbooks, manuals, and journals, to identify symptoms, make diagnoses, and develop approach to treatment. Plans and develops accredited psychological service programs in psychiatric center or hospital in collaboration with psychiatrists and other professional staff. Selects, administers, scores, and interprets psychological tests to obtain information on individual's intelligence, achievement, interest, and personality. Develops treatment plan, including type, frequency, intensity, and duration of therapy, in collaboration with psychiatrist and other specialists. Conducts individual and group counseling sessions regarding psychological or emotional problems, such as stress, substance abuse, and family situations. Responds to client reactions, evaluates effectiveness of counseling or treatment, and modifies plan as needed. Interviews individuals, couples, or families and reviews records to obtain information on medical, psychological, emotional, relationship, or other problems. Analyzes information to assess client problems, determine advisability of counseling, and refer client to other specialists, institutions, or support services. **SKILLS**—Social Perceptiveness: Being aware of others' reactions and understanding why they react as they do. Active Listening: Giving full attention to what other people are saying, taking time to understand the points being made, asking questions as appropriate, and not interrupting at inappropriate times. Reading Comprehension: Understanding written sentences and paragraphs in work-related documents. Speaking: Talking to others to convey information effectively. Critical Thinking: Using logic and reasoning to identify the strengths and weaknesses of alternative solutions, conclusions, or approaches to problems. Writing: Communicating effectively in writing as appropriate for the needs of the audience.

GOE INFORMATION—**Interest Area:** 12. Education and Social Service. **Work Group:** 12.02. Social Services. **Other Job Titles in This Work Group:**

Child, Family, and School Social Workers; Clergy; Clinical, Counseling, and School Psychologists; Community and Social Service Specialists, All Other; Counseling Psychologists; Counselors, All Other; Directors, Religious Activities and Education; Marriage and Family Therapists; Medical and Public Health Social Workers; Mental Health and Substance Abuse Social Workers; Mental Health Counselors; Probation Officers and Correctional Treatment Specialists; Rehabilitation Counselors; Religious Workers, All Other; Residential Advisors; Social and Human Service Assistants; Social Workers, All Other; Substance Abuse and Behavioral Disorder Counselors. **PERSONALITY TYPE**—Investigative. Investigative occupations frequently involve working with ideas and require an extensive amount of thinking. These occupations can involve searching for facts and figuring out problems mentally.

EDUCATION/TRAINING PROGRAM(S)—Clinical Psychology; Counseling Psychology; Developmental and Child Psychology; Educational Psychology; Psychology, General; School Psychology. **RELATED KNOWLEDGE/COURSES**—Psychology: Knowledge of human behavior and performance; individual differences in ability, personality, and interests; learning and motivation; psychological research methods; and the assessment and treatment of behavioral and affective disorders. **Therapy and Counseling:** Knowledge of principles, methods, and procedures for diagnosis, treatment, and rehabilitation of physical and mental dysfunctions and for career counseling and guidance. **English Language:** Knowledge of the structure and content of the English language, including the meaning and spelling of words, rules of composition, and grammar. **Customer and Personal Service:** Knowledge of principles and processes for providing customer and personal services. This includes customer needs assessment, meeting quality standards for services, and evaluation of customer satisfaction. **Administration and Management:** Knowledge of business and management principles involved in strategic planning, resource allocation, human resources modeling, leadership technique, production methods, and coordination of people and resources.

Clinical, Counseling, and School Psychologists

- ▲ Education/Training Required: Master's degree
- ▲ Annual Earnings: $48,320
- ▲ Growth: 18%
- ▲ Annual Job Openings: 18,000
- ▲ Self-Employed: 43.7%
- ▲ Part-Time: 23.4%

Diagnose and treat mental disorders; learning disabilities; and cognitive, behavioral, and emotional problems using individual, child, family, and group therapies. May design and implement behavior modification programs. SKILLS—No data available.

GOE INFORMATION—Interest Area: 12. Education and Social Service. Work Group: 12.02. Social Services. Other Job Titles in This Work Group: Child, Family, and School Social Workers; Clergy; Clinical Psychologists; Community and Social Service Specialists, All Other; Counseling Psychologists; Counselors, All Other; Directors, Religious Activities and Education; Marriage and Family Therapists; Medical and Public Health Social Workers; Mental Health and Substance Abuse Social Workers; Mental Health Counselors; Probation Officers and Correctional Treatment Specialists; Rehabilitation Counselors; Religious Workers, All Other; Residential Advisors; Social and Human Service Assistants; Social Workers, All Other; Substance Abuse and Behavioral Disorder Counselors. PERSONALITY TYPE—No data available.

EDUCATION/TRAINING PROGRAM(S)— Clinical Psychology; Counseling Psychology; Developmental and Child Psychology; Educational Psychology; Psychology, General; School Psychology. RELATED KNOWLEDGE/COURSES—No data available.

Commercial and Industrial Designers

- ▲ Education/Training Required: Bachelor's degree
- ▲ Annual Earnings: $48,780
- ▲ Growth: 24%
- ▲ Annual Job Openings: 7,000
- ▲ Self-Employed: 31.9%
- ▲ Part-Time: 20%

Develop and design manufactured products, such as cars, home appliances, and children's toys. Combine artistic talent with research on product use, marketing, and materials to create the most functional and appealing product design. Confers with engineering, marketing, production, or sales department or customer to establish design concepts for manufactured products. Integrates findings and concepts and sketches design ideas. Designs packaging and containers for products such as foods, beverages, toiletries, or medicines. Prepares itemized production requirements to produce item. Fabricates model or sample in paper, wood, glass, fabric, plastic, or metal, using hand and power tools. Directs and coordinates preparation of detailed drawings from sketches or fabrication of models or samples. Reads publications, attends showings, and studies traditional, period, and contemporary design styles and motifs to obtain perspective and design concepts. Modifies design to conform with customer specifications, production limitations, or changes in design trends. Presents design to customer or design committee for approval and discusses need for modification. Creates and designs graphic material for use as ornamentation, illustration, or advertising on manufactured materials and packaging. Evaluates design ideas for feasibility based on factors such as appearance, function, serviceability, budget, production costs/methods, and market characteristics. Prepares detailed drawings, illustrations, artwork, or blueprints, using drawing instruments or paints and brushes. **SKILLS**—Reading Comprehension: Understanding written sentences and paragraphs in work-related documents. Active Learning: Understanding the implications of new information for both current and future problem-solving and decision-making. Critical Thinking: Using logic and reasoning to identify the strengths and weaknesses of alternative solutions, conclusions, or approaches to problems. Equipment Selection: Determining the kind of tools and equipment needed to do a job. Operations Analysis: Analyzing needs and product requirements to create a design. Coordination: Adjusting actions in relation to others' actions. Monitoring: Monitoring/Assessing your performance or that of other individuals or organizations to make improvements or take corrective action.

GOE INFORMATION—**Interest Area:** 01. Arts, Entertainment, and Media. **Work Group:** 01.04. Visual Arts. **Other Job Titles in This Work Group:** Cartoonists; Designers, All Other; Exhibit Designers; Fashion Designers; Fine Artists, Including Painters, Sculptors, and Illustrators; Floral Designers; Graphic Designers; Interior Designers; Merchandise Displayers and Window Trimmers; Multi-Media Artists and Animators; Painters and Illustrators; Sculptors; Set and Exhibit Designers; Set Designers; Sketch Artists. **PERSONALITY TYPE**—Artistic. Artistic occupations frequently involve working with forms, designs, and patterns. They often require self-expression, and the work can be done without following a clear set of rules.

EDUCATION/TRAINING PROGRAM(S)— Design and Applied Arts, Other; Design and Visual Communications; Industrial Design. **RELATED KNOWLEDGE/COURSES**—**Design:** Knowledge of design techniques, tools, and principles involved in production of precision technical plans, blueprints, drawings, and models. **Sales and Marketing:** Knowledge of principles and methods for showing, promoting, and selling products or services. This includes marketing strategy and tactics, product demonstration, sales techniques, and sales control systems. **Fine Arts:** Knowledge of the theory and techniques required to compose, produce, and perform works of music, dance, visual arts, drama, and sculpture. **Production and Processing:** Knowledge of raw materials, production processes, quality control, costs, and other techniques for maximizing the effective manufacture and distribution of goods. **Principles of Mechanical Devices:** Knowledge of machines and tools, including their designs, uses, repair, and maintenance.

Communications Teachers, Postsecondary

- ▲ Education/Training Required: Master's degree
- ▲ Annual Earnings: $45,540
- ▲ Growth: 24% for all Postsecondary Teachers
- ▲ Annual Job Openings: 184,000 for all Postsecondary Teachers
- ▲ Self-Employed: 0%
- ▲ Part-Time: 32.3% for all Postsecondary Teachers

Teach courses in communications, such as organizational communications, public relations, radio/television broadcasting, and journalism. **SKILLS**—No data available.

GOE INFORMATION—**Interest Area:** 12. Education and Social Service. **Work Group:** 12.03. Educational Services. **Other Job Titles in This Work Group:** Adult Literacy, Remedial Education, and GED

Teachers and Instructors; Agricultural Sciences Teachers, Postsecondary; Anthropology and Archeology Teachers, Postsecondary; Architecture Teachers, Postsecondary; Archivists; Area, Ethnic, and Cultural Studies Teachers, Postsecondary; Art, Drama, and Music Teachers, Postsecondary; Atmospheric, Earth, Marine, and Space Sciences Teachers, Postsecondary; Audio-Visual Collections Specialists; Biological Science Teachers, Postsecondary; Business Teachers, Postsecondary; Chemistry Teachers, Postsecondary; Child Care Workers; Computer Science Teachers, Postsecondary; Criminal Justice and Law Enforcement Teachers, Postsecondary; Curators; Economics Teachers, Postsecondary; Education Teachers, Postsecondary; Educational Psychologists; Educational, Vocational, and School Counselors; Elementary School Teachers, Except Special Education; Engineering Teachers, Postsecondary; English Language and Literature Teachers, Postsecondary; Environmental Science Teachers,

Postsecondary; Farm and Home Management Advisors; Foreign Language and Literature Teachers, Postsecondary; Forestry and Conservation Science Teachers, Postsecondary; Geography Teachers, Postsecondary; Graduate Teaching Assistants; Health Specialties Teachers, Postsecondary; History Teachers, Postsecondary; Home Economics Teachers, Postsecondary; Kindergarten Teachers, Except Special Education; Law Teachers, Postsecondary; Librarians; Library Assistants, Clerical; Library Science Teachers, Postsecondary; others. **PERSONALITY TYPE**—No data available.

EDUCATION/TRAINING PROGRAM(S)—Advertising; Broadcast Journalism; Communications, General; Journalism; Journalism and Mass Communication, Other; Mass Communications; Public Relations and Organizational Communications; Radio and Television Broadcasting. **RELATED KNOWLEDGE/COURSES**—No data available.

Compensation, Benefits, and Job Analysis Specialists

- ▲ Education/Training Required: Bachelor's degree
- ▲ Annual Earnings: $41,660
- ▲ Growth: 16%
- ▲ Annual Job Openings: 8,000
- ▲ Self-Employed: 2.6%
- ▲ Part-Time: 6.9%

Conduct programs of compensation and benefits and job analysis for employer. May specialize in specific areas, such as position classification and pension programs. Analyzes organizational, occupational, and industrial data to facilitate organizational functions and provide technical information to business, industry, and government. Evaluates and improves methods and techniques for selecting, promoting, evaluating, and training workers. Plans and develops curricula and materials for training programs and conducts training. Determines need for and develops job analysis instruments and materials. Researches job and worker requirements, structural and functional relationships among jobs and occupations, and occupational trends. Prepares reports, such as job descriptions, organization and flow charts, and career path reports, to summarize job analysis informa-

tion. Consults with business, industry, government, and union officials to arrange for, plan, and design occupational studies and surveys. Prepares research results for publication in form of journals, books, manuals, and film. Observes and interviews employees to collect job, organizational, and occupational information. **SKILLS**—Writing: Communicating effectively in writing as appropriate for the needs of the audience. Reading Comprehension: Understanding written sentences and paragraphs in work-related documents. Systems Evaluation: Identifying measures or indicators of system performance and the actions needed to improve or correct performance relative to the goals of the system. Speaking: Talking to others to convey information effectively. Learning Strategies: Selecting and using training/instructional methods and procedures appropriate for the situation when learning or teaching new things. Active Listening: Giving full attention to what other people are saying, taking time to understand the points being made, asking questions as appropriate, and not interrupting at inappropriate times. Coordination: Adjusting actions in relation to others' actions.

GOE INFORMATION—Interest Area: 13. General Management and Support. **Work Group:** 13.02. Management Support. **Other Job Titles in This Work Group:** Accountants; Accountants and Auditors; Appraisers and Assessors of Real Estate; Appraisers, Real Estate; Assessors; Auditors; Budget Analysts; Claims Adjusters, Examiners, and Investigators; Claims Examiners, Property and Casualty Insurance; Cost Estimators; Credit Analysts; Employment Interviewers, Private or Public Employment Service; Employment, Recruitment, and Placement Specialists; Financial Analysts; Human Resources, Training, and Labor Relations Specialists, All Other; Insurance Adjusters, Examiners, and Investigators; Insurance Appraisers, Auto Damage; Insurance Underwriters; Loan Counselors; Loan Officers; Logisticians; Management Analysts; Market Research Analysts; Personnel Recruiters; Purchasing Agents and Buyers, Farm Products; Purchasing Agents, Except Wholesale, Retail, and Farm Products; Tax Examiners, Collectors, and Revenue Agents; Training and Development Specialists; Wholesale and Retail Buyers, Except Farm Products. **PERSONALITY TYPE—**In-

vestigative. Investigative occupations frequently involve working with ideas and require an extensive amount of thinking. These occupations can involve searching for facts and figuring out problems mentally.

EDUCATION/TRAINING PROGRAM(S)— Human Resources Management; Human Resources Management, Other; Labor/Personnel Relations and Studies; Organizational Behavior Studies. **RELATED KNOWLEDGE/COURSES—Mathematics:** Knowledge of arithmetic, algebra, geometry, calculus, and statistics and their applications. **English Language:** Knowledge of the structure and content of the English language, including the meaning and spelling of words, rules of composition, and grammar. **Psychology:** Knowledge of human behavior and performance; individual differences in ability, personality, and interests; learning and motivation; psychological research methods; and the assessment and treatment of behavioral and affective disorders. **Personnel and Human Resources:** Knowledge of principles and procedures for personnel recruitment, selection, training, compensation and benefits, labor relations and negotiation, and personnel information systems. **Computers and Electronics:** Knowledge of circuit boards, processors, chips, electronic equipment, and computer hardware and software, including applications and programming.

Composers

- ▲ Education/Training Required: Master's degree
- ▲ Annual Earnings: $31,510
- ▲ Growth: 13%
- ▲ Annual Job Openings: 9,000
- ▲ Self-Employed: 25.8%
- ▲ Part-Time: 53.5%

Compose music for orchestra, choral group, or band. Creates original musical form or writes within circumscribed musical form, such as sonata, symphony, or opera. Transcribes or records musical ideas into notes on scored music paper. Develops pattern of harmony, applying knowledge of music theory. Synthesizes ideas for melody of musical scores for choral group or band. Creates musical

and tonal structure, applying elements of music theory, such as instrumental and vocal capabilities. Determines basic pattern of melody, applying knowledge of music theory. **SKILLS—**Equipment Selection: Determining the kind of tools and equipment needed to do a job. Complex Problem Solving: Identifying complex problems and reviewing related information to develop and evaluate options and implement solutions. Monitoring: Monitoring/Assessing your performance or that of other individuals or organizations to make improvements or take corrective action. Writing: Communicating effectively in writing as appropriate for the needs of the audience. Reading Comprehension: Understanding written sentences and paragraphs in work-related documents.

GOE INFORMATION—**Interest Area:** 01. Arts, Entertainment, and Media. **Work Group:** 01.05. Performing Arts. **Other Job Titles in This Work Group:** Actors; Choreographers; Dancers; Directors—Stage, Motion Pictures, Television, and Radio; Music Arrangers and Orchestrators; Music Directors; Music Directors and Composers; Musicians and Singers; Musicians, Instrumental; Public Address System and Other Announcers; Radio and Television Announcers; Singers; Talent Directors. **PERSONALITY TYPE**—Artistic. Artistic occupations frequently involve working with forms, designs, and patterns. They often require self-expression, and the work can be done without following a clear set of rules.

EDUCATION/TRAINING PROGRAM(S)—Music—General Performance; Music—Voice and Choral/Opera Performance; Music Business Management and Merchandising; Music Conducting; Music Theory and Composition; Music, General; Music, Other; Musicology and Ethnomusicology; Religious/Sacred Music. **RELATED KNOWLEDGE/COURSES**—**Fine Arts:** Knowledge of the theory and techniques required to compose, produce, and perform works of music, dance, visual arts, drama, and sculpture. **Mathematics:** Knowledge of arithmetic, algebra, geometry, calculus, and statistics and their applications. **English Language:** Knowledge of the structure and content of the English language, including the meaning and spelling of words, rules of composition, and grammar. **Clerical Studies:** Knowledge of administrative and clerical procedures and systems such as word processing, managing files and records, stenography and transcription, designing forms, and other office procedures and terminology. **Communications and Media:** Knowledge of media production, communication, and dissemination techniques and methods. This includes alternative ways to inform and entertain via written, oral, and visual media.

Computer and Information Scientists, Research

- ▲ Education/Training Required: Doctoral degree
- ▲ Annual Earnings: $70,590
- ▲ Growth: 40%
- ▲ Annual Job Openings: 2,000
- ▲ Self-Employed: 2.7%
- ▲ Part-Time: 5.7%

Conduct research into fundamental computer and information science as theorists, designers, or inventors. Solve or develop solutions to problems in the field of computer hardware and software. SKILLS—No data available.

GOE INFORMATION—**Interest Area:** 02. Science, Math, and Engineering. **Work Group:** 02.06. Mathematics and Computers. **Other Job Titles in This Work Group:** Actuaries; Computer Programmers; Computer Security Specialists; Computer Specialists, All Other; Computer Support Specialists; Computer Systems Analysts; Database Administrators; Mathematical Science

Occupations, All Other; Mathematical Technicians; Mathematicians; Network and Computer Systems Administrators; Network Systems and Data Communications Analysts; Operations Research Analysts; Statistical Assistants; Statisticians. **PERSONALITY TYPE**—No data available.

EDUCATION/TRAINING PROGRAM(S)—Computer and Information Sciences, General; Computer and Information Sciences, Other; Computer Science; Computer Systems Analysis; Information Sciences and Systems; Mathematics and Computer Science; Science, Technology and Society. **RELATED KNOWLEDGE/COURSES**—No data available.

Computer and Information Systems Managers

▲ Education/Training Required: Work experience, plus degree

▲ Annual Earnings: $78,830

▲ Growth: 48%

▲ Annual Job Openings: 28,000

▲ Self-Employed: 0%

▲ Part-Time: 6.1%

Plan, direct, or coordinate activities in such fields as electronic data processing, information systems, systems analysis, and computer programming. Evaluates data processing project proposals and assesses project feasibility. Directs daily operations of department and coordinates project activities with other departments. Directs training of subordinates. Participates in staffing decisions. Develops and interprets organizational goals, policies, and procedures and reviews project plans. Develops performance standards and evaluates work in light of established standards. Analyzes workflow and assigns or schedules work to meet priorities and goals. Meets with department heads, managers, supervisors, vendors, and others to solicit cooperation and resolve problems. Approves, prepares, monitors, and adjusts operational budget. Consults with users, management, vendors, and technicians to determine computing needs and system requirements. Prepares and reviews operational reports or project progress reports. **SKILLS**—Management of Material Resources: Obtaining and seeing to the appropriate use of equipment, facilities, and materials needed to do certain work. Coordination: Adjusting actions in relation to others' actions. Management of Personnel Resources: Motivating, developing, and directing people as they work, identifying the best people for the job. Reading Comprehension: Understanding written sentences and paragraphs in work-related documents. Systems Evaluation: Identifying measures or indicators of system performance and the actions needed to improve or correct performance relative to the goals of the system. Judgment and Decision Making: Considering the relative costs and benefits of potential actions to choose the most appropriate one.

GOE INFORMATION—Interest Area: 02. Science, Math, and Engineering. **Work Group:** 02.01. Managerial Work in Science, Math, and Engineering. **Other**

Job Titles in This Work Group: Engineering Managers; Natural Sciences Managers. **PERSONALITY TYPE**—Enterprising. Enterprising occupations frequently involve starting up and carrying out projects. These occupations can involve leading people and making many decisions. They sometimes require risk taking and often deal with business.

EDUCATION/TRAINING PROGRAM(S)—Business Administration and Management, General; Business Computer Programming/Programmer; Business Systems Analysis and Design; Business Systems Networking and Telecommunications; Computer and Information Sciences, General; Computer Science; Enterprise Management and Operation, General; Information Sciences and Systems; Logistics and Materials Management; Management Information Systems and Business Data Processing; Operations Management and Supervision. **RELATED KNOWLEDGE/COURSES**—**Administration and Management:** Knowledge of business and management principles involved in strategic planning, resource allocation, human resources modeling, leadership technique, production methods, and coordination of people and resources. **Computers and Electronics:** Knowledge of circuit boards, processors, chips, electronic equipment, and computer hardware and software, including applications and programming. **Mathematics:** Knowledge of arithmetic, algebra, geometry, calculus, and statistics and their applications. **English Language:** Knowledge of the structure and content of the English language, including the meaning and spelling of words, rules of composition, and grammar. **Economics and Accounting:** Knowledge of economic and accounting principles and practices, the financial markets, banking, and the analysis and reporting of financial data.

Computer Hardware Engineers

▲ Education/Training Required: Bachelor's degree

▲ Annual Earnings: $67,300

▲ Growth: 25%

▲ Annual Job Openings: 3,000

▲ Self-Employed: 2.9%

▲ Part-Time: 2.6%

Research, design, develop, and test computer or computer-related equipment for commercial, industrial, military, or scientific use. May supervise the manufacturing and installation of computer or computer-related equipment and components. Analyzes software requirements to determine feasibility of design within time and cost constraints. Trains users to use new or modified equipment. Recommends purchase of equipment to control dust, temperature, and humidity in area of system installation. Enters data into computer terminal to store, retrieve, and manipulate data for analysis of system capabilities and requirements. Specifies power supply requirements and configuration. Consults with customer concerning maintenance of software system. Monitors functioning of equipment to ensure system operates in conformance with specifications. Evaluates factors such as reporting formats required, cost constraints, and need for security restrictions to determine hardware configuration. Formulates and designs software system, using scientific analysis and mathematical models to predict and measure outcome and consequences of design. Confers with data processing and project managers to obtain information on limitations and capabilities for data processing projects. Coordinates installation of software system. Develops and directs software system testing procedures, programming, and documentation. Consults with engineering staff to evaluate interface between hardware and software and operational and performance requirements of overall system. Analyzes information to determine, recommend, and plan layout for type of computers and peripheral equipment modifications to existing systems. **SKILLS**—Troubleshooting: Determining causes of operating errors and deciding what to do about them. Programming: Writing computer programs for various purposes. Active Learning: Understanding the implications of new information for both current and future problem-solving and decision-making. Mathematics: Using mathematics to solve problems. Installation: Installing equipment, machines, wiring, or programs to meet specifications. Operations Analysis: Analyzing needs and product requirements to create a design.

GOE INFORMATION—Interest Area: 02. Science, Math, and Engineering. **Work Group:** 02.07. Engineering. **Other Job Titles in This Work Group:** Aerospace Engineers; Agricultural Engineers; Architects, Except Landscape and Naval; Biomedical Engineers; Chemical Engineers; Civil Engineers; Computer Software Engineers, Applications; Computer Software Engineers, Systems Software; Electrical Engineers; Electronics Engineers, Except Computer; Engineers, All Other; Environmental Engineers; Fire-Prevention and Protection Engineers; Health and Safety Engineers, Except Mining Safety Engineers and Inspectors; Industrial Engineers; Industrial Safety and Health Engineers; Landscape Architects; Marine Architects; Marine Engineers; Marine Engineers and Naval Architects; Materials Engineers; Mechanical Engineers; Mining and Geological Engineers, Including Mining Safety Engineers; Nuclear Engineers; Petroleum Engineers; Product Safety Engineers; Sales Engineers. **PERSONALITY TYPE**—Investigative. Investigative occupations frequently involve working with ideas and require an extensive amount of thinking. These occupations can involve searching for facts and figuring out problems mentally.

EDUCATION/TRAINING PROGRAM(S)— Computer Engineering; Electrical, Electronics and Communication Engineering. **RELATED KNOWLEDGE/COURSES**—**Computers and Electronics:** Knowledge of circuit boards, processors, chips, electronic equipment, and computer hardware and software, including applications and programming. **Mathematics:** Knowledge of arithmetic, algebra, geometry, calculus, and statistics and their applications. **Engineering and Technology:** Knowledge of the practical application of engineering science and technology. This includes applying principles, techniques, procedures, and equipment to the design and production of various goods and services. **English Language:** Knowledge of the structure and content of the English language, including the meaning and spelling of words, rules of composition, and grammar. **Education and Training:** Knowledge of principles and methods for curriculum and training design, teaching and instruction for individuals and groups, and the measurement of training effects. **Administration and Management:** Knowledge of business and management principles involved in strategic planning, resource allocation, human resources modeling, leadership technique, production methods, and coordination of people and resources. **Design:** Knowledge of design techniques, tools, and principles involved in production of precision technical plans, blueprints, drawings, and models.

Computer Programmers

▲ Education/Training Required: Bachelor's degree

▲ Annual Earnings: $57,590

▲ Growth: 16%

▲ Annual Job Openings: 36,000

▲ Self-Employed: 4.8%

▲ Part-Time: 7.3%

Convert project specifications and statements of problems and procedures to detailed logical flow charts for coding into computer language. Develop and write computer programs to store, locate, and retrieve specific documents, data, and information. May program web sites. Analyzes, reviews, and rewrites programs, using workflow chart and diagram, applying knowledge of computer capabilities, subject matter, and symbolic logic. Converts detailed logical flow chart to language processible by computer. Resolves symbolic formulations, prepares flow charts and block diagrams, and encodes resultant equations for processing. Develops programs from workflow charts or diagrams, considering computer storage capacity, speed, and intended use of output data. Consults with managerial and engineering and technical personnel to clarify program intent, identify problems, and suggest changes. Prepares records and reports. Assists computer operators or system analysts to resolve problems in running computer program. Trains subordinates in programming and program coding. Assigns, coordinates, and reviews work and activities of programming personnel. Collaborates with computer manufacturers and other users to develop new programming methods. Writes instructions to guide operating personnel during production runs. Revises or directs revision of existing programs to increase operating efficiency or adapt to new requirements. Compiles and writes documentation of program development and subsequent revisions. Prepares or receives detailed workflow chart and diagram to illustrate sequence of steps to describe input, output, and logical operation. **SKILLS**—Programming: Writing computer programs for various purposes. Reading Comprehension: Understanding written sentences and paragraphs in work-related documents. Troubleshooting: Determining causes of operating errors and deciding what to do about them. Writing: Communicating effectively in writing as appropriate for the needs of the audience. Active Learning: Understanding the implications of new information for both current and future problem-solving and decision-making.

GOE INFORMATION—Interest Area: 02. Science, Math, and Engineering. **Work Group:** 02.06. Mathematics and Computers. **Other Job Titles in This Work Group:** Actuaries; Computer and Information Scientists, Research; Computer Security Specialists; Computer Specialists, All Other; Computer Support Specialists; Computer Systems Analysts; Database Administrators; Mathematical Science Occupations, All Other; Mathematical Technicians; Mathematicians; Network and Computer Systems Administrators; Network Systems and Data Communications Analysts; Operations Research Analysts; Statistical Assistants; Statisticians. **PERSONALITY TYPE**—Investigative. Investigative occupations frequently involve working with ideas and require an extensive amount of thinking. These occupations can involve searching for facts and figuring out problems mentally.

EDUCATION/TRAINING PROGRAM(S)— Business Computer Programming/Programmer; Computer Programming; Management Information Systems and Business Data Processing. **RELATED KNOWLEDGE/ COURSES—Computers and Electronics:** Knowledge of circuit boards, processors, chips, electronic equipment, and computer hardware and software, including applications and programming. **Mathematics:** Knowledge of arithmetic, algebra, geometry, calculus, and statistics and their applications. **Education and Training:** Knowledge of principles and methods for curriculum and training design, teaching and instruction for individuals and groups, and the measurement of training effects. **English Language:** Knowledge of the structure and content of the English language, including the meaning and spelling of words, rules of composition, and grammar. **Clerical Studies:** Knowledge of administrative and clerical procedures and systems such as word processing, managing files and records, stenography and transcription, designing forms, and other office procedures and terminology.

Computer Science Teachers, Postsecondary

- ▲ Education/Training Required: Master's degree
- ▲ Annual Earnings: $46,890
- ▲ Growth: 24% for all Postsecondary Teachers
- ▲ Annual Job Openings: 184,000 for all Postsecondary Teachers
- ▲ Self-Employed: 0%
- ▲ Part-Time: 32.3% for all Postsecondary Teachers

Teach courses in computer science. May specialize in a field of computer science, such as the design and function of computers or operations and research analysis. Prepares and delivers lectures to students. Compiles, administers, and grades examinations or assigns this work to others. Directs research of other teachers or graduate students working for advanced academic degrees. Compiles bibliographies of specialized materials for outside reading assignments. Stimulates class discussions. Conducts research in particular field of knowledge and publishes findings in professional journals. Acts as adviser to student organizations. Serves on faculty committee providing professional consulting services to government and industry. Advises students on academic and vocational curricula. **SKILLS—Reading Comprehension:** Understanding written sentences and paragraphs in work-related documents. **Instructing:** Teaching others how to do something. **Writing:** Communicating effectively in writing as appropriate for the needs of the audience. **Active Learning:** Understanding the implications of new information for both current and future problem-solving and decision-making. **Learning Strategies:** Selecting and using training/instructional methods and procedures appropriate for the situation when learning or teaching new things.

GOE INFORMATION—Interest Area: 12. Education and Social Service. **Work Group:** 12.03. Educational Services. **Other Job Titles in This Work Group:** Adult Literacy, Remedial Education, and GED Teachers and Instructors; Agricultural Sciences Teachers, Postsecondary; Anthropology and Archeology Teachers, Postsecondary; Architecture Teachers, Postsecondary; Archivists; Area, Ethnic, and Cultural Studies Teachers, Postsecondary; Art, Drama, and Music Teachers, Postsecondary; Atmospheric, Earth, Marine, and Space Sciences Teachers, Postsecondary; Audio-Visual

Collections Specialists; Biological Science Teachers, Postsecondary; Business Teachers, Postsecondary; Chemistry Teachers, Postsecondary; Child Care Workers; Communications Teachers, Postsecondary; Criminal Justice and Law Enforcement Teachers, Postsecondary; Curators; Economics Teachers, Postsecondary; Education Teachers, Postsecondary; Educational Psychologists; Educational, Vocational, and School Counselors; Elementary School Teachers, Except Special Education; Engineering Teachers, Postsecondary; English Language and Literature Teachers, Postsecondary; Environmental Science Teachers, Postsecondary; Farm and Home Management Advisors; Foreign Language and Literature Teachers, Postsecondary; Forestry and Conservation Science Teachers, Postsecondary; Geography Teachers, Postsecondary; Graduate Teaching Assistants; Health Specialties Teachers, Postsecondary; History Teachers, Postsecondary; Home Economics Teachers, Postsecondary; Kindergarten Teachers, Except Special Education; Law Teachers, Postsecondary; Librarians; Library Assistants, Clerical; Library Science Teachers, Postsecondary; others. **PERSONALITY TYPE**—Investigative. Investigative occupations frequently involve working with ideas and require an extensive amount of thinking. These occupations can involve searching for facts and figuring out problems mentally.

EDUCATION/TRAINING PROGRAM(S)—Business Computer Programming/Programmer; Business Systems Analysis and Design; Business Systems Networking and Telecommunications; Computer and Information Sciences, General; Computer Programming; Computer Science; Computer Systems Analysis; Information Sciences and Systems; Management Information Systems and Business Data Processing. **RELATED KNOWLEDGE/ COURSES**—**Computers and Electronics:** Knowledge of circuit boards, processors, chips, electronic equipment, and computer hardware and software, including applications and programming. **Education and Training:** Knowledge of principles and methods for curriculum and training design, teaching and instruction for individuals and groups, and the measurement of training effects. **Mathematics:** Knowledge of arithmetic, algebra, geometry, calculus, and statistics and their applications. **English Language:** Knowledge of the structure and content of the English language, including the meaning and spelling of words, rules of composition, and grammar. **Administration and Management:** Knowledge of business and management principles involved in strategic planning, resource allocation, human resources modeling, leadership technique, production methods, and coordination of people and resources.

Computer Security Specialists

▲ Education/Training Required: Bachelor's degree

▲ Annual Earnings: $51,280

▲ Growth: 82%

▲ Annual Job Openings: 18,000

▲ Self-Employed: 2.7%

▲ Part-Time: 5.7%

Plan, coordinate, and implement security measures for information systems to regulate access to computer data files and prevent unauthorized modification, destruction, or disclosure of information. Develops plans to safeguard computer files against accidental or unauthorized modification, destruction, or disclosure and to meet emergency data processing needs. Writes reports to document computer security and emergency measures policies, procedures, and test results. Tests data processing system to ensure functioning of data pro-

cessing activities and security measures. Modifies computer security files to incorporate new software, correct errors, or change individual access status. Monitors use of data files and regulates access to safeguard information in computer files. Confers with personnel to discuss issues such as computer data access needs, security violations, and programming changes. Coordinates implementation of computer system plan with establishment personnel and outside vendors. **SKILLS**—Programming: Writing computer programs for various purposes. Operations Analysis:

Analyzing needs and product requirements to create a design. Writing: Communicating effectively in writing as appropriate for the needs of the audience. Mathematics: Using mathematics to solve problems. Technology Design: Generating or adapting equipment and technology to serve user needs.

GOE INFORMATION—Interest Area: 02. Science, Math, and Engineering. Work Group: 02.06. Mathematics and Computers. Other Job Titles in This Work Group: Actuaries; Computer and Information Scientists, Research; Computer Programmers; Computer Specialists, All Other; Computer Support Specialists; Computer Systems Analysts; Database Administrators; Mathematical Science Occupations, All Other; Mathematical Technicians; Mathematicians; Network and Computer Systems Administrators; Network Systems and Data Communications Analysts; Operations Research Analysts; Statistical Assistants; Statisticians. PERSONALITY TYPE—Investigative. Investigative occupations frequently involve working with ideas and require an extensive amount of thinking. These occupations can involve searching for facts and figuring out problems mentally.

EDUCATION/TRAINING PROGRAM(S)— Business Systems Networking and Telecommunications; Computer and Information Sciences, General; Computer and Information Sciences, Other; Computer Systems Analysis; Information Sciences and Systems. RELATED KNOWLEDGE/COURSES—Computers and Electronics: Knowledge of circuit boards, processors, chips, electronic equipment, and computer hardware and software, including applications and programming. English Language: Knowledge of the structure and content of the English language, including the meaning and spelling of words, rules of composition, and grammar. Public Safety and Security: Knowledge of relevant equipment, policies, procedures, and strategies to promote effective local, state, or national security operations for the protection of people, data, property, and institutions. Administration and Management: Knowledge of business and management principles involved in strategic planning, resource allocation, human resources modeling, leadership technique, production methods, and coordination of people and resources. Mathematics: Knowledge of arithmetic, algebra, geometry, calculus, and statistics and their applications.

Computer Software Engineers, Applications

- ▲ Education/Training Required: Bachelor's degree
- ▲ Annual Earnings: $67,670
- ▲ Growth: 100%
- ▲ Annual Job Openings: 28,000
- ▲ Self-Employed: 4.1%
- ▲ Part-Time: 5.7%

Develop, create, and modify general computer applications software or specialized utility programs. Analyze user needs and develop software solutions. Design software or customize software for client use with the aim of optimizing operational efficiency. May analyze and design databases within an application area, working individually or coordinating database development as part of a team. Analyzes software requirements to determine feasibility of design within time and cost constraints. Specifies power supply requirements and configuration. Consults with customer concerning maintenance of software system. Monitors functioning of equipment to ensure system operates in conformance with specifications. Evaluates factors such as reporting formats required, cost constraints, and need for security restrictions to determine hardware configuration. Formulates and designs software system, using scientific analysis and mathematical models to predict and measure outcome and consequences of design. Confers with data processing and project managers to obtain information on limitations and capabilities for data processing projects. Coordinates installation of software system. Develops and directs software system testing procedures, programming, and documentation. Consults with engineering staff to evaluate interface between hardware and software and operational and performance requirements of overall system. Analyzes information to determine, recommend, and plan layout for type of computers and peripheral equipment modifications to existing systems. Enters data into computer terminal to store, retrieve, and manipulate data for analysis of system capabilities and requirements. Recommends purchase of equipment to control dust, temperature, and humidity in area of system installation. Trains users to use new or modified equipment. **SKILLS**— Troubleshooting: Determining causes of operating errors and deciding what to do about them. Programming: Writing computer programs for various purposes. Active Learning: Understanding the implications of new information for both current and future problem-solving and decision-making. Mathematics: Using mathematics to solve problems. Installation: Installing equipment, machines, wiring, or programs to meet specifications. Operations Analysis: Analyzing needs and product requirements to create a design.

GOE INFORMATION—Interest Area: 02. Science, Math, and Engineering. **Work Group:** 02.07. Engineering. **Other Job Titles in This Work Group:** Aerospace Engineers; Agricultural Engineers; Architects, Except Landscape and Naval; Biomedical Engineers; Chemical Engineers; Civil Engineers; Computer Hardware Engineers; Computer Software Engineers, Systems Software; Electrical Engineers; Electronics Engineers, Except Computer; Engineers, All Other; Environmental Engineers; Fire-Prevention and Protection Engineers; Health and Safety Engineers, Except Mining Safety Engineers and Inspectors; Industrial Engineers; Industrial Safety and Health Engineers; Landscape Architects; Marine Architects; Marine Engineers; Marine Engineers and Naval Architects; Materials Engineers; Mechanical Engineers; Mining and Geological Engineers, Including Mining Safety Engineers; Nuclear Engineers; Petroleum Engineers; Product Safety Engineers; Sales Engineers. **PERSONALITY TYPE**— Investigative. Investigative occupations frequently involve working with ideas and require an extensive amount of thinking. These occupations can involve searching for facts and figuring out problems mentally.

EDUCATION/TRAINING PROGRAM(S)— Computer Engineering; Computer Science; Electrical, Electronics and Communication Engineering. **RELATED KNOWLEDGE/COURSES—Computers and Electronics:** Knowledge of circuit boards, processors, chips, electronic equipment, and computer hardware and software, including applications and programming. **Mathematics:** Knowledge of arithmetic, algebra, geometry, calculus, and statistics and their applications. **Engineering and Technology:** Knowledge of the practical application of engineering science and technology. This includes applying principles, techniques, procedures, and equipment to the design and production of various goods and services. **English Language:** Knowledge of the structure and content of the English language, including the meaning and spelling of words, rules of composition, and grammar. **Administration and Management:** Knowledge of business and management principles involved in strategic planning, resource allocation, human resources modeling, leadership technique, production methods, and coordination of people and resources. **Education and Training:** Knowledge of principles and methods for curriculum and training design, teaching and instruction for individuals and groups, and the measurement of training effects. **Design:** Knowledge of design techniques, tools, and principles involved in production of precision technical plans, blueprints, drawings, and models.

Computer Software Engineers, Systems Software

- Education/Training Required: Bachelor's degree
- Annual Earnings: $69,530
- Growth: 90%
- Annual Job Openings: 23,000
- Self-Employed: 4.1%
- Part-Time: 5.7%

Research, design, develop, and test operating systems-level software, compilers, and network distribution software for medical, industrial, military, communications, aerospace, business, scientific, and general computing applications. Set operational specifications and formulate and analyze software requirements. Apply principles and techniques of computer science, engineering, and mathematical analysis. Analyzes software requirements to determine feasibility of design within time and cost constraints. Coordinates installation of software system. Consults with customer concerning maintenance of software system. Trains users to use new or modified equipment. Recommends purchase of equipment to control dust, temperature, and humidity in area of system installation. Enters data into computer terminal to store, retrieve, and manipulate data for analysis of system capabilities and requirements. Specifies power supply requirements and configuration. Monitors functioning of equipment to ensure system operates in conformance with specifications. Develops and directs software system testing procedures, programming, and documentation. Consults with engineering staff to evaluate interface between hardware and software and operational and performance requirements of overall system. Evaluates factors such as reporting formats required, cost constraints, and need for security restrictions to determine hardware configuration. Confers with data processing and project managers to obtain information on limitations and capabilities for data processing projects. Formulates and designs software system, using scientific analysis and mathematical models to predict and measure outcome and consequences of design. Analyzes information to determine, recommend, and plan layout for type of computers and peripheral equipment modifications to existing systems. **SKILLS—Troubleshooting:** Determining causes of operating errors and deciding what to do about them. Programming: Writing computer programs for various purposes. Active Learning: Understanding the implications of new information for both current and future problem-solving and decision-making. Mathematics: Using mathematics to solve problems. Operations Analysis: Analyzing needs and product requirements to create a design. Installation: Installing equipment, machines, wiring, or programs to meet specifications.

GOE INFORMATION—Interest Area: 02. Science, Math, and Engineering. **Work Group:** 02.07. Engineering. **Other Job Titles in This Work Group:** Aerospace Engineers; Agricultural Engineers; Architects, Except Landscape and Naval; Biomedical Engineers; Chemical Engineers; Civil Engineers; Computer Hardware Engineers; Computer Software Engineers, Applications; Electrical Engineers; Electronics Engineers, Except Computer; Engineers, All Other; Environmental Engineers; Fire-Prevention and Protection Engineers; Health and Safety Engineers, Except Mining Safety Engineers and Inspectors; Industrial Engineers; Industrial Safety and Health Engineers; Landscape Architects; Marine Architects; Marine Engineers; Marine Engineers and Naval Architects; Materials Engineers; Mechanical Engineers; Mining and Geological Engineers, Including Mining Safety Engineers; Nuclear Engineers; Petroleum Engineers; Product Safety Engineers; Sales Engineers. **PERSONALITY TYPE—** Investigative. Investigative occupations frequently involve working with ideas and require an extensive amount of thinking. These occupations can involve searching for facts and figuring out problems mentally.

EDUCATION/TRAINING PROGRAM(S)— Computer Engineering; Computer Science; Electrical, Electronics and Communication Engineering; Information Sciences and Systems. **RELATED KNOWLEDGE/ COURSES—Computers and Electronics:** Knowledge of circuit boards, processors, chips, electronic equipment, and computer hardware and software, including applications and programming. **Engineering and Technology:** Knowledge of the practical application of engineering science and technology. This includes applying principles, techniques, procedures, and equipment to the design and production of various goods and services. **Mathematics:** Knowledge of arithmetic, algebra, geometry, calculus, and statistics and their applications. **English Language:** Knowledge of the structure and content of the English language, including the meaning and spelling of words, rules of composition, and grammar. **Administration and Management:** Knowledge of business and management principles involved in strategic planning, resource allocation, human resources modeling, leadership technique, production methods, and coordination of people and resources. **Design:** Knowledge of design techniques, tools, and principles involved in production of precision technical plans, blueprints, drawings, and models. **Educa-**

tion and Training: Knowledge of principles and methods for curriculum and training design, teaching and instruction for individuals and groups, and the measurement of training effects.

Computer Support Specialists

- ▲ Education/Training Required: Associate's degree
- ▲ Annual Earnings: $36,460
- ▲ Growth: 97%
- ▲ Annual Job Openings: 40,000
- ▲ Self-Employed: No data available
- ▲ Part-Time: No data available

Provide technical assistance to computer system users. Answer questions or resolve computer problems for clients in person, via telephone, or from remote location. May provide assistance concerning the use of computer hardware and software, including printing, installation, word processing, electronic mail, and operating systems. Installs and performs minor repairs to hardware, software, and peripheral equipment, following design or installation specifications. Confers with staff, users, and management to determine requirements for new systems or modifications. Reads technical manuals, confers with users, and conducts computer diagnostics to determine nature of problems and provide technical assistance. Develops training materials and procedures and conducts training programs. Refers major hardware or software problems or defective products to vendors or technicians for service. Conducts office automation feasibility studies, including workflow analysis, space design, and cost comparison analysis. Supervises and coordinates workers engaged in problem-solving, monitoring, and installing data communication equipment and software. Inspects equipment and reads order sheets to prepare for delivery to users. Reads trade magazines and technical manuals and attends conferences and seminars to maintain knowledge of hardware and software. Maintains record of daily data communication transactions, problems and remedial action taken, and installation activities. Prepares evaluations of software and hardware and submits recommendations to management for review. Tests and monitors software, hardware, and peripheral equipment to evaluate use, effectiveness, and adequacy of product for user. Enters commands and observes system functioning to verify correct operations and detect errors.

SKILLS—Reading Comprehension: Understanding written sentences and paragraphs in work-related documents. Active Learning: Understanding the implications of new information for both current and future problem-solving and decision-making. Programming: Writing computer programs for various purposes. Troubleshooting: Determining causes of operating errors and deciding what to do about them. Writing: Communicating effectively in writing as appropriate for the needs of the audience. Judgment and Decision Making: Considering the relative costs and benefits of potential actions to choose the most appropriate one.

GOE INFORMATION—**Interest Area:** 02. Science, Math, and Engineering. **Work Group:** 02.06. Mathematics and Computers. **Other Job Titles in This Work Group:** Actuaries; Computer and Information Scientists, Research; Computer Programmers; Computer Security Specialists; Computer Specialists, All Other; Computer Systems Analysts; Database Administrators; Mathematical Science Occupations, All Other; Mathematical Technicians; Mathematicians; Network and Computer Systems Administrators; Network Systems and Data Communications Analysts; Operations Research Analysts; Statistical Assistants; Statisticians. **PERSONALITY TYPE**—Investigative. Investigative occupations frequently involve working with ideas and require an extensive amount of thinking. These occupations can involve searching for facts and figuring out problems mentally.

EDUCATION/TRAINING PROGRAM(S)—Business Systems Networking and Telecommunications; Data Processing Technologist/Technician. **RELATED KNOWLEDGE/COURSES**—Computers and

Electronics: Knowledge of circuit boards, processors, chips, electronic equipment, and computer hardware and software, including applications and programming. Education and Training: Knowledge of principles and methods for curriculum and training design, teaching and instruction for individuals and groups, and the measurement of training effects. Mathematics: Knowledge of arithmetic, algebra, geometry, calculus, and statistics and their applications. Telecommunications: Knowledge of transmission, broadcasting, switching, control, and operation of telecommunications systems. English Language: Knowledge of the structure and content of the English language, including the meaning and spelling of words, rules of composition, and grammar. Engineering and Technology: Knowledge of the practical application of engineering science and technology. This includes applying principles, techniques, procedures, and equipment to the design and production of various goods and services.

Computer Systems Analysts

▲ Education/Training Required: Bachelor's degree

▲ Annual Earnings: $59,330

▲ Growth: 60%

▲ Annual Job Openings: 34,000

▲ Self-Employed: 7.7%

▲ Part-Time: 5.7%

Analyze science, engineering, business, and all other data processing problems for application to electronic data processing systems. Analyze user requirements, procedures, and problems to automate or improve existing systems and review computer system capabilities, workflow, and scheduling limitations. May analyze or recommend commercially available software. May supervise computer programmers. Analyzes and tests computer programs or system to identify errors and ensure conformance to standard. Consults with staff and users to identify operating procedure problems. Formulates and reviews plans outlining steps required to develop programs to meet staff and user requirements. Coordinates installation of computer programs and operating systems and tests, maintains, and monitors computer system. Writes documentation to describe and develop installation and operating procedures of programs. Devises flow charts and diagrams to illustrate steps and to describe logical operational steps of program. Reads manuals, periodicals, and technical reports to learn how to develop programs to meet staff and user requirements. Reviews and analyzes computer printouts and performance indications to locate code problems. Assists staff and users to solve computer-related problems, such as malfunctions and program problems. Trains staff and users to use computer system and its programs. Modifies program to correct errors by correcting computer codes. Writes and revises program and system design procedures, test procedures, and quality standards. SKILLS—Troubleshooting: Determining causes of operating errors and deciding what to do about them. Programming: Writing computer programs for various purposes. Reading Comprehension: Understanding written sentences and paragraphs in work-related documents. Writing: Communicating effectively in writing as appropriate for the needs of the audience. Quality Control Analysis: Conducting tests and inspections of products, services, or processes to evaluate quality or performance.

GOE INFORMATION—Interest Area: 02. Science, Math, and Engineering. Work Group: 02.06. Mathematics and Computers. Other Job Titles in This Work Group: Actuaries; Computer and Information Scientists, Research; Computer Programmers; Computer Security Specialists; Computer Specialists, All Other; Computer Support Specialists; Database Administrators; Mathematical Science Occupations, All Other; Mathematical Technicians; Mathematicians; Network and Computer Systems Administrators; Network Systems and Data Communications Analysts; Operations Research Analysts; Statistical Assistants; Statisticians. **PERSONALITY TYPE**—Investigative. Investigative occupations frequently involve working with ideas and require an extensive amount of thinking. These occupations can involve searching for facts and figuring out problems mentally.

EDUCATION/TRAINING PROGRAM(S)—Business Systems Analysis and Design; Computer and Information Sciences, General; Computer Systems Analysis. **RELATED KNOWLEDGE/COURSES—Computers and Electronics:** Knowledge of circuit boards, processors, chips, electronic equipment, and computer hardware and software, including applications and programming. **English Language:** Knowledge of the structure and content of the English language, including the meaning and spelling of words, rules of composition, and grammar. **Education and Training:** Knowledge of principles and methods for curriculum and training design, teaching and instruction for individuals and groups, and the measurement of training effects. **Mathematics:** Knowledge of arithmetic, algebra, geometry, calculus, and statistics and their applications. **Customer and Personal Service:** Knowledge of principles and processes for providing customer and personal services. This includes customer needs assessment, meeting quality standards for services, and evaluation of customer satisfaction.

Conservation Scientists

- ▲ Education/Training Required: Bachelor's degree
- ▲ Annual Earnings: $47,140
- ▲ Growth: 8%
- ▲ Annual Job Openings: 1,000
- ▲ Self-Employed: 2.4%
- ▲ Part-Time: 6.6%

Manage, improve, and protect natural resources to maximize their use without damaging the environment. May conduct soil surveys and develop plans to eliminate soil erosion or to protect rangelands from fire and rodent damage. May instruct farmers, agricultural production managers, or ranchers in best ways to use crop rotation, contour plowing, or terracing to conserve soil and water; in the number and kind of livestock and forage plants best suited to particular ranges; and in range and farm improvements, such as fencing and reservoirs for stock watering. **SKILLS—** No data available.

GOE INFORMATION—Interest Area: 02. Science, Math, and Engineering. **Work Group:** 02.03. Life Sciences. **Other Job Titles in This Work Group:** Agricultural and Food Science Technicians; Agricultural Technicians; Animal Scientists; Biochemists; Biochemists and Biophysicists; Biological Scientists, All Other; Biolo-

gists; Biophysicists; Environmental Scientists and Specialists, Including Health; Epidemiologists; Food Science Technicians; Food Scientists and Technologists; Foresters; Life Scientists, All Other; Medical Scientists, Except Epidemiologists; Microbiologists; Plant Scientists; Range Managers; Soil and Plant Scientists; Soil Conservationists; Soil Scientists; Zoologists and Wildlife Biologists. **PERSONALITY TYPE**—No data available.

EDUCATION/TRAINING PROGRAM(S)—Conservation and Renewable Natural Resources, Other; Forest Management; Forestry and Related Sciences, Other; Forestry Sciences; Forestry, General; Natural Resources Conservation, General; Natural Resources Law Enforcement and Protective Services; Natural Resources Management and Policy; Natural Resources Management and Protective Services, Other; Wildlife and Wildlands Management. **RELATED KNOWLEDGE/ COURSES—**No data available.

Construction Managers

- ▲ Education/Training Required: Bachelor's degree
- ▲ Annual Earnings: $58,250
- ▲ Growth: 16%
- ▲ Annual Job Openings: 26,000
- ▲ Self-Employed: 1%
- ▲ Part-Time: 6.1%

Plan, direct, coordinate, or budget, usually through subordinate supervisory personnel, activities concerned with the construction and maintenance of structures, facilities, and systems. Participate in the conceptual development of a construction project and oversee its organization, scheduling, and implementation. Plans, organizes, and directs activities concerned with construction and maintenance of structures, facilities, and systems. Investigates reports of damage at construction sites to ensure proper procedures are being carried out. Dispatches workers to construction sites to work on specified project. Formulates reports concerning such areas as work progress, costs, and scheduling. Studies job specifications to plan and approve construction of project. Directs and supervises workers on construction site to ensure project meets specifications. Contracts workers to perform construction work in accordance with specifications. Interprets and explains plans and contract terms to administrative staff, workers, and clients. Requisitions supplies and materials to complete construction project. Inspects and reviews construction work, repair projects, and reports to ensure work conforms to specifications. Confers with supervisory personnel to discuss such matters as work procedures, complaints, and construction problems. **SKILLS—** Coordination: Adjusting actions in relation to others' actions. Management of Personnel Resources: Motivating, developing, and directing people as they work, identifying the best people for the job. Time Management: Managing one's own time and the time of others. Mathematics: Using mathematics to solve problems. Management of Financial Resources: Determining how money will be spent to get the work done and accounting for these expenditures. Judgment and Decision Making: Considering the relative costs and benefits of potential actions to choose the most

appropriate one. Reading Comprehension: Understanding written sentences and paragraphs in work-related documents.

GOE INFORMATION—Interest Area: 06. Construction, Mining, and Drilling. **Work Group:** 06.01. Managerial Work in Construction, Mining, and Drilling. **Other Job Titles in This Work Group:** First-Line Supervisors and Manager/Supervisors—Construction Trades Workers; First-Line Supervisors and Manager/Supervisors—Extractive Workers; First-Line Supervisors/Managers of Construction Trades and Extraction Workers. **PERSONALITY TYPE—**Enterprising. Enterprising occupations frequently involve starting up and carrying out projects. These occupations can involve leading people and making many decisions. They sometimes require risk taking and often deal with business.

EDUCATION/TRAINING PROGRAM(S)— Business Administration and Management, General; Construction/Building Technologist/Technician; Enterprise Management and Operation, General; Entrepreneurship; Operations Management and Supervision. **RELATED KNOWLEDGE/COURSES—Administration and Management:** Knowledge of business and management principles involved in strategic planning, resource allocation, human resources modeling, leadership technique, production methods, and coordination of people and resources. **Building and Construction:** Knowledge of materials, methods, and tools involved in the construction or repair of houses, buildings, or other structures, such as highways and roads. **Personnel and Human Resources:** Knowledge of principles and procedures for personnel recruitment, selection, training, compensation and benefits, labor relations and negotiation, and personnel information systems. **Public Safety and Security:**

Knowledge of relevant equipment, policies, procedures, and strategies to promote effective local, state, or national security operations for the protection of people, data, property, and institutions. **Principles of Mechanical Devices:** Knowledge of machines and tools, including their designs, uses, repair, and maintenance.

Copy Writers

- ▲ Education/Training Required: Bachelor's degree
- ▲ Annual Earnings: $42,270
- ▲ Growth: 28%
- ▲ Annual Job Openings: 18,000
- ▲ Self-Employed: 31.2%
- ▲ Part-Time: 18.5%

Write advertising copy for use by publication or broadcast media to promote sale of goods and services. Writes advertising copy for use by publication or broadcast media and revises copy according to supervisor's instructions. Writes articles, bulletins, sales letters, speeches, and other related informative and promotional material. Prepares advertising copy, using computer. Consults with sales media and marketing representatives to obtain information on product or service and discuss style and length of advertising copy. Reviews advertising trends, consumer surveys, and other data regarding marketing of goods and services to formulate approach. Obtains additional background and current development information through research and interview. **SKILLS**—Writing: Communicating effectively in writing as appropriate for the needs of the audience. Reading Comprehension: Understanding written sentences and paragraphs in work-related documents. Active Learning: Understanding the implications of new information for both current and future problem-solving and decision-making. Critical Thinking: Using logic and reasoning to identify the strengths and weaknesses of alternative solutions, conclusions, or approaches to problems. Active Listening: Giving full attention to what other people are saying, taking time to understand the points being made, asking questions as appropriate, and not interrupting at inappropriate times.

GOE INFORMATION—**Interest Area:** 01. Arts, Entertainment, and Media. **Work Group:** 01.02. Writing and Editing. **Other Job Titles in This Work Group:** Creative Writers; Editors; Poets and Lyricists; Technical Writers; Writers and Authors. **PERSONALITY TYPE**—Artistic. Artistic occupations frequently involve working with forms, designs, and patterns. They often require self-expression, and the work can be done without following a clear set of rules.

EDUCATION/TRAINING PROGRAM(S)— Broadcast Journalism; Business Communications; Communications, Other; English Creative Writing; Journalism; Mass Communications; Playwriting and Screenwriting; Technical and Business Writing. **RELATED KNOWLEDGE/COURSES**—**Sales and Marketing:** Knowledge of principles and methods for showing, promoting, and selling products or services. This includes marketing strategy and tactics, product demonstration, sales techniques, and sales control systems. **English Language:** Knowledge of the structure and content of the English language, including the meaning and spelling of words, rules of composition, and grammar. **Computers and Electronics:** Knowledge of circuit boards, processors, chips, electronic equipment, and computer hardware and software, including applications and programming. **Communications and Media:** Knowledge of media production, communication, and dissemination techniques and methods. This includes alternative ways to inform and entertain via written, oral, and visual media. **Clerical Studies:** Knowledge of administrative and clerical procedures and systems such as word processing, managing files and records, stenography and transcription, designing forms, and other office procedures and terminology.

Cost Estimators

▲ Education/Training Required: Bachelor's degree

▲ Annual Earnings: $45,800

▲ Growth: 16%

▲ Annual Job Openings: 28,000

▲ Self-Employed: 0%

▲ Part-Time: 9.4%

Prepare cost estimates for product manufacturing, construction projects, or services to aid management in bidding on or determining price of product or service. May specialize according to particular service performed or type of product manufactured. Analyzes blueprints, specifications, proposals, and other documentation to prepare time, cost, and labor estimates. Prepares estimates for selecting vendors or subcontractors and determining cost-effectiveness. Prepares time, cost, and labor estimates for products, projects, or services, applying specialized methodologies, techniques, or processes. Computes cost factors used for preparing estimates for management and determining cost-effectiveness. Prepares estimates used for management purposes, such as planning, organizing, and scheduling work. Reviews data to determine material and labor requirements and prepares itemized list. Conducts special studies to develop and establish standard hour and related cost data or to effect cost reduction. Consults with clients, vendors, or other individuals to discuss and formulate estimates and resolve issues. **SKILLS—Mathematics:** Using mathematics to solve problems. Reading Comprehension: Understanding written sentences and paragraphs in work-related documents. Writing: Communicating effectively in writing as appropriate for the needs of the audience. Active Learning: Understanding the implications of new information for both current and future problem-solving and decision-making. Complex Problem Solving: Identifying complex problems and reviewing related information to develop and evaluate options and implement solutions.

GOE INFORMATION—Interest Area: 13. General Management and Support. **Work Group:** 13.02. Management Support. **Other Job Titles in This Work Group:** Accountants; Accountants and Auditors; Appraisers and Assessors of Real Estate; Appraisers, Real Estate; Assessors; Auditors; Budget Analysts; Claims Adjusters, Examiners, and Investigators; Claims Examiners, Property and Casualty Insurance; Compensation, Benefits, and Job Analysis Specialists; Credit Analysts; Employment Interviewers, Private or Public Employment Service; Employment, Recruitment, and Placement Specialists; Financial Analysts; Human Resources, Training, and Labor Relations Specialists, All Other; Insurance Adjusters, Examiners, and Investigators; Insurance Appraisers, Auto Damage; Insurance Underwriters; Loan Counselors; Loan Officers; Logisticians; Management Analysts; Market Research Analysts; Personnel Recruiters; Purchasing Agents and Buyers, Farm Products; Purchasing Agents, Except Wholesale, Retail, and Farm Products; Tax Examiners, Collectors, and Revenue Agents; Training and Development Specialists; Wholesale and Retail Buyers, Except Farm Products. **PERSONALITY TYPE—Conventional.** Conventional occupations frequently involve following set procedures and routines. These occupations can include working with data and details more than with ideas. Usually there is a clear line of authority to follow.

EDUCATION/TRAINING PROGRAM(S)— Community Organization, Resources and Services; Operations Management and Supervision; Public Administration. **RELATED KNOWLEDGE/COURSES—Mathematics:** Knowledge of arithmetic, algebra, geometry, calculus, and statistics and their applications. **Production and Processing:** Knowledge of raw materials, production processes, quality control, costs, and other techniques for maximizing the effective manufacture and distribution of goods. **Economics and Accounting:** Knowledge of economic and accounting principles and practices, the financial markets, banking, and the analysis and reporting of financial data. **Building and Construction:** Knowledge of materials, methods, and tools involved in the construction or repair of houses, buildings, or other structures, such as highways and roads. **Administration and Management:** Knowledge of business and management principles involved in strategic planning, resource allocation, human resources modeling, leadership technique, production methods, and coordination of people and resources.

Counseling Psychologists

- ▲ Education/Training Required: Master's degree
- ▲ Annual Earnings: $48,320
- ▲ Growth: 18%
- ▲ Annual Job Openings: 18,000
- ▲ Self-Employed: 43.7%
- ▲ Part-Time: 23.4%

Assess and evaluate individuals' problems through the use of case history, interview, and observation and provide individual or group counseling services to assist individuals in achieving more effective personal, social, educational, and vocational development and adjustment. Counsels clients to assist them in understanding personal or interactive problems, defining goals, and developing realistic action plans. Collects information about individuals or clients, using interviews, case histories, observational techniques, and other assessment methods. Selects, administers, or interprets psychological tests to assess intelligence, aptitude, ability, or interests. Evaluates results of counseling methods to determine the reliability and validity of treatments. Analyzes data, such as interview notes, test results, and reference manuals and texts, to identify symptoms and diagnose the nature of client's problems. Advises clients on the potential benefits of counseling or makes referrals to specialists or other institutions for non-counseling problems. Develops therapeutic and treatment plans based on individual interests, abilities, or needs of clients. Consults with other professionals to discuss therapy or treatment and counseling resources or techniques and to share occupational information. Conducts research to develop or improve diagnostic or therapeutic counseling techniques. **SKILLS—Social Perceptiveness:** Being aware of others' reactions and understanding why they react as they do. Active Listening: Giving full attention to what other people are saying, taking time to understand the points being made, asking questions as appropriate, and not interrupting at inappropriate times. Reading Comprehension: Understanding written sentences and paragraphs in work-related documents. Critical Thinking: Using logic and reasoning to identify the strengths and weaknesses of alternative solutions, conclusions, or approaches to problems. Active Learning: Understanding the implications of new information for both current and future problem-solving and decision-making. Learning Strategies: Selecting and using training/instructional methods and procedures appropriate for the situation when learning or teaching new things.

GOE INFORMATION—Interest Area: 12. Education and Social Service. **Work Group:** 12.02. Social Services. **Other Job Titles in This Work Group:** Child, Family, and School Social Workers; Clergy; Clinical Psychologists; Clinical, Counseling, and School Psychologists; Community and Social Service Specialists, All Other; Counselors, All Other; Directors, Religious Activities and Education; Marriage and Family Therapists; Medical and Public Health Social Workers; Mental Health and Substance Abuse Social Workers; Mental Health Counselors; Probation Officers and Correctional Treatment Specialists; Rehabilitation Counselors; Religious Workers, All Other; Residential Advisors; Social and Human Service Assistants; Social Workers, All Other; Substance Abuse and Behavioral Disorder Counselors. **PERSONALITY TYPE—Social.** Social occupations frequently involve working with, communicating with, and teaching people. These occupations often involve helping or providing service to others.

EDUCATION/TRAINING PROGRAM(S)— Clinical Psychology; Counseling Psychology; Developmental and Child Psychology; Educational Psychology; Psychology, General; School Psychology. **RELATED KNOWLEDGE/COURSES—Therapy and Counseling:** Knowledge of principles, methods, and procedures for diagnosis, treatment, and rehabilitation of physical and mental dysfunctions and for career counseling and guidance. **Psychology:** Knowledge of human behavior and performance; individual differences in ability, personality, and interests; learning and motivation; psychological research methods; and the assessment and treatment of behavioral and affective disorders. **Mathematics:** Knowledge of arithmetic, algebra, geometry, calculus, and statistics and their applications. **Communications and Media:** Knowledge of media production, communication, and dissemination techniques and methods. This includes alternative ways to inform and entertain via written, oral, and visual media. **English Language:** Knowledge of the structure and content of the English language, including the meaning and spelling of words, rules of composition, and grammar.

Creative Writers

▲ Education/Training Required: Bachelor's degree

▲ Annual Earnings: $42,270

▲ Growth: 28%

▲ Annual Job Openings: 18,000

▲ Self-Employed: 31.2%

▲ Part-Time: 18.5%

Create original written works, such as plays or prose, for publication or performance. Writes fiction or nonfiction prose work, such as short story, novel, biography, article, descriptive or critical analysis, or essay. Writes play or script for moving pictures or television, based on original ideas or adapted from fictional, historical, or narrative sources. Organizes material for project, plans arrangement or outline, and writes synopsis. Collaborates with other writers on specific projects. Confers with client, publisher, or producer to discuss development changes or revisions. Conducts research to obtain factual information and authentic detail, utilizing sources such as newspaper accounts, diaries, and interviews. Reviews, submits for approval, and revises written material to meet personal standards and satisfy needs of client, publisher, director, or producer. Selects subject or theme for writing project based on personal interest and writing specialty or assignment from publisher, client, producer, or director. Develops factors, such as theme, plot, characterization, psychological analysis, historical environment, action, and dialogue, to create material. Writes humorous material for publication or performance, such as comedy routines, gags, comedy shows, or scripts for entertainers. **SKILLS—Writing:** Communicating effectively in writing as appro-priate for the needs of the audience. Reading Comprehension: Understanding written sentences and paragraphs in work-related documents. Coordination: Adjusting actions in relation to others' actions. Critical Thinking: Using logic and reasoning to identify the strengths and weaknesses of alternative solutions, conclusions, or approaches to problems. Complex Problem Solving: Identifying complex problems and reviewing related information to develop and evaluate options and implement solutions.

GOE INFORMATION—Interest Area: 01. Arts, Entertainment, and Media. **Work Group:** 01.02. Writing and Editing. **Other Job Titles in This Work Group:** Copy Writers; Editors; Poets and Lyricists; Technical Writers; Writers and Authors. **PERSONALITY TYPE—Artistic.** Artistic occupations frequently involve working with forms, designs, and patterns. They often require self-expression, and the work can be done without following a clear set of rules.

EDUCATION/TRAINING PROGRAM(S)— Broadcast Journalism; Business Communications; Communications, Other; English Creative Writing; Journalism; Mass Communications; Playwriting and Screenwriting; Technical and Business Writing. **RELATED KNOWL-**

EDGE/COURSES—**English Language:** Knowledge of the structure and content of the English language, including the meaning and spelling of words, rules of composition, and grammar. **Communications and Media:** Knowledge of media production, communication, and dissemination techniques and methods. This includes alternative ways to inform and entertain via written, oral, and visual media. **Computers and Electronics:** Knowledge of circuit boards, processors, chips, electronic equipment, and computer hardware and software, including applications and programming. **Fine Arts:** Knowledge of

the theory and techniques required to compose, produce, and perform works of music, dance, visual arts, drama, and sculpture. **Psychology:** Knowledge of human behavior and performance; individual differences in ability, personality, and interests; learning and motivation; psychological research methods; and the assessment and treatment of behavioral and affective disorders. **Clerical Studies:** Knowledge of administrative and clerical procedures and systems such as word processing, managing files and records, stenography and transcription, designing forms, and other office procedures and terminology.

Credit Analysts

- ▲ Education/Training Required: Bachelor's degree
- ▲ Annual Earnings: $40,180
- ▲ Growth: 16%
- ▲ Annual Job Openings: 7,000
- ▲ Self-Employed: 0%
- ▲ Part-Time: 7.2%

Analyze current credit data and financial statements of individuals or firms to determine the degree of risk involved in extending credit or lending money. Prepare reports with this credit information for use in decision-making. Analyzes credit data and financial statements to determine degree of risk involved in extending credit or lending money. Compares liquidity, profitability, and credit history with similar establishments of same industry and geographic location. Consults with customers to resolve complaints, verify financial and credit transactions, and adjust accounts as needed. Reviews individual or commercial customer files to identify and select delinquent accounts for collection. Confers with credit association and other business representatives to exchange credit information. Completes loan application, including credit analysis and summary of loan request, and submits to loan committee for approval. Evaluates customer records and recommends payment plan based on earnings, savings data, payment history, and purchase activity. Analyzes financial data, such as income growth, quality of management, and market share, to determine profitability of loan. Generates financial ratios, using computer program, to evaluate customer's financial status. **SKILLS**—Reading Comprehension: Understanding writ-

ten sentences and paragraphs in work-related documents. Critical Thinking: Using logic and reasoning to identify the strengths and weaknesses of alternative solutions, conclusions, or approaches to problems. Active Listening: Giving full attention to what other people are saying, taking time to understand the points being made, asking questions as appropriate, and not interrupting at inappropriate times. Judgment and Decision Making: Considering the relative costs and benefits of potential actions to choose the most appropriate one. Speaking: Talking to others to convey information effectively. Mathematics: Using mathematics to solve problems.

GOE INFORMATION—Interest Area: 13. General Management and Support. **Work Group:** 13.02. Management Support. **Other Job Titles in This Work Group:** Accountants; Accountants and Auditors; Appraisers and Assessors of Real Estate; Appraisers, Real Estate; Assessors; Auditors; Budget Analysts; Claims Adjusters, Examiners, and Investigators; Claims Examiners, Property and Casualty Insurance; Compensation, Benefits, and Job Analysis Specialists; Cost Estimators; Employment Interviewers, Private or Public Employment Service; Employment, Recruitment, and Placement Specialists; Financial

Analysts; Human Resources, Training, and Labor Relations Specialists, All Other; Insurance Adjusters, Examiners, and Investigators; Insurance Appraisers, Auto Damage; Insurance Underwriters; Loan Counselors; Loan Officers; Logisticians; Management Analysts; Market Research Analysts; Personnel Recruiters; Purchasing Agents and Buyers, Farm Products; Purchasing Agents, Except Wholesale, Retail, and Farm Products; Tax Examiners, Collectors, and Revenue Agents; Training and Development Specialists; Wholesale and Retail Buyers, Except Farm Products. **PERSONALITY TYPE**—Conventional. Conventional occupations frequently involve following set procedures and routines. These occupations can include working with data and details more than with ideas. Usually there is a clear line of authority to follow.

EDUCATION/TRAINING PROGRAM(S)— Accounting; Finance, General. **RELATED KNOWLEDGE/COURSES**—**Economics and Accounting:** Knowledge of economic and accounting principles and practices, the financial markets, banking, and the analysis and reporting of financial data. **Mathematics:** Knowledge of arithmetic, algebra, geometry, calculus, and statistics and their applications. **English Language:** Knowledge of the structure and content of the English language, including the meaning and spelling of words, rules of composition, and grammar. **Computers and Electronics:** Knowledge of circuit boards, processors, chips, electronic equipment, and computer hardware and software, including applications and programming. **Law and Government:** Knowledge of laws, legal codes, court procedures, precedents, government regulations, executive orders, agency rules, and the democratic political process. **Customer and Personal Service:** Knowledge of principles and processes for providing customer and personal services. This includes customer needs assessment, meeting quality standards for services, and evaluation of customer satisfaction. **Geography:** Knowledge of principles and methods for describing the features of land, sea, and air masses, including their physical characteristics, locations, interrelationships, and distribution of plant, animal, and human life.

Criminal Justice and Law Enforcement Teachers, Postsecondary

- ▲ Education/Training Required: Master's degree
- ▲ Annual Earnings: $41,350
- ▲ Growth: 24% for all Postsecondary Teachers
- ▲ Annual Job Openings: 184,000 for all Postsecondary Teachers
- ▲ Self-Employed: 0%
- ▲ Part-Time: 32.3% for all Postsecondary Teachers

Teach courses in criminal justice, corrections, and law enforcement administration. **SKILLS**— No data available.

GOE INFORMATION—**Interest Area:** 12. Education and Social Service. **Work Group:** 12.03. Educational Services. **Other Job Titles in This Work Group:** Adult Literacy, Remedial Education, and GED Teachers and Instructors; Agricultural Sciences Teachers, Postsecondary; Anthropology and Archeology Teachers, Postsecondary; Architecture Teachers, Postsecondary; Archivists; Area, Ethnic, and Cultural Studies Teachers, Postsecondary; Art, Drama, and Music Teachers, Postsecondary; Atmospheric, Earth, Marine, and Space Sciences Teachers, Postsecondary; Audio-Visual Collections Specialists; Biological Science Teachers, Postsecondary; Business Teachers, Postsecondary; Chemistry Teachers, Postsecondary; Child Care Workers; Communications Teachers, Postsecondary; Computer Science Teachers, Postsecondary; Curators; Economics Teachers, Postsecondary; Education Teachers, Postsecondary; Educational Psychologists; Educational, Vocational, and School Counselors; Elementary School Teachers, Except Special

Education; Engineering Teachers, Postsecondary; English Language and Literature Teachers, Postsecondary; Environmental Science Teachers, Postsecondary; Farm and Home Management Advisors; Foreign Language and Literature Teachers, Postsecondary; Forestry and Conservation Science Teachers, Postsecondary; Geography Teachers, Postsecondary; Graduate Teaching Assistants; Health Specialties Teachers, Postsecondary; History Teachers, Postsecondary; Home Economics Teachers, Postsecondary; Kindergarten Teachers, Except Special Education; Law Teachers, Postsecondary; Librarians; Library Assistants, Clerical; Library Science Teachers, Postsecondary; Library Technicians; others. **PERSONALITY TYPE**—No data available.

EDUCATION/TRAINING PROGRAM(S)—Criminal Justice/Law Enforcement Administration; Teacher Education, Specific Academic and Vocational Programs. **RELATED KNOWLEDGE/COURSES**—No data available.

Database Administrators

- ▲ Education/Training Required: Bachelor's degree
- ▲ Annual Earnings: $51,990
- ▲ Growth: 66%
- ▲ Annual Job Openings: 8,000
- ▲ Self-Employed: 2.7%
- ▲ Part-Time: 5.7%

Coordinate changes to computer databases; test and implement the database, applying knowledge of database management systems. May plan, coordinate, and implement security measures to safeguard computer databases. Writes logical and physical database descriptions including location, space, access method, and security. Trains users and answers questions. Specifies user and user access levels for each segment of database. Revises company definition of data as defined in data dictionary. Confers with coworkers to determine scope and limitations of project. Reviews procedures in database management system manuals for making changes to database. Reviews workflow charts developed by programmer analyst to understand tasks computer will perform, such as updating records. Codes database descriptions and specifies identifiers of database to management system or directs others in coding descriptions. Tests, corrects errors, and modifies changes to programs or to database. Reviews project request describing database user needs, estimating time and cost required to accomplish project. Directs programmers and analysts to make changes to database management system. Selects and enters codes to monitor database performance and to create production database. Develops data model describing data elements and how they are used, following procedures and using pen, template or computer software. Establishes and calculates optimum values for database parameters, using manuals and calculator. **SKILLS**—Programming: Writing computer programs for various purposes. Mathematics: Using mathematics to solve problems. Operations Analysis: Analyzing needs and product requirements to create a design. Reading Comprehension: Understanding written sentences and paragraphs in work-related documents. Critical Thinking: Using logic and reasoning to identify the strengths and weaknesses of alternative solutions, conclusions, or approaches to problems.

GOE INFORMATION—**Interest Area:** 02. Science, Math, and Engineering. **Work Group:** 02.06. Mathematics and Computers. **Other Job Titles in This Work Group:** Actuaries; Computer and Information Scientists, Research; Computer Programmers; Computer Security Specialists; Computer Specialists, All Other; Computer Support Specialists; Computer Systems Analysts; Mathematical Science Occupations, All Other; Mathematical Technicians; Mathematicians; Network and Computer Systems Administrators; Network Systems and Data Communications Analysts; Operations Research Analysts; Statistical Assistants; Statisticians. **PERSONALITY TYPE**—Investigative. Investigative occupations frequently involve working with ideas and require an extensive amount of thinking. These occupations can involve searching for facts and figuring out problems mentally.

EDUCATION/TRAINING PROGRAM(S)— Business Systems Analysis and Design; Computer and Information Sciences, General; Computer Systems Analysis; Management Information Systems and Business Data Processing. **RELATED KNOWLEDGE/ COURSES—Computers and Electronics:** Knowledge of circuit boards, processors, chips, electronic equipment, and computer hardware and software, including applications and programming. **Administration and**

Management: Knowledge of business and management principles involved in strategic planning, resource allocation, human resources modeling, leadership technique, production methods, and coordination of people and resources. **Mathematics:** Knowledge of arithmetic, algebra, geometry, calculus, and statistics and their applications. **English Language:** Knowledge of the structure and content of the English language, including the meaning and spelling of words, rules of composition, and grammar. **Education and Training:** Knowledge of principles and methods for curriculum and training design, teaching and instruction for individuals and groups, and the measurement of training effects.

Dental Hygienists

- ▲ Education/Training Required: Associate's degree
- ▲ Annual Earnings: $51,330
- ▲ Growth: 37%
- ▲ Annual Job Openings: 5,000
- ▲ Self-Employed: 1.6%
- ▲ Part-Time: 22.9%

Clean teeth and examine oral areas, head, and neck for signs of oral disease. May educate patients on oral hygiene, take and develop X rays, or apply fluoride or sealants. Cleans calcareous deposits, accretions, and stains from teeth and beneath margins of gums, using dental instruments. Charts conditions of decay and disease for diagnosis and treatment by dentist. Examines gums, using probes, to locate periodontal recessed gums and signs of gum disease. Administers local anesthetic agents. Exposes and develops X-ray film. Applies fluorides and other cavity preventing agents to arrest dental decay. Removes sutures and dressings. Makes impressions for study casts. Places, carves, and finishes amalgam restorations. Feels and visually examines gums for sores and signs of disease. Feels lymph nodes under patient's chin to detect swelling or tenderness that could indicate presence of oral cancer. Places and removes rubber dams, matrices, and temporary restorations. Removes excess cement from coronal surfaces of teeth. Conducts dental health clinics for community groups to augment services of dentist. Provides clinical services and health education to improve and maintain oral health of schoolchildren.

SKILLS—Reading Comprehension: Understanding written sentences and paragraphs in work-related documents. **Active Learning:** Understanding the implications of new information for both current and future problem-solving and decision-making. **Speaking:** Talking to others to convey information effectively. **Critical Thinking:** Using logic and reasoning to identify the strengths and weaknesses of alternative solutions, conclusions, or approaches to problems. **Service Orientation:** Actively looking for ways to help people. **Science:** Using scientific rules and methods to solve problems.

GOE INFORMATION—Interest Area: 14. Medical and Health Services. **Work Group:** 14.03. Dentistry. **Other Job Titles in This Work Group:** Dental Assistants; Dentists, All Other Specialists; Dentists, General; Oral and Maxillofacial Surgeons; Orthodontists; Prosthodontists. **PERSONALITY TYPE—Social.** Social occupations frequently involve working with, communicating with, and teaching people. These occupations often involve helping or providing service to others.

EDUCATION/TRAINING PROGRAM(S)—Dental Hygienist. **RELATED KNOWLEDGE/ COURSES—Medicine and Dentistry:** Knowledge of the information and techniques needed to diagnose and treat human injuries, diseases, and deformities. This includes symptoms, treatment alternatives, drug properties and interactions, and preventive health-care measures. **Biology:** Knowledge of plant and animal organisms and their tissues, cells, functions, interdependencies, and interactions with each other and the environment. **Education and Training:** Knowledge of principles and methods for curriculum and training design, teaching and instruction for individuals and groups, and the measurement of training effects. **English Language:** Knowledge of the structure and content of the English language, including the meaning and spelling of words, rules of composition, and grammar. **Customer and Personal Service:** Knowledge of principles and processes for providing customer and personal services. This includes customer needs assessment, meeting quality standards for services, and evaluation of customer satisfaction.

Diagnostic Medical Sonographers

- ▲ Education/Training Required: Associate's degree
- ▲ Annual Earnings: $44,820
- ▲ Growth: 26%
- ▲ Annual Job Openings: 3,000
- ▲ Self-Employed: 4%
- ▲ Part-Time: 22.3%

Produce ultrasonic recordings of internal organs for use by physicians. SKILLS—No data available.

GOE INFORMATION—Interest Area: 14. Medical and Health Services. **Work Group:** 14.05. Medical Technology. **Other Job Titles in This Work Group:** Cardiovascular Technologists and Technicians; Health Technologists and Technicians, All Other; Medical and Clinical Laboratory Technicians; Medical and Clinical Laboratory Technologists; Medical Equipment Preparers; Nuclear Medicine Technologists; Orthotists and Prosthetists; Radiologic Technicians; Radiologic Technologists; Radiologic Technologists and Technicians. **PERSONALITY TYPE—**No data available.

EDUCATION/TRAINING PROGRAM(S)—Diagnostic Medical Sonography; Health and Medical Diagnostic and Treatment Services, Other. **RELATED KNOWLEDGE/COURSES—**No data available.

Dietitians and Nutritionists

- ▲ Education/Training Required: Bachelor's degree
- ▲ Annual Earnings: $38,450
- ▲ Growth: 15%
- ▲ Annual Job Openings: 5,000
- ▲ Self-Employed: 13.2%
- ▲ Part-Time: 29.1%

Plan and conduct food service or nutritional programs to assist in the promotion of health and control of disease. May supervise activities of a department providing quantity food services, counsel individuals, or conduct nutritional research. Develops and implements dietary-care plans based on assessments of nutritional needs, diet restrictions, and other current health plans. Instructs patients and their families in nutritional principles, dietary plans, and food selection and preparation. Confers with design, building, and equipment personnel to plan for construction and remodeling of food service units. Plans and prepares grant proposals to request program funding. Writes research reports and other publications to document and communicate research findings. Develops curriculum and prepares manuals, visual aids, course outlines, and other materials used in teaching. Inspects meals served for conformance to prescribed diets and standards of palatability and appearance. Plans, conducts, and evaluates dietary, nutritional, and epidemiological research and analyzes findings for practical applications. Evaluates nutritional care plans and provides follow-up on continuity of care. Supervises activities of workers engaged in planning, preparing, and serving meals. Plans, organizes, and conducts training programs in dietetics, nutrition, and institutional management and administration for medical students and hospital personnel. Monitors food service operations and ensures conformance to nutritional and quality standards. Consults with physicians and health care personnel to determine nutritional needs and diet restrictions of patient or client. **SKILLS**—Writing: Communicating effectively in writing as appropriate for the needs of the audience. Reading Comprehension: Understanding written sentences and paragraphs in work-related documents. Management of Financial Resources: Determining how money will be spent to get the work done and accounting for these expenditures. Critical Thinking: Using logic and reasoning to identify the strengths and weaknesses of alternative solutions, conclusions, or approaches to problems. Active Learning: Understanding the implications of new information for

both current and future problem-solving and decision-making.

GOE INFORMATION—**Interest Area:** 14. Medical and Health Services. **Work Group:** 14.08. Health Protection and Promotion. **Other Job Titles in This Work Group:** Athletic Trainers; Dietetic Technicians; Health Educators. **PERSONALITY TYPE**—Investigative. Investigative occupations frequently involve working with ideas and require an extensive amount of thinking. These occupations can involve searching for facts and figuring out problems mentally.

EDUCATION/TRAINING PROGRAM(S)—Dietetics/Human Nutritional Services; Food Systems Administration; Foods and Nutrition Science; Foods and Nutrition Studies, General; Foods and Nutrition Studies, Other; Medical Dietician. **RELATED KNOWLEDGE/COURSES**—**English Language:** Knowledge of the structure and content of the English language, including the meaning and spelling of words, rules of composition, and grammar. **Education and Training:** Knowledge of principles and methods for curriculum and training design, teaching and instruction for individuals and groups, and the measurement of training effects. **Biology:** Knowledge of plant and animal organisms and their tissues, cells, functions, interdependencies, and interactions with each other and the environment. **Administration and Management:** Knowledge of business and management principles involved in strategic planning, resource allocation, human resources modeling, leadership technique, production methods, and coordination of people and resources. **Food Production:** Knowledge of techniques and equipment for planting, growing, and harvesting food products (both plant and animal) for consumption, including storage/handling techniques.

Directors—Stage, Motion Pictures, Television, and Radio

- ▲ Education/Training Required: Work experience, plus degree
- ▲ Annual Earnings: $41,030
- ▲ Growth: 27%
- ▲ Annual Job Openings: 11,000
- ▲ Self-Employed: 23.7%
- ▲ Part-Time: 25.3%

Interpret script, conduct rehearsals, and direct activities of cast and technical crew for stage, motion pictures, television, or radio programs. Reads and rehearses cast to develop performance based on script interpretations. Directs cast, crew, and technicians during production or recording and filming in studio or on location. Directs live broadcasts, films and recordings, or non-broadcast programming for public entertainment or education. Establishes pace of program and sequences of scenes according to time requirements and cast and set accessibility. Approves equipment and elements required for production, such as scenery, lights, props, costumes, choreography, and music. Auditions and selects cast and technical staff. Cuts and edits film or tape to integrate component parts of film into desired sequence. Reviews educational material to gather information for scripts. Writes and compiles letters, memos, notes, scripts, and other program material, using computer. Compiles cue words and phrases and cues announcers, cast members, and technicians during performances. Interprets stage-set diagrams to determine stage layout and supervises placement of equipment and scenery. Coaches performers in acting techniques to develop and improve performance and image. Confers with technical directors, managers, and writers to discuss details of production, such as photography, script, music, sets, and costumes. **SKILLS—** Coordination: Adjusting actions in relation to others' actions. Reading Comprehension: Understanding written sentences and paragraphs in work-related documents. Instructing: Teaching others how to do something. Speaking: Talking to others to convey information effectively. Management of Personnel Resources: Motivating, developing, and directing people as they work, identifying the best people for the job. Critical Thinking: Using logic and reasoning to identify the strengths and weaknesses of alternative solutions, conclusions, or approaches to problems.

GOE INFORMATION—Interest Area: 01. Arts, Entertainment, and Media. **Work Group:** 01.05. Per-

forming Arts. **Other Job Titles in This Work Group:** Actors; Choreographers; Composers; Dancers; Music Arrangers and Orchestrators; Music Directors; Music Directors and Composers; Musicians and Singers; Musicians, Instrumental; Public Address System and Other Announcers; Radio and Television Announcers; Singers; Talent Directors. **PERSONALITY TYPE—**Artistic. Artistic occupations frequently involve working with forms, designs, and patterns. They often require self-expression, and the work can be done without following a clear set of rules.

EDUCATION/TRAINING PROGRAM(S)— Acting and Directing; Drama/Theater Arts, General; Drama/Theater Literature, History and Criticism; Dramatic/Theater Arts and Stagecraft, Other; Film/Cinema Studies; Film-Video Making/Cinematography and Production; Radio and Television Broadcasting. **RELATED KNOWLEDGE/COURSES—Fine Arts:** Knowledge of the theory and techniques required to compose, produce, and perform works of music, dance, visual arts, drama, and sculpture. **Administration and Management:** Knowledge of business and management principles involved in strategic planning, resource allocation, human resources modeling, leadership technique, production methods, and coordination of people and resources. **Communications and Media:** Knowledge of media production, communication, and dissemination techniques and methods. This includes alternative ways to inform and entertain via written, oral, and visual media. **English Language:** Knowledge of the structure and content of the English language, including the meaning and spelling of words, rules of composition, and grammar. **Computers and Electronics:** Knowledge of circuit boards, processors, chips, electronic equipment, and computer hardware and software, including applications and programming. **Clerical Studies:** Knowledge of administrative and clerical procedures and systems such as word processing, managing files and records, stenography and transcription, designing forms, and other office procedures and terminology.

Directors, Religious Activities and Education

- ▲ Education/Training Required: Bachelor's degree
- ▲ Annual Earnings: $27,000
- ▲ Growth: 16%
- ▲ Annual Job Openings: 23,000
- ▲ Self-Employed: 1.2%
- ▲ Part-Time: 14%

Direct and coordinate activities of a denominational group to meet religious needs of students. Plan, direct, or coordinate church school programs designed to promote religious education among church membership. May provide counseling and guidance relative to marital, health, financial, and religious problems. Coordinates activities with religious advisers, councils, and university officials to meet religious needs of students. Assists and advises groups in promoting interfaith understanding. Solicits support, participation, and interest in religious education programs from congregation members, organizations, officials, and clergy. Orders and distributes school supplies. Analyzes revenue and program cost data to determine budget priorities. Interprets religious education to public through speaking, leading discussions, and writing articles for local and national publications. Interprets policies of university to community religious workers. Analyzes member participation and changes in congregation emphasis to determine needs for religious education. Plans and conducts conferences dealing with interpretation of religious ideas and convictions. Promotes student participation in extracurricular congregational activities. Counsels individuals regarding marital, health, financial, and religious problems. Plans congregational activities and projects to encourage participation in religious education programs. Supervises instructional staff in religious education program. Develops, organizes, and directs study courses and religious education programs within congregation. **SKILLS**—Social Perceptiveness: Being aware of others' reactions and understanding why they react as they do. Reading Comprehension: Understanding written sentences and paragraphs in work-related documents. Writing: Communicating effectively in writing as appropriate for the needs of the audience. Active Listening: Giving full attention to what other people are saying, taking time to understand the

points being made, asking questions as appropriate, and not interrupting at inappropriate times. Service Orientation: Actively looking for ways to help people. Speaking: Talking to others to convey information effectively.

GOE INFORMATION—**Interest Area:** 12. Education and Social Service. **Work Group:** 12.02. Social Services. **Other Job Titles in This Work Group:** Child, Family, and School Social Workers; Clergy; Clinical Psychologists; Clinical, Counseling, and School Psychologists; Community and Social Service Specialists, All Other; Counseling Psychologists; Counselors, All Other; Marriage and Family Therapists; Medical and Public Health Social Workers; Mental Health and Substance Abuse Social Workers; Mental Health Counselors; Probation Officers and Correctional Treatment Specialists; Rehabilitation Counselors; Religious Workers, All Other; Residential Advisors; Social and Human Service Assistants; Social Workers, All Other; Substance Abuse and Behavioral Disorder Counselors. **PERSONALITY TYPE**—Social. Social occupations frequently involve working with, communicating with, and teaching people. These occupations often involve helping or providing service to others.

EDUCATION/TRAINING PROGRAM(S)—Bible/Biblical Studies; Missions/Missionary Studies and Misology; Religious Education. **RELATED KNOWLEDGE/COURSES**—**Administration and Management:** Knowledge of business and management principles involved in strategic planning, resource allocation, human resources modeling, leadership technique, production methods, and coordination of people and resources. **Therapy and Counseling:** Knowledge of principles, methods, and procedures for diagnosis, treatment, and rehabilitation of physical and mental dysfunctions and for career counseling and guidance. **Psychology:** Knowledge of human behavior and performance; individual differences in ability, personality, and interests; learning and motivation; psychological research methods; and the assessment and treatment of behavioral and affective disorders. **Education and Training:** Knowledge of principles and methods for curriculum and training design, teaching and instruction for individuals and groups, and the measurement of training effects. **Sociology and Anthropology:** Knowledge of group behavior and dynamics, societal trends and influences, human migrations, ethnicity, cultures, and their history and origins. **Philosophy and Theology:** Knowledge of different philosophical systems and religions. This includes their basic principles, values, ethics, ways of thinking, customs, and practices and their impact on human culture. **English Language:** Knowledge of the structure and content of the English language, including the meaning and spelling of words, rules of composition, and grammar.

Economics Teachers, Postsecondary

▲ Education/Training Required: Master's degree

▲ Annual Earnings: $61,180

▲ Growth: 24% for all Postsecondary Teachers

▲ Annual Job Openings: 184,000 for all Postsecondary Teachers

▲ Self-Employed: 0%

▲ Part-Time: 32.3% for all Postsecondary Teachers

Teach courses in economics. Prepares and delivers lectures to students. Compiles bibliographies of specialized materials for outside reading assignments. Directs research of other teachers or graduate students working for advanced academic degrees. Serves on faculty committee providing professional consulting services to government and industry. Acts as adviser to student organizations. Conducts research in particular field of knowledge and publishes findings in professional journals. Advises students on academic and vocational curricula. Stimulates class discussions. Compiles, administers, and grades examinations or assigns this work to others. **SKILLS**—Reading Comprehension: Understanding written sentences and paragraphs in work-related documents. Instructing: Teaching others how to do something. Active Learning: Understanding the implications of new information for both current and future problem-solving and decision-making. Speaking: Talking to others to convey information effectively. Learning Strategies: Selecting and using training/instructional methods and procedures appropriate for the situation when learning or teaching new things. Active Listening: Giving full attention to what other people are saying, taking time to understand the points being made, asking questions as appropriate, and not interrupting at inappropriate times. Writing: Communicating effectively in writing as appropriate for the needs of the audience.

GOE INFORMATION—Interest Area: 12. Education and Social Service. **Work Group:** 12.03. Educational Services. **Other Job Titles in This Work Group:** Adult Literacy, Remedial Education, and GED Teachers and Instructors; Agricultural Sciences Teachers, Postsecondary; Anthropology and Archeology Teachers, Postsecondary; Architecture Teachers, Postsecondary; Archivists; Area, Ethnic, and Cultural Studies Teachers, Postsecondary; Art, Drama, and Music Teachers, Postsecondary; Atmospheric, Earth, Marine, and Space Sciences Teachers, Postsecondary; Audio-Visual Collections Specialists; Biological Science Teachers, Postsecondary; Business Teachers, Postsecondary; Chemistry Teachers, Postsecondary; Child Care Workers; Communications Teachers, Postsecondary; Computer Science Teachers, Postsecondary; Criminal Justice and Law Enforcement Teachers, Postsecondary; Curators; Education Teachers, Postsecondary; Educational Psychologists; Educational, Vocational, and School Counselors; Elementary School Teachers, Except Special Education; Engineering

Teachers, Postsecondary; English Language and Literature Teachers, Postsecondary; Environmental Science Teachers, Postsecondary; Farm and Home Management Advisors; Foreign Language and Literature Teachers, Postsecondary; Forestry and Conservation Science Teachers, Postsecondary; Geography Teachers, Postsecondary; Graduate Teaching Assistants; Health Specialties Teachers, Postsecondary; History Teachers, Postsecondary; Home Economics Teachers, Postsecondary; Kindergarten Teachers, Except Special Education; Law Teachers, Postsecondary; Librarians; Library Assistants, Clerical; Library Science Teachers, Postsecondary; others. **PERSONALITY TYPE**—Social. Social occupations frequently involve working with, communicating with, and teaching people. These occupations often involve helping or providing service to others.

EDUCATION/TRAINING PROGRAM(S)— Applied and Resource Economics; Business/Managerial Economics; Development Economics and International Development; Econometrics and Quantitative Economics; Economics, General; Economics, Other; International Economics; Social Science Teacher Education. **RELATED KNOWLEDGE/COURSES—Education and Training:** Knowledge of principles and methods for curriculum and training design, teaching and instruction for individuals and groups, and the measurement of training effects. **Sociology and Anthropology:** Knowledge of group behavior and dynamics, societal trends and influences, human migrations, ethnicity, cultures, and their history and origins. **Psychology:** Knowledge of human behavior and performance; individual differences in ability, personality, and interests; learning and motivation; psychological research methods; and the assessment and treatment of behavioral and affective disorders. **History and Archeology:** Knowledge of historical events and their causes, indicators, and effects on civilizations and cultures. **English Language:** Knowledge of the structure and content of the English language, including the meaning and spelling of words, rules of composition, and grammar.

Economists

▲ Education/Training Required: Bachelor's degree

▲ Annual Earnings: $64,830

▲ Growth: 18%

▲ Annual Job Openings: 3,000

▲ Self-Employed: 18.9%

▲ Part-Time: 8.8%

Conduct research, prepare reports, or formulate plans to aid in solution of economic problems arising from production and distribution of goods and services. May collect and process economic and statistical data using econometric and sampling techniques. Studies economic and statistical data in area of specialization, such as finance, labor, or agriculture. Supervises research projects and students' study projects. Assigns work to staff. Teaches theories, principles, and methods of economics. Testifies at regulatory or legislative hearings to present recommendations. Provides advice and consultation to business and public and private agencies. Develops economic guidelines and standards and prepares points of view used in forecasting trends and formulating economic policy. Reviews and analyzes data to prepare reports, to forecast future marketing trends, and to stay abreast of economic changes. Compiles data relating to research area, such as employment, productivity, and wages and hours. Formulates recommendations, policies, or plans to interpret markets or solve economic problems. Devises methods and procedures for collecting and processing data, using various econometric and sampling techniques. Organizes research data into report format, including graphic illustrations of research findings. **SKILLS—Systems Evaluation:** Identifying measures or indicators of system performance and the actions needed to improve or correct performance relative to the goals of the system. Systems Analysis: Determining how a system should work and how changes in conditions, operations, and the environment will affect outcomes. Judgment and

Decision Making: Considering the relative costs and benefits of potential actions to choose the most appropriate one. Writing: Communicating effectively in writing as appropriate for the needs of the audience. Complex Problem Solving: Identifying complex problems and reviewing related information to develop and evaluate options and implement solutions.

GOE INFORMATION—Interest Area: 02. Science, Math, and Engineering. Work Group: 02.04. Social Sciences. Other Job Titles in This Work Group: Anthropologists; Anthropologists and Archeologists; Archeologists; City Planning Aides; Historians; Industrial-Organizational Psychologists; Political Scientists; Psychologists, All Other; Social Science Research Assistants; Social Scientists and Related Workers, All Other; Sociologists; Survey Researchers; Urban and Regional Planners. PERSONALITY TYPE—Investigative. Investigative occupations frequently involve working with ideas and require an extensive amount of thinking. These occupations can involve searching for facts and figuring out problems mentally.

EDUCATION/TRAINING PROGRAM(S)—Agricultural Economics; Applied and Resource Economics; Business/Managerial Economics; Development Economics and International Development; Economet-rics and Quantitative Economics; Economics, General; Economics, Other; International Economics. RELATED KNOWLEDGE/COURSES—Mathematics: Knowledge of arithmetic, algebra, geometry, calculus, and statistics and their applications. Economics and Accounting: Knowledge of economic and accounting principles and practices, the financial markets, banking, and the analysis and reporting of financial data. English Language: Knowledge of the structure and content of the English language, including the meaning and spelling of words, rules of composition, and grammar. Education and Training: Knowledge of principles and methods for curriculum and training design, teaching and instruction for individuals and groups, and the measurement of training effects. Computers and Electronics: Knowledge of circuit boards, processors, chips, electronic equipment, and computer hardware and software, including applications and programming. Administration and Management: Knowledge of business and management principles involved in strategic planning, resource allocation, human resources modeling, leadership technique, production methods, and coordination of people and resources. Production and Processing: Knowledge of raw materials, production processes, quality control, costs, and other techniques for maximizing the effective manufacture and distribution of goods.

Editors

▲ Education/Training Required: Bachelor's degree

▲ Annual Earnings: $39,370

▲ Growth: 23%

▲ Annual Job Openings: 14,000

▲ Self-Employed: 31.2%

▲ Part-Time: 18.5%

Perform variety of editorial duties, such as laying out, indexing, and revising content of written materials, in preparation for final publication. Plans and prepares page layouts to position and space articles and photographs or illustrations. Determines placement of stories based on relative significance, available space, and knowledge of layout principles. Confers with management and editorial staff members regarding placement of developing news stories. Writes and rewrites head-lines, captions, columns, articles, and stories to conform to publication's style, editorial policy, and publishing requirements. Reads and evaluates manuscripts or other materials submitted for publication and confers with authors regarding changes or publication. Reads copy or proof to detect and correct errors in spelling, punctuation, and syntax and indicates corrections, using standard proofreading and typesetting symbols. Reviews and approves proofs submitted by composing room. Selects local, state, national, and international news items received by wire from press associations. Compiles index cross-references and related items, such as glossaries, bibliographies, and footnotes. Verifies facts, dates, and statistics, using standard reference sources. Arranges topical or alphabetical list of index items according to page or chapter, indicating location of item in text. Reads material to determine items to be included in index of book or other publication. Selects and crops photographs and illustrative materials to conform to space and subject matter requirements. **SKILLS**—Writing: Communicating effectively in writing as appropriate for the needs of the audience. Reading Comprehension: Understanding written sentences and paragraphs in work-related documents. Critical Thinking: Using logic and reasoning to identify the strengths and weaknesses of alternative solutions, conclusions, or approaches to problems. Coordination: Adjusting actions in relation to others' actions. Active Learning: Understanding the implications of new information for both current and future problem-solving and decision-making.

GOE INFORMATION—**Interest Area:** 01. Arts, Entertainment, and Media. **Work Group:** 01.02. Writing and Editing. **Other Job Titles in This Work Group:** Copy Writers; Creative Writers; Poets and Lyricists; Technical Writers; Writers and Authors. **PERSONALITY TYPE**—Artistic. Artistic occupations frequently involve working with forms, designs, and patterns. They often require self-expression, and the work can be done without following a clear set of rules.

EDUCATION/TRAINING PROGRAM(S)— Broadcast Journalism; Business Communications; Communications, Other; English Creative Writing; Journalism; Mass Communications; Technical and Business Writing. **RELATED KNOWLEDGE/COURSES**—**English Language:** Knowledge of the structure and content of the English language, including the meaning and spelling of words, rules of composition, and grammar. **Communications and Media:** Knowledge of media production, communication, and dissemination techniques and methods. This includes alternative ways to inform and entertain via written, oral, and visual media. **Administration and Management:** Knowledge of business and management principles involved in strategic planning, resource allocation, human resources modeling, leadership technique, production methods, and coordination of people and resources. **Computers and Electronics:** Knowledge of circuit boards, processors, chips, electronic equipment, and computer hardware and software, including applications and programming. **Clerical Studies:** Knowledge of administrative and clerical procedures and systems such as word processing, managing files and records, stenography and transcription, designing forms, and other office procedures and terminology.

Education Administrators, Elementary and Secondary School

- ▲ Education/Training Required: Work experience, plus degree
- ▲ Annual Earnings: $66,930
- ▲ Growth: 13%
- ▲ Annual Job Openings: 35,000
- ▲ Self-Employed: 13.8%
- ▲ Part-Time: 9.8%

Plan, direct, or coordinate the academic, clerical, or auxiliary activities of public or private elementary or secondary level schools. Establishes program philosophy plans, policies, and academic codes of ethics to maintain educational standards for student screening, placement, and training. Teaches classes or courses to students. Completes, maintains, or assigns preparation of attendance, activity, planning, or personnel reports and records for officials and agencies. Reviews and interprets government codes and develops programs to ensure facility safety, security, and maintenance. Counsels and provides guidance to students regarding personal, academic, or behavioral problems. Confers with parents and staff to discuss educational activities, policies, and student behavioral or learning problems. Writes articles, manuals, and other publications and assists in the distribution of promotional literature. Contacts and addresses commercial, community, or political groups to promote educational programs and services or lobby for legislative changes. Recruits, hires, trains, and evaluates primary and supplemental staff and recommends personnel actions for programs and services. Plans and coordinates consumer research and educational services to assist organizations in product development and marketing. Organizes and directs committees of specialists, volunteers, and staff to provide technical and advisory assistance for programs. Determines allocations of funds for staff, supplies, materials, and equipment and authorizes purchases. Directs and coordinates activities of teachers or administrators at daycare centers, schools, public agencies, and institutions. Evaluates programs to determine effectiveness, efficiency, and utilization and to ensure activities comply with federal, state, and local regulations. Prepares and submits budget requests or grant proposals to solicit program funding. Determines scope of educational program offerings and prepares drafts of course schedules and descriptions to estimate staffing and facility requirements. Collects and analyzes survey data, regulatory information, and demographic and employment trends to forecast enrollment patterns and curriculum changes. Coordinates outreach activities with businesses, communities, and other institutions or organizations to identify educational needs and establish and coordinate programs. Reviews and approves new programs or recommends modifications to existing programs. Plans, directs, and monitors instructional methods and content for educational, vocational, or student activity programs. **SKILLS**—Coordination: Adjusting actions in relation to others' actions. Writing: Communicating effectively in writing as appropriate for the needs of the audience. Reading Comprehension: Understanding written sentences and paragraphs in work-related documents. Learning Strategies: Selecting and using training/instructional methods and procedures appropriate for the situation when learning or teaching new things. Management of Personnel Resources: Motivating, developing, and directing people as they work, identifying the best people for the job.

GOE INFORMATION—**Interest Area:** 12. Education and Social Service. **Work Group:** 12.01. Managerial Work in Education and Social Service. **Other Job Titles in This Work Group:** Education Administrators, All Other; Education Administrators, Postsecondary; Education Administrators, Preschool and Child Care Center/Program; Instructional Coordinators; Park Naturalists; Social and Community Service Managers. **PERSONALITY TYPE**—Social. Social occupations frequently involve working with, communicating with, and teaching people. These occupations often involve helping or providing service to others.

EDUCATION/TRAINING PROGRAM(S)—Administration of Special Education; Community and Junior College Administration; Education Administration and Supervision, General; Education Administration and Supervision, Other; Educational Supervision; Elementary, Middle and Secondary Education Administration. **RELATED KNOWLEDGE/COURSES**—**Education and Training:** Knowledge of principles and methods for curriculum and training design, teaching and instruction for individuals and groups, and the measurement of training effects. **Administration and Management:** Knowledge of business and management principles involved in strategic planning, resource allocation, human resources modeling, leadership technique, production methods, and coordination of people and resources. **English Language:** Knowledge of the structure and content of the English language, including the meaning and spelling of words, rules of composition, and grammar. **Personnel and Human Resources:** Knowledge of principles and procedures for personnel recruitment, selection, training, compensation and benefits, labor relations and negotiation, and personnel information systems. **Sales and Marketing:** Knowledge of principles and methods for showing, promoting, and selling products or services. This includes marketing strategy and tactics, product demonstration, sales techniques, and sales control systems.

E

Education Administrators, Postsecondary

▲ Education/Training Required: Work experience, plus degree

▲ Annual Earnings: $59,480

▲ Growth: 13%

▲ Annual Job Openings: 35,000

▲ Self-Employed: 13.8%

▲ Part-Time: 9.8%

Plan, direct, or coordinate research, instructional, student administration and services, and other educational activities at postsecondary institutions, including universities, colleges, and junior and community colleges. Establishes operational policies and procedures and develops academic objectives. Selects and counsels candidates for financial aid and coordinates issuing and collecting student aid payments. Advises student organizations, sponsors faculty activities, and arranges for caterers, entertainers, and decorators at scheduled events. Audits financial status of student organization and facility accounts and certifies income reports from event ticket sales. Assists faculty and staff to conduct orientation programs, teach classes, issue student transcripts, and prepare commencement lists. Plans and promotes athletic policies, sports events, ticket sales, and student participation in social, cultural, and recreational activities. Coordinates alumni functions and encourages alumni endorsement of recruiting and fundraising activities. Reviews student misconduct reports requiring disciplinary action and counsels students to ensure conformance to university policies. Recruits, employs, trains, and terminates department personnel. Negotiates with foundation and industry representatives to secure loans for university and identify costs and materials for building construction. Confers with other academic staff to explain admission requirements and transfer credit policies and compares course equivalencies to university/college curriculum. Determines course schedules and correlates room assignments to ensure optimum use of buildings and equipment. Represents college/university as liaison officer with accrediting agencies and to exchange information between academic institutions and in community. Evaluates personnel and physical plant operations, student programs, and statistical and research data to implement procedures or modifications to administrative policies. Advises staff and students on problems relating to policies, program administration, and financial and personal matters and recommends solutions. Estimates and allocates department funding based on financial success of previous courses and other pertinent factors. Consults with staff, students, alumni, and subject experts to determine needs/feasibility and to formulate admission policies and educational programs. Completes and submits operating budget for approval, controls expenditures, and maintains financial reports and records. Meets with academic and administrative personnel to disseminate information, identify problems, monitor progress reports, and ensure adherence to goals/objectives. Directs work activities of personnel engaged in administration of academic institutions, departments, and alumni organizations. **SKILLS**—Coordination: Adjusting actions in relation to others' actions. Management of Financial Resources: Determining how money will be spent to get the work done and accounting for these expenditures. Systems Evaluation: Identifying measures or indicators of system performance and the actions needed to improve or correct performance relative to the goals of the system. Reading Comprehension: Understanding written sentences and paragraphs in work-related documents. Monitoring: Monitoring/Assessing your performance or that of other individuals or organizations to make improvements or take corrective action. Judgment and Decision Making: Considering the relative costs and benefits of potential actions to choose the most appropriate one.

GOE INFORMATION—**Interest Area:** 12. Education and Social Service. **Work Group:** 12.01. Managerial Work in Education and Social Service. **Other Job Titles in This Work Group:** Education Administrators, All Other; Education Administrators, Elementary and Secondary School; Education Administrators, Preschool and Child Care Center/Program; Instructional Coordinators; Park Naturalists; Social and Community Service Managers. **PERSONALITY TYPE—Enterprising.** Enterprising occupations frequently involve starting up and carrying out projects. These occupations can involve leading people and making many decisions. They sometimes require risk taking and often deal with business.

EDUCATION/TRAINING PROGRAM(S)— Administration of Special Education; Community and Junior College Administration; Education Administration and Supervision, General; Education Administration and Supervision, Other; Educational Supervision; Higher Education Administration. **RELATED KNOWLEDGE/ COURSES—Administration and Management:** Knowledge of business and management principles involved in strategic planning, resource allocation, human resources

modeling, leadership technique, production methods, and coordination of people and resources. **Education and Training:** Knowledge of principles and methods for curriculum and training design, teaching and instruction for individuals and groups, and the measurement of training effects. **Economics and Accounting:** Knowledge of economic and accounting principles and practices, the financial markets, banking, and the analysis and reporting of financial data. **Personnel and Human Resources:** Knowledge of principles and procedures for personnel recruitment, selection, training, compensation and benefits, labor relations and negotiation, and personnel information systems. **English Language:** Knowledge of the structure and content of the English language, including the meaning and spelling of words, rules of composition, and grammar.

Education Administrators, Preschool and Child Care Center/Program

- ▲ Education/Training Required: Work experience, plus degree
- ▲ Annual Earnings: $30,420
- ▲ Growth: 13%
- ▲ Annual Job Openings: 35,000
- ▲ Self-Employed: 13.8%
- ▲ Part-Time: 9.8%

Plan, direct, or coordinate the academic and nonacademic activities of preschool and child care centers or programs. Establishes program philosophy plans, policies, and academic codes of ethics to maintain educational standards for student screening, placement, and training. Determines scope of educational program offerings and prepares drafts of course schedules and descriptions to estimate staffing and facility requirements. Collects and analyzes survey data, regulatory information, and demographic and employment trends to forecast enrollment patterns and curriculum changes. Determines allocations of funds for staff, supplies, materials, and equipment and authorizes purchases. Plans and coordinates consumer research and educational services to assist organizations in product development and marketing. Teaches classes or courses to students. Completes, maintains, or assigns preparation of attendance, activity, planning, or personnel reports and records for officials and agencies. Reviews and interprets government codes and

develops programs to ensure facility safety, security, and maintenance. Counsels and provides guidance to students regarding personal, academic, or behavioral problems. Confers with parents and staff to discuss educational activities, policies, and student behavioral or learning problems. Writes articles, manuals, and other publications and assists in the distribution of promotional literature. Contacts and addresses commercial, community, or political groups to promote educational programs and services or lobby for legislative changes. Recruits, hires, trains, and evaluates primary and supplemental staff and recommends personnel actions for programs and services. Organizes and directs committees of specialists, volunteers, and staff to provide technical and advisory assistance for programs. Directs and coordinates activities of teachers or administrators at daycare centers, schools, public agencies, and institutions. Coordinates outreach activities with businesses, communities, and other institutions or organizations to identify educational needs and establish and coordinate programs. Prepares and submits budget requests or grant proposals to solicit program funding. Plans, directs, and monitors instructional methods and content for educational, vocational, or student activity programs. Evaluates programs to determine effectiveness, efficiency, and utilization and to ensure activities comply with federal, state, and local regulations. Reviews and approves new programs or recommends modifications to existing programs. **SKILLS**—Writing: Communicating effectively in writing as appropriate for the needs of the audience. Coordination: Adjusting actions in relation to others' actions. Reading Comprehension: Understanding written sentences and paragraphs in work-related documents. Learning Strategies: Selecting and using training/instructional methods and procedures appropriate for the situation when learning or teaching new things. Management of Personnel Resources: Motivating, developing, and directing people as they work, identifying the best people for the job.

GOE INFORMATION—Interest Area: 12. Education and Social Service. **Work Group:** 12.01. Managerial Work in Education and Social Service. **Other Job Titles in This Work Group:** Education Administrators, All Other; Education Administrators, Elementary and Secondary School; Education Administrators, Postsecondary; Instructional Coordinators; Park Naturalists; Social and Community Service Managers. **PERSONALITY TYPE**—Social. Social occupations frequently involve working with, communicating with, and teaching people. These occupations often involve helping or providing service to others.

EDUCATION/TRAINING PROGRAM(S)—Administration of Special Education; Community and Junior College Administration; Education Administration and Supervision, General; Education Administration and Supervision, Other; Educational Supervision; Elementary, Middle and Secondary Education Administration. **RELATED KNOWLEDGE/COURSES—Education and Training:** Knowledge of principles and methods for curriculum and training design, teaching and instruction for individuals and groups, and the measurement of training effects. **Administration and Management:** Knowledge of business and management principles involved in strategic planning, resource allocation, human resources modeling, leadership technique, production methods, and coordination of people and resources. **English Language:** Knowledge of the structure and content of the English language, including the meaning and spelling of words, rules of composition, and grammar. **Personnel and Human Resources:** Knowledge of principles and procedures for personnel recruitment, selection, training, compensation and benefits, labor relations and negotiation, and personnel information systems. **Sales and Marketing:** Knowledge of principles and methods for showing, promoting, and selling products or services. This includes marketing strategy and tactics, product demonstration, sales techniques, and sales control systems.

Education Teachers, Postsecondary

- ▲ Education/Training Required: Master's degree
- ▲ Annual Earnings: $44,840
- ▲ Growth: 24% for all Postsecondary Teachers
- ▲ Annual Job Openings: 184,000 for all Postsecondary Teachers
- ▲ Self-Employed: 0%
- ▲ Part-Time: 32.3% for all Postsecondary Teachers

Teach courses pertaining to education, such as counseling, curriculum, guidance, instruction, teacher education, and teaching English as a second language. SKILLS—No data available.

GOE INFORMATION—Interest Area: 12. Education and Social Service. **Work Group:** 12.03. Educational Services. **Other Job Titles in This Work Group:** Adult Literacy, Remedial Education, and GED

Teachers and Instructors; Agricultural Sciences Teachers, Postsecondary; Anthropology and Archeology Teachers, Postsecondary; Architecture Teachers, Postsecondary; Archivists; Area, Ethnic, and Cultural Studies Teachers, Postsecondary; Art, Drama, and Music Teachers, Postsecondary; Atmospheric, Earth, Marine, and Space Sciences Teachers, Postsecondary; Audio-Visual Collections Specialists; Biological Science Teachers, Postsecondary; Business Teachers, Postsecondary; Chemistry Teachers, Postsecondary; Child Care Workers; Communications Teachers, Postsecondary; Computer Science Teachers, Postsecondary; Criminal Justice and Law Enforcement Teachers, Postsecondary; Curators; Economics Teachers, Postsecondary; Educational Psychologists; Educational, Vocational, and School Counselors; Elementary School Teachers, Except Special Education; Engineering Teachers, Postsecondary; English Language and Literature

Teachers, Postsecondary; Environmental Science Teachers, Postsecondary; Farm and Home Management Advisors; Foreign Language and Literature Teachers, Postsecondary; Forestry and Conservation Science Teachers, Postsecondary; Geography Teachers, Postsecondary; Graduate Teaching Assistants; Health Specialties Teachers, Postsecondary; History Teachers, Postsecondary; Home Economics Teachers, Postsecondary; Kindergarten Teachers, Except Special Education; Law Teachers, Postsecondary; Librarians; Library Assistants, Clerical; Library Science Teachers, Postsecondary; others. **PERSONALITY TYPE**—No data available.

EDUCATION/TRAINING PROGRAM(S)— Agricultural Teacher Education (Vocational); Education, General; Teacher Education, Specific Academic and Vocational Programs. **RELATED KNOWLEDGE/ COURSES**—No data available.

Educational Psychologists

▲ Education/Training Required: Master's degree

▲ Annual Earnings: $48,320

▲ Growth: 18%

▲ Annual Job Openings: 18,000

▲ Self-Employed: 43.7%

▲ Part-Time: 23.4%

Investigate processes of learning and teaching and develop psychological principles and techniques applicable to educational problems. Conducts experiments to study educational problems, such as motivation, adjustment, teacher training, and individual differences in mental abilities. Formulates achievement, diagnostic, and predictive tests to aid teachers in planning methods and content of instruction. Plans remedial classes and testing programs designed to meet needs of special students. Analyzes characteristics and adjustment needs of students having various mental abilities and recommends educational program to promote maximum adjustment. Administers standardized tests to evaluate intelligence, achievement, and personality and to diagnose disabilities and difficulties among students. Recommends placement of students in classes and treatment programs based on individual needs. Refers individuals to community agencies to obtain medical, vocational, or social services for

child or family. Advises school board, superintendent, administrative committees, and parent-teacher groups regarding provision of psychological services within educational system or school. Counsels pupils individually and in groups to assist pupils to achieve personal, social, and emotional adjustment. Collaborates with education specialists in developing curriculum content and methods of organizing and conducting classroom work. Evaluates needs, limitations, and potentials of child through observation, review of school records, and consultation with parents and school personnel. Advises teachers and other school personnel on methods to enhance school and classroom atmosphere to maximize student learning and motivation. Interprets and explains test results in terms of norms, reliability, and validity to teachers, counselors, students, and other entitled parties. Investigates traits, attitudes, and feelings of teachers to predict conditions that affect teachers' mental health and success with students. Conducts research to aid introduction of programs in schools to meet current psychological, educational, and sociological needs of children. **SKILLS**—Social Perceptiveness: Being aware of others' reactions and understanding why they react as they do. Writing: Communicating effectively in writing as appropriate for the needs of the audience. Learning Strategies: Selecting and using training/instructional methods and procedures appropriate for the situation when learning or teaching new things. Reading Comprehension: Understanding written sentences and paragraphs in work-related documents. Systems Evaluation: Identifying measures or indicators of system performance and the actions needed to improve or correct performance relative to the goals of the system.

GOE INFORMATION—Interest Area: 12. Education and Social Service. **Work Group:** 12.03. Educational Services. **Other Job Titles in This Work Group:** Adult Literacy, Remedial Education, and GED Teachers and Instructors; Agricultural Sciences Teachers, Postsecondary; Anthropology and Archeology Teachers, Postsecondary; Architecture Teachers, Postsecondary; Archivists; Area, Ethnic, and Cultural Studies Teachers, Postsecondary; Art, Drama, and Music Teachers, Postsecondary; Atmospheric, Earth, Marine, and Space Sciences Teachers, Postsecondary; Audio-Visual Collections Specialists; Biological Science Teachers, Postsecondary; Business Teachers, Postsecondary; Chemistry Teachers, Postsecondary; Child Care Workers; Communications Teachers, Postsecondary; Computer Science Teachers, Postsecondary; Criminal Justice and Law Enforcement Teachers, Postsecondary; Curators; Economics Teachers, Postsecondary; Education Teachers, Postsecondary; Educational, Vocational, and School Counselors; Elementary School Teachers, Except Special Education; Engineering Teachers, Postsecondary; English Language and Literature Teachers, Postsecondary; Envi-

ronmental Science Teachers, Postsecondary; Farm and Home Management Advisors; Foreign Language and Literature Teachers, Postsecondary; Forestry and Conservation Science Teachers, Postsecondary; Geography Teachers, Postsecondary; Graduate Teaching Assistants; Health Specialties Teachers, Postsecondary; History Teachers, Postsecondary; Home Economics Teachers, Postsecondary; Kindergarten Teachers, Except Special Education; Law Teachers, Postsecondary; Librarians; Library Assistants, Clerical; Library Science Teachers, Postsecondary; others. **PERSONALITY TYPE**—Investigative. Investigative occupations frequently involve working with ideas and require an extensive amount of thinking. These occupations can involve searching for facts and figuring out problems mentally.

EDUCATION/TRAINING PROGRAM(S)— Clinical Psychology; Counseling Psychology; Developmental and Child Psychology; Educational Psychology; Psychology, General; School Psychology. **RELATED KNOWLEDGE/COURSES—Psychology:** Knowledge of human behavior and performance; individual differences in ability, personality, and interests; learning and motivation; psychological research methods; and the assessment and treatment of behavioral and affective disorders. **Education and Training:** Knowledge of principles and methods for curriculum and training design, teaching and instruction for individuals and groups, and the measurement of training effects. **English Language:** Knowledge of the structure and content of the English language, including the meaning and spelling of words, rules of composition, and grammar. **Therapy and Counseling:** Knowledge of principles, methods, and procedures for diagnosis, treatment, and rehabilitation of physical and mental dysfunctions and for career counseling and guidance. **Mathematics:** Knowledge of arithmetic, algebra, geometry, calculus, and statistics and their applications.

Educational, Vocational, and School Counselors

- ▲ Education/Training Required: Master's degree
- ▲ Annual Earnings: $42,110
- ▲ Growth: 25%
- ▲ Annual Job Openings: 22,000
- ▲ Self-Employed: 0.6%
- ▲ Part-Time: 18%

Counsel individuals and provide group educational and vocational guidance services. Advises counselees to assist them in developing their educational and vocational objectives. Advises counselees to assist them in understanding and overcoming personal and social problems. Collects and evaluates information about counselees' abilities, interests, and personality characteristics, using records, tests, and interviews. Compiles and studies occupational, educational, and economic information to assist counselees in making and carrying out vocational and educational objectives. Interprets program regulations or benefit requirements and assists counselees in obtaining needed supportive services. Refers qualified counselees to employer or employment service for placement. Conducts follow-up interviews with counselees and maintains case records. Establishes and maintains relationships with employers and personnel from supportive service agencies to develop opportunities for counselees. Plans and conducts orientation programs and group conferences to promote adjustment of individuals to new life experiences. Teaches vocational and educational guidance classes. Addresses community groups and faculty members to explain counseling services. **SKILLS**—Active Listening: Giving full attention to what other people are saying, taking time to understand the points being made, asking questions as appropriate, and not interrupting at inappropriate times. Reading Comprehension: Understanding written sentences and paragraphs in work-related documents. Social Perceptiveness: Being aware of others' reactions and understanding why they react as they do. Speaking: Talking to others to convey information effectively. Service Orientation: Actively looking for ways to help people.

GOE INFORMATION—Interest Area: 12. Education and Social Service. **Work Group:** 12.03. Educational Services. **Other Job Titles in This Work Group:** Adult Literacy, Remedial Education, and GED Teachers and Instructors; Agricultural Sciences Teachers, Postsecondary; Anthropology and Archeology Teachers, Postsecondary; Architecture Teachers, Postsecondary; Archivists; Area, Ethnic, and Cultural Studies Teachers, Postsecondary; Art, Drama, and Music Teachers, Postsecondary; Atmospheric, Earth, Marine, and Space Sciences Teachers, Postsecondary; Audio-Visual Collections Specialists; Biological Science Teachers, Postsecondary; Business Teachers, Postsecondary; Chemistry Teachers, Postsecondary; Child Care Workers; Com-

munications Teachers, Postsecondary; Computer Science Teachers, Postsecondary; Criminal Justice and Law Enforcement Teachers, Postsecondary; Curators; Economics Teachers, Postsecondary; Education Teachers, Postsecondary; Educational Psychologists; Elementary School Teachers, Except Special Education; Engineering Teachers, Postsecondary; English Language and Literature Teachers, Postsecondary; Environmental Science Teachers, Postsecondary; Farm and Home Management Advisors; Foreign Language and Literature Teachers, Postsecondary; Forestry and Conservation Science Teachers, Postsecondary; Geography Teachers, Postsecondary; Graduate Teaching Assistants; Health Specialties Teachers, Postsecondary; History Teachers, Postsecondary; Home Economics Teachers, Postsecondary; Kindergarten Teachers, Except Special Education; Law Teachers, Postsecondary; Librarians; Library Assistants, Clerical; Library Science Teachers, Postsecondary; others. **PERSONALITY TYPE**—Social. Social occupations frequently involve working with, communicating with, and teaching people. These occupations often involve helping or providing service to others.

EDUCATION/TRAINING PROGRAM(S)—College/Postsecondary Student Counseling and Personnel Services; Counselor Education Counseling and Guidance Services. **RELATED KNOWLEDGE/COURSES—Therapy and Counseling:** Knowledge of principles, methods, and procedures for diagnosis, treatment, and rehabilitation of physical and mental dysfunctions and for career counseling and guidance. **Education and Training:** Knowledge of principles and methods for curriculum and training design, teaching and instruction for individuals and groups, and the measurement of training effects. **Psychology:** Knowledge of human behavior and performance; individual differences in ability, personality, and interests; learning and motivation; psychological research methods; and the assessment and treatment of behavioral and affective disorders. **English Language:** Knowledge of the structure and content of the English language, including the meaning and spelling of words, rules of composition, and grammar. **Personnel and Human Resources:** Knowledge of principles and procedures for personnel recruitment, selection, training, compensation and benefits, labor relations and negotiation, and personnel information systems.

Electrical and Electronic Engineering Technicians

- ▲ Education/Training Required: Associate's degree
- ▲ Annual Earnings: $40,020
- ▲ Growth: 11%
- ▲ Annual Job Openings: 22,000
- ▲ Self-Employed: 1.9%
- ▲ Part-Time: 7.4%

Apply electrical and electronic theory and related knowledge, usually under the direction of engineering staff, to design, build, repair, calibrate, and modify electrical components, circuitry, controls, and machinery for subsequent evaluation and use by engineering staff in making engineering design decisions. SKILLS—No data available.

GOE INFORMATION—Interest Area: 02. Science, Math, and Engineering. Work Group: 02.08. Engineering Technology. Other Job Titles in This Work Group: Aerospace Engineering and Operations Technicians; Architectural and Civil Drafters; Architectural Drafters; Calibration and Instrumentation Technicians; Cartographers and Photogrammetrists; Civil Drafters; Civil Engineering Technicians; Construction and Building Inspectors; Drafters, All Other; Electrical and Electronics Drafters; Electrical Drafters; Electrical Engineering Technicians; Electro-Mechanical Technicians; Electronic Drafters; Electronics Engineering Technicians; Engineering Technicians, Except Drafters, All Other; Environmental Engineering Technicians; Industrial Engineering Technicians; Mapping Technicians; Mechanical Drafters; Mechanical Engineering Technicians; Numerical Tool and Process Control Programmers; Pressure Vessel Inspectors; Surveying and Mapping Technicians; Surveying Technicians; Surveyors. PERSONALITY TYPE—No data available.

EDUCATION/TRAINING PROGRAM(S)—Computer Engineering Technologist/Technician; Electrical and Electronic Engineering-Related Technologist/Technician; Electrical, Electronic and Communications Engineering Technologist/Technician. RELATED KNOWLEDGE/COURSES—No data available.

Electrical and Electronics Drafters

- ▲ Education/Training Required: Associate's degree
- ▲ Annual Earnings: $38,210
- ▲ Growth: 23%
- ▲ Annual Job Openings: 5,000
- ▲ Self-Employed: 3%
- ▲ Part-Time: 7.9%

Prepare wiring diagrams, circuit board assembly diagrams, and layout drawings used for manufacture, installation, and repair of electrical equipment in factories, power plants, and buildings. SKILLS—No data available.

GOE INFORMATION—Interest Area: 02. Science, Math, and Engineering. Work Group: 02.08. Engineering Technology. Other Job Titles in This Work Group: Aerospace Engineering and Operations Technicians; Architectural and Civil Drafters; Architectural Drafters; Calibration and Instrumentation Technicians; Cartographers and Photogrammetrists; Civil Drafters; Civil Engineering Technicians; Construction and Building Inspectors; Drafters, All Other; Electrical and Electronic Engineering Technicians; Electrical Drafters; Electrical Engineering Technicians; Electro-Mechanical Technicians; Electronic Drafters; Electronics Engineering Technicians; Engineering Technicians, Except Drafters, All Other; Environmental Engineering Technicians; Industrial Engineering Technicians; Mapping Technicians; Mechanical Drafters; Mechanical Engineering Technicians; Numerical Tool and Process Control Programmers; Pressure Vessel Inspectors; Surveying and Mapping Technicians; Surveying Technicians; Surveyors. **PERSONALITY TYPE**—No data available.

EDUCATION/TRAINING PROGRAM(S)— Electrical/Electronics Drafting. **RELATED KNOWLEDGE/COURSES**—No data available.

Electrical Drafters

▲ Education/Training Required: Associate's degree

▲ Annual Earnings: $38,210

▲ Growth: 23%

▲ Annual Job Openings: 5,000

▲ Self-Employed: 3%

▲ Part-Time: 7.9%

Develop specifications and instructions for installation of voltage transformers, overhead or underground cables, and related electrical equipment used to conduct electrical energy from transmission lines or high-voltage distribution lines to consumers. Drafts working drawing, wiring diagrams, wiring connections, or cross section of underground cables as required for instructions to installation crew. Takes measurements, such as distances to be spanned by wire and cable, which affect installation and arrangement of equipment. Reviews completed construction drawings and cost estimates for accuracy and conformity to standards and regulations. Draws master sketch showing relation of proposed installation to existing facilities. Drafts sketches to scale. Studies work order request to determine type of service, such as lighting or power, demanded by installation. Estimates labor and material costs for installation of electrical equipment and distribution systems. Confers with engineering staff and other personnel to resolve problems. Visits site of proposed installation and draws rough sketch of location. **SKILLS**—Operations Analysis: Analyzing needs and product requirements to create a design. Judgment and Decision Making: Considering the relative costs and benefits of potential actions to choose the most appropriate one. Mathematics: Using mathematics to solve problems. Equipment Selection: Determining the kind of tools and equipment needed to do a job. Management of Personnel Resources: Motivating, developing, and directing people as they work, identifying the best people for the job. Reading Comprehension: Understanding written sentences and paragraphs in work-related documents.

GOE INFORMATION—**Interest Area:** 02. Science, Math, and Engineering. **Work Group:** 02.08. Engineering Technology. **Other Job Titles in This Work Group:** Aerospace Engineering and Operations Technicians; Architectural and Civil Drafters; Architectural Drafters; Calibration and Instrumentation Technicians; Cartographers and Photogrammetrists; Civil Drafters; Civil Engineering Technicians; Construction and Building Inspectors; Drafters, All Other; Electrical and Electronic Engineering Technicians; Electrical and Electronics Drafters; Electrical Engineering Technicians; Electro-Mechanical Technicians; Electronic Drafters; Electronics Engineering Technicians; Engineering Technicians, Except Drafters, All Other; Environmental Engineering Technicians; Industrial Engineering Technicians; Mapping Technicians; Mechanical Drafters; Mechanical Engineering Technicians; Numerical Tool and Process Control Programmers; Pressure Vessel Inspectors; Surveying and

Mapping Technicians; Surveying Technicians; Surveyors. **PERSONALITY TYPE**—Conventional. Conventional occupations frequently involve following set procedures and routines. These occupations can include working with data and details more than with ideas. Usually there is a clear line of authority to follow.

EDUCATION/TRAINING PROGRAM(S)—Electrical/Electronics Drafting. **RELATED KNOWLEDGE/COURSES**—**Design:** Knowledge of design techniques, tools, and principles involved in production of precision technical plans, blueprints, drawings, and models. **Engineering and Technology:** Knowledge of the practical application of engineering science and technology. This includes applying principles, techniques, procedures, and equipment to the design and production of various goods and services. **Mathematics:** Knowledge of arithmetic, algebra, geometry, calculus, and statistics and their applications. **Administration and Management:** Knowledge of business and management principles involved in strategic planning, resource allocation, human resources modeling, leadership technique, production methods, and coordination of people and resources. **Building and Construction:** Knowledge of materials, methods, and tools involved in the construction or repair of houses, buildings, or other structures, such as highways and roads.

Electrical Engineering Technicians

- ▲ Education/Training Required: Associate's degree
- ▲ Annual Earnings: $40,020
- ▲ Growth: 11%
- ▲ Annual Job Openings: 22,000
- ▲ Self-Employed: 2.2%
- ▲ Part-Time: 3.1%

Apply electrical theory and related knowledge to test and modify developmental or operational electrical machinery and electrical control equipment and circuitry in industrial or commercial plants and laboratories. Usually work under direction of engineering staff. Sets up and operates test equipment to evaluate performance of developmental parts, assemblies, or systems under simulated operating conditions. Maintains and repairs testing equipment. Plans method and sequence of operations for testing and developing experimental electronic and electrical equipment. Assembles electrical and electronic systems and prototypes according to engineering data and knowledge of electrical principles, using hand tools and measuring instruments. Analyzes and interprets test information. Collaborates with electrical engineer and other personnel to solve developmental problems. Draws diagrams and writes engineering specifications to clarify design details and functional criteria of experimental electronics units. Modifies electrical prototypes, parts, assemblies, and systems to correct functional deviations. **SKILLS**—Technology Design: Generating or adapting equipment and technology to serve user needs. Active Learning: Understanding the implications of new information for both current and future problem-solving and decision-making. Troubleshooting: Determining causes of operating errors and deciding what to do about them. Operations Analysis: Analyzing needs and product requirements to create a design. Reading Comprehension: Understanding written sentences and paragraphs in work-related documents. Equipment Selection: Determining the kind of tools and equipment needed to do a job.

GOE INFORMATION—**Interest Area:** 02. Science, Math, and Engineering. **Work Group:** 02.08. Engineering Technology. **Other Job Titles in This Work Group:** Aerospace Engineering and Operations Technicians; Architectural and Civil Drafters; Architectural Drafters; Calibration and Instrumentation Technicians; Cartographers and Photogrammetrists; Civil Drafters; Civil Engineering Technicians; Construction and Building Inspectors; Drafters, All Other; Electrical and Electronic Engineering Technicians; Electrical and Electronics Drafters; Electrical Drafters; Electro-Mechanical Technicians;

Electronic Drafters; Electronics Engineering Technicians; Engineering Technicians, Except Drafters, All Other; Environmental Engineering Technicians; Industrial Engineering Technicians; Mapping Technicians; Mechanical Drafters; Mechanical Engineering Technicians; Numerical Tool and Process Control Programmers; Pressure Vessel Inspectors; Surveying and Mapping Technicians; Surveying Technicians; Surveyors. **PERSONALITY TYPE**—Realistic. Realistic occupations frequently involve work activities that include practical, hands-on problems and solutions. They often deal with plants, animals, and real-world materials like wood, tools, and machinery. Many of the occupations require working outside and do not involve a lot of paperwork or working closely with others.

EDUCATION/TRAINING PROGRAM(S)— Computer Engineering Technologist/Technician; Electrical and Electronic Engineering-Related Technologist/Technician; Electrical, Electronic and Communications Engineering Technologist/Technician. **RELATED**

KNOWLEDGE/COURSES—**Engineering and Technology:** Knowledge of the practical application of engineering science and technology. This includes applying principles, techniques, procedures, and equipment to the design and production of various goods and services. **Mathematics:** Knowledge of arithmetic, algebra, geometry, calculus, and statistics and their applications. **Design:** Knowledge of design techniques, tools, and principles involved in production of precision technical plans, blueprints, drawings, and models. **Computers and Electronics:** Knowledge of circuit boards, processors, chips, electronic equipment, and computer hardware and software, including applications and programming. **Physics:** Knowledge and prediction of physical principles and laws and their interrelationships and applications to understanding fluid, material, and atmospheric dynamics and mechanical, electrical, atomic, and sub-atomic structures and processes.

Electrical Engineers

- ▲ Education/Training Required: Bachelor's degree
- ▲ Annual Earnings: $64,910
- ▲ Growth: 11%
- ▲ Annual Job Openings: 8,000
- ▲ Self-Employed: 2.9%
- ▲ Part-Time: 2.6%

Design, develop, test, or supervise the manufacturing and installation of electrical equipment, components, or systems for commercial, industrial, military, or scientific use. Designs electrical instruments, equipment, facilities, components, products, and systems for commercial, industrial, and domestic purposes. Plans and implements research methodology and procedures to apply principles of electrical theory to engineering projects. Prepares and studies technical drawings, specifications of electrical systems, and topographical maps to ensure installation and operations conform to standards and customer requirements. Develops applications of controls, instruments, and systems for new commercial, domestic, and industrial uses. Plans layout of electric power generating plants and distribution lines and stations. Op-

erates computer-assisted engineering and design software and equipment to perform engineering tasks. Compiles data and writes reports regarding existing and potential engineering studies and projects. Collects data relating to commercial and residential development, population, and power system interconnection to determine operating efficiency of electrical systems. Estimates labor, material, and construction costs and prepares specifications for purchase of materials and equipment. Evaluates and analyzes data regarding electric power systems and stations and recommends changes to improve operating efficiency. Inspects completed installations and observes operations for conformance to design and equipment specifications and operational and safety standards. Confers with engineers, customers, and others to discuss existing or potential engi-

E

neering projects and products. Performs detailed calculations to compute and establish manufacturing, construction, and installation standards and specifications. Conducts field surveys and studies maps, graphs, diagrams, and other data to identify and correct power system problems. Investigates customer or public complaints, determines nature and extent of problem, and recommends remedial measures. Directs operations and coordinates manufacturing, construction, installation, maintenance, and testing activities to ensure compliance with specifications, codes, and customer requirements. **SKILLS**—Mathematics: Using mathematics to solve problems. Critical Thinking: Using logic and reasoning to identify the strengths and weaknesses of alternative solutions, conclusions, or approaches to problems. Reading Comprehension: Understanding written sentences and paragraphs in work-related documents. Active Learning: Understanding the implications of new information for both current and future problem-solving and decision-making. Writing: Communicating effectively in writing as appropriate for the needs of the audience.

GOE INFORMATION—**Interest Area:** 02. Science, Math, and Engineering. **Work Group:** 02.07. Engineering. **Other Job Titles in This Work Group:** Aerospace Engineers; Agricultural Engineers; Architects, Except Landscape and Naval; Biomedical Engineers; Chemical Engineers; Civil Engineers; Computer Hardware Engineers; Computer Software Engineers, Applications; Computer Software Engineers, Systems Software; Electronics Engineers, Except Computer; Engineers, All Other; Environmental Engineers; Fire-Prevention and Protection Engineers; Health and Safety Engineers, Except Mining Safety Engineers and Inspectors; Industrial Engineers; Industrial Safety and Health Engineers; Landscape Architects; Marine Architects; Marine Engineers; Marine Engineers and Naval Architects; Materials Engineers; Mechanical Engineers; Mining and Geological Engineers, Including Mining Safety Engineers; Nuclear Engineers; Petroleum Engineers; Product Safety Engineers; Sales Engineers. **PERSONALITY TYPE**—Investigative. Investigative occupations frequently involve working with ideas and require an extensive amount of thinking. These occupations can involve searching for facts and figuring out problems mentally.

EDUCATION/TRAINING PROGRAM(S)—Electrical, Electronics and Communication Engineering. **RELATED KNOWLEDGE/COURSES**—**Engineering and Technology:** Knowledge of the practical application of engineering science and technology. This includes applying principles, techniques, procedures, and equipment to the design and production of various goods and services. **Mathematics:** Knowledge of arithmetic, algebra, geometry, calculus, and statistics and their applications. **Computers and Electronics:** Knowledge of circuit boards, processors, chips, electronic equipment, and computer hardware and software, including applications and programming. **Design:** Knowledge of design techniques, tools, and principles involved in production of precision technical plans, blueprints, drawings, and models. **Building and Construction:** Knowledge of materials, methods, and tools involved in the construction or repair of houses, buildings, or other structures, such as highways and roads. **Production and Processing:** Knowledge of raw materials, production processes, quality control, costs, and other techniques for maximizing the effective manufacture and distribution of goods.

Electro-Mechanical Technicians

▲ Education/Training Required: Associate's degree

▲ Annual Earnings: $36,150

▲ Growth: 14%

▲ Annual Job Openings: 4,000

▲ Self-Employed: 0%

▲ Part-Time: 3.8%

Operate, test, and maintain unmanned, automated, servo-mechanical, or electromechanical equipment. May operate unmanned submarines, aircraft, or other equipment at worksites, such as oil rigs, deep ocean exploration, or hazardous waste removal. May assist engineers in testing and designing robotics equipment. Operates metal-working machines to fabricate housings, jigs, fittings, and fixtures. Aligns, fits, and assembles component parts, using hand tools, power tools, fixtures, templates, and microscope. Installs electrical and electronic parts and hardware in housing or assembly, using soldering equipment and hand tools. Tests performance of electromechanical assembly, using test instruments such as oscilloscope, electronic voltmeter, and bridge. Analyzes and records test results and prepares written documentation. Reads blueprints, schematics, diagrams, and technical orders to determine method and sequence of assembly. Inspects parts for surface defects. Verifies dimensions and clearances of parts to ensure conformance to specifications, using precision measuring instruments. Repairs, reworks, and calibrates assemblies to meet operational specifications and tolerances. **SKILLS**—Troubleshooting: Determining causes of operating errors and deciding what to do about them. Repairing: Repairing machines or systems using the needed tools. Quality Control Analysis: Conducting tests and inspections of products, services, or processes to evaluate quality or performance. Equipment Maintenance: Performing routine maintenance on equipment and determining when and what kind of maintenance is needed. Operation and Control: Controlling operations of equipment or systems.

GOE INFORMATION—**Interest Area:** 02. Science, Math, and Engineering. **Work Group:** 02.08. Engineering Technology. **Other Job Titles in This Work Group:** Aerospace Engineering and Operations Technicians; Architectural and Civil Drafters; Architectural Drafters; Calibration and Instrumentation Technicians; Cartographers and Photogrammetrists; Civil Drafters; Civil Engineering Technicians; Construction and Building Inspectors; Drafters, All Other; Electrical and Electronic Engineering Technicians; Electrical and Electronics Drafters; Electrical Drafters; Electrical Engineering Technicians; Electronic Drafters; Electronics Engineering Technicians; Engineering Technicians, Except Drafters, All Other; Environmental Engineering Technicians; Industrial Engineering Technicians; Mapping Technicians; Mechanical Drafters; Mechanical Engineering Technicians; Numerical Tool and Process Control Programmers; Pressure Vessel Inspectors; Surveying and Mapping Technicians; Surveying Technicians; Surveyors. **PERSONALITY TYPE**—Realistic. Realistic occupations frequently involve work activities that include practical, hands-on problems and solutions. They often deal with plants, animals, and real-world materials like wood, tools, and machinery. Many of the occupations require working outside and do not involve a lot of paperwork or working closely with others.

EDUCATION/TRAINING PROGRAM(S)—Computer Engineering Technologist/Technician; Electrical and Electronic Engineering-Related Technologist/Technician; Electrical, Electronic and Communications Engineering Technologist/Technician; Electromechanical Instrumentation and Maintenance Technologist/Technician; Electromechanical Technologist/Technician; Engineering-Related Technologist/Technician, General; Engineering-Related Technologists/Technicians, Other; Mechanical Engineering/Mechanical Technologist/Technician; Robotics Technologist/Technician; Solar Technologist/Technician. **RELATED KNOWLEDGE/COURSES**—**Principles of Mechanical Devices:** Knowledge of machines and tools, including their designs, uses, repair, and maintenance. **Engineering and Technology:** Knowledge of the practical application of engineering science and technology. This includes applying principles, techniques, procedures, and equipment to the design and production of various goods and services. **Production and Processing:** Knowledge of raw materials, production processes, quality control, costs, and other techniques for maximizing the effective manufacture and distribution of goods. **Computers and Electronics:** Knowledge of circuit boards, processors, chips, electronic equipment, and computer hardware and software, including applications and programming. **Design:** Knowledge of design techniques, tools, and principles involved in production of precision technical plans, blueprints, drawings, and models.

Electronics Engineering Technicians

▲ Education/Training Required: Associate's degree

▲ Annual Earnings: $40,020

▲ Growth: 11%

▲ Annual Job Openings: 22,000

▲ Self-Employed: 2.2%

▲ Part-Time: 3.1%

Lay out, build, test, troubleshoot, repair, and modify developmental and production electronic components, parts, equipment, and systems, such as computer equipment, missile control instrumentation, electron tubes, test equipment, and machine tool numerical controls, applying principles and theories of electronics, electrical circuitry, engineering mathematics, electronic and electrical testing, and physics. Usually work under direction of engineering staff. Reads blueprints, wiring diagrams, schematic drawings, and engineering instructions for assembling electronics units, applying knowledge of electronic theory and components. Assembles circuitry or electronic components, according to engineering instructions, technical manuals, and knowledge of electronics using hand tools and power tools. Tests electronics unit, using standard test equipment, to evaluate performance and determine needs for adjustments. Adjusts and replaces defective or improperly functioning circuitry and electronics components, using hand tools and soldering iron. Assists engineers in development of testing techniques, laboratory equipment, and circuitry or installation specifications, by writing reports and recording data. Designs basic circuitry and sketches for design documentation, as directed by engineers, using drafting instruments and computer aided design equipment. Fabricates parts, such as coils, terminal boards, and chassis, using bench lathes, drills, or other machine tools. **SKILLS**—Mathematics: Using mathematics to solve problems. Active Learning: Understanding the implications of new information for both current and future problem-solving and decision-making. Operations Analysis: Analyzing needs and product requirements to create a design. Troubleshooting: Determining causes of operating errors and deciding what to do about them. Technology Design: Generating or adapting equipment and technology to serve user needs. Critical Thinking: Using logic and reasoning to identify the strengths and weaknesses of alternative solutions, conclusions, or approaches to problems. Installation: Installing equipment, machines, wiring, or programs to meet specifications.

GOE INFORMATION—**Interest Area:** 02. Science, Math, and Engineering. **Work Group:** 02.08. Engineering Technology. **Other Job Titles in This Work Group:** Aerospace Engineering and Operations Technicians; Architectural and Civil Drafters; Architectural Drafters; Calibration and Instrumentation Technicians; Cartographers and Photogrammetrists; Civil Drafters; Civil Engineering Technicians; Construction and Building Inspectors; Drafters, All Other; Electrical and Electronic Engineering Technicians; Electrical and Electronics Drafters; Electrical Drafters; Electrical Engineering Technicians; Electro-Mechanical Technicians; Electronic Drafters; Engineering Technicians, Except Drafters, All Other; Environmental Engineering Technicians; Industrial Engineering Technicians; Mapping Technicians; Mechanical Drafters; Mechanical Engineering Technicians; Numerical Tool and Process Control Programmers; Pressure Vessel Inspectors; Surveying and Mapping Technicians; Surveying Technicians; Surveyors. **PERSONALITY TYPE**—Realistic. Realistic occupations frequently involve work activities that include practical, hands-on problems and solutions. They often deal with plants, animals, and real-world materials like wood, tools, and machinery. Many of the occupations require working outside and do not involve a lot of paperwork or working closely with others.

EDUCATION/TRAINING PROGRAM(S)—Computer Engineering Technologist/Technician; Electrical and Electronic Engineering-Related Technologist/Technician; Electrical, Electronic and Communications

Engineering Technologist/Technician. **RELATED KNOWLEDGE/COURSES—Computers and Electronics:** Knowledge of circuit boards, processors, chips, electronic equipment, and computer hardware and software, including applications and programming. **Engineering and Technology:** Knowledge of the practical application of engineering science and technology. This includes applying principles, techniques, procedures, and equipment to the design and production of various goods and services. **Design:** Knowledge of design techniques, tools, and principles involved in production of precision technical plans, blueprints, drawings, and models. **Mathematics:** Knowledge of arithmetic, algebra, geometry, calculus, and statistics and their applications. **English Language:** Knowledge of the structure and content of the English language, including the meaning and spelling of words, rules of composition, and grammar.

Electronics Engineers, Except Computer

▲ Education/Training Required: Bachelor's degree

▲ Annual Earnings: $64,830

▲ Growth: 10%

▲ Annual Job Openings: 6,000

▲ Self-Employed: 2.9%

▲ Part-Time: 2.6%

Research, design, develop, and test electronic components and systems for commercial, industrial, military, or scientific use utilizing knowledge of electronic theory and materials properties. Design electronic circuits and components for use in fields such as telecommunications, aerospace guidance and propulsion control, acoustics, or instruments and controls. Designs electronic components, products, and systems for commercial, industrial, medical, military, and scientific applications. Investigates causes of personal injury resulting from contact with high-voltage communications equipment. Determines material and equipment needs and orders supplies. Reviews or prepares budget and cost estimates for equipment, construction, and installation projects and controls expenditures. Prepares, reviews, and maintains maintenance schedules and operational reports and charts. Provides technical assistance to field and laboratory staff regarding equipment standards and problems and applications of transmitting and receiving methods. Operates computer-assisted engineering and design software and equipment to perform engineering tasks. Confers with engineers, customers, and others to discuss existing and potential engineering projects or products. Prepares engineering sketches and specifications for construction, relocation, and installation of transmitting and receiving equipment, facilities, products, and systems. Inspects electronic equipment, instruments, products, and systems to ensure conformance to specifications, safety standards, and applicable codes and regulations. Plans and implements research, methodology, and procedures to apply principles of electronic theory to engineering projects. Directs and coordinates activities concerned with manufacture, construction, installation, maintenance, operation, and modification of electronic equipment, products, and systems. Evaluates operational systems and recommends repair or design modifications based on factors such as environment, service, cost, and system capabilities. Conducts studies to gather information regarding current services, equipment capacities, traffic data, and acquisition and installation costs. Analyzes system requirements, capacity, cost, and customer needs to determine feasibility of project and develop system plan. Plans and develops applications and modifications for electronic properties used in components, products, and systems to improve technical performance. Develops operational, maintenance, and testing procedures for electronic products, components, equipment, and systems. **SKILLS—Mathematics:** Using mathematics to solve problems. **Reading Comprehension:** Understanding written sentences and paragraphs in work-related documents. **Writing:** Communicating effectively in writing as appropriate for the needs of the audience. **Science:** Using scientific rules and methods to solve problems. Judgment and Decision Making: Considering the relative costs and benefits of potential actions to choose the most appropriate one.

GOE INFORMATION—Interest Area: 02. Science, Math, and Engineering. Work Group: 02.07. Engineering. Other Job Titles in This Work Group: Aerospace Engineers; Agricultural Engineers; Architects, Except Landscape and Naval; Biomedical Engineers; Chemical Engineers; Civil Engineers; Computer Hardware Engineers; Computer Software Engineers, Applications; Computer Software Engineers, Systems Software; Electrical Engineers; Engineers, All Other; Environmental Engineers; Fire-Prevention and Protection Engineers; Health and Safety Engineers, Except Mining Safety Engineers and Inspectors; Industrial Engineers; Industrial Safety and Health Engineers; Landscape Architects; Marine Architects; Marine Engineers; Marine Engineers and Naval Architects; Materials Engineers; Mechanical Engineers; Mining and Geological Engineers, Including Mining Safety Engineers; Nuclear Engineers; Petroleum Engineers; Product Safety Engineers; Sales Engineers. PERSONALITY TYPE—Investigative. Investigative occupations frequently involve working with ideas and require an exten-

sive amount of thinking. These occupations can involve searching for facts and figuring out problems mentally.

EDUCATION/TRAINING PROGRAM(S)— Electrical, Electronics and Communication Engineering. RELATED KNOWLEDGE/COURSES—Engineering and Technology: Knowledge of the practical application of engineering science and technology. This includes applying principles, techniques, procedures, and equipment to the design and production of various goods and services. Mathematics: Knowledge of arithmetic, algebra, geometry, calculus, and statistics and their applications. Design: Knowledge of design techniques, tools, and principles involved in production of precision technical plans, blueprints, drawings, and models. Computers and Electronics: Knowledge of circuit boards, processors, chips, electronic equipment, and computer hardware and software, including applications and programming. Production and Processing: Knowledge of raw materials, production processes, quality control, costs, and other techniques for maximizing the effective manufacture and distribution of goods. Telecommunications: Knowledge of transmission, broadcasting, switching, control, and operation of telecommunications systems.

Elementary School Teachers, Except Special Education

▲ Education/Training Required: Bachelor's degree
▲ Annual Earnings: $39,700
▲ Growth: 13%
▲ Annual Job Openings: 144,000
▲ Self-Employed: 0%
▲ Part-Time: 11.7%

Teach pupils in public or private schools at the elementary level basic academic, social, and other formative skills. Lectures, demonstrates, and uses audiovisual aids and computers to present academic, social, and motor skill subject matter to class. Teaches subjects such as math, science, or social studies. Prepares course objectives and outline for course of study, following curriculum guidelines or requirements of state and school. Prepares, administers, and corrects tests and records results. Assigns lessons, corrects papers, and hears oral pre-

sentations. Teaches rules of conduct and maintains discipline and suitable learning environment in classroom and on playground. Evaluates student performance and discusses pupil academic and behavioral attitudes and achievements with parents. Keeps attendance and grade records and prepares reports as required by school. Counsels pupils when adjustment and academic problems arise. Supervises outdoor and indoor play activities. Teaches combined grade classes. Attends staff meetings, serves on committees, and attends workshops or in-service training activities. Coordinates class field trips. Prepares bulletin boards. **SKILLS**—Learning Strategies: Selecting and using training/instructional methods and procedures appropriate for the situation when learning or teaching new things. Social Perceptiveness: Being aware of others' reactions and understanding why they react as they do. Instructing: Teaching others how to do something. Reading Comprehension: Understanding written sentences and paragraphs in work-related documents. Speaking: Talking to others to convey information effectively.

GOE INFORMATION—Interest Area: 12. Education and Social Service. **Work Group:** 12.03. Educational Services. **Other Job Titles in This Work Group:** Adult Literacy, Remedial Education, and GED Teachers and Instructors; Agricultural Sciences Teachers, Postsecondary; Anthropology and Archeology Teachers, Postsecondary; Architecture Teachers, Postsecondary; Archivists; Area, Ethnic, and Cultural Studies Teachers, Postsecondary; Art, Drama, and Music Teachers, Postsecondary; Atmospheric, Earth, Marine, and Space Sciences Teachers, Postsecondary; Audio-Visual Collections Specialists; Biological Science Teachers, Postsecondary; Business Teachers, Postsecondary; Chemistry Teachers, Postsecondary; Child Care Workers; Communications Teachers, Postsecondary; Computer Science Teachers, Postsecondary; Criminal Justice and Law Enforcement Teachers, Postsecondary; Curators; Economics Teachers, Postsecondary; Education Teachers, Postsecondary; Educational Psychologists; Educational, Vocational, and School Counselors; Engineering Teachers, Postsecondary; English Language and Literature Teachers, Postsecondary; Environmental Science Teachers, Postsecondary; Farm and Home Management Advisors; Foreign Language and Literature Teachers, Postsecondary;

Forestry and Conservation Science Teachers, Postsecondary; Geography Teachers, Postsecondary; Graduate Teaching Assistants; Health Specialties Teachers, Postsecondary; History Teachers, Postsecondary; Home Economics Teachers, Postsecondary; Kindergarten Teachers, Except Special Education; Law Teachers, Postsecondary; Librarians; Library Assistants, Clerical; Library Science Teachers, Postsecondary; others. **PERSONALITY TYPE**—Social. Social occupations frequently involve working with, communicating with, and teaching people. These occupations often involve helping or providing service to others.

EDUCATION/TRAINING PROGRAM(S)— Elementary Teacher Education. **RELATED KNOWLEDGE/COURSES—Education and Training:** Knowledge of principles and methods for curriculum and training design, teaching and instruction for individuals and groups, and the measurement of training effects. **English Language:** Knowledge of the structure and content of the English language, including the meaning and spelling of words, rules of composition, and grammar. **Psychology:** Knowledge of human behavior and performance; individual differences in ability, personality, and interests; learning and motivation; psychological research methods; and the assessment and treatment of behavioral and affective disorders. **Mathematics:** Knowledge of arithmetic, algebra, geometry, calculus, and statistics and their applications. **History and Archeology:** Knowledge of historical events and their causes, indicators, and effects on civilizations and cultures. **Customer and Personal Service:** Knowledge of principles and processes for providing customer and personal services. This includes customer needs assessment, meeting quality standards for services, and evaluation of customer satisfaction.

Employment Interviewers, Private or Public Employment Service

- ▲ Education/Training Required: Bachelor's degree
- ▲ Annual Earnings: $36,480
- ▲ Growth: 18%
- ▲ Annual Job Openings: 19,000
- ▲ Self-Employed: 0%
- ▲ Part-Time: 6.9%

Interview job applicants in employment office and refer them to prospective employers for consideration. Search application files, notify selected applicants of job openings, and refer qualified applicants to prospective employers. Contact employers to verify referral results. Record and evaluate various pertinent data. Interviews job applicants to select people meeting employer qualifications. Reviews employment applications and evaluates work history, education and training, job skills, compensation needs, and other qualifications of applicants. Records additional knowledge, skills, abilities, interests, test results, and other data pertinent to selection and referral of applicants. Informs applicants of job duties and responsibilities, compensation and benefits, work schedules, working conditions, promotional opportunities, and other related information. Searches for and recruits applicants for open positions. Performs reference and background checks on applicants. Contacts employers to solicit orders for job vacancies and records information on forms to describe duties, hiring requirements, and related data. Refers applicants to vocational counseling services. Evaluates selection and testing techniques by conducting research or follow-up activities and conferring with management and supervisory personnel. Conducts or arranges for skills, intelligence, or psychological testing of applicants. Keeps records of applicants not selected for employment. Reviews job orders and matches applicants with job requirements, utilizing manual or computerized file search. Refers selected applicants to person placing job order, according to policy of organization. **SKILLS**—Reading Comprehension: Understanding written sentences and paragraphs in work-related documents. Active Listening: Giving full attention to what other people are saying, taking time to understand the points being made, asking questions as appropriate, and not interrupting at inappropriate times. Speaking: Talking to others to convey information effectively. Writing: Communicating effectively in writing as appropriate for the needs of the audience. Judgment and Decision Making: Considering the relative costs and benefits of potential actions to choose the most appropriate one.

GOE INFORMATION—**Interest Area:** 13. General Management and Support. **Work Group:** 13.02. Management Support. **Other Job Titles in This Work Group:** Accountants; Accountants and Auditors; Appraisers and Assessors of Real Estate; Appraisers, Real Estate; Assessors; Auditors; Budget Analysts; Claims Adjusters, Examiners, and Investigators; Claims Examiners, Property and Casualty Insurance; Compensation, Benefits, and Job Analysis Specialists; Cost Estimators; Credit Analysts; Employment, Recruitment, and Placement Specialists; Financial Analysts; Human Resources, Training, and Labor Relations Specialists, All Other; Insurance Adjusters, Examiners, and Investigators; Insurance Appraisers, Auto Damage; Insurance Underwriters; Loan Counselors; Loan Officers; Logisticians; Management Analysts; Market Research Analysts; Personnel Recruiters; Purchasing Agents and Buyers, Farm Products; Purchasing Agents, Except Wholesale, Retail, and Farm Products; Tax Examiners, Collectors, and Revenue Agents; Training and Development Specialists; Wholesale and Retail Buyers, Except Farm Products. **PERSONALITY TYPE**—Social. Social occupations frequently involve working with, communicating with, and teaching people. These occupations often involve helping or providing service to others.

EDUCATION/TRAINING PROGRAM(S)—Human Resources Management; Human Resources Management, Other; Labor/Personnel Relations and Studies; Organizational Behavior Studies. **RELATED KNOWLEDGE/COURSES**—**Personnel and Human Resources:** Knowledge of principles and procedures for personnel recruitment, selection, training, compensation and benefits, labor relations and negotiation, and personnel information systems. **Therapy and Counseling:** Knowledge of principles, methods, and procedures for diagnosis, treatment, and rehabilitation of physical and mental dysfunctions and for career counseling and guidance. **English Language:** Knowledge of the structure and content of the English language, including the meaning and spelling of words, rules of composition, and grammar. **Administration and Management:** Knowledge of business and management principles involved in strategic planning, resource allocation, human resources modeling, leadership technique, production methods, and coordination of people and resources. **Clerical Studies:** Knowledge of administrative and clerical procedures and systems such as word processing, managing files and records, stenography and transcription, designing forms, and other office procedures and terminology.

Employment, Recruitment, and Placement Specialists

▲ Education/Training Required: Bachelor's degree
▲ Annual Earnings: $36,480
▲ Growth: 18%
▲ Annual Job Openings: 19,000
▲ Self-Employed: 2.6%
▲ Part-Time: 6.9%

Recruit and place workers. SKILLS—No data available.

GOE INFORMATION—Interest Area: 13. General Management and Support. **Work Group:** 13.02. Management Support. **Other Job Titles in This Work Group:** Accountants; Accountants and Auditors; Appraisers and Assessors of Real Estate; Appraisers, Real Estate; Assessors; Auditors; Budget Analysts; Claims Adjusters, Examiners, and Investigators; Claims Examiners, Property and Casualty Insurance; Compensation, Benefits, and Job Analysis Specialists; Cost Estimators; Credit Analysts; Employment Interviewers, Private or Public Employment Service; Financial Analysts; Human Resources, Training, and Labor Relations Specialists, All Other; Insurance Adjusters, Examiners, and Investigators; Insurance Apprais-ers, Auto Damage; Insurance Underwriters; Loan Counselors; Loan Officers; Logisticians; Management Analysts; Market Research Analysts; Personnel Recruiters; Purchasing Agents and Buyers, Farm Products; Purchasing Agents, Except Wholesale, Retail, and Farm Products; Tax Examiners, Collectors, and Revenue Agents; Training and Development Specialists; Wholesale and Retail Buyers, Except Farm Products. **PERSONALITY TYPE**—No data available.

EDUCATION/TRAINING PROGRAM(S)—Human Resources Management; Human Resources Management, Other; Labor/Personnel Relations and Studies; Organizational Behavior Studies. **RELATED KNOWLEDGE/COURSES**—No data available.

Engineering Managers

▲ Education/Training Required: Work experience, plus degree
▲ Annual Earnings: $84,070
▲ Growth: 8%
▲ Annual Job Openings: 24,000
▲ Self-Employed: 0%
▲ Part-Time: 6.1%

Plan, direct, or coordinate activities in such fields as architecture and engineering or research and development in these fields. Establishes procedures and directs testing, operation, maintenance, and repair of transmitter equipment. Plans and directs oil field development, gas and oil production, and geothermal drilling. Plans, directs, and coordinates survey work with activities of other staff, certifies survey work, and writes land legal descriptions. Analyzes technology, resource needs, and market demand and confers with management, production, and marketing staff to plan and assess feasibility of project. Plans, coordinates, and directs engineering project; organizes and assigns staff; and directs integration of technical activities with products. Evaluates contract proposals, directs negotiation of research contracts, and prepares bids and contracts. Directs, reviews, and approves product design and changes and directs testing. Plans and directs installation, maintenance, testing, and repair of facilities and equipment. Administers highway planning, construction, and maintenance and reviews and recommends or approves contracts and cost estimates. Directs engineering of water control, treatment, and distribution projects. Confers with and prepares reports for officials and speaks to public to solicit support. **SKILLS—Coordination:** Adjusting actions in relation to others' actions. Operations Analysis: Analyzing needs and product requirements to create a design. Science: Using scientific rules and methods to solve problems. Troubleshooting: Determining causes of operating errors and deciding what to do about them. Reading Comprehension: Understanding written sentences and paragraphs in work-related documents.

GOE INFORMATION—Interest Area: 02. Science, Math, and Engineering. **Work Group:** 02.01. Managerial Work in Science, Math, and Engineering. **Other Job Titles in This Work Group:** Computer and Information Systems Managers; Natural Sciences Managers. **PERSONALITY TYPE—**Enterprising. Enterprising occupations frequently involve starting up and carrying out projects. These occupations can involve leading people and making many decisions. They sometimes require risk taking and often deal with business.

EDUCATION/TRAINING PROGRAM(S)— Aerospace, Aeronautical and Astronautical Engineering; Agricultural Engineering; Architectural Engineering; Architectural Environmental Design; Architectural Urban Design and Planning; Architecture; Bioengineering and Biomedical Engineering; Ceramic Sciences and Engineering; Chemical Engineering; City/Urban, Community and Regional Planning; Civil Engineering, General; Civil Engineering, Other; Computer Engineering; Electrical, Electronics and Communication Engineering; Engineering Design; Engineering Mechanics; Engineering Physics; Engineering Science; Engineering, General; Engineering, Other; Engineering/Industrial Management; Environmental/Environmental Health Engineering; Geological Engineering; Geophysical Engineering; Geotechnical Engineering; Industrial/Manufacturing Engineering; Interior Architecture; Landscape Architecture; Material Engineering; Materials Science; Mechanical Engineering; Metallurgical Engineering; Mining and Mineral Engineering; Naval Architecture and Marine Engineering; Nuclear Engineering; Ocean Engineering; Petroleum Engineering; Polymer/Plastics Engineering; Structural Engineering; Systems Engineering; Textile Sciences and Engineering; Transportation and Highway Engineering; Water Resources Engineering. **RELATED KNOWLEDGE/ COURSES—Engineering and Technology:** Knowledge of the practical application of engineering science and technology. This includes applying principles, techniques, procedures, and equipment to the design and production of various goods and services. **Administration and Management:** Knowledge of business and management principles involved in strategic planning, resource allocation, human resources modeling, leadership technique, production methods, and coordination of people and resources. **Design:** Knowledge of design techniques, tools, and principles involved in production of precision technical plans, blueprints, drawings, and models. **Physics:** Knowledge and prediction of physical principles and laws and their interrelationships and applications to understanding fluid, material, and atmospheric dynamics and mechanical, electrical, atomic, and sub-atomic structures and processes. **Mathematics:** Knowledge of arithmetic, algebra, geometry, calculus, and statistics and their applications.

Engineering Teachers, Postsecondary

- ▲ Education/Training Required: Master's degree
- ▲ Annual Earnings: $65,640
- ▲ Growth: 24% for all Postsecondary Teachers
- ▲ Annual Job Openings: 184,000 for all Postsecondary Teachers
- ▲ Self-Employed: 0%
- ▲ Part-Time: 32.3% for all Postsecondary Teachers

Teach courses pertaining to the application of physical laws and principles of engineering for the development of machines, materials, instruments, processes, and services. Includes teachers of subjects such as chemical, civil, electrical, industrial, mechanical, mineral, and petroleum engineering. Includes both teachers primarily engaged in teaching and those who do a combination of both teaching and research. Prepares and delivers lectures to students. Serves on faculty committee providing professional consulting services to government and industry. Acts as adviser to student organizations. Conducts research in particular field of knowledge and publishes findings in professional journals. Stimulates class discussions. Compiles, administers, and grades examinations or assigns this work to others. Advises students on academic and vocational curricula. Directs research of other teachers or graduate students working for advanced academic degrees. Compiles bibliographies of specialized materials for outside reading assignments. **SKILLS**—Mathematics: Using mathematics to solve problems. Active Learning: Understanding the implications of new information for both current and future problem-solving and decision-making. Reading Comprehension: Understanding written sentences and paragraphs in work-related documents. Critical Thinking: Using logic and reasoning to identify the strengths and weaknesses of alternative solutions, conclusions, or approaches to problems. Science: Using scientific rules and methods to solve problems.

GOE INFORMATION—**Interest Area:** 12. Education and Social Service. **Work Group:** 12.03. Educational Services. **Other Job Titles in This Work Group:** Adult Literacy, Remedial Education, and GED Teachers and Instructors; Agricultural Sciences Teachers, Postsecondary; Anthropology and Archeology Teachers, Postsecondary; Architecture Teachers, Postsecondary; Archivists; Area, Ethnic, and Cultural Studies Teachers, Postsecondary; Art, Drama, and Music Teachers, Postsecondary; Atmospheric, Earth, Marine, and Space Sciences Teachers, Postsecondary; Audio-Visual Collections Specialists; Biological Science Teachers, Postsecondary; Business Teachers, Postsecondary; Chemistry Teachers, Postsecondary; Child Care Workers; Communications Teachers, Postsecondary; Computer Science Teachers, Postsecondary; Criminal Justice and Law En-

forcement Teachers, Postsecondary; Curators; Economics Teachers, Postsecondary; Education Teachers, Postsecondary; Educational Psychologists; Educational, Vocational, and School Counselors; Elementary School Teachers, Except Special Education; English Language and Literature Teachers, Postsecondary; Environmental Science Teachers, Postsecondary; Farm and Home Management Advisors; Foreign Language and Literature Teachers, Postsecondary; Forestry and Conservation Science Teachers, Postsecondary; Geography Teachers, Postsecondary; Graduate Teaching Assistants; Health Specialties Teachers, Postsecondary; History Teachers, Postsecondary; Home Economics Teachers, Postsecondary; Kindergarten Teachers, Except Special Education; Law Teachers, Postsecondary; Librarians; Library Assistants, Clerical; Library Science Teachers, Postsecondary; others. **PERSONALITY TYPE**—Investigative. Investigative occupations frequently involve working with ideas and require an extensive amount of thinking. These occupations can involve searching for facts and figuring out problems mentally.

EDUCATION/TRAINING PROGRAM(S)—Aerospace, Aeronautical and Astronautical Engineering; Agricultural Engineering; Architectural Engineering; Bioengineering and Biomedical Engineering; Ceramic Sciences and Engineering; Chemical Engineering; Civil Engineering, General; Civil Engineering, Other; Computer Engineering; Electrical, Electronics and Communication Engineering; Engineering Design; Engineering Mechanics; Engineering Physics; Engineering Science; Engineering, General; Engineering, Other; Engineering/Industrial Management; Environmental/Environmental Health Engineering; Geological Engineering; Geophysical Engineering; Geotechnical Engineering; Industrial/Manufacturing Engineering; Material Engineering; Materials Science; Mechanical Engineering; Metallurgical Engineering; Mining and Mineral Engineering; Naval Architecture and Marine Engineering; Nuclear Engineering; Ocean Engineering; Petroleum Engineering; Polymer/Plastics Engineering; Structural Engineering; Systems Engineering; Teacher Education, Specific Academic and Vocational Programs; Textile Sciences and Engineering; Transportation and Highway Engineering; Water Resources Engineering. **RELATED KNOWLEDGE/COURSES—Engineering and Technology:** Knowledge of the practical application of engineering science and technology. This includes applying

E

principles, techniques, procedures, and equipment to the design and production of various goods and services. **Education and Training:** Knowledge of principles and methods for curriculum and training design, teaching and instruction for individuals and groups, and the measurement of training effects. **Mathematics:** Knowledge of arithmetic, algebra, geometry, calculus, and statistics and their applications. **Physics:** Knowledge and prediction of physical principles and laws and their interrelationships and applications to understanding fluid, material, and at-

mospheric dynamics and mechanical, electrical, atomic, and sub-atomic structures and processes. **English Language:** Knowledge of the structure and content of the English language, including the meaning and spelling of words, rules of composition, and grammar. **Design:** Knowledge of design techniques, tools, and principles involved in production of precision technical plans, blueprints, drawings, and models.

English Language and Literature Teachers, Postsecondary

▲ Education/Training Required: Master's degree

▲ Annual Earnings: $44,310

▲ Growth: 24% for all Postsecondary Teachers

▲ Annual Job Openings: 184,000 for all Postsecondary Teachers

▲ Self-Employed: 0%

▲ Part-Time: 32.3% for all Postsecondary Teachers

Teach courses in English language and literature, including linguistics and comparative literature. Prepares and delivers lectures to students. Stimulates class discussions. Advises students on academic and vocational curricula. Conducts research in particular field of knowledge and publishes findings in professional journals. Serves on faculty committee providing professional consulting services to government and industry. Acts as adviser to student organizations. Directs research of other teachers or graduate students working for advanced academic degrees. Compiles, administers, and grades examinations or assigns this work to others. Compiles bibliographies of specialized materials for outside reading assignments. **SKILLS—Reading Comprehension:** Understanding written sentences and paragraphs in work-related documents. **Instructing:** Teaching others how to do something. **Speaking:** Talking to others to convey information effectively. **Learning Strategies:** Selecting and using training/instructional methods and procedures appropriate for the situation when learning or teaching new things. **Writing:** Communicating effectively in writing as appropriate for the needs of the audience.

GOE INFORMATION—Interest Area: 12. Education and Social Service. **Work Group:** 12.03. Educational Services. **Other Job Titles in This Work Group:** Adult Literacy, Remedial Education, and GED Teachers and Instructors; Agricultural Sciences Teachers, Postsecondary; Anthropology and Archeology Teachers, Postsecondary; Architecture Teachers, Postsecondary; Archivists; Area, Ethnic, and Cultural Studies Teachers, Postsecondary; Art, Drama, and Music Teachers, Postsecondary; Atmospheric, Earth, Marine, and Space Sciences Teachers, Postsecondary; Audio-Visual Collections Specialists; Biological Science Teachers, Postsecondary; Business Teachers, Postsecondary; Chemistry Teachers, Postsecondary; Child Care Workers; Communications Teachers, Postsecondary; Computer Science Teachers, Postsecondary; Criminal Justice and Law Enforcement Teachers, Postsecondary; Curators; Economics Teachers, Postsecondary; Education Teachers, Postsecondary; Educational Psychologists; Educational, Vocational, and School Counselors; Elementary School Teachers, Except Special Education; Engineering Teachers, Postsecondary; Environmental Science Teachers,

Postsecondary; Farm and Home Management Advisors; Foreign Language and Literature Teachers, Postsecondary; Forestry and Conservation Science Teachers, Postsecondary; Geography Teachers, Postsecondary; Graduate Teaching Assistants; Health Specialties Teachers, Postsecondary; History Teachers, Postsecondary; Home Economics Teachers, Postsecondary; Kindergarten Teachers, Except Special Education; Law Teachers, Postsecondary; Librarians; Library Assistants, Clerical; Library Science Teachers, Postsecondary; others. **PERSONALITY TYPE**—Artistic. Artistic occupations frequently involve working with forms, designs, and patterns. They often require self-expression, and the work can be done without following a clear set of rules.

EDUCATION/TRAINING PROGRAM(S)— American Literature (United States); Arabic Language and Literature; Classical and Ancient Near Eastern Languages and Literatures; Classics and Classical Languages and Literatures; Comparative Literature; English Language and Literature, General; English Language and Literature/Letters, Other; English Literature (British and Commonwealth); Foreign Languages and Literatures, Other; Greek Language and Literature (Ancient and Medieval); Hebrew Language and Literature; Latin Language and Literature

(Ancient and Medieval); Middle Eastern Languages and Literatures, Other; Speech and Rhetorical Studies. **RELATED KNOWLEDGE/COURSES**—**Education and Training:** Knowledge of principles and methods for curriculum and training design, teaching and instruction for individuals and groups, and the measurement of training effects. **English Language:** Knowledge of the structure and content of the English language, including the meaning and spelling of words, rules of composition, and grammar. **Foreign Language:** Knowledge of the structure and content of a foreign (non-English) language, including the meaning and spelling of words, rules of composition and grammar, and pronunciation. **Communications and Media:** Knowledge of media production, communication, and dissemination techniques and methods. This includes alternative ways to inform and entertain via written, oral, and visual media. **Computers and Electronics:** Knowledge of circuit boards, processors, chips, electronic equipment, and computer hardware and software, including applications and programming. **Clerical Studies:** Knowledge of administrative and clerical procedures and systems such as word processing, managing files and records, stenography and transcription, designing forms, and other office procedures and terminology.

Environmental Engineering Technicians

- ▲ Education/Training Required: Associate's degree
- ▲ Annual Earnings: $34,000
- ▲ Growth: 29%
- ▲ Annual Job Openings: 2,000
- ▲ Self-Employed: 1.9%
- ▲ Part-Time: 7.4%

Apply theory and principles of environmental engineering to modify, test, and operate equipment and devices used in the prevention, control, and remediation of environmental pollution, including waste treatment and site remediation. May assist in the development of environmental pollution remediation devices under direction of engineer. **SKILLS**—No data available.

GOE INFORMATION—**Interest Area:** 02. Science, Math, and Engineering. **Work Group:** 02.08. En-

gineering Technology. **Other Job Titles in This Work Group:** Aerospace Engineering and Operations Technicians; Architectural and Civil Drafters; Architectural Drafters; Calibration and Instrumentation Technicians; Cartographers and Photogrammetrists; Civil Drafters; Civil Engineering Technicians; Construction and Building Inspectors; Drafters, All Other; Electrical and Electronic Engineering Technicians; Electrical and Electronics Drafters; Electrical Drafters; Electrical Engineering Technicians; Electro-Mechanical Technicians; Electronic Drafters; Electronics Engineering Technicians; Engineering Technicians, Except Drafters, All Other; Industrial Engineering Technicians; Mapping Technicians; Mechanical Drafters; Mechanical Engineering Technicians; Numerical Tool and Process Control Programmers; Pressure Vessel Inspectors; Surveying and Mapping Technicians; Surveying Technicians; Surveyors. **PERSONALITY TYPE**—No data available.

EDUCATION/TRAINING PROGRAM(S)— Environmental and Pollution Control Technologist/Technician; Solar Technologist/Technician. **RELATED KNOWLEDGE/COURSES**—No data available.

Environmental Engineers

▲ Education/Training Required: Bachelor's degree
▲ Annual Earnings: $57,780
▲ Growth: 26%
▲ Annual Job Openings: 3,000
▲ Self-Employed: 2.7%
▲ Part-Time: 4.5%

Design, plan, or perform engineering duties in the prevention, control, and remediation of environmental health hazards utilizing various engineering disciplines. Work may include waste treatment, site remediation, or pollution control technology. **SKILLS**—No data available.

GOE INFORMATION—**Interest Area:** 02. Science, Math, and Engineering. **Work Group:** 02.07. Engineering. **Other Job Titles in This Work Group:** Aerospace Engineers; Agricultural Engineers; Architects, Except Landscape and Naval; Biomedical Engineers; Chemical Engineers; Civil Engineers; Computer Hardware Engineers; Computer Software Engineers, Applications; Computer Software Engineers, Systems Software; Electrical Engineers; Electronics Engineers, Except Computer;

Engineers, All Other; Fire-Prevention and Protection Engineers; Health and Safety Engineers, Except Mining Safety Engineers and Inspectors; Industrial Engineers; Industrial Safety and Health Engineers; Landscape Architects; Marine Architects; Marine Engineers; Marine Engineers and Naval Architects; Materials Engineers; Mechanical Engineers; Mining and Geological Engineers, Including Mining Safety Engineers; Nuclear Engineers; Petroleum Engineers; Product Safety Engineers; Sales Engineers. **PERSONALITY TYPE**—No data available.

EDUCATION/TRAINING PROGRAM(S)— Engineering Design; Environmental/Environmental Health Engineering; Geophysical Engineering. **RELATED KNOWLEDGE/COURSES**—No data available.

Environmental Science and Protection Technicians, Including Health

▲ Education/Training Required: Associate's degree
▲ Annual Earnings: $33,830
▲ Growth: 24%
▲ Annual Job Openings: 3,000
▲ Self-Employed: 0.9%
▲ Part-Time: 11.7%

Perform laboratory and field tests to monitor the environment and investigate sources of pollution, including those that affect health. Under direction of an environmental scientist or specialist, may collect samples of gases, soil, water, and other materials for testing and take corrective actions as assigned. Collects samples of gases, soils, water, industrial wastewater, and asbestos products to conduct tests on pollutant levels. Discusses test results and analyses with customers. Calibrates microscopes and test instruments. Develops procedures and directs activities of workers in laboratory. Records test data and prepares reports, summaries, and charts that interpret test results and recommend changes. Sets up equipment or station to monitor and collect pollutants from sites such as smokestacks, manufacturing plants, or mechanical equipment. Determines amounts and kinds of chemicals to use in destroying harmful organisms and removing impurities from purification systems. Conducts standardized tests to ensure materials and supplies used throughout power supply system meet processing and safety specifications. Examines and analyzes material for presence and concentration of contaminants such as asbestos in environment, using variety of microscopes. Weighs, analyzes, and measures collected sample particles, such as lead, coal dust, or rock, to determine concentration of pollutants. Prepares samples or photomicrographs for testing and analysis. Calculates amount of pollutant in samples or computes air pollution or gas flow in industrial processes, using chemical and mathematical formulas. Performs chemical and physical laboratory and field tests on collected samples to assess compliance with pollution standards, using test instruments. SKILLS—Science: Using scientific rules and methods to solve problems. Mathematics: Using mathematics to solve problems. Reading Comprehension: Understanding written sentences and paragraphs in work-related documents. Writing: Communicating effectively in writing as appropriate for the needs of the audience. Critical Thinking: Using logic and reasoning to identify the strengths and weaknesses of alternative solutions, conclusions, or approaches to problems.

GOE INFORMATION—Interest Area: 02. Science, Math, and Engineering. Work Group: 02.05. Laboratory Technology. Other Job Titles in This Work Group: Biological Technicians; Chemical Technicians; Geological and Petroleum Technicians; Geological Data Technicians; Geological Sample Test Technicians; Nuclear Equipment Operation Technicians; Nuclear Technicians; Photographers, Scientific. PERSONALITY TYPE—Investigative. Investigative occupations frequently involve working with ideas and require an extensive amount of thinking. These occupations can involve searching for facts and figuring out problems mentally.

EDUCATION/TRAINING PROGRAM(S)—Aeronautical and Aerospace Engineering Technologist/Technician; Architectural Engineering Technologist/Technician; Chemical Technologist/Technician; Communications Technologists/Technicians, Other; Energy Management and Systems Technologist/Technician; Engineering-Related Technologist/Technician, General; Engineering-Related Technologists/Technicians, Other; Environmental and Pollution Control Technologist/Technician; Environmental Control Technologists/Technicians, Other; Environmental Science/Studies; Hydraulic Technologist/Technician; Industrial Production Technologists/Technicians, Other; Laser and Optical Technologist/Technician; Mechanical Engineering-Related Technologists/Technicians, Other; Metallurgical Technologist/Technician; Mining and Petroleum Technologists/Technicians, Other; Mining Technologist/Technician; Physical Science Technologists/Technicians, Other; Plastics Technologist/Technician; Radio and Television Broadcasting Technologist/Technician; Science Technologists/Technicians, Other; Solar Technologist/Technician. RELATED KNOWLEDGE/COURSES—Chemistry: Knowledge of the chemical composition, structure, and properties of substances and of the chemical processes and transformations that they undergo. This includes uses of chemicals and their interactions, danger signs, production techniques, and disposal methods. Mathematics: Knowledge of arithmetic, algebra, geometry, calculus, and statistics and their applications. Public Safety and Security: Knowledge of relevant equipment, policies, procedures, and strategies to promote effective local, state, or national security operations for the protection of people, data, property, and institutions. English Language: Knowledge of the structure and content of the English language, including the meaning and spelling of words, rules of composition, and grammar. **Computers and Electronics:** Knowledge of circuit boards, processors, chips, electronic equipment, and computer hardware and software, including applications and programming.

Environmental Science Teachers, Postsecondary

▲ Education/Training Required: Master's degree

▲ Annual Earnings: $54,410

▲ Growth: 24% for all Postsecondary Teachers

▲ Annual Job Openings: 184,000 for all Postsecondary Teachers

▲ Self-Employed: 0%

▲ Part-Time: 32.3% for all Postsecondary Teachers

Teach courses in environmental science. **SKILLS**—No data available.

GOE INFORMATION—**Interest Area:** 12. Education and Social Service. **Work Group:** 12.03. Educational Services. **Other Job Titles in This Work Group:** Adult Literacy, Remedial Education, and GED Teachers and Instructors; Agricultural Sciences Teachers, Postsecondary; Anthropology and Archeology Teachers, Postsecondary; Architecture Teachers, Postsecondary; Archivists; Area, Ethnic, and Cultural Studies Teachers, Postsecondary; Art, Drama, and Music Teachers, Postsecondary; Atmospheric, Earth, Marine, and Space Sciences Teachers, Postsecondary; Audio-Visual Collections Specialists; Biological Science Teachers, Postsecondary; Business Teachers, Postsecondary; Chemistry Teachers, Postsecondary; Child Care Workers; Communications Teachers, Postsecondary; Computer Science Teachers, Postsecondary; Criminal Justice and Law Enforcement Teachers, Postsecondary; Curators; Economics Teachers, Postsecondary; Education Teachers, Postsecondary; Educational Psychologists; Educational, Vocational, and School Counselors; Elementary School Teachers, Except Special Education; Engineering Teachers, Postsecondary; English Language and Literature Teachers, Postsecondary; Farm and Home Management Advisors; Foreign Language and Literature Teachers, Postsecondary; Forestry and Conservation Science Teachers, Postsecondary; Geography Teachers, Postsecondary; Graduate Teaching Assistants; Health Specialties Teachers, Postsecondary; History Teachers, Postsecondary; Home Economics Teachers, Postsecondary; Kindergarten Teachers, Except Special Education; Law Teachers, Postsecondary; Librarians; Library Assistants, Clerical; Library Science Teachers, Postsecondary; others. **PERSONALITY TYPE**—No data available.

EDUCATION/TRAINING PROGRAM(S)— Earth and Planetary Sciences; Environmental Science/Studies; Oceanography; Physical Sciences, General; Science Teacher Education, General. **RELATED KNOWLEDGE/COURSES**—No data available.

Environmental Scientists and Specialists, Including Health

▲ Education/Training Required: Bachelor's degree

▲ Annual Earnings: $44,180

▲ Growth: 22%

▲ Annual Job Openings: 4,000

▲ Self-Employed: 7.6%

▲ Part-Time: 6.6%

Conduct research or perform investigation for the purpose of identifying, abating, or eliminating sources of pollutants or hazards that affect either the environment or the health of the population. Utilizing knowledge of various scientific disciplines, may collect, synthesize, study, report, and take action based on data derived from measurements or observations of air, food, soil, water, and other sources. Plans and develops research models using knowledge of mathematical and statistical concepts. Collects, identifies, and analyzes data to assess sources of pollution, determine their effects, and establish standards. Prepares graphs or charts from data samples and advises enforcement personnel on proper standards and regulations. Determines data collection methods to be employed in research projects and surveys. **SKILLS**—Active Learning: Understanding the implications of new information for both current and future problem-solving and decision-making. Mathematics: Using mathematics to solve problems. Science: Using scientific rules and methods to solve problems. Reading Comprehension: Understanding written sentences and paragraphs in work-related documents. Complex Problem Solving: Identifying complex problems and reviewing related information to develop and evaluate options and implement solutions.

GOE INFORMATION—**Interest Area:** 02. Science, Math, and Engineering. **Work Group:** 02.03. Life Sciences. **Other Job Titles in This Work Group:** Agricultural and Food Science Technicians; Agricultural Technicians; Animal Scientists; Biochemists; Biochemists and Biophysicists; Biological Scientists, All Other; Biologists; Biophysicists; Conservation Scientists; Epidemiologists; Food Science Technicians; Food Scientists and Technologists; Foresters; Life Scientists, All Other; Medical Scientists, Except Epidemiologists; Microbiologists; Plant Scientists; Range Managers; Soil and Plant Scientists; Soil Conservationists; Soil Scientists; Zoologists and Wildlife Biologists. **PERSONALITY TYPE**—Investigative. Investigative occupations frequently involve working with ideas and require an extensive amount of thinking. These occupations can involve searching for facts and figuring out problems mentally.

EDUCATION/TRAINING PROGRAM(S)—Conservation and Renewable Natural Resources, Other; Environmental Science/Studies; Forest Management; Forestry and Related Sciences, Other; Forestry Sciences; Forestry, General; Natural Resources Conservation, General; Natural Resources Law Enforcement and Protective Services; Natural Resources Management and Policy; Natural Resources Management and Protective Services, Other; Wood Science and Pulp/Paper Technology. **RELATED KNOWLEDGE/COURSES**—**Mathematics:** Knowledge of arithmetic, algebra, geometry, calculus, and statistics and their applications. **Biology:** Knowledge of plant and animal organisms and their tissues, cells, functions, interdependencies, and interactions with each other and the environment. **Chemistry:** Knowledge of the chemical composition, structure, and properties of substances and of the chemical processes and transformations that they undergo. This includes uses of chemicals and their interactions, danger signs, production techniques, and disposal methods. **English Language:** Knowledge of the structure and content of the English language, including the meaning and spelling of words, rules of composition, and grammar. **Physics:** Knowledge and prediction of physical principles and laws and their interrelationships and applications to understanding fluid, material, and atmospheric dynamics and mechanical, electrical, atomic, and sub-atomic structures and processes.

Epidemiologists

▲ Education/Training Required: Doctoral degree

▲ Annual Earnings: $48,390

▲ Growth: 26%

▲ Annual Job Openings: 2,000

▲ Self-Employed: 2.8%

▲ Part-Time: 6.6%

Investigate and describe the determinants and distribution of disease, disability, and other health outcomes and develop the means for prevention and control. Plans and directs studies to investigate human or animal disease, preventive methods, and treatments for disease. Studies effects of drugs, gases, pesticides, parasites, or micro-organisms or health and physiological processes of animals and humans. Plans methodological design of research study and arranges for data collection. Consults with and advises physicians, educators, researchers, and others regarding medical applications of sciences, such as physics, biology, and chemistry. Confers with health department, industry personnel, physicians, and others to develop health safety standards and programs to improve public health. Teaches principles of medicine and medical and laboratory procedures to physicians, residents, students, and technicians. Supervises activities of clerical and statistical or laboratory personnel. Standardizes drug dosages, methods of immunization, and procedures for manufacture of drugs and medicinal compounds. Prepares and analyzes samples for toxicity, bacteria, or microorganisms or to study cell structure and properties. Examines organs, tissues, cell structures, or micro-organisms by systematic observation or using microscope. Conducts research to develop methodologies; instrumentation; or identification, diagnosing, and treatment procedures for medical application. Investigates cause, progress, life cycle, or mode of transmission of diseases or parasites. Analyzes data, applying statistical techniques and scientific knowledge; prepares reports; and presents findings. **SKILLS—** Instructing: Teaching others how to do something. Active Learning: Understanding the implications of new information for both current and future problem-solving and decision-making. Reading Comprehension: Understanding written sentences and paragraphs in work-related documents. Writing: Communicating effectively in writing as appropriate for the needs of the audience. Science: Using scientific rules and methods to solve problems.

GOE INFORMATION—Interest Area: 02. Science, Math, and Engineering. **Work Group:** 02.03. Life

Sciences. **Other Job Titles in This Work Group:** Agricultural and Food Science Technicians; Agricultural Technicians; Animal Scientists; Biochemists; Biochemists and Biophysicists; Biological Scientists, All Other; Biologists; Biophysicists; Conservation Scientists; Environmental Scientists and Specialists, Including Health; Food Science Technicians; Food Scientists and Technologists; Foresters; Life Scientists, All Other; Medical Scientists, Except Epidemiologists; Microbiologists; Plant Scientists; Range Managers; Soil and Plant Scientists; Soil Conservationists; Soil Scientists; Zoologists and Wildlife Biologists. **PERSONALITY TYPE—Investigative.** Investigative occupations frequently involve working with ideas and require an extensive amount of thinking. These occupations can involve searching for facts and figuring out problems mentally.

EDUCATION/TRAINING PROGRAM(S)— Epidemiology; Medical Cell Biology; Medical Physics/Biophysics. **RELATED KNOWLEDGE/ COURSES—Mathematics:** Knowledge of arithmetic, algebra, geometry, calculus, and statistics and their applications. **Biology:** Knowledge of plant and animal organisms and their tissues, cells, functions, interdependencies, and interactions with each other and the environment. **Chemistry:** Knowledge of the chemical composition, structure, and properties of substances and of the chemical processes and transformations that they undergo. This includes uses of chemicals and their interactions, danger signs, production techniques, and disposal methods. **Computers and Electronics:** Knowledge of circuit boards, processors, chips, electronic equipment, and computer hardware and software, including applications and programming. **Medicine and Dentistry:** Knowledge of the information and techniques needed to diagnose and treat human injuries, diseases, and deformities. This includes symptoms, treatment alternatives, drug properties and interactions, and preventive health-care measures. **English Language:** Knowledge of the structure and content of the English language, including the meaning and spelling of words, rules of composition, and grammar.

Exhibit Designers

- ▲ Education/Training Required: Bachelor's degree
- ▲ Annual Earnings: $31,440
- ▲ Growth: 27%
- ▲ Annual Job Openings: 2,000
- ▲ Self-Employed: 31.9%
- ▲ Part-Time: 20%

Plan, design, and oversee construction and installation of permanent and temporary exhibits and displays. Prepares preliminary drawings of proposed exhibit, including detailed construction, layout, material specifications, or special-effects diagrams. Arranges for acquisition of specimens or graphics or building of exhibit structures by outside contractors to complete exhibit. Inspects installed exhibit for conformance to specifications and satisfactory operation of special effects components. Submits plans for approval and adapts plan to serve intended purpose or to conform to budget or fabrication restrictions. Designs, draws, paints, or sketches backgrounds and fixtures for use in windows or interior displays. Oversees preparation of artwork, construction of exhibit components, and placement of collection to ensure intended interpretation of concepts and conformance to specifications. Confers with client or staff regarding theme, interpretive or informational purpose, planned location, budget, materials, or promotion. Designs display to decorate streets, fairgrounds, building, or other places for celebrations, using paper, cloth, plastic, or other materials. **SKILLS**—Writing: Communicating effectively in writing as appropriate for the needs of the audience. Coordination: Adjusting actions in relation to others' actions. Time Management: Managing one's own time and the time of others. Reading Comprehension: Understanding written sentences and paragraphs in work-related documents. Management of Material Resources: Obtaining and seeing to the appropriate use of equipment, facilities, and materials needed to do certain work. Mathematics: Using mathematics to solve problems. Active Learning: Understanding the implications of new information for both current and future problem-solving and decision-making.

GOE INFORMATION—**Interest Area:** 01. Arts, Entertainment, and Media. **Work Group:** 01.04. Visual Arts. **Other Job Titles in This Work Group:** Cartoonists; Commercial and Industrial Designers; Designers, All Other; Fashion Designers; Fine Artists, Including Painters, Sculptors, and Illustrators; Floral Designers; Graphic Designers; Interior Designers; Merchandise Displayers and Window Trimmers; Multi-Media Artists and Animators; Painters and Illustrators; Sculptors; Set and Exhibit Designers; Set Designers; Sketch Artists. **PERSONALITY TYPE**—Artistic. Artistic occupations frequently involve working with forms, designs, and patterns. They often require self-expression, and the work can be done without following a clear set of rules.

EDUCATION/TRAINING PROGRAM(S)—Design and Applied Arts, Other; Design and Visual Communications; Technical Theater/Theater Design and Stagecraft. **RELATED KNOWLEDGE/COURSES**—**Design:** Knowledge of design techniques, tools, and principles involved in production of precision technical plans, blueprints, drawings, and models. **Fine Arts:** Knowledge of the theory and techniques required to compose, produce, and perform works of music, dance, visual arts, drama, and sculpture. **Building and Construction:** Knowledge of materials, methods, and tools involved in the construction or repair of houses, buildings, or other structures, such as highways and roads. **Psychology:** Knowledge of human behavior and performance; individual differences in ability, personality, and interests; learning and motivation; psychological research methods; and the assessment and treatment of behavioral and affective disorders. **Mathematics:** Knowledge of arithmetic, algebra, geometry, calculus, and statistics and their applications. **Principles of Mechanical Devices:** Knowledge of machines and tools, including their designs, uses, repair, and maintenance. **English Language:** Knowledge of the structure and content of the English language, including the meaning and spelling of words, rules of composition, and grammar.

Family and General Practitioners

- ▲ Education/Training Required: First professional degree
- ▲ Annual Earnings: $ 114,170
- ▲ Growth: 18%
- ▲ Annual Job Openings: 27,000
- ▲ Self-Employed: 20.4%
- ▲ Part-Time: 7.2%

Diagnose, treat, and help prevent diseases and injuries that commonly occur in the general population. Examines or conducts tests on patient to provide information on medical condition. Analyzes records, reports, test results, or examination information to diagnose medical condition of patient. Prescribes or administers treatment, therapy, medication, vaccination, and other specialized medical care to treat or prevent illness, disease, or injury. Explains procedures and discusses test results on prescribed treatments with patents. Advises patients and community concerning diet, activity, hygiene, and disease prevention. Directs and coordinates activities of nurses, students, assistants, specialists, therapists, and other medical staff. Conducts research to study anatomy and develop or test medications, treatments, or procedures to prevent or control disease or injury. Prepares reports for government or management of birth, death, and disease statistics, workforce evaluations, or medical status of individuals. Plans, implements, or administers health programs or standards in hospital, business, or community for information, prevention, or treatment of injury or illness. Refers patient to medical specialist or other practitioner when necessary. Collects, records, and maintains patient information, such as medical history, reports, and examination results. Operates on patients to remove, repair, or improve functioning of diseased or injured body parts and systems and delivers babies. **SKILLS**—Reading Comprehension: Understanding written sentences and paragraphs in work-related documents. Active Learning: Understanding the implications of new information for both current and future problem-solving and decision-making. Science: Using scientific rules and methods to solve problems. Judgment and Decision

Making: Considering the relative costs and benefits of potential actions to choose the most appropriate one. Critical Thinking: Using logic and reasoning to identify the strengths and weaknesses of alternative solutions, conclusions, or approaches to problems. Speaking: Talking to others to convey information effectively. Writing: Communicating effectively in writing as appropriate for the needs of the audience.

GOE INFORMATION—Interest Area: 14. Medical and Health Services. **Work Group:** 14.02. Medicine and Surgery. **Other Job Titles in This Work Group:** Anesthesiologists; Internists, General; Medical Assistants; Obstetricians and Gynecologists; Pediatricians, General; Pharmacists; Pharmacy Aides; Pharmacy Technicians; Physician Assistants; Physicians and Surgeons, All Other; Psychiatrists; Registered Nurses; Surgeons; Surgical Technologists. **PERSONALITY TYPE**—Investigative. Investigative occupations frequently involve working with ideas and require an extensive amount of thinking. These occupations can involve searching for facts and figuring out problems mentally.

EDUCATION/TRAINING PROGRAM(S)— Family Medicine Residency; Medicine (M.D.); Osteopathic Medicine (D.O.). **RELATED KNOWLEDGE/ COURSES—Medicine and Dentistry:** Knowledge of the information and techniques needed to diagnose and treat human injuries, diseases, and deformities. This includes symptoms, treatment alternatives, drug properties and interactions, and preventive health-care measures. **Biology:** Knowledge of plant and animal organisms and their tissues, cells, functions, interdependencies, and interactions with each other and the environment. **English Language:** Knowledge of the structure and content of the English language, including the meaning and spelling of words, rules of composition, and grammar. **Therapy and Counseling:** Knowledge of principles, methods, and procedures for diagnosis, treatment, and rehabilitation of physical and mental dysfunctions and for career counseling and guidance. **Administration and Management:** Knowledge of business and management principles involved in strategic planning, resource allocation, human resources modeling, leadership technique, production methods, and coordination of people and resources.

Farm and Home Management Advisors

- ▲ Education/Training Required: Bachelor's degree
- ▲ Annual Earnings: $36,290
- ▲ Growth: 6%
- ▲ Annual Job Openings: 2,000
- ▲ Self-Employed: 0%
- ▲ Part-Time: 42.5%

Advise, instruct, and assist individuals and families engaged in agriculture, agricultural-related processes, or home economics activities. Demonstrate procedures and apply research findings to solve problems; instruct and train in product development, sales, and the utilization of machinery and equipment to promote general welfare. Includes county agricultural agents, feed and farm management advisers, home economists, and extension service advisors. Advises farmers in matters such as feeding and health maintenance of livestock, cultivation, growing and harvesting practices, and budgeting. Advises individuals and families on home management practices, such as budget planning, meal preparation, energy conservation, clothing, and home furnishings. Plans, develops, organizes, and evaluates training programs in subjects such as home management, horticulture, and consumer information. Collects and evaluates data to ascertain needs and develop programs beneficial to community. Conducts classes to educate others in subjects such as nutrition, home management, home furnishing, child care, and farming techniques. Delivers lectures to organizations or talks over radio and television to disseminate information and promote objectives of program. Prepares leaflets, pamphlets, and visual aids for educational and informational purposes. Organizes, advises, and participates in community activities and organizations such as county and state fair events and 4-H Clubs. **SKILLS**—Reading Comprehension: Understanding written sentences and paragraphs in work-related documents. Writing: Communicating effectively in writing as appropriate for the needs of the audience. Persuasion: Persuading others to change their minds or behavior. Instructing: Teaching others how to do something. Learning Strategies: Selecting and using training/instructional methods and procedures appropriate for the situation when learning or teaching new things. Active Learning: Understanding the implications of new information for both current and future problem-solving and decision-making. Speaking: Talking to others to convey information effectively.

GOE INFORMATION—Interest Area: 12. Education and Social Service. **Work Group:** 12.03. Educational Services. **Other Job Titles in This Work Group:** Adult Literacy, Remedial Education, and GED Teachers and Instructors; Agricultural Sciences Teachers, Postsecondary; Anthropology and Archeology Teachers, Postsecondary; Architecture Teachers, Postsecondary; Archivists; Area, Ethnic, and Cultural Studies Teachers, Postsecondary; Art, Drama, and Music Teachers, Postsecondary; Atmospheric, Earth, Marine, and Space Sciences Teachers, Postsecondary; Audio-Visual Collections Specialists; Biological Science Teachers, Postsecondary; Business Teachers, Postsecondary; Chemistry Teachers, Postsecondary; Child Care Workers; Communications Teachers, Postsecondary; Computer Science Teachers, Postsecondary; Criminal Justice and Law Enforcement Teachers, Postsecondary; Curators; Economics

Teachers, Postsecondary; Education Teachers, Postsecondary; Educational Psychologists; Educational, Vocational, and School Counselors; Elementary School Teachers, Except Special Education; Engineering Teachers, Postsecondary; English Language and Literature Teachers, Postsecondary; Environmental Science Teachers, Postsecondary; Foreign Language and Literature Teachers, Postsecondary; Forestry and Conservation Science Teachers, Postsecondary; Geography Teachers, Postsecondary; Graduate Teaching Assistants; Health Specialties Teachers, Postsecondary; History Teachers, Postsecondary; Home Economics Teachers, Postsecondary; Kindergarten Teachers, Except Special Education; Law Teachers, Postsecondary; Librarians; Library Assistants, Clerical; Library Science Teachers, Postsecondary; others. **PERSONALITY TYPE**—Social. Social occupations frequently involve working with, communicating with, and teaching people. These occupations often involve helping or providing service to others.

EDUCATION/TRAINING PROGRAM(S)— Agricultural Animal Husbandry and Production Management; Agricultural Animal Nutrition; Agricultural Extension; Business Home Economics; Child Growth, Care and Development Studies; Clothing/Apparel and Textile Studies; Consumer Economics and Science; Crop Production Operations and Management; Family and Community Studies; Family and Marriage Counseling; Family Life and Relations Studies; Family Resource Management Studies; Family/Consumer Resource Management, Other; Farm and Ranch Management; Gerontological Services; Home Economics Communications; Home Economics, General; Home Economics, Other; Housing Studies, General; Housing Studies, Other; Individual and Family Development Studies, General; Individual and Family Development Studies, Other; Vocational Home Economics, Other. **RELATED KNOWLEDGE/COURSES—Food Production:** Knowledge of techniques and equipment for planting, growing, and harvesting food products (both plant and animal) for consumption, including storage/handling techniques. **Education and Training:** Knowledge of principles and methods for curriculum and training design, teaching and instruction for individuals and groups, and the measurement of training effects. **Economics and Accounting:** Knowledge of economic and accounting principles and practices, the financial markets, banking, and the analysis and reporting of financial data. **Administration and Management:** Knowledge of business and management principles involved in strategic planning, resource allocation, human resources modeling, leadership technique, production methods, and coordination of people and resources. **Mathematics:** Knowledge of arithmetic, algebra, geometry, calculus, and statistics and their applications.

Fashion Designers

- ▲ Education/Training Required: Bachelor's degree
- ▲ Annual Earnings: $48,530
- ▲ Growth: 20%
- ▲ Annual Job Openings: 2,000
- ▲ Self-Employed: 31.9%
- ▲ Part-Time: 20%

Design clothing and accessories. Create original garments or design garments that follow well-established fashion trends. May develop the line of color and kinds of materials. Designs custom garments for clients. Attends fashion shows and reviews garment magazines and manuals to analyze fashion trends, predictions, and consumer preferences. Sews together sections to form mockup or sample of garment or article, using sewing equipment. Directs and coordinates workers who draw and cut patterns and construct sample or finished garment. Arranges for showing of sample garments at sales meetings or fashion shows. Confers with sales and management executives or clients regarding design ideas. Examines sample garment on and off model and modifies design to achieve desired effect. Integrates findings of analysis and discussion and personal tastes and knowledge of design to originate design ideas. Sketches rough and detailed drawings of apparel or accessories and writes specifications, such as color scheme, construction, or material type. Draws pattern for article designed, cuts pattern, and cuts material according to pattern, using measuring and drawing instruments and scissors. **SKILLS**—Coordination: Adjusting actions in relation to others' actions. Operations Analysis: Analyzing needs and product requirements to create a design. Persuasion: Persuading others to change their minds or behavior. Active Learning: Understanding the implications of new information for both current and future problem-solving and decision-making. Judgment and Decision Making: Considering the relative costs and benefits of potential actions to choose the most appropriate one.

GOE INFORMATION—**Interest Area:** 01. Arts, Entertainment, and Media. **Work Group:** 01.04. Visual Arts. **Other Job Titles in This Work Group:** Cartoonists; Commercial and Industrial Designers; Designers, All Other; Exhibit Designers; Fine Artists, Including Painters, Sculptors, and Illustrators; Floral Designers; Graphic Designers; Interior Designers; Merchandise Displayers and Window Trimmers; Multi-Media Artists and Animators; Painters and Illustrators; Sculptors; Set and Exhibit Designers; Set Designers; Sketch Artists. **PERSONALITY TYPE**—Artistic. Artistic occupations frequently involve working with forms, designs, and patterns. They often re-

quire self-expression, and the work can be done without following a clear set of rules.

EDUCATION/TRAINING PROGRAM(S)—Fashion Design and Illustration. **RELATED KNOWLEDGE/COURSES**—**Design:** Knowledge of design techniques, tools, and principles involved in production of precision technical plans, blueprints, drawings, and models. **Fine Arts:** Knowledge of the theory and techniques required to compose, produce, and perform works of music, dance, visual arts, drama, and sculpture. **Sales and Marketing:** Knowledge of principles and methods for showing, promoting, and selling products or services. This includes marketing strategy and tactics, product demonstration, sales techniques, and sales control systems. **Psychology:** Knowledge of human behavior and performance; individual differences in ability, personality, and interests; learning and motivation; psychological research methods; and the assessment and treatment of behavioral and affective disorders. **Sociology and Anthropology:** Knowledge of group behavior and dynamics, societal trends and influences, human migrations, ethnicity, cultures, and their history and origins. **Customer and Personal Service:** Knowledge of principles and processes for providing customer and personal services. This includes customer needs assessment, meeting quality standards for services, and evaluation of customer satisfaction.

Film and Video Editors

- ▲ Education/Training Required: Bachelor's degree
- ▲ Annual Earnings: $34,160
- ▲ Growth: 26%
- ▲ Annual Job Openings: 2,000
- ▲ Self-Employed: 23.7%
- ▲ Part-Time: 25.3%

Edit motion picture soundtracks, film, and video. Edits film and videotape to insert music, dialogue, and sound effects and to correct errors, using editing equipment. Reviews assembled film or edited videotape on screen or monitor and makes corrections. Trims film segments to specified lengths and reassembles segments in sequence that presents story with maximum effect. Evaluates and

selects scenes in terms of dramatic and entertainment value and story continuity. Supervises and coordinates activities of workers engaged in editing and assembling filmed scenes photographed by others. Studies script and confers with producers and directors concerning layout or editing to increase dramatic or entertainment value of production. **SKILLS**—Monitoring: Monitoring/Assessing your performance or that of other individuals or organizations to make improvements or take corrective action. Critical Thinking: Using logic and reasoning to identify the strengths and weaknesses of alternative solutions, conclusions, or approaches to problems. Reading Comprehension: Understanding written sentences and paragraphs in work-related documents. Active Listening: Giving full attention to what other people are saying, taking time to understand the points being made, asking questions as appropriate, and not interrupting at inappropriate times. Coordination: Adjusting actions in relation to others' actions. Active Learning: Understanding the implications of new information for both current and future problem-solving and decision-making.

GOE INFORMATION—Interest Area: 01. Arts, Entertainment, and Media. **Work Group:** 01.08. Media Technology. **Other Job Titles in This Work Group:** Audio and Video Equipment Technicians; Broadcast Technicians; Camera Operators, Television, Video, and Motion Picture; Media and Communication Equipment Workers, All Other; Photographers; Professional Photographers; Radio Operators; Sound Engineering Technicians. **PERSONALITY TYPE**—Artistic. Artistic occupations frequently involve working with forms, designs, and

patterns. They often require self-expression, and the work can be done without following a clear set of rules.

EDUCATION/TRAINING PROGRAM(S)— Communications Technologists/Technicians, Other; Film-Video Making/Cinematography and Production; Radio and Television Broadcasting; Radio and Television Broadcasting Technologist/Technician. **RELATED KNOWLEDGE/COURSES—Communications and Media:** Knowledge of media production, communication, and dissemination techniques and methods. This includes alternative ways to inform and entertain via written, oral, and visual media. **Fine Arts:** Knowledge of the theory and techniques required to compose, produce, and perform works of music, dance, visual arts, drama, and sculpture. **Computers and Electronics:** Knowledge of circuit boards, processors, chips, electronic equipment, and computer hardware and software, including applications and programming. **English Language:** Knowledge of the structure and content of the English language, including the meaning and spelling of words, rules of composition, and grammar. **Telecommunications:** Knowledge of transmission, broadcasting, switching, control, and operation of telecommunications systems.

Financial Analysts

- ▲ Education/Training Required: Bachelor's degree
- ▲ Annual Earnings: $52,420
- ▲ Growth: 26%
- ▲ Annual Job Openings: 20,000
- ▲ Self-Employed: 0%
- ▲ Part-Time: 5.2%

Conduct quantitative analyses of information affecting investment programs of public or private institutions. Analyzes financial information to forecast business, industry, and economic conditions for use in making investment decisions. Interprets data concerning price, yield, stability, and future trends in investment risks and economic influences pertinent to investments. Gathers information such as industry, regulatory, and economic information, company financial statements, financial periodicals, and newspapers. Calls brokers and purchases in-

vestments for company according to company policy. Draws charts and graphs to illustrate reports, using computer. Recommends investment timing and buy-and-sell orders to company or to staff of investment establishment. **SKILLS**—Judgment and Decision Making: Considering the relative costs and benefits of potential actions to choose the most appropriate one. Reading Comprehension: Understanding written sentences and paragraphs in work-related documents. Critical Thinking: Using logic and reasoning to identify the strengths and weaknesses of alternative solutions, conclusions, or approaches to problems. Active Learning: Understanding the implications of new information for both current and future problem-solving and decision-making. Mathematics: Using mathematics to solve problems.

GOE INFORMATION—**Interest Area:** 13. General Management and Support. **Work Group:** 13.02. Management Support. **Other Job Titles in This Work Group:** Accountants; Accountants and Auditors; Appraisers and Assessors of Real Estate; Appraisers, Real Estate; Assessors; Auditors; Budget Analysts; Claims Adjusters, Examiners, and Investigators; Claims Examiners, Property and Casualty Insurance; Compensation, Benefits, and Job Analysis Specialists; Cost Estimators; Credit Analysts; Employment Interviewers, Private or Public Employment Service; Employment, Recruitment, and Placement Specialists; Human Resources, Training, and Labor Relations Specialists, All Other; Insurance Adjusters, Examiners, and Investigators; Insurance Appraisers, Auto Damage; Insurance Underwriters; Loan Counselors; Loan Officers; Logisticians; Management Analysts; Market Research Analysts; Personnel Recruiters; Purchasing Agents and Buyers, Farm Products; Purchasing Agents, Except Wholesale, Retail, and Farm Products; Tax Examiners, Collectors, and Revenue Agents; Training and Development Specialists; Wholesale and Retail Buyers, Except Farm Products. **PERSONALITY TYPE**—Investigative. Investigative occupations frequently involve working with ideas and require an extensive amount of thinking. These occupations can involve searching for facts and figuring out problems mentally.

EDUCATION/TRAINING PROGRAM(S)—Finance, General. **RELATED KNOWLEDGE/ COURSES**—**Economics and Accounting:** Knowledge of economic and accounting principles and practices, the financial markets, banking, and the analysis and reporting of financial data. **Mathematics:** Knowledge of arithmetic, algebra, geometry, calculus, and statistics and their applications. **Computers and Electronics:** Knowledge of circuit boards, processors, chips, electronic equipment, and computer hardware and software, including applications and programming. **English Language:** Knowledge of the structure and content of the English language, including the meaning and spelling of words, rules of composition, and grammar. **Law and Government:** Knowledge of laws, legal codes, court procedures, precedents, government regulations, executive orders, agency rules, and the democratic political process.

Financial Examiners

- ▲ Education/Training Required: Bachelor's degree
- ▲ Annual Earnings: $53,060
- ▲ Growth: 10%
- ▲ Annual Job Openings: 2,000
- ▲ Self-Employed: 1.3%
- ▲ Part-Time: 2.9%

Enforce or ensure compliance with laws and regulations governing financial and securities institutions and financial and real estate transactions. May examine, verify correctness of, or establish authenticity of records. Investigates activities of institutions to enforce laws and regulations and to ensure legality of transactions and operations or financial solvency. Conducts or arranges for educational classes and training programs. Directs workers engaged in designing, writing, and publishing guidelines, manuals, bulletins, and reports.

Recommends action to ensure compliance with laws and regulations or to protect solvency of institution. Reviews applications for merger, acquisition, establishment of new institution, acceptance in Federal Reserve System, or registration of securities sales. Determines if application action is in public interest and in accordance with regulations and recommends acceptance or rejection of application. Confers with officials of real estate, securities, or financial institution industries to exchange views and discuss issues or pending cases. Schedules audits and examines records and reports to determine regulatory compliance. Establishes guidelines for and directs implementation of procedures and policies to comply with new and revised regulations. Reviews, analyzes, and interprets new, proposed, or revised laws, regulations, policies, and procedures. **SKILLS**—Reading Comprehension: Understanding written sentences and paragraphs in work-related documents. Writing: Communicating effectively in writing as appropriate for the needs of the audience. Judgment and Decision Making: Considering the relative costs and benefits of potential actions to choose the most appropriate one. Mathematics: Using mathematics to solve problems. Active Listening: Giving full attention to what other people are saying, taking time to understand the points being made, asking questions as appropriate, and not interrupting at inappropriate times. Speaking: Talking to others to convey information effectively.

GOE INFORMATION—Interest Area: 04. Law, Law Enforcement, and Public Safety. **Work Group:** 04.04. Public Safety. **Other Job Titles in This Work Group:** Agricultural Inspectors; Aviation Inspectors; Compliance Officers, Except Agriculture, Construction, Health and Safety, and Transportation; Emergency Medical Technicians and Paramedics; Environmental Compliance Inspectors; Equal Opportunity Representatives and Officers; Fire Fighters; Fire Inspectors; Fire Inspectors and Investigators; Forest Fire Fighters; Forest Fire Inspectors and Prevention Specialists; Government Property Inspectors and

Investigators; Licensing Examiners and Inspectors; Marine Cargo Inspectors; Municipal Fire Fighters; Nuclear Monitoring Technicians; Occupational Health and Safety Specialists; Occupational Health and Safety Technicians; Public Transportation Inspectors. **PERSONALITY TYPE**—Enterprising. Enterprising occupations frequently involve starting up and carrying out projects. These occupations can involve leading people and making many decisions. They sometimes require risk taking and often deal with business.

EDUCATION/TRAINING PROGRAM(S)—Accounting; Taxation. **RELATED KNOWLEDGE/ COURSES**—**Economics and Accounting:** Knowledge of economic and accounting principles and practices, the financial markets, banking, and the analysis and reporting of financial data. **Mathematics:** Knowledge of arithmetic, algebra, geometry, calculus, and statistics and their applications. **English Language:** Knowledge of the structure and content of the English language, including the meaning and spelling of words, rules of composition, and grammar. **Education and Training:** Knowledge of principles and methods for curriculum and training design, teaching and instruction for individuals and groups, and the measurement of training effects. **Law and Government:** Knowledge of laws, legal codes, court procedures, precedents, government regulations, executive orders, agency rules, and the democratic political process.

Financial Managers

- ▲ Education/Training Required: Work experience, plus degree
- ▲ Annual Earnings: $67,020
- ▲ Growth: 18%
- ▲ Annual Job Openings: 53,000
- ▲ Self-Employed: 1.4%
- ▲ Part-Time: 2.6%

Plan, direct, and coordinate accounting, investing, banking, insurance, securities, and other financial activities of a branch, office, or department of an establishment. **SKILLS**—No data available.

GOE INFORMATION—Interest Area: 13. General Management and Support. **Work Group:** 13.01. General Management Work and Management of Support Functions. **Other Job Titles in This Work Group:** Chief Executives; Compensation and Benefits Managers;

Farm, Ranch, and Other Agricultural Managers; Financial Managers, Branch or Department; Funeral Directors; General and Operations Managers; Government Service Executives; Human Resources Managers; Human Resources Managers, All Other; Legislators; Managers, All Other; Postmasters and Mail Superintendents; Private Sector Executives; Property, Real Estate, and Community Association Managers; Public Relations Managers; Purchasing Managers; Storage and Distribution Managers; Training and Development Managers; Transportation, Storage, and Distribution Managers; Treasurers, Controllers, and Chief Financial Officers. **PERSONALITY TYPE**—No data available.

EDUCATION/TRAINING PROGRAM(S)— Finance, General; Financial Management and Services, Other; International Finance; Public Finance. **RELATED KNOWLEDGE/COURSES**—No data available.

Financial Managers, Branch or Department

- ▲ Education/Training Required: Work experience, plus degree
- ▲ Annual Earnings: $67,020
- ▲ Growth: 18%
- ▲ Annual Job Openings: 53,000
- ▲ Self-Employed: 1.4%
- ▲ Part-Time: 2.6%

Direct and coordinate financial activities of workers in a branch, office, or department of an establishment, such as branch bank, brokerage firm, risk and insurance department, or credit department. Directs and coordinates activities of workers engaged in conducting credit investigations and collecting delinquent accounts of customers. Directs and coordinates activities to implement institution policies, procedures, and practices concerning granting or extending lines of credit and loans. Prepares financial and regulatory reports required by law, regulations, and board of directors. Selects appropriate technique to minimize loss, such as avoidance and loss prevention and reduction. Directs floor operations of brokerage firm engaged in buying and selling securities at exchange. Evaluates effectiveness of current collection policies and procedures. Evaluates data pertaining to costs to plan budget. Monitors order flow and transactions that brokerage firm executes on floor of exchange. Submits delinquent accounts to attorney or outside agency for collection. Examines, evaluates, and processes loan applications. Establishes credit limitations on customer account. Reviews reports of securities transactions and price lists to analyze market conditions. Reviews collection reports to ascertain status of collections and balances outstanding. Directs insurance negotiations, selects insurance brokers and carriers, and places insurance. Establishes procedures for custody and control of assets, records, loan collateral, and securities to ensure safekeeping. Prepares operational and risk reports for management analysis. Analyzes and classifies risks as to frequency and financial impact of risk on company. Plans, directs, and coordinates risk and insurance programs of establishment to control risks and losses. Manages branch or office of financial institution. **SKILLS**—Writing: Communicating effectively in writing as appropriate for the needs of the audience. Monitoring: Monitoring/Assessing your performance or that of other individuals or organizations to make improvements or take corrective action. Management of Financial Resources: Determining how money will be spent to get the work done and accounting for these expenditures. Critical Thinking: Using logic and reasoning to identify the strengths and weaknesses of alternative solutions, conclusions, or approaches to problems. Judgment and Decision Making: Considering the relative costs and benefits of potential actions to choose the most appropriate one.

GOE INFORMATION—**Interest Area:** 13. General Management and Support. **Work Group:** 13.01. General Management Work and Management of Support

Functions. **Other Job Titles in This Work Group:** Chief Executives; Compensation and Benefits Managers; Farm, Ranch, and Other Agricultural Managers; Financial Managers; Funeral Directors; General and Operations Managers; Government Service Executives; Human Resources Managers; Human Resources Managers, All Other; Legislators; Managers, All Other; Postmasters and Mail Superintendents; Private Sector Executives; Property, Real Estate, and Community Association Managers; Public Relations Managers; Purchasing Managers; Storage and Distribution Managers; Training and Development Managers; Transportation, Storage, and Distribution Managers; Treasurers, Controllers, and Chief Financial Officers. **PERSONALITY TYPE**—Enterprising. Enterprising occupations frequently involve starting up and carrying out projects. These occupations can involve leading people and making many decisions. They sometimes require risk taking and often deal with business.

EDUCATION/TRAINING PROGRAM(S)— Finance, General; Financial Management and Services,

Other; International Finance; Public Finance. **RELATED KNOWLEDGE/COURSES—Economics and Accounting:** Knowledge of economic and accounting principles and practices, the financial markets, banking, and the analysis and reporting of financial data. **Administration and Management:** Knowledge of business and management principles involved in strategic planning, resource allocation, human resources modeling, leadership technique, production methods, and coordination of people and resources. **Mathematics:** Knowledge of arithmetic, algebra, geometry, calculus, and statistics and their applications. **English Language:** Knowledge of the structure and content of the English language, including the meaning and spelling of words, rules of composition, and grammar. **Law and Government:** Knowledge of laws, legal codes, court procedures, precedents, government regulations, executive orders, agency rules, and the democratic political process.

Fire Investigators

- ▲ Education/Training Required: Bachelor's degree
- ▲ Annual Earnings: $41,630
- ▲ Growth: 15%
- ▲ Annual Job Openings: 1,000
- ▲ Self-Employed: 0%
- ▲ Part-Time: 1.9%

Conduct investigations to determine causes of fires and explosions. Examines site and collects evidence to gather information relating to cause of fire, explosion, or false alarm. Photographs damage and evidence relating to cause of fire or explosion for future reference. Instructs children about dangers of fire. Swears out warrants and arrests, logs, fingerprints, and detains suspected arsonists. Testifies in court for cases involving fires, suspected arson, and false alarms. Prepares and maintains reports of investigation results and records of convicted arsonists and arson suspects. Conducts internal investigation to determine negligence and violation of laws and regulations by fire department employees. Subpoenas and interviews witnesses, property owners, and building occu-

pants to obtain information and sworn testimony. Analyzes evidence and other information to determine probable cause of fire or explosion. Tests site and materials to establish facts such as burn patterns and flash points of materials, using test equipment. **SKILLS—Active Listening:** Giving full attention to what other people are saying, taking time to understand the points being made, asking questions as appropriate, and not interrupting at inappropriate times. Critical Thinking: Using logic and reasoning to identify the strengths and weaknesses of alternative solutions, conclusions, or approaches to problems. Writing: Communicating effectively in writing as appropriate for the needs of the audience. Speaking: Talking to others to convey information effectively. Reading Comprehension: Understanding written sentences and paragraphs in work-related documents. Judgment and Decision Making: Considering the relative costs and benefits of potential actions to choose the most appropriate one.

GOE INFORMATION—Interest Area: 04. Law, Law Enforcement, and Public Safety. **Work Group:** 04.03. Law Enforcement. **Other Job Titles in This Work Group:** Animal Control Workers; Bailiffs; Child Support, Missing Persons, and Unemployment Insurance Fraud Investigators; Correctional Officers and Jailers; Criminal Investigators and Special Agents; Crossing Guards; Detectives and Criminal Investigators; Fish and Game Wardens; Forensic Science Technicians; Gaming Surveillance Officers and Gaming Investigators; Highway Patrol Pilots; Immigration and Customs Inspectors; Lifeguards, Ski Patrol, and Other Recreational Protective Service Workers; Parking Enforcement Workers; Police and Sheriff's Patrol Officers; Police Detectives; Police Identification and Records Officers; Police Patrol Officers; Private Detectives and Investigators; Security Guards; Sheriffs and Deputy Sheriffs; Transit and Railroad Police. **PERSONALITY TYPE**—Investigative. Investigative occupations frequently involve working with ideas and require an extensive amount of thinking. These occupations can involve searching for facts and figuring out problems mentally.

EDUCATION/TRAINING PROGRAM(S)— Fire Protection and Safety Technologist/Technician; Fire Science/Firefighting. **RELATED KNOWLEDGE/ COURSES—Public Safety and Security:** Knowledge of relevant equipment, policies, procedures, and strategies to promote effective local, state, or national security operations for the protection of people, data, property, and institutions. **English Language:** Knowledge of the structure and content of the English language, including the meaning and spelling of words, rules of composition, and grammar. **Law and Government:** Knowledge of laws, legal codes, court procedures, precedents, government regulations, executive orders, agency rules, and the democratic political process. **Chemistry:** Knowledge of the chemical composition, structure, and properties of substances and of the chemical processes and transformations that they undergo. This includes uses of chemicals and their interactions, danger signs, production techniques, and disposal methods. **Building and Construction:** Knowledge of materials, methods, and tools involved in the construction or repair of houses, buildings, or other structures, such as highways and roads.

Fire-Prevention and Protection Engineers

- ▲ Education/Training Required: Bachelor's degree
- ▲ Annual Earnings: $54,630
- ▲ Growth: 11%
- ▲ Annual Job Openings: 3,000
- ▲ Self-Employed: 2.7%
- ▲ Part-Time: 4.5%

Research causes of fires, determine fire protection methods, and design or recommend materials or equipment such as structural components or fire-detection equipment to assist organizations in safeguarding life and property against fire, explosion, and related hazards. Determines fire causes and methods of fire prevention. Conducts research on fire retardants and fire safety of materials and devices to determine cause and methods of fire prevention. Studies build-ings to evaluate fire prevention factors, resistance of construction, contents, water supply and delivery, and exits. Recommends and advises on use of fire detection equipment, extinguishing devices, or methods to alleviate conditions conducive to fire. Advises and plans for prevention of destruction by fire, wind, water, or other causes of damage. Organizes and trains personnel to carry out fire protection programs. Designs fire detection equipment, alarm systems, fire extinguishing devices and systems, or structural components protection. Evaluates fire departments and laws and regulations affecting fire prevention or fire safety. **SKILLS**—Technology Design: Generating or adapting equipment and technology to serve user needs. Instructing: Teaching others how to do something. Reading Comprehension: Understanding written sentences and paragraphs in work-related documents. Active Learning: Understanding the implications of new information for both current and future problem-solving and decision-making. Speaking: Talking to others to convey information effectively. Operations Analysis: Analyzing needs and product requirements to create a design.

GOE INFORMATION—**Interest Area:** 02. Science, Math, and Engineering. **Work Group:** 02.07. Engineering. **Other Job Titles in This Work Group:** Aerospace Engineers; Agricultural Engineers; Architects, Except Landscape and Naval; Biomedical Engineers; Chemical Engineers; Civil Engineers; Computer Hardware Engineers; Computer Software Engineers, Applications; Computer Software Engineers, Systems Software; Electrical Engineers; Electronics Engineers, Except Computer; Engineers, All Other; Environmental Engineers; Health and Safety Engineers, Except Mining Safety Engineers and Inspectors; Industrial Engineers; Industrial Safety and Health Engineers; Landscape Architects; Marine Architects; Marine Engineers; Marine Engineers and Naval Architects; Materials Engineers; Mechanical Engineers; Mining and Geological Engineers, Including Mining Safety Engineers; Nuclear Engineers; Petroleum Engineers; Prod-

uct Safety Engineers; Sales Engineers. **PERSONALITY TYPE**—Investigative. Investigative occupations frequently involve working with ideas and require an extensive amount of thinking. These occupations can involve searching for facts and figuring out problems mentally.

EDUCATION/TRAINING PROGRAM(S)— Engineering/Industrial Management; Environmental/Environmental Health Engineering; Systems Engineering. **RELATED KNOWLEDGE/COURSES**—**Public Safety and Security:** Knowledge of relevant equipment, policies, procedures, and strategies to promote effective local, state, or national security operations for the protection of people, data, property, and institutions. **Education and Training:** Knowledge of principles and methods for curriculum and training design, teaching and instruction for individuals and groups, and the measurement of training effects. **Chemistry:** Knowledge of the chemical composition, structure, and properties of substances and of the chemical processes and transformations that they undergo. This includes uses of chemicals and their interactions, danger signs, production techniques, and disposal methods. **Engineering and Technology:** Knowledge of the practical application of engineering science and technology. This includes applying principles, techniques, procedures, and equipment to the design and production of various goods and services. **Law and Government:** Knowledge of laws, legal codes, court procedures, precedents, government regulations, executive orders, agency rules, and the democratic political process.

Food Science Technicians

▲ Education/Training Required: Associate's degree
▲ Annual Earnings: $27,080
▲ Growth: 15%
▲ Annual Job Openings: 3,000
▲ Self-Employed: 0.9%
▲ Part-Time: 11.7%

Perform standardized qualitative and quantitative tests to determine physical or chemical properties of food or beverage products. Conducts standardized tests on food, beverages, additives, and preservatives to ensure compliance to standards for factors

such as color, texture, nutrients, and coloring. Prepares slides and incubates slides with cell cultures. Cleans and sterilizes laboratory equipment. Orders supplies to maintain inventory in laboratory or in storage facility of food or beverage processing plant. Measures, tests, and weighs bottles, cans, and other containers to ensure hardness, strength, and dimensions meet specifications. Records and compiles test results and prepares graphs, charts, and reports. Tastes or smells food or beverages to ensure flavor meets specifications or to select samples with specific characteristics. Computes moisture or salt content, percentage of ingredients, formulas, or other product factors, using mathematical and chemical procedures. Examines chemical and biological samples to identify cell structure, bacteria, or extraneous material, using microscope. Mixes, blends, or cultivates ingredients to make reagents or to manufacture food or beverage products. Analyzes test results to classify product or compares results with standard tables. **SKILLS**—Mathematics: Using mathematics to solve problems. Reading Comprehension: Understanding written sentences and paragraphs in work-related documents. Writing: Communicating effectively in writing as appropriate for the needs of the audience. Active Learning: Understanding the implications of new information for both current and future problem-solving and decision-making. Science: Using scientific rules and methods to solve problems.

GOE INFORMATION—**Interest Area:** 02. Science, Math, and Engineering. **Work Group:** 02.03. Life Sciences. **Other Job Titles in This Work Group:** Agricultural and Food Science Technicians; Agricultural Technicians; Animal Scientists; Biochemists; Biochemists and Biophysicists; Biological Scientists, All Other; Biologists; Biophysicists; Conservation Scientists; Environmental Scientists and Specialists, Including Health; Epidemiologists; Food Scientists and Technologists; Foresters; Life Scientists, All Other; Medical Scientists, Except Epidemiologists; Microbiologists; Plant Scientists;

Range Managers; Soil and Plant Scientists; Soil Conservationists; Soil Scientists; Zoologists and Wildlife Biologists. **PERSONALITY TYPE**—Realistic. Realistic occupations frequently involve work activities that include practical, hands-on problems and solutions. They often deal with plants, animals, and real-world materials like wood, tools, and machinery. Many of the occupations require working outside and do not involve a lot of paperwork or working closely with others.

EDUCATION/TRAINING PROGRAM(S)—Agricultural Animal Breeding and Genetics; Agricultural Animal Husbandry and Production Management; Agricultural Animal Nutrition; Agronomy and Crop Science; Animal Sciences, General; Crop Production Operations and Management; Dairy Science; Food Sciences and Technology. **RELATED KNOWLEDGE/COURSES**—**Chemistry:** Knowledge of the chemical composition, structure, and properties of substances and of the chemical processes and transformations that they undergo. This includes uses of chemicals and their interactions, danger signs, production techniques, and disposal methods. **Biology:** Knowledge of plant and animal organisms and their tissues, cells, functions, interdependencies, and interactions with each other and the environment. **Mathematics:** Knowledge of arithmetic, algebra, geometry, calculus, and statistics and their applications. **English Language:** Knowledge of the structure and content of the English language, including the meaning and spelling of words, rules of composition, and grammar. **Food Production:** Knowledge of techniques and equipment for planting, growing, and harvesting food products (both plant and animal) for consumption, including storage/handling techniques.

Foreign Language and Literature Teachers, Postsecondary

- ▲ Education/Training Required: Master's degree
- ▲ Annual Earnings: $44,380
- ▲ Growth: 24% for all Postsecondary Teachers
- ▲ Annual Job Openings: 184,000 for all Postsecondary Teachers
- ▲ Self-Employed: 0%
- ▲ Part-Time: 32.3% for all Postsecondary Teachers

Teach courses in foreign (i.e., other than English) languages and literature. Prepares and delivers lectures to students. Compiles, administers, and grades examinations or assigns this work to others. Compiles bibliographies of specialized materials for outside reading assignments. Stimulates class discussions. Advises students on academic and vocational curricula. Directs research of other teachers or graduate students working for advanced academic degrees. Conducts research in particular field of knowledge and publishes findings in professional journals. Acts as adviser to student organizations. Serves on faculty committee providing professional consulting services to government and industry. **SKILLS**—Reading Comprehension: Understanding written sentences and paragraphs in work-related documents. Speaking: Talking to others to convey information effectively. Instructing: Teaching others how to do something. Writing: Communicating effectively in writing as appropriate for the needs of the audience. Learning Strategies: Selecting and using training/instructional methods and procedures appropriate for the situation when learning or teaching new things.

GOE INFORMATION—**Interest Area:** 12. Education and Social Service. **Work Group:** 12.03. Educational Services. **Other Job Titles in This Work Group:** Adult Literacy, Remedial Education, and GED Teachers and Instructors; Agricultural Sciences Teachers, Postsecondary; Anthropology and Archeology Teachers, Postsecondary; Architecture Teachers, Postsecondary; Archivists; Area, Ethnic, and Cultural Studies Teachers, Postsecondary; Art, Drama, and Music Teachers, Postsecondary; Atmospheric, Earth, Marine, and Space Sciences Teachers, Postsecondary; Audio-Visual Collections Specialists; Biological Science Teachers, Postsecondary; Business Teachers, Postsecondary; Chemistry Teachers, Postsecondary; Child Care Workers; Communications Teachers, Postsecondary; Computer Science Teachers, Postsecondary; Criminal Justice and Law Enforcement Teachers, Postsecondary; Curators; Economics Teachers, Postsecondary; Education Teachers, Postsecondary; Educational Psychologists; Educational, Vocational, and School Counselors; Elementary School Teachers, Except Special Education; Engineering Teachers, Postsecondary; English Language and Literature Teachers, Postsecondary; Environmental Science Teachers, Postsecondary; Farm and Home Management Advisors;

Forestry and Conservation Science Teachers, Postsecondary; Geography Teachers, Postsecondary; Graduate Teaching Assistants; Health Specialties Teachers, Postsecondary; History Teachers, Postsecondary; Home Economics Teachers, Postsecondary; Kindergarten Teachers, Except Special Education; Law Teachers, Postsecondary; Librarians; Library Assistants, Clerical; Library Science Teachers, Postsecondary; others. **PERSONALITY TYPE**—Artistic. Artistic occupations frequently involve working with forms, designs, and patterns. They often require self-expression, and the work can be done without following a clear set of rules.

EDUCATION/TRAINING PROGRAM(S)—Chinese Language and Literature; East and Southeast Asian Languages and Literatures, Other; East European Languages and Literatures, Other; Foreign Language Interpretation and Translation; Foreign Languages and Literatures, General; French Language and Literature; German Language and Literature; Germanic Languages and Literatures, Other; Greek Language and Literature (Modern); Italian Language and Literature; Japanese Language and Literature; Portuguese Language and Literature; Romance Languages and Literatures, Other; Russian Language and Literature; Scandinavian Languages and Literatures; Slavic Languages and Literatures (Other Than Russian); South Asian Languages and Literatures; Spanish Language and Literature. **RELATED KNOWLEDGE/COURSES**—**English Language:** Knowledge of the structure and content of the English language, including the meaning and spelling of words, rules of composition, and grammar. **Education and Training:** Knowledge of principles and methods for curriculum and training design, teaching and instruction for individuals and groups, and the measurement of training effects. **Foreign Language:** Knowledge of the structure and content of a foreign (non-English) language, including the meaning and spelling of words, rules of composition and grammar, and pronunciation. **Communications and Media:** Knowledge of media production, communication, and dissemination techniques and methods. This includes alternative ways to inform and entertain via written, oral, and visual media. **Clerical Studies:** Knowledge of administrative and clerical procedures and systems such as word processing, managing files and records, stenography and transcription, designing forms, and other office procedures and terminology. **Computers and Electronics:** Knowledge of circuit boards, processors, chips, electronic equipment, and computer hardware and software, including applications and programming.

Forensic Science Technicians

- ▲ Education/Training Required: Associate's degree
- ▲ Annual Earnings: $37,520
- ▲ Growth: 13%
- ▲ Annual Job Openings: 1,000
- ▲ Self-Employed: 0.9%
- ▲ Part-Time: 11.7%

Collect, identify, classify, and analyze physical evidence related to criminal investigations. Perform tests on weapons or substances such as fiber, hair, and tissue to determine significance to investigation. May testify as expert witnesses on evidence or crime laboratory techniques. May serve as specialists in area of expertise, such as ballistics, fingerprinting, handwriting, or biochemistry. Examines, tests, and analyzes tissue samples, chemical substances, physical materials, and ballistics evidence, using recording, measuring, and testing equipment. Interprets laboratory findings and test results to identify and classify substances, materials, and other evidence collected at crime scene. Collects and preserves criminal evidence used to solve cases. Confers with ballistics, fingerprinting, handwriting, documents, electronics, medical, chemical, or metallurgical experts concerning evidence and its interpretation. Reconstructs crime scene to determine relationships among pieces of evidence. Prepares reports or presentations of findings, investigative methods, or laboratory techniques. Testifies as expert witness on evidence or laboratory techniques in trials or hearings. **SKILLS**—Science: Using scientific rules and methods to solve problems. Reading Comprehension: Understanding written sentences and paragraphs in work-related documents. Critical Thinking: Using logic and reasoning to identify the strengths and weaknesses of alternative solutions, conclusions, or approaches to problems. Mathematics: Using mathematics to solve problems. Writing: Communicating effectively in writing as appropriate for the needs of the audience. Speaking: Talking to others to convey information effectively.

GOE INFORMATION—Interest Area: 04. Law, Law Enforcement, and Public Safety. **Work Group:** 04.03. Law Enforcement. **Other Job Titles in This Work Group:** Animal Control Workers; Bailiffs; Child Support, Missing Persons, and Unemployment Insurance Fraud Investigators; Correctional Officers and Jailers; Criminal Investigators and Special Agents; Crossing Guards; Detectives and Criminal Investigators; Fire Investigators; Fish and Game Wardens; Gaming Surveillance Officers and Gaming Investigators; Highway Patrol Pilots; Immigration and Customs Inspectors; Lifeguards, Ski Patrol, and Other Recreational Protective Service Workers; Parking Enforcement Workers; Police and Sheriff's Patrol Officers; Police Detectives; Police Identification and Records Officers; Police Patrol Officers; Private Detectives and Investigators; Security Guards; Sheriffs and Deputy Sheriffs; Transit and Railroad Police. **PERSONALITY TYPE**—Investigative. Investigative occupations frequently involve working with ideas and require an extensive amount of thinking. These occupations can involve searching for facts and figuring out problems mentally.

EDUCATION/TRAINING PROGRAM(S)—Forensic Technologist/Technician. **RELATED KNOWLEDGE/COURSES**—Public Safety and Security: Knowledge of relevant equipment, policies, procedures, and strategies to promote effective local, state, or national security operations for the protection of people, data, property, and institutions. **Chemistry:** Knowledge of the chemical composition, structure, and properties of substances and of the chemical processes and transformations that they undergo. This includes uses of chemicals and their interactions, danger signs, production techniques, and disposal methods. **English Language:** Knowledge of the structure and content of the English language, including the meaning and spelling of words, rules of composition, and grammar. **Law and Government:** Knowledge of laws, legal codes, court procedures, precedents, government regulations, executive orders, agency rules, and the democratic political process. **Computers and Electronics:** Knowledge of circuit boards, processors, chips, electronic equipment, and computer hardware and software, including applications and programming.

Forest and Conservation Technicians

- ▲ Education/Training Required: Associate's degree
- ▲ Annual Earnings: $29,580
- ▲ Growth: 3%
- ▲ Annual Job Openings: 2,000
- ▲ Self-Employed: 12%
- ▲ Part-Time: 17.5%

Compile data pertaining to size, content, condition, and other characteristics of forest tracts under direction of foresters; train and lead forest workers in forest propagation and fire prevention and suppression. May assist conservation scientists in managing, improving, and protecting rangelands and wildlife habitats and help provide technical assistance regarding the conservation of soil, water, and related natural resources. **SKILLS**—No data available.

GOE INFORMATION—**Interest Area:** 03. Plants and Animals. **Work Group:** 03.03. Hands-on Work in Plants and Animals. **Other Job Titles in This Work Group:** Agricultural Equipment Operators; Fallers; Farmworkers and Laborers, Crop, Nursery, and Greenhouse; Farmworkers, Farm and Ranch Animals; Fishers and Related Fishing Workers; Forest and Conservation Workers; General Farmworkers; Grounds Maintenance Workers, All Other; Hunters and Trappers; Landscaping and Groundskeeping Workers; Logging Equipment Operators; Logging Tractor Operators; Logging Workers, All Other; Nursery Workers; Pest Control Workers; Pesticide Handlers, Sprayers, and Applicators, Vegetation; Tree Trimmers and Pruners. **PERSONALITY TYPE**—No data available.

EDUCATION/TRAINING PROGRAM(S)— Conservation and Renewable Natural Resources, Other; Forest Management; Forestry and Related Sciences, Other; Forestry Sciences; Forestry, General; Natural Resources Conservation, General; Natural Resources Law Enforcement and Protective Services; Natural Resources Management and Policy; Natural Resources Management and Protective Services, Other; Wood Science and Pulp/Paper Technology. **RELATED KNOWLEDGE/COURSES**—No data available.

Foresters

- ▲ Education/Training Required: Bachelor's degree
- ▲ Annual Earnings: $43,640
- ▲ Growth: 7%
- ▲ Annual Job Openings: 1,000
- ▲ Self-Employed: 2.4%
- ▲ Part-Time: 6.6%

Manage forested lands for economic, recreational, and conservation purposes. **May inventory the type, amount, and location of standing timber, appraise the timber's worth, negotiate the purchase, and draw up contracts for procurement. May determine how to conserve wildlife habitats, creek beds, water quality, and soil stability and how best to comply with environmental regulations. May devise plans for planting and growing new trees, monitor trees for healthy growth, and determine the best time for harvesting. Develop forest management plans for public and privately owned forested lands.** Manages tree nurseries and thins forest to encourage natural growth of sprouts or seedlings of desired varieties. Participates in environmental studies and prepares environmental reports. Assists in planning and implementing projects for control of floods, soil erosion, tree diseases, infestation, and forest fire. Develops techniques for measuring and identifying trees. Advises landowners on forestry management techniques. Suggests methods of processing wood for various uses. Supervises activities of other forestry workers. Conducts public educational programs on forest care and conservation. Directs suppression of forest fires and fights forest fires. Plans and directs construction and maintenance of recreation facilities, fire towers, trails, roads, and fire breaks. Plans and directs forestation and reforestation projects. Plans cutting programs to assure continuous production or to assist timber companies to achieve production goals. Researches forest propagation and culture affecting tree growth rates, yield, and duration and seed production, growth viability, and germination of different species. Analyzes forest conditions to determine reason for prevalence of different variety of trees. Maps forest areas and estimates standing timber and future growth. Studies classification, life history, light and soil requirements, and resistance to disease and insects of different tree species. Determines methods of cutting and removing timber with minimum waste and environmental damage. Investigates adaptability of different tree species to new environmental conditions, such as soil type, climate, and altitude. **SKILLS**—Systems Analysis: Determining how a system should work and how changes in conditions, operations, and the environment will affect outcomes. Judgment and Decision Making: Considering the relative costs and benefits of potential actions to choose the most appropriate one. Active Learning: Understanding the implications of new information for both current and future problem-solving and decision-making. Complex Problem Solving: Identifying complex problems and reviewing related information to develop and evaluate options and implement solutions. Speaking: Talking to others to convey information effectively. Reading Comprehension: Understanding written sentences and paragraphs in work-related documents.

GOE INFORMATION—**Interest Area:** 02. Science, Math, and Engineering. **Work Group:** 02.03. Life Sciences. **Other Job Titles in This Work Group:** Agricultural and Food Science Technicians; Agricultural Technicians; Animal Scientists; Biochemists; Biochemists and Biophysicists; Biological Scientists, All Other; Biologists; Biophysicists; Conservation Scientists; Environmental Scientists and Specialists, Including Health; Epidemiologists; Food Science Technicians; Food Scientists and Technologists; Life Scientists, All Other; Medical Scientists, Except Epidemiologists; Microbiologists; Plant Scientists; Range Managers; Soil and Plant Scientists; Soil Conservationists; Soil Scientists; Zoologists and Wildlife Biologists. **PERSONALITY TYPE**—Realistic. Realistic occupations frequently involve work activities that include practical, hands-on problems and solutions. They often deal with plants, animals, and real-world materials like wood, tools, and machinery. Many of the occupations require working outside and do not involve a lot of paperwork or working closely with others.

EDUCATION/TRAINING PROGRAM(S)—Conservation and Renewable Natural Resources, Other; Forest Harvesting and Production Technologist/Technician; Forest Management; Forestry and Related Sciences, Other; Forestry Sciences; Forestry, General; Natural Resources Conservation, General; Natural Resources Law Enforcement and Protective Services; Natural Resources Management and Policy; Natural Resources Management and Protective Services, Other; Wood Science and Pulp/Paper Technology. **RELATED KNOWLEDGE/COURSES**—**Biology:** Knowledge of plant and animal organisms and their tissues, cells, functions, interdependencies, and interactions with each other and the environment. **Administration and Management:** Knowledge of business and management principles involved in strategic planning, resource allocation, human resources modeling, leadership technique, production methods, and coordination of people and resources. **English Language:** Knowledge of the structure and content of the English language, including the meaning and spelling of words, rules of composition, and grammar. **Chemistry:** Knowledge of the chemical composition, structure, and properties of substances and of the chemical processes and transformations that they undergo. This includes uses of chemicals and their interactions, danger signs, production techniques, and disposal methods. **Education and Training:** Knowledge of principles and methods for curriculum and training design, teaching and instruction for individuals and groups, and the measurement of training effects. **Mathematics:** Knowledge of arithmetic, algebra, geometry, calculus, and statistics and their applications.

Forestry and Conservation Science Teachers, Postsecondary

- ▲ Education/Training Required: Master's degree
- ▲ Annual Earnings: $58,110
- ▲ Growth: 24% for all Postsecondary Teachers
- ▲ Annual Job Openings: 184,000 for all Postsecondary Teachers
- ▲ Self-Employed: 0%
- ▲ Part-Time: 32.3% for all Postsecondary Teachers

Teach courses in environmental and conservation science. Prepares and delivers lectures to students. Compiles, administers, and grades examinations or assigns this work to others. Advises students on academic and vocational curricula. Conducts research in particular field of knowledge and publishes findings in professional journals. Serves on faculty committee providing professional consulting services to government and industry. Acts as adviser to student organizations. Directs research of other teachers or graduate students working for advanced academic degrees. Stimulates class discussions. Compiles bibliographies of specialized materials for outside reading assignments. **SKILLS**—Reading Comprehension: Understanding written sentences and paragraphs in work-related documents. Instructing: Teaching others how to do something. Learning Strategies: Selecting and using training/instructional methods and procedures appropriate for the situation when learning or teaching new things. Writing: Communicating effectively in writing as appropriate for the needs of the audience. Science: Using scientific rules and methods to solve problems. Critical Thinking: Using logic and reasoning to identify the strengths and weaknesses of alternative solutions, conclusions, or approaches to problems. Active Learning: Understanding the implications of new information for both current and future problem-solving and decision-making.

GOE INFORMATION—**Interest Area:** 12. Education and Social Service. **Work Group:** 12.03. Educational Services. **Other Job Titles in This Work Group:** Adult Literacy, Remedial Education, and GED Teachers and Instructors; Agricultural Sciences Teachers, Postsecondary; Anthropology and Archeology Teachers, Postsecondary; Architecture Teachers, Postsecondary; Archivists; Area, Ethnic, and Cultural Studies Teachers, Postsecondary; Art, Drama, and Music Teachers, Postsecondary; Atmospheric, Earth, Marine, and Space Sciences Teachers, Postsecondary; Audio-Visual Collections Specialists; Biological Science Teachers, Postsecondary; Business Teachers, Postsecondary; Chemistry Teachers, Postsecondary; Child Care Workers; Communications Teachers, Postsecondary; Computer Science Teachers, Postsecondary; Criminal Justice and Law Enforcement Teachers, Postsecondary; Curators; Economics Teachers, Postsecondary; Education Teachers, Postsecondary; Educational Psychologists; Educational, Vocational, and School Counselors; Elementary School Teachers, Except Special Education; Engineering Teachers, Postsecondary; English Language and Literature Teachers, Postsecondary; Environmental Science Teachers, Postsecondary; Farm and Home Management Advisors; Foreign Language and Literature Teachers, Postsecondary; Geography Teachers, Postsecondary; Graduate Teaching Assistants; Health Specialties Teachers, Postsecondary; History Teachers, Postsecondary; Home Economics Teachers, Postsecondary; Kindergarten Teachers, Except Special Education; Law Teachers, Postsecondary; Librarians; Library Assistants, Clerical; Library Science Teachers, Postsecondary; Library Technicians; others. **PERSONALITY TYPE**—Investigative. Investigative occupations frequently involve working with ideas and require an extensive amount of thinking. These occupations can involve searching for facts and figuring out problems mentally.

EDUCATION/TRAINING PROGRAM(S)—No data available. **RELATED KNOWLEDGE/COURSES—Education and Training:** Knowledge of principles and methods for curriculum and training design, teaching and instruction for individuals and groups, and the measurement of training effects. **Biology:** Knowledge of plant and animal organisms and their tissues, cells, functions, interdependencies, and interactions with each other and the environment. **Psychology:** Knowledge of human behavior and performance; individual differences in ability, personality, and interests; learning and motivation; psychological research methods; and the assessment and treatment of behavioral and affective disorders. **Chemistry:** Knowledge of the chemical composition, structure, and properties of substances and of the chemical processes and transformations that they undergo. This includes uses of chemicals and their interactions, danger signs, production techniques, and disposal methods. **English Language:** Knowledge of the structure and content of the English language, including the meaning and spelling of words, rules of composition, and grammar.

Funeral Directors

- ▲ Education/Training Required: Associate's degree
- ▲ Annual Earnings: $41,110
- ▲ Growth: 3%
- ▲ Annual Job Openings: 3,000
- ▲ Self-Employed: 11.6%
- ▲ Part-Time: 7.4%

Perform various tasks to arrange and direct funeral services, such as coordinating transportation of body to mortuary for embalming, interviewing family or other authorized person to arrange details, selecting pallbearers, procuring official for religious rites, and providing transportation for mourners. Arranges and directs funeral services. Interviews family or other authorized person to arrange details, such as selection of casket and location and time of burial. Closes casket and leads funeral cortege to church or burial site. Directs placement and removal of casket from hearse. Plans placement of casket in parlor or chapel and adjusts lights, fixtures, and floral displays. Directs preparations and shipment of body for out-of-state burial. **SKILLS—Social Perceptiveness:** Being aware of others' reactions and understanding why they react as they do. Active Listening: Giving full attention to what other people are saying, taking time to understand the points being made, asking questions as appropriate, and not interrupting at inappropriate times. Coordination: Adjusting actions in relation to others' actions. Speaking: Talking to others to convey information effectively. Reading Comprehension: Understanding written sentences and paragraphs in work-related documents. Service Orientation: Actively looking for ways to help people.

GOE INFORMATION—Interest Area: 13. General Management and Support. **Work Group:** 13.01. General Management Work and Management of Support Functions. **Other Job Titles in This Work Group:** Chief Executives; Compensation and Benefits Managers; Farm, Ranch, and Other Agricultural Managers; Financial Managers; Financial Managers, Branch or Department;

General and Operations Managers; Government Service Executives; Human Resources Managers; Human Resources Managers, All Other; Legislators; Managers, All Other; Postmasters and Mail Superintendents; Private Sector Executives; Property, Real Estate, and Community Association Managers; Public Relations Managers; Purchasing Managers; Storage and Distribution Managers; Training and Development Managers; Transportation, Storage, and Distribution Managers; Treasurers, Controllers, and Chief Financial Officers. **PERSONALITY TYPE**—Enterprising. Enterprising occupations frequently involve starting up and carrying out projects. These occupations can involve leading people and making many decisions. They sometimes require risk taking and often deal with business.

EDUCATION/TRAINING PROGRAM(S)— Funeral Services and Mortuary Science. **RELATED KNOWLEDGE/COURSES—Administration and Management:** Knowledge of business and management principles involved in strategic planning, resource allocation, human resources modeling, leadership tech-

nique, production methods, and coordination of people and resources. **Customer and Personal Service:** Knowledge of principles and processes for providing customer and personal services. This includes customer needs assessment, meeting quality standards for services, and evaluation of customer satisfaction. **Transportation:** Knowledge of principles and methods for moving people or goods by air, rail, sea, or road, including the relative costs and benefits. **Sales and Marketing:** Knowledge of principles and methods for showing, promoting, and selling products or services. This includes marketing strategy and tactics, product demonstration, sales techniques, and sales control systems. **Psychology:** Knowledge of human behavior and performance; individual differences in ability, personality, and interests; learning and motivation; psychological research methods; and the assessment and treatment of behavioral and affective disorders. **English Language:** Knowledge of the structure and content of the English language, including the meaning and spelling of words, rules of composition, and grammar.

Gaming Managers

- ▲ Education/Training Required: Work experience, plus degree
- ▲ Annual Earnings: $53,380
- ▲ Growth: 30%
- ▲ Annual Job Openings: Fewer than 500
- ▲ Self-Employed: 49.4%
- ▲ Part-Time: 7.2%

Plan, organize, direct, control, or coordinate gaming operations in a casino. Formulate gaming policies for their area of responsibility. Reviews operational expenses, budget estimates, betting accounts, and collection reports for accuracy. Observes and supervises operation to ensure that employees render prompt and courteous service to patrons. Establishes policies on types of gambling offered, odds, extension of credit, and serving food and beverages. Directs workers compiling summary sheets for each race or event to show amount wagered and amount to be paid to winners. Trains new workers and evaluates their performance. Records, issues receipts for, and pays off bets. Explains and interprets house rules,

such as game rules and betting limits, to patrons. Interviews and hires workers. Resolves customer complaints regarding service. Prepares work schedules, assigns work stations, and keeps attendance records. **SKILLS**—Management of Personnel Resources: Motivating, developing, and directing people as they work, identifying the best people for the job. Management of Financial Resources: Determining how money will be spent to get the work done and accounting for these expenditures. Critical Thinking: Using logic and reasoning to identify the strengths and weaknesses of alternative solutions, conclusions, or approaches to problems. Speaking: Talking to others to convey information effectively. Reading Comprehension:

Understanding written sentences and paragraphs in work-related documents. Mathematics: Using mathematics to solve problems. Time Management: Managing one's own time and the time of others.

GOE INFORMATION—Interest Area: 11. Recreation, Travel, and Other Personal Services. Work Group: 11.01. Managerial Work in Recreation, Travel, and Other Personal Services. Other Job Titles in This Work Group: Aircraft Cargo Handling Supervisors; First-Line Supervisors/Managers of Food Preparation and Serving Workers; First-Line Supervisors/Managers of Housekeeping and Janitorial Workers; First-Line Supervisors/Managers of Personal Service Workers; Food Service Managers; Gaming Supervisors; Housekeeping Supervisors; Janitorial Supervisors; Lodging Managers; Meeting and Convention Planners. PERSONALITY TYPE—Enterprising. Enterprising occupations frequently involve starting up and carrying out projects. These occupations can involve leading people and making many decisions. They sometimes require risk taking and often deal with business.

EDUCATION/TRAINING PROGRAM(S)—Arts Management; Business Administration and Management, General; Business Administration and Management, Other; Business Management and Administrative Services, Other; Business, General; Community Organization, Resources and Services; Enterprise Management and Operation, General; Enterprise Management and Operation, Other; Entrepreneurship; Franchise Operation; Hospitality and Recreation Marketing Operations, General; Hospitality Services Management, Other; Non-Profit and Public Management; Public Administration; Travel-Tourism Management. RELATED KNOWLEDGE/COURSES—Administration and Management: Knowledge of business and management principles involved in strategic planning, resource allocation, human resources modeling, leadership technique, production methods, and coordination of people and resources. Economics and Accounting: Knowledge of economic and accounting principles and practices, the financial markets, banking, and the analysis and reporting of financial data. Personnel and Human Resources: Knowledge of principles and procedures for personnel recruitment, selection, training, compensation and benefits, labor relations and negotiation, and personnel information systems. Mathematics: Knowledge of arithmetic, algebra, geometry, calculus, and statistics and their applications. Customer and Personal Service: Knowledge of principles and processes for providing customer and personal services. This includes customer needs assessment, meeting quality standards for services, and evaluation of customer satisfaction.

General and Operations Managers

- ▲ Education/Training Required: Work experience, plus degree
- ▲ Annual Earnings: $61,160
- ▲ Growth: 15%
- ▲ Annual Job Openings: 235,000
- ▲ Self-Employed: 49.4%
- ▲ Part-Time: 7.2%

Plan, direct, or coordinate the operations of companies or public and private sector organizations. Duties and responsibilities include formulating policies, managing daily operations, and planning the use of materials and human resources, but are too diverse and general in nature to be classified in any one functional area of management or administration, such as personnel, purchasing, or administrative services. Includes owners and managers who head small business establishments whose duties are primarily managerial. SKILLS—No data available.

GOE INFORMATION—Interest Area: 13. General Management and Support. Work Group: 13.01. General Management Work and Management of Support

Functions. **Other Job Titles in This Work Group:** Chief Executives; Compensation and Benefits Managers; Farm, Ranch, and Other Agricultural Managers; Financial Managers; Financial Managers, Branch or Department; Funeral Directors; Government Service Executives; Human Resources Managers; Human Resources Managers, All Other; Legislators; Managers, All Other; Postmasters and Mail Superintendents; Private Sector Executives; Property, Real Estate, and Community Association Managers; Public Relations Managers; Purchasing Managers; Storage and Distribution Managers; Training and Development Managers; Transportation, Storage, and Distribution Managers; Treasurers, Controllers, and Chief Financial Officers. **PERSONALITY TYPE**—No data available.

EDUCATION/TRAINING PROGRAM(S)—Business Administration and Management, General; Enterprise Management and Operation, General; International Business; Public Administration; Public Administration and Services, Other; Public Policy Analysis. **RELATED KNOWLEDGE/COURSES**—No data available.

Geographers

- ▲ Education/Training Required: Bachelor's degree
- ▲ Annual Earnings: $46,690
- ▲ Growth: 17%
- ▲ Annual Job Openings: 2,000
- ▲ Self-Employed: 7.6%
- ▲ Part-Time: 6.6%

Study nature and use of areas of earth's surface, relating and interpreting interactions of physical and cultural phenomena. Conduct research on physical aspects of a region, including land forms, climates, soils, plants, and animals, and conduct research on the spatial implications of human activities within a given area, including social characteristics, economic activities, and political organization, as well as researching interdependence between regions at scales ranging from local to global. Collects data on physical characteristics of specified area, such as geological formation, climate, and vegetation, using surveying or meteorological equipment. Advises governments and organizations on ethnic and natural boundaries between nation or administrative areas. Studies population characteristics within area, such as ethnic distribution and economic activity. Constructs and interprets maps, graphs, and diagrams. Prepares environmental impact reports based on results of study. Uses surveying equipment to assess geology, physics, and biology within given area. **SKILLS**—Writing: Communicating effectively in writing as appropriate for the needs of the audience.

Reading Comprehension: Understanding written sentences and paragraphs in work-related documents. Mathematics: Using mathematics to solve problems. Critical Thinking: Using logic and reasoning to identify the strengths and weaknesses of alternative solutions, conclusions, or approaches to problems. Speaking: Talking to others to convey information effectively. Active Learning: Understanding the implications of new information for both current and future problem-solving and decision-making.

GOE INFORMATION—**Interest Area:** 02. Science, Math, and Engineering. **Work Group:** 02.02. Physical Sciences. **Other Job Titles in This Work Group:** Astronomers; Atmospheric and Space Scientists; Chemists; Geologists; Geoscientists, Except Hydrologists and Geographers; Hydrologists; Materials Scientists; Physical Scientists, All Other; Physicists. **PERSONALITY TYPE**—Investigative. Investigative occupations frequently involve working with ideas and require an extensive amount of thinking. These occupations can involve searching for facts and figuring out problems mentally.

EDUCATION/TRAINING PROGRAM(S)—Geography. **RELATED KNOWLEDGE/ COURSES—Geography:** Knowledge of principles and methods for describing the features of land, sea, and air masses, including their physical characteristics, locations, interrelationships, and distribution of plant, animal, and human life. **Sociology and Anthropology:** Knowledge of group behavior and dynamics, societal trends and influences, human migrations, ethnicity, cultures, and their history and origins. **Biology:** Knowledge of plant and animal organisms and their tissues, cells, functions, interdependencies, and interactions with each other and the environment. **Physics:** Knowledge and prediction of physical principles and laws and their interrelationships and applications to understanding fluid, material, and atmospheric dynamics and mechanical, electrical, atomic, and sub-atomic structures and processes. **Mathematics:** Knowledge of arithmetic, algebra, geometry, calculus, and statistics and their applications.

Geography Teachers, Postsecondary

- ▲ Education/Training Required: Master's degree
- ▲ Annual Earnings: $54,080
- ▲ Growth: 24% for all Postsecondary Teachers
- ▲ Annual Job Openings: 184,000 for all Postsecondary Teachers
- ▲ Self-Employed: 0%
- ▲ Part-Time: 32.3% for all Postsecondary Teachers

Teach courses in geography. **SKILLS**—No data available.

GOE INFORMATION—Interest Area: 12. Education and Social Service. **Work Group:** 12.03. Educational Services. **Other Job Titles in This Work Group:** Adult Literacy, Remedial Education, and GED Teachers and Instructors; Agricultural Sciences Teachers, Postsecondary; Anthropology and Archeology Teachers, Postsecondary; Architecture Teachers, Postsecondary; Archivists; Area, Ethnic, and Cultural Studies Teachers, Postsecondary; Art, Drama, and Music Teachers, Postsecondary; Atmospheric, Earth, Marine, and Space Sciences Teachers, Postsecondary; Audio-Visual Collections Specialists; Biological Science Teachers, Postsecondary; Business Teachers, Postsecondary; Chemistry Teachers, Postsecondary; Child Care Workers; Communications Teachers, Postsecondary; Computer Science Teachers, Postsecondary; Criminal Justice and Law Enforcement Teachers, Postsecondary; Curators; Economics Teachers, Postsecondary; Education Teachers, Postsecondary; Educational Psychologists; Educational, Vocational, and School Counselors; Elementary School Teachers, Except Special Education; Engineering Teachers, Postsecondary; English Language and Literature Teachers, Postsecondary; Environmental Science Teachers, Postsecondary; Farm and Home Management Advisors; Foreign Language and Literature Teachers, Postsecondary; Forestry and Conservation Science Teachers, Postsecondary; Graduate Teaching Assistants; Health Specialties Teachers, Postsecondary; History Teachers, Postsecondary; Home Economics Teachers, Postsecondary; Kindergarten Teachers, Except Special Education; Law Teachers, Postsecondary; Librarians; Library Assistants, Clerical; Library Science Teachers, Postsecondary; others. **PERSONALITY TYPE**—No data available.

EDUCATION/TRAINING PROGRAM(S)—Geography. **RELATED KNOWLEDGE/ COURSES**—No data available.

Geological and Petroleum Technicians

▲ Education/Training Required: Associate's degree

▲ Annual Earnings: $36,490

▲ Growth: 6%

▲ Annual Job Openings: 2,000

▲ Self-Employed: 1.9%

▲ Part-Time: 7.4%

Assist scientists in the use of electrical, sonic, or nuclear measuring instruments in both laboratory and production activities to obtain data indicating potential sources of metallic ore, gas, or petroleum. Analyze mud and drill cuttings. Chart pressure, temperature, and other characteristics of wells or bore holes. Investigate and collect information leading to the possible discovery of new oil fields. **SKILLS**—No data available.

GOE INFORMATION—**Interest Area:** 02. Science, Math, and Engineering. **Work Group:** 02.05. Laboratory Technology. **Other Job Titles in This Work Group:** Biological Technicians; Chemical Technicians; Environmental Science and Protection Technicians, Including Health; Geological Data Technicians; Geological Sample Test Technicians; Nuclear Equipment Operation Technicians; Nuclear Technicians; Photographers, Scientific. **PERSONALITY TYPE**—No data available.

EDUCATION/TRAINING PROGRAM(S)—Aeronautical and Aerospace Engineering Technologist/Technician; Architectural Engineering Technologist/Technician; Communications Technologists/Technicians, Other; Energy Management and Systems Technologist/Technician; Engineering-Related Technologist/Technician, General; Engineering-Related Technologists/Technicians, Other; Environmental and Pollution Control Technologist/Technician; Environmental Control Technologists/Technicians, Other; Hydraulic Technologist/Technician; Industrial Production Technologists/Technicians, Other; Laser and Optical Technologist/Technician; Mechanical Engineering-Related Technologists/Technicians, Other; Metallurgical Technologist/Technician; Mining and Petroleum Technologists/Technicians, Other; Mining Technologist/Technician; Petroleum Technologist/Technician; Plastics Technologist/Technician; Radio and Television Broadcasting Technologist/Technician; Solar Technologist/Technician. **RELATED KNOWLEDGE/COURSES**—No data available.

Geological Data Technicians

▲ Education/Training Required: Associate's degree

▲ Annual Earnings: $36,490

▲ Growth: 6%

▲ Annual Job Openings: 2,000

▲ Self-Employed: 0.9%

▲ Part-Time: 11.7%

Measure, record, and evaluate geological data, using sonic, electronic, electrical, seismic, or gravity-measuring instruments to prospect for oil or gas. May collect and evaluate core samples and cuttings. Measures geological characteristics used in prospecting for oil or gas, using measuring instruments. Prepares and attaches packing instructions to shipping container. Develops and designs packing materials and handling procedures for shipping of objects. Diagnoses and repairs malfunctioning instruments and equipment, using manufacturers' manuals and hand tools. Develops and prints photographic recordings of information, using equipment. Plans and directs activities of workers who operate equipment to collect data or operates equipment. Assembles, maintains, and distributes information for library or record system. Operates and adjusts equipment and apparatus to obtain geological data. Reads and studies reports to compile information and data for geological and geophysical prospecting. Sets up or directs setup of instruments used to collect geological data. Interviews individuals and researches public databases to obtain information. Collects samples and cuttings, using equipment and hand tools. Evaluates and interprets core samples, cuttings, and other geological data used in prospecting for oil or gas. Records readings to obtain data used in prospecting for oil or gas. **SKILLS**—Reading Comprehension: Understanding written sentences and paragraphs in work-related documents. Mathematics: Using mathematics to solve problems. Speaking: Talking to others to convey information effectively. Science: Using scientific rules and methods to solve problems. Writing: Communicating effectively in writing as appropriate for the needs of the audience. Active Listening: Giving full attention to what other people are saying, taking time to understand the points being made, asking questions as appropriate, and not interrupting at inappropriate times.

GOE INFORMATION—**Interest Area:** 02. Science, Math, and Engineering. **Work Group:** 02.05. Laboratory Technology. **Other Job Titles in This Work Group:** Biological Technicians; Chemical Technicians; Environmental Science and Protection Technicians, Including Health; Geological and Petroleum Technicians; Geological Sample Test Technicians; Nuclear Equipment Operation Technicians; Nuclear Technicians; Photographers, Scientific. **PERSONALITY TYPE**—Realistic. Realistic occupations frequently involve work activities that include practical, hands-on problems and solutions. They often deal with plants, animals, and real-world materials like wood, tools, and machinery. Many of the occupations require working outside and do not involve a lot of paperwork or working closely with others.

EDUCATION/TRAINING PROGRAM(S)—Aeronautical and Aerospace Engineering Technologist/Technician; Architectural Engineering Technologist/Technician; Communications Technologists/Technicians, Other; Energy Management and Systems Technologist/Technician; Engineering-Related Technologist/Technician, General; Engineering-Related Technologists/Technicians, Other; Environmental and Pollution Control Technologist/Technician; Environmental Control Technologists/Technicians, Other; Hydraulic Technologist/Technician; Industrial Production Technologists/Technicians, Other; Laser and Optical Technologist/Technician; Mechanical Engineering-Related Technologists/Technicians, Other; Metallurgical Technologist/Technician; Mining and Petroleum Technologists/Technicians, Other; Mining Technologist/Technician; Petroleum Technologist/Technician; Plastics Technologist/Technician; Radio and Television Broadcasting Technologist/Technician; Solar Technologist/Technician. **RELATED KNOWLEDGE/COURSES**—**Physics:** Knowledge and prediction of physical principles and laws and their interrelationships and applications to understanding fluid, material, and atmospheric dynamics and mechanical, electrical, atomic, and sub-atomic structures and processes. **Mathematics:** Knowledge of arithmetic, algebra, geometry, calculus, and statistics and their applications. **Engineering and Technology:** Knowledge of the practical application of engineering science and technology. This includes applying principles, techniques, procedures, and equipment to the design and production of various goods and services. **Principles of Mechanical Devices:** Knowledge of machines and tools, including their designs, uses, repair, and maintenance. **Production and Processing:** Knowledge of raw materials, production processes, quality control, costs, and other techniques for maximizing the effective manufacture and distribution of goods. **English Language:** Knowledge of the structure and content of the English language, including the meaning and spelling of words, rules of composition, and grammar. **Administration and Management:** Knowledge of business and management principles involved in strategic planning, resource allocation, human resources modeling, leadership technique, production methods, and coordination of people and resources.

Geological Sample Test Technicians

- ▲ Education/Training Required: Associate's degree
- ▲ Annual Earnings: $36,490
- ▲ Growth: 6%
- ▲ Annual Job Openings: 2,000
- ▲ Self-Employed: 0.9%
- ▲ Part-Time: 11.7%

Test and analyze geological samples, crude oil, or petroleum products to detect presence of petroleum, gas, or mineral deposits indicating potential for exploration and production or to determine physical and chemical properties to ensure that products meet quality standards. Tests samples for content and characteristics, using laboratory apparatus and testing equipment. Records testing and operational data for review and further analysis. Assembles and disassembles testing, measuring, and mechanical equipment and devices. Inspects engines for wear and defective parts, using equipment and measuring devices. Supervises and coordinates activities of workers, including initiating and recommending personnel actions. Adjusts and repairs testing, electrical, and mechanical equipment and devices. Collects solid and fluid samples from oil-or-gas bearing formations for analysis. Analyzes samples to determine presence, quantity, and quality of products, such as oil or gases. **SKILLS**—Science: Using scientific rules and methods to solve problems. Coordination: Adjusting actions in relation to others' actions. Mathematics: Using mathematics to solve problems. Quality Control Analysis: Conducting tests and inspections of products, services, or processes to evaluate quality or performance. Management of Personnel Resources: Motivating, developing, and directing people as they work, identifying the best people for the job. Equipment Maintenance: Performing routine maintenance on equipment and determining when and what kind of maintenance is needed.

GOE INFORMATION—Interest Area: 02. Science, Math, and Engineering. **Work Group:** 02.05. Laboratory Technology. **Other Job Titles in This Work Group:** Biological Technicians; Chemical Technicians; Environmental Science and Protection Technicians, Including Health; Geological and Petroleum Technicians;

Geological Data Technicians; Nuclear Equipment Operation Technicians; Nuclear Technicians; Photographers, Scientific. **PERSONALITY TYPE**—Realistic. Realistic occupations frequently involve work activities that include practical, hands-on problems and solutions. They often deal with plants, animals, and real-world materials like wood, tools, and machinery. Many of the occupations require working outside and do not involve a lot of paperwork or working closely with others.

EDUCATION/TRAINING PROGRAM(S)— Aeronautical and Aerospace Engineering Technologist/ Technician; Architectural Engineering Technologist/Technician; Communications Technologists/Technicians, Other; Energy Management and Systems Technologist/Technician; Engineering-Related Technologist/Technician, General; Engineering-Related Technologists/Technicians, Other; Environmental and Pollution Control Technologist/Technician; Environmental Control Technologists/ Technicians, Other; Hydraulic Technologist/Technician; Industrial Production Technologists/Technicians, Other; Laser and Optical Technologist/Technician; Mechanical Engineering-Related Technologists/Technicians, Other; Metallurgical Technologist/Technician; Mining and Petroleum Technologists/Technicians, Other; Mining Technologist/Technician; Petroleum Technologist/Technician; Plastics Technologist/Technician; Radio and Television Broadcasting Technologist/Technician; Solar Technologist/ Technician. **RELATED KNOWLEDGE/ COURSES—Principles of Mechanical Devices:** Knowledge of machines and tools, including their designs, uses, repair, and maintenance. **Physics:** Knowledge and prediction of physical principles and laws and their interrelationships and applications to understanding fluid, material, and atmospheric dynamics and mechanical, electrical, atomic, and sub-atomic structures and processes. **Engi-**

neering and Technology: Knowledge of the practical application of engineering science and technology. This includes applying principles, techniques, procedures, and equipment to the design and production of various goods and services. **Mathematics:** Knowledge of arithmetic, algebra, geometry, calculus, and statistics and their applications. **Personnel and Human Resources:** Knowledge of principles and procedures for personnel recruitment, selection, training, compensation and benefits, labor relations and negotiation, and personnel information systems.

Geologists

- ▲ Education/Training Required: Bachelor's degree
- ▲ Annual Earnings: $56,230
- ▲ Growth: 18%
- ▲ Annual Job Openings: 2,000
- ▲ Self-Employed: 15.1%
- ▲ Part-Time: 6.3%

Study composition, structure, and history of the earth's crust; examine rocks, minerals, and fossil remains to identify and determine the sequence of processes affecting the development of the earth; apply knowledge of chemistry, physics, biology, and mathematics to explain these phenomena and to help locate mineral and petroleum deposits and underground water resources; prepare geologic reports and maps; and interpret research data to recommend further action for study. Studies, examines, measures, and classifies composition, structure, and history of earth's crust, including rocks, minerals, fossils, soil, and ocean floor. Prepares geological reports, maps, charts, and diagrams. Analyzes engineering problems at construction projects, such as dams, tunnels, and large buildings, applying geological knowledge. Inspects proposed construction site and sets up test equipment and drilling machinery. Recommends and prepares reports on foundation design, acquisition, retention, or release of property leases or areas of further research. Develops instruments for geological work, such as diamond tool and dies, jeweled bearings, and grinding laps and wheels. Measures characteristics of earth, using seismograph, gravimeter, torsion balance, magnetometer, pendulum devices, and electrical resistivity apparatus. Tests industrial diamonds and abrasives, soil, or rocks to determine geological characteristics, using optical, X-ray, heat, acid, and precision instruments. Interprets research data and recommends further study or action. Locates and estimates probable gas and oil deposits, using aerial photographs, charts, and research and survey results. Identifies and determines sequence of processes affecting development of earth. **SKILLS—Mathematics:** Using mathematics to solve problems. Technology Design: Generating or adapting equipment and technology to serve user needs. Reading Comprehension: Understanding written sentences and paragraphs in work-related documents. Writing: Communicating effectively in writing as appropriate for the needs of the audience. Active Learning: Understanding the implications of new information for both current and future problem-solving and decision-making.

GOE INFORMATION—Interest Area: 02. Science, Math, and Engineering. **Work Group:** 02.02. Physical Sciences. **Other Job Titles in This Work Group:** Astronomers; Atmospheric and Space Scientists; Chemists; Geographers; Geoscientists, Except Hydrologists and Geographers; Hydrologists; Materials Scientists; Physical Scientists, All Other; Physicists. **PERSONALITY TYPE—Investigative.** Investigative occupations frequently involve working with ideas and require an extensive amount of thinking. These occupations can involve searching for facts and figuring out problems mentally.

EDUCATION/TRAINING PROGRAM(S)— Earth and Planetary Sciences; Geochemistry; Geological and Related Sciences, Other; Geology; Geophysics and Seismology; Miscellaneous Physical Sciences, Other; Oceanography; Paleontology. **RELATED KNOWLEDGE/COURSES—Physics:** Knowledge and prediction of physical principles and laws and their interrelationships and applications to understanding fluid, material, and atmospheric dynamics and mechanical, electrical, atomic, and sub-atomic structures and processes. **Mathematics:** Knowledge of arithmetic, algebra, geometry, calculus, and statistics and their applications. **Engineering and Technology:** Knowledge of the practical application of engineering science and technology. This includes applying principles, techniques, procedures, and equipment to the design and production of various goods and services. **Chemistry:** Knowledge of the chemical composition, structure, and properties of substances and of the chemical processes and transformations that they undergo. This includes uses of chemicals and their interactions, danger signs, production techniques, and disposal methods. **English Language:** Knowledge of the structure and content of the English language, including the meaning and spelling of words, rules of composition, and grammar.

Geoscientists, Except Hydrologists and Geographers

▲ Education/Training Required: Bachelor's degree

▲ Annual Earnings: $56,230

▲ Growth: 18%

▲ Annual Job Openings: 2,000

▲ Self-Employed: 15.1%

▲ Part-Time: 6.3%

Study the composition, structure, and other physical aspects of the earth. May use geological, physics, and mathematics knowledge in exploration for oil, gas, minerals, or underground water or in waste disposal, land reclamation, or other environmental problems. May study the earth's internal composition, atmospheres, and oceans and its magnetic, electrical, and gravitational forces. Includes mineralogists, crystallographers, paleontologists, stratigraphers, geodesists, and seismologists. **SKILLS**—No data available.

GOE INFORMATION—**Interest Area:** 02. Science, Math, and Engineering. **Work Group:** 02.02. Physical Sciences. **Other Job Titles in This Work Group:** Astronomers; Atmospheric and Space Scientists; Chemists; Geographers; Geologists; Hydrologists; Materials Scientists; Physical Scientists, All Other; Physicists. **PERSONALITY TYPE**—No data available.

EDUCATION/TRAINING PROGRAM(S)— Earth and Planetary Sciences; Geochemistry; Geological and Related Sciences, Other; Geology; Geophysics and Seismology; Miscellaneous Physical Sciences, Other; Oceanography; Paleontology. **RELATED KNOWLEDGE/COURSES**—No data available.

Government Service Executives

▲ Education/Training Required: Work experience, plus degree

▲ Annual Earnings: $113,810

▲ Growth: 17%

▲ Annual Job Openings: 48,000

▲ Self-Employed: 0%

▲ Part-Time: 5.8%

Determine and formulate policies and provide overall direction of federal, state, local, or international government activities. Plan, direct, and coordinate operational activities at the highest level of management with the help of subordinate managers. Directs organization charged with administering and monitoring regulated activities to interpret and clarify laws and ensure compliance with laws. Administers, interprets, and explains policies, rules, regulations, and laws to organizations and individuals under authority of commission or applicable legislation. Develops, plans, organizes, and administers policies and procedures for organization to ensure administrative and operational objectives are met. Directs and coordinates activities of workers in public organization to ensure continuing operations, maximize returns on investments, and increase productivity. Negotiates contracts and agreements with federal and state agencies and other organizations and prepares budget for funding and implementation of programs. Implements corrective action plan to solve problems. Reviews and analyzes legislation, laws, and public policy and recommends changes to promote and support interests of general population, as well as special groups. Develops, directs, and coordinates testing, hiring, training, and evaluation of staff personnel. Establishes and maintains comprehensive and current record-keeping system of activities and operational procedures in business office. Testifies in court, before control or review board, or at legislature. Participates in activities to promote business and expand services and provides technical assistance in conducting of conferences, seminars, and workshops. Delivers speeches, writes articles, and presents information for organization at meetings or conventions to promote services, exchange ideas, and accomplish objectives. Plans, promotes, organizes, and coordinates public community service program and maintains cooperative working relationships among public and agency participants. Conducts or directs investigations or hearings to resolve complaints and violations of laws. Prepares, reviews, and submits reports concerning activities, expenses, budget, government statutes and rulings, and other items affecting business or program services. Directs, coordinates, and conducts activities between United States Government and foreign entities to provide information to promote international interest and harmony. Evaluates findings of investigations, surveys, and studies to formulate policies and techniques and recommend improvements for personnel actions, programs, or business services. Consults with staff and others in government, business, and private organizations to discuss issues, coordinate activities, and resolve problems. Directs and conducts studies and research and prepares reports and other publications relating to operational trends and program objectives and accomplishments. Prepares budget and directs and monitors expenditures of department funds. **SKILLS**—Coordination: Adjusting actions in relation to others' actions. Judgment and Decision Making: Considering the relative costs and benefits of potential actions to choose the most appropriate one. Monitoring: Monitoring/Assessing your performance or that of other individuals or organizations to make improvements or take corrective action. Critical Thinking: Using logic and reasoning to identify the strengths and weaknesses of alternative solutions, conclusions, or approaches to problems. Systems Evaluation: Identifying measures or indicators of system performance and the actions needed to improve or correct performance relative to the goals of the system.

GOE INFORMATION—**Interest Area:** 13. General Management and Support. **Work Group:** 13.01. General Management Work and Management of Support Functions. **Other Job Titles in This Work Group:** Chief Executives; Compensation and Benefits Managers; Farm, Ranch, and Other Agricultural Managers; Financial Managers; Financial Managers, Branch or Department; Funeral Directors; General and Operations Managers; Human Resources Managers; Human Resources Managers, All Other; Legislators; Managers, All Other; Postmasters and Mail Superintendents; Private Sector Executives; Property, Real Estate, and Community Association Managers; Public Relations Managers; Purchasing Managers; Storage and Distribution Managers; Training and Development Managers; Transportation, Storage, and Distribution Managers; Treasurers, Controllers, and Chief Financial Officers. **PERSONALITY TYPE**—Enterprising. Enterprising occupations frequently involve starting up and carrying out projects. These occupations can involve leading people and making many decisions. They sometimes require risk taking and often deal with business.

EDUCATION/TRAINING PROGRAM(S)— Business Administration and Management, General; Enterprise Management and Operation, General; International Business; Public Administration; Public Administration and Services, Other; Public Policy Analysis. **RELATED KNOWLEDGE/COURSES—Administration and Management:** Knowledge of business and management principles involved in strategic planning, resource allocation, human resources modeling, leadership technique, production methods, and coordination of people and resources. **Law and Government:** Knowledge of laws, legal codes, court procedures, precedents, government regulations, executive orders, agency rules, and the democratic political process. **English Language:** Knowledge of the structure and content of the English language, including the meaning and spelling of words, rules of composition, and grammar. **Education and Training:** Knowledge of principles and methods for curriculum and training design, teaching and instruction for individuals and groups, and the measurement of training effects. **Economics and Accounting:** Knowledge of economic and accounting principles and practices, the financial markets, banking, and the analysis and reporting of financial data. **Personnel and Human Resources:** Knowledge of principles and procedures for personnel recruitment, selection, training, compensation and benefits, labor relations and negotiation, and personnel information systems.

Graduate Teaching Assistants

- ▲ Education/Training Required: Master's degree
- ▲ Annual Earnings: $21,960
- ▲ Growth: 24% for all Postsecondary Teachers
- ▲ Annual Job Openings: 184,000 for all Postsecondary Teachers
- ▲ Self-Employed: 0%
- ▲ Part-Time: 32.3% for all Postsecondary Teachers

Assist department chairperson, faculty members, or other professional staff members in college or university by performing teaching or teaching-related duties, such as teaching lower-level courses, developing teaching materials, preparing and giving examinations, and grading examinations or papers. Graduate assistants must be enrolled in a graduate school program. Graduate assistants who primarily perform non-teaching duties, such as laboratory research, should be reported in the occupational category related to the work performed. Develops teaching materials, such as syllabi and visual aids. Assists faculty member or staff with student conferences. Assists library staff in maintaining library collection. Assists faculty member or staff with laboratory or field research. Teaches lower-level courses. Prepares and gives examinations. Grades examinations and papers. **SKILLS—Reading Comprehension:** Understanding written sentences and paragraphs in work-related documents. **Instructing:** Teaching others how to do something.

Speaking: Talking to others to convey information effectively. Writing: Communicating effectively in writing as appropriate for the needs of the audience. Learning Strategies: Selecting and using training/instructional methods and procedures appropriate for the situation when learning or teaching new things.

GOE INFORMATION—Interest Area: 12. Education and Social Service. **Work Group:** 12.03. Educational Services. **Other Job Titles in This Work Group:** Adult Literacy, Remedial Education, and GED Teachers and Instructors; Agricultural Sciences Teachers, Postsecondary; Anthropology and Archeology Teachers, Postsecondary; Architecture Teachers, Postsecondary; Archivists; Area, Ethnic, and Cultural Studies Teachers, Postsecondary; Art, Drama, and Music Teachers, Postsecondary; Atmospheric, Earth, Marine, and Space Sciences Teachers, Postsecondary; Audio-Visual Collections Specialists; Biological Science Teachers, Postsecondary; Business Teachers, Postsecondary; Chemistry Teachers, Postsecondary; Child Care Workers; Communications Teachers, Postsecondary; Computer Science Teachers, Postsecondary; Criminal Justice and Law Enforcement Teachers, Postsecondary; Curators; Economics Teachers, Postsecondary; Education Teachers, Postsecondary; Educational Psychologists; Educational, Vocational, and School Counselors; Elementary School Teachers, Except Special Education; Engineering Teachers, Postsecondary; English Language and Literature Teachers, Postsecondary; Environmental Science Teachers, Postsecondary; Farm and Home Management Advisors; Foreign Language and Literature Teachers, Postsecondary; Forestry and Conservation Science Teachers, Postsecondary; Geography Teachers, Postsecondary; Health Specialties Teachers, Postsecondary; History Teachers, Postsecondary; Home Economics Teachers, Postsecondary; Kindergarten Teachers, Except Special Education; Law Teachers, Postsecondary; Librarians; Library Assistants, Clerical; Library Science Teachers, Postsecondary; others. **PERSONALITY TYPE**—Social. Social occupations frequently involve working with, communicating with, and teaching people. These occupations often involve helping or providing service to others.

EDUCATION/TRAINING PROGRAM(S)— Education, General. **RELATED KNOWLEDGE/ COURSES—Education and Training:** Knowledge of principles and methods for curriculum and training design, teaching and instruction for individuals and groups, and the measurement of training effects. **English Language:** Knowledge of the structure and content of the English language, including the meaning and spelling of words, rules of composition, and grammar. **Mathematics:** Knowledge of arithmetic, algebra, geometry, calculus, and statistics and their applications. **Clerical Studies:** Knowledge of administrative and clerical procedures and systems such as word processing, managing files and records, stenography and transcription, designing forms, and other office procedures and terminology. **Computers and Electronics:** Knowledge of circuit boards, processors, chips, electronic equipment, and computer hardware and software, including applications and programming.

Graphic Designers

- ▲ Education/Training Required: Bachelor's degree
- ▲ Annual Earnings: $34,570
- ▲ Growth: 27%
- ▲ Annual Job Openings: 28,000
- ▲ Self-Employed: 60.9%
- ▲ Part-Time: 24%

Design or create graphics to meet specific commercial or promotional needs, such as packaging, displays, or logos. May use a variety of mediums to achieve artistic or decorative effects. Draws sample of finished layout and presents sample to art director for approval. Produces still and animated graphic formats for on-air and taped portions of television news broadcasts, using electronic video equipment. Reviews final layout and suggests improvements as needed. Develops negatives and prints, using negative and print developing equipment, tools, and work aids to produce layout photographs. Prepares notes and instructions for workers who assemble and prepare final layouts for printing. Photographs layouts, using camera, to make layout prints for supervisor or client. Confers with client regarding layout design. Prepares series of drawings to illustrate sequence and timing of story development for television production. Studies illustrations and photographs to plan presentation of material, product, or service. Prepares illustrations or rough sketches of material according to instructions of client or supervisor. Arranges layout based upon available space, knowledge of layout principles, and esthetic design concepts. Marks up, pastes, and assembles final layouts to prepare layouts for printer. Determines size and arrangement of illustrative material and copy and selects style and size of type. Keys information into computer equipment to create layouts for client or supervisor. Draws and prints charts, graphs, illustrations, and other artwork, using computer. **SKILLS**—Reading Comprehension: Understanding written sentences and paragraphs in work-related documents. Active Listening: Giving full attention to what other people are saying, taking time to understand the points being made, asking questions as appropriate, and not interrupting at inappropriate times. Speaking: Talking to others to convey information effectively. Equipment Selection: Determining the kind of tools and equipment needed to do a job. Writing: Communicating effectively in writing as appropriate for the needs of the audience.

GOE INFORMATION—**Interest Area:** 01. Arts, Entertainment, and Media. **Work Group:** 01.04. Visual Arts. **Other Job Titles in This Work Group:** Cartoonists; Commercial and Industrial Designers; Designers, All Other; Exhibit Designers; Fashion Designers; Fine Artists, Including Painters, Sculptors, and Illustrators; Floral Designers; Interior Designers; Merchandise Displayers and Window Trimmers; Multi-Media Artists and Animators; Painters and Illustrators; Sculptors; Set and Exhibit Designers; Set Designers; Sketch Artists. **PERSONALITY TYPE**—Artistic. Artistic occupations frequently involve working with forms, designs, and patterns. They often require self-expression, and the work can be done without following a clear set of rules.

EDUCATION/TRAINING PROGRAM(S)—Design and Visual Communications; Graphic Design, Commercial Art and Illustration; Industrial Design. **RELATED KNOWLEDGE/COURSES**—**Fine Arts:** Knowledge of the theory and techniques required to compose, produce, and perform works of music, dance, visual arts, drama, and sculpture. **Communications and Media:** Knowledge of media production, communication, and dissemination techniques and methods. This includes alternative ways to inform and entertain via written, oral, and visual media. **Design:** Knowledge of design techniques, tools, and principles involved in production of precision technical plans, blueprints, drawings, and models. **Computers and Electronics:** Knowledge of circuit boards, processors, chips, electronic equipment, and computer hardware and software, including applications and programming. **English Language:** Knowledge of the structure and content of the English language, including the meaning and spelling of words, rules of composition, and grammar.

Health and Safety Engineers, Except Mining Safety Engineers and Inspectors

- ▲ Education/Training Required: Bachelor's degree
- ▲ Annual Earnings: $54,630
- ▲ Growth: 11%
- ▲ Annual Job Openings: 3,000
- ▲ Self-Employed: 2.7%
- ▲ Part-Time: 4.5%

Promote worksite or product safety by applying knowledge of industrial processes, mechanics, chemistry, psychology, and industrial health and safety laws. SKILLS—No data available.

GOE INFORMATION—**Interest Area:** 02. Science, Math, and Engineering. **Work Group:** 02.07. Engineering. **Other Job Titles in This Work Group:** Aerospace Engineers; Agricultural Engineers; Architects, Except Landscape and Naval; Biomedical Engineers; Chemical Engineers; Civil Engineers; Computer Hardware Engineers; Computer Software Engineers, Applications; Computer Software Engineers, Systems Software; Electrical Engineers; Electronics Engineers, Except Computer; Engineers, All Other; Environmental Engineers; Fire-Prevention and Protection Engineers; Industrial Engineers; Industrial Safety and Health Engineers; Landscape Architects; Marine Architects; Marine Engineers; Marine Engineers and Naval Architects; Materials Engineers; Mechanical Engineers; Mining and Geological Engineers, Including Mining Safety Engineers; Nuclear Engineers; Petroleum Engineers; Product Safety Engineers; Sales Engineers. **PERSONALITY TYPE**—No data available.

EDUCATION/TRAINING PROGRAM(S)—
Engineering/Industrial Management; Environmental/

Environmental Health Engineering; Systems Engineering. **RELATED KNOWLEDGE/COURSES**—No data available.

Health Educators

- ▲ Education/Training Required: Master's degree
- ▲ Annual Earnings: $33,860
- ▲ Growth: 24%
- ▲ Annual Job Openings: 7,000
- ▲ Self-Employed: 3.9%
- ▲ Part-Time: 39.7%

Promote, maintain, and improve individual and community health by assisting individuals and communities to adopt healthy behaviors. Collect and analyze data to identify community needs prior to planning, implementing, monitoring, and evaluating programs designed to encourage healthy lifestyles, policies, and environments. May also serve as a resource to assist individuals, other professionals, or the community and may administer fiscal resources for health education programs. Plans and provides educational opportunities for health personnel. Collaborates with health specialists and civic groups to ascertain community health needs, determine availability of services, and develop goals. Promotes health discussions in schools, industry, and community agencies. Conducts community surveys to ascertain health needs, develop desirable health goals, and determine availability of professional health services. Prepares and disseminates educational and informational materials. Develops and maintains cooperation between public, civic, professional, and voluntary agencies. **SKILLS**—Speaking: Talking to others to convey information effectively. Writing: Communicating effectively in writing as appropriate for the needs of the audience. Coordination: Adjusting actions in relation to others' actions. Active Listening: Giving full attention to what other people are saying, taking time to understand the points being made, asking questions as appropriate, and not interrupting at inappropriate times. Active Learning: Understanding the implications of new information for both current and future problem-solving and decision-making. Reading Com-

prehension: Understanding written sentences and paragraphs in work-related documents.

GOE INFORMATION—**Interest Area:** 14. Medical and Health Services. **Work Group:** 14.08. Health Protection and Promotion. **Other Job Titles in This Work Group:** Athletic Trainers; Dietetic Technicians; Dietitians and Nutritionists. **PERSONALITY TYPE**—Social. Social occupations frequently involve working with, communicating with, and teaching people. These occupations often involve helping or providing service to others.

EDUCATION/TRAINING PROGRAM(S)—Community Health Liaison; Curriculum and Instruction; Educational/Instructional Media Design; Public Health Education and Promotion. **RELATED KNOWLEDGE/COURSES**—Education and Training: Knowledge of principles and methods for curriculum and training design, teaching and instruction for individuals and groups, and the measurement of training effects. **English Language:** Knowledge of the structure and content of the English language, including the meaning and spelling of words, rules of composition, and grammar. **Communications and Media:** Knowledge of media production, communication, and dissemination techniques and methods. This includes alternative ways to inform and entertain via written, oral, and visual media. **Customer and Personal Service:** Knowledge of principles and processes for providing customer and personal services. This includes customer needs assessment, meeting quality standards for services, and evaluation of customer satisfaction. **Medicine and Dentistry:** Knowledge of the information and techniques needed to diagnose and treat human injuries, diseases, and deformities. This includes symptoms, treatment alternatives, drug properties and interactions, and preventive health-care measures. **Therapy** **and Counseling:** Knowledge of principles, methods, and procedures for diagnosis, treatment, and rehabilitation of physical and mental dysfunctions and for career counseling and guidance.

Health Specialties Teachers, Postsecondary

- ▲ Education/Training Required: Master's degree
- ▲ Annual Earnings: $59,220
- ▲ Growth: 24% for all Postsecondary Teachers
- ▲ Annual Job Openings: 184,000 for all Postsecondary Teachers
- ▲ Self-Employed: 0%
- ▲ Part-Time: 32.3% for all Postsecondary Teachers

Teach courses in health specialties, such as veterinary medicine, dentistry, pharmacy, therapy, laboratory technology, and public health. Prepares and delivers lectures to students. Compiles bibliographies of specialized materials for outside reading assignments. Stimulates class discussions. Compiles, administers, and grades examinations or assigns this work to others. Directs research of other teachers or graduate students working for advanced academic degrees. Serves on faculty committee providing professional consulting services to government and industry. Acts as adviser to student organizations. Conducts research in particular field of knowledge and publishes findings in professional journals. Advises students on academic and vocational curricula. **SKILLS**—Reading Comprehension: Understanding written sentences and paragraphs in work-related documents. Science: Using scientific rules and methods to solve problems. Writing: Communicating effectively in writing as appropriate for the needs of the audience. Instructing: Teaching others how to do something. Critical Thinking: Using logic and reasoning to identify the strengths and weaknesses of alternative solutions, conclusions, or approaches to problems. Active Listening: Giving full attention to what other people are saying, taking time to understand the points being made, asking questions as appropriate, and not interrupting at inappropriate times. Active Learning: Understanding the implications of new information for both current and future problem-solving and decision-making.

GOE INFORMATION—**Interest Area:** 12. Education and Social Service. **Work Group:** 12.03. Educational Services. **Other Job Titles in This Work Group:** Adult Literacy, Remedial Education, and GED Teachers and Instructors; Agricultural Sciences Teachers, Postsecondary; Anthropology and Archeology Teachers, Postsecondary; Architecture Teachers, Postsecondary; Archivists; Area, Ethnic, and Cultural Studies Teachers, Postsecondary; Art, Drama, and Music Teachers, Postsecondary; Atmospheric, Earth, Marine, and Space Sciences Teachers, Postsecondary; Audio-Visual Collections Specialists; Biological Science Teachers, Postsecondary; Business Teachers, Postsecondary; Chemistry Teachers, Postsecondary; Child Care Workers; Communications Teachers, Postsecondary; Computer Science Teachers, Postsecondary; Criminal Justice and Law Enforcement Teachers, Postsecondary; Curators; Economics Teachers, Postsecondary; Education Teachers, Postsecondary; Educational Psychologists; Educational, Vocational, and School Counselors; Elementary School Teachers, Except Special Education; Engineering Teachers, Postsecondary; English Language and Literature Teachers, Postsecondary; Environmental Science Teachers, Postsecondary; Farm and Home Management Advisors;

Foreign Language and Literature Teachers, Postsecondary; Forestry and Conservation Science Teachers, Postsecondary; Geography Teachers, Postsecondary; Graduate Teaching Assistants; History Teachers, Postsecondary; Home Economics Teachers, Postsecondary; Kindergarten Teachers, Except Special Education; Law Teachers, Postsecondary; Librarians; Library Assistants, Clerical; Library Science Teachers, Postsecondary; others. **PERSONALITY TYPE**—Investigative. Investigative occupations frequently involve working with ideas and require an extensive amount of thinking. These occupations can involve searching for facts and figuring out problems mentally.

EDUCATION/TRAINING PROGRAM(S)— Health Occupations Teacher Education (Vocational). **RELATED KNOWLEDGE/COURSES**—Education and Training: Knowledge of principles and methods for curriculum and training design, teaching and instruction for individuals and groups, and the measurement of training effects. **Biology:** Knowledge of plant and animal organisms and their tissues, cells, functions, interdependencies, and interactions with each other and the environment. **Medicine and Dentistry:** Knowledge of the information and techniques needed to diagnose and treat human injuries, diseases, and deformities. This includes symptoms, treatment alternatives, drug properties and interactions, and preventive health-care measures. **English Language:** Knowledge of the structure and content of the English language, including the meaning and spelling of words, rules of composition, and grammar. **Therapy and Counseling:** Knowledge of principles, methods, and procedures for diagnosis, treatment, and rehabilitation of physical and mental dysfunctions and for career counseling and guidance.

Historians

- ▲ Education/Training Required: Bachelor's degree
- ▲ Annual Earnings: $39,860
- ▲ Growth: 17%
- ▲ Annual Job Openings: 2,000
- ▲ Self-Employed: 5.2%
- ▲ Part-Time: 18.1%

Research, analyze, record, and interpret the past as recorded in sources, such as government and institutional records, newspapers and other periodicals, photographs, interviews, films, and unpublished manuscripts, such as personal diaries and letters. Conducts historical research on subjects of import to society and presents finding and theories in textbooks, journals, and other publications. Assembles historical data by consulting sources such as archives, court records, diaries, news files, and miscellaneous published and unpublished materials. Organizes and evaluates data on basis of authenticity and relative significance. Consults with or advises other individuals on historical authenticity of various materials. Consults experts or witnesses of historical events. Reviews and collects data, such as books, pamphlets, periodicals, and rare newspapers, to provide source material for research. Traces historical development in fields such as economics, sociology, or philosophy. Reviews publications and exhibits prepared by others prior to public release in order to ensure historical accuracy of presentations. Coordinates activities of workers engaged in cataloging and filing materials. Edits society publications. Speaks before various groups, organizations, and clubs to promote societal aims and activities. Translates or requests translation of reference materials. Advises or consults with individuals, institutions, and commercial organizations on technological evolution or customs peculiar to certain historical period. **SKILLS**—Writing: Communicating effectively in writing as appropriate for the needs of the audience. Reading Comprehension: Understanding written sentences and paragraphs in work-related documents. Speaking: Talking to others to convey information effectively. Critical Thinking: Using logic and reasoning to identify the strengths and weaknesses of alternative solutions, conclusions, or approaches to problems. Active Learning: Understanding the implications of new information for both current and future problem-solving and decision-making.

GOE INFORMATION—Interest Area: 02. Science, Math, and Engineering. **Work Group:** 02.04. Social Sciences. **Other Job Titles in This Work Group:** Anthropologists; Anthropologists and Archeologists; Archeologists; City Planning Aides; Economists; Industrial-Organizational Psychologists; Political Scientists; Psychologists, All Other; Social Science Research Assistants; Social Scientists and Related Workers, All Other; Sociologists; Survey Researchers; Urban and Regional Planners. **PERSONALITY TYPE**—Investigative. Investigative occupations frequently involve working with ideas and require an extensive amount of thinking. These occupations can involve searching for facts and figuring out problems mentally.

EDUCATION/TRAINING PROGRAM(S)—American (United States) History; European History;

History and Philosophy of Science and Technology; History, General; History, Other; Social Sciences and History, Other. **RELATED KNOWLEDGE/COURSES—History and Archeology:** Knowledge of historical events and their causes, indicators, and effects on civilizations and cultures. **English Language:** Knowledge of the structure and content of the English language, including the meaning and spelling of words, rules of composition, and grammar. **Administration and Management:** Knowledge of business and management principles involved in strategic planning, resource allocation, human resources modeling, leadership technique, production methods, and coordination of people and resources. **Sociology and Anthropology:** Knowledge of group behavior and dynamics, societal trends and influences, human migrations, ethnicity, cultures, and their history and origins. **Communications and Media:** Knowledge of media production, communication, and dissemination techniques and methods. This includes alternative ways to inform and entertain via written, oral, and visual media.

History Teachers, Postsecondary

- ▲ Education/Training Required: Master's degree
- ▲ Annual Earnings: $49,080
- ▲ Growth: 24% for all Postsecondary Teachers
- ▲ Annual Job Openings: 184,000 for all Postsecondary Teachers
- ▲ Self-Employed: 0%
- ▲ Part-Time: 32.3% for all Postsecondary Teachers

Teach courses in human history and historiography. Prepares and delivers lectures to students. Compiles bibliographies of specialized materials for outside reading assignments. Advises students on academic and vocational curricula. Compiles, administers, and grades examinations or assigns this work to others. Stimulates class discussions. Directs research of other teachers or graduate students working for advanced academic degrees. Serves on faculty committee providing professional consulting services to government and industry. Acts as adviser to student orga-

nizations. Conducts research in particular field of knowledge and publishes findings in professional journals. **SKILLS—Reading Comprehension:** Understanding written sentences and paragraphs in work-related documents. **Instructing:** Teaching others how to do something. **Speaking:** Talking to others to convey information effectively. **Active Learning:** Understanding the implications of new information for both current and future problem-solving and decision-making. **Active Listening:** Giving full attention to what other people are saying, taking time to understand the points being made, asking questions as appropriate, and not interrupting at inappropriate times. Writing: Communicating effectively in writing as appropriate for the needs of the audience. Learning Strategies: Selecting and using training/instructional methods and procedures appropriate for the situation when learning or teaching new things.

GOE INFORMATION—Interest Area: 12. Education and Social Service. Work Group: 12.03. Educational Services. Other Job Titles in This Work Group: Adult Literacy, Remedial Education, and GED Teachers and Instructors; Agricultural Sciences Teachers, Postsecondary; Anthropology and Archeology Teachers, Postsecondary; Architecture Teachers, Postsecondary; Archivists; Area, Ethnic, and Cultural Studies Teachers, Postsecondary; Art, Drama, and Music Teachers, Postsecondary; Atmospheric, Earth, Marine, and Space Sciences Teachers, Postsecondary; Audio-Visual Collections Specialists; Biological Science Teachers, Postsecondary; Business Teachers, Postsecondary; Chemistry Teachers, Postsecondary; Child Care Workers; Communications Teachers, Postsecondary; Computer Science Teachers, Postsecondary; Criminal Justice and Law Enforcement Teachers, Postsecondary; Curators; Economics Teachers, Postsecondary; Education Teachers, Postsecondary; Educational Psychologists; Educational, Vocational, and School Counselors; Elementary School Teachers, Except Special Education; Engineering Teachers, Postsecondary; English Language and Literature Teachers, Postsecondary; Environmental Science Teachers, Postsecondary; Farm and Home Management Advisors;

Foreign Language and Literature Teachers, Postsecondary; Forestry and Conservation Science Teachers, Postsecondary; Geography Teachers, Postsecondary; Graduate Teaching Assistants; Health Specialties Teachers, Postsecondary; Home Economics Teachers, Postsecondary; Kindergarten Teachers, Except Special Education; Law Teachers, Postsecondary; Librarians; Library Assistants, Clerical; Library Science Teachers, Postsecondary; others. **PERSONALITY TYPE**—Social. Social occupations frequently involve working with, communicating with, and teaching people. These occupations often involve helping or providing service to others.

EDUCATION/TRAINING PROGRAM(S)— History, General. RELATED KNOWLEDGE/ COURSES—**Education and Training:** Knowledge of principles and methods for curriculum and training design, teaching and instruction for individuals and groups, and the measurement of training effects. **Sociology and Anthropology:** Knowledge of group behavior and dynamics, societal trends and influences, human migrations, ethnicity, cultures, and their history and origins. **English Language:** Knowledge of the structure and content of the English language, including the meaning and spelling of words, rules of composition, and grammar. **History and Archeology:** Knowledge of historical events and their causes, indicators, and effects on civilizations and cultures. **Psychology:** Knowledge of human behavior and performance; individual differences in ability, personality, and interests; learning and motivation; psychological research methods; and the assessment and treatment of behavioral and affective disorders.

Home Economics Teachers, Postsecondary

- ▲ Education/Training Required: Master's degree
- ▲ Annual Earnings: $46,500
- ▲ Growth: 24% for all Postsecondary Teachers
- ▲ Annual Job Openings: 184,000 for all Postsecondary Teachers
- ▲ Self-Employed: 0%
- ▲ Part-Time: 32.3% for all Postsecondary Teachers

Teach courses in child care, family relations, finance, nutrition, and related subjects as pertaining to home management. SKILLS—No data available.

GOE INFORMATION—Interest Area: 12. Education and Social Service. Work Group: 12.03. Educational Services. Other Job Titles in This Work Group: Adult Literacy, Remedial Education, and GED Teachers and Instructors; Agricultural Sciences Teachers, Postsecondary; Anthropology and Archeology Teachers, Postsecondary; Architecture Teachers, Postsecondary; Archivists; Area, Ethnic, and Cultural Studies Teachers, Postsecondary; Art, Drama, and Music Teachers, Postsecondary; Atmospheric, Earth, Marine, and Space Sciences Teachers, Postsecondary; Audio-Visual Collections Specialists; Biological Science Teachers, Postsecondary; Business Teachers, Postsecondary; Chemistry Teachers, Postsecondary; Child Care Workers; Communications Teachers, Postsecondary; Computer Science Teachers, Postsecondary; Criminal Justice and Law Enforcement Teachers, Postsecondary; Curators; Economics Teachers, Postsecondary; Education Teachers, Postsecondary; Educational Psychologists; Educational, Vocational, and School Counselors; Elementary School Teachers, Except Special Education; Engineering Teachers, Postsecondary; English Language and Literature Teachers, Postsecondary; Environmental Science Teachers, Postsecondary; Farm and Home Management Advisors; Foreign Language and Literature Teachers, Postsecondary; Forestry and Conservation Science Teachers, Postsecondary; Geography Teachers, Postsecondary; Graduate Teaching Assistants; Health Specialties Teachers, Postsecondary; History Teachers, Postsecondary; Kindergarten Teachers, Except Special Education; Law Teachers, Postsecondary; Librarians; Library Assistants, Clerical; Library Science Teachers, Postsecondary; others. PERSONALITY TYPE—No data available.

EDUCATION/TRAINING PROGRAM(S)— Home Economics, General. RELATED KNOWLEDGE/COURSES—No data available.

Human Resources Managers

- ▲ Education/Training Required: Work experience, plus degree
- ▲ Annual Earnings: $59,000
- ▲ Growth: 13%
- ▲ Annual Job Openings: 14,000
- ▲ Self-Employed: 0.5%
- ▲ Part-Time: 3.6%

Plan, direct, and coordinate human resource management activities of an organization to maximize the strategic use of human resources and maintain functions such as employee compensation, recruitment, personnel policies, and regulatory compliance. Formulates policies and procedures for recruitment, testing, placement, classification, orientation, benefits, and labor and industrial relations. Plans, directs, supervises, and coordinates work activities of subordinates and staff relating to employment, compensation, labor relations, and employee relations. Analyzes compensation policies, government regulations, and prevailing wage rates to develop competitive compensation plan. Develops methods to improve employment policies, processes, and practices and recommends changes to management. Prepares personnel forecast to project employment needs. Prepares budget for personnel operations. Prepares and delivers presentations and reports to corporate officers or other management regarding human resource management policies and practices and recommendations for change. Negotiates bargaining agreements and resolves labor disputes. Meets with shop stewards and supervisors to resolve grievances. Conducts exit interviews to identify reasons for employee termination and writes separation notices. Plans and conducts new employee orientation to foster positive attitude toward organizational objectives. Writes directives advising department managers of organization policy in personnel matters such as equal employment opportunity, sexual harassment, and discrimination. Studies legislation, arbitration decisions, and collective bargaining contracts to assess industry trends. Maintains records and compiles statistical reports concerning personnel-related data such as hires, transfers, performance appraisals, and absenteeism rates. Analyzes statistical data and reports to identify and determine causes of personnel problems and develop recommendations for improvement of organization's personnel policies and practices. Represents organization at personnel-related hearings and investigations. Contracts with vendors to provide employee services, such as canteen, transportation, or relocation service. Investigates industrial accidents and prepares reports for insurance carrier. **SKILLS**—Management of Personnel Resources: Motivating, developing, and directing people as they work, identifying the best people for the job. Systems Analysis: Determining how a system should work and how changes in conditions, operations, and the environment will affect outcomes. Systems Evaluation: Identifying measures or indicators of system performance and the actions needed to improve or correct performance relative to the goals of the system. Active Learning: Understanding the implications of new information for both current and future problem-solving and decision-making. Coordination: Adjusting actions in relation to others' actions. Speaking: Talking to others to convey information effectively. Reading Comprehension: Understanding written sentences and paragraphs in work-related documents.

GOE INFORMATION—**Interest Area:** 13. General Management and Support. **Work Group:** 13.01. General Management Work and Management of Support Functions. **Other Job Titles in This Work Group:** Chief Executives; Compensation and Benefits Managers;

Farm, Ranch, and Other Agricultural Managers; Financial Managers; Financial Managers, Branch or Department; Funeral Directors; General and Operations Managers; Government Service Executives; Human Resources Managers, All Other; Legislators; Managers, All Other; Postmasters and Mail Superintendents; Private Sector Executives; Property, Real Estate, and Community Association Managers; Public Relations Managers; Purchasing Managers; Storage and Distribution Managers; Training and Development Managers; Transportation, Storage, and Distribution Managers; Treasurers, Controllers, and Chief Financial Officers. **PERSONALITY TYPE**— Enterprising. Enterprising occupations frequently involve starting up and carrying out projects. These occupations can involve leading people and making many decisions. They sometimes require risk taking and often deal with business.

EDUCATION/TRAINING PROGRAM(S)— Human Resources Management. **RELATED KNOWLEDGE/COURSES**—**Personnel and Human Resources:** Knowledge of principles and procedures for personnel recruitment, selection, training, compensation and benefits, labor relations and negotiation, and personnel information systems. **Administration and Management:** Knowledge of business and management principles involved in strategic planning, resource allocation, human resources modeling, leadership technique, production methods, and coordination of people and resources. **Mathematics:** Knowledge of arithmetic, algebra, geometry, calculus, and statistics and their applications. **English Language:** Knowledge of the structure and content of the English language, including the meaning and spelling of words, rules of composition, and grammar. **Education and Training:** Knowledge of principles and methods for curriculum and training design, teaching and instruction for individuals and groups, and the measurement of training effects.

Hydrologists

▲ Education/Training Required: Bachelor's degree

▲ Annual Earnings: $55,410

▲ Growth: 26%

▲ Annual Job Openings: 1,000

▲ Self-Employed: 15.1%

▲ Part-Time: 6.3%

Research the distribution, circulation, and physical properties of underground and surface waters; study the form and intensity of precipitation, its rate of infiltration into the soil, movement through the earth, and its return to the ocean and atmosphere. Studies and analyzes physical aspects of earth, including atmosphere, hydrosphere, and interior structure. Studies waters of land areas to determine modes of return to ocean and atmosphere. Compiles and evaluates data to prepare navigational charts and maps, predict atmospheric conditions, and prepare environmental reports. Prepares and issues maps and reports indicating areas of seismic risk to existing or proposed construction or development. Evaluates data in reference to project planning, such as flood and drought control, water power and supply, drainage, irrigation, and inland navigation. Investigates origin and activity of glaciers, volcanoes, and earthquakes. Studies, maps, and charts distribution, disposition, and development of waters of land areas, including form and intensity of precipitation. Studies, measures, and interprets seismic, gravitational, electrical, thermal, and magnetic forces and data affecting the earth. **SKILLS—** Mathematics: Using mathematics to solve problems. Science: Using scientific rules and methods to solve problems. Writing: Communicating effectively in writing as appropriate for the needs of the audience. Active Learning: Understanding the implications of new information for both current and future problem-solving and decision-making. Critical Thinking: Using logic and reasoning to identify the strengths and weaknesses of alternative solutions, conclusions, or approaches to problems.

GOE INFORMATION—Interest Area: 02. Science, Math, and Engineering. **Work Group:** 02.02. Physi-

cal Sciences. **Other Job Titles in This Work Group:** Astronomers; Atmospheric and Space Scientists; Chemists; Geographers; Geologists; Geoscientists, Except Hydrologists and Geographers; Materials Scientists; Physical Scientists, All Other; Physicists. **PERSONALITY TYPE**—Investigative. Investigative occupations frequently involve working with ideas and require an extensive amount of thinking. These occupations can involve searching for facts and figuring out problems mentally.

EDUCATION/TRAINING PROGRAM(S)— Earth and Planetary Sciences; Geology; Miscellaneous Physical Sciences, Other; Oceanography. **RELATED KNOWLEDGE/COURSES—Physics:** Knowledge and prediction of physical principles and laws and their interrelationships and applications to understanding fluid, material, and atmospheric dynamics and mechanical, electrical, atomic, and sub-atomic structures and processes. **Mathematics:** Knowledge of arithmetic, algebra, geometry, calculus, and statistics and their applications. **Geography:** Knowledge of principles and methods for describing the features of land, sea, and air masses, including their physical characteristics, locations, interrelationships, and distribution of plant, animal, and human life. **Chemistry:** Knowledge of the chemical composition, structure, and properties of substances and of the chemical processes and transformations that they undergo. This includes uses of chemicals and their interactions, danger signs, production techniques, and disposal methods. **English Language:** Knowledge of the structure and content of the English language, including the meaning and spelling of words, rules of composition, and grammar.

Industrial Engineering Technicians

- ▲ Education/Training Required: Associate's degree
- ▲ Annual Earnings: $40,910
- ▲ Growth: 10%
- ▲ Annual Job Openings: 5,000
- ▲ Self-Employed: 1.9%
- ▲ Part-Time: 7.4%

Apply engineering theory and principles to problems of industrial layout or manufacturing production, usually under the direction of engineering staff. May study and record time, motion, method, and speed involved in performance of production, maintenance, clerical, and other worker operations for such purposes as establishing standard production rates or improving efficiency. Studies time, motion, methods, and speed involved in maintenance, production, and other operations to establish standard production rate and improve efficiency. Prepares charts, graphs, and diagrams to illustrate workflow, routing, floor layouts, material handling, and machine utilization. Observes workers operating equipment or performing tasks to determine time involved and fatigue rate, using timing devices. Recommends revision to methods of operation, material handling, equipment layout, or other changes to increase production or improve standards. Observes worker using equipment to verify that equipment is being operated and maintained according to quality assurance standards. Evaluates data and writes reports to validate or indicate deviations from existing standards. Prepares graphs or charts of data or enters data into computer for analysis. Selects products for tests at specified stages in production process and tests products for performance characteristics and adherence to specifications. Compiles and evaluates statistical data to determine and maintain quality and reliability of products. Reads worker logs, product processing sheets, and specification sheets to verify that records adhere to quality assurance specifications. Interprets engineering drawings, schematic diagrams, or formulas and confers with management or engineering staff to determine quality and reliability standards. Aids in planning work assignments in accordance with worker performance, machine capacity, production schedules, and anticipated delays. Recommends modifications to existing quality or production standards to achieve optimum quality within limits of equipment capability. Records test data, applying statistical quality control procedures. **SKILLS**—Reading Comprehension: Understanding written sentences and paragraphs in work-related documents. Mathematics: Using mathematics to solve problems. Quality Control Analysis: Conducting tests and inspections of products, services, or processes to evaluate quality or performance. Writing: Communicating effectively in writing as appropriate for the needs of the audience. Critical Thinking: Using logic and reasoning to identify the strengths and weaknesses of alternative solutions, conclusions, or approaches to problems. Systems Evaluation: Identifying measures or indicators of system performance and the actions needed to improve or correct performance relative to the goals of the system. Monitoring: Monitoring/Assessing your performance or that of other individuals or organizations to make improvements or take corrective action.

GOE INFORMATION—Interest Area: 02. Science, Math, and Engineering. **Work Group:** 02.08. Engineering Technology. **Other Job Titles in This Work Group:** Aerospace Engineering and Operations Technicians; Architectural and Civil Drafters; Architectural Drafters; Calibration and Instrumentation Technicians; Cartographers and Photogrammetrists; Civil Drafters; Civil Engineering Technicians; Construction and Building Inspectors; Drafters, All Other; Electrical and Electronic Engineering Technicians; Electrical and Electronics Drafters; Electrical Drafters; Electrical Engineering Technicians; Electro-Mechanical Technicians; Electronic Drafters; Electronics Engineering Technicians; Engineering Technicians, Except Drafters, All Other; Environmental Engineering

Technicians; Mapping Technicians; Mechanical Drafters; Mechanical Engineering Technicians; Numerical Tool and Process Control Programmers; Pressure Vessel Inspectors; Surveying and Mapping Technicians; Surveying Technicians; Surveyors. **PERSONALITY TYPE**—Investigative. Investigative occupations frequently involve working with ideas and require an extensive amount of thinking. These occupations can involve searching for facts and figuring out problems mentally.

EDUCATION/TRAINING PROGRAM(S)—Industrial/Manufacturing Technologist/Technician. **RELATED KNOWLEDGE/COURSES—Engineering and Technology:** Knowledge of the practical application of engineering science and technology. This includes applying principles, techniques, procedures, and equipment to the design and production of various goods and services. **Production and Processing:** Knowledge of raw materials, production processes, quality control, costs, and other techniques for maximizing the effective manufacture and distribution of goods. **Mathematics:** Knowledge of arithmetic, algebra, geometry, calculus, and statistics and their applications. **Design:** Knowledge of design techniques, tools, and principles involved in production of precision technical plans, blueprints, drawings, and models. **English Language:** Knowledge of the structure and content of the English language, including the meaning and spelling of words, rules of composition, and grammar.

Industrial Engineers

▲ Education/Training Required: Bachelor's degree
▲ Annual Earnings: $58,580
▲ Growth: 4%
▲ Annual Job Openings: 10,000
▲ Self-Employed: 0.9%
▲ Part-Time: 2.4%

Design, develop, test, and evaluate integrated systems for managing industrial production processes, including human work factors, quality control, inventory control, logistics and material flow, cost analysis, and production coordination. Analyzes statistical data and product specifications to determine standards and establish quality and reliability objectives of finished product. Reviews production schedules, engineering specifications, orders, and related information to obtain knowledge of manufacturing methods, procedures, and activities. Directs workers engaged in product measurement, inspection, and testing activities to ensure quality control and reliability. Completes production reports, purchase orders, and material, tool, and equipment lists. Estimates production cost and effect of product design changes for management review, action, and control. Recommends methods for improving utilization of personnel, material, and utilities. Communicates with management and user personnel to develop production and design standards. Coordinates quality control objectives and activities to resolve production problems, maximize product reliability, and minimize cost. Applies statistical methods and performs mathematical calculations to determine manufacturing processes, staff requirements, and production standards. Formulates sampling procedures and designs and develops forms and instructions for recording, evaluating, and reporting quality and reliability data. Studies operations sequence, material flow, functional statements, organization charts, and project information to determine worker functions and responsibilities. Schedules deliveries based on production forecasts, material substitutions, storage and handling facilities, and maintenance requirements. Confers with vendors, staff, and management personnel regarding purchases, procedures, product specifications, manufacturing capabilities, and project status. Evaluates precision and accuracy of production and testing equipment and engineering drawings to formulate corrective action plan. Implements methods and procedures for disposition of discrepant material and defective or damaged parts and assesses cost and responsibility. Regulates and alters workflow schedules according to established manufacturing sequences and lead times to expedite production operations. Records or oversees recording of information to ensure currency of engineering drawings and documentation of production problems. Plans and establishes sequence of operations to fabricate and assemble parts or products and to promote efficient utilization of resources. Develops manufacturing methods, labor utilization standards, and cost analysis systems to promote efficient staff and facility utilization. Drafts and designs layout of equipment, materials, and workspace to illustrate maximum efficiency, using drafting tools and computer. **SKILLS**—Mathematics: Using mathematics to solve problems. Reading Comprehension: Understanding written sentences and paragraphs in work-related documents. Management of Material Resources: Obtaining and seeing to the appropriate use of equipment, facilities, and materials needed to do certain work. Operations Analysis: Analyzing needs and product requirements to create a design. Critical Thinking: Using logic and reasoning to identify the strengths and weaknesses of alternative solutions, conclusions, or approaches to problems.

GOE INFORMATION—Interest Area: 02. Science, Math, and Engineering. **Work Group:** 02.07. Engineering. **Other Job Titles in This Work Group:** Aerospace Engineers; Agricultural Engineers; Architects, Except Landscape and Naval; Biomedical Engineers; Chemical Engineers; Civil Engineers; Computer Hardware Engineers; Computer Software Engineers, Applications; Computer Software Engineers, Systems Software; Electrical Engineers; Electronics Engineers, Except Computer; Engineers, All Other; Environmental Engineers; Fire-Prevention and Protection Engineers; Health and Safety Engineers, Except Mining Safety Engineers and Inspectors; Industrial Safety and Health Engineers; Landscape Architects; Marine Architects; Marine Engineers; Marine

Engineers and Naval Architects; Materials Engineers; Mechanical Engineers; Mining and Geological Engineers, Including Mining Safety Engineers; Nuclear Engineers; Petroleum Engineers; Product Safety Engineers; Sales Engineers. **PERSONALITY TYPE**—Enterprising. Enterprising occupations frequently involve starting up and carrying out projects. These occupations can involve leading people and making many decisions. They sometimes require risk taking and often deal with business.

EDUCATION/TRAINING PROGRAM(S)—Architectural Engineering; Bioengineering and Biomedical Engineering; Engineering Design; Engineering Mechanics; Engineering Physics; Engineering Science; Engineering, General; Engineering, Other; Engineering/Industrial Management; Environmental/Environmental Health Engineering; Geological Engineering; Geophysical Engineering; Industrial/Manufacturing Engineering; Ocean Engineering; Polymer/Plastics Engineering; Systems Engineering; Textile Sciences and Engineering. **RELATED KNOWLEDGE/COURSES**—**Mathematics:** Knowledge of arithmetic, algebra, geometry, calculus, and statistics and their applications. **Production and Processing:** Knowledge of raw materials, production processes, quality control, costs, and other techniques for maximizing the effective manufacture and distribution of goods. **Engineering and Technology:** Knowledge of the practical application of engineering science and technology. This includes applying principles, techniques, procedures, and equipment to the design and production of various goods and services. **Administration and Management:** Knowledge of business and management principles involved in strategic planning, resource allocation, human resources modeling, leadership technique, production methods, and coordination of people and resources. **Design:** Knowledge of design techniques, tools, and principles involved in production of precision technical plans, blueprints, drawings, and models.

Industrial Production Managers

▲ Education/Training Required: Bachelor's degree

▲ Annual Earnings: $61,660

▲ Growth: 6%

▲ Annual Job Openings: 22,000

▲ Self-Employed: 0%

▲ Part-Time: 6.1%

Plan, direct, or coordinate the work activities and resources necessary for manufacturing products in accordance with cost, quality, and quantity specifications. Directs and coordinates production, processing, distribution, and marketing activities of industrial organization. Reviews processing schedules and production orders to determine staffing requirements, work procedures, and duty assignments. Reviews plans and confers with research and support staff to develop new products and processes or the quality of existing products. Initiates and coordinates inventory and cost control programs. Develops budgets and approves expenditures for supplies, materials, and human resources. Examines samples of raw products or directs testing during processing to ensure finished products conform to prescribed quality standards. Hires, trains, evaluates, and discharges staff. Resolves personnel grievances. Prepares and maintains production reports and personnel records. Coordinates and recommends procedures for facility and equipment maintenance or modification. Negotiates materials prices with suppliers. Reviews operations and confers with technical or administrative staff to resolve production or processing problems. Analyzes production, quality control, maintenance, and other operational reports to detect production problems. **SKILLS**—Coordination: Adjusting actions in relation to others' actions. Judgment and Decision Making: Considering the relative costs and benefits of potential actions to choose the most appropriate one. Management of Personnel Resources: Motivating, developing, and directing people as they work, identifying the best people for the job. Systems Evaluation: Identifying measures or indicators of system performance and the actions needed to improve or correct performance relative to the goals of the system. Management of Material Resources: Obtaining and seeing to the appropriate use of equipment, facilities, and materials needed to do certain work. Monitoring: Monitoring/Assessing your performance or that of other individuals or organizations to make improvements or take corrective action.

GOE INFORMATION—**Interest Area:** 08. Industrial Production. **Work Group:** 08.01. Managerial Work in Industrial Production. **Other Job Titles in This Work Group:** First-Line Supervisors/Managers of Helpers, Laborers, and Material Movers, Hand; First-Line Supervisors/Managers of Production and Operating Workers. **PERSONALITY TYPE**—Enterprising. Enterprising occupations frequently involve starting up and carrying out projects. These occupations can involve leading people and making many decisions. They sometimes require risk taking and often deal with business.

EDUCATION/TRAINING PROGRAM(S)—Business Administration and Management, General; Operations Management and Supervision. **RELATED KNOWLEDGE/COURSES**—**Production and Processing:** Knowledge of raw materials, production processes, quality control, costs, and other techniques for maximizing the effective manufacture and distribution of goods. **Administration and Management:** Knowledge of business and management principles involved in strategic planning, resource allocation, human resources modeling, leadership technique, production methods, and coordination of people and resources. **Personnel and Human Resources:** Knowledge of principles and procedures for personnel recruitment, selection, training, compensation and benefits, labor relations and negotiation, and personnel information systems. **English Language:** Knowledge of the structure and content of the English language, including the meaning and spelling of words, rules of composition, and grammar. **Food Production:** Knowledge of techniques and equipment for planting, grow-ing, and harvesting food products (both plant and animal) for consumption, including storage/handling techniques.

Industrial Safety and Health Engineers

- ▲ Education/Training Required: Bachelor's degree
- ▲ Annual Earnings: $54,630
- ▲ Growth: 11%
- ▲ Annual Job Openings: 3,000
- ▲ Self-Employed: 2.7%
- ▲ Part-Time: 4.5%

Plan, implement, and coordinate safety programs requiring application of engineering principles and technology to prevent or correct unsafe environmental working conditions. Devises and implements safety or industrial health program to prevent, correct, or control unsafe environmental conditions. Installs or directs installation of safety devices on machinery. Maintains liaison with outside organizations, such as fire departments, mutual aid societies, and rescue teams. Prepares reports of findings from investigation of accidents, inspection of facilities, or testing of environment. Designs and builds safety devices for machinery or safety clothing. Checks floors of plant to ensure they are strong enough to support heavy machinery. Conducts plant or area surveys to determine safety levels for exposure to materials and conditions. Investigates causes of industrial accidents or injuries to develop solutions to minimize or prevent recurrence. Compiles, analyzes, and interprets statistical data related to exposure factors concerning occupational illnesses and accidents. Examines plans and specifications for new machinery or equipment to determine if all safety requirements have been included. Inspects facilities, machinery, and safety equipment to identify and correct potential hazards and ensure compliance with safety regulations. Conducts or directs testing of air quality, noise, temperature, or radiation to verify compliance with health and safety regulations. Provides technical guidance to organizations regarding how to handle health-related problems, such as water and air pollution. Conducts or coordinates training of workers concerning safety laws and regulations; use of safety equipment, devices, and clothing; and first aid.

SKILLS—Mathematics: Using mathematics to solve problems. Operations Analysis: Analyzing needs and product requirements to create a design. Instructing: Teaching others how to do something. Monitoring: Monitoring/Assessing your performance or that of other individuals or organizations to make improvements or take corrective action. Critical Thinking: Using logic and reasoning to identify the strengths and weaknesses of alternative solutions, conclusions, or approaches to problems. Reading Comprehension: Understanding written sentences and paragraphs in work-related documents. Technology Design: Generating or adapting equipment and technology to serve user needs.

GOE INFORMATION—Interest Area: 02. Science, Math, and Engineering. **Work Group:** 02.07. Engineering. **Other Job Titles in This Work Group:** Aerospace Engineers; Agricultural Engineers; Architects, Except Landscape and Naval; Biomedical Engineers; Chemical Engineers; Civil Engineers; Computer Hardware Engineers; Computer Software Engineers, Applications; Computer Software Engineers, Systems Software; Electrical Engineers; Electronics Engineers, Except Computer; Engineers, All Other; Environmental Engineers; Fire-Prevention and Protection Engineers; Health and Safety Engineers, Except Mining Safety Engineers and Inspectors; Industrial Engineers; Landscape Architects; Marine Architects; Marine Engineers; Marine Engineers and Naval Architects; Materials Engineers; Mechanical Engineers; Mining and Geological Engineers, Including Mining Safety Engineers; Nuclear Engineers; Petroleum Engineers; Product Safety Engineers; Sales Engineers. **PERSONALITY**

TYPE—Investigative. Investigative occupations frequently involve working with ideas and require an extensive amount of thinking. These occupations can involve searching for facts and figuring out problems mentally.

EDUCATION/TRAINING PROGRAM(S)—Engineering/Industrial Management; Environmental/Environmental Health Engineering; Systems Engineering. RELATED KNOWLEDGE/COURSES—Engineering and Technology: Knowledge of the practical application of engineering science and technology. This includes applying principles, techniques, procedures, and equipment to the design and production of various goods and services. Public Safety and Security: Knowledge of relevant equipment, policies, procedures, and strategies to promote effective local, state, or national security operations for the protection of people, data, property, and institutions. Design: Knowledge of design techniques, tools, and principles involved in production of precision technical plans, blueprints, drawings, and models. Physics: Knowledge and prediction of physical principles and laws and their interrelationships and applications to understanding fluid, material, and atmospheric dynamics and mechanical, electrical, atomic, and sub-atomic structures and processes. Administration and Management: Knowledge of business and management principles involved in strategic planning, resource allocation, human resources modeling, leadership technique, production methods, and coordination of people and resources.

Industrial-Organizational Psychologists

- ▲ Education/Training Required: Master's degree
- ▲ Annual Earnings: $66,880
- ▲ Growth: 18%
- ▲ Annual Job Openings: 18,000
- ▲ Self-Employed: 43.7%
- ▲ Part-Time: 23.4%

Apply principles of psychology to personnel, administration, management, sales, and marketing problems. Activities may include policy planning; employee screening, training and development; and organizational development and analysis. May work with management to reorganize the work setting to improve worker productivity. Develops interview techniques, rating scales, and psychological tests to assess skills, abilities, and interests as aids in selection, placement and promotion. Analyzes data, using statistical methods and applications, to evaluate and measure the effectiveness of program implementation or training. Plans, develops, and organizes training programs, applying principles of learning and individual differences. Studies consumer reaction to new products and package designs, using surveys and tests, and measures the effectiveness of advertising media. Advises management in strategic changes to personnel, managerial, and marketing policies and practices to improve organizational effectiveness and efficiency. Conducts research studies of physical work environments, organizational structure, communication systems, group interaction, morale, and motivation to assess organizational functioning. Analyzes job requirements to establish criteria for classification, selection, training, and other related personnel functions. Observes and interviews workers to identify the physical, mental, and educational requirements of job. SKILLS—Systems Evaluation: Identifying measures or indicators of system performance and the actions needed to improve or correct performance relative to the goals of the system. Reading Comprehension: Understanding written sentences and paragraphs in work-related documents. Active Learning: Understanding the implications of new information for both current and future problem-solving and decision-making. Mathematics: Using mathematics to solve problems. Writing: Communicating effectively in writing as appropriate for the needs of the audience.

GOE INFORMATION—Interest Area: 02. Science, Math, and Engineering. Work Group: 02.04. Social Sciences. Other Job Titles in This Work Group:

Anthropologists; Anthropologists and Archeologists; Archeologists; City Planning Aides; Economists; Historians; Political Scientists; Psychologists, All Other; Social Science Research Assistants; Social Scientists and Related Workers, All Other; Sociologists; Survey Researchers; Urban and Regional Planners. **PERSONALITY TYPE—** Investigative. Investigative occupations frequently involve working with ideas and require an extensive amount of thinking. These occupations can involve searching for facts and figuring out problems mentally.

EDUCATION/TRAINING PROGRAM(S)— Industrial and Organizational Psychology; Psychology, General. **RELATED KNOWLEDGE/ COURSES—Psychology:** Knowledge of human behavior and performance; individual differences in ability, personality, and interests; learning and motivation; psy-chological research methods; and the assessment and treatment of behavioral and affective disorders. **Personnel and Human Resources:** Knowledge of principles and procedures for personnel recruitment, selection, training, compensation and benefits, labor relations and negotiation, and personnel information systems. **Education and Training:** Knowledge of principles and methods for curriculum and training design, teaching and instruction for individuals and groups, and the measurement of training effects. **Mathematics:** Knowledge of arithmetic, algebra, geometry, calculus, and statistics and their applications. **Administration and Management:** Knowledge of business and management principles involved in strategic planning, resource allocation, human resources modeling, leadership technique, production methods, and coordination of people and resources.

Instructional Coordinators

- ▲ Education/Training Required: Master's degree
- ▲ Annual Earnings: $44,230
- ▲ Growth: 25%
- ▲ Annual Job Openings: 15,000
- ▲ Self-Employed: 13.8%
- ▲ Part-Time: 9.8%

Develop instructional material, coordinate educational content, and incorporate current technology in specialized fields that provide guidelines to educators and instructors for developing curricula and conducting courses. Researches, evaluates, and prepares recommendations on curricula, instructional methods, and materials for school system. Develops tests, questionnaires, and procedures to measure effectiveness of curriculum and to determine if program objectives are being met. Prepares or approves manuals, guidelines, and reports on state educational policies and practices for distribution to school districts. Orders or authorizes purchase of instructional materials, supplies, equipment, and visual aids designed to meet educational needs of students. Confers with school officials, teachers, and administrative staff to plan and develop curricula and establish guidelines for educational programs. Confers with educational committees and advisory groups to gather information on instructional methods and materials related to specific academic subjects. Advises teaching and administrative staff in assessment, curriculum development, management of student behavior, and use of materials and equipment. Observes, evaluates, and recommends changes in work of teaching staff to strengthen teaching skills in classroom. Plans, conducts, and evaluates training programs and conferences for teachers to study new classroom procedures, instructional materials, and teaching aids. Advises school officials on implementation of state and federal programs and procedures. Conducts or participates in workshops, committees, and conferences designed to promote intellectual, social, and physical welfare of students. Coordinates activities of workers engaged in cataloging, distributing, and maintaining educational materials and equipment in curriculum library and laboratory. Interprets and enforces provisions of state education codes and rules and regulations of State Board of Education. Prepares or assists in preparation of grant proposals, budgets, and program policies and goals. Addresses public audiences to explain and elicit support for program objectives. Reviews student files and confers with educators, parents, and other concerned parties to decide student placement and provision of services. Inspects and authorizes repair of instructional equipment, such as musical instruments. **SKILLS**—Learning Strategies: Selecting and using training/instructional methods and procedures appropriate for the situation when learning or teaching new things. Speaking: Talking to others to convey information effectively. Instructing: Teaching others how to do something. Reading Comprehension: Understanding written sentences and paragraphs in work-related documents. Writing: Communicating effectively in writing as appropriate for the needs of the audience.

GOE INFORMATION—**Interest Area:** 12. Education and Social Service. **Work Group:** 12.01. Managerial Work in Education and Social Service. **Other Job Titles in This Work Group:** Education Administrators, All Other; Education Administrators, Elementary and Secondary School; Education Administrators, Postsecondary; Education Administrators, Preschool and Child Care Center/Program; Park Naturalists; Social and Community Service Managers. **PERSONALITY TYPE**—Social. Social occupations frequently involve working with, communicating with, and teaching people. These occupations often involve helping or providing service to others.

EDUCATION/TRAINING PROGRAM(S)—Curriculum and Instruction; Education of the Gifted and Talented; Educational/Instructional Media Design. **RELATED KNOWLEDGE/COURSES**—**Education and Training:** Knowledge of principles and methods for curriculum and training design, teaching and instruction for individuals and groups, and the measurement of training effects. **English Language:** Knowledge of the structure and content of the English language, including the meaning and spelling of words, rules of composition, and grammar. **Administration and Management:** Knowledge of business and management principles involved in strategic planning, resource allocation, human resources modeling, leadership technique, production methods, and coordination of people and resources. **Psychology:** Knowledge of human behavior and performance; individual differences in ability, personality, and interests; learning and motivation; psychological research methods; and the assessment and treatment of behavioral and affective disorders. **Personnel and Human Resources:** Knowledge of principles and procedures for personnel recruitment, selection, training, compensation and benefits, labor relations and negotiation, and personnel information systems.

Insurance Sales Agents

- ▲ Education/Training Required: Bachelor's degree
- ▲ Annual Earnings: $38,750
- ▲ Growth: 3%
- ▲ Annual Job Openings: 43,000
- ▲ Self-Employed: 30.1%
- ▲ Part-Time: 9.3%

Sell life, property, casualty, health, automotive, or other types of insurance. May refer clients to independent brokers, work as independent broker, or be employed by an insurance company. Advises clients of broker (independent agent) in selecting casualty, life, or property insurance. Explains group insurance programs to promote sale of insurance plan. Selects company that offers type of coverage requested by client to underwrite policy. Discusses advantages and disadvantages of various policies. Calls on policyholders to deliver and explain policy, to suggest additions or changes in insurance program, or to change beneficiaries. Explains necessary bookkeeping requirements for customer to implement and provide group insurance program. Establishes client's method of payment. Installs bookkeeping systems and resolves system problems. Plans and oversees incorporation of insurance program into bookkeeping system of company. Contacts underwriter and submits forms to obtain binder coverage. **SKILLS**—Speaking: Talking to others to convey information effectively. Reading Comprehension: Understanding written sentences and paragraphs in work-related documents. Persuasion: Persuading others to change their minds or behavior. Critical Thinking: Using logic and reasoning to identify the strengths and weaknesses of alternative solutions, conclusions, or approaches to problems. Active Listening: Giving full attention to what other people are saying, taking time to understand the points being made, asking questions as appropriate, and not interrupting at inappropriate times.

GOE INFORMATION—**Interest Area:** 10. Sales and Marketing. **Work Group:** 10.02. Sales Technology. **Other Job Titles in This Work Group:** Advertising Sales Agents; Sales Agents, Financial Services; Sales Agents, Securities and Commodities; Sales Representatives, Agricultural; Sales Representatives, Chemical and Pharmaceutical; Sales Representatives, Electrical/Electronic; Sales Representatives, Instruments; Sales Representatives, Mechanical Equipment and Supplies; Sales Representatives, Medical; Sales Representatives, Services, All Other; Sales Representatives, Wholesale and Manufacturing, Technical and Scientific Products; Securities, Commodities, and Financial Services Sales Agents. **PERSONALITY**

TYPE—Enterprising. Enterprising occupations frequently involve starting up and carrying out projects. These occupations can involve leading people and making many decisions. They sometimes require risk taking and often deal with business.

EDUCATION/TRAINING PROGRAM(S)— Insurance and Risk Management; Insurance Marketing Operations. **RELATED KNOWLEDGE/ COURSES**—**Sales and Marketing:** Knowledge of principles and methods for showing, promoting, and selling products or services. This includes marketing strategy and tactics, product demonstration, sales techniques, and sales control systems. **Clerical Studies:** Knowledge of administrative and clerical procedures and systems such as word processing, managing files and records, stenography and transcription, designing forms, and other office procedures and terminology. **English Language:** Knowledge of the structure and content of the English language, including the meaning and spelling of words, rules of composition, and grammar. **Mathematics:** Knowledge of arithmetic, algebra, geometry, calculus, and statistics and their applications. **Administration and Management:** Knowledge of business and management principles involved in strategic planning, resource allocation, human resources modeling, leadership technique, production methods, and coordination of people and resources.

Insurance Underwriters

- ▲ Education/Training Required: Bachelor's degree
- ▲ Annual Earnings: $43,150
- ▲ Growth: 2%
- ▲ Annual Job Openings: 11,000
- ▲ Self-Employed: 0%
- ▲ Part-Time: 8.4%

Review individual applications for insurance to evaluate degree of risk involved and determine acceptance of applications. Examines documents to determine degree of risk from such factors as applicant financial standing and value and condition of property. Writes to field representatives, medical personnel, and others to obtain further information, quote rates, or explain company underwriting policies. Evaluates possibility of losses due to catastrophe or excessive insurance. Authorizes reinsurance of policy when risk is high. Decreases value of policy when risk is substandard and specifies applicable endorsements or applies rating to ensure safe profitable distribution of risks, using reference materials. Reviews company records to determine amount of insurance in force on single risk or group of closely related risks. Declines excessive risks. **SKILLS**—Judgment and Decision

Making: Considering the relative costs and benefits of potential actions to choose the most appropriate one. Mathematics: Using mathematics to solve problems. Reading Comprehension: Understanding written sentences and paragraphs in work-related documents. Critical Thinking: Using logic and reasoning to identify the strengths and weaknesses of alternative solutions, conclusions, or approaches to problems. Writing: Communicating effectively in writing as appropriate for the needs of the audience.

GOE INFORMATION—Interest Area: 13. General Management and Support. Work Group: 13.02. Management Support. Other Job Titles in This Work Group: Accountants; Accountants and Auditors; Appraisers and Assessors of Real Estate; Appraisers, Real Estate; Assessors; Auditors; Budget Analysts; Claims Adjusters, Examiners, and Investigators; Claims Examiners, Property and Casualty Insurance; Compensation, Benefits, and Job Analysis Specialists; Cost Estimators; Credit Analysts; Employment Interviewers, Private or Public Employment Service; Employment, Recruitment, and Placement Specialists; Financial Analysts; Human Resources, Training, and Labor Relations Specialists, All Other; Insurance Adjusters, Examiners, and Investigators; Insurance Appraisers, Auto Damage; Loan Counselors; Loan Officers; Logisticians; Management Analysts; Market Research Analysts; Personnel Recruiters; Purchasing Agents and Buyers, Farm Products; Purchasing Agents, Except Wholesale, Retail, and Farm Products; Tax Examiners, Collectors, and

Revenue Agents; Training and Development Specialists; Wholesale and Retail Buyers, Except Farm Products. **PERSONALITY TYPE**—Conventional. Conventional occupations frequently involve following set procedures and routines. These occupations can include working with data and details more than with ideas. Usually there is a clear line of authority to follow.

EDUCATION/TRAINING PROGRAM(S)— Insurance and Risk Management. RELATED KNOWLEDGE/COURSES—Mathematics: Knowledge of arithmetic, algebra, geometry, calculus, and statistics and their applications. English Language: Knowledge of the structure and content of the English language, including the meaning and spelling of words, rules of composition, and grammar. Economics and Accounting: Knowledge of economic and accounting principles and practices, the financial markets, banking, and the analysis and reporting of financial data. Clerical Studies: Knowledge of administrative and clerical procedures and systems such as word processing, managing files and records, stenography and transcription, designing forms, and other office procedures and terminology. Administration and Management: Knowledge of business and management principles involved in strategic planning, resource allocation, human resources modeling, leadership technique, production methods, and coordination of people and resources.

Interior Designers

- ▲ Education/Training Required: Bachelor's degree
- ▲ Annual Earnings: $36,540
- ▲ Growth: 17%
- ▲ Annual Job Openings: 7,000
- ▲ Self-Employed: 46.3%
- ▲ Part-Time: 20%

Plan, design, and furnish interiors of residential, commercial, or industrial buildings. Formulate design which is practical, aesthetic, and conducive to intended purposes, such as raising productivity, selling merchandise, or improving

lifestyle. May specialize in a particular field, style, or phase of interior design. Formulates environmental plan to be practical, esthetic, and conducive to intended purposes, such as raising productivity or selling merchandise. Estimates material requirements and costs and presents design to client for approval. Subcontracts fabrication, installation, and arrangement of carpeting, fixtures, accessories, draperies, paint and wall coverings, artwork, furniture, and related items. Renders design ideas in form of paste-ups or drawings. Confers with client to determine factors affecting planning interior environments, such as budget, architectural preferences, and purpose and function. Plans and designs interior environments for boats, planes, buses, trains, and other enclosed spaces. Advises client on interior design factors, such as space planning, layout and utilization of furnishings and equipment, and color coordination. Selects or designs and purchases furnishings, artwork, and accessories. **SKILLS**—Coordination: Adjusting actions in relation to others' actions. Active Listening: Giving full attention to what other people are saying, taking time to understand the points being made, asking questions as appropriate, and not interrupting at inappropriate times. Operations Analysis: Analyzing needs and product requirements to create a design. Management of Financial Resources: Determining how money will be spent to get the work done and accounting for these expenditures. Speaking: Talking to others to convey information effectively. Mathematics: Using mathematics to solve problems.

GOE INFORMATION—Interest Area: 01. Arts, Entertainment, and Media. **Work Group:** 01.04. Visual Arts. **Other Job Titles in This Work Group:** Cartoonists; Commercial and Industrial Designers; Designers, All Other; Exhibit Designers; Fashion Designers; Fine Artists, Including Painters, Sculptors, and Illustrators; Floral Designers; Graphic Designers; Merchandise Displayers and Window Trimmers; Multi-Media Artists and Animators; Painters and Illustrators; Sculptors; Set and Exhibit Designers; Set Designers; Sketch Artists. **PERSONALITY TYPE**—Artistic. Artistic occupations frequently involve working with forms, designs, and patterns. They often require self-expression, and the work can be done without following a clear set of rules.

EDUCATION/TRAINING PROGRAM(S)— Home Furnishings and Equipment Installers and Consultants, G; Home Furnishings and Equipment Installers and Consultants, O; Interior Architecture; Interior Design; Interior Environments. **RELATED KNOWLEDGE/ COURSES—Design:** Knowledge of design techniques, tools, and principles involved in production of precision technical plans, blueprints, drawings, and models. **Administration and Management:** Knowledge of business and management principles involved in strategic planning, resource allocation, human resources modeling, leadership technique, production methods, and coordination of people and resources. **Sales and Marketing:** Knowledge of principles and methods for showing, promoting, and selling products or services. This includes marketing strategy and tactics, product demonstration, sales techniques, and sales control systems. **Mathematics:** Knowledge of arithmetic, algebra, geometry, calculus, and statistics and their applications. **Fine Arts:** Knowledge of the theory and techniques required to compose, produce, and perform works of music, dance, visual arts, drama, and sculpture.

Internists, General

- ▲ Education/Training Required: First professional degree
- ▲ Annual Earnings: $142,400
- ▲ Growth: 18%
- ▲ Annual Job Openings: 27,000
- ▲ Self-Employed: 20.4%
- ▲ Part-Time: 7.2%

Diagnose and provide non-surgical treatment of diseases and injuries of internal organ systems. Provide care mainly for adults who have a wide range of problems associated with the internal organs. Examines or conducts tests on patient to provide information on medical condition. Analyzes records, reports, test results, or examination information to diagnose medical condition of patient. Explains procedures and discusses test results on prescribed treatments with patents. Prescribes or administers treatment, therapy, medication, vaccination, and other specialized medical care to treat or prevent illness, disease, or injury. Refers patient to medical specialist or other practitioner when necessary. Plans, implements, or administers health programs or standards in hospital, business, or community for information, prevention, or treatment of injury or illness. Prepares reports for government or management of birth, death, and disease statistics, workforce evaluations, or medical status of individuals. Conducts research to study anatomy and develop or test medications, treatments, or procedures to prevent or control disease or injury. Directs and coordinates activities of nurses, students, assistants, specialists, therapists, and other medical staff. Advises patients and community concerning diet, activity, hygiene, and disease prevention. Collects, records, and maintains patient information, such as medical history, reports, and examination results. Operates on patients to remove, repair, or improve functioning of diseased or injured body parts and systems and delivers babies. Monitors patients' condition and progress and re-evaluates treatments as necessary. **SKILLS**—Reading Comprehension: Understanding written sentences and paragraphs in work-related documents. Science: Using scientific rules and methods to solve problems. Active Learning: Understanding the implications of new information for both current and future problem-solving and decision-making. Judgment and Decision Making: Considering the relative costs and benefits of potential actions to choose the most appropriate one. Mathematics: Using mathematics to solve problems. Writing: Communicating effectively in writing as appropriate for the needs of the audience. Active Listening: Giving full attention to what other people are saying, taking time to understand the points being made, asking questions as appropriate, and not interrupting at inappropriate times.

GOE INFORMATION—**Interest Area:** 14. Medical and Health Services. **Work Group:** 14.02. Medicine and Surgery. **Other Job Titles in This Work Group:** Anesthesiologists; Family and General Practitioners; Medical Assistants; Obstetricians and Gynecologists; Pediatricians, General; Pharmacists; Pharmacy Aides; Pharmacy Technicians; Physician Assistants; Physicians and Surgeons, All Other; Psychiatrists; Registered Nurses; Surgeons; Surgical Technologists. **PERSONALITY TYPE**—Investigative. Investigative occupations frequently involve working with ideas and require an extensive amount of thinking. These occupations can involve searching for facts and figuring out problems mentally.

EDUCATION/TRAINING PROGRAM(S)— Critical Care Medicine Residency; Endocrinology and Metabolism Residency; Gastroenterology Residency; Geriatric Medicine Residency; Hematology Residency; Infectious Disease Residency; Internal Medicine Residency; Nephrology Residency; Neurology Residency; Nuclear Medicine Residency; Oncology Residency; Pulmonary Disease Residency; Rheumatology Residency. **RELATED KNOWLEDGE/COURSES**—**Medicine and Dentistry:** Knowledge of the information and techniques needed to diagnose and treat human injuries, diseases, and deformities. This includes symptoms, treatment alternatives, drug properties and interactions, and preventive health-care measures. **Biology:** Knowledge of plant and animal organisms and their tissues, cells, functions, interdependencies, and interactions with each other and the environment. **English Language:** Knowledge of the structure and content of the English language, including the meaning and spelling of words, rules of composition, and grammar. **Therapy and Counseling:** Knowledge of principles, methods, and procedures for diagnosis, treatment, and rehabilitation of physical and mental dysfunctions and for career counseling and guidance. **Administration and Management:** Knowledge of business and management principles involved in strategic planning, resource allocation, human resources modeling, leadership technique, production methods, and coordination of people and resources.

Judges, Magistrate Judges, and Magistrates

▲ Education/Training Required: Work experience, plus degree
▲ Annual Earnings: $86,760
▲ Growth: 1%
▲ Annual Job Openings: 2,000
▲ Self-Employed: 0%
▲ Part-Time: 7.8%

Arbitrate, advise, adjudicate, or administer justice in a court of law. May sentence defendant in criminal cases according to government statutes. May determine liability of defendant in civil cases. May issue marriage licenses and perform wedding ceremonies. Listens to presentation of case or allegations of plaintiff. Instructs jury on applicable law and directs jury to deduce facts from evidence presented. Sentences defendant in criminal cases, on conviction by jury, according to statutes of state or federal government. Establishes rules of procedure on questions for which standard procedures have not been established by law or by superior court. Conducts preliminary hearings in felony cases to determine reasonable and probable cause to hold defendant for further proceedings or trial. Awards judicial relief to litigants in civil cases in relation to findings by jury or by court. Examines evidence in criminal cases to determine if evidence will support charges. Performs wedding ceremonies. Rules on admissibility of evidence and methods of conducting testimony. Settles disputes between opposing attorneys. **SKILLS**—Judgment and Decision Making: Considering the relative costs and benefits of potential actions to choose the most appropriate one. Reading Comprehension: Understanding written sentences and paragraphs in work-related documents. Active Listening: Giving full attention to what other people are saying, taking time to understand the points being made, asking questions as appropriate, and not interrupting at inappropriate times. Critical Thinking: Using logic and reasoning to identify the strengths and weaknesses of alternative solutions, conclusions, or approaches to problems. Active Learning: Understanding the implications of new information for both current and future problem-solving and decision-making.

GOE INFORMATION—Interest Area: 04. Law, Law Enforcement, and Public Safety. **Work Group:** 04.02. Law. **Other Job Titles in This Work Group:** Administrative Law Judges, Adjudicators, and Hearing Officers; Arbitrators, Mediators, and Conciliators; Law Clerks; Lawyers; Legal Support Workers, All Other; Paralegals and Legal Assistants; Title Examiners and Abstractors; Title Examiners, Abstractors, and Searchers; Title Searchers. **PERSONALITY TYPE**—Enterprising. Enterprising occupations frequently involve starting up and carrying out projects. These occupations can involve leading people and making many decisions. They sometimes require risk taking and often deal with business.

EDUCATION/TRAINING PROGRAM(S)—Law (LL.B., J.D.); Law and Legal Studies, Other. **RELATED KNOWLEDGE/COURSES**—**Law and Government:** Knowledge of laws, legal codes, court procedures, precedents, government regulations, executive orders, agency rules, and the democratic political process. **English Language:** Knowledge of the structure and content of the English language, including the meaning and spelling of words, rules of composition, and grammar. **Public Safety and Security:** Knowledge of relevant equipment, policies, procedures, and strategies to promote effective local, state, or national security operations for the protection of people, data, property, and institutions. **Administration and Management:** Knowledge of business and management principles involved in strategic planning, resource allocation, human resources modeling, leadership technique, production methods, and coordination of people and resources. **Sociology and Anthropology:** Knowledge of group behavior and dynamics, societal trends and influences, human migrations, ethnicity, cultures, and their history and origins.

Kindergarten Teachers, Except Special Education

▲ Education/Training Required: Bachelor's degree
▲ Annual Earnings: $37,610
▲ Growth: 14%
▲ Annual Job Openings: 23,000
▲ Self-Employed: 1.5%
▲ Part-Time: 32.4%

Teach elemental natural and social science, personal hygiene, music, art, and literature to children from 4 to 6 years old. Promote physical, mental, and social development. May be required to hold state certification. Teaches elemental science, personal hygiene, and humanities to children to promote physical, mental, and social development. Supervises student activities, such as field visits, to stimulate student interest and broaden understanding of physical and social environment. Organizes and conducts games and group projects to develop cooperative behavior and assist children in forming satisfying relationships. Encourages students in activities, such as singing, dancing, and rhythmic activities, to promote self- expression and appreciation of esthetic experience. Instructs children in practices of personal cleanliness and self care. Observes children to detect signs of ill health or emotional disturbance and to evaluate progress. Discusses student problems and progress with parents. Alternates periods of strenuous activity with periods of rest or light activity to avoid overstimulation and fatigue. **SKILLS**—Learning Strategies: Selecting and using training/instructional methods and procedures appropriate for the situation when learning or teaching new things. Monitoring: Monitoring/Assessing your performance or that of other individuals or organizations to make improvements or take corrective action. Speaking: Talking to others to convey information effectively. Reading Comprehension: Understanding written sentences and paragraphs in work-related documents. Active Listening: Giving full attention to what other people are saying, taking time to understand the points being made, asking questions as appropriate, and not interrupting at inappropriate times.

GOE INFORMATION—Interest Area: 12. Education and Social Service. **Work Group:** 12.03. Educational Services. **Other Job Titles in This Work**

Group: Adult Literacy, Remedial Education, and GED Teachers and Instructors; Agricultural Sciences Teachers, Postsecondary; Anthropology and Archeology Teachers, Postsecondary; Architecture Teachers, Postsecondary; Archivists; Area, Ethnic, and Cultural Studies Teachers, Postsecondary; Art, Drama, and Music Teachers, Postsecondary; Atmospheric, Earth, Marine, and Space Sciences Teachers, Postsecondary; Audio-Visual Collections Specialists; Biological Science Teachers, Postsecondary; Business Teachers, Postsecondary; Chemistry Teachers, Postsecondary; Child Care Workers; Communications Teachers, Postsecondary; Computer Science Teachers, Postsecondary; Criminal Justice and Law Enforcement Teachers, Postsecondary; Curators; Economics Teachers, Postsecondary; Education Teachers, Postsecondary; Educational Psychologists; Educational, Vocational, and School Counselors; Elementary School Teachers, Except Special Education; Engineering Teachers, Postsecondary; English Language and Literature Teachers, Postsecondary; Environmental Science Teachers, Postsecondary; Farm and Home Management Advisors; Foreign Language and Literature Teachers, Postsecondary; Forestry and Conservation Science Teachers, Postsecondary; Geography Teachers, Postsecondary; Graduate Teaching Assistants; Health Specialties Teachers, Postsecondary; History Teachers, Postsecondary; Home Economics Teachers, Postsecondary; Law Teachers, Postsecondary; Librarians; Library Assistants, Clerical; Library Science Teachers, Postsecondary; others. **PERSONALITY TYPE**—Social. Social occupations frequently involve working with, communicating with, and teaching people. These occupations often involve helping or providing service to others.

EDUCATION/TRAINING PROGRAM(S)— Pre-Elementary/Early Childhood/Kindergarten Teacher Education. **RELATED KNOWLEDGE/**

COURSES—Education and Training: Knowledge of principles and methods for curriculum and training design, teaching and instruction for individuals and groups, and the measurement of training effects. **Customer and Personal Service:** Knowledge of principles and processes for providing customer and personal services. This includes customer needs assessment, meeting quality standards for services, and evaluation of customer satisfaction. **English Language:** Knowledge of the structure and content of the English language, including the meaning and spelling of words, rules of composition, and grammar. **Psychology:** Knowledge of human behavior and performance; individual differences in ability, personality, and interests; learning and motivation; psychological research methods; and the assessment and treatment of behavioral and affective disorders. **Fine Arts:** Knowledge of the theory and techniques required to compose, produce, and perform works of music, dance, visual arts, drama, and sculpture.

Landscape Architects

- ▲ Education/Training Required: Bachelor's degree
- ▲ Annual Earnings: $43,540
- ▲ Growth: 31%
- ▲ Annual Job Openings: 1,000
- ▲ Self-Employed: 21.6%
- ▲ Part-Time: 8%

Plan and design land areas for such projects as parks and other recreational facilities, airports, highways, hospitals, schools, land subdivisions, and commercial, industrial, and residential sites. Prepares site plans, specifications, and cost estimates for land development, coordinating arrangement of existing and proposed land features and structures. Compiles and analyzes data on conditions, such as location, drainage, and location of structures for environmental reports and landscaping plans. Confers with clients, engineering personnel, and architects on overall program. Inspects landscape work to ensure compliance with specifications, approve quality of materials and work, and advise client and construction personnel. **SKILLS**—Judgment and Decision Making: Considering the relative costs and benefits of potential actions to choose the most appropriate one. Critical Thinking: Using logic and reasoning to identify the strengths and weaknesses of alternative solutions, conclusions, or approaches to problems. Active Listening: Giving full attention to what other people are saying, taking time to understand the points being made, asking questions as appropriate, and not interrupting at inappropriate times. Active Learning: Understanding the implications of new information for both current and future problem-solving and decision-making. Complex Problem Solving:

Identifying complex problems and reviewing related information to develop and evaluate options and implement solutions.

GOE INFORMATION—Interest Area: 02. Science, Math, and Engineering. **Work Group:** 02.07. Engineering. **Other Job Titles in This Work Group:** Aerospace Engineers; Agricultural Engineers; Architects, Except Landscape and Naval; Biomedical Engineers; Chemical Engineers; Civil Engineers; Computer Hardware Engineers; Computer Software Engineers, Applications; Computer Software Engineers, Systems Software; Electrical Engineers; Electronics Engineers, Except Computer; Engineers, All Other; Environmental Engineers; Fire-Prevention and Protection Engineers; Health and Safety Engineers, Except Mining Safety Engineers and Inspectors; Industrial Engineers; Industrial Safety and Health Engineers; Marine Architects; Marine Engineers; Marine Engineers and Naval Architects; Materials Engineers; Mechanical Engineers; Mining and Geological Engineers, Including Mining Safety Engineers; Nuclear Engineers; Petroleum Engineers; Product Safety Engineers; Sales Engineers. **PERSONALITY TYPE**—Artistic. Artistic occupations frequently involve working with forms, designs, and patterns. They often require self-expression, and the work can be done without following a clear set of rules.

EDUCATION/TRAINING PROGRAM(S)—Landscape Architecture. **RELATED KNOWLEDGE/COURSES—Design:** Knowledge of design techniques, tools, and principles involved in production of precision technical plans, blueprints, drawings, and models. **Mathematics:** Knowledge of arithmetic, algebra, geometry, calculus, and statistics and their applications. **Engineering and Technology:** Knowledge of the practical application of engineering science and technology. This includes applying principles, techniques, procedures, and equipment to the design and production of various goods and services. **Administration and Management:** Knowledge of business and management principles involved in strategic planning, resource allocation, human resources modeling, leadership technique, production methods, and coordination of people and resources. **Biology:** Knowledge of plant and animal organisms and their tissues, cells, functions, interdependencies, and interactions with each other and the environment.

Law Clerks

- ▲ Education/Training Required: Bachelor's degree
- ▲ Annual Earnings: $28,510
- ▲ Growth: 13%
- ▲ Annual Job Openings: 3,000
- ▲ Self-Employed: 2.5%
- ▲ Part-Time: 9.6%

Assist lawyers or judges by researching or preparing legal documents. May meet with clients or assist lawyers and judges in court. Researches and analyzes law sources to prepare legal documents for review, approval, and use by attorney. Files pleadings with court clerk. Prepares affidavits of documents and maintains document file. Investigates facts and law of case to determine causes of action and to prepare case accordingly. Delivers or directs delivery of subpoenas to witness and parties to action. Searches patent files to ascertain originality of patent application. Stores, catalogs, and maintains currency of legal volumes. Appraises and inventories real and personal property for estate planning. Prepares real estate closing statement and assists in closing process. Communicates and arbitrates disputes between disputing parties. **SKILLS—Reading Comprehension:** Understanding written sentences and paragraphs in work-related documents. **Critical Thinking:** Using logic and reasoning to identify the strengths and weaknesses of alternative solutions, conclusions, or approaches to problems. **Writing:** Communicating effectively in writing as appropriate for the needs of the audience. **Active Listening:** Giving full attention to what other people are saying, taking time to understand the points being made, asking questions as appropriate, and not interrupting at inappropriate times. **Active Learning:** Understanding the implications of new information for both current and future problem-solving and decision-making.

GOE INFORMATION—Interest Area: 04. Law, Law Enforcement, and Public Safety. **Work Group:** 04.02. Law. **Other Job Titles in This Work Group:** Administrative Law Judges, Adjudicators, and Hearing Officers; Arbitrators, Mediators, and Conciliators; Judges, Magistrate Judges, and Magistrates; Lawyers; Legal Support Workers, All Other; Paralegals and Legal Assistants; Title Examiners and Abstractors; Title Examiners, Abstractors, and Searchers; Title Searchers. **PERSONALITY TYPE—**Enterprising. Enterprising occupations frequently involve starting up and carrying out projects. These occupations can involve leading people and making many decisions. They sometimes require risk taking and often deal with business.

EDUCATION/TRAINING PROGRAM(S)—Law (LL.B., J.D.). **RELATED KNOWLEDGE/COURSES—English Language:** Knowledge of the structure and content of the English language, including the meaning and spelling of words, rules of composition, and grammar. **Law and Government:** Knowledge of laws, legal codes, court procedures, precedents, government regulations, executive orders, agency rules, and the democratic political process. **Clerical Studies:** Knowledge of administrative and clerical procedures and systems such as word processing, managing files and records, stenography and transcription, designing forms, and other office procedures and terminology. **Mathematics:** Knowledge of arithmetic, algebra, geometry, calculus, and statistics and their applications. **Communications and Media:** Knowledge of media production, communication, and dissemination techniques and methods. This includes alternative ways to inform and entertain via written, oral, and visual media. **Computers and Electronics:** Knowledge of circuit boards, processors, chips, electronic equipment, and computer hardware and software, including applications and programming.

Law Teachers, Postsecondary

- ▲ Education/Training Required: First professional degree
- ▲ Annual Earnings: $75,190
- ▲ Growth: 24% for all Postsecondary Teachers
- ▲ Annual Job Openings: 184,000 for all Postsecondary Teachers
- ▲ Self-Employed: 0%
- ▲ Part-Time: 32.3% for all Postsecondary Teachers

Teach courses in law. **SKILLS**—No data available.

GOE INFORMATION—Interest Area: 12. Education and Social Service. **Work Group:** 12.03. Educational Services. **Other Job Titles in This Work Group:** Adult Literacy, Remedial Education, and GED Teachers and Instructors; Agricultural Sciences Teachers, Postsecondary; Anthropology and Archeology Teachers, Postsecondary; Architecture Teachers, Postsecondary; Archivists; Area, Ethnic, and Cultural Studies Teachers, Postsecondary; Art, Drama, and Music Teachers, Postsecondary; Atmospheric, Earth, Marine, and Space Sciences Teachers, Postsecondary; Audio-Visual Collections Specialists; Biological Science Teachers, Postsecondary; Business Teachers, Postsecondary; Chemistry Teachers, Postsecondary; Child Care Workers; Communications Teachers, Postsecondary; Computer Science Teachers, Postsecondary; Criminal Justice and Law Enforcement Teachers, Postsecondary; Curators; Economics Teachers, Postsecondary; Education Teachers, Postsecondary; Educational Psychologists; Educational, Vocational, and School Counselors; Elementary School Teachers, Except Special Education; Engineering Teachers, Postsecondary; English Language and Literature Teachers, Postsecondary; Environmental Science Teachers, Postsecondary; Farm and Home Management Advisors; Foreign Language and Literature Teachers, Postsecondary; Forestry and Conservation Science Teachers, Postsecondary; Geography Teachers, Postsecondary; Graduate Teaching Assistants; Health Specialties Teachers, Postsecondary; History Teachers, Postsecondary; Home Economics Teachers, Postsecondary; Kindergarten Teachers, Except Special Education; Librarians; Library Assistants, Clerical; Library Science Teachers, Postsecondary; others. **PERSONALITY TYPE**—No data available.

EDUCATION/TRAINING PROGRAM(S)— Law (LL.B., J.D.). **RELATED KNOWLEDGE/COURSES**—No data available.

Lawyers

▲ Education/Training Required: First professional degree

▲ Annual Earnings: $88,280

▲ Growth: 18%

▲ Annual Job Openings: 35,000

▲ Self-Employed: 36%

▲ Part-Time: 7%

Represent clients in criminal and civil litigation and other legal proceedings, draw up legal documents, and manage or advise clients on legal transactions. May specialize in a single area or may practice broadly in many areas of law. Conducts case, examining and cross examining witnesses, and summarizes case to judge or jury. Examines legal data to determine advisability of defending or prosecuting lawsuit. Studies Constitution, statutes, decisions, regulations, and ordinances of quasi-judicial bodies. Interprets laws, rulings, and regulations for individuals and business. Presents evidence to defend client in civil or criminal litigation. Presents evidence to prosecute defendant in civil or criminal litigation. Represents client in court or before government agency. Searches for and examines public and other legal records to write opinions or establish ownership. Acts as agent, trustee, guardian, or executor for business or individuals. Probates wills and represents and advises executors and administrators of estates. Prepares opinions on legal issues. Prepares and drafts legal documents, such as wills, deeds, patent applications, mortgages, leases, and contracts. Prepares and files legal briefs. Confers with colleagues with specialty in area of legal issue to establish and verify basis for legal proceeding. Evaluates findings and develops strategy and arguments in preparation for presentation of case. Gathers evidence to formulate defense or to initiate legal actions. Advises clients concerning business transactions, claim liability, advisability of prosecuting or defending lawsuits, or legal rights and obligations. Interviews clients and witnesses to ascertain facts of case. **SKILLS—Reading Comprehension:** Understanding written sentences and paragraphs in work-related documents. **Persuasion:** Persuading others to change their minds or behavior. **Speaking:** Talking to others to convey information effectively. **Critical Thinking:** Using logic and reasoning to identify the strengths and weaknesses of alternative solutions, conclusions, or approaches to problems. **Writing:** Communicating effectively in writing as appropriate for the needs of the audience.

GOE INFORMATION—Interest Area: 04. Law, Law Enforcement, and Public Safety. **Work Group:** 04.02. Law. **Other Job Titles in This Work Group:** Administrative Law Judges, Adjudicators, and Hearing Officers; Arbitrators, Mediators, and Conciliators; Judges, Magistrate Judges, and Magistrates; Law Clerks; Legal Support Workers, All Other; Paralegals and Legal Assistants; Title Examiners and Abstractors; Title Examiners, Abstractors, and Searchers; Title Searchers. **PERSONALITY TYPE—Enterprising.** Enterprising occupations frequently involve starting up and carrying out projects. These occupations can involve leading people and making many decisions. They sometimes require risk taking and often deal with business.

EDUCATION/TRAINING PROGRAM(S)— Juridical Science/Legal Specialization (LL.M., M.C.L., J.S.D./S; Law (LL.B., J.D.); Law and Legal Studies, Other. **RELATED KNOWLEDGE/COURSES—Law and Government:** Knowledge of laws, legal codes, court procedures, precedents, government regulations, executive orders, agency rules, and the democratic political process. **English Language:** Knowledge of the structure and content of the English language, including the meaning and spelling of words, rules of composition, and grammar. **Administration and Management:** Knowledge of business and management principles involved in strategic planning, resource allocation, human resources modeling, leadership technique, production methods, and coordination of people and resources. **Education and Training:** Knowledge of principles and methods for curriculum and training design, teaching and instruction for individuals and groups, and the measurement of training effects. **Clerical Studies:** Knowledge of administrative and clerical procedures and systems such as word processing, managing files and records, stenography and transcription, designing forms, and other office procedures and terminology.

Librarians

▲ Education/Training Required: Master's degree

▲ Annual Earnings: $41,700

▲ Growth: 7%

▲ Annual Job Openings: 6,000

▲ Self-Employed: 0%

▲ Part-Time: 22.4%

Administer libraries and perform related library services. Work in a variety of settings, including public libraries, schools, colleges and universities, museums, corporations, government agencies, law firms, non-profit organizations, and health-care providers. Tasks may include selecting, acquiring, cataloguing, classifying, circulating, and maintaining library materials and furnishing reference, bibliographical, and readers' advisory services. May perform in-depth, strategic research and synthesize, analyze, edit, and filter information. May set up or work with databases and information systems to catalogue and access information. Organizes collections of books, publications, documents, audiovisual aids, and other reference materials for convenient access. Assists patrons in selecting books and informational material and in research problems. Researches, retrieves, and disseminates information from books, periodicals, reference materials, or commercial databases in response to requests. Reviews, compiles, and publishes listing of library materials, including bibliographies and book reviews, to notify users. Confers with teachers, parents, and community organizations to develop, plan, and conduct programs in reading, viewing, and communication skills. Compiles lists of overdue materials and notifies borrowers. Keys information into computer to store or search for selected material or databases. Directs and trains library staff in duties, including receiving, shelving, researching, cataloging, and equipment use. Assembles and arranges display materials. Manages library program for children and other special groups. Explains use of library facilities, resources, equipment, and services and provides information governing library use and policies. Manages library resources stored in files, on film, or in computer databases for research information. Codes, classifies, and catalogs books, publications, films, audiovisual aids, and other library materials. Reviews and evaluates resource material to select and order books, periodicals, audiovisual aids, and other materials for acquisition. **SKILLS**—Reading Comprehension: Understanding written sentences and paragraphs in work-related documents. Active Listening: Giving full attention to what other people are saying, taking time to understand the points being made, asking questions as appropriate, and not interrupting at inappropriate times. Speaking: Talking to others to convey information effectively. Writing: Communicating effectively in writing as appropriate for the needs of the audience. Learning Strategies: Selecting and using training/instructional methods and procedures appropriate for the situation when learning or teaching new things.

GOE INFORMATION—Interest Area: 12. Education and Social Service. **Work Group:** 12.03. Educational Services. **Other Job Titles in This Work Group:** Adult Literacy, Remedial Education, and GED Teachers and Instructors; Agricultural Sciences Teachers, Postsecondary; Anthropology and Archeology Teachers, Postsecondary; Architecture Teachers, Postsecondary; Archivists; Area, Ethnic, and Cultural Studies Teachers, Postsecondary; Art, Drama, and Music Teachers, Postsecondary; Atmospheric, Earth, Marine, and Space Sciences Teachers, Postsecondary; Audio-Visual Collections Specialists; Biological Science Teachers, Postsecondary; Business Teachers, Postsecondary; Chemistry Teachers, Postsecondary; Child Care Workers; Communications Teachers, Postsecondary; Computer Science Teachers, Postsecondary; Criminal Justice and Law Enforcement Teachers, Postsecondary; Curators; Economics Teachers, Postsecondary; Education Teachers, Postsecondary; Educational Psychologists; Educational, Vocational, and School Counselors; Elementary School Teachers, Except Special Education; Engineering Teachers, Postsecondary; English Language and Literature Teachers, Postsecondary; Environmental Science Teachers, Postsecondary; Farm and Home Management Advisors; Foreign Language and Literature Teachers, Postsecondary; Forestry and Conservation Science Teachers, Postsecondary; Geography Teachers, Postsecondary; Graduate Teaching Assistants; Health Specialties Teachers, Postsecondary; History Teachers, Postsecondary; Home Economics Teachers, Postsecondary; Kindergarten Teachers, Except Special Education; Law Teachers, Postsecondary; Library Assistants, Clerical; others. **PERSONALITY TYPE**—Artistic. Artistic occupations frequently involve working with forms, designs, and patterns. They often require self-expression, and the work can be done without following a clear set of rules.

EDUCATION/TRAINING PROGRAM(S)— Library Science, Other; Library Science/Librarianship. **RELATED KNOWLEDGE/COURSES**—**English Language:** Knowledge of the structure and content of the English language, including the meaning and spelling of words, rules of composition, and grammar. **Education and Training:** Knowledge of principles and methods for curriculum and training design, teaching and instruction for individuals and groups, and the measurement of training effects. **Clerical Studies:** Knowledge of administrative and clerical procedures and systems such as word processing, managing files and records, stenography and transcription, designing forms, and other office procedures and terminology. **Customer and Personal Service:** Knowledge of principles and processes for providing customer and personal services. This includes customer needs assessment, meeting quality standards for services, and evaluation of customer satisfaction. **Administration and Management:** Knowledge of business and management principles involved in strategic planning, resource allocation, human resources modeling, leadership technique, production methods, and coordination of people and resources.

Library Science Teachers, Postsecondary

▲ Education/Training Required: Master's degree

▲ Annual Earnings: $49,370

▲ Growth: 24% for all Postsecondary Teachers

▲ Annual Job Openings: 184,000 for all Postsecondary Teachers

▲ Self-Employed: 0%

▲ Part-Time: 32.3% for all Postsecondary Teachers

Teach courses in library science. **SKILLS**—No data available.

GOE INFORMATION—**Interest Area:** 12. Education and Social Service. **Work Group:** 12.03. Educational Services. **Other Job Titles in This Work Group:** Adult Literacy, Remedial Education, and GED Teachers and Instructors; Agricultural Sciences Teachers, Postsecondary; Anthropology and Archeology Teachers, Postsecondary; Architecture Teachers, Postsecondary; Ar-

chivists; Area, Ethnic, and Cultural Studies Teachers, Postsecondary; Art, Drama, and Music Teachers, Postsecondary; Atmospheric, Earth, Marine, and Space Sciences Teachers, Postsecondary; Audio-Visual Collections Specialists; Biological Science Teachers, Postsecondary; Business Teachers, Postsecondary; Chemistry Teachers, Postsecondary; Child Care Workers; Communications Teachers, Postsecondary; Computer Science Teachers, Postsecondary; Criminal Justice and Law Enforcement Teachers, Postsecondary; Curators; Economics Teachers, Postsecondary; Education Teachers, Postsecondary; Educational Psychologists; Educational, Vocational, and School Counselors; Elementary School Teachers, Except Special Education; Engineering Teachers, Postsecondary; English Language and Literature Teachers, Postsecondary; Environmental Science Teachers, Postsecondary; Farm and Home Management Advisors; Foreign Language and Literature Teachers, Postsecondary; Forestry and Conservation Science Teachers, Postsecondary; Geography Teachers, Postsecondary; Graduate Teaching Assistants; Health Specialties Teachers, Postsecondary; History Teachers, Postsecondary; Home Economics Teachers, Postsecondary; Kindergarten Teachers, Except Special Education; Law Teachers, Postsecondary; Librarians; Library Assistants, Clerical; others. **PERSONALITY TYPE**—No data available.

EDUCATION/TRAINING PROGRAM(S)— Library Science/Librarianship; Teacher Education, Specific Academic and Vocational Programs. **RELATED KNOWLEDGE/COURSES**—No data available.

Loan Counselors

- ▲ Education/Training Required: Bachelor's degree
- ▲ Annual Earnings: $32,160
- ▲ Growth: 16%
- ▲ Annual Job Openings: 3,000
- ▲ Self-Employed: 0%
- ▲ Part-Time: 7.2%

Provide guidance to prospective loan applicants who have problems qualifying for traditional loans. Guidance may include determining the best type of loan and explaining loan requirements or restrictions. Analyzes applicant's financial status, credit, and property evaluation to determine feasibility of granting loan. Interviews applicant and requests specified information for loan application. Ensures loan agreements are complete and accurate according to policy. Submits application to credit analyst for verification and recommendation. Confers with underwriters to aid in resolving mortgage application problems. Arranges for maintenance and liquidation of delinquent property. Supervises loan personnel. Negotiates payment arrangements with customers for delinquent loan balance. Analyzes potential loan markets to develop prospects for loans. Petitions court to transfer title and deeds of collateral to bank. Computes payment schedule. Contacts applicant or creditors to resolve questions regarding application information. Approves loan within specified limits. Refers loan to loan committee for approval. **SKILLS**—Reading Comprehension: Understanding written sentences and paragraphs in work-related documents. Speaking: Talking to others to convey information effectively. Active Listening: Giving full attention to what other people are saying, taking time to understand the points being made, asking questions as appropriate, and not interrupting at inappropriate times. Mathematics: Using mathematics to solve problems. Judgment and Decision Making: Considering the relative costs and benefits of potential actions to choose the most appropriate one. Writing: Communicating effectively in writing as appropriate for the needs of the audience.

GOE INFORMATION—**Interest Area:** 13. General Management and Support. **Work Group:** 13.02. Management Support. **Other Job Titles in This Work Group:** Accountants; Accountants and Auditors; Appraisers and Assessors of Real Estate; Appraisers, Real Estate; Assessors; Auditors; Budget Analysts; Claims Adjusters, Examiners, and Investigators; Claims Examiners, Property and Casualty Insurance; Compensation, Benefits, and Job Analysis Specialists; Cost Estimators; Credit Analysts; Employment Interviewers, Private or Public Employment Service; Employment, Recruitment, and Placement Specialists; Financial Analysts; Human Resources, Training, and Labor Relations Specialists, All Other; Insurance Adjusters, Examiners, and Investigators; Insurance Appraisers, Auto Damage; Insurance Underwriters; Loan Officers;

Logisticians; Management Analysts; Market Research Analysts; Personnel Recruiters; Purchasing Agents and Buyers, Farm Products; Purchasing Agents, Except Wholesale, Retail, and Farm Products; Tax Examiners, Collectors, and Revenue Agents; Training and Development Specialists; Wholesale and Retail Buyers, Except Farm Products. **PERSONALITY TYPE**—Enterprising. Enterprising occupations frequently involve starting up and carrying out projects. These occupations can involve leading people and making many decisions. They sometimes require risk taking and often deal with business.

EDUCATION/TRAINING PROGRAM(S)— Banking and Financial Support Services; Financial Management and Services, Other. **RELATED KNOWLEDGE/COURSES—Economics and Accounting:** Knowledge of economic and accounting principles and practices, the financial markets, banking, and the analysis and reporting of financial data. **Mathematics:** Knowledge of arithmetic, algebra, geometry, calculus, and statistics and their applications. **English Language:** Knowledge of the structure and content of the English language, including the meaning and spelling of words, rules of composition, and grammar. **Clerical Studies:** Knowledge of administrative and clerical procedures and systems such as word processing, managing files and records, stenography and transcription, designing forms, and other office procedures and terminology. **Customer and Personal Service:** Knowledge of principles and processes for providing customer and personal services. This includes customer needs assessment, meeting quality standards for services, and evaluation of customer satisfaction. **Law and Government:** Knowledge of laws, legal codes, court procedures, precedents, government regulations, executive orders, agency rules, and the democratic political process.

Loan Officers

- ▲ Education/Training Required: Bachelor's degree
- ▲ Annual Earnings: $41,420
- ▲ Growth: 5%
- ▲ Annual Job Openings: 28,000
- ▲ Self-Employed: 0%
- ▲ Part-Time: 7.2%

Evaluate, authorize, or recommend approval of commercial, real estate, or credit loans. Advise borrowers on financial status and methods of payments. Includes mortgage loan officers and agents, collection analysts, loan servicing officers, and loan underwriters. Analyzes applicant's financial status, credit, and property evaluation to determine feasibility of granting loan. Approves loan within specified limits. Refers loan to loan committee for approval. Interviews applicant and requests specified information for loan application. Submits application to credit analyst for verification and recommendation. Confers with underwriters to aid in resolving mortgage application problems. Arranges for maintenance and liquidation of delinquent property. Supervises loan personnel. Negotiates payment arrangements with customers for delinquent loan balance. Analyzes potential loan markets to develop prospects for loans.

Petitions court to transfer title and deeds of collateral to bank. Computes payment schedule. Ensures loan agreements are complete and accurate according to policy. Contacts applicant or creditors to resolve questions regarding application information. **SKILLS**—Reading Comprehension: Understanding written sentences and paragraphs in work-related documents. Speaking: Talking to others to convey information effectively. Active Listening: Giving full attention to what other people are saying, taking time to understand the points being made, asking questions as appropriate, and not interrupting at inappropriate times. Writing: Communicating effectively in writing as appropriate for the needs of the audience. Mathematics: Using mathematics to solve problems. Judgment and Decision Making: Considering the relative costs and benefits of potential actions to choose the most appropriate one.

GOE INFORMATION—**Interest Area:** 13. General Management and Support. **Work Group:** 13.02. Management Support. **Other Job Titles in This Work Group:** Accountants; Accountants and Auditors; Appraisers and Assessors of Real Estate; Appraisers, Real Estate; Assessors; Auditors; Budget Analysts; Claims Adjusters, Examiners, and Investigators; Claims Examiners, Property and Casualty Insurance; Compensation, Benefits, and Job Analysis Specialists; Cost Estimators; Credit Analysts; Employment Interviewers, Private or Public Employment Service; Employment, Recruitment, and Placement Specialists; Financial Analysts; Human Resources, Training, and Labor Relations Specialists, All Other; Insurance Adjusters, Examiners, and Investigators; Insurance Appraisers, Auto Damage; Insurance Underwriters; Loan Counselors; Logisticians; Management Analysts; Market Research Analysts; Personnel Recruiters; Purchasing Agents and Buyers, Farm Products; Purchasing Agents, Except Wholesale, Retail, and Farm Products; Tax Examiners, Collectors, and Revenue Agents; Training and Development Specialists; Wholesale and Retail Buyers, Except Farm Products. **PERSONALITY TYPE**—Enterprising. Enterprising occupations frequently involve starting up and carrying out projects. These occupations can involve leading people and making many decisions. They sometimes require risk taking and often deal with business.

EDUCATION/TRAINING PROGRAM(S)—Finance, General. **RELATED KNOWLEDGE/COURSES**—**Economics and Accounting:** Knowledge of economic and accounting principles and practices, the financial markets, banking, and the analysis and reporting of financial data. **Mathematics:** Knowledge of arithmetic, algebra, geometry, calculus, and statistics and their applications. **English Language:** Knowledge of the structure and content of the English language, including the meaning and spelling of words, rules of composition, and grammar. **Clerical Studies:** Knowledge of administrative and clerical procedures and systems such as word processing, managing files and records, stenography and transcription, designing forms, and other office procedures and terminology. **Law and Government:** Knowledge of laws, legal codes, court procedures, precedents, government regulations, executive orders, agency rules, and the democratic political process. **Customer and Personal Service:** Knowledge of principles and processes for providing customer and personal services. This includes customer needs assessment, meeting quality standards for services, and evaluation of customer satisfaction.

Management Analysts

- ▲ Education/Training Required: Work experience, plus degree
- ▲ Annual Earnings: $55,040
- ▲ Growth: 29%
- ▲ Annual Job Openings: 50,000
- ▲ Self-Employed: 46.4%
- ▲ Part-Time: 19.5%

Conduct organizational studies and evaluations, design systems and procedures, conduct work simplifications and measurement studies, and prepare operations and procedures manuals to assist management in operating more efficiently and effectively. Includes program analysts and management consultants. Reviews forms and reports and confers with management and users about format, distribution, and purpose and to identify problems and improvements. Gathers and organizes information on problems or procedures. Confers with personnel concerned to ensure successful functioning of newly implemented systems or procedures. Documents findings of study and prepares recommendations for implementation of new systems, procedures, or organizational changes. Analyzes data gathered and develops solutions or alternative methods of proceeding. Plans study of work problems and procedures, such as organizational change, communications, information flow, integrated production methods, inventory control, or cost analysis. Develops and implements records management program for filing, protection, and retrieval of records and assures compliance with program. Prepares manuals and trains workers in use of new forms, reports, procedures, or equipment according to organizational policy. Designs, evaluates, recommends, and approves changes of forms and reports. Recommends purchase of storage equipment and designs area layout to locate equipment in space available. Interviews personnel and conducts on-site observation to ascertain unit functions, work performed, and methods, equipment, and personnel used. **SKILLS**— Systems Evaluation: Identifying measures or indicators of system performance and the actions needed to improve or correct performance relative to the goals of the system. Writing: Communicating effectively in writing as appropriate for the needs of the audience. Monitoring: Monitoring/Assessing your performance or that of other individuals or organizations to make improvements or take corrective action. Judgment and Decision Making: Considering the relative costs and benefits of potential actions to choose the most appropriate one. Reading Comprehension: Understanding written sentences and paragraphs in work-related documents.

GOE INFORMATION—Interest Area: 13. General Management and Support. **Work Group:** 13.02. Management Support. **Other Job Titles in This Work Group:** Accountants; Accountants and Auditors; Appraisers and Assessors of Real Estate; Appraisers, Real Estate; Assessors; Auditors; Budget Analysts; Claims Adjusters, Examiners, and Investigators; Claims Examiners, Property and Casualty Insurance; Compensation, Benefits, and Job Analysis Specialists; Cost Estimators; Credit Analysts; Employment Interviewers, Private or Public Employment Service; Employment, Recruitment, and Placement Specialists; Financial Analysts; Human Resources, Training,

and Labor Relations Specialists, All Other; Insurance Adjusters, Examiners, and Investigators; Insurance Appraisers, Auto Damage; Insurance Underwriters; Loan Counselors; Loan Officers; Logisticians; Market Research Analysts; Personnel Recruiters; Purchasing Agents and Buyers, Farm Products; Purchasing Agents, Except Wholesale, Retail, and Farm Products; Tax Examiners, Collectors, and Revenue Agents; Training and Development Specialists; Wholesale and Retail Buyers, Except Farm Products. **PERSONALITY TYPE**—Enterprising. Enterprising occupations frequently involve starting up and carrying out projects. These occupations can involve leading people and making many decisions. They sometimes require risk taking and often deal with business.

EDUCATION/TRAINING PROGRAM(S)— Business Administration and Management, General. **RELATED KNOWLEDGE/COURSES—Administration and Management:** Knowledge of business and management principles involved in strategic planning, resource allocation, human resources modeling, leadership technique, production methods, and coordination of people and resources. **English Language:** Knowledge of the structure and content of the English language, including the meaning and spelling of words, rules of composition, and grammar. **Education and Training:** Knowledge of principles and methods for curriculum and training design, teaching and instruction for individuals and groups, and the measurement of training effects. **Mathematics:** Knowledge of arithmetic, algebra, geometry, calculus, and statistics and their applications. **Personnel and Human Resources:** Knowledge of principles and procedures for personnel recruitment, selection, training, compensation and benefits, labor relations and negotiation, and personnel information systems.

Marine Architects

▲ Education/Training Required: Bachelor's degree

▲ Annual Earnings: $60,890

▲ Growth: 2%

▲ Annual Job Openings: Fewer than 500

▲ Self-Employed: No data available

▲ Part-Time: No data available

Design and oversee construction and repair of marine craft and floating structures such as ships, barges, tugs, dredges, submarines, torpedoes, floats, and buoys. May confer with marine engineers. Oversees construction and testing of prototype in model basin and develops sectional and waterline curves of hull to establish center of gravity, ideal hull form, and buoyancy and stability data. Designs complete hull and superstructure according to specifications and test data and in conformity with standards of safety, efficiency, and economy. Designs layout of craft interior, including cargo space, passenger compartments, ladder wells, and elevators. Evaluates performance of craft during dock and sea trials to determine design changes and conformance with national and international standards. Studies design proposals and specifications to establish basic characteristics of craft, such as size, weight, speed, propulsion, displacement, and draft. Confers with marine engineering personnel to establish arrangement of boiler room equipment and propulsion machinery, heating and ventilating systems, refrigeration equipment, piping, and other functional equipment. **SKILLS**—Mathematics: Using mathematics to solve problems. Active Learning: Understanding the implications of new information for both current and future problem-solving and decision-making. Monitoring: Monitoring/Assessing your performance or that of other individuals or organizations to make improvements or take corrective action. Quality Control Analysis: Conducting tests and inspections of products, services, or processes to evaluate quality or performance. Critical Thinking: Using logic and reasoning to identify the strengths and weaknesses of alternative solutions, conclusions, or approaches to problems. Reading Comprehension: Understanding written sentences and paragraphs in work-related documents.

GOE INFORMATION—**Interest Area:** 02. Science, Math, and Engineering. **Work Group:** 02.07. Engineering. **Other Job Titles in This Work Group:** Aerospace Engineers; Agricultural Engineers; Architects, Except Landscape and Naval; Biomedical Engineers; Chemical Engineers; Civil Engineers; Computer Hardware Engineers; Computer Software Engineers, Applications; Computer Software Engineers, Systems Software; Electrical Engineers; Electronics Engineers, Except Computer; Engineers, All Other; Environmental Engineers; Fire-Prevention and Protection Engineers; Health and Safety Engineers, Except Mining Safety Engineers and Inspectors; Industrial Engineers; Industrial Safety and Health Engineers; Landscape Architects; Marine Engineers; Marine Engineers and Naval Architects; Materials Engineers; Mechanical Engineers; Mining and Geological Engineers, Including Mining Safety Engineers; Nuclear Engineers; Petroleum Engineers; Product Safety Engineers; Sales Engineers. **PERSONALITY TYPE**—Realistic. Realistic occupations frequently involve work activities that include practical, hands-on problems and solutions. They often deal with plants, animals, and real-world materials like wood, tools, and machinery. Many of the occupations require working outside and do not involve a lot of paperwork or working closely with others.

EDUCATION/TRAINING PROGRAM(S)— Naval Architecture and Marine Engineering. **RELATED KNOWLEDGE/COURSES—Design:** Knowledge of design techniques, tools, and principles involved in production of precision technical plans, blueprints, drawings, and models. **Engineering and Technology:** Knowledge of the practical application of engineering science and technology. This includes applying principles, techniques, procedures, and equipment to the design and production of various goods and services. **Mathematics:** Knowledge of arithmetic, algebra, geometry, calculus, and statistics and their applications. **Physics:** Knowledge and prediction of physical principles and laws and their interrelationships and applications to understanding fluid, material, and atmospheric dynamics and mechanical, electrical, atomic, and sub-atomic structures and processes. **Building and Construction:** Knowledge of materials, methods, and tools involved in the construction or repair of houses, buildings, or other structures, such as highways and roads.

Marine Engineers

▲ Education/Training Required: Bachelor's degree

▲ Annual Earnings: $60,890

▲ Growth: 2%

▲ Annual Job Openings: Fewer than 500

▲ Self-Employed: 2.7%

▲ Part-Time: 4.5%

Design, develop, and take responsibility for the installation of ship machinery and related equipment, including propulsion machines and power supply systems. Designs and oversees testing, installation, and repair of marine apparatus and equipment. Conducts analytical, environmental, operational, or performance studies to develop design for products such as marine engines, equipment, and structures. Prepares or directs preparation of product or system layout and detailed drawings and schematics. Analyzes data to determine feasibility of product proposal. Investigates and observes tests on machinery and equipment for compliance with standards. Determines conditions under which tests are to be conducted and sequences and phases of test operations. Inspects marine equipment and machinery to draw up work requests and job specifications. Prepares technical reports for use by engineering, management, or sales personnel. Coordinates activities with those of regulatory bodies to ensure repairs and alterations are at minimum cost and consistent with safety. Procures materials needed to repair marine equipment and machinery. Maintains contact and formulates reports for contractors and clients to ensure completion of work at minimum cost. Reviews work requests and compares them with previous work completed on ship to ensure costs are economically sound. Maintains and coordinates repair of marine machinery and equipment for installation on vessels. Conducts environmental, operational, or performance tests on marine machinery and equipment. Confers with research personnel to clarify or resolve problems and develop or modify design. Evaluates operation of marine equipment during acceptance testing and shakedown cruises. **SKILLS**—Mathematics: Using mathematics to solve problems. Reading Comprehension: Understanding written sentences and paragraphs in work-related documents. Writing: Communicating effectively in writing as appropriate for the needs of the audience. Science: Using scientific rules and methods to solve problems. Coordination: Adjusting actions in relation to others' actions. Equipment Selection: Determining the kind of tools and equipment needed to do a job.

GOE INFORMATION—Interest Area: 02. Science, Math, and Engineering. **Work Group:** 02.07. Engineering. **Other Job Titles in This Work Group:** Aerospace Engineers; Agricultural Engineers; Architects, Except Landscape and Naval; Biomedical Engineers; Chemical Engineers; Civil Engineers; Computer Hardware Engineers; Computer Software Engineers, Applications; Computer Software Engineers, Systems Software; Electrical Engineers; Electronics Engineers, Except Computer; Engineers, All Other; Environmental Engineers; Fire-Prevention and Protection Engineers; Health and Safety Engineers, Except Mining Safety Engineers and Inspectors; Industrial Engineers; Industrial Safety and Health Engineers; Landscape Architects; Marine Architects; Marine Engineers and Naval Architects; Materials Engineers; Mechanical Engineers; Mining and Geological Engineers, Including Mining Safety Engineers; Nuclear Engineers; Petroleum Engineers; Product Safety Engineers; Sales Engineers. **PERSONALITY TYPE**—Realistic. Realistic occupations frequently involve work activities that include practical, hands-on problems and solutions. They often deal with plants, animals, and real-world materials like wood, tools, and machinery. Many of the occupations require working outside and do not involve a lot of paperwork or working closely with others.

EDUCATION/TRAINING PROGRAM(S)—Naval Architecture and Marine Engineering. **RELATED KNOWLEDGE/COURSES**—Engineering and Technology: Knowledge of the practical application of engineering science and technology. This includes applying principles, techniques, procedures, and equipment to the design and production of various goods and services. **Principles of Mechanical Devices:** Knowledge of machines and tools, including their designs, uses, repair, and maintenance. **Mathematics:** Knowledge of arithmetic, algebra, geometry, calculus, and statistics and their applications. **Physics:** Knowledge and prediction of physical principles and laws and their interrelationships and applications to understanding fluid, material, and atmospheric dynamics and mechanical, electrical, atomic, and sub-atomic structures and processes. **Design:** Knowledge of design techniques, tools, and principles involved in production of precision technical plans, blueprints, drawings, and models. **Administration and Management:** Knowledge of business and management principles involved in strategic planning, resource allocation, human resources modeling, leadership technique, production methods, and coordination of people and resources.

Marine Engineers and Naval Architects

▲ Education/Training Required: Bachelor's degree
▲ Annual Earnings: $60,890
▲ Growth: 2%
▲ Annual Job Openings: Fewer than 500
▲ Self-Employed: 2.7%
▲ Part-Time: 4.5%

Design, develop, and evaluate the operation of marine vessels, ship machinery, and related equipment, such as power supply and propulsion systems. **SKILLS**—No data available.

GOE INFORMATION—Interest Area: 02. Science, Math, and Engineering. **Work Group:** 02.07. Engineering. **Other Job Titles in This Work Group:** Aerospace Engineers; Agricultural Engineers; Architects, Except Landscape and Naval; Biomedical Engineers; Chemical Engineers; Civil Engineers; Computer Hardware Engineers; Computer Software Engineers, Applications; Computer Software Engineers, Systems Software; Electrical Engineers; Electronics Engineers, Except Computer; Engineers, All Other; Environmental Engineers; Fire-Prevention and Protection Engineers; Health and Safety Engineers, Except Mining Safety Engineers and Inspectors; Industrial Engineers; Industrial Safety and Health Engineers; Landscape Architects; Marine Architects; Marine Engineers; Materials Engineers; Mechanical Engineers; Mining and Geological Engineers, Including Mining Safety Engineers; Nuclear Engineers; Petroleum Engineers; Product Safety Engineers; Sales Engineers. **PERSONALITY TYPE**—No data available.

EDUCATION/TRAINING PROGRAM(S)—Naval Architecture and Marine Engineering. **RELATED KNOWLEDGE/COURSES**—No data available.

Market Research Analysts

▲ Education/Training Required: Bachelor's degree
▲ Annual Earnings: $51,190
▲ Growth: 24%
▲ Annual Job Openings: 13,000
▲ Self-Employed: 18.9%
▲ Part-Time: 8.8%

Research market conditions in local, regional, or national areas to determine potential sales of a product or service. May gather information on competitors, prices, sales, and methods of marketing and distribution. May use survey results to create a marketing campaign based on regional preferences and buying habits. Examines and analyzes statistical data to forecast future marketing trends and to identify potential markets. Collects data on customer preferences and buying habits. Prepares reports and graphic illustrations of findings. Translates complex numerical data into nontechnical, written text. Attends staff conferences to submit findings and proposals to management for consideration. Checks consumer reaction to new or improved products or services. Establishes research methodology and designs format for data gathering, such as surveys, opinion polls, or questionnaires. Gathers data on competitors and analyzes prices, sales, and method of marketing and distribution. **SKILLS**—Writing: Communicating effectively in writing as appropriate for the needs of the audience. Mathematics: Using mathematics to solve problems. Reading Comprehension: Understanding written sentences and paragraphs in work-related documents. Monitoring: Monitoring/Assessing your performance or that of other individuals or organizations to make improvements or take corrective action. Active Listening: Giving full attention to what other people are saying, taking time to understand the points being made, asking questions as appropriate, and not interrupting at inappropriate times.

GOE INFORMATION—**Interest Area:** 13. General Management and Support. **Work Group:** 13.02. Management Support. **Other Job Titles in This Work Group:** Accountants; Accountants and Auditors; Appraisers and Assessors of Real Estate; Appraisers, Real Estate; Assessors; Auditors; Budget Analysts; Claims Adjusters, Examiners, and Investigators; Claims Examiners, Property and Casualty Insurance; Compensation, Benefits, and Job Analysis Specialists; Cost Estimators; Credit Analysts; Employment Interviewers, Private or Public Employment Service; Employment, Recruitment, and Placement Spe-

cialists; Financial Analysts; Human Resources, Training, and Labor Relations Specialists, All Other; Insurance Adjusters, Examiners, and Investigators; Insurance Appraisers, Auto Damage; Insurance Underwriters; Loan Counselors; Loan Officers; Logisticians; Management Analysts; Personnel Recruiters; Purchasing Agents and Buyers, Farm Products; Purchasing Agents, Except Wholesale, Retail, and Farm Products; Tax Examiners, Collectors, and Revenue Agents; Training and Development Specialists; Wholesale and Retail Buyers, Except Farm Products. **PERSONALITY TYPE**—Investigative. Investigative occupations frequently involve working with ideas and require an extensive amount of thinking. These occupations can involve searching for facts and figuring out problems mentally.

EDUCATION/TRAINING PROGRAM(S)—Applied and Resource Economics; Business/Managerial Economics; Econometrics and Quantitative Economics; Economics, General; International Economics; Marketing Research. **RELATED KNOWLEDGE/COURSES**—**Mathematics:** Knowledge of arithmetic, algebra, geometry, calculus, and statistics and their applications. **Sales and Marketing:** Knowledge of principles and methods for showing, promoting, and selling products or services. This includes marketing strategy and tactics, product demonstration, sales techniques, and sales control systems. **English Language:** Knowledge of the structure and content of the English language, including the meaning and spelling of words, rules of composition, and grammar. **Computers and Electronics:** Knowledge of circuit boards, processors, chips, electronic equipment, and computer hardware and software, including applications and programming. **Geography:** Knowledge of principles and methods for describing the features of land, sea, and air masses, including their physical characteristics, locations, interrelationships, and distribution of plant, animal, and human life. **Economics and Accounting:** Knowledge of economic and accounting principles and practices, the financial markets, banking, and the analysis and reporting of financial data.

Marketing Managers

- ▲ Education/Training Required: Work experience, plus degree
- ▲ Annual Earnings: $71,240
- ▲ Growth: 29%
- ▲ Annual Job Openings: 12,000
- ▲ Self-Employed: 2.4%
- ▲ Part-Time: 2.6%

Determine the demand for products and services offered by a firm and its competitors and identify potential customers. Develop pricing strategies with the goal of maximizing the firm's profits or share of the market while ensuring the firm's customers are satisfied. Oversee product development or monitor trends that indicate the need for new products and services. Develops marketing strategy, based on knowledge of establishment policy, nature of market, and cost and markup factors. Coordinates and publicizes marketing activities to promote products and services. Conducts economic and commercial surveys to identify potential markets for products and services. Analyzes business developments and consults trade journals to monitor market trends and determine market opportunities for products. Advises business and other groups on local, national, and international factors affecting the buying and selling of products and services. Selects products and accessories to be displayed at trade or special production shows. Compiles list describing product or service offerings and sets prices or fees. Prepares report of marketing activities. Confers with legal staff to resolve problems, such as copyright infringement and royalty sharing, with outside producers and distributors. Consults with buying personnel to gain advice regarding the types of products or services that are expected to be in demand. Coordinates promotional activities and shows to market products and services. **SKILLS**—Systems Analysis: Determining how a system should work and how changes in conditions, operations, and the environment will affect outcomes. Judgment and Decision Making: Considering the relative costs and benefits of potential actions to choose the most appropriate one. Coordination: Adjusting actions in relation to others' actions. Speaking: Talking to others to convey information effectively. Complex Problem Solving: Identifying complex problems and reviewing related information to develop and evaluate options and implement solutions.

GOE INFORMATION—**Interest Area:** 10. Sales and Marketing. **Work Group:** 10.01. Managerial Work in Sales and Marketing. **Other Job Titles in This Work Group:** Advertising and Promotions Managers; First-Line Supervisors/Managers of Non-Retail Sales Workers; First-Line Supervisors/Managers of Retail Sales Workers; Sales Managers. **PERSONALITY TYPE**—Enterprising. Enterprising occupations frequently involve starting up and carrying out projects. These occupations can involve leading people and making many decisions. They sometimes require risk taking and often deal with business.

EDUCATION/TRAINING PROGRAM(S)—Business Marketing and Marketing Management; International Business Marketing; Marketing Management and Research, Other; Marketing Research. **RELATED KNOWLEDGE/COURSES**—**Sales and Marketing:** Knowledge of principles and methods for showing, promoting, and selling products or services. This includes marketing strategy and tactics, product demonstration, sales techniques, and sales control systems. **Administration and Management:** Knowledge of business and management principles involved in strategic planning, resource allocation, human resources modeling, leadership technique, production methods, and coordination of people and resources. **Mathematics:** Knowledge of arithmetic, algebra, geometry, calculus, and statistics and their applications. **Communications and Media:** Knowledge of media production, communication, and dissemination techniques and methods. This includes alternative ways to inform and entertain via written, oral, and visual media. **English Language:** Knowledge of the structure and content of the English language, including the meaning and spelling of words, rules of composition, and grammar.

Marriage and Family Therapists

▲ Education/Training Required: Master's degree
▲ Annual Earnings: $34,660
▲ Growth: 30%
▲ Annual Job Openings: 2,000
▲ Self-Employed: 0.6%
▲ Part-Time: 18%

Diagnose and treat mental and emotional disorders, whether cognitive, affective, or behavioral, within the context of marriage and family systems. Apply psychotherapeutic and family systems theories and techniques in the delivery of professional services to individuals, couples, and families for the purpose of treating such diagnosed nervous and mental disorders. SKILLS— No data available.

GOE INFORMATION—Interest Area: 12. Education and Social Service. Work Group: 12.02. Social Services. Other Job Titles in This Work Group: Child, Family, and School Social Workers; Clergy; Clinical Psychologists; Clinical, Counseling, and School Psycholo-

gists; Community and Social Service Specialists, All Other; Counseling Psychologists; Counselors, All Other; Directors, Religious Activities and Education; Medical and Public Health Social Workers; Mental Health and Substance Abuse Social Workers; Mental Health Counselors; Probation Officers and Correctional Treatment Specialists; Rehabilitation Counselors; Religious Workers, All Other; Residential Advisors; Social and Human Service Assistants; Social Workers, All Other; Substance Abuse and Behavioral Disorder Counselors. PERSONALITY TYPE— No data available.

EDUCATION/TRAINING PROGRAM(S)— Social Work. RELATED KNOWLEDGE/ COURSES—No data available.

Materials Engineers

▲ Education/Training Required: Bachelor's degree
▲ Annual Earnings: $59,100
▲ Growth: 5%
▲ Annual Job Openings: 2,000
▲ Self-Employed: 5.4%
▲ Part-Time: 3.1%

Evaluate materials and develop machinery and processes to manufacture materials for use in products that must meet specialized design and performance specifications. Develop new uses for known materials. Includes those working with composite materials or specializing in one type of material, such as graphite, metal and metal alloys, ceramics and glass, plastics and polymers, and naturally occurring materials. Reviews new prod-

uct plans and makes recommendations for material selection based on design objectives and cost. Confers with producers of material during investigation and evaluation of material for product applications. Reviews product failure data and interprets laboratory test results to determine material or process causes. Plans and implements laboratory operations to develop material and fabrication procedures that maintain cost and performance standards. Evaluates technical and economic factors relating to process or product design objectives. **SKILLS**—Mathematics: Using mathematics to solve problems. Science: Using scientific rules and methods to solve problems. Judgment and Decision Making: Considering the relative costs and benefits of potential actions to choose the most appropriate one. Operations Analysis: Analyzing needs and product requirements to create a design. Reading Comprehension: Understanding written sentences and paragraphs in work-related documents. Active Learning: Understanding the implications of new information for both current and future problem-solving and decision-making.

GOE INFORMATION—**Interest Area:** 02. Science, Math, and Engineering. **Work Group:** 02.07. Engineering. **Other Job Titles in This Work Group:** Aerospace Engineers; Agricultural Engineers; Architects, Except Landscape and Naval; Biomedical Engineers; Chemical Engineers; Civil Engineers; Computer Hardware Engineers; Computer Software Engineers, Applications; Computer Software Engineers, Systems Software; Electrical Engineers; Electronics Engineers, Except Computer; Engineers, All Other; Environmental Engineers; Fire-Prevention and Protection Engineers; Health and Safety Engineers, Except Mining Safety Engineers and Inspectors; Industrial Engineers; Industrial Safety and Health Engineers; Landscape Architects; Marine Architects; Marine Engineers; Marine Engineers and Naval Architects; Mechanical Engineers; Mining and Geological Engineers,

Including Mining Safety Engineers; Nuclear Engineers; Petroleum Engineers; Product Safety Engineers; Sales Engineers. **PERSONALITY TYPE**—Investigative. Investigative occupations frequently involve working with ideas and require an extensive amount of thinking. These occupations can involve searching for facts and figuring out problems mentally.

EDUCATION/TRAINING PROGRAM(S)—Ceramic Sciences and Engineering; Material Engineering; Metallurgical Engineering; Metallurgy. **RELATED KNOWLEDGE/COURSES**—**Engineering and Technology:** Knowledge of the practical application of engineering science and technology. This includes applying principles, techniques, procedures, and equipment to the design and production of various goods and services. **Design:** Knowledge of design techniques, tools, and principles involved in production of precision technical plans, blueprints, drawings, and models. **Mathematics:** Knowledge of arithmetic, algebra, geometry, calculus, and statistics and their applications. **English Language:** Knowledge of the structure and content of the English language, including the meaning and spelling of words, rules of composition, and grammar. **Production and Processing:** Knowledge of raw materials, production processes, quality control, costs, and other techniques for maximizing the effective manufacture and distribution of goods.

Materials Scientists

- ▲ Education/Training Required: Bachelor's degree
- ▲ Annual Earnings: $60,620
- ▲ Growth: 20%
- ▲ Annual Job Openings: 1,000
- ▲ Self-Employed: 7.6%
- ▲ Part-Time: 6.6%

Research and study the structures and chemical properties of various natural and man-made materials, including metals, alloys, rubber, ceramics, semiconductors, polymers, and glass. Determine ways to strengthen or combine materials or develop new materials with new or specific properties for use in a variety of products and

applications. Plans laboratory experiments to confirm feasibility of processes and techniques to produce materials having special characteristics. Guides technical staff engaged in developing materials for specific use in projected product or device. Reports materials study findings for other scientists and requesters. Studies structures and properties of materials such as metals, alloys, polymers, and ceramics to obtain research data. **SKILLS**—Science: Using scientific rules and methods to solve problems. Active Learning: Understanding the implications of new information for both current and future problem-solving and decision-making. Writing: Communicating effectively in writing as appropriate for the needs of the audience. Reading Comprehension: Understanding written sentences and paragraphs in work-related documents. Mathematics: Using mathematics to solve problems.

GOE INFORMATION—Interest Area: 02. Science, Math, and Engineering. **Work Group:** 02.02. Physical Sciences. **Other Job Titles in This Work Group:** Astronomers; Atmospheric and Space Scientists; Chemists; Geographers; Geologists; Geoscientists, Except Hydrologists and Geographers; Hydrologists; Physical Scientists, All Other; Physicists. **PERSONALITY TYPE**—Investigative. Investigative occupations frequently involve working with ideas and require an extensive amount of thinking. These occupations can involve searching for facts and figuring out problems mentally.

Mathematical Science Teachers, Postsecondary

EDUCATION/TRAINING PROGRAM(S)—Materials Science. **RELATED KNOWLEDGE/ COURSES**—**Engineering and Technology:** Knowledge of the practical application of engineering science and technology. This includes applying principles, techniques, procedures, and equipment to the design and production of various goods and services. **Mathematics:** Knowledge of arithmetic, algebra, geometry, calculus, and statistics and their applications. **Chemistry:** Knowledge of the chemical composition, structure, and properties of substances and of the chemical processes and transformations that they undergo. This includes uses of chemicals and their interactions, danger signs, production techniques, and disposal methods. **English Language:** Knowledge of the structure and content of the English language, including the meaning and spelling of words, rules of composition, and grammar. **Physics:** Knowledge and prediction of physical principles and laws and their interrelationships and applications to understanding fluid, material, and atmospheric dynamics and mechanical, electrical, atomic, and sub-atomic structures and processes.

▲ Education/Training Required: Master's degree

▲ Annual Earnings: $47,440

▲ Growth: 24% for all Postsecondary Teachers

▲ Annual Job Openings: 184,000 for all Postsecondary Teachers

▲ Self-Employed: 0%

▲ Part-Time: 32.3% for all Postsecondary Teachers

Teach courses pertaining to mathematical concepts, statistics, and actuarial science and to the application of original and standardized mathematical techniques in solving specific problems and situations. Prepares and delivers lectures to students. Acts as adviser to student organizations. Serves on faculty committee providing professional consulting services to government and industry. Advises students on academic and vocational curricula. Compiles, administers, and grades examinations or assigns this work to others. Directs research of other teachers or graduate students working for

advanced academic degrees. Compiles bibliographies of specialized materials for outside reading assignments. Conducts research in particular field of knowledge and publishes findings in professional journals. Stimulates class discussions. **SKILLS**—Mathematics: Using mathematics to solve problems. Reading Comprehension: Understanding written sentences and paragraphs in work-related documents. Instructing: Teaching others how to do something. Learning Strategies: Selecting and using training/ instructional methods and procedures appropriate for the situation when learning or teaching new things. Writing:

Communicating effectively in writing as appropriate for the needs of the audience. Active Learning: Understanding the implications of new information for both current and future problem-solving and decision-making.

GOE INFORMATION—Interest Area: 12. Education and Social Service. Work Group: 12.03. Educational Services. Other Job Titles in This Work Group: Adult Literacy, Remedial Education, and GED Teachers and Instructors; Agricultural Sciences Teachers, Postsecondary; Anthropology and Archeology Teachers, Postsecondary; Architecture Teachers, Postsecondary; Archivists; Area, Ethnic, and Cultural Studies Teachers, Postsecondary; Art, Drama, and Music Teachers, Postsecondary; Atmospheric, Earth, Marine, and Space Sciences Teachers, Postsecondary; Audio-Visual Collections Specialists; Biological Science Teachers, Postsecondary; Business Teachers, Postsecondary; Chemistry Teachers, Postsecondary; Child Care Workers; Communications Teachers, Postsecondary; Computer Science Teachers, Postsecondary; Criminal Justice and Law Enforcement Teachers, Postsecondary; Curators; Economics Teachers, Postsecondary; Education Teachers, Postsecondary; Educational Psychologists; Educational, Vocational, and School Counselors; Elementary School Teachers, Except Special Education; Engineering Teachers, Postsecondary; English Language and Literature Teachers, Postsecondary; Environmental Science Teachers, Postsecondary; Farm and Home Management Advisors; Foreign Language and Literature Teachers, Postsecondary; Forestry and Conservation Science Teachers, Postsecondary; Geography Teachers, Postsecondary; Graduate Teaching Assistants; Health Specialties Teachers, Postsecondary; History Teachers, Postsecondary; Home Economics Teachers, Postsecondary; Kindergarten Teachers, Except Special Education; Law Teachers, Postsecondary; Librarians; Library Assistants, Clerical; others. PERSONALITY TYPE—Investigative. Investigative occupations frequently involve working with ideas and require an extensive amount of thinking. These occupations can involve searching for facts and figuring out problems mentally.

EDUCATION/TRAINING PROGRAM(S)— Applied Mathematics, General; Business Statistics; Mathematical Statistics; Mathematics; Mathematics and Computer Science; Mathematics, Other. RELATED KNOWLEDGE/COURSES—Mathematics: Knowledge of arithmetic, algebra, geometry, calculus, and statistics and their applications. Education and Training: Knowledge of principles and methods for curriculum and training design, teaching and instruction for individuals and groups, and the measurement of training effects. English Language: Knowledge of the structure and content of the English language, including the meaning and spelling of words, rules of composition, and grammar. Computers and Electronics: Knowledge of circuit boards, processors, chips, electronic equipment, and computer hardware and software, including applications and programming. Administration and Management: Knowledge of business and management principles involved in strategic planning, resource allocation, human resources modeling, leadership technique, production methods, and coordination of people and resources. Clerical Studies: Knowledge of administrative and clerical procedures and systems such as word processing, managing files and records, stenography and transcription, designing forms, and other office procedures and terminology.

Mathematicians

- ▲ Education/Training Required: Master's degree
- ▲ Annual Earnings: $68,640
- ▲ Growth: –2%
- ▲ Annual Job Openings: Fewer than 500
- ▲ Self-Employed: 0%
- ▲ Part-Time: 5.2%

Conduct research in fundamental mathematics or in application of mathematical techniques to science, management, and other fields. Solve or direct solutions to problems in various fields by mathematical methods. Conducts research in fundamental mathematics and in application of mathematical techniques to science, management, and other fields. Conducts research in such branches of mathematics as algebra, geometry, number theory, logic, and topology. Performs computations and applies methods of numerical analysis. Conceives or directs ideas for application of mathematics to wide variety of fields, including science, engineering, military planning, electronic data processing, and management. Studies and test hypotheses and alternative theories. Utilizes knowledge of such subjects or fields as physics, engineering, astronomy, biology, economics, business and industrial management, or cryptography. Acts as advisor or consultant to research personnel concerning mathematical methods and applications. Operates or directs operation of desk calculators and mechanical and electronic computation machines, analyzers, and plotters in solving problem support of mathematical, scientific, or industrial research. Applies mathematics or mathematical methods of numerical analysis and operates or directs operation of desk calculators and mechanical and other functional areas. **SKILLS—Mathematics:** Using mathematics to solve problems. **Active Learning:** Understanding the implications of new information for both current and future problem-solving and decision-making. **Learning Strategies:** Selecting and using training/instructional methods and procedures appropriate for the situation when learning or teaching new things. **Critical Thinking:** Using logic and reasoning to identify the strengths and weaknesses of alternative solutions, conclusions, or approaches to problems. **Reading Comprehension:** Understanding written sentences and paragraphs in work-related documents.

GOE INFORMATION—Interest Area: 02. Science, Math, and Engineering. **Work Group:** 02.06. Mathematics and Computers. **Other Job Titles in This Work Group:** Actuaries; Computer and Information Scientists, Research; Computer Programmers; Computer Security Specialists; Computer Specialists, All Other; Computer Support Specialists; Computer Systems Analysts; Database Administrators; Mathematical Science Occupations, All Other; Mathematical Technicians; Network and Computer Systems Administrators; Network Systems and Data Communications Analysts; Operations Research Analysts; Statistical Assistants; Statisticians. **PERSONALITY TYPE—Investigative.** Investigative occupations frequently involve working with ideas and require an extensive amount of thinking. These occupations can involve searching for facts and figuring out problems mentally.

EDUCATION/TRAINING PROGRAM(S)— Applied Mathematics, General; Applied Mathematics, Other; Mathematics; Mathematics and Computer Science; Mathematics, Other. **RELATED KNOWLEDGE/ COURSES—Mathematics:** Knowledge of arithmetic, algebra, geometry, calculus, and statistics and their applications. **Computers and Electronics:** Knowledge of circuit boards, processors, chips, electronic equipment, and computer hardware and software, including applications and programming. **Administration and Management:** Knowledge of business and management principles involved in strategic planning, resource allocation, human resources modeling, leadership technique, production methods, and coordination of people and resources. **Physics:** Knowledge and prediction of physical principles and laws and their interrelationships and applications to understanding fluid, material, and atmospheric dynamics and mechanical, electrical, atomic, and sub-atomic structures and processes. **English Language:** Knowledge of the structure and content of the English language, including the meaning and spelling of words, rules of composition, and grammar. **Engineering and Technology:** Knowledge of the practical application of engineering science and technology. This includes applying principles, techniques, procedures, and equipment to the design and production of various goods and services.

Mechanical Engineering Technicians

- ▲ Education/Training Required: Associate's degree
- ▲ Annual Earnings: $39,570
- ▲ Growth: 14%
- ▲ Annual Job Openings: 5,000
- ▲ Self-Employed: 1.9%
- ▲ Part-Time: 7.4%

Apply theory and principles of mechanical engineering to modify, develop, and test machinery and equipment under direction of engineering staff or physical scientists. Reviews project instructions and blueprints to ascertain test specifications, procedures, and objectives and tests nature of technical problems, such as redesign. Estimates cost factors, including labor and material for purchased and fabricated parts and costs for assembly, testing, and installing. Inspects lines and figures for clarity and returns erroneous drawings to designer for correction. Prepares parts sketches and writes work orders and purchase requests to be furnished by outside contractors. Reads dials and meters to determine amperage, voltage, and electrical out- and input at specific operating temperature to analyze parts performance. Operates drill press, grinders, engine lathe, or other machines to modify parts tested or to fabricate experimental parts for testing. Evaluates tool drawing designs by measuring drawing dimensions and comparing with original specifications for form and function, using engineering skills. Confers with technicians and submits reports of test results to engineering department and recommends design or material changes. Records test procedures and results, numerical and graphical data, and recommendations for changes in product or test methods. Drafts detail drawing or sketch for drafting room completion or to request parts fabrication by machine, sheet, or wood shops. Calculates required capacities for equipment of proposed system to obtain specified performance and submits data to engineering personnel for approval. Discusses changes in design, method of manufacture and assembly, and drafting techniques and procedures with staff and coordinates corrections. Devises, fabricates, and assembles new or modified mechanical components for products such as industrial machinery or equipment and measuring instruments. Analyzes tests results in relation to design or rated specifications and test objectives and modifies or adjusts equipment to meet specifications. Tests equipment, using test devices attached to generator, voltage regulator, or other electrical parts, such as generators or spark plugs. Reviews project instructions and specifications to identify, modify and plan requirements fabrication, assembly, and testing. Sets up prototype and test apparatus and operates test controlling equipment to observe and record prototype test results. Sets up and conducts tests of complete units and components under operational conditions to investigate proposals for improving equipment performance. **SKILLS**—Mathematics: Using mathematics to solve problems. Technology Design: Generating or adapting equipment and technology to serve user needs. Reading Comprehension: Understanding written sentences and paragraphs in work-related documents. Operation and Control: Controlling operations of equipment or systems. Active Learning: Understanding the implications of new information for both current and future problem-solving and decision-making. Active Listening: Giving full attention to what other people are saying, taking time to understand the points being made, asking questions as appropriate, and not interrupting at inappropriate times.

GOE INFORMATION—**Interest Area:** 02. Science, Math, and Engineering. **Work Group:** 02.08. Engineering Technology. **Other Job Titles in This Work Group:** Aerospace Engineering and Operations Technicians; Architectural and Civil Drafters; Architectural Drafters; Calibration and Instrumentation Technicians; Cartographers and Photogrammetrists; Civil Drafters; Civil Engineering Technicians; Construction and Building Inspectors; Drafters, All Other; Electrical and Electronic Engineering Technicians; Electrical and Electronics Drafters; Electrical Drafters; Electrical Engineering Technicians; Electro-Mechanical Technicians; Electronic Drafters; Electronics Engineering Technicians; Engineering Technicians, Except Drafters, All Other; Environmental Engineering Technicians; Industrial Engineering Technicians; Mapping Technicians; Mechanical Drafters; Numerical Tool and Process Control Programmers; Pressure Vessel Inspectors; Surveying and Mapping Technicians; Surveying Technicians; Surveyors. **PERSONALITY TYPE**—Realistic. Realistic occupations frequently involve work activities that include practical, hands-on problems and solutions. They often deal with plants, animals, and real-world materials like wood, tools, and machinery. Many of the occupations require working outside and do not involve a lot of paperwork or working closely with others.

EDUCATION/TRAINING PROGRAM(S)— Mechanical Engineering/Mechanical Technologist/ Technician. **RELATED KNOWLEDGE/**

COURSES—Engineering and Technology: Knowledge of the practical application of engineering science and technology. This includes applying principles, techniques, procedures, and equipment to the design and production of various goods and services. **Principles of Mechanical Devices:** Knowledge of machines and tools, including their designs, uses, repair, and maintenance. **Design:** Knowledge of design techniques, tools, and principles involved in production of precision technical plans, blueprints, drawings, and models. **Mathematics:** Knowledge of arithmetic, algebra, geometry, calculus, and statistics and their applications. **Physics:** Knowledge and prediction of physical principles and laws and their interrelationships and applications to understanding fluid, material, and atmospheric dynamics and mechanical, electrical, atomic, and sub-atomic structures and processes.

Mechanical Engineers

- ▲ Education/Training Required: Bachelor's degree
- ▲ Annual Earnings: $58,710
- ▲ Growth: 13%
- ▲ Annual Job Openings: 7,000
- ▲ Self-Employed: 3.5%
- ▲ Part-Time: 2.1%

Perform engineering duties in planning and designing tools, engines, machines, and other mechanically functioning equipment. Oversee installation, operation, maintenance, and repair of such equipment as centralized heat, gas, water, and steam systems. Designs products and systems to meet process requirements, applying knowledge of engineering principles. Oversees installation to ensure machines and equipment are installed and functioning according to specifications. Specifies system components or directs modification of products to ensure conformance with engineering design and performance specifications. Alters or modifies design to obtain specified functional and operational performance. Assists drafter in developing structural design of product, using drafting tools or computer-assisted design/drafting equipment and software. Selects or designs tools to meet specifications, using manuals, drafting tools, computer, and specialized software programs.

Tests ability of machines to perform tasks. Develops models of alternate processing methods to test feasibility or new applications of system components and recommends implementation of procedures. Confers with establishment personnel and engineers to implement operating procedures and resolve system malfunctions and to provide technical information. Plans and directs engineering personnel in fabrication of test control apparatus and equipment and develops procedures for testing products. Researches and analyzes data, such as customer design proposal, specifications, and manuals, to determine feasibility of design or application. Studies industrial processes to determine where and how application of equipment can be made. Investigates equipment failures and difficulties, diagnoses faulty operation, and makes recommendations to maintenance crew. Determines parts supply, maintenance tasks, safety procedures, and service schedule required to maintain machines and equipment in prescribed condition. Conducts experiments to test and analyze existing designs and equipment to obtain data on performance of product and prepares reports. Inspects, evaluates, and arranges field installations and recommends design modifications to eliminate machine or system malfunctions. Coordinates building, fabrication, and installation of product design and operation, maintenance, and repair activities to utilize machines and equipment. **SKILLS**—Mathematics: Using mathematics to solve problems. Active Learning: Understanding the implications of new information for both current and future problem-solving and decision-making. Reading Comprehension: Understanding written sentences and paragraphs in work-related documents. Science: Using scientific rules and methods to solve problems. Technology Design: Generating or adapting equipment and technology to serve user needs.

GOE INFORMATION—**Interest Area:** 02. Science, Math, and Engineering. **Work Group:** 02.07. Engineering. **Other Job Titles in This Work Group:** Aerospace Engineers; Agricultural Engineers; Architects, Except Landscape and Naval; Biomedical Engineers; Chemical Engineers; Civil Engineers; Computer Hardware Engineers; Computer Software Engineers, Applications; Computer Software Engineers, Systems Software; Electrical Engineers; Electronics Engineers, Except Computer; Engineers, All Other; Environmental Engineers; Fire-Prevention and Protection Engineers; Health and Safety Engineers, Except Mining Safety Engineers and Inspectors; Industrial Engineers; Industrial Safety and Health Engineers; Landscape Architects; Marine Architects;

Marine Engineers; Marine Engineers and Naval Architects; Materials Engineers; Mining and Geological Engineers, Including Mining Safety Engineers; Nuclear Engineers; Petroleum Engineers; Product Safety Engineers; Sales Engineers. **PERSONALITY TYPE**—Realistic. Realistic occupations frequently involve work activities that include practical, hands-on problems and solutions. They often deal with plants, animals, and real-world materials like wood, tools, and machinery. Many of the occupations require working outside and do not involve a lot of paperwork or working closely with others.

EDUCATION/TRAINING PROGRAM(S)— Mechanical Engineering. **RELATED KNOWLEDGE/COURSES**—**Engineering and Technology:** Knowledge of the practical application of engineering science and technology. This includes applying principles, techniques, procedures, and equipment to the design and production of various goods and services. **Design:** Knowledge of design techniques, tools, and principles involved in production of precision technical plans, blueprints, drawings, and models. **Mathematics:** Knowledge of arithmetic, algebra, geometry, calculus, and statistics and their applications. **Computers and Electronics:** Knowledge of circuit boards, processors, chips, electronic equipment, and computer hardware and software, including applications and programming. **Physics:** Knowledge and prediction of physical principles and laws and their interrelationships and applications to understanding fluid, material, and atmospheric dynamics and mechanical, electrical, atomic, and sub-atomic structures and processes.

Medical and Clinical Laboratory Technicians

- ▲ Education/Training Required: Associate's degree
- ▲ Annual Earnings: $27,540
- ▲ Growth: 19%
- ▲ Annual Job Openings: 19,000
- ▲ Self-Employed: 0.7%
- ▲ Part-Time: 19.5%

Perform routine medical laboratory tests for the diagnosis, treatment, and prevention of disease. May work under the supervision of a medical technologist. Conducts quantitative and qualitative

chemical analyses of body fluids, such as blood, urine, and spinal fluid. Conducts blood tests for transfusion purposes. Tests vaccines for sterility and virus inactivity. Draws blood from patient, observing principles of asepsis to obtain blood sample. Prepares standard volumetric solutions and reagents used in testing. Inoculates fertilized eggs, broths, or other bacteriological media with organisms. Incubates bacteria for specified period and prepares vaccines and serums by standard laboratory methods. Performs blood counts, using microscope. **SKILLS**—Science: Using scientific rules and methods to solve problems. Reading Comprehension: Understanding written sentences and paragraphs in work-related documents. Quality Control Analysis: Conducting tests and inspections of products, services, or processes to evaluate quality or performance. Mathematics: Using mathematics to solve problems. Equipment Selection: Determining the kind of tools and equipment needed to do a job.

GOE INFORMATION—Interest Area: 14. Medical and Health Services. **Work Group:** 14.05. Medical Technology. **Other Job Titles in This Work Group:** Cardiovascular Technologists and Technicians; Diagnostic Medical Sonographers; Health Technologists and Technicians, All Other; Medical and Clinical Laboratory Technologists; Medical Equipment Preparers; Nuclear Medicine Technologists; Orthotists and Prosthetists; Radiologic Technicians; Radiologic Technologists; Radiologic Technologists and Technicians. **PERSONALITY TYPE—** Realistic. Realistic occupations frequently involve work activities that include practical, hands-on problems and solutions. They often deal with plants, animals, and real-world materials like wood, tools, and machinery. Many of the occupations require working outside and do not involve a lot of paperwork or working closely with others.

EDUCATION/TRAINING PROGRAM(S)— Blood Bank Technologist/Technician; Hematology Technologist/Technician; Medical Laboratory Assistant; Medical Laboratory Technician. **RELATED KNOWLEDGE/ COURSES—Chemistry:** Knowledge of the chemical composition, structure, and properties of substances and of the chemical processes and transformations that they undergo. This includes uses of chemicals and their interactions, danger signs, production techniques, and disposal methods. **Biology:** Knowledge of plant and animal organisms and their tissues, cells, functions, interdependencies, and interactions with each other and the environment. **Medicine and Dentistry:** Knowledge of the information and techniques needed to diagnose and treat human injuries, diseases, and deformities. This includes symptoms, treatment alternatives, drug properties and interactions, and preventive health-care measures. **Mathematics:** Knowledge of arithmetic, algebra, geometry, calculus, and statistics and their applications. **Public Safety and Security:** Knowledge of relevant equipment, policies, procedures, and strategies to promote effective local, state, or national security operations for the protection of people, data, property, and institutions.

Medical and Clinical Laboratory Technologists

- ▲ Education/Training Required: Bachelor's degree
- ▲ Annual Earnings: $40,510
- ▲ Growth: 17%
- ▲ Annual Job Openings: 19,000
- ▲ Self-Employed: 0.7%
- ▲ Part-Time: 19.5%

Perform complex medical laboratory tests for diagnosis, treatment, and prevention of disease. May train or supervise staff. Cuts, stains, and mounts biological material on slides for microscopic study and diagnosis, following standard laboratory procedures. Analyzes samples of biological material for chemical content or reaction. Harvests cell culture at optimum time sequence based on knowledge of cell cycle differences and culture conditions. Cultivates, isolates, and assists in identifying microbial organisms and performs various tests on these micro-organisms. Conducts chemical analysis of body fluids, including blood, urine, and spinal fluid, to determine presence of normal and abnormal components. Sets up, cleans, and maintains laboratory equipment. Enters analysis of medical tests and clinical results into computer for storage. Calibrates and maintains equipment used in quantitative and qualitative analysis, such as spectrophotometers, calorimeters, flame photometers, and computer-controlled analyzers. Communicates with physicians, family members, and researchers requesting technical information regarding test results. Conducts research under direction of Microbiologist or Biochemist. Cuts images of chromosomes from photograph and identifies and arranges them in numbered pairs on karyotype chart, using standard practices. Studies blood cells, number of blood cells, and morphology, using microscopic technique. Performs tests to determine blood group, type, and compatibility for transfusion purposes. Examines and tests human, animal, or other materials for microbial organisms. Prepares slide of cell culture to identify chromosomes, views and photographs slide under photo-microscope, and prints picture. Selects and prepares specimen and media for cell culture, using aseptic technique and knowledge of medium components and cell requirements. Examines slides under microscope to detect deviations from norm and to report abnormalities for further study. **SKILLS**—Reading Comprehension: Understanding written sentences and paragraphs in work-related documents. Science: Using scientific rules and methods to solve problems. Writing: Communicating effectively in writing as appropriate for the needs of the audience. Active Learning: Understanding the implications of new information for both current and future problem-solving and decision-making. Speaking: Talking to others to convey information effectively.

GOE INFORMATION—**Interest Area:** 14. Medical and Health Services. **Work Group:** 14.05. Medical Technology. **Other Job Titles in This Work Group:** Cardiovascular Technologists and Technicians; Diagnostic

Medical Sonographers; Health Technologists and Technicians, All Other; Medical and Clinical Laboratory Technicians; Medical Equipment Preparers; Nuclear Medicine Technologists; Orthotists and Prosthetists; Radiologic Technicians; Radiologic Technologists; Radiologic Technologists and Technicians. **PERSONALITY TYPE**—Investigative. Investigative occupations frequently involve working with ideas and require an extensive amount of thinking. These occupations can involve searching for facts and figuring out problems mentally.

EDUCATION/TRAINING PROGRAM(S)—Cytotechnologist; Health and Medical Laboratory Technologists/Technicians, Other; Medical Technology. **RELATED KNOWLEDGE/COURSES**—Biology: Knowledge of plant and animal organisms and their tissues, cells, functions, interdependencies, and interactions with each other and the environment. **Chemistry:** Knowledge of the chemical composition, structure, and properties of substances and of the chemical processes and transformations that they undergo. This includes uses of chemicals and their interactions, danger signs, production techniques, and disposal methods. **English Language:** Knowledge of the structure and content of the English language, including the meaning and spelling of words, rules of composition, and grammar. **Medicine and Dentistry:** Knowledge of the information and techniques needed to diagnose and treat human injuries, diseases, and deformities. This includes symptoms, treatment alternatives, drug properties and interactions, and preventive health-care measures. **Education and Training:** Knowledge of principles and methods for curriculum and training design, teaching and instruction for individuals and groups, and the measurement of training effects.

Medical and Health Services Managers

- ▲ Education/Training Required: Work experience, plus degree
- ▲ Annual Earnings: $56,370
- ▲ Growth: 32%
- ▲ Annual Job Openings: 27,000
- ▲ Self-Employed: 49.4%
- ▲ Part-Time: 7.2%

Plan, direct, or coordinate medicine and health services in hospitals, clinics, managed care organizations, public health agencies, or similar organizations. Administers fiscal operations, such as planning budgets, authorizing expenditures, and coordinating financial reporting. Develops organizational policies and procedures and establishes evaluative or operational criteria for facility or medical unit. Develops or expands medical programs or health services for research, rehabilitation, and community health promotion. Directs and coordinates activities of medical, nursing, technical, clerical, service, and maintenance personnel of health-care facility or mobile unit. Implements and administers programs and services for health-care or medical facility. Prepares activity reports to inform management of the status and implementation plans of programs, services, and quality initiatives. Reviews and analyzes facility activities and data to aid planning and cash and risk management and to improve service utilization. Develops and maintains computerized records management system to store or process activity or personnel data. Inspects facilities for emergency readiness and compliance of access, safety, and sanitation regulations and recommends building or equipment modifications. Develops instructional materials and conducts in-service and community-based educational programs. Consults with medical, business, and community groups to discuss service problems, coordinate activities and plans, and promote health programs. Recruits, hires, and evaluates the performance of medical staff and auxiliary personnel. Establishes work schedules and assignments for staff, according to workload, space, and equipment availability. **SKILLS**—Systems Evaluation: Identifying measures or indicators of system performance and the actions needed to improve or correct performance relative to the goals of the system. Management of Financial Resources: Determining how money will be spent to get the work done and accounting for these expenditures. Reading Comprehension: Understanding written sentences and paragraphs in work-related documents. Coordination: Adjusting actions in relation to others' actions. Management of Personnel Resources: Motivating, developing, and directing people as they work, identifying the best people for the job. Writing: Communicating effectively in writing as appropriate for the needs of the audience. Systems Analysis: Determining how a system should work and how changes in conditions, operations, and the environment will affect outcomes.

GOE INFORMATION—**Interest Area:** 14. Medical and Health Services. **Work Group:** 14.01. Managerial Work in Medical and Health Services. **Other Job Titles in This Work Group:** Coroners. **PERSONALITY TYPE**—Enterprising. Enterprising occupations frequently involve starting up and carrying out projects. These occupations can involve leading people and making many decisions. They sometimes require risk taking and often deal with business.

EDUCATION/TRAINING PROGRAM(S)—Analytical Chemistry; Anatomy; Biochemistry; Biological and Physical Sciences; Biological Immunology; Biological Sciences/Life Sciences, Other; Biology, General; Biometrics; Biophysics; Biostatistics; Biotechnology Research; Botany, General; Botany, Other; Cell and Molecular Biology, Other; Cell Biology; Chemistry, General; Chemistry, Other; Entomology; Evolutionary Biology; Genetics, Plant and Animal; Health and Medical Administrative Services, Other; Health System/Health Services Administration; Health Unit Manager/Ward Supervisor; Hospital/Health Facilities Administration; Inorganic Chemistry; Marine/Aquatic Biology; Medical Records Administration; Medicinal/Pharmaceutical Chemistry; Microbiology/Bacteriology; Miscellaneous Biological Specializations, Other; Molecular Biology; Neuroscience; Nursing Administration (Post-R.N.); Nutritional Sciences; Organic Chemistry; Parasitology; Pathology, Human and Animal; Pharmacology, Human and Animal; Physical and Theoretical Chemistry; Physiology, Human and Animal; Plant Pathology; Plant Physiology; Public Health, General; Radiation Biology/Radiobiology; Toxicology; Virology. **RELATED KNOWLEDGE/COURSES**—**Administration and Management:** Knowledge of business and management principles involved in strategic planning, resource allocation, human resources modeling, leadership technique, production methods, and coordination of people and resources. **Personnel and Human Resources:** Knowledge of principles and procedures for personnel recruitment, selection, training, compensation and benefits, labor relations and negotiation, and personnel information systems. **Education and Training:** Knowledge of principles and methods for curriculum and training design, teaching and instruction for individuals and groups, and the measurement of training effects. **Economics and Accounting:** Knowledge of economic and accounting principles and practices, the financial markets, banking, and the analysis and reporting of financial data. **Math-** **ematics:** Knowledge of arithmetic, algebra, geometry, calculus, and statistics and their applications.

Medical and Public Health Social Workers

- ▲ Education/Training Required: Bachelor's degree
- ▲ Annual Earnings: $34,790
- ▲ Growth: 32%
- ▲ Annual Job Openings: 13,000
- ▲ Self-Employed: 3.1%
- ▲ Part-Time: 11.9%

Provide persons, families, or vulnerable populations with the psychosocial support needed to cope with chronic, acute, or terminal illnesses, such as Alzheimer's, cancer, or AIDS. Services include advising family caregivers, providing patient education and counseling, and making necessary referrals for other social services. Counsels clients and patients, individually and in group sessions, to assist in overcoming dependencies, adjusting to life, and making changes. Monitors, evaluates, and records client progress according to measurable goals described in treatment and care plan. Refers patient, client, or family to community resources to assist in recovery from mental or physical illness. Plans and conducts programs to prevent substance abuse or improve health and counseling services in community. Supervises and directs other workers providing services to client or patient. Intervenes as advocate for client or patient to resolve emergency problems in crisis situation. Modifies treatment plan to comply with changes in client's status. Formulates or coordinates program plan for treatment, care, and rehabilitation of client or patient, based on social work experience and knowledge. Counsels family members to assist in understanding, dealing with, and supporting client or patient. Interviews clients, reviews records, and confers with other professionals to evaluate mental or physical condition of client or patient. **SKILLS—Social Perceptiveness:** Being aware of others' reactions and understanding why they react as they do. Critical Thinking: Using logic and reasoning to identify the strengths and weaknesses of alternative solutions, conclusions, or approaches to problems. Management of Financial Resources: Determining how money will be spent to get the work done and accounting for these expenditures.

Reading Comprehension: Understanding written sentences and paragraphs in work-related documents. Active Listening: Giving full attention to what other people are saying, taking time to understand the points being made, asking questions as appropriate, and not interrupting at inappropriate times. Service Orientation: Actively looking for ways to help people.

GOE INFORMATION—Interest Area: 12. Education and Social Service. **Work Group:** 12.02. Social Services. **Other Job Titles in This Work Group:** Child, Family, and School Social Workers; Clergy; Clinical Psychologists; Clinical, Counseling, and School Psychologists; Community and Social Service Specialists, All Other; Counseling Psychologists; Counselors, All Other; Directors, Religious Activities and Education; Marriage and Family Therapists; Mental Health and Substance Abuse Social Workers; Mental Health Counselors; Probation Officers and Correctional Treatment Specialists; Rehabilitation Counselors; Religious Workers, All Other; Residential Advisors; Social and Human Service Assistants; Social Workers, All Other; Substance Abuse and Behavioral Disorder Counselors. **PERSONALITY TYPE—Social.** Social occupations frequently involve working with, communicating with, and teaching people. These occupations often involve helping or providing service to others.

EDUCATION/TRAINING PROGRAM(S)— Clinical and Medical Social Work. **RELATED KNOWLEDGE/COURSES—Therapy and Counseling:** Knowledge of principles, methods, and procedures for diagnosis, treatment, and rehabilitation of physical and mental dysfunctions and for career counseling and guidance. **Customer and Personal Service:** Knowledge of principles and processes for providing customer and personal services. This includes customer needs assessment, meeting quality standards for services, and evaluation of customer satisfaction. **Psychology:** Knowledge of human behavior and performance; individual differences in ability, personality, and interests; learning and motivation; psychological research methods; and the assessment and treatment of behavioral and affective disorders. **Educa-** **tion and Training:** Knowledge of principles and methods for curriculum and training design, teaching and instruction for individuals and groups, and the measurement of training effects. **English Language:** Knowledge of the structure and content of the English language, including the meaning and spelling of words, rules of composition, and grammar.

Medical Records and Health Information Technicians

- ▲ Education/Training Required: Associate's degree
- ▲ Annual Earnings: $22,750
- ▲ Growth: 49%
- ▲ Annual Job Openings: 14,000
- ▲ Self-Employed: 0%
- ▲ Part-Time: 22.9%

Compile, process, and maintain medical records of hospital and clinic patients in a manner consistent with medical, administrative, ethical, legal, and regulatory requirements of the health-care system. Process, maintain, compile, and report patient information for health requirements and standards. Compiles and maintains medical records of patients to document condition and treatment and to provide data for research studies. Maintains variety of health record indexes and storage and retrieval systems. Enters data, such as demographic characteristics, history and extent of disease, diagnostic procedures, and treatment, into computer. Prepares statistical reports, narrative reports, and graphic presentations of tumor registry data for use by hospital staff, researchers, and other users. Assists in special studies or research as needed. Contacts discharged patients, their families, and physicians to maintain registry with follow-up information, such as quality of life and length of survival of cancer patients. Reviews records for completeness and to abstract and code data, using standard classification systems, and to identify and compile patient data. Compiles medical care and census data for statistical reports on diseases treated, surgery performed, and use of hospital beds. **SKILLS—Reading Compre-** hension: Understanding written sentences and paragraphs in work-related documents. Writing: Communicating effectively in writing as appropriate for the needs of the audience. Speaking: Talking to others to convey information effectively. Active Listening: Giving full attention to what other people are saying, taking time to understand the points being made, asking questions as appropriate, and not interrupting at inappropriate times. Mathematics: Using mathematics to solve problems.

GOE INFORMATION—Interest Area: 09. Business Detail. **Work Group:** 09.07. Records Processing. **Other Job Titles in This Work Group:** Correspondence Clerks; Court Reporters; Credit Authorizers; Credit Authorizers, Checkers, and Clerks; Credit Checkers; File Clerks; Human Resources Assistants, Except Payroll and Timekeeping; Information and Record Clerks, All Other; Insurance Claims and Policy Processing Clerks; Insurance Claims Clerks; Insurance Policy Processing Clerks; Medical Transcriptionists; Office Clerks, General; Procurement Clerks; Proofreaders and Copy Markers. **PERSONALITY TYPE—**Conventional. Conventional occupations frequently involve following set procedures and routines. These occupations can include working with data and details more than with ideas. Usually there is a clear line of authority to follow.

EDUCATION/TRAINING PROGRAM(S)— Medical Records Technologist/Technician. **RELATED KNOWLEDGE/COURSES—Clerical Studies:** Knowledge of administrative and clerical procedures and systems such as word processing, managing files and records, stenography and transcription, designing forms, and other office procedures and terminology. **Computers and Electronics:** Knowledge of circuit boards, processors, chips, electronic equipment, and computer hardware and software, including applications and programming. **Mathematics:** Knowledge of arithmetic, algebra, geometry, calculus, and statistics and their applications. **English**

Language: Knowledge of the structure and content of the English language, including the meaning and spelling of words, rules of composition, and grammar. **Medicine and Dentistry:** Knowledge of the information and techniques needed to diagnose and treat human injuries, diseases, and deformities. This includes symptoms, treatment alternatives, drug properties and interactions, and preventive health-care measures.

Medical Scientists, Except Epidemiologists

▲ Education/Training Required: Doctoral degree

▲ Annual Earnings: $57,810

▲ Growth: 26%

▲ Annual Job Openings: 2,000

▲ Self-Employed: 2.8%

▲ Part-Time: 6.6%

Conduct research dealing with the understanding of human diseases and the improvement of human health. Engage in clinical investigation or other research, production, technical writing, or related activities. Plans and directs studies to investigate human or animal disease, preventive methods, and treatments for disease. Consults with and advises physicians, educators, researchers, and others regarding medical applications of sciences, such as physics, biology, and chemistry. Confers with health department, industry personnel, physicians, and others to develop health safety standards and programs to improve public health. Supervises activities of clerical and statistical or laboratory personnel. Teaches principles of medicine and medical and laboratory procedures to physicians, residents, students, and technicians. Standardizes drug dosages, methods of immunization, and procedures for manufacture of drugs and medicinal compounds. Prepares and analyzes samples for toxicity, bacteria, or microorganisms or to study cell structure and properties. Examines organs, tissues, cell structures, or micro-organisms by systematic observation or using microscope. Investigates cause, progress, life cycle, or mode of transmission of diseases or parasites. Studies effects of drugs, gases, pesticides, parasites, or micro-organisms or health and physiological processes of animals and humans. Plans methodological design of research study and arranges for data collection. Conducts research to develop method-

ologies, instrumentation, or identification, diagnosing, and treatment procedures for medical application. Analyzes data, applying statistical techniques and scientific knowledge, prepares reports, and presents findings. **SKILLS**— Instructing: Teaching others how to do something. Active Learning: Understanding the implications of new information for both current and future problem-solving and decision-making. Reading Comprehension: Understanding written sentences and paragraphs in work-related documents. Writing: Communicating effectively in writing as appropriate for the needs of the audience. Science: Using scientific rules and methods to solve problems.

GOE INFORMATION—Interest Area: 02. Science, Math, and Engineering. **Work Group:** 02.03. Life Sciences. **Other Job Titles in This Work Group:** Agricultural and Food Science Technicians; Agricultural Technicians; Animal Scientists; Biochemists; Biochemists and Biophysicists; Biological Scientists, All Other; Biologists; Biophysicists; Conservation Scientists; Environmental Scientists and Specialists, Including Health; Epidemiologists; Food Science Technicians; Food Scientists and Technologists; Foresters; Life Scientists, All Other; Microbiologists; Plant Scientists; Range Managers; Soil and Plant Scientists; Soil Conservationists; Soil Scientists; Zoologists and Wildlife Biologists. **PERSONALITY TYPE**—Investigative. Investigative occupations frequently involve working with ideas and require an extensive amount of thinking. These occupations can involve searching for facts and figuring out problems mentally.

EDUCATION/TRAINING PROGRAM(S)— Basic Medical Sciences, Other; Medical Anatomy; Medical Biochemistry; Medical Biomathematics and Biometrics; Medical Cell Biology; Medical Clinical Sciences (M.S., Ph.D.); Medical Genetics; Medical Immunology; Medical Microbiology; Medical Molecular Biology; Medical Neurobiology; Medical Nutrition; Medical Pathology; Medical Physics/Biophysics; Medical Physiology; Medical Toxicology. **RELATED KNOWLEDGE/ COURSES—Mathematics:** Knowledge of arithmetic, algebra, geometry, calculus, and statistics and their applications. **Biology:** Knowledge of plant and animal organisms and their tissues, cells, functions, interdependencies, and interactions with each other and the environment. **Chemistry:** Knowledge of the chemical composition, structure, and properties of substances and of the chemical processes and transformations that they undergo. This includes uses of chemicals and their interactions, danger signs, production techniques, and disposal methods. **Computers and Electronics:** Knowledge of circuit boards, processors, chips, electronic equipment, and computer hardware and software, including applications and programming. **English Language:** Knowledge of the structure and content of the English language, including the meaning and spelling of words, rules of composition, and grammar. **Medicine and Dentistry:** Knowledge of the information and techniques needed to diagnose and treat human injuries, diseases, and deformities. This includes symptoms, treatment alternatives, drug properties and interactions, and preventive health-care measures.

Medical Transcriptionists

- ▲ Education/Training Required: Associate's degree
- ▲ Annual Earnings: $25,270
- ▲ Growth: 30%
- ▲ Annual Job Openings: 15,000
- ▲ Self-Employed: No data available
- ▲ Part-Time: No data available

Use transcribing machines with headset and foot pedal to listen to recordings by physicians and other health-care professionals dictating a variety of medical reports, such as emergency room visits, diagnostic imaging studies, operations, chart reviews, and final summaries. Transcribe dictated reports and translate medical jargon and abbreviations into their expanded forms. Edit as necessary and return reports in either printed or electronic form to the dictator for review and signature or correction. **SKILLS—**No data available.

GOE INFORMATION—Interest Area: 09. Business Detail. **Work Group:** 09.07. Records Processing.

Other Job Titles in This Work Group: Correspondence Clerks; Court Reporters; Credit Authorizers; Credit Authorizers, Checkers, and Clerks; Credit Checkers; File Clerks; Human Resources Assistants, Except Payroll and Timekeeping; Information and Record Clerks, All Other; Insurance Claims and Policy Processing Clerks; Insurance Claims Clerks; Insurance Policy Processing Clerks; Medical Records and Health Information Technicians; Office Clerks, General; Procurement Clerks; Proofreaders and Copy Markers. **PERSONALITY TYPE—** No data available.

EDUCATION/TRAINING PROGRAM(S)— Medical Transcription. **RELATED KNOWLEDGE/ COURSES—**No data available.

Meeting and Convention Planners

- ▲ Education/Training Required: Bachelor's degree
- ▲ Annual Earnings: $35,540
- ▲ Growth: 23%
- ▲ Annual Job Openings: 3,000
- ▲ Self-Employed: 5.4%
- ▲ Part-Time: 7.7%

Coordinate activities of staff and convention personnel to make arrangements for group meetings and conventions. Directs and coordinates activities of staff and convention personnel to make arrangements, prepare facilities, and provide services for events. Reads trade publications, attends seminars, and consults with other meeting professionals to keep abreast of meeting management standards and trends. Maintains records of events. Reviews bills for accuracy and approves payment. Obtains permits from fire and health departments to erect displays and exhibits and serve food at events. Speaks with attendees and resolves complaints to maintain goodwill. Inspects rooms and displays for conformance to customer requirements and conducts post-meeting evaluations to improve future events. Negotiates contracts with such providers as hotels, convention centers, and speakers. Evaluates and selects providers of services, such as meeting facilities, speakers, and transportation, according to customer requirements. Consults with customer to determine objectives and requirements for events, such as meetings, conferences, and conventions. Plans and develops programs, budgets, and services, such as lodging, catering, and entertainment, according to customer requirements. **SKILLS**—Coordination: Adjusting actions in relation to others' actions. Management of Personnel Resources: Motivating, developing, and directing people as they work, identifying the best people for the job. Service Orientation: Actively looking for ways to help people. Speaking: Talking to others to convey information effectively. Writing: Communicating effectively in writing as appropriate for the needs of the audience. Active Listening: Giving full attention to what other people are saying, taking time to understand the points being made, asking questions as appropriate, and not interrupting at inappropriate times.

GOE INFORMATION—**Interest Area:** 11. Recreation, Travel, and Other Personal Services. **Work Group:** 11.01. Managerial Work in Recreation, Travel, and Other Personal Services. **Other Job Titles in This Work Group:** Aircraft Cargo Handling Supervisors; First-Line Supervisors/Managers of Food Preparation and Serving Workers; First-Line Supervisors/Managers of Housekeeping and Janitorial Workers; First-Line Supervisors/Managers of Personal Service Workers; Food Service Managers; Gaming Managers; Gaming Supervisors; Housekeeping Supervisors; Janitorial Supervisors; Lodging Managers. **PERSONALITY TYPE**—Enterprising. Enterprising occupations frequently involve starting up and carrying out projects. These occupations can involve leading people and making many decisions. They sometimes require risk taking and often deal with business.

EDUCATION/TRAINING PROGRAM(S)—Hotel/Motel Services Marketing Operations; Travel Services Marketing Operations. **RELATED KNOWLEDGE/COURSES**—**Administration and Management:** Knowledge of business and management principles involved in strategic planning, resource allocation, human resources modeling, leadership technique, production methods, and coordination of people and resources. **Customer and Personal Service:** Knowledge of principles and processes for providing customer and personal services. This includes customer needs assessment, meeting quality standards for services, and evaluation of customer satisfaction. **English Language:** Knowledge of the structure and content of the English language, including the meaning and spelling of words, rules of composition, and grammar. **Sales and Marketing:** Knowledge of principles and methods for showing, promoting, and selling products or services. This includes marketing strategy and tactics, product demonstration, sales techniques, and sales control systems. **Communications and Media:** Knowledge of media production, communication, and dissemination techniques and methods. This includes alternative ways to inform and entertain via written, oral, and visual media.

Mental Health and Substance Abuse Social Workers

- ▲ Education/Training Required: Master's degree
- ▲ Annual Earnings: $30,170
- ▲ Growth: 39%
- ▲ Annual Job Openings: 10,000
- ▲ Self-Employed: 3.1%
- ▲ Part-Time: 11.9%

Assess and treat individuals with mental, emotional, or substance abuse problems, including abuse of alcohol, tobacco, and/or other drugs. Activities may include individual and group therapy, crisis intervention, case management, client advocacy, prevention, and education. Counsels clients and patients, individually and in group sessions, to assist in overcoming dependencies, adjusting to life, and making changes. Refers patient, client, or family to community resources to assist in recovery from mental or physical illness. Plans and conducts programs to prevent substance abuse or improve health and counseling services in community. Supervises and directs other workers providing services to client or patient. Intervenes as advocate for client or patient to resolve emergency problems in crisis situation. Modifies treatment plan to comply with changes in client's status. Interviews clients, reviews records, and confers with other professionals to evaluate mental or physical condition of client or patient. Formulates or coordinates program plan for treatment, care, and rehabilitation of client or patient based on social work experience and knowledge. Monitors, evaluates, and records client progress according to measurable goals described in treatment and care plan. Counsels family members to assist in understanding, dealing with, and supporting client or patient. **SKILLS—Social Perceptiveness:** Being aware of others' reactions and understanding why they react as they do. Service Orientation: Actively looking for ways to help people. Critical Thinking: Using logic and reasoning to identify the strengths and weaknesses of alternative solutions, conclusions, or approaches to problems. Management of Financial Resources: Determining how money will

be spent to get the work done and accounting for these expenditures. Active Listening: Giving full attention to what other people are saying, taking time to understand the points being made, asking questions as appropriate, and not interrupting at inappropriate times. Reading Comprehension: Understanding written sentences and paragraphs in work-related documents.

GOE INFORMATION—Interest Area: 12. Education and Social Service. **Work Group:** 12.02. Social Services. **Other Job Titles in This Work Group:** Child, Family, and School Social Workers; Clergy; Clinical Psychologists; Clinical, Counseling, and School Psychologists; Community and Social Service Specialists, All Other; Counseling Psychologists; Counselors, All Other; Directors, Religious Activities and Education; Marriage and Family Therapists; Medical and Public Health Social Workers; Mental Health Counselors; Probation Officers and Correctional Treatment Specialists; Rehabilitation Counselors; Religious Workers, All Other; Residential Advisors; Social and Human Service Assistants; Social Workers, All Other; Substance Abuse and Behavioral Disorder Counselors. **PERSONALITY TYPE—Social.** Social occupations frequently involve working with, communicating with, and teaching people. These occupations often involve helping or providing service to others.

EDUCATION/TRAINING PROGRAM(S)— Clinical and Medical Social Work. **RELATED KNOWLEDGE/COURSES—Therapy and Counseling:** Knowledge of principles, methods, and procedures for diagnosis, treatment, and rehabilitation of physical and mental dysfunctions and for career counseling and guidance. **Psychology:** Knowledge of human behavior and performance; individual differences in ability, personality, and interests; learning and motivation; psychological research methods; and the assessment and treatment of behavioral and affective disorders. **Customer and Personal Service:** Knowledge of principles and processes for providing customer and personal services. This includes customer needs assessment, meeting quality standards for services, and evaluation of customer satisfaction. **Education and Training:** Knowledge of principles and methods for curriculum and training design, teaching and instruction for individuals and groups, and the measurement of training effects. **English Language:** Knowledge of the structure and content of the English language, including the meaning and spelling of words, rules of composition, and grammar.

Mental Health Counselors

- ▲ Education/Training Required: Master's degree
- ▲ Annual Earnings: $27,570
- ▲ Growth: 22%
- ▲ Annual Job Openings: 7,000
- ▲ Self-Employed: 0.6%
- ▲ Part-Time: 18%

Counsel with emphasis on prevention. Work with individuals and groups to promote optimum mental health. May help individuals deal with addictions and substance abuse; family, parenting, and marital problems; suicide; stress management; problems with self-esteem; and issues associated with aging and mental and emotional health. Counsels clients and patients, individually and in group sessions, to assist in overcoming dependencies, adjusting to life, and making changes. Modifies treatment plan to comply with changes in client's status. Intervenes as advocate for client or patient to resolve emergency problems in crisis situation. Supervises and directs other workers providing services to client or patient. Plans and conducts programs to prevent substance abuse or improve health and counseling services in community. Refers patient, client, or family to community resources to assist in recovery from mental or physical illness. Monitors, evaluates, and records client progress according to measurable goals described in treatment and care plan. Counsels family members to assist in understanding, dealing with, and supporting client or patient. Formulates or coordinates program plan for treatment, care, and rehabilitation of client or patient, based on social work experience and knowledge. Interviews clients, reviews records, and confers with other professionals to evaluate mental or physical condition of client or patient. **SKILLS—Social Perceptiveness:** Being aware of others' reactions and understanding why they react as they do. Service Orientation: Actively looking for ways to help people. Management of Financial Resources: Determining how money will be spent to get the work done and accounting for these expenditures. Critical Thinking: Using logic and reasoning to identify the strengths and weaknesses of alternative solutions, conclusions, or approaches to problems. Active Listening: Giving full attention to what other people are saying, taking time to understand the points being made, asking questions as appropriate, and not interrupting at inappropriate times. Reading Comprehension: Understanding written sentences and paragraphs in work-related documents.

GOE INFORMATION—Interest Area: 12. Education and Social Service. **Work Group:** 12.02. Social Services. **Other Job Titles in This Work Group:** Child, Family, and School Social Workers; Clergy; Clinical Psychologists; Clinical, Counseling, and School Psychologists; Community and Social Service Specialists, All Other; Counseling Psychologists; Counselors, All Other; Directors, Religious Activities and Education; Marriage and Family Therapists; Medical and Public Health Social Workers; Mental Health and Substance Abuse Social Workers; Probation Officers and Correctional Treatment Specialists; Rehabilitation Counselors; Religious Workers, All Other; Residential Advisors; Social and Human Service Assistants;

Social Workers, All Other; Substance Abuse and Behavioral Disorder Counselors. **PERSONALITY TYPE**—Social. Social occupations frequently involve working with, communicating with, and teaching people. These occupations often involve helping or providing service to others.

EDUCATION/TRAINING PROGRAM(S)—Alcohol/Drug Abuse Counseling; Clinical and Medical Social Work; Mental Health Services, Other. **RELATED KNOWLEDGE/COURSES—Therapy and Counseling:** Knowledge of principles, methods, and procedures for diagnosis, treatment, and rehabilitation of physical and mental dysfunctions and for career counseling and guidance. **Customer and Personal Service:** Knowledge of principles and processes for providing customer and personal services. This includes customer needs assessment, meeting quality standards for services, and evaluation of customer satisfaction. **Psychology:** Knowledge of human behavior and performance; individual differences in ability, personality, and interests; learning and motivation; psychological research methods; and the assessment and treatment of behavioral and affective disorders. **Education and Training:** Knowledge of principles and methods for curriculum and training design, teaching and instruction for individuals and groups, and the measurement of training effects. **English Language:** Knowledge of the structure and content of the English language, including the meaning and spelling of words, rules of composition, and grammar.

Microbiologists

- ▲ Education/Training Required: Doctoral degree
- ▲ Annual Earnings: $48,890
- ▲ Growth: 21%
- ▲ Annual Job Openings: 5,000
- ▲ Self-Employed: 4.9%
- ▲ Part-Time: 6.6%

Investigate the growth, structure, development, and other characteristics of microscopic organisms, such as bacteria, algae, or fungi. Includes medical microbiologists who study the relationship between organisms and disease or the effects of antibiotics on microorganisms. Studies growth, structure, development, and general characteristics of bacteria and other micro-organisms. Studies growth structure and development of viruses and rickettsiae. Examines physiological, morphological, and cultural characteristics, using microscope, to identify micro-organisms. Observes action of micro-organisms upon living tissues of plants, higher animals, and other micro-organisms and on dead organic matter. Conducts chemical analyses of substances, such as acids, alcohols, and enzymes. Prepares technical reports and recommendations based upon research outcomes. Researches use of bacteria and micro-organisms to develop vitamins, antibiotics, amino acids, grain alcohol, sugars, and polymers. Isolates and makes cultures of bacteria or other micro-organisms in prescribed media, controlling moisture, aeration, temperature, and nutrition. **SKILLS—Science:** Using scientific rules and methods to solve problems. **Reading Comprehension:** Understanding written sentences and paragraphs in work-related documents. **Writing:** Communicating effectively in writing as appropriate for the needs of the audience. **Active Learning:** Understanding the implications of new information for both current and future problem-solving and decision-making. **Mathematics:** Using mathematics to solve problems.

GOE INFORMATION—Interest Area: 02. Science, Math, and Engineering. **Work Group:** 02.03. Life Sciences. **Other Job Titles in This Work Group:** Agricultural and Food Science Technicians; Agricultural Technicians; Animal Scientists; Biochemists; Biochemists and Biophysicists; Biological Scientists, All Other; Biologists; Biophysicists; Conservation Scientists; Environmental Scientists and Specialists, Including Health; Epidemiologists; Food Science Technicians; Food Scientists and Technologists; Foresters; Life Scientists, All Other; Medical Scientists, Except Epidemiologists; Plant Scientists; Range Managers; Soil and Plant Scientists; Soil Conservationists; Soil Scientists; Zoologists and Wildlife Biologists. **PERSONALITY TYPE**—Investigative. Investigative occupations frequently involve working with ideas and require an extensive amount of thinking. These occupations can involve searching for facts and figuring out problems mentally.

EDUCATION/TRAINING PROGRAM(S)— Cell and Molecular Biology, Other; Microbiology/Bacteriology. **RELATED KNOWLEDGE/COURSES—Biology:** Knowledge of plant and animal organisms and their tissues, cells, functions, interdependencies, and interactions with each other and the environment. **Mathematics:** Knowledge of arithmetic, algebra, geometry, calculus, and statistics and their applications. **Chemistry:** Knowledge of the chemical composition, structure, and properties of substances and of the chemical processes and transformations that they undergo. This includes uses of chemicals and their interactions, danger signs, production techniques, and disposal methods. **Administration and Management:** Knowledge of business and management principles involved in strategic planning, resource allocation, human resources modeling, leadership technique, production methods, and coordination of people and resources. **English Language:** Knowledge of the structure and content of the English language, including the meaning and spelling of words, rules of composition, and grammar.

Middle School Teachers, Except Special and Vocational Education

- ▲ Education/Training Required: Bachelor's degree
- ▲ Annual Earnings: $39,750
- ▲ Growth: 10%
- ▲ Annual Job Openings: 54,000
- ▲ Self-Employed: 0%
- ▲ Part-Time: 10.6%

Teach students in public or private schools in one or more subjects at the middle, intermediate, or junior high level, which falls between elementary and senior high school as defined by applicable state laws and regulations. Instructs students, using various teaching methods such as lecture and demonstration. Prepares course outlines and objectives according to curriculum guidelines or state and local requirements. Evaluates, records, and reports student progress. Maintains discipline in classroom. Selects, stores, orders, issues, and inventories classroom equipment, materials, and supplies. Performs advisory duties, such as sponsoring student organizations or clubs, helping students select courses, and counseling students with problems. Keeps attendance records. Participates in faculty and professional meetings, educational conferences, and teacher training workshops. Confers with students, parents, and school counselors to resolve behavioral and academic problems. Uses audiovisual aids and other materials to supplement presentations. Assigns lessons and corrects homework.

Develops and administers tests. **SKILLS**—Learning Strategies: Selecting and using training/instructional methods and procedures appropriate for the situation when learning or teaching new things. Speaking: Talking to others to convey information effectively. Reading Comprehension: Understanding written sentences and paragraphs in work-related documents. Mathematics: Using mathematics to solve problems. Instructing: Teaching others how to do something.

GOE INFORMATION—Interest Area: 12. Education and Social Service. **Work Group:** 12.03. Educational Services. **Other Job Titles in This Work Group:** Adult Literacy, Remedial Education, and GED Teachers and Instructors; Agricultural Sciences Teachers, Postsecondary; Anthropology and Archeology Teachers, Postsecondary; Architecture Teachers, Postsecondary; Archivists; Area, Ethnic, and Cultural Studies Teachers, Postsecondary; Art, Drama, and Music Teachers, Postsecondary; Atmospheric, Earth, Marine, and Space

Sciences Teachers, Postsecondary; Audio-Visual Collections Specialists; Biological Science Teachers, Postsecondary; Business Teachers, Postsecondary; Chemistry Teachers, Postsecondary; Child Care Workers; Communications Teachers, Postsecondary; Computer Science Teachers, Postsecondary; Criminal Justice and Law Enforcement Teachers, Postsecondary; Curators; Economics Teachers, Postsecondary; Education Teachers, Postsecondary; Educational Psychologists; Educational, Vocational, and School Counselors; Elementary School Teachers, Except Special Education; Engineering Teachers, Postsecondary; English Language and Literature Teachers, Postsecondary; Environmental Science Teachers, Postsecondary; Farm and Home Management Advisors; Foreign Language and Literature Teachers, Postsecondary; Forestry and Conservation Science Teachers, Postsecondary; Geography Teachers, Postsecondary; Graduate Teaching Assistants; Health Specialties Teachers, Postsecondary; History Teachers, Postsecondary; Home Economics Teachers, Postsecondary; Kindergarten Teachers, Except Special Education; Law Teachers, Postsecondary; Librarians; Library Assistants, Clerical; others. **PERSONALITY TYPE**—Social. Social occupations frequently involve working with, communicating with, and teaching people. These occupations often involve helping or providing service to others.

EDUCATION/TRAINING PROGRAM(S)— Art Teacher Education; Computer Teacher Education; English Teacher Education; Foreign Languages Teacher Education; Health Occupations Teacher Education (Vocational); Health Teacher Education; History Teacher Education; Home Economics Teacher Education (Vocational); Junior High/Intermediate/Middle School Teacher Education; Mathematics Teacher Education; Music Teacher Education; Physical Education Teaching and Coaching; Reading Teacher Education; Science Teacher Education, General; Social Science Teacher Education; Social Studies Teacher Education; Teacher Education, Specific Academic and Vocational Programs; Technology Teacher Education/Industrial Arts Teacher Education. **RELATED KNOWLEDGE/COURSES—Education and Training:** Knowledge of principles and methods for curriculum and training design, teaching and instruction for individuals and groups, and the measurement of training effects. **English Language:** Knowledge of the structure and content of the English language, including the meaning and spelling of words, rules of composition, and grammar. **Mathematics:** Knowledge of arithmetic, algebra, geometry, calculus, and statistics and their applications. **Therapy and Counseling:** Knowledge of principles, methods, and procedures for diagnosis, treatment, and rehabilitation of physical and mental dysfunctions and for career counseling and guidance. **Clerical Studies:** Knowledge of administrative and clerical procedures and systems such as word processing, managing files and records, stenography and transcription, designing forms, and other office procedures and terminology. **Psychology:** Knowledge of human behavior and performance; individual differences in ability, personality, and interests; learning and motivation; psychological research methods; and the assessment and treatment of behavioral and affective disorders.

Mining and Geological Engineers, Including Mining Safety Engineers

▲ Education/Training Required: Bachelor's degree

▲ Annual Earnings: $60,820

▲ Growth: -1%

▲ Annual Job Openings: Fewer than 500

▲ Self-Employed: 0%

▲ Part-Time: 3.1%

Determine the location and plan the extraction of coal, metallic ores, nonmetallic minerals, and building materials, such as stone and gravel. Work involves conducting preliminary surveys of deposits or undeveloped mines and planning their development; examining deposits or mines to determine whether they can be worked at a profit; making geological and topographical surveys; evolving methods of mining best suited to character, type, and size of deposits; and supervising mining operations. Lays out and directs mine construction operations. Evaluates data to develop new mining products, equipment, or processes. Designs, implements, and monitors facility projects, such as water, communication, ventilation, drainage, power supply, and conveyor systems. Prepares technical reports for use by mining, engineering, and management personnel. Conducts or collaborates in geological exploration and reviews maps and drilling logs to determine location, size, accessibility, and value of mineral deposits or optimal oil and gas reservoir locations. Provides technical consultation during drilling operations. Tests air to detect toxic gases and recommends alterations or installation of ventilation shafts, partitions, or equipment to remedy problem. Trains mine personnel in safe working practices and first aid. Monitors production rate of gas, oil, or minerals from wells or mines. Determines methods to extract minerals, considering factors such as safety, optimal costs, and deposit characteristics. Designs and maintains protective and rescue equipment and safety devices. Inspects mining areas for unsafe structures, equipment, and working conditions. Devises methods to solve environmental problems and reclaim mine sites. Plans and coordinates mining processes and labor utilization. Plans, conducts, or directs others in performing mining experiments to test or prove research findings. **SKILLS**—Operations Analysis: Analyzing needs and product requirements to create a design. Judgment and Decision Making: Considering the relative costs and benefits of potential actions to choose the most appropriate one. Equipment Selection: Determining the kind of tools and equipment needed to do a job. Mathematics: Using mathematics to solve problems. Active Learning: Understanding the implications of new information for both current and future problem-solving and decision-making.

GOE INFORMATION—Interest Area: 02. Science, Math, and Engineering. **Work Group:** 02.07. Engineering. **Other Job Titles in This Work Group:** Aerospace Engineers; Agricultural Engineers; Architects, Except Landscape and Naval; Biomedical Engineers; Chemical Engineers; Civil Engineers; Computer Hardware Engineers; Computer Software Engineers, Applications; Computer Software Engineers, Systems Software; Electrical Engineers; Electronics Engineers, Except Computer; Engineers, All Other; Environmental Engineers; Fire-Prevention and Protection Engineers; Health and Safety Engineers, Except Mining Safety Engineers and Inspectors; Industrial Engineers; Industrial Safety and Health Engineers; Landscape Architects; Marine Architects; Marine Engineers; Marine Engineers and Naval Architects; Materials Engineers; Mechanical Engineers; Nuclear Engineers; Petroleum Engineers; Product Safety Engineers; Sales Engineers. **PERSONALITY TYPE**—Investigative. Investigative occupations frequently involve working with ideas and require an extensive amount of thinking. These occupations can involve searching for facts and figuring out problems mentally.

EDUCATION/TRAINING PROGRAM(S)—Architectural Engineering; Bioengineering and Biomedical Engineering; Engineering Design; Engineering Mechanics; Engineering Physics; Engineering Science; Engineering, General; Engineering, Other; Engineering/Industrial Management; Environmental/Environmental Health Engineering; Geological Engineering; Geophysical Engineering; Mining and Mineral Engineering; Ocean Engineering; Systems Engineering; Textile Sciences and Engineering. **RELATED KNOWLEDGE/COURSES—Engineering and Technology:** Knowledge of the practical application of engineering science and technology. This includes applying principles, techniques, procedures, and equipment to the design and production of various goods and services. **Mathematics:** Knowledge of arithmetic, algebra, geometry, calculus, and statistics and their applications. **Physics:** Knowledge and prediction of physical principles and laws and their interrelationships and applications to understanding fluid, material, and atmospheric dynamics and mechanical, electrical, atomic, and sub-atomic structures and processes. **Administration and Management:** Knowledge of business and management principles involved in strategic planning, resource allocation, human resources modeling, leadership technique, production methods, and coordination of people and resources. **Design:** Knowledge of design techniques, tools, and principles involved in production of precision technical plans, blueprints, drawings, and models.

Multi-Media Artists and Animators

- ▲ Education/Training Required: Bachelor's degree
- ▲ Annual Earnings: $41,130
- ▲ Growth: 22%
- ▲ Annual Job Openings: 8,000
- ▲ Self-Employed: 60.9%
- ▲ Part-Time: 24%

Create special effects, animation, or other visual images using film, video, computers, or other electronic tools and media for use in products or creations such as computer games, movies, music videos, and commercials. SKILLS—No data available.

GOE INFORMATION—Interest Area: 01. Arts, Entertainment, and Media. Work Group: 01.04. Visual Arts. Other Job Titles in This Work Group: Cartoonists; Commercial and Industrial Designers; Designers, All Other; Exhibit Designers; Fashion Designers; Fine Artists, Including Painters, Sculptors, and Illustrators; Floral Designers; Graphic Designers; Interior Designers; Merchandise Displayers and Window Trimmers; Painters and Illustrators; Sculptors; Set and Exhibit Designers; Set Designers; Sketch Artists. PERSONALITY TYPE—No data available.

EDUCATION/TRAINING PROGRAM(S)—Art, General; Drawing; Graphic Design, Commercial Art and Illustration; Intermedia; Painting; Printmaking. RELATED KNOWLEDGE/COURSES—No data available.

Music Arrangers and Orchestrators

- ▲ Education/Training Required: Bachelor's degree
- ▲ Annual Earnings: $31,510
- ▲ Growth: 13%
- ▲ Annual Job Openings: 9,000
- ▲ Self-Employed: 25.8%
- ▲ Part-Time: 53.5%

Write and transcribe musical scores. Composes musical scores for orchestra, band, choral group, or individual instrumentalist or vocalist, using knowledge of music theory and instrumental and vocal capabilities. Transposes music from one voice or instrument to another to accommodate particular musician in musical group. Adapts musical composition for orchestra, band, choral group, or individual to style for which it was not originally written. Copies parts from score for individual performers. Determines voice, instrument, harmonic structure, rhythm, tempo, and tone balance to achieve desired effect. Transcribes musical parts from score written by arranger or orchestrator for each instrument or voice, using knowl-edge of music composition. SKILLS—Coordination: Adjusting actions in relation to others' actions. Writing: Communicating effectively in writing as appropriate for the needs of the audience. Active Listening: Giving full attention to what other people are saying, taking time to understand the points being made, asking questions as appropriate, and not interrupting at inappropriate times. Complex Problem Solving: Identifying complex problems and reviewing related information to develop and evaluate options and implement solutions. Reading Comprehension: Understanding written sentences and paragraphs in work-related documents.

GOE INFORMATION—**Interest Area:** 01. Arts, Entertainment, and Media. **Work Group:** 01.05. Performing Arts. **Other Job Titles in This Work Group:** Actors; Choreographers; Composers; Dancers; Directors—Stage, Motion Pictures, Television, and Radio; Music Directors; Music Directors and Composers; Musicians and Singers; Musicians, Instrumental; Public Address System and Other Announcers; Radio and Television Announcers; Singers; Talent Directors. **PERSONALITY TYPE**—Artistic. Artistic occupations frequently involve working with forms, designs, and patterns. They often require self-expression, and the work can be done without following a clear set of rules.

EDUCATION/TRAINING PROGRAM(S)—Music—General Performance; Music—Voice and Choral/Opera Performance; Music Business Management and Merchandising; Music Conducting; Music Theory and Composition; Music, General; Music, Other; Musicology and Ethnomusicology; Religious/Sacred Music. **RELATED KNOWLEDGE/COURSES—Fine Arts:** Knowledge of the theory and techniques required to compose, produce, and perform works of music, dance, visual arts, drama, and sculpture. **English Language:** Knowledge of the structure and content of the English language, including the meaning and spelling of words, rules of composition, and grammar.

> ▲ Education/Training Required: Master's degree
> ▲ Annual Earnings: $31,510
> ▲ Growth: 13%
> ▲ Annual Job Openings: 9,000
> ▲ Self-Employed: 25.8%
> ▲ Part-Time: 53.5%

Music Directors

Direct and conduct instrumental or vocal performances by musical groups, such as orchestras or choirs. Directs group at rehearsals and live or recorded performances to achieve desired effects, such as tonal and harmonic balance, dynamics, rhythm, and tempo. Positions members within group to obtain balance among instrumental sections. Auditions and selects vocal and instrumental groups for musical presentations. Transcribes musical compositions and melodic lines to adapt them to or create particular style for group. Engages services of composer to write score. Issues assignments and reviews work of staff in such areas as scoring, arranging, and copying music and lyric and vocal coaching. Selects vocal, instrumental, and recorded music suitable to type of performance requirements to accommodate ability of group. **SKILLS**—Coordination: Adjusting actions in relation to others' actions. Time Management: Managing one's own time and the time of others. Management of Personnel Resources: Motivating, developing, and directing people as they work, identifying the best people for the job. Monitoring: Monitoring/Assessing your performance or that of other individuals or organizations to make improvements or take corrective action. Instructing: Teaching others how to do something.

GOE INFORMATION—**Interest Area:** 01. Arts, Entertainment, and Media. **Work Group:** 01.05. Performing Arts. **Other Job Titles in This Work Group:** Actors; Choreographers; Composers; Dancers; Directors—Stage, Motion Pictures, Television, and Radio; Music Arrangers and Orchestrators; Music Directors and Composers; Musicians and Singers; Musicians, Instrumental; Public Address System and Other Announcers; Radio and Television Announcers; Singers; Talent Directors. **PERSONALITY TYPE**—Artistic. Artistic occupations frequently involve working with forms, designs, and patterns. They often require self-expression, and the work can be done without following a clear set of rules.

EDUCATION/TRAINING PROGRAM(S)—Music—General Performance; Music—Voice and Choral/Opera Performance; Music Business Management and Merchandising; Music Conducting; Music Theory and Composition; Music, General; Music, Other; Musicology and Ethnomusicology; Religious/Sacred Music.

RELATED KNOWLEDGE/COURSES—Fine Arts: Knowledge of the theory and techniques required to compose, produce, and perform works of music, dance, visual arts, drama, and sculpture. **Administration and Management:** Knowledge of business and management principles involved in strategic planning, resource allocation, human resources modeling, leadership technique, production methods, and coordination of people and resources. **Personnel and Human Resources:** Knowledge of principles and procedures for personnel recruitment, selection, training, compensation and benefits, labor relations and negotiation, and personnel information systems. **English Language:** Knowledge of the structure and content of the English language, including the meaning and spelling of words, rules of composition, and grammar. **Transportation:** Knowledge of principles and methods for moving people or goods by air, rail, sea, or road, including the relative costs and benefits. **Psychology:** Knowledge of human behavior and performance; individual differences in ability, personality, and interests; learning and motivation; psychological research methods; and the assessment and treatment of behavioral and affective disorders. **Education and Training:** Knowledge of principles and methods for curriculum and training design, teaching and instruction for individuals and groups, and the measurement of training effects.

Music Directors and Composers

- ▲ Education/Training Required: Master's degree
- ▲ Annual Earnings: $31,510
- ▲ Growth: 13%
- ▲ Annual Job Openings: 9,000
- ▲ Self-Employed: 25.8%
- ▲ Part-Time: 53.5%

Conduct, direct, plan, and lead instrumental or vocal performances by musical groups, such as orchestras, choirs, and glee clubs. Includes arrangers, composers, choral directors, and orchestrators. SKILLS—No data available.

GOE INFORMATION—**Interest Area:** 01. Arts, Entertainment, and Media. **Work Group:** 01.05. Performing Arts. **Other Job Titles in This Work Group:** Actors; Choreographers; Composers; Dancers; Directors—Stage, Motion Pictures, Television, and Radio; Music Arrangers and Orchestrators; Music Directors; Musicians and Singers; Musicians, Instrumental; Public Address System and Other Announcers; Radio and Television Announcers; Singers; Talent Directors. PERSONALITY TYPE—No data available.

EDUCATION/TRAINING PROGRAM(S)—Music—General Performance; Music—Voice and Choral/Opera Performance; Music Business Management and Merchandising; Music Conducting; Music Theory and Composition; Music, General; Music, Other; Musicology and Ethnomusicology; Religious/Sacred Music. RELATED KNOWLEDGE/COURSES—No data available.

Natural Sciences Managers

▲ Education/Training Required: Work experience, plus degree
▲ Annual Earnings: $75,880
▲ Growth: 8%
▲ Annual Job Openings: 4,000
▲ Self-Employed: 0%
▲ Part-Time: 6.1%

Plan, direct, or coordinate activities in such fields as life sciences, physical sciences, mathematics, and statistics and research and development in these fields. Schedules, directs, and assigns duties to engineers, technicians, researchers, and other staff. Prepares and administers budget, approves and reviews expenditures, and prepares financial reports. Confers with scientists, engineers, regulators, and others to plan and review projects and to provide technical assistance. Provides technical assistance to agencies conducting environmental studies. Advises and assists in obtaining patents or other legal requirements. Reviews project activities and prepares and reviews research, testing, and operational reports. Coordinates successive phases of problem analysis, solution proposals, and testing. Plans and directs research, development, and production activities of chemical plant. **SKILLS**—Coordination: Adjusting actions in relation to others' actions. Reading Comprehension: Understanding written sentences and paragraphs in work-related documents. Science: Using scientific rules and methods to solve problems. Management of Material Resources: Obtaining and seeing to the appropriate use of equipment, facilities, and materials needed to do certain work. Time Management: Managing one's own time and the time of others. Critical Thinking: Using logic and reasoning to identify the strengths and weaknesses of alternative solutions, conclusions, or approaches to problems. Active Learning: Understanding the implications of new information for both current and future problem-solving and decision-making.

GOE INFORMATION—**Interest Area:** 02. Science, Math, and Engineering. **Work Group:** 02.01. Managerial Work in Science, Math, and Engineering. **Other Job Titles in This Work Group:** Computer and Information Systems Managers; Engineering Managers. **PERSONALITY TYPE**—Investigative. Investigative occupations frequently involve working with ideas and require an extensive amount of thinking. These occupations can involve searching for facts and figuring out problems mentally.

EDUCATION/TRAINING PROGRAM(S)—Acoustics; Analytical Chemistry; Anatomy; Applied Mathematics, General; Applied Mathematics, Other; Astronomy; Astrophysics; Atmospheric Sciences and Meteorology; Biochemistry; Biological and Physical Sciences; Biological Immunology; Biological Sciences/Life Sciences, Other; Biology, General; Biometrics; Biophysics; Biopsychology; Biostatistics; Biotechnology Research; Botany, General; Botany, Other; Business Administration and Management, General; Cell and Molecular Biology, Other; Cell Biology; Chemical and Atomic/Molecular Physics; Chemistry, General; Chemistry, Other; Earth and Planetary Sciences; Ecology; Elementary Particle Physics; Entomology; Environmental Science/Studies; Evolutionary Biology; Genetics, Plant and Animal; Geochemistry; Geological and Related Sciences, Other; Geology; Geophysics and Seismology; Inorganic Chemistry; Marine/Aquatic Biology; Mathematical Statistics; Mathematics; Mathematics and Computer Science; Mathematics, Other; Medicinal/Pharmaceutical Chemistry; Metallurgy; Microbiology/Bacteriology; Miscellaneous Biological Specializations, Other; Miscellaneous Physical Sciences, Other; Molecular Biology; Natural Resources Conservation, General; Neuroscience; Nuclear Physics; Nutritional Sciences; Oceanography; Operations Research; Optics; Organic Chemistry; Paleontology; Parasitology; Pathology, Human and Animal; Pharmacology, Human and Animal; Physical and Theoretical Chemistry; Physical Sciences, General; Physical Sciences, Other; Physics, General; Physics, Other; Physiology, Human and Animal; Plant Pathology; Plant Physiology; Plasma and High-Temperature Physics; Polymer Chemistry; Radiation Biology/Radiobiology; Science, Technology and Society; Solid State and Low-Temperature Physics; Theoretical and Mathematical Physics; Toxicology; Virology; Zoology, General; Zoology, Other. **RELATED KNOWLEDGE/COURSES—Administration and Management:** Knowledge of business and management principles involved in strategic planning, resource allocation, human resources modeling, leadership technique, production methods, and coordination of people and resources. **Mathematics:** Knowledge of arithmetic, algebra, geometry, calculus, and statistics and their applications. **English Language:** Knowledge of the structure and content of the English language, including the meaning and spelling of words, rules of composition, and grammar. **Chemistry:** Knowledge of the chemical composition, structure, and properties of substances and of the chemical processes and transformations that they undergo. This includes uses of chemicals and their interactions, danger signs, production techniques, and disposal methods. **Economics and Accounting:** Knowledge of economic and accounting principles and practices, the financial markets, banking, and the analysis and reporting of financial data.

Network and Computer Systems Administrators

- ▲ Education/Training Required: Bachelor's degree
- ▲ Annual Earnings: $51,280
- ▲ Growth: 82%
- ▲ Annual Job Openings: 18,000
- ▲ Self-Employed: 49.4%
- ▲ Part-Time: 7.2%

Install, configure, and support an organization's local area network (LAN), wide area network (WAN), and Internet system or a segment of a network system. Maintain network hardware and software. Monitor network to ensure network availability to all system users and perform necessary maintenance to support network availability. May supervise other network support and client server specialists and plan, coordinate, and implement network security measures. **SKILLS**—No data available.

GOE INFORMATION—Interest Area: 02. Science, Math, and Engineering. **Work Group:** 02.06. Mathematics and Computers. **Other Job Titles in This Work Group:** Actuaries; Computer and Information Scientists, Research; Computer Programmers; Computer Security Specialists; Computer Specialists, All Other; Computer Support Specialists; Computer Systems Analysts; Database Administrators; Mathematical Science Occupations, All Other; Mathematical Technicians; Mathematicians; Network Systems and Data Communications Analysts; Operations Research Analysts; Statistical Assistants; Statisticians. **PERSONALITY TYPE**—No data available.

EDUCATION/TRAINING PROGRAM(S)—Business Systems Networking and Telecommunications; Computer and Information Sciences, General; Computer and Information Sciences, Other; Computer Systems Analysis; Information Sciences and Systems. **RELATED KNOWLEDGE/COURSES**—No data available.

Network Systems and Data Communications Analysts

- ▲ Education/Training Required: Bachelor's degree
- ▲ Annual Earnings: $54,510
- ▲ Growth: 78%
- ▲ Annual Job Openings: 9,000
- ▲ Self-Employed: 49.4%
- ▲ Part-Time: 7.2%

Analyze, design, test, and evaluate network systems, such as local area networks (LAN), wide area networks (WAN), Internet, intranet, and other data communications systems. Perform network modeling, analysis, and planning. Research and recommend network and data communications hardware and software. Includes telecommunications specialists who deal with the interfacing of computer and communications equipment. May supervise computer programmers. Analyzes test data and recommends hardware or software for purchase. Develops and writes procedures for installation, use, and solving problems of communications hardware and software. Assists users to identify and solve data communication problems. Trains users in use of equipment. Visits vendors to learn about available products or services. Conducts survey to determine user needs. Tests and evaluates hardware and software to determine efficiency, reliability, and compatibility with existing system. Reads technical manuals and brochures to determine equipment which meets establishment requirements. Monitors system performance. Identifies areas of operation which need upgraded equipment, such as modems, fiber-optic cables, and telephone wires. **SKILLS**—Reading Comprehension: Understanding written sentences and paragraphs in work-related documents. Troubleshooting: Determining causes of operating errors and deciding what to do about them. Management of Material Resources: Obtaining and seeing to the appropriate use of equipment, facilities, and materials needed to do certain work. Writing: Communicating effectively in writing as appropriate for the needs of the audience. Active Learning: Understanding the implications of new information for both current and future problem-solving and decision-making. Operations Analysis: Analyzing needs and product require-

ments to create a design. Active Listening: Giving full attention to what other people are saying, taking time to understand the points being made, asking questions as appropriate, and not interrupting at inappropriate times.

GOE INFORMATION—**Interest Area:** 02. Science, Math, and Engineering. **Work Group:** 02.06. Mathematics and Computers. **Other Job Titles in This Work Group:** Actuaries; Computer and Information Scientists, Research; Computer Programmers; Computer Security Specialists; Computer Specialists, All Other; Computer Support Specialists; Computer Systems Analysts; Database Administrators; Mathematical Science Occupations, All Other; Mathematical Technicians; Mathematicians; Network and Computer Systems Administrators; Operations Research Analysts; Statistical Assistants; Statisticians. **PERSONALITY TYPE**—Investigative. Investigative occupations frequently involve working with ideas and require an extensive amount of thinking. These occupations can involve searching for facts and figuring out problems mentally.

EDUCATION/TRAINING PROGRAM(S)—Business Information and Data Processing Services, Other; Business Systems Analysis and Design; Business Systems Networking and Telecommunications; Computer and Information Sciences, General; Computer and Information Sciences, Other; Computer Science; Computer Systems Analysis; Data Processing Technologist/Technician; Information Sciences and Systems. **RELATED KNOWLEDGE/COURSES**—Telecommunications: Knowledge of transmission, broadcasting, switching, control, and operation of telecommunications systems. **Computers and Electronics:** Knowledge of circuit boards, processors, chips, electronic equipment, and computer hardware and software, including applications and programming. **Mathematics:** Knowledge of arithmetic, algebra, geometry, calculus, and statistics and their applications. **Education and Training:** Knowledge of principles and methods for curriculum and training design, teaching and instruction for individuals and groups, and the measurement of training effects. **Public Safety and Security:** Knowledge of relevant equipment, policies, procedures, and strategies to promote effective local, state, or national security operations for the protection of people, data, property, and institutions.

Nuclear Engineers

- ▲ Education/Training Required: Bachelor's degree
- ▲ Annual Earnings: $79,360
- ▲ Growth: 2%
- ▲ Annual Job Openings: 1,000
- ▲ Self-Employed: 0%
- ▲ Part-Time: 3.1%

Conduct research on nuclear engineering problems or apply principles and theory of nuclear science to problems concerned with release, control, and utilization of nuclear energy and nuclear waste disposal. Determines potential hazard and accident conditions which may exist in fuel handling and storage and recommends preventive measures. Performs experiments to determine acceptable methods of nuclear material usage, nuclear fuel reclamation, and waste disposal. Plans and designs nuclear research to discover facts or to test, prove, or modify known nuclear theories. Conducts tests to research nuclear fuel behavior and nuclear machinery and equipment performance. Analyzes available data and consults with other scientists to determine parameters of experimentation and suitability of analytical models. Formulates equations that describe phenomena occurring during fission of nuclear fuels and develops analytical models for research. Examines accidents and obtains data to formulate preventive measures. Synthesizes analyses of test results and prepares technical reports of findings and recommendations. Directs operating and maintenance activities of operational nuclear facility. Writes operational instructions relative to nuclear plant operation and nuclear fuel and waste handling and disposal. Maintains reports to summarize work and document plant operations. Formulates and initiates corrective actions and orders plant shutdown in emergency situations. Computes cost estimates of construction projects, prepares project proposals, and discusses projects with vendors, contractors, and nuclear facility's review board. Designs and over-sees construction and operation of nuclear fuels reprocessing systems and reclamation systems. Designs and develops nuclear machinery and equipment, such as reactor cores, radiation shielding, and associated instrumentation and control mechanisms. Monitors nuclear operations to identify potential or inherent design, construction, or operational problems to ensure safe operations. Inspects nuclear fuels, waste, equipment, test-reactor vessel and related systems, and control instrumentation to identify potential problems or hazards. Evaluates research findings to develop new concepts of thermonuclear analysis and new uses of radioactive models. **SKILLS—Science:** Using scientific rules and methods to solve problems. **Mathematics:** Using mathematics to solve problems. **Operations Analysis:** Analyzing needs and product requirements to create a design. **Active Learning:** Understanding the implications of new information for both current and future problem-solving and decision-making. **Judgment and Decision Making:** Considering the relative costs and benefits of potential actions to choose the most appropriate one.

GOE INFORMATION—Interest Area: 02. Science, Math, and Engineering. **Work Group:** 02.07. Engineering. **Other Job Titles in This Work Group:** Aerospace Engineers; Agricultural Engineers; Architects, Except Landscape and Naval; Biomedical Engineers; Chemical Engineers; Civil Engineers; Computer Hardware Engineers; Computer Software Engineers, Applications; Computer Software Engineers, Systems Software; Electrical Engineers; Electronics Engineers, Except Computer;

Engineers, All Other; Environmental Engineers; Fire-Prevention and Protection Engineers; Health and Safety Engineers, Except Mining Safety Engineers and Inspectors; Industrial Engineers; Industrial Safety and Health Engineers; Landscape Architects; Marine Architects; Marine Engineers; Marine Engineers and Naval Architects; Materials Engineers; Mechanical Engineers; Mining and Geological Engineers, Including Mining Safety Engineers; Petroleum Engineers; Product Safety Engineers; Sales Engineers. **PERSONALITY TYPE**—Investigative. Investigative occupations frequently involve working with ideas and require an extensive amount of thinking. These occupations can involve searching for facts and figuring out problems mentally.

EDUCATION/TRAINING PROGRAM(S)—Nuclear Engineering. **RELATED KNOWLEDGE/COURSES**—**Engineering and Technology:** Knowledge of the practical application of engineering science and technology. This includes applying principles, techniques,

procedures, and equipment to the design and production of various goods and services. **Physics:** Knowledge and prediction of physical principles and laws and their interrelationships and applications to understanding fluid, material, and atmospheric dynamics and mechanical, electrical, atomic, and sub-atomic structures and processes. **Mathematics:** Knowledge of arithmetic, algebra, geometry, calculus, and statistics and their applications. **Design:** Knowledge of design techniques, tools, and principles involved in production of precision technical plans, blueprints, drawings, and models. **Administration and Management:** Knowledge of business and management principles involved in strategic planning, resource allocation, human resources modeling, leadership technique, production methods, and coordination of people and resources. **English Language:** Knowledge of the structure and content of the English language, including the meaning and spelling of words, rules of composition, and grammar.

Nuclear Equipment Operation Technicians

▲ Education/Training Required: Associate's degree

▲ Annual Earnings: $59,160

▲ Growth: 21%

▲ Annual Job Openings: Fewer than 500

▲ Self-Employed: 0.9%

▲ Part-Time: 11.7%

Operate equipment used for the release, control, and utilization of nuclear energy to assist scientists in laboratory and production activities. Sets control panel switches and activates equipment, such as nuclear reactor, particle accelerator, or gamma radiation equipment, according to specifications. Adjusts controls of equipment to control particle beam, chain reaction, or radiation, according to specifications. Installs instrumentation leads in reactor core to measure operating temperature and pressure according to mockups, blueprints, and diagrams. Controls laboratory compounding equipment enclosed in protective hot cell to prepare radioisotopes and other radioactive materials. Sets up and operates machines to saw fuel elements to size or to cut and polish test pieces, following blueprints and other specifications. Tests

physical, chemical, or metallurgical properties of experimental materials according to standardized procedures, using test equipment and measuring instruments. Modifies, devises, and maintains equipment used in operations. Disassembles, cleans, and decontaminates hot cells and reactor parts during maintenance shutdown, using slave manipulators, crane, and hand tools. Writes summary of activities or records experiment data in log for further analysis by engineers, scientists, or customers or for future reference. Communicates with maintenance personnel to ensure readiness of support systems and to warn of radiation hazards. Withdraws radioactive sample for analysis, fills container with prescribed quantity of material for shipment, or removes spent fuel elements. Transfers experimental materials to and from specified containers and to tube, chamber, or tunnel, using slave manipulators or extension tools. Positions fuel elements in reactor or environmental chamber according to specified configuration, using slave manipulators or extension tools. Reviews experiment schedule to determine specifications such as subatomic particle parameters, radiation time, dosage, and gamma intensity. Monitors instruments, gauges, and recording devices in control room during operation of equipment under direction of nuclear experimenter. Calculates equipment operating factors, such as radiation time, dosage, temperature, and pressure, using standard formulas and conversion tables. **SKILLS**—Mathematics: Using mathematics to solve problems. Science: Using scientific rules and methods to solve problems. Installation: Installing equipment, machines, wiring, or programs to meet specifications. Operation and Control: Controlling operations of equipment or systems. Reading Comprehension: Understanding written sentences and paragraphs in work-related documents.

GOE INFORMATION—**Interest Area:** 02. Science, Math, and Engineering. **Work Group:** 02.05. Laboratory Technology. **Other Job Titles in This Work Group:** Biological Technicians; Chemical Technicians; Environmental Science and Protection Technicians, Including Health; Geological and Petroleum Technicians; Geological Data Technicians; Geological Sample Test Technicians; Nuclear Technicians; Photographers, Scientific. **PERSONALITY TYPE**—Realistic. Realistic occupations frequently involve work activities that include prac-

tical, hands-on problems and solutions. They often deal with plants, animals, and real-world materials like wood, tools, and machinery. Many of the occupations require working outside and do not involve a lot of paperwork or working closely with others.

EDUCATION/TRAINING PROGRAM(S)— Industrial Radiologic Technologist/Technician; Nuclear and Industrial Radiologic Technologists/Technicians, Other; Nuclear/Nuclear Power Technologist/Technician. **RELATED KNOWLEDGE/COURSES**—**Engineering and Technology:** Knowledge of the practical application of engineering science and technology. This includes applying principles, techniques, procedures, and equipment to the design and production of various goods and services. **Physics:** Knowledge and prediction of physical principles and laws and their interrelationships and applications to understanding fluid, material, and atmospheric dynamics and mechanical, electrical, atomic, and sub-atomic structures and processes. **Public Safety and Security:** Knowledge of relevant equipment, policies, procedures, and strategies to promote effective local, state, or national security operations for the protection of people, data, property, and institutions. **Mathematics:** Knowledge of arithmetic, algebra, geometry, calculus, and statistics and their applications. **Chemistry:** Knowledge of the chemical composition, structure, and properties of substances and of the chemical processes and transformations that they undergo. This includes uses of chemicals and their interactions, danger signs, production techniques, and disposal methods.

Nuclear Medicine Technologists

▲ Education/Training Required: Associate's degree
▲ Annual Earnings: $44,130
▲ Growth: 22%
▲ Annual Job Openings: 1,000
▲ Self-Employed: 0%
▲ Part-Time: 17.5%

Prepare, administer, and measure radioactive isotopes in therapeutic, diagnostic, and tracer studies utilizing a variety of radioisotope equipment. Prepare stock solutions of radioactive materials

and calculate doses to be administered by radiologists. Subject patients to radiation. Execute blood volume, red cell survival, and fat absorption studies following standard laboratory techniques. Administers radiopharmaceuticals or radiation to patient to detect or treat diseases, using radioisotope equipment, under direction of physician. Measures glandular activity, blood volume, red cell survival, and radioactivity of patient, using scanners, Geiger counters, scintillometers, and other laboratory equipment. Maintains and calibrates radioisotope and laboratory equipment. Disposes of radioactive materials and stores radiopharmaceuticals, following radiation safety procedures. Develops treatment procedures for nuclear medicine treatment programs. Positions radiation fields, radiation beams, and patient to develop most effective treatment of patient's disease, using computer. Calculates, measures, prepares, and records radiation dosage or radiopharmaceuticals, using computer and following physician's prescription and X rays. SKILLS—Reading Comprehension: Understanding written sentences and paragraphs in work-related documents. Mathematics: Using mathematics to solve problems. Instructing: Teaching others how to do something. Science: Using scientific rules and methods to solve problems. Speaking: Talking to others to convey information effectively. Active Listening: Giving full attention to what other people are saying, taking time to understand the points being made, asking questions as appropriate, and not interrupting at inappropriate times.

GOE INFORMATION—Interest Area: 14. Medical and Health Services. Work Group: 14.05. Medical Technology. Other Job Titles in This Work Group: Cardiovascular Technologists and Technicians; Diagnostic Medical Sonographers; Health Technologists and Techni-

cians, All Other; Medical and Clinical Laboratory Technicians; Medical and Clinical Laboratory Technologists; Medical Equipment Preparers; Orthotists and Prosthetists; Radiologic Technicians; Radiologic Technologists; Radiologic Technologists and Technicians. PERSONALITY TYPE—Investigative. Investigative occupations frequently involve working with ideas and require an extensive amount of thinking. These occupations can involve searching for facts and figuring out problems mentally.

EDUCATION/TRAINING PROGRAM(S)— Nuclear Medical Technologist/Technician. RELATED KNOWLEDGE/COURSES—Medicine and Dentistry: Knowledge of the information and techniques needed to diagnose and treat human injuries, diseases, and deformities. This includes symptoms, treatment alternatives, drug properties and interactions, and preventive health-care measures. Biology: Knowledge of plant and animal organisms and their tissues, cells, functions, interdependencies, and interactions with each other and the environment. Computers and Electronics: Knowledge of circuit boards, processors, chips, electronic equipment, and computer hardware and software, including applications and programming. Mathematics: Knowledge of arithmetic, algebra, geometry, calculus, and statistics and their applications. Chemistry: Knowledge of the chemical composition, structure, and properties of substances and of the chemical processes and transformations that they undergo. This includes uses of chemicals and their interactions, danger signs, production techniques, and disposal methods.

Nuclear Monitoring Technicians

▲ Education/Training Required: Associate's degree
▲ Annual Earnings: $59,160
▲ Growth: 21%
▲ Annual Job Openings: Fewer than 500
▲ Self-Employed: 0.9%
▲ Part-Time: 11.7%

Collect and test samples to monitor results of nuclear experiments and contamination of humans, facilities, and environment. Measures intensity and identifies type of radiation in work areas, equipment,

and materials, using radiation detectors and other instruments. Calculates safe radiation exposure time for personnel, using plant contamination readings and prescribed safe levels of radiation. Scans photographic emulsions exposed to direct radiation to compute track properties from standard formulas, using microscope with scales and protractors. Calibrates and maintains chemical instrumentation sensing elements and sampling system equipment, using calibrations instruments and hand tools. Prepares reports on contamination tests, material and equipment decontaminated, and methods used in decontamination process. Instructs personnel in radiation safety procedures and demonstrates use of protective clothing and equipment. Places radioactive waste, such as sweepings and broken sample bottles, into containers for disposal. Decontaminates objects by cleaning with soap or solvents or by abrading, using wire brush, buffing wheel or sandblasting machine. Enters data into computer to record characteristics of nuclear events and locating coordinates of particles. Weighs and mixes decontamination chemical solutions in tank and immerses objects in solution for specified time, using hoist. Determines or recommends radioactive decontamination procedures according to size and nature of equipment and degree of contamination. Confers with scientist directing project to determine significant events to watch for during test. Informs supervisors to take action when individual exposures or area radiation levels approach maximum permissible limits. Monitors personnel for length and intensity of exposure to radiation for health and safety purposes. Observes projected photographs to locate particle tracks and events and compiles lists of events from particle detectors. Assists in setting up equipment that automatically detects area radiation deviations and tests detection equipment to ensure accuracy. Collects samples of air, water, gases, and solids to determine radioactivity levels of contamination. **SKILLS**—Science: Using scientific rules and methods to solve problems. Mathematics: Using mathematics to solve problems. Reading Comprehension: Understanding written sentences and paragraphs in work-related documents. Speaking: Talking to others to convey information effectively. Operation Monitoring: Watching gauges, dials, or other indicators to make sure a machine is working properly. Critical Thinking: Using logic and reasoning to identify the strengths and weaknesses of alternative solutions, conclusions, or approaches to problems. Writing: Communicating effectively in writing as appropriate for the needs of the audience.

GOE INFORMATION—Interest Area: 04. Law, Law Enforcement, and Public Safety. **Work Group:** 04.04. Public Safety. **Other Job Titles in This Work Group:** Agricultural Inspectors; Aviation Inspectors; Compliance Officers, Except Agriculture, Construction, Health and Safety, and Transportation; Emergency Medical Technicians and Paramedics; Environmental Compliance Inspectors; Equal Opportunity Representatives and Officers; Financial Examiners; Fire Fighters; Fire Inspectors; Fire Inspectors and Investigators; Forest Fire Fighters; Forest Fire Inspectors and Prevention Specialists; Government Property Inspectors and Investigators; Licensing Examiners and Inspectors; Marine Cargo Inspectors; Municipal Fire Fighters; Occupational Health and Safety Specialists; Occupational Health and Safety Technicians; Public Transportation Inspectors. **PERSONALITY TYPE**—Realistic. Realistic occupations frequently involve work activities that include practical, hands-on problems and solutions. They often deal with plants, animals, and real-world materials like wood, tools, and machinery. Many of the occupations require working outside and do not involve a lot of paperwork or working closely with others.

EDUCATION/TRAINING PROGRAM(S)—Industrial Radiologic Technologist/Technician; Nuclear and Industrial Radiologic Technologists/Technicians, Other; Nuclear/Nuclear Power Technologist/Technician. **RELATED KNOWLEDGE/COURSES**—Physics: Knowledge and prediction of physical principles and laws and their interrelationships and applications to understanding fluid, material, and atmospheric dynamics and mechanical, electrical, atomic, and sub-atomic structures and processes. **Mathematics:** Knowledge of arithmetic, algebra, geometry, calculus, and statistics and their applications. **Public Safety and Security:** Knowledge of relevant equipment, policies, procedures, and strategies to promote effective local, state, or national security operations for the protection of people, data, property, and institutions. **Chemistry:** Knowledge of the chemical composition, structure, and properties of substances and of the chemical processes and transformations that they undergo. This includes uses of chemicals and their interactions, danger signs, production techniques, and disposal methods. **Education and Training:** Knowledge of principles and methods for curriculum and training design, teaching and instruction for individuals and groups, and the measurement of training effects.

Nuclear Technicians

- ▲ Education/Training Required: Associate's degree
- ▲ Annual Earnings: $59,160
- ▲ Growth: 21%
- ▲ Annual Job Openings: Fewer than 500
- ▲ Self-Employed: 0.9%
- ▲ Part-Time: 11.7%

Assist scientists in both laboratory and production activities by performing technical tasks involving nuclear physics, primarily in operation, maintenance, production, and quality control support activities. **SKILLS**—No data available.

GOE INFORMATION—**Interest Area:** 02. Science, Math, and Engineering. **Work Group:** 02.05. Laboratory Technology. **Other Job Titles in This Work Group:** Biological Technicians; Chemical Technicians; Environmental Science and Protection Technicians, Including Health; Geological and Petroleum Technicians; Geological Data Technicians; Geological Sample Test Technicians; Nuclear Equipment Operation Technicians; Photographers, Scientific. **PERSONALITY TYPE**—No data available.

EDUCATION/TRAINING PROGRAM(S)—Industrial Radiologic Technologist/Technician; Nuclear and Industrial Radiologic Technologists/Technicians, Other; Nuclear/Nuclear Power Technologist/Technician. **RELATED KNOWLEDGE/COURSES**—No data available.

Nursing Instructors and Teachers, Postsecondary

- ▲ Education/Training Required: Master's degree
- ▲ Annual Earnings: $47,650
- ▲ Growth: 24% for all Postsecondary Teachers
- ▲ Annual Job Openings: 184,000 for all Postsecondary Teachers
- ▲ Self-Employed: 0%
- ▲ Part-Time: 32.3% for all Postsecondary Teachers

Demonstrate and teach patient care in classroom and clinical units to nursing students. Includes both teachers primarily engaged in teaching and those who do a combination of both teaching and research. Instructs and lectures nursing students in principles and application of physical, biological, and psychological subjects related to nursing. Conducts and supervises laboratory work. Issues assignments to students. Participates in planning curriculum, teaching schedule, and course outline with medical and nursing personnel. Directs seminars and panels. Supervises student nurses and demonstrates patient care in clinical units of hospital. Cooperates with medical and nursing personnel in evaluating and improving teaching and nursing practices. Prepares and administers examinations to nursing students. Evaluates student progress and maintains records of student classroom and clinical experience. Conducts classes for patients in health practices and procedures. **SKILLS**—Learning Strategies: Selecting and using training/instructional methods and procedures appropriate for the situation when learning or teaching new things. Instructing: Teaching others how to do something. Reading Comprehension: Understanding written sentences and paragraphs in work-related documents. Speaking: Talking to others to convey information effectively. Science: Using scientific rules and methods to solve problems.

GOE INFORMATION—**Interest Area:** 12. Education and Social Service. **Work Group:** 12.03. Educational Services. **Other Job Titles in This Work Group:** Adult Literacy, Remedial Education, and GED Teachers and Instructors; Agricultural Sciences Teachers, Postsecondary; Anthropology and Archeology Teachers, Postsecondary; Architecture Teachers, Postsecondary; Archivists; Area, Ethnic, and Cultural Studies Teachers, Postsecondary; Art, Drama, and Music Teachers, Postsecondary; Atmospheric, Earth, Marine, and Space Sciences Teachers, Postsecondary; Audio-Visual Collections Specialists; Biological Science Teachers, Postsecondary; Business Teachers, Postsecondary; Chemistry Teachers, Postsecondary; Child Care Workers; Communications Teachers, Postsecondary; Computer Science Teachers, Postsecondary; Criminal Justice and Law Enforcement Teachers, Postsecondary; Curators; Economics Teachers, Postsecondary; Education Teachers, Postsecondary; Educational Psychologists; Educational, Vocational, and School Counselors; Elementary School Teachers, Except Special Education; Engineering Teachers, Postsecondary; English Language and Literature Teachers, Postsecondary; Environmental Science Teachers, Postsecondary; Farm and Home Management Advisors; Foreign Language and Literature Teachers, Postsecondary; Forestry and Conservation Science Teachers, Postsecondary; Geography Teachers, Postsecondary; Graduate Teaching Assistants; Health Specialties Teachers, Postsecondary; History Teachers, Postsecondary; Home Economics Teach-

ers, Postsecondary; Kindergarten Teachers, Except Special Education; Law Teachers, Postsecondary; Librarians; Library Assistants, Clerical; others. **PERSONALITY TYPE**—Social. Social occupations frequently involve working with, communicating with, and teaching people. These occupations often involve helping or providing service to others.

EDUCATION/TRAINING PROGRAM(S)— Nursing (R.N. Training); Nursing Anesthetist (Post-R.N.); Nursing Midwifery (Post-R.N.); Nursing Science (Post-R.N.); Nursing, Adult Health (Post-R.N.); Nursing, Family Practice (Post-R.N.); Nursing, Maternal/Child Health (Post-R.N.); Nursing, Other; Nursing, Pediatric (Post-R.N.); Nursing, Psychiatric/Mental Health (Post-R.N.); Nursing, Public Health (Post-R.N.); Nursing, Surgical (Post-R.N.). **RELATED KNOWLEDGE/ COURSES—Education and Training:** Knowledge of principles and methods for curriculum and training design, teaching and instruction for individuals and groups, and the measurement of training effects. **Medicine and Dentistry:** Knowledge of the information and techniques needed to diagnose and treat human injuries, diseases, and deformities. This includes symptoms, treatment alternatives, drug properties and interactions, and preventive health-care measures. **Biology:** Knowledge of plant and animal organisms and their tissues, cells, functions, interdependencies, and interactions with each other and the environment. **English Language:** Knowledge of the structure and content of the English language, including the meaning and spelling of words, rules of composition, and grammar. **Psychology:** Knowledge of human behavior and performance; individual differences in ability, personality, and interests; learning and motivation; psychological research methods; and the assessment and treatment of behavioral and affective disorders.

Occupational Health and Safety Specialists

▲ Education/Training Required: Master's degree

▲ Annual Earnings: $42,750

▲ Growth: 15%

▲ Annual Job Openings: 4,000

▲ Self-Employed: 4%

▲ Part-Time: 22.3%

Review, evaluate, and analyze work environments and design programs and procedures to control, eliminate, and prevent disease or injury caused by chemical, physical, and biological agents or ergonomic factors. **May conduct inspections and enforce adherence to laws and regulations governing the health and safety of individuals. May be employed in the public or private sector.** Investigates adequacy of ventilation, exhaust equipment, lighting, and other conditions which may affect employee health, comfort, or efficiency. Conducts evaluations of exposure to ionizing and nonionizing radiation and to noise. Collects samples of dust, gases, vapors, and other potentially toxic materials for analysis. Recommends measures to ensure maximum employee protection. Collaborates with engineers and physicians to institute control and remedial measures for hazardous and potentially hazardous conditions of equipment. Participates in educational meetings to instruct employees in matters pertaining to occupational health and prevention of accidents. Prepares reports including observations, analysis of contaminants, and recommendation for control and correction of hazards. Reviews physicians' reports and conducts worker studies to determine if diseases or illnesses are job related. Prepares and calibrates equipment used to collect and analyze samples. Prepares documents to be used in legal proceedings and gives testimony in court proceedings. Uses cost-benefit analysis to justify money spent. **SKILLS**—Reading Comprehension: Understanding written sentences and paragraphs in work-related documents. Writing: Communicating effectively in writing as appropriate for the needs of the audience. Speaking: Talking to others to convey information effectively. Science: Using scientific rules and methods to solve problems. Mathematics: Using mathematics to solve problems.

GOE INFORMATION—**Interest Area:** 04. Law, Law Enforcement, and Public Safety. **Work Group:** 04.04. Public Safety. **Other Job Titles in This Work Group:** Agricultural Inspectors; Aviation Inspectors; Compliance Officers, Except Agriculture, Construction, Health and Safety, and Transportation; Emergency Medical Technicians and Paramedics; Environmental Compliance Inspectors; Equal Opportunity Representatives and Officers; Financial Examiners; Fire Fighters; Fire Inspectors; Fire Inspectors and Investigators; Forest Fire Fighters; Forest Fire Inspectors and Prevention Specialists; Government Property Inspectors and Investigators; Licensing Examiners and Inspectors; Marine Cargo Inspectors; Municipal Fire Fighters; Nuclear Monitoring Technicians; Occupational Health and Safety Technicians; Public Transportation Inspectors. **PERSONALITY TYPE**—Social. Social occupations frequently involve working with, communicating with, and teaching people. These occupations often involve helping or providing service to others.

EDUCATION/TRAINING PROGRAM(S)—Environmental Health; Occupational Health and Industrial Hygiene; Occupational Safety and Health Technologist/Technician; Quality Control and Safety Technologists/Technicians, Other. **RELATED KNOWLEDGE/COURSES**—**Public Safety and Security:** Knowledge of relevant equipment, policies, procedures, and strategies to promote effective local, state, or national security operations for the protection of people, data, property, and institutions. **Chemistry:** Knowledge of the chemical composition, structure, and properties of substances and of the chemical processes and transformations that they undergo. This includes uses of chemicals and their interactions, danger signs, production techniques, and disposal methods. **Law and Government:** Knowledge of laws, legal codes, court procedures, precedents, government regulations, executive orders, agency rules, and the democratic political process. **Physics:** Knowledge and prediction of physical principles and laws and their interrelationships and applications to understanding fluid, material, and atmospheric dynamics and mechanical, electrical, atomic, and sub-atomic structures and processes. **Education and Training:** Knowledge of principles and methods for curriculum and training design, teaching and instruction for individuals and groups, and the measurement of training effects. **Medicine and Dentistry:** Knowledge of the information and techniques needed to diagnose and treat human injuries, diseases, and deformities. This includes symptoms, treatment alternatives, drug properties and interactions, and preventive health-care measures.

Occupational Health and Safety Technicians

▲ Education/Training Required: Associate's degree
▲ Annual Earnings: $42,750
▲ Growth: 15%
▲ Annual Job Openings: 4,000
▲ Self-Employed: 4%
▲ Part-Time: 22.3%

Collect data on work environments for analysis by occupational health and safety specialists. Implement and conduct evaluation of programs designed to limit chemical, physical, biological, and ergonomic risks to workers. **SKILLS**—No data available.

GOE INFORMATION—**Interest Area:** 04. Law, Law Enforcement, and Public Safety. **Work Group:** 04.04. Public Safety. **Other Job Titles in This Work Group:** Agricultural Inspectors; Aviation Inspectors; Compliance Officers, Except Agriculture, Construction, Health and Safety, and Transportation; Emergency Medical Technicians and Paramedics; Environmental Compliance Inspectors; Equal Opportunity Representatives and Officers;

Financial Examiners; Fire Fighters; Fire Inspectors; Fire Inspectors and Investigators; Forest Fire Fighters; Forest Fire Inspectors and Prevention Specialists; Government Property Inspectors and Investigators; Licensing Examiners and Inspectors; Marine Cargo Inspectors; Municipal Fire Fighters; Nuclear Monitoring Technicians; Occupational Health and Safety Specialists; Public Transportation Inspectors. **PERSONALITY TYPE**—No data available.

EDUCATION/TRAINING PROGRAM(S)—Environmental Health; Occupational Health and Industrial Hygiene. **RELATED KNOWLEDGE/ COURSES**—No data available.

Occupational Therapist Assistants

▲ Education/Training Required: Associate's degree
▲ Annual Earnings: $34,340
▲ Growth: 40%
▲ Annual Job Openings: 3,000
▲ Self-Employed: 0%
▲ Part-Time: 24.9%

Assist occupational therapists in providing occupational therapy treatments and procedures. May, in accordance with state laws, assist in development of treatment plans, carry out routine functions, direct activity programs, and document the progress of treatments. Generally requires formal training. Assists occupational therapist to plan, implement, and administer educational, vocational, and recreational activities to restore, reinforce,

and enhance task performances. Reports information and observations to supervisor verbally. Transports patient to and from occupational therapy work area. Maintains observed information in client records and prepares written reports. Prepares work material, assembles and maintains equipment, and orders supplies. Fabricates splints and other assistant devices. Assists educational specialist or clinical psychologist in administering situational or diagnostic tests to measure client's abilities or progress. Designs and adapts equipment and working-living environment. Helps professional staff demonstrate therapy techniques, such as manual and creative arts and games. Instructs or assists in instructing patient and family in home programs and basic living skills as well as care and use of adaptive equipment. Assists in evaluation of physically, developmentally, mentally retarded, or emotionally disabled client's daily living skills and capacities. **SKILLS**—Social Perceptiveness: Being aware of others' reactions and understanding why they react as they do. Reading Comprehension: Understanding written sentences and paragraphs in work-related documents. Active Listening: Giving full attention to what other people are saying, taking time to understand the points being made, asking questions as appropriate, and not interrupting at inappropriate times. Speaking: Talking to others to convey information effectively. Service Orientation: Actively looking for ways to help people.

GOE INFORMATION—**Interest Area:** 14. Medical and Health Services. **Work Group:** 14.06. Medical Therapy. **Other Job Titles in This Work Group:** Audiologists; Massage Therapists; Occupational Therapist Aides; Occupational Therapists; Physical Therapist Aides; Physical Therapist Assistants; Physical Therapists; Radiation Therapists; Recreational Therapists; Respiratory Therapists; Respiratory Therapy Technicians; Speech-Language Pathologists; Therapists, All Other. **PERSONALITY TYPE**—Social. Social occupations frequently involve working with, communicating with,

and teaching people. These occupations often involve helping or providing service to others.

EDUCATION/TRAINING PROGRAM(S)— Occupational Therapy Assistant. **RELATED KNOWLEDGE/COURSES**—**Therapy and Counseling:** Knowledge of principles, methods, and procedures for diagnosis, treatment, and rehabilitation of physical and mental dysfunctions and for career counseling and guidance. **Education and Training:** Knowledge of principles and methods for curriculum and training design, teaching and instruction for individuals and groups, and the measurement of training effects. **Medicine and Dentistry:** Knowledge of the information and techniques needed to diagnose and treat human injuries, diseases, and deformities. This includes symptoms, treatment alternatives, drug properties and interactions, and preventive health-care measures. **Psychology:** Knowledge of human behavior and performance; individual differences in ability, personality, and interests; learning and motivation; psychological research methods; and the assessment and treatment of behavioral and affective disorders. **English Language:** Knowledge of the structure and content of the English language, including the meaning and spelling of words, rules of composition, and grammar. **Customer and Personal Service:** Knowledge of principles and processes for providing customer and personal services. This includes customer needs assessment, meeting quality standards for services, and evaluation of customer satisfaction.

Occupational Therapists

- ▲ Education/Training Required: Bachelor's degree
- ▲ Annual Earnings: $49,450
- ▲ Growth: 34%
- ▲ Annual Job Openings: 4,000
- ▲ Self-Employed: 5.6%
- ▲ Part-Time: 20.8%

Assess, plan, organize, and participate in rehabilitative programs that help restore vocational, homemaking, and daily living skills, as well as general independence, to disabled persons. Plans, organizes, and conducts occupational therapy program in

hospital, institutional, or community setting. Plans programs and social activities to help patients learn work skills and adjust to handicaps. Teaches individuals skills and techniques required for participation in activities and evaluates individual's progress. Consults with rehabilitation team to select activity programs and coordinate occupational therapy with other therapeutic activities. Requisitions supplies and equipment. Completes and maintains necessary records. Trains nurses and other medical staff in therapy techniques and objectives. Designs and constructs special equipment, such as splints and braces. Lays out materials for individual's use and cleans and repairs tools after therapy sessions. Recommends changes in individual's work or living environment consistent with needs and capabilities. Selects activities which will help individual learn work skills within limits of individual's mental and physical capabilities. **SKILLS**—Instructing: Teaching others how to do something. Active Listening: Giving full attention to what other people are saying, taking time to understand the points being made, asking questions as appropriate, and not interrupting at inappropriate times. Social Perceptiveness: Being aware of others' reactions and understanding why they react as they do. Speaking: Talking to others to convey information effectively. Reading Comprehension: Understanding written sentences and paragraphs in work-related documents.

GOE INFORMATION—**Interest Area:** 14. Medical and Health Services. **Work Group:** 14.06. Medical Therapy. **Other Job Titles in This Work Group:** Audiologists; Massage Therapists; Occupational Therapist Aides; Occupational Therapist Assistants; Physical Therapist Aides; Physical Therapist Assistants; Physical Therapists; Radiation Therapists; Recreational Therapists; Respiratory Therapists; Respiratory Therapy Technicians; Speech-Language Pathologists; Therapists, All Other. **PERSONALITY TYPE**—Social. Social occupations frequently involve working with, communicating with, and teaching people. These occupations often involve helping or providing service to others.

EDUCATION/TRAINING PROGRAM(S)—Occupational Therapy. **RELATED KNOWLEDGE/COURSES**—**Therapy and Counseling:** Knowledge of principles, methods, and procedures for diagnosis, treatment, and rehabilitation of physical and mental dysfunctions and for career counseling and guidance. **Education and Training:** Knowledge of principles and methods for curriculum and training design, teaching and instruction for individuals and groups, and the measurement of training effects. **Administration and Management:** Knowledge of business and management principles involved in strategic planning, resource allocation, human resources modeling, leadership technique, production methods, and coordination of people and resources. **Psychology:** Knowledge of human behavior and performance; individual differences in ability, personality, and interests; learning and motivation; psychological research methods; and the assessment and treatment of behavioral and affective disorders. **Clerical Studies:** Knowledge of administrative and clerical procedures and systems such as word processing, managing files and records, stenography and transcription, designing forms, and other office procedures and terminology. **Customer and Personal Service:** Knowledge of principles and processes for providing customer and personal services. This includes customer needs assessment, meeting quality standards for services, and evaluation of customer satisfaction. **Medicine and Dentistry:** Knowledge of the information and techniques needed to diagnose and treat human injuries, diseases, and deformities. This includes symptoms, treatment alternatives, drug properties and interactions, and preventive health-care measures.

Operations Research Analysts

- ▲ Education/Training Required: Master's degree
- ▲ Annual Earnings: $53,420
- ▲ Growth: 8%
- ▲ Annual Job Openings: 4,000
- ▲ Self-Employed: 0%
- ▲ Part-Time: 2.8%

Formulate and apply mathematical modeling and other optimizing methods using a computer to develop and interpret information that assists management with decision making, policy formulation, or other managerial functions. May develop related software, service, or products. Frequently concentrates on collecting and analyzing data and developing decision support software. May develop and supply optimal time, cost, or logistics networks for program evaluation, review, or implementation. Analyzes problem in terms of management information and conceptualizes and defines problem. Prepares model of problem in form of one or several equations that relates constants and variables, restrictions, alternatives, conflicting objectives, and their numerical parameters. Specifies manipulative or computational methods to be applied to model. Evaluates implementation and effectiveness of research. Develops and applies time and cost networks to plan and control large projects. Prepares for management reports defining problem, evaluation, and possible solution. Studies information and selects plan from competitive proposals that afford maximum probability of profit or effectiveness relating to cost or risk. Defines data requirements and gathers and validates information, applying judgment and statistical tests. Designs, conducts, and evaluates experimental operational models where insufficient data exists to formulate model. Performs validation and testing of model to ensure adequacy or determines need for reformulation. SKILLS—Mathematics: Using mathematics to solve problems. Systems Evaluation: Identifying measures or indicators of system performance and the actions needed to improve or correct performance relative to the goals of the system. Critical Thinking: Using logic and reasoning to identify the strengths and weaknesses of alternative solutions, conclusions, or approaches to problems. Judgment and Decision Making: Considering the relative costs and benefits of potential actions to choose the most appropriate one. Monitoring: Monitoring/Assessing your performance or that of other individuals or organizations to make improvements or take corrective action.

GOE INFORMATION—Interest Area: 02. Science, Math, and Engineering. Work Group: 02.06. Mathematics and Computers. Other Job Titles in This Work Group: Actuaries; Computer and Information Scientists, Research; Computer Programmers; Computer Security Specialists; Computer Specialists, All Other; Computer Support Specialists; Computer Systems Analysts; Database Administrators; Mathematical Science Occupations, All Other; Mathematical Technicians; Mathematicians; Network and Computer Systems Administrators; Network Systems and Data Communications Analysts; Statistical Assistants; Statisticians. PERSONALITY TYPE—Investigative. Investigative occupations frequently involve working with ideas and require an extensive amount of thinking. These occupations can involve searching for facts and figuring out problems mentally.

EDUCATION/TRAINING PROGRAM(S)— Business Administration and Management, General; Business Quantitative Methods and Management Science, Other; Management Science; Operations Research. RELATED KNOWLEDGE/COURSES—Mathematics: Knowledge of arithmetic, algebra, geometry, calculus, and statistics and their applications. Administration and Management: Knowledge of business and management principles involved in strategic planning, resource allocation, human resources modeling, leadership technique, production methods, and coordination of people and resources. Computers and Electronics: Knowledge of circuit boards, processors, chips, electronic equipment, and computer hardware and software, including applications and programming. Economics and Accounting: Knowledge of economic and accounting principles and practices, the financial markets, banking, and the analysis and reporting of financial data. English Language: Knowledge of the structure and content of the English language, including the meaning and spelling of words, rules of composition, and grammar.

Optometrists

▲ Education/Training Required: First professional degree

▲ Annual Earnings: $82,860

▲ Growth: 19%

▲ Annual Job Openings: 1,000

▲ Self-Employed: 37.5%

▲ Part-Time: 10.5%

Diagnose, manage, and treat conditions and diseases of the human eye and visual system. Examine eyes and visual system, diagnose problems or impairments, prescribe corrective lenses, and provide treatment. May prescribe therapeutic drugs to treat specific eye conditions. Prescribes eyeglasses, contact lenses, and other vision aids or therapeutic procedures to correct or conserve vision. Consults with and refers patients to ophthalmologist or other health care practitioner if additional medical treatment is determined necessary. Examines eyes to determine visual acuity and perception and to diagnose diseases and other abnormalities, such as glaucoma and color blindness. Prescribes medications to treat eye diseases if state laws permit. **SKILLS**—Reading Comprehension: Understanding written sentences and paragraphs in work-related documents. Active Listening: Giving full attention to what other people are saying, taking time to understand the points being made, asking questions as appropriate, and not interrupting at inappropriate times. Mathematics: Using mathematics to solve problems. Science: Using scientific rules and methods to solve problems. Instructing: Teaching others how to do something. Writing: Communicating effectively in writing as appropriate for the needs of the audience.

GOE INFORMATION—**Interest Area:** 14. Medical and Health Services. **Work Group:** 14.04. Health Specialties. **Other Job Titles in This Work Group:** Chiropractors; Opticians, Dispensing; Podiatrists. **PERSONALITY TYPE**—Investigative. Investigative occupations frequently involve working with ideas and require an extensive amount of thinking. These occupations can involve searching for facts and figuring out problems mentally.

EDUCATION/TRAINING PROGRAM(S)—Optometry (O.D.). **RELATED KNOWLEDGE/COURSES**—**Medicine and Dentistry:** Knowledge of the information and techniques needed to diagnose and treat human injuries, diseases, and deformities. This includes symptoms, treatment alternatives, drug properties and interactions, and preventive health-care measures. **Biology:** Knowledge of plant and animal organisms and their tissues, cells, functions, interdependencies, and interactions with each other and the environment. **English Language:** Knowledge of the structure and content of the English language, including the meaning and spelling of words, rules of composition, and grammar. **Customer and Personal Service:** Knowledge of principles and processes for providing customer and personal services. This includes customer needs assessment, meeting quality standards for services, and evaluation of customer satisfaction. **Mathematics:** Knowledge of arithmetic, algebra, geometry, calculus, and statistics and their applications. **Chemistry:** Knowledge of the chemical composition, structure, and properties of substances and of the chemical processes and transformations that they undergo. This includes uses of chemicals and their interactions, danger signs, production techniques, and disposal methods.

Orthotists and Prosthetists

- ▲ Education/Training Required: Bachelor's degree
- ▲ Annual Earnings: $45,740
- ▲ Growth: 17%
- ▲ Annual Job Openings: 1,000
- ▲ Self-Employed: 4%
- ▲ Part-Time: 22.3%

Assist patients with disabling conditions of limbs and spine or with partial or total absence of limb by fitting and preparing orthopedic braces or prostheses. Fits patients for device, using static and dynamic alignments. Selects materials and components and makes cast measurements, model modifications, and layouts, using measuring equipment. Instructs patients in use of orthopedic or prosthetic devices. Maintains patients' records. Participates in research to modify design, fit, and function of orthopedic or prosthetic devices. Lectures and demonstrates to colleagues and other professionals concerned with orthopedics or prosthetics. Supervises laboratory activities or activities of prosthetic assistants and support staff relating to development of orthopedic or prosthetic devices. Repairs and maintains orthopedic prosthetic devices, using hand tools. Examines, measures, and evaluates patients' needs in relation to disease and functional loss. Evaluates device on patient and makes adjustments to assure fit, function, comfort, and quality. Designs orthopedic and prosthetic devices according to physician's prescription. Assists physician in formulating specifications and prescription for orthopedic and/or prosthetic devices. **SKILLS—Speaking:** Talking to others to convey information effectively. Reading Comprehension: Understanding written sentences and paragraphs in work-related documents. Active Listening: Giving full attention to what other people are saying, taking time to understand the points being made, asking questions as appropriate, and not interrupting at inappropriate times. Technology Design: Generating or adapting equipment and technology to serve user needs. Social Perceptiveness: Being aware of others' reactions and understanding why they react as they do.

GOE INFORMATION—Interest Area: 14. Medical and Health Services. **Work Group:** 14.05. Medical Technology. **Other Job Titles in This Work Group:** Cardiovascular Technologists and Technicians; Diagnostic Medical Sonographers; Health Technologists and Technicians, All Other; Medical and Clinical Laboratory Technicians; Medical and Clinical Laboratory Technologists; Medical Equipment Preparers; Nuclear Medicine Technologists; Radiologic Technicians; Radiologic Technologists; Radiologic Technologists and Technicians. **PERSONALITY TYPE—Social.** Social occupations frequently involve working with, communicating with, and teaching people. These occupations often involve helping or providing service to others.

EDUCATION/TRAINING PROGRAM(S)— Orthotics/Prosthetics. **RELATED KNOWLEDGE/ COURSES—Medicine and Dentistry:** Knowledge of the information and techniques needed to diagnose and treat human injuries, diseases, and deformities. This includes symptoms, treatment alternatives, drug properties and interactions, and preventive health-care measures. **Design:** Knowledge of design techniques, tools, and principles involved in production of precision technical plans, blueprints, drawings, and models. **Therapy and Counseling:** Knowledge of principles, methods, and procedures for diagnosis, treatment, and rehabilitation of physical and mental dysfunctions and for career counseling and guidance. **Education and Training:** Knowledge of principles and methods for curriculum and training design, teaching and instruction for individuals and groups, and the measurement of training effects. **Customer and Personal Service:** Knowledge of principles and processes for providing customer and personal services. This includes customer needs assessment, meeting quality standards for services, and evaluation of customer satisfaction. **Building and Construction:** Knowledge of

materials, methods, and tools involved in the construction or repair of houses, buildings, or other structures, such as highways and roads.

Paralegals and Legal Assistants

- ▲ Education/Training Required: Associate's degree
- ▲ Annual Earnings: $35,360
- ▲ Growth: 33%
- ▲ Annual Job Openings: 23,000
- ▲ Self-Employed: 0.9%
- ▲ Part-Time: 12.5%

Assist lawyers by researching legal precedent, investigating facts, or preparing legal documents. Conduct research to support a legal proceeding, to formulate a defense, or to initiate legal action. Gathers and analyzes research data, such as statutes, decisions, and legal articles, codes, and documents. Prepares legal documents, including briefs, pleadings, appeals, wills, contracts, and real estate closing statements. Prepares affidavits or other documents, maintains document file, and files pleadings with court clerk. Arbitrates disputes between parties and assists in real estate closing process. Answers questions regarding legal issues pertaining to civil service hearings. Presents arguments and evidence to support appeal at appeal hearing. Keeps and monitors legal volumes to ensure that law library is up-to-date. Directs and coordinates law office activity, including delivery of subpoenas. Calls upon witnesses to testify at hearing. Appraises and inventories real and personal property for estate planning. Investigates facts and law of cases to determine causes of action and to prepare cases. **SKILLS—Reading Comprehension:** Understanding written sentences and paragraphs in work-related documents. **Critical Thinking:** Using logic and reasoning to identify the strengths and weaknesses of alternative solutions, conclusions, or approaches to problems. **Speaking:** Talking to others to convey information effectively. **Writing:** Communicating effectively in writing as appropriate for the needs of the audience. **Negotiation:** Bringing others together and trying to reconcile differences. **Persuasion:** Persuading others to change their minds or behavior. **Active Listening:** Giving full attention to what other people are saying, taking time

to understand the points being made, asking questions as appropriate, and not interrupting at inappropriate times.

GOE INFORMATION—Interest Area: 04. Law, Law Enforcement, and Public Safety. **Work Group:** 04.02. Law. **Other Job Titles in This Work Group:** Administrative Law Judges, Adjudicators, and Hearing Officers; Arbitrators, Mediators, and Conciliators; Judges, Magistrate Judges, and Magistrates; Law Clerks; Lawyers; Legal Support Workers, All Other; Title Examiners and Abstractors; Title Examiners, Abstractors, and Searchers; Title Searchers. **PERSONALITY TYPE**—Enterprising. Enterprising occupations frequently involve starting up and carrying out projects. These occupations can involve leading people and making many decisions. They sometimes require risk taking and often deal with business.

EDUCATION/TRAINING PROGRAM(S)— Paralegal/Legal Assistant. **RELATED KNOWLEDGE/COURSES—Law and Government:** Knowledge of laws, legal codes, court procedures, precedents, government regulations, executive orders, agency rules, and the democratic political process. **Clerical Studies:** Knowledge of administrative and clerical procedures and systems such as word processing, managing files and records, stenography and transcription, designing forms, and other office procedures and terminology. **English Language:** Knowledge of the structure and content of the English language, including the meaning and spelling of words, rules of composition, and grammar. **Computers and Electronics:** Knowledge of circuit boards, processors, chips, electronic equipment, and computer hardware and software, including applications and programming. **Administration and Management:** Knowledge of business and management principles involved in strategic planning, resource allocation, human resources modeling, leadership technique, production methods, and coordination of people and resources.

Park Naturalists

- ▲ Education/Training Required: Bachelor's degree
- ▲ Annual Earnings: $47,140
- ▲ Growth: 8%
- ▲ Annual Job Openings: 1,000
- ▲ Self-Employed: 2.4%
- ▲ Part-Time: 6.6%

Plan, develop, and conduct programs to inform public of historical, natural, and scientific features of national, state, or local park. Conducts field trips to point out scientific, historic, and natural features of park. Plans and develops audiovisual devices for public programs. Confers with park staff to determine subjects to be presented to public. Interviews specialists in desired fields to obtain and develop data for park information programs. Prepares and presents illustrated lectures of park features. Takes photographs and motion pictures to illustrate lectures and publications and to develop displays. Surveys park to determine distribution and abundance of fauna and flora. Maintains official park photographic and information files. Performs emergency duties to protect human life, government property, and natural features of park. Plans and organizes activities of seasonal staff members. Surveys park to determine forest conditions. Constructs historical, scientific, and nature visitor-center displays. **SKILLS—Speaking:** Talking to others to convey information effectively. **Writing:** Communicating effectively in writing as appropriate for the needs of the audience. **Service Orientation:** Actively looking for ways to help people. **Active Listening:** Giving full attention to what other people are saying, taking time to understand the points being made, asking questions as appropriate, and not interrupting at inappropriate times. **Reading Comprehension:** Understanding written sentences and paragraphs in work-related documents.

GOE INFORMATION—Interest Area: 12. Education and Social Service. **Work Group:** 12.01. Managerial Work in Education and Social Service. **Other Job**

Titles in This Work Group: Education Administrators, All Other; Education Administrators, Elementary and Secondary School; Education Administrators, Postsecondary; Education Administrators, Preschool and Child Care Center/Program; Instructional Coordinators; Social and Community Service Managers. **PERSONALITY TYPE—Social.** Social occupations frequently involve working with, communicating with, and teaching people. These occupations often involve helping or providing service to others.

EDUCATION/TRAINING PROGRAM(S)— Conservation and Renewable Natural Resources, Other; Forest Management; Forestry and Related Sciences, Other; Forestry Sciences; Forestry, General; Natural Resources Conservation, General; Natural Resources Law Enforcement and Protective Services; Natural Resources Management and Policy; Natural Resources Management and Protective Services, Other; Wildlife and Wildlands Management. **RELATED KNOWLEDGE/ COURSES—Biology:** Knowledge of plant and animal organisms and their tissues, cells, functions, interdependencies, and interactions with each other and the environment. **English Language:** Knowledge of the structure and content of the English language, including the meaning and spelling of words, rules of composition, and grammar. **Education and Training:** Knowledge of principles and methods for curriculum and training design, teaching and instruction for individuals and groups, and the measurement of training effects. **Communications and Media:** Knowledge of media production, communication, and dissemination techniques and methods. This includes alternative ways to inform and entertain via written, oral, and visual media. **Administration and Management:** Knowledge of business and management principles involved in strategic planning, resource allocation, human resources modeling, leadership technique, production methods, and coordination of people and resources. **History and Archeology:** Knowledge of historical events and

their causes, indicators, and effects on civilizations and cultures. **Geography:** Knowledge of principles and methods for describing the features of land, sea, and air masses, including their physical characteristics, locations, interrelationships, and distribution of plant, animal, and human life.

Pediatricians, General

- ▲ Education/Training Required: First professional degree
- ▲ Annual Earnings: $125,970
- ▲ Growth: 18%
- ▲ Annual Job Openings: 27,000
- ▲ Self-Employed: 20.4%
- ▲ Part-Time: 7.2%

Diagnose, treat, and help prevent children's diseases and injuries. Examines or conducts tests on patient to provide information on medical condition. Conducts research to study anatomy and develop or test medications, treatments, or procedures to prevent or control disease or injury. Prepares reports for government or management of birth, death, and disease statistics, workforce evaluations, or medical status of individuals. Directs and coordinates activities of nurses, students, assistants, specialists, therapists, and other medical staff. Plans, implements, or administers health programs or standards in hospital, business, or community for information, prevention, or treatment of injury or illness. Explains procedures and discusses test results on prescribed treatments with patents. Operates on patients to remove, repair, or improve functioning of diseased or injured body parts and systems and delivers babies. Collects, records, and maintains patient information, such as medical history, reports, and examination results. Advises patients and community concerning diet, activity, hygiene, and disease prevention. Refers patient to medical specialist or other practitioner when necessary. Prescribes or administers treatment, therapy, medication, vaccination, and other specialized medical care to treat or prevent illness, disease, or injury. Analyzes records, reports, test results, or examination information to diagnose medical condition of patient. Monitors patients' condition and progress and re-evaluates treatments as necessary. **SKILLS**—Reading Comprehen-

sion: Understanding written sentences and paragraphs in work-related documents. Active Learning: Understanding the implications of new information for both current and future problem-solving and decision-making. Science: Using scientific rules and methods to solve problems. Judgment and Decision Making: Considering the relative costs and benefits of potential actions to choose the most appropriate one. Mathematics: Using mathematics to solve problems. Active Listening: Giving full attention to what other people are saying, taking time to understand the points being made, asking questions as appropriate, and not interrupting at inappropriate times. Writing: Communicating effectively in writing as appropriate for the needs of the audience.

GOE INFORMATION—Interest Area: 14. Medical and Health Services. **Work Group:** 14.02. Medicine and Surgery. **Other Job Titles in This Work Group:** Anesthesiologists; Family and General Practitioners; Internists, General; Medical Assistants; Obstetricians and Gynecologists; Pharmacists; Pharmacy Aides; Pharmacy Technicians; Physician Assistants; Physicians and Surgeons, All Other; Psychiatrists; Registered Nurses; Surgeons; Surgical Technologists. **PERSONALITY TYPE**—Investigative. Investigative occupations frequently involve working with ideas and require an extensive amount of thinking. These occupations can involve searching for facts and figuring out problems mentally.

EDUCATION/TRAINING PROGRAM(S)—Child/Pediatric Neurology Residency; Family Medicine Residency; Neonatal-Perinatal Medicine Residency; Pediatric Hemato-Oncology Residency; Pediatric Nephrology Residency; Pediatric Orthopedics Residency; Pediatric Surgery Residency; Pediatrics Residency. **RELATED KNOWLEDGE/COURSES—Medicine and Dentistry:** Knowledge of the information and techniques needed to diagnose and treat human injuries, diseases, and deformities. This includes symptoms, treatment alternatives, drug properties and interactions, and preventive health-care measures. **Biology:** Knowledge of plant and animal organisms and their tissues, cells, functions, inter-dependencies, and interactions with each other and the environment. **English Language:** Knowledge of the structure and content of the English language, including the meaning and spelling of words, rules of composition, and grammar. **Therapy and Counseling:** Knowledge of principles, methods, and procedures for diagnosis, treatment, and rehabilitation of physical and mental dysfunctions and for career counseling and guidance. **Administration and Management:** Knowledge of business and management principles involved in strategic planning, resource allocation, human resources modeling, leadership technique, production methods, and coordination of people and resources.

Personal Financial Advisors

▲ Education/Training Required: Bachelor's degree

▲ Annual Earnings: $55,320

▲ Growth: 34%

▲ Annual Job Openings: 13,000

▲ Self-Employed: 5.4%

▲ Part-Time: 7.7%

Advise clients on financial plans utilizing knowledge of tax and investment strategies, securities, insurance, pension plans, and real estate. Duties include assessing clients' assets, liabilities, cash flow, insurance coverage, tax status, and financial objectives to establish investment strategies. Interviews client with debt problems to determine available monthly income after living expenses to meet credit obligations. Establishes payment priorities to plan payoff method and estimate time for debt liquidation. Explains to individuals and groups financial assistance available to college and university students, such as loans, grants, and scholarships. Interviews students to obtain information and compares data on students' applications with eligibility requirements to determine eligibility for assistance program. Contacts creditors to arrange for payment adjustments so that payments are feasible for client and agreeable to creditors. Prepares required records and reports. Assists in selection of candidates for specific financial awards or aid. Authorizes release of funds to students. Opens account for client and disburses funds from account to creditors as agent for client. Determines amount of aid to be granted, considering such factors as funds available, extent of demand, and needs of students. Calculates amount of debt and funds available. Counsels client on financial problems, such as excessive spending and borrowing of funds. **SKILLS—Active Listening:** Giving full attention to what other people are saying, taking time to understand the points being made, asking questions as appropriate, and not interrupting at inappropriate times. Speaking: Talking to others to convey information effectively. Reading Comprehension: Understanding written sentences and paragraphs in work-related documents. Mathematics: Using mathematics to solve problems. Critical Thinking: Using logic and reasoning to identify the strengths and weaknesses of alternative solutions, conclusions, or approaches to problems. Judgment and Decision Making: Considering the relative costs and benefits of potential actions to choose the most appropriate one. Service Orientation: Actively looking for ways to help people.

GOE INFORMATION—Interest Area: 12. Education and Social Service. **Work Group:** 12.03. Educational Services. **Other Job Titles in This Work**

Group: Adult Literacy, Remedial Education, and GED Teachers and Instructors; Agricultural Sciences Teachers, Postsecondary; Anthropology and Archeology Teachers, Postsecondary; Architecture Teachers, Postsecondary; Archivists; Area, Ethnic, and Cultural Studies Teachers, Postsecondary; Art, Drama, and Music Teachers, Postsecondary; Atmospheric, Earth, Marine, and Space Sciences Teachers, Postsecondary; Audio-Visual Collections Specialists; Biological Science Teachers, Postsecondary; Business Teachers, Postsecondary; Chemistry Teachers, Postsecondary; Child Care Workers; Communications Teachers, Postsecondary; Computer Science Teachers, Postsecondary; Criminal Justice and Law Enforcement Teachers, Postsecondary; Curators; Economics Teachers, Postsecondary; Education Teachers, Postsecondary; Educational Psychologists; Educational, Vocational, and School Counselors; Elementary School Teachers, Except Special Education; Engineering Teachers, Postsecondary; English Language and Literature Teachers, Postsecondary; Environmental Science Teachers, Postsecondary; Farm and Home Management Advisors; Foreign Language and Literature Teachers, Postsecondary; Forestry and Conservation Science Teachers, Postsecondary; Geography Teachers, Postsecondary; Graduate Teaching Assistants; Health Specialties Teachers, Postsecondary; History Teachers, Postsecondary; Home Economics Teachers, Postsecondary; Kindergarten Teachers, Except Special Education; Law Teachers, Postsecondary; Librarians; Library Assistants, Clerical; others. **PERSONALITY TYPE**—Social. Social occupations frequently involve working with, communicating with, and teaching people. These occupations often involve helping or providing service to others.

EDUCATION/TRAINING PROGRAM(S)—Finance, General; Financial Planning. **RELATED KNOWLEDGE/COURSES**—**Economics and Accounting:** Knowledge of economic and accounting principles and practices, the financial markets, banking, and the analysis and reporting of financial data. **Mathematics:** Knowledge of arithmetic, algebra, geometry, calculus, and statistics and their applications. **Administration and Management:** Knowledge of business and management principles involved in strategic planning, resource allocation, human resources modeling, leadership technique, production methods, and coordination of people and resources. **Customer and Personal Service:** Knowledge of principles and processes for providing customer and personal services. This includes customer needs assessment, meeting quality standards for services, and evaluation of customer satisfaction. **English Language:** Knowledge of the structure and content of the English language, including the meaning and spelling of words, rules of composition, and grammar.

Personnel Recruiters

- ▲ Education/Training Required: Bachelor's degree
- ▲ Annual Earnings: $36,480
- ▲ Growth: 18%
- ▲ Annual Job Openings: 19,000
- ▲ Self-Employed: 2.6%
- ▲ Part-Time: 6.9%

Seek out, interview, and screen applicants to fill existing and future job openings and promote career opportunities within an organization. Interviews applicants to obtain work history, training, education, job skills, and other background information. Arranges for interviews and travel and lodging for selected applicants at company expense. Projects yearly recruitment expenditures for budgetary consideration and control. Corrects and scores portions of examinations used to screen and select applicants. Prepares and maintains employment records and authorizes paperwork assigning applicant to positions. Speaks to civic, social, and other groups to provide information concerning job possibilities and career opportunities. Assists and advises establishment management in organizing, preparing, and implementing recruiting and retention programs. Evaluates recruitment and selection criteria to ensure conformance to professional, statistical, and testing standards and recommends revision as needed. Hires or refers applicant to other hiring personnel in organization. Provides potential applicants with information regarding facilities, operations, benefits, and job or career opportunities in organization. Contacts college representatives to arrange for and schedule on-campus interviews with students. Reviews and evaluates applicant qualifications or eligibility for specified licensing according to established guidelines and designated licensing codes. Notifies applicants by mail or telephone to inform them of employment possibilities, consideration, and selection. Conducts reference and background checks on applicants. **SKILLS**—Active Listening: Giving full attention to what other people are saying, taking time to understand the points being made, asking questions as appropriate, and not interrupting at inappropriate times. Reading Comprehension: Understanding written sentences and paragraphs in work-related documents. Writing: Communicating effectively in writing as appropriate for the needs of the audience. Speaking: Talking to others to convey information effectively. Management of Personnel Resources: Motivating, developing, and directing people as they work, identifying the best people for the job. Judgment and Decision Making: Considering the relative costs and benefits of potential actions to choose the most appropriate one.

GOE INFORMATION—**Interest Area:** 13. General Management and Support. **Work Group:** 13.02. Management Support. **Other Job Titles in This Work Group:** Accountants; Accountants and Auditors; Appraisers and Assessors of Real Estate; Appraisers, Real Estate; Assessors; Auditors; Budget Analysts; Claims Adjusters, Examiners, and Investigators; Claims Examiners, Property and Casualty Insurance; Compensation, Benefits, and Job Analysis Specialists; Cost Estimators; Credit Analysts; Employment Interviewers, Private or Public Employment Service; Employment, Recruitment, and Placement Specialists; Financial Analysts; Human Resources, Training,

and Labor Relations Specialists, All Other; Insurance Adjusters, Examiners, and Investigators; Insurance Appraisers, Auto Damage; Insurance Underwriters; Loan Counselors; Loan Officers; Logisticians; Management Analysts; Market Research Analysts; Purchasing Agents and Buyers, Farm Products; Purchasing Agents, Except Wholesale, Retail, and Farm Products; Tax Examiners, Collectors, and Revenue Agents; Training and Development Specialists; Wholesale and Retail Buyers, Except Farm Products. **PERSONALITY TYPE**—Enterprising. Enterprising occupations frequently involve starting up and carrying out projects. These occupations can involve leading people and making many decisions. They sometimes require risk taking and often deal with business.

EDUCATION/TRAINING PROGRAM(S)—Human Resources Management; Human Resources Management, Other; Labor/Personnel Relations and Studies; Organizational Behavior Studies. **RELATED KNOWLEDGE/COURSES**—**Personnel and Human Resources:** Knowledge of principles and procedures for personnel recruitment, selection, training, compensation and benefits, labor relations and negotiation, and personnel information systems. **Psychology:** Knowledge of human behavior and performance; individual differences in ability, personality, and interests; learning and motivation; psychological research methods; and the assessment and treatment of behavioral and affective disorders. **English Language:** Knowledge of the structure and content of the English language, including the meaning and spelling of words, rules of composition, and grammar. **Administration and Management:** Knowledge of business and management principles involved in strategic planning, resource allocation, human resources modeling, leadership technique, production methods, and coordination of people and resources. **Sales and Marketing:** Knowledge of principles and methods for showing, promoting, and selling products or services. This includes marketing strategy and tactics, product demonstration, sales techniques, and sales control systems. **Mathematics:** Knowledge of arithmetic, algebra, geometry, calculus, and statistics and their applications.

Petroleum Engineers

▲ Education/Training Required: Bachelor's degree

▲ Annual Earnings: $78,910

▲ Growth: –7%

▲ Annual Job Openings: Fewer than 500

▲ Self-Employed: 0%

▲ Part-Time: 3.1%

Devise methods to improve oil and gas well production and determine the need for new or modified tool designs. Oversee drilling and offer technical advice to achieve economical and satisfactory progress. Designs or modifies mining and oil field machinery and tools, applying engineering principles. Confers with scientific, engineering, and technical personnel to resolve design, research, and testing problems. Evaluates findings to develop, design, or test equipment or processes. Analyzes data to recommend placement of wells and supplementary processes to enhance production. Coordinates activities of workers engaged in research, planning, and development. Assigns work to staff to obtain maximum utilization of personnel. Tests machinery and equipment to ensure conformance to performance specifications and to ensure safety. Writes technical reports for engineering and management personnel. Interprets drilling and testing information for personnel. Inspects oil and gas wells to determine that installations are completed. Assists engineering and other personnel to solve operating problems. Monitors production rates and plans rework processes to improve production. Conducts engineering research experiments to improve or modify mining and oil machinery and operations. Develops plans for oil and gas field drilling and for product recovery and treatment. **SKILLS—Mathematics:** Using mathematics to solve problems. **Writing:** Communicating effectively in writing as appropriate for the needs of the audience. **Operations Analysis:** Analyzing needs and product requirements to create a design. **Reading Comprehension:** Understanding written sentences and paragraphs in work-related documents. **Science:** Using scientific rules and methods to solve problems. **Critical Thinking:** Using logic and reasoning to identify the strengths and weaknesses of alternative solutions, conclusions, or approaches to problems. **Judgment**

and Decision Making: Considering the relative costs and benefits of potential actions to choose the most appropriate one.

GOE INFORMATION—Interest Area: 02. Science, Math, and Engineering. **Work Group:** 02.07. Engineering. **Other Job Titles in This Work Group:** Aerospace Engineers; Agricultural Engineers; Architects, Except Landscape and Naval; Biomedical Engineers; Chemical Engineers; Civil Engineers; Computer Hardware Engineers; Computer Software Engineers, Applications; Computer Software Engineers, Systems Software; Electrical Engineers; Electronics Engineers, Except Computer; Engineers, All Other; Environmental Engineers; Fire-Prevention and Protection Engineers; Health and Safety Engineers, Except Mining Safety Engineers and Inspectors; Industrial Engineers; Industrial Safety and Health Engineers; Landscape Architects; Marine Architects; Marine Engineers; Marine Engineers and Naval Architects; Materials Engineers; Mechanical Engineers; Mining and Geological Engineers, Including Mining Safety Engineers; Nuclear Engineers; Product Safety Engineers; Sales Engineers. **PERSONALITY TYPE—**Realistic. Realistic occupations frequently involve work activities that include practical, hands-on problems and solutions. They often deal with plants, animals, and real-world materials like wood, tools, and machinery. Many of the occupations require working outside and do not involve a lot of paperwork or working closely with others.

EDUCATION/TRAINING PROGRAM(S)— Petroleum Engineering. **RELATED KNOWLEDGE/ COURSES—Engineering and Technology:** Knowledge of the practical application of engineering science and technology. This includes applying principles, techniques, procedures, and equipment to the design and production of various goods and services. **Physics:** Knowledge and prediction of physical principles and laws and their interrelationships and applications to understanding fluid, material, and atmospheric dynamics and mechanical, electrical, atomic, and sub-atomic structures and processes. **English Language:** Knowledge of the structure and content of the English language, including the meaning and spelling of words, rules of composition, and grammar. **Administra-**

tion and Management: Knowledge of business and management principles involved in strategic planning, resource allocation, human resources modeling, leadership technique, production methods, and coordination of people and resources. **Mathematics:** Knowledge of arithmetic, algebra, geometry, calculus, and statistics and their applications.

Pharmacists

▲ Education/Training Required: First professional degree
▲ Annual Earnings: $70,950
▲ Growth: 24%
▲ Annual Job Openings: 20,000
▲ Self-Employed: 4.2%
▲ Part-Time: 24.6%

Compound and dispense medications following prescriptions issued by physicians, dentists, or other authorized medical practitioners. Compounds medications, using standard formulas and processes, such as weighing, measuring, and mixing ingredients. Compounds radioactive substances and reagents to prepare radiopharmaceutical, following radiopharmacy laboratory procedures. Plans and implements procedures in pharmacy, such as mixing, packaging, and labeling pharmaceuticals according to policies and legal requirements. Reviews prescription to assure accuracy and determine ingredients needed and suitability of radiopharmaceutical prescriptions. Consults medical staff to advise on drug applications and characteristics and to review and evaluate quality and effectiveness of radiopharmaceuticals. Maintains records, such as pharmacy files, charge system, inventory, and control records for radioactive nuclei. Verifies that specified radioactive substance and reagent will give desired results in examination or treatment procedures. Analyzes records to indicate prescribing trends and excessive usage. Oversees preparation and dispensation of experimental drugs. Maintains established procedures concerning quality assurance, security of controlled substances, and disposal of hazardous waste. Calculates volume of radioactive pharmaceutical required to provide patient desired level of radioactivity at prescribed time. Assays prepared radiopharmaceutical, using instruments and equipment to verify

rate of drug disintegration and ensure patient receives required dose. Answers questions and provides information to pharmacy customers on drug interactions, side effects, dosage, and storage of pharmaceuticals. **SKILLS**—Reading Comprehension: Understanding written sentences and paragraphs in work-related documents. Writing: Communicating effectively in writing as appropriate for the needs of the audience. Mathematics: Using mathematics to solve problems. Science: Using scientific rules and methods to solve problems. Instructing: Teaching others how to do something. Active Learning: Understanding the implications of new information for both current and future problem-solving and decision-making.

GOE INFORMATION—**Interest Area:** 14. Medical and Health Services. **Work Group:** 14.02. Medicine and Surgery. **Other Job Titles in This Work Group:** Anesthesiologists; Family and General Practitioners; Internists, General; Medical Assistants; Obstetricians and Gynecologists; Pediatricians, General; Pharmacy Aides; Pharmacy Technicians; Physician Assistants; Physicians and Surgeons, All Other; Psychiatrists; Registered Nurses; Surgeons; Surgical Technologists. **PERSONALITY TYPE**—Investigative. Investigative occupations frequently involve working with ideas and require an extensive amount of thinking. These occupations can involve searching for facts and figuring out problems mentally.

EDUCATION/TRAINING PROGRAM(S)— Medical Pharmacology and Pharmaceutical Sciences; Medicinal/Pharmaceutical Chemistry; Pharmacy (B. Pharm., Pharm.D.); Pharmacy Administration and Pharmaceutics; Pharmacy, Other. **RELATED KNOWLEDGE/ COURSES—Chemistry:** Knowledge of the chemical composition, structure, and properties of substances and of the chemical processes and transformations that they undergo. This includes uses of chemicals and their interactions, danger signs, production techniques, and disposal methods. **Medicine and Dentistry:** Knowledge of the information and techniques needed to diagnose and treat human injuries, diseases, and deformities. This includes symptoms, treatment alternatives, drug properties and interactions, and preventive health-care measures. **Admin-** istration and Management: Knowledge of business and management principles involved in strategic planning, resource allocation, human resources modeling, leadership technique, production methods, and coordination of people and resources. **Biology:** Knowledge of plant and animal organisms and their tissues, cells, functions, interdependencies, and interactions with each other and the environment. **Computers and Electronics:** Knowledge of circuit boards, processors, chips, electronic equipment, and computer hardware and software, including applications and programming. **English Language:** Knowledge of the structure and content of the English language, including the meaning and spelling of words, rules of composition, and grammar.

Philosophy and Religion Teachers, Postsecondary

- ▲ Education/Training Required: Master's degree
- ▲ Annual Earnings: $46,170
- ▲ Growth: 24% for all Postsecondary Teachers
- ▲ Annual Job Openings: 184,000 for all Postsecondary Teachers
- ▲ Self-Employed: 0%
- ▲ Part-Time: 32.3% for all Postsecondary Teachers

Teach courses in philosophy, religion, and theology. **SKILLS—**No data available.

GOE INFORMATION—Interest Area: 12. Education and Social Service. **Work Group:** 12.03. Educational Services. **Other Job Titles in This Work Group:** Adult Literacy, Remedial Education, and GED Teachers and Instructors; Agricultural Sciences Teachers, Postsecondary; Anthropology and Archeology Teachers, Postsecondary; Architecture Teachers, Postsecondary; Archivists; Area, Ethnic, and Cultural Studies Teachers, Postsecondary; Art, Drama, and Music Teachers, Postsecondary; Atmospheric, Earth, Marine, and Space Sciences Teachers, Postsecondary; Audio-Visual Collections Specialists; Biological Science Teachers, Postsecondary; Business Teachers, Postsecondary; Chemistry Teachers, Postsecondary; Child Care Workers; Com- munications Teachers, Postsecondary; Computer Science Teachers, Postsecondary; Criminal Justice and Law Enforcement Teachers, Postsecondary; Curators; Economics Teachers, Postsecondary; Education Teachers, Postsecondary; Educational Psychologists; Educational, Vocational, and School Counselors; Elementary School Teachers, Except Special Education; Engineering Teachers, Postsecondary; English Language and Literature Teachers, Postsecondary; Environmental Science Teachers, Postsecondary; Farm and Home Management Advisors; Foreign Language and Literature Teachers, Postsecondary; Forestry and Conservation Science Teachers, Postsecondary; Geography Teachers, Postsecondary; Graduate Teaching Assistants; Health Specialties Teachers, Postsecondary; History Teachers, Postsecondary; Home Economics Teachers, Postsecondary; Kindergarten Teachers, Except Special Education; Law Teachers, Postsecondary; Librarians; Library Assistants, Clerical; others. **PERSONALITY TYPE**—No data available.

Physical Therapist Aides

> ▲ Education/Training Required: Associate's degree
> ▲ Annual Earnings: $19,670
> ▲ Growth: 46%
> ▲ Annual Job Openings: 7,000
> ▲ Self-Employed: 0%
> ▲ Part-Time: 34.5%

EDUCATION/TRAINING PROGRAM(S)—Philosophy and Religion. **RELATED KNOWLEDGE/COURSES**—No data available.

Under close supervision of a physical therapist or physical therapy assistant, perform only delegated, selected, or routine tasks in specific situations. These duties include preparing the patient and the treatment area. Observes patients during treatment, compiles and evaluates data on patients' responses to treatments and progress, and reports to physical therapist. Administers active and passive manual therapeutic exercises, therapeutic massage, and heat, light, sound, water, and electrical modality treatments, such as ultrasound. Administers traction to relieve neck and back pain, using intermittent and static traction equipment. Provides routine treatments, such as hydrotherapy, hot and cold packs, and paraffin bath. Secures patients into or onto therapy equipment. Measures patient's range-of-joint motion, body parts, and vital signs to determine effects of treatments or for patient evaluations. Records treatment given and equipment used. Performs clerical duties, such as taking inventory, ordering supplies, answering telephone, taking messages, and filling out forms. Cleans work area and equipment after treatment. Transports patients to and from treatment area. Fits patients for orthopedic braces, prostheses, and supportive devices, such as crutches. Assists patients to dress, undress, and put on and remove supportive devices, such as braces, splints, and slings. Confers with physical therapy staff and others to discuss and evaluate patient information for planning, modifying, and coordinating treatment. Adjusts fit of supportive devices for patients as instructed. Trains patients in use and care of orthopedic braces, prostheses, and supportive devices, such as crutches. Safeguards, motivates, and assists patients practicing exercises and functional activities under direction of profes-

sional staff. Instructs, motivates, and assists patients to learn and improve functional activities, such as perambulation, transfer, ambulation, and daily-living activities. **SKILLS**—Reading Comprehension: Understanding written sentences and paragraphs in work-related documents. Learning Strategies: Selecting and using training/instructional methods and procedures appropriate for the situation when learning or teaching new things. Service Orientation: Actively looking for ways to help people. Active Listening: Giving full attention to what other people are saying, taking time to understand the points being made, asking questions as appropriate, and not interrupting at inappropriate times. Instructing: Teaching others how to do something.

GOE INFORMATION—**Interest Area:** 14. Medical and Health Services. **Work Group:** 14.06. Medical Therapy. **Other Job Titles in This Work Group:** Audiologists; Massage Therapists; Occupational Therapist Aides; Occupational Therapist Assistants; Occupational Therapists; Physical Therapist Assistants; Physical Therapists; Radiation Therapists; Recreational Therapists; Respiratory Therapists; Respiratory Therapy Technicians; Speech-Language Pathologists; Therapists, All Other. **PERSONALITY TYPE**—Social. Social occupations frequently involve working with, communicating with, and teaching people. These occupations often involve helping or providing service to others.

EDUCATION/TRAINING PROGRAM(S)—Physical Therapy Assistant. **RELATED KNOWLEDGE/COURSES**—**Therapy and Counseling:** Knowledge of principles, methods, and procedures for diagnosis, treatment, and rehabilitation of physical and mental dysfunctions and for career counseling and guidance. **Customer and Personal Service:** Knowledge of principles and processes for providing customer and personal services. This includes customer needs assessment, meeting quality standards for services, and evaluation of customer satisfaction. **Education and Training:** Knowledge of principles and methods for curriculum and training design, teaching and instruction for individuals and groups, and the measurement of training effects. **Clerical Studies:** Knowledge of administrative and clerical procedures and systems such as word processing, managing files and records, stenography and transcription, designing forms, and other office procedures and terminology. **Psychology:** Knowledge of human behavior and performance; individual differences in ability, personality, and interests; learning and motivation; psychological research methods; and the assessment and treatment of behavioral and affective disorders. **Biology:** Knowledge of plant and animal organisms and their tissues, cells, functions, interdependencies, and interactions with each other and the environment.

Physical Therapist Assistants

- ▲ Education/Training Required: Associate's degree
- ▲ Annual Earnings: $33,870
- ▲ Growth: 45%
- ▲ Annual Job Openings: 9,000
- ▲ Self-Employed: 0%
- ▲ Part-Time: 34.5%

Assist physical therapists in providing physical therapy treatments and procedures. May, in accordance with state laws, assist in the development of treatment plans, carry out routine functions, document the progress of treatment, and modify specific treatments in accordance with patient status and within the scope of treatment plans established by a physical therapist. Generally requires formal training. Records treatment given and equipment used. Fits patients for orthopedic braces, prostheses, and supportive devices, such as crutches. Transports patients to and from treatment area. Cleans work area and equipment after treatment. Performs clerical duties, such as taking inventory, ordering supplies, answering telephone, taking messages, and filling out forms. Administers active and passive manual therapeutic exercises, therapeutic massage, and heat, light, sound, water, and electrical modality treatments, such as ultrasound. Instructs, motivates, and assists patients to learn and improve functional activities, such as perambulation, transfer, ambulation, and daily-living activities. Safeguards, motivates, and assists patients practicing exercises and functional activities under direction of professional staff. Administers traction to relieve neck and back pain, using intermittent and static traction equipment. Secures patients into or onto therapy equipment. Measures patient's range-of-joint motion, body parts, and vital signs to determine effects of treatments or for patient evaluations. Assists patients to dress, undress, and put on and remove supportive devices, such as braces, splints, and slings. Confers with physical therapy staff and others to discuss and evaluate patient information for planning, modifying, and coordinating treatment. Adjusts fit of supportive devices for patients as instructed. Provides routine treatments, such as hydrotherapy, hot and cold packs, and paraffin bath. Trains patients in use and care of orthopedic braces, prostheses, and supportive devices, such as crutches. Observes patients during treatments, compiles and evaluates data on patients' responses to treatments and progress, and reports to physical therapist. **SKILLS**— Reading Comprehension: Understanding written sentences and paragraphs in work-related documents. Learning Strategies: Selecting and using training/instructional methods and procedures appropriate for the situation when learning or teaching new things. Service Orientation: Actively looking for ways to help people. Instructing: Teaching others how to do something. Active Listening: Giving full attention to what other people are saying, taking time to understand the points being made, asking questions as appropriate, and not interrupting at inappropriate times.

GOE INFORMATION—Interest Area: 14. Medical and Health Services. **Work Group:** 14.06. Medical Therapy. **Other Job Titles in This Work Group:** Audiologists; Massage Therapists; Occupational Therapist Aides; Occupational Therapist Assistants; Occupational Therapists; Physical Therapist Aides; Physical Therapists; Radiation Therapists; Recreational Therapists; Respiratory Therapists; Respiratory Therapy Technicians; Speech-Language Pathologists; Therapists, All Other. **PERSONALITY TYPE**—Social. Social occupations frequently involve working with, communicating with, and teaching people. These occupations often involve helping or providing service to others.

EDUCATION/TRAINING PROGRAM(S)— Physical Therapy Assistant. **RELATED KNOWLEDGE/COURSES—Therapy and Counseling:** Knowledge of principles, methods, and procedures for diagnosis, treatment, and rehabilitation of physical and

mental dysfunctions and for career counseling and guidance. **Customer and Personal Service:** Knowledge of principles and processes for providing customer and personal services. This includes customer needs assessment, meeting quality standards for services, and evaluation of customer satisfaction. **Education and Training:** Knowledge of principles and methods for curriculum and training design, teaching and instruction for individuals and groups, and the measurement of training effects. **Clerical Studies:** Knowledge of administrative and clerical procedures and systems such as word processing, managing files and records, stenography and transcription, designing forms, and other office procedures and terminology. **Psychology:** Knowledge of human behavior and performance; individual differences in ability, personality, and interests; learning and motivation; psychological research methods; and the assessment and treatment of behavioral and affective disorders. **Biology:** Knowledge of plant and animal organisms and their tissues, cells, functions, interdependencies, and interactions with each other and the environment.

Physical Therapists

- ▲ Education/Training Required: Master's degree
- ▲ Annual Earnings: $54,810
- ▲ Growth: 33%
- ▲ Annual Job Openings: 6,000
- ▲ Self-Employed: 5.9%
- ▲ Part-Time: 20.8%

Assess, plan, organize, and participate in rehabilitative programs that improve mobility, relieve pain, increase strength, and decrease or prevent deformity of patients suffering from disease or injury. Administers manual exercises to improve and maintain function. Administers treatment involving application of physical agents, using equipment, moist packs, ultraviolet and infrared lamps, and ultrasound machines. Administers traction to relieve pain, using traction equipment. Evaluates effects of treatment at various stages and adjusts treatments to achieve maximum benefit. Instructs, motivates, and assists patient to perform various physical activities and use supportive devices, such as crutches, canes,

and prostheses. Administers massage, applying knowledge of massage techniques and body physiology. Tests and measures patient's strength, motor development, sensory perception, functional capacity, and respiratory and circulatory efficiency and records data. Reviews physician's referral and patient's condition and medical records to determine physical therapy treatment required. Plans and prepares written treatment program based on evaluation of patient data. Evaluates, fits, and adjusts prosthetic and orthotic devices and recommends modification to orthotist. Records treatment, response, and progress in patient's chart or enters information into computer. Confers with medical practitioners to obtain additional information, suggest revisions in treatment, and integrate physical therapy into patient's care. Instructs patient and family in treatment procedures to be continued at home. **SKILLS**—Reading Comprehension: Understanding written sentences and paragraphs in work-related documents. Writing: Communicating effectively in writing as appropriate for the needs of the audience. Judgment and Decision Making: Considering the relative costs and benefits of potential actions to choose the most appropriate one. Active Listening: Giving full attention to what other people are saying, taking time to understand the points being made, asking questions as appropriate, and not interrupting at inappropriate times. Critical Thinking: Using logic and reasoning to identify the strengths and weaknesses of alternative solutions, conclusions, or approaches to problems. Speaking: Talking to others to convey information effectively. Instructing: Teaching others how to do something.

GOE INFORMATION—**Interest Area:** 14. Medical and Health Services. **Work Group:** 14.06. Medical Therapy. **Other Job Titles in This Work Group:** Audiologists; Massage Therapists; Occupational Therapist Aides; Occupational Therapist Assistants; Occupational Therapists; Physical Therapist Aides; Physical Therapist Assistants; Radiation Therapists; Recreational Therapists; Respiratory Therapists; Respiratory Therapy Technicians; Speech-Language Pathologists; Therapists, All Other. **PERSONALITY TYPE**—Social. Social occupations frequently involve working with, communicating with, and teaching people. These occupations often involve helping or providing service to others.

EDUCATION/TRAINING PROGRAM(S)— Physical Therapy. **RELATED KNOWLEDGE/ COURSES**—**Therapy and Counseling:** Knowledge of principles, methods, and procedures for diagnosis, treatment, and rehabilitation of physical and mental dysfunctions and for career counseling and guidance. **Medicine and Dentistry:** Knowledge of the information and techniques needed to diagnose and treat human injuries, diseases, and deformities. This includes symptoms, treatment alternatives, drug properties and interactions, and preventive health-care measures. **English Language:** Knowledge of the structure and content of the English language, including the meaning and spelling of words, rules of composition, and grammar. **Psychology:** Knowledge of human behavior and performance; individual differences in ability, personality, and interests; learning and motivation; psychological research methods; and the assessment and treatment of behavioral and affective disorders. **Administration and Management:** Knowledge of business and management principles involved in strategic planning, resource allocation, human resources modeling, leadership technique, production methods, and coordination of people and resources.

Physician Assistants

- ▲ Education/Training Required: Bachelor's degree
- ▲ Annual Earnings: $61,910
- ▲ Growth: 54%
- ▲ Annual Job Openings: 5,000
- ▲ Self-Employed: 0%
- ▲ Part-Time: 24.6%

Provide health-care services typically performed by a physician under the supervision of a physician. Conduct complete physicals, provide treatment, and counsel patients. May, in some cases, prescribe medication. Must graduate from an accredited educational program for physician assistants. Examines patient. Interprets diagnostic test results for deviations from normal. Counsels patients regarding prescribed therapeutic regimens, normal growth and development, family planning, emotional problems of daily living, and health maintenance. Develops and implements patient management plans, records progress notes, and assists in provision of continuity of care. Performs therapeutic procedures, such as injections, immunizations, suturing and wound care, and managing infection. Compiles patient medical data, including health history and results of physical examination. Administers or orders diagnostic tests, such as X-ray, electrocardiogram, and laboratory tests. **SKILLS—Reading Comprehension:** Understanding written sentences and paragraphs in work-related documents. Active Learning: Understanding the implications of new information for both current and future problem-solving and decision-making. Active Listening: Giving full attention to what other people are saying, taking time to understand the points being made, asking questions as appropriate, and not interrupting at inappropriate times. Speaking: Talking to others to convey information effectively. Science: Using scientific rules and methods to solve problems. Critical Thinking: Using logic and reasoning to identify the strengths and weaknesses of alternative solutions, conclusions, or approaches to problems. Service Orientation: Actively looking for ways to help people.

GOE INFORMATION—Interest Area: 14. Medical and Health Services. **Work Group:** 14.02. Medicine and Surgery. **Other Job Titles in This Work Group:** Anesthesiologists; Family and General Practitioners; Internists, General; Medical Assistants; Obstetricians and Gynecologists; Pediatricians, General; Pharmacists; Pharmacy Aides; Pharmacy Technicians; Physicians and Surgeons, All Other; Psychiatrists; Registered Nurses; Surgeons; Surgical Technologists. **PERSONALITY TYPE—**Investi-

gative. Investigative occupations frequently involve working with ideas and require an extensive amount of thinking. These occupations can involve searching for facts and figuring out problems mentally.

EDUCATION/TRAINING PROGRAM(S)— Physician Assistant. **RELATED KNOWLEDGE/ COURSES—Medicine and Dentistry:** Knowledge of the information and techniques needed to diagnose and treat human injuries, diseases, and deformities. This includes symptoms, treatment alternatives, drug properties and interactions, and preventive health-care measures. **Biology:** Knowledge of plant and animal organisms and their tissues, cells, functions, interdependencies, and interactions with each other and the environment. **Chemistry:** Knowledge of the chemical composition, structure, and properties of substances and of the chemical processes and transformations that they undergo. This includes uses of chemicals and their interactions, danger signs, production techniques, and disposal methods. **Therapy and Counseling:** Knowledge of principles, methods, and procedures for diagnosis, treatment, and rehabilitation of physical and mental dysfunctions and for career counseling and guidance. **Psychology:** Knowledge of human behavior and performance; individual differences in ability, personality, and interests; learning and motivation; psychological research methods; and the assessment and treatment of behavioral and affective disorders.

▲ Education/Training Required: Doctoral degree

▲ Annual Earnings: $83,310

▲ Growth: 10%

▲ Annual Job Openings: 1,000

▲ Self-Employed: 5%

▲ Part-Time: 6.6%

Physicists

Conduct research into the phases of physical phenomena, develop theories and laws on the basis of observation and experiments, and devise methods to apply laws and theories to industry and other fields. Observes structure and properties of matter and transformation and propagation of energy, us-

ing masers, lasers, telescopes, and other equipment. Assists in developing standards of permissible concentrations of radioisotopes in liquids and gases. Assists with development of manufacturing, assembly, and fabrication processes of lasers, masers, infrared, and other light-emitting and light-sensitive devices. Directs testing and monitoring of contamination of radioactive equipment and recording of personnel and plant area radiation exposure data. Advises authorities in procedures to be followed in radiation incidents or hazards and assists in civil defense planning. Incorporates methods for maintenance and repair of components and designs and develops test instrumentation and test procedures. Consults other scientists regarding innovations to ensure equipment or plant design conforms to health physics standards for protection of personnel. Conducts research pertaining to potential environmental impact of proposed atomic energy–related industrial development to determine qualifications for licensing. Designs electronic circuitry and optical components with scientific characteristics to fit within specified mechanical limits and perform according to specifications. Conducts application analysis to determine commercial, industrial, scientific, medical, military, or other uses for electro-optical devices. Analyzes results of experiments designed to detect and measure previously unobserved physical phenomena. Conducts instrumental analyses to determine physical properties of materials. Describes and expresses observations and conclusions in mathematical terms. **SKILLS**—Mathematics: Using mathematics to solve problems. Science: Using scientific rules and methods to solve problems. Writing: Communicating effectively in writing as appropriate for the needs of the audience. Reading Comprehension: Understanding written sentences and paragraphs in work-related documents. Active Learning: Understanding the implications of new information for both current and future problem-solving and decision-making.

GOE INFORMATION—**Interest Area:** 02. Science, Math, and Engineering. **Work Group:** 02.02. Physical Sciences. **Other Job Titles in This Work Group:**

Astronomers; Atmospheric and Space Scientists; Chemists; Geographers; Geologists; Geoscientists, Except Hydrologists and Geographers; Hydrologists; Materials Scientists; Physical Scientists, All Other. **PERSONALITY TYPE**—Investigative. Investigative occupations frequently involve working with ideas and require an extensive amount of thinking. These occupations can involve searching for facts and figuring out problems mentally.

EDUCATION/TRAINING PROGRAM(S)— Acoustics; Astrophysics; Chemical and Atomic/Molecular Physics; Elementary Particle Physics; Health Physics/ Radiologic Health; Nuclear Physics; Optics; Physics, General; Physics, Other; Plasma and High-Temperature Physics; Solid State and Low-Temperature Physics; Theoretical and Mathematical Physics. **RELATED KNOWLEDGE/COURSES**—**Physics:** Knowledge and prediction of physical principles and laws and their interrelationships and applications to understanding fluid, material, and atmospheric dynamics and mechanical, electrical, atomic, and sub-atomic structures and processes. **Mathematics:** Knowledge of arithmetic, algebra, geometry, calculus, and statistics and their applications. **English Language:** Knowledge of the structure and content of the English language, including the meaning and spelling of words, rules of composition, and grammar. **Education and Training:** Knowledge of principles and methods for curriculum and training design, teaching and instruction for individuals and groups, and the measurement of training effects. **Engineering and Technology:** Knowledge of the practical application of engineering science and technology. This includes applying principles, techniques, procedures, and equipment to the design and production of various goods and services.

Physics Teachers, Postsecondary

- ▲ Education/Training Required: Master's degree
- ▲ Annual Earnings: $58,500
- ▲ Growth: 24% for all Postsecondary Teachers
- ▲ Annual Job Openings: 184,000 for all Postsecondary Teachers
- ▲ Self-Employed: 0%
- ▲ Part-Time: 32.3% for all Postsecondary Teachers

Teach courses pertaining to the laws of matter and energy. Includes both teachers primarily engaged in teaching and those who do a combination of both teaching and research. Prepares and delivers lectures to students. Compiles bibliographies of specialized materials for outside reading assignments. Stimulates class discussions. Compiles, administers, and grades examinations or assigns this work to others. Advises students on academic and vocational curricula. Conducts research in particular field of knowledge and publishes findings in professional journals. Acts as adviser to student organizations. Serves on faculty committee providing professional consulting services to government and industry. Directs research of other teachers or graduate students working for advanced academic degrees. **SKILLS**—Reading Comprehension: Understanding written sentences and paragraphs in work-related documents. Writing: Communicating effectively in writing as appropriate for the needs of the audience. Instructing: Teaching others how to do something. Science: Using scientific rules and methods to solve problems. Learning Strategies: Selecting and using training/instructional methods and procedures appropriate for the situation when learning or teaching new things.

GOE INFORMATION—**Interest Area:** 12. Education and Social Service. **Work Group:** 12.03. Educational Services. **Other Job Titles in This Work Group:** Adult Literacy, Remedial Education, and GED Teachers and Instructors; Agricultural Sciences Teachers, Postsecondary; Anthropology and Archeology Teachers, Postsecondary; Architecture Teachers, Postsecondary; Archivists; Area, Ethnic, and Cultural Studies Teachers, Postsecondary; Art, Drama, and Music Teachers, Postsecondary; Atmospheric, Earth, Marine, and Space Sciences Teachers, Postsecondary; Audio-Visual Collections Specialists; Biological Science Teachers, Postsecondary; Business Teachers, Postsecondary; Chemistry Teachers, Postsecondary; Child Care Workers; Communications Teachers, Postsecondary; Computer Science Teachers, Postsecondary; Criminal Justice and Law Enforcement Teachers, Postsecondary; Curators; Economics Teachers, Postsecondary; Education Teachers, Postsecondary; Educational Psychologists; Educational, Vocational, and School Counselors; Elementary School Teachers, Except Special Education; Engineering Teachers, Postsecondary; English Language and Literature Teachers, Postsecondary; Environmental Science Teachers, Postsecondary; Farm and Home Management Advisors; Foreign Language and Literature Teachers, Postsecondary; Forestry and Conservation Science Teachers, Postsecondary; Geography Teachers, Postsecondary; Graduate Teaching Assistants; Health Specialties Teachers, Postsecondary; History Teachers, Postsecondary; Home Economics Teachers, Postsecondary; Kindergarten Teachers, Except Special Education; Law Teachers, Postsecondary; Librarians; Library Assistants, Clerical; others. **PERSONALITY TYPE**—Investigative. Investigative occupations frequently involve working with ideas and require an extensive amount of thinking. These occupations can involve searching for facts and figuring out problems mentally.

EDUCATION/TRAINING PROGRAM(S)—Acoustics; Chemical and Atomic/Molecular Physics; Elementary Particle Physics; Nuclear Physics; Optics; Physics, General; Physics, Other; Plasma and High-Temperature Physics; Solid State and Low-Temperature Physics; Theoretical and Mathematical Physics. **RELATED KNOWLEDGE/COURSES**—**Physics:** Knowledge and prediction of physical principles and laws and their interrelationships and applications to understanding fluid, material, and atmospheric dynamics and mechanical, electrical, atomic, and sub-atomic structures and processes. **Education and Training:** Knowledge of principles and methods for curriculum and training design, teaching and instruction for individuals and groups, and the measurement of training effects. **Mathematics:** Knowledge of arithmetic, algebra, geometry, calculus, and statistics and their applications. **English Language:** Knowledge of the structure and content of the English language, including the meaning and spelling of words, rules of composition, and grammar. **Administration and Management:** Knowledge of business and management principles involved in strategic planning, resource allocation, human resources modeling, leadership technique, production methods, and coordination of people and resources.

P

Pilots, Ship

> ▲ Education/Training Required: Work experience, plus degree
> ▲ Annual Earnings: $47,510
> ▲ Growth: 3%
> ▲ Annual Job Openings: 2,000
> ▲ Self-Employed: 7.9%
> ▲ Part-Time: 3%

Command ships to steer them into and out of harbors, estuaries, straits, and sounds and on rivers, lakes, and bays. Must be licensed by U.S. Coast Guard with limitations indicating class and tonnage of vessels for which license is valid and route and waters that may be piloted. Directs course and speed of ship on basis of specialized knowledge of local winds, weather, tides, and current. Orders worker at helm to steer ship. Navigates ship to avoid reefs, outlying shoals, and other hazards, utilizing aids to navigation, such as lighthouses and buoys. Signals tugboat captain to berth and unberth ship. **SKILLS—Operation and Control:** Controlling operations of equipment or systems. **Judgment and Decision Making:** Considering the relative costs and benefits of potential actions to choose the most appropriate one. **Monitoring:** Monitoring/Assessing your performance or that of other individuals or organizations to make improvements or take corrective action. **Mathematics:** Using mathematics to solve problems. **Active Listening:** Giving full attention to what other people are saying, taking time to understand the points being made, asking questions as appropriate, and not interrupting at inappropriate times.

GOE INFORMATION—**Interest Area:** 07. Transportation. **Work Group:** 07.04. Water Vehicle Operation. **Other Job Titles in This Work Group:** Able Seamen; Captains, Mates, and Pilots of Water Vessels; Dredge Operators; Mates—Ship, Boat, and Barge; Motorboat Operators; Ordinary Seamen and Marine Oilers; Sailors and Marine Oilers; Ship and Boat Captains. **PERSONALITY TYPE**—Realistic. Realistic occupations frequently involve work activities that include practical, hands-on problems and solutions. They often deal with plants, animals, and real-world materials like wood, tools, and machinery. Many of the occupations require working outside and do not involve a lot of paperwork or working closely with others.

EDUCATION/TRAINING PROGRAM(S)—Fishing Technology/Commercial Fishing; Marine Science/Merchant Marine Officer; Water Transportation Workers, Other. **RELATED KNOWLEDGE/COURSES**—**Transportation:** Knowledge of principles and methods for moving people or goods by air, rail, sea, or road, including the relative costs and benefits. **Geography:** Knowledge of principles and methods for describing the features of land, sea, and air masses, including their physical characteristics, locations, interrelationships, and distribution of plant, animal, and human life. **Telecommunications:** Knowledge of transmission, broadcasting, switching, control, and operation of telecommunications systems. **Engineering and Technology:** Knowledge of the practical application of engineering science and technology. This includes applying principles, techniques, procedures, and equipment to the design and production of various goods and services. **Mathematics:** Knowledge of arithmetic, algebra, geometry, calculus, and statistics and their applications.

Podiatrists

▲ Education/Training Required: First professional degree

▲ Annual Earnings: $107,560

▲ Growth: 14%

▲ Annual Job Openings: 1,000

▲ Self-Employed: 46.6%

▲ Part-Time: 10.5%

Diagnose and treat diseases and deformities of the human foot. Diagnoses ailments, such as tumors, ulcers, fractures, skin or nail diseases, and deformities, utilizing urinalysis, blood tests, and X rays. Treats conditions such as corns, calluses, ingrown nails, tumors, shortened tendons, bunions, cysts, and abscesses by surgical methods. Corrects deformities by means of plaster casts and strapping. Treats bone, muscle, and joint disorders. Treats deformities by mechanical and electrical methods, such as whirlpool or paraffin baths and shortwave and low voltage currents. Prescribes corrective footwear. Prescribes drugs. Makes and fits prosthetic appliances. Performs surgery. Advises patients concerning continued treatment of disorders and foot care to prevent recurrence of disorders. Refers patients to physician when symptoms indicative of systemic disorders, such as arthritis or diabetes, are observed in feet and legs. **SKILLS**—Reading Comprehension: Understanding written sentences and paragraphs in work-related documents. Active Learning: Understanding the implications of new information for both current and future problem-solving and decision-making. Judgment and Decision Making: Considering the relative costs and benefits of potential actions to choose the most appropriate one. Active Listening: Giving full attention to what other people are saying, taking time to understand the points being made, asking questions as appropriate, and not interrupting at inappropriate times. Critical Thinking: Using logic and reasoning to identify the strengths and weaknesses of alternative solutions, conclusions, or approaches to problems.

GOE INFORMATION—Interest Area: 14. Medical and Health Services. **Work Group:** 14.04. Health Specialties. **Other Job Titles in This Work Group:** Chiropractors; Opticians, Dispensing; Optometrists. **PERSONALITY TYPE**—Social. Social occupations frequently involve working with, communicating with, and teaching people. These occupations often involve helping or providing service to others.

EDUCATION/TRAINING PROGRAM(S)— Podiatry (D.P.M., D.P., Pod.D.). **RELATED KNOWLEDGE/COURSES—Medicine and Dentistry:** Knowledge of the information and techniques needed to diagnose and treat human injuries, diseases, and deformities. This includes symptoms, treatment alternatives, drug properties and interactions, and preventive health-care measures. **Biology:** Knowledge of plant and animal organisms and their tissues, cells, functions, interdependencies, and interactions with each other and the environment. **Chemistry:** Knowledge of the chemical composition, structure, and properties of substances and of the chemical processes and transformations that they undergo. This includes uses of chemicals and their interactions, danger signs, production techniques, and disposal methods. **Therapy and Counseling:** Knowledge of principles, methods, and procedures for diagnosis, treatment, and rehabilitation of physical and mental dysfunctions and for career counseling and guidance. **English Language:** Knowledge of the structure and content of the English language, including the meaning and spelling of words, rules of composition, and grammar.

P

Poets and Lyricists

▲ Education/Training Required: Bachelor's degree

▲ Annual Earnings: $42,270

▲ Growth: 28%

▲ Annual Job Openings: 18,000

▲ Self-Employed: 31.2%

▲ Part-Time: 18.5%

Write poetry or song lyrics for publication or performance. Writes words to fit musical compositions, including lyrics for operas, musical plays, and choral works. Chooses subject matter and suitable form to express personal feeling and experience or ideas or to narrate story or event. Adapts text to accommodate musical requirements of composer and singer. Writes narrative, dramatic, lyric, or other types of poetry for publication. **SKILLS**—Writing: Communicating effectively in writing as appropriate for the needs of the audience. Reading Comprehension: Understanding written sentences and paragraphs in work-related documents. Learning Strategies: Selecting and using training/instructional methods and procedures appropriate for the situation when learning or teaching new things. Monitoring: Monitoring/Assessing your performance or that of other individuals or organizations to make improvements or take corrective action.

GOE INFORMATION—**Interest Area:** 01. Arts, Entertainment, and Media. **Work Group:** 01.02. Writing and Editing. **Other Job Titles in This Work Group:** Copy Writers; Creative Writers; Editors; Technical Writers; Writers and Authors. **PERSONALITY TYPE**—Artistic. Artistic occupations frequently involve working with forms, designs, and patterns. They often require self-expression, and the work can be done without following a clear set of rules.

EDUCATION/TRAINING PROGRAM(S)—Broadcast Journalism; Business Communications; Communications, Other; English Creative Writing; Journalism; Mass Communications; Playwriting and Screenwriting; Technical and Business Writing. **RELATED KNOWLEDGE/COURSES**—**Fine Arts:** Knowledge of the theory and techniques required to compose, produce, and perform works of music, dance, visual arts, drama, and sculpture. **English Language:** Knowledge of the structure and content of the English language, including the meaning and spelling of words, rules of composition, and grammar. **Communications and Media:** Knowledge of media production, communication, and dissemination techniques and methods. This includes alternative ways to inform and entertain via written, oral, and visual media. **Customer and Personal Service:** Knowledge of principles and processes for providing customer and personal services. This includes customer needs assessment, meeting quality standards for services, and evaluation of customer satisfaction.

Political Science Teachers, Postsecondary

▲ Education/Training Required: Master's degree

▲ Annual Earnings: $53,520

▲ Growth: 24% for all Postsecondary Teachers

▲ Annual Job Openings: 184,000 for all Postsecondary Teachers

▲ Self-Employed: 0%

▲ Part-Time: 32.3% for all Postsecondary Teachers

Teach courses in political science, international affairs, and international relations. Acts as adviser to student organizations. Compiles bibliographies of specialized materials for outside reading assignments. Directs research of other teachers or graduate students working for advanced academic degrees. Serves on faculty committee providing professional consulting services to government and industry. Conducts research in particular field of knowledge and publishes findings in professional journals. Advises students on academic and vocational curricula. Compiles, administers, and grades examinations or assigns this work to others. Prepares and delivers lectures to students. Stimulates class discussions. **SKILLS**—Reading Comprehension: Understanding written sentences and paragraphs in work-related documents. Instructing: Teaching others how to do something. Speaking: Talking to others to convey information effectively. Active Learning: Understanding the implications of new information for both current and future problem-solving and decision-making. Active Listening: Giving full attention to what other people are saying, taking time to understand the points being made, asking questions as appropriate, and not interrupting at inappropriate times. Writing: Communicating effectively in writing as appropriate for the needs of the audience. Learning Strategies: Selecting and using training/instructional methods and procedures appropriate for the situation when learning or teaching new things.

GOE INFORMATION—Interest Area: 12. Education and Social Service. **Work Group:** 12.03. Educational Services. **Other Job Titles in This Work Group:** Adult Literacy, Remedial Education, and GED Teachers and Instructors; Agricultural Sciences Teachers, Postsecondary; Anthropology and Archeology Teachers, Postsecondary; Architecture Teachers, Postsecondary; Archivists; Area, Ethnic, and Cultural Studies Teachers, Postsecondary; Art, Drama, and Music Teachers, Postsecondary; Atmospheric, Earth, Marine, and Space Sciences Teachers, Postsecondary; Audio-Visual Collections Specialists; Biological Science Teachers, Postsecondary; Business Teachers, Postsecondary; Chemistry Teachers, Postsecondary; Child Care Workers; Communications Teachers, Postsecondary; Computer Science Teachers, Postsecondary; Criminal Justice and Law Enforcement Teachers, Postsecondary; Curators; Economics Teachers, Postsecondary; Education Teachers, Postsecondary; Educational Psychologists; Educational, Vocational, and School Counselors; Elementary School Teachers, Except Special Education; Engineering Teachers, Postsecondary; English Language and Literature Teachers, Postsecondary; Environmental Science Teachers, Postsecondary; Farm and Home Management Advisors; Foreign Language and Literature Teachers, Postsecondary; Forestry and Conservation Science Teachers, Postsecondary; Geography Teachers, Postsecondary; Graduate Teaching Assistants; Health Specialties Teachers, Postsecondary; History Teachers, Postsecondary; Home Economics Teachers, Postsecondary; Kindergarten Teachers, Except Special Education; Law Teachers, Postsecondary; Librarians; Library Assistants, Clerical; others. **PERSONALITY TYPE**—Social. Social occupations frequently involve working with, communicating with, and teaching people. These occupations often involve helping or providing service to others.

EDUCATION/TRAINING PROGRAM(S)—American Government; Political Science, General; Social Science Teacher Education. **RELATED KNOWLEDGE/COURSES**—Education and Training: Knowledge of principles and methods for curriculum and training design, teaching and instruction for individuals and groups, and the measurement of training effects. **Sociology and Anthropology:** Knowledge of group behavior and dynamics, societal trends and influences, human migrations, ethnicity, cultures, and their history and origins. **History and Archeology:** Knowledge of historical events and their causes, indicators, and effects on civilizations and cultures. **Psychology:** Knowledge of human behavior and performance; individual differences in ability, personality, and interests; learning and motivation; psychological research methods; and the assessment and treatment of behavioral and affective disorders. **English Language:** Knowledge of the structure and content of the English language, including the meaning and spelling of words, rules of composition, and grammar.

Political Scientists

▲ Education/Training Required: Master's degree

▲ Annual Earnings: $81,040

▲ Growth: 17%

▲ Annual Job Openings: 2,000

▲ Self-Employed: 5.2%

▲ Part-Time: 18.1%

Study the origin, development, and operation of political systems. Research a wide range of subjects, such as relations between the United States and foreign countries, the beliefs and institutions of foreign nations, or the politics of small towns or a major metropolis. May study topics such as public opinion, political decision-making, and ideology. May analyze the structure and operation of governments, as well as various political entities. May conduct public opinion surveys, analyze election results, or analyze public documents. Conducts research into political philosophy and theories of political systems, such as governmental institutions, public laws, and international law. Analyzes and interprets results of studies and prepares reports detailing findings, recommendations, or conclusions. Organizes and conducts public opinion surveys and interprets results. Recommends programs and policies to institutions and organizations. Prepares reports detailing findings and conclusions. Consults with government officials, civic bodies, research agencies, and political parties. SKILLS—Writing: Communicating effectively in writing as appropriate for the needs of the audience. Reading Comprehension: Understanding written sentences and paragraphs in work-related documents. Mathematics: Using mathematics to solve problems. Active Learning: Understanding the implications of new information for both current and future problem-solving and decision-making. Speaking: Talking to others to convey information effectively. Active Listening: Giving full attention to what other people are saying, taking time to understand the points being made, asking questions as appropriate, and not interrupting at inappropriate times.

GOE INFORMATION—Interest Area: 02. Science, Math, and Engineering. Work Group: 02.04. Social Sciences. Other Job Titles in This Work Group: Anthropologists; Anthropologists and Archeologists; Archeologists; City Planning Aides; Economists; Historians; Industrial-Organizational Psychologists; Psychologists, All Other; Social Science Research Assistants; Social Scientists and Related Workers, All Other; Sociologists; Survey Researchers; Urban and Regional Planners. PERSONALITY TYPE—Investigative. Investigative occupations frequently involve working with ideas and require an extensive amount of thinking. These occupations can involve searching for facts and figuring out problems mentally.

EDUCATION/TRAINING PROGRAM(S)— American Government; International Relations and Affairs; Political Science and Government, Other; Political Science, General. RELATED KNOWLEDGE/ COURSES—Law and Government: Knowledge of laws, legal codes, court procedures, precedents, government regulations, executive orders, agency rules, and the democratic political process. English Language: Knowledge of the structure and content of the English language, including the meaning and spelling of words, rules of composition, and grammar. Communications and Media: Knowledge of media production, communication, and dissemination techniques and methods. This includes alternative ways to inform and entertain via written, oral, and visual media. Mathematics: Knowledge of arithmetic, algebra, geometry, calculus, and statistics and their applications. Philosophy and Theology: Knowledge of different philosophical systems and religions. This includes their basic principles, values, ethics, ways of thinking, customs, and practices and their impact on human culture.

Postsecondary Teachers

- ▲ Education/Training Required: Master's degree
- ▲ Annual Earnings: $46,330
- ▲ Growth: 23%
- ▲ Annual Job Openings: 184,000
- ▲ Self-Employed: 0%
- ▲ Part-Time: 32.3%

For detailed information, see

- Agricultural Sciences Teachers, Postsecondary
- Anthropology and Archeology Teachers, Postsecondary
- Architecture Teachers, Postsecondary
- Area, Ethnic, and Cultural Studies Teachers, Postsecondary
- Art, Drama, and Music Teachers, Postsecondary
- Atmospheric, Earth, Marine, and Space Sciences Teachers, Postsecondary
- Biological Science Teachers, Postsecondary
- Business Teachers, Postsecondary
- Chemistry Teachers, Postsecondary
- Communications Teachers, Postsecondary
- Computer Science Teachers, Postsecondary
- Criminal Justice and Law Enforcement Teachers, Postsecondary
- Economics Teachers, Postsecondary
- Education Administrators, Postsecondary
- Education Teachers, Postsecondary
- Engineering Teachers, Postsecondary
- English Language and Literature Teachers, Postsecondary
- Environmental Science Teachers, Postsecondary
- Foreign Language and Literature Teachers, Postsecondary
- Forestry and Conservation Science Teachers, Postsecondary
- Geography Teachers, Postsecondary
- Graduate Teaching Assistants
- Health Specialties Teachers, Postsecondary
- History Teachers, Postsecondary
- Home Economics Teachers, Postsecondary
- Law Teachers, Postsecondary
- Library Science Teachers, Postsecondary
- Mathematical Science Teachers, Postsecondary
- Nursing Instructors and Teachers, Postsecondary
- Philosophy and Religion Teachers, Postsecondary
- Physics Teachers, Postsecondary
- Political Science Teachers, Postsecondary
- Psychology Teachers, Postsecondary
- Recreation and Fitness Studies Teachers, Postsecondary
- Social Work Teachers, Postsecondary
- Sociology Teachers, Postsecondary

P

Preschool Teachers, Except Special Education

▲ Education/Training Required: Bachelor's degree
▲ Annual Earnings: $17,810
▲ Growth: 20%
▲ Annual Job Openings: 55,000
▲ Self-Employed: 1.5%
▲ Part-Time: 32.4%

Instruct children (normally up to 5 years of age) in activities designed to promote social, physical, and intellectual growth needed for primary school in preschool, daycare center, or other child development facility. May be required to hold state certification. Instructs children in activities designed to promote social, physical, and intellectual growth in facility such as preschool or daycare center. Plans individual and group activities for children, such as learning to listen to instructions, playing with others, and using play equipment. Demonstrates activity. Structures play activities to instill concepts of respect and concern for others. Monitors individual and/or group activities to prevent accidents and promote social skills. Reads books to entire class or to small groups. Confers with parents to explain preschool program and to discuss ways they can develop their child's interest. Plans instructional activities for teacher aide. Administers tests to determine each child's level of development according to design of test. Attends staff meetings. **SKILLS**—Learning Strategies: Selecting and using training/instructional methods and procedures appropriate for the situation when learning or teaching new things. Monitoring: Monitoring/Assessing your performance or that of other individuals or organizations to make improvements or take corrective action. Social Perceptiveness: Being aware of others' reactions and understanding why they react as they do. Active Listening: Giving full attention to what other people are saying, taking time to understand the points being made, asking questions as appropriate, and not interrupting at inappropriate times. Reading Comprehension: Understanding written sentences and paragraphs in work-related documents. Speaking: Talking to others to convey information effectively.

GOE INFORMATION—**Interest Area:** 12. Education and Social Service. **Work Group:** 12.03. Educational Services. **Other Job Titles in This Work Group:** Adult Literacy, Remedial Education, and GED Teachers and Instructors; Agricultural Sciences Teachers, Postsecondary; Anthropology and Archeology Teachers, Postsecondary; Architecture Teachers, Postsecondary; Archivists; Area, Ethnic, and Cultural Studies Teachers, Postsecondary; Art, Drama, and Music Teachers, Postsecondary; Atmospheric, Earth, Marine, and Space Sciences Teachers, Postsecondary; Audio-Visual Collections Specialists; Biological Science Teachers, Postsecondary; Business Teachers, Postsecondary; Chemistry Teachers, Postsecondary; Child Care Workers; Communications Teachers, Postsecondary; Computer Science Teachers, Postsecondary; Criminal Justice and Law Enforcement Teachers, Postsecondary; Curators; Economics Teachers, Postsecondary; Education Teachers, Postsecondary; Educational Psychologists; Educational, Vocational, and School Counselors; Elementary School Teachers, Except Special Education; Engineering Teachers, Postsecondary; English Language and Literature Teachers, Postsecondary; Environmental Science Teachers, Postsecondary; Farm and Home Management Advisors; Foreign Language and Literature Teachers, Postsecondary; Forestry and Conservation Science Teachers, Postsecondary; Geography Teachers, Postsecondary; Graduate Teaching Assistants; Health Specialties Teachers, Postsecondary; History Teachers, Postsecondary; Home Economics Teachers, Postsecondary; Kindergarten Teachers, Except Special Education; Law Teachers, Postsecondary; Librarians; Library Assistants, Clerical; others. **PERSONALITY TYPE**—Social. Social occupations frequently involve working with, communicating with, and teaching people.

These occupations often involve helping or providing service to others.

EDUCATION/TRAINING PROGRAM(S)— Pre-Elementary/Early Childhood/Kindergarten Teacher Education. **RELATED KNOWLEDGE/ COURSES—Education and Training:** Knowledge of principles and methods for curriculum and training design, teaching and instruction for individuals and groups, and the measurement of training effects. **Customer and Personal Service:** Knowledge of principles and processes for providing customer and personal services. This includes customer needs assessment, meeting quality standards for services, and evaluation of customer satisfaction. **English Language:** Knowledge of the structure and content of the English language, including the meaning and spelling of words, rules of composition, and grammar. **Psychology:** Knowledge of human behavior and performance; individual differences in ability, personality, and interests; learning and motivation; psychological research methods; and the assessment and treatment of behavioral and affective disorders. **Fine Arts:** Knowledge of the theory and techniques required to compose, produce, and perform works of music, dance, visual arts, drama, and sculpture.

Private Sector Executives

- ▲ Education/Training Required: Work experience, plus degree
- ▲ Annual Earnings: $ 113,810
- ▲ Growth: 17%
- ▲ Annual Job Openings: 48,000
- ▲ Self-Employed: 0%
- ▲ Part-Time: 6.1%

Determine and formulate policies and business strategies and provide overall direction of private sector organizations. Plan, direct, and coordinate operational activities at the highest level of management with the help of subordinate managers. Directs, plans, and implements policies and objectives of organization or business in accordance with charter and board of directors. Directs activities of organization to plan procedures, establish responsibilities, and coordinate functions among departments and sites. Analyzes operations to evaluate performance of company and staff and to determine areas of cost reduction and program improvement. Confers with board members, organization officials, and staff members to establish policies and formulate plans. Reviews financial statements and sales and activity reports to ensure that organization's objectives are achieved. Assigns or delegates responsibilities to subordinates. Directs and coordinates activities of business involved with buying and selling investment products and financial services. Establishes internal control procedures. Presides over or serves on board of directors, management committees, or other governing boards. Directs inservice training of staff. Administers program for selection of sites, construction of buildings, and provision of equipment and supplies. Screens, selects, hires, transfers, and discharges employees. Promotes objectives of institution or business before associations, public, government agencies, or community groups. Negotiates or approves contracts with suppliers and distributors and with maintenance, janitorial, and security providers. Prepares reports and budgets. Directs non-merchandising departments of business, such as advertising, purchasing, credit, and accounting. Directs and coordinates activities of business or department concerned with production, pricing, sales, and/or distribution of products. Directs and coordinates organization's financial and budget activities to fund operations, maximize investments, and increase efficiency. **SKILLS—Judgment and Decision Making:** Considering the relative costs and benefits of potential actions to choose the most appropriate one. **Coordination:** Adjusting actions in relation to others' actions. **Systems Evaluation:** Identifying measures or indicators of system performance and the actions needed to improve or correct performance relative to the goals of the system. **Systems Analysis:** Determining how a system should work and how changes in conditions, operations, and the environment will affect outcomes. Management of Financial Resources: Determining how money will be spent to get the work done and accounting for these expenditures.

GOE INFORMATION—Interest Area: 13. General Management and Support. **Work Group:** 13.01. General Management Work and Management of Support Functions. **Other Job Titles in This Work Group:** Chief Executives; Compensation and Benefits Managers; Farm, Ranch, and Other Agricultural Managers; Financial Managers; Financial Managers, Branch or Department; Funeral Directors; General and Operations Managers; Government Service Executives; Human Resources Managers; Human Resources Managers, All Other; Legislators; Managers, All Other; Postmasters and Mail Superintendents; Property, Real Estate, and Community Association Managers; Public Relations Managers; Purchasing Managers; Storage and Distribution Managers; Training and Development Managers; Transportation, Storage, and Distribution Managers; Treasurers, Controllers, and Chief Financial Officers. **PERSONALITY TYPE**—Enterprising. Enterprising occupations frequently involve starting up and carrying out projects. These occupations can involve leading people and making many decisions. They sometimes require risk taking and often deal with business.

EDUCATION/TRAINING PROGRAM(S)— Business Administration and Management, General; Enterprise Management and Operation, General; International Business; Public Administration; Public Administration and Services, Other; Public Policy Analysis. **RELATED KNOWLEDGE/COURSES—Administration and Management:** Knowledge of business and management principles involved in strategic planning, resource allocation, human resources modeling, leadership technique, production methods, and coordination of people and resources. **English Language:** Knowledge of the structure and content of the English language, including the meaning and spelling of words, rules of composition, and grammar. **Economics and Accounting:** Knowledge of economic and accounting principles and practices, the financial markets, banking, and the analysis and reporting of financial data. **Mathematics:** Knowledge of arithmetic, algebra, geometry, calculus, and statistics and their applications. **Sales and Marketing:** Knowledge of principles and methods for showing, promoting, and selling products or services. This includes marketing strategy and tactics, product demonstration, sales techniques, and sales control systems. **Production and Processing:** Knowledge of raw materials, production processes, quality control, costs, and other techniques for maximizing the effective manufacture and distribution of goods.

Probation Officers and Correctional Treatment Specialists

▲ Education/Training Required: Bachelor's degree
▲ Annual Earnings: $38,150
▲ Growth: 24%
▲ Annual Job Openings: 14,000
▲ Self-Employed: 3.1%
▲ Part-Time: 11.9%

Provide social services to assist in rehabilitation of law offenders in custody or on probation or parole. Make recommendations for actions involving formulation of rehabilitation plan and treatment of offender, including conditional release and education and employment stipulations. Counsels offender and refers offender to social resources of community for assistance. Interviews offender or inmate to determine social progress, individual problems, needs, interests, and attitude. Conducts follow-up interview with offender or inmate to ascertain progress made. Reviews and evaluates legal and social history and progress of offender or inmate. Conducts prehearing or presentencing investigations and testifies in court. Prepares and maintains case folder for each assigned inmate or offender. Develops and prepares informational packets of social agencies and assistance organizations and programs for inmate or offender. Assists offender or inmate with matters concerning detainers, sentences in other jurisdictions, writs, and applications for social assistance. Makes recommendations concerning conditional release or institutionalization of offender or inmate. Confers with inmate's or offender's family to identify needs and problems and to ensure that family and business are attended to. Informs offender or inmate of requirements of conditional release, such as office visits, restitution payments, or educational and employment stipulations. Determines nature and extent of inmate's or offender's criminal record and current and prospective social problems. Consults with attorneys, judges, and institution personnel to evaluate inmate's social progress. Formulates rehabilitation plan for each assigned offender or inmate. Provides guidance to inmates or offenders, such as development of vocational and educational plans and available social services. **SKILLS**—Active Listening: Giving full attention to what other people are saying, taking time to understand the points being made, asking questions as appropriate, and not interrupting at inappropriate times. Speaking: Talking to others to convey information effectively. Judgment and Decision Making: Considering the relative costs and benefits of potential actions to choose the most appropriate one. Reading Comprehension: Understanding written sentences and paragraphs in work-related documents. Service Orientation: Actively looking for ways to help people.

GOE INFORMATION—**Interest Area:** 12. Education and Social Service. **Work Group:** 12.02. Social Services. **Other Job Titles in This Work Group:** Child, Family, and School Social Workers; Clergy; Clinical Psychologists; Clinical, Counseling, and School Psychologists; Community and Social Service Specialists, All Other; Counseling Psychologists; Counselors, All Other; Directors, Religious Activities and Education; Marriage and Family Therapists; Medical and Public Health Social Workers; Mental Health and Substance Abuse Social Workers; Mental Health Counselors; Rehabilitation Counselors; Religious Workers, All Other; Residential Advisors; Social and Human Service Assistants; Social Workers, All Other; Substance Abuse and Behavioral Disorder Counselors. **PERSONALITY TYPE**—Social. Social occupations frequently involve working with, communicating with, and teaching people. These occupations often involve helping or providing service to others.

EDUCATION/TRAINING PROGRAM(S)—Corrections/Correctional Administration; Criminal Justice and Corrections, Other; Forensic Technologist/Technician; Protective Services, Other; Social Work. **RELATED KNOWLEDGE/COURSES**—**Therapy and Counseling:** Knowledge of principles, methods, and procedures for diagnosis, treatment, and rehabilitation of physical and mental dysfunctions and for career counseling and guidance. **Psychology:** Knowledge of human behavior and performance; individual differences in ability, personality, and interests; learning and motivation; psychological research methods; and the assessment and treatment of behavioral and affective disorders. **Law and Government:** Knowledge of laws, legal codes, court procedures, precedents, government regulations, executive orders, agency rules, and the democratic political process. **Public Safety and Security:** Knowledge of relevant equipment, policies, procedures, and strategies to promote effective local, state, or national security operations for the protection of people, data, property, and institutions. **English Language:** Knowledge of the structure and content of the English language, including the meaning and spelling of words, rules of composition, and grammar.

Producers

- ▲ Education/Training Required: Work experience, plus degree
- ▲ Annual Earnings: $41,030
- ▲ Growth: 27%
- ▲ Annual Job Openings: 11,000
- ▲ Self-Employed: 23.7%
- ▲ Part-Time: 25.3%

Plan and coordinate various aspects of radio, television, stage, or motion picture production, such as selecting script; coordinating writing, directing, and editing; and arranging financing. Coordinates various aspects of production, such as audio and camera work, music, timing, writing, and staging. Represents network or company in negotiations with independent producers. Selects scenes from taped program to be used for promotional purposes. Reads manuscript and selects play for stage performance. Times scene and calculates program timing. Distributes rehearsal call sheets and copies of script, arranges for rehearsal quarters, and contacts cast members to verify readiness for rehearsal. Establishes management policies, production schedules, and operating budgets for production. Directs activities of one or more departments of motion picture studio and prepares rehearsal call sheets and reports of activities and operating costs. Reviews film, recordings, or rehearsals to ensure conformance to production and broadcast standards. Produces shows for special occasions, such as holiday or testimonial. Obtains and distributes costumes, props, music, and studio equipment to complete production. Composes and edits script or outlines story for screenwriter to write script. Selects and hires cast and staff members and arbitrates personnel disputes. Conducts meetings with staff to discuss production progress and to ensure production objectives are attained. **SKILLS**—Coordination: Adjusting actions in relation to others' actions. Reading Comprehension: Understanding written sentences and paragraphs in work-related documents. Management of Personnel Resources: Motivating, developing, and directing people as they work, identifying the best people for the job. Speaking: Talking to others to convey information effectively. Writing: Communicating effectively in writing as appropriate for the needs of the audience.

GOE INFORMATION—Interest Area: 01. Arts, Entertainment, and Media. **Work Group:** 01.01. Managerial Work in Arts, Entertainment, and Media. **Other Job Titles in This Work Group:** Agents and Business Managers of Artists, Performers, and Athletes; Art Directors; Producers and Directors; Program Directors; Technical Directors/Managers. **PERSONALITY TYPE**—Artistic. Artistic occupations frequently involve working with forms, designs, and patterns. They often require self-expression, and the work can be done without following a clear set of rules.

EDUCATION/TRAINING PROGRAM(S)— Acting and Directing; Drama/Theater Arts, General; Drama/Theater Literature, History and Criticism; Dramatic/Theater Arts and Stagecraft, Other; Film/Cinema Studies; Film-Video Making/Cinematography and Production; Radio and Television Broadcasting. **RELATED KNOWLEDGE/COURSES**—**Communications and Media:** Knowledge of media production, communication, and dissemination techniques and methods. This includes alternative ways to inform and entertain via written, oral, and visual media. **Administration and Management:** Knowledge of business and management principles involved in strategic planning, resource allocation, human resources modeling, leadership technique, production methods, and coordination of people and resources. **Personnel and Human Resources:** Knowledge of principles and procedures for personnel recruitment, selection, training, compensation and benefits, labor relations and negotiation, and personnel information systems. **English Language:** Knowledge of the structure and content of the English language, including the meaning and spelling of words, rules of composition, and grammar. **Fine Arts:** Knowledge of the theory and techniques required to compose, produce, and perform works of music, dance, visual arts, drama, and sculpture.

Producers and Directors

- ▲ Education/Training Required: Work experience, plus degree
- ▲ Annual Earnings: $41,030
- ▲ Growth: 27%
- ▲ Annual Job Openings: 11,000
- ▲ Self-Employed: 23.7%
- ▲ Part-Time: 25.3%

Produce or direct stage, television, radio, video, or motion picture productions for entertainment, information, or instruction. Responsible for creative decisions, such as interpretation of script, choice of guests, set design, sound, special effects, and choreography. **SKILLS**—No data available.

GOE INFORMATION—**Interest Area:** 01. Arts, Entertainment, and Media. **Work Group:** 01.01. Managerial Work in Arts, Entertainment, and Media. **Other Job Titles in This Work Group:** Agents and Business Managers of Artists, Performers, and Athletes; Art Directors; Producers; Program Directors; Technical Directors/Managers. **PERSONALITY TYPE**—No data available.

EDUCATION/TRAINING PROGRAM(S)—Acting and Directing; Drama/Theater Arts, General; Drama/Theater Literature, History and Criticism; Dramatic/Theater Arts and Stagecraft, Other; Film/Cinema Studies; Film-Video Making/Cinematography and Production; Radio and Television Broadcasting. **RELATED KNOWLEDGE/COURSES**—No data available.

Product Safety Engineers

- ▲ Education/Training Required: Bachelor's degree
- ▲ Annual Earnings: $54,630
- ▲ Growth: 11%
- ▲ Annual Job Openings: 3,000
- ▲ Self-Employed: 2.7%
- ▲ Part-Time: 4.5%

Develop and conduct tests to evaluate product safety levels and recommend measures to reduce or eliminate hazards. Conducts research to evaluate safety levels for products. Advises and recommends procedures for detection, prevention, and elimination of physical, chemical, or other product hazards. Participates in preparation of product usage and precautionary label instructions. Prepares reports of findings from investigation of accidents. Investigates causes of accidents, injuries, or illnesses from product usage to develop solutions to minimize or prevent recurrence. Evaluates potential health hazards or damage which could occur from misuse of product and engineers solutions to improve safety. **SKILLS**—Mathematics: Using mathematics to solve problems. Active Learning: Understanding the implications of new information for both current and future problem-solving and decision-making. Writing: Communicating effectively in writing as appropriate for the needs of the audience. Quality Control Analysis: Conducting tests and inspections of products, services, or processes to evaluate quality or performance. Critical Thinking: Using logic and reasoning to identify the strengths and weaknesses of alternative solutions, conclusions, or approaches to problems.

GOE INFORMATION—**Interest Area:** 02. Science, Math, and Engineering. **Work Group:** 02.07. Engineering. **Other Job Titles in This Work Group:** Aerospace Engineers; Agricultural Engineers; Architects, Except Landscape and Naval; Biomedical Engineers; Chemical Engineers; Civil Engineers; Computer Hardware Engineers; Computer Software Engineers, Applications; Computer Software Engineers, Systems Software; Electrical Engineers; Electronics Engineers, Except Computer; Engineers, All Other; Environmental Engineers; Fire-Prevention and Protection Engineers; Health and Safety Engineers, Except Mining Safety Engineers and Inspectors; Industrial Engineers; Industrial Safety and Health Engineers; Landscape Architects; Marine Architects; Marine Engineers; Marine Engineers and Naval Architects; Materials Engineers; Mechanical Engineers; Mining and Geological Engineers, Including Mining Safety Engineers; Nuclear Engineers; Petroleum Engineers; Sales Engineers. **PERSONALITY TYPE**—Investigative. Investigative occupations frequently involve working with ideas and require an extensive amount of thinking. These occupations can involve searching for facts and figuring out problems mentally.

EDUCATION/TRAINING PROGRAM(S)— Engineering/Industrial Management; Environmental/ Environmental Health Engineering; Systems Engineering. **RELATED KNOWLEDGE/COURSES—** **Chemistry:** Knowledge of the chemical composition, structure, and properties of substances and of the chemical processes and transformations that they undergo. This includes uses of chemicals and their interactions, danger signs, production techniques, and disposal methods. **Public Safety and Security:** Knowledge of relevant equipment, policies, procedures, and strategies to promote effective local, state, or national security operations for the protection of people, data, property, and institutions. **Engineer-** **ing and Technology:** Knowledge of the practical application of engineering science and technology. This includes applying principles, techniques, procedures, and equipment to the design and production of various goods and services. **English Language:** Knowledge of the structure and content of the English language, including the meaning and spelling of words, rules of composition, and grammar. **Physics:** Knowledge and prediction of physical principles and laws and their interrelationships and applications to understanding fluid, material, and atmospheric dynamics and mechanical, electrical, atomic, and sub-atomic structures and processes.

Program Directors

- ▲ Education/Training Required: Work experience, plus degree
- ▲ Annual Earnings: $41,030
- ▲ Growth: 27%
- ▲ Annual Job Openings: 11,000
- ▲ Self-Employed: 23.7%
- ▲ Part-Time: 25.3%

Direct and coordinate activities of personnel engaged in preparation of radio or television station program schedules and programs, such as sports or news. Directs and coordinates activities of personnel engaged in broadcast news, sports, or programming. Establishes work schedules and hires, assigns, and evaluates staff. Originates feature ideas and researches program topics for implementation. Writes news copy, notes, letters, and memos, using computer. Examines expenditures to ensure programming and broadcasting activities are within budget. Monitors and reviews news and programming copy and film, using audio or video equipment. Directs setup of remote facilities and installs or cancels programs at remote stations. Evaluates length, content, and suitability of programs for broadcast. Reviews, corrects, and advises member stations concerning programs and schedules. Confers with directors and production staff to discuss issues such as production and casting problems, budget, policy, and news coverage. Coordinates activities between departments, such as news and programming. Plans and schedules programming and event coverage based on length of broadcast and available station or network time.

SKILLS—Coordination: Adjusting actions in relation to others' actions. **Writing:** Communicating effectively in writing as appropriate for the needs of the audience. **Management of Personnel Resources:** Motivating, developing, and directing people as they work, identifying the best people for the job. **Reading Comprehension:** Understanding written sentences and paragraphs in work-related documents. **Time Management:** Managing one's own time and the time of others. **Active Learning:** Understanding the implications of new information for both current and future problem-solving and decision-making.

GOE INFORMATION—Interest Area: 01. Arts, Entertainment, and Media. **Work Group:** 01.01. Managerial Work in Arts, Entertainment, and Media. **Other Job Titles in This Work Group:** Agents and Business Managers of Artists, Performers, and Athletes; Art Directors; Producers; Producers and Directors; Technical Directors/Managers. **PERSONALITY TYPE—Enterprising.** Enterprising occupations frequently involve starting up and carrying out projects. These occupations can involve leading people and making many decisions. They sometimes require risk taking and often deal with business.

EDUCATION/TRAINING PROGRAM(S)— Acting and Directing; Drama/Theater Arts, General; Drama/Theater Literature, History and Criticism; Dramatic/Theater Arts and Stagecraft, Other; Film/Cinema Studies; Film-Video Making/Cinematography and Production; Radio and Television Broadcasting. **RELATED KNOWLEDGE/COURSES—Communications and Media:** Knowledge of media production, communication, and dissemination techniques and methods. This includes alternative ways to inform and entertain via written, oral, and visual media. **Administration and Management:** Knowledge of business and management principles involved in strategic planning, resource allocation, human resources modeling, leadership technique, production methods, and coordination of people and resources. **Personnel and Human Resources:** Knowledge of principles and procedures for personnel recruitment, selection, training, compensation and benefits, labor relations and negotiation, and personnel information systems. **English Language:** Knowledge of the structure and content of the English language, including the meaning and spelling of words, rules of composition, and grammar. **Economics and Accounting:** Knowledge of economic and accounting principles and practices, the financial markets, banking, and the analysis and reporting of financial data.

Property, Real Estate, and Community Association Managers

- ▲ Education/Training Required: Bachelor's degree
- ▲ Annual Earnings: $36,020
- ▲ Growth: 23%
- ▲ Annual Job Openings: 24,000
- ▲ Self-Employed: 40.2%
- ▲ Part-Time: 21.9%

Plan, direct, or coordinate selling, buying, leasing, or governance activities of commercial, industrial, or residential real estate properties. Manages and oversees operations, maintenance, and administrative functions for commercial, industrial, or residential properties. Plans, schedules, and coordinates general maintenance, major repairs, and remodeling or construction projects for commercial or residential property. Recruits, hires, and trains managerial, clerical, and maintenance staff or contracts with vendors for security, maintenance, extermination, or groundskeeping personnel. Maintains records of sales, rental or usage activity, special permits issued, maintenance and operating costs, or property availability. Develops and administers annual operating budget. Inspects facilities and equipment and inventories building contents to document damage and determine repair needs. Meets with prospective leasers to show property, explain terms of occupancy, and provide information about local area. Prepares reports summarizing financial and operational status of property or facility. Maintains contact with insurance carrier, fire and police departments, and other agencies to ensure protection and compliance with codes and regulations. Confers with legal authority to ensure transactions and terminations of contracts and agreements are in accordance with court orders, laws, and regulations. Assembles and analyzes construction and vendor service contract bids. Negotiates for sale, lease, or development of property and completes or reviews appropriate documents and forms. Purchases building and maintenance supplies, equipment, or furniture. Directs and coordinates the activities of staff and contract personnel and evaluates performance. Investigates complaints, disturbances, and violations and resolves problems following management rules and regulations. Meets with clients to negotiate management and service contracts, determine priorities, and discuss financial and operational status of property. Directs collection of monthly assessments, rental fees, and deposits and payment of insurance premiums, mortgage, taxes, and incurred operating expenses. **SKILLS—Management of Financial Resources:** Determining how money will be spent to get the work done and accounting for these expenditures. Coordination: Adjusting actions in relation

P

to others' actions. Active Listening: Giving full attention to what other people are saying, taking time to understand the points being made, asking questions as appropriate, and not interrupting at inappropriate times. Management of Personnel Resources: Motivating, developing, and directing people as they work, identifying the best people for the job. Writing: Communicating effectively in writing as appropriate for the needs of the audience. Reading Comprehension: Understanding written sentences and paragraphs in work-related documents. Judgment and Decision Making: Considering the relative costs and benefits of potential actions to choose the most appropriate one.

GOE INFORMATION—Interest Area: 13. General Management and Support. Work Group: 13.01. General Management Work and Management of Support Functions. Other Job Titles in This Work Group: Chief Executives; Compensation and Benefits Managers; Farm, Ranch, and Other Agricultural Managers; Financial Managers; Financial Managers, Branch or Department; Funeral Directors; General and Operations Managers; Government Service Executives; Human Resources Managers; Human Resources Managers, All Other; Legislators; Managers, All Other; Postmasters and Mail Superintendents; Private Sector Executives; Public Relations Managers; Purchasing Managers; Storage and Distribution Managers; Training and Development Managers; Transportation, Storage, and Distribution Managers; Trea-

surers, Controllers, and Chief Financial Officers. **PERSONALITY TYPE**—Enterprising. Enterprising occupations frequently involve starting up and carrying out projects. These occupations can involve leading people and making many decisions. They sometimes require risk taking and often deal with business.

EDUCATION/TRAINING PROGRAM(S)—Business Administration and Management, General; Public Administration; Purchasing, Procurement and Contracts Management; Real Estate. **RELATED KNOWLEDGE/COURSES—Administration and Management:** Knowledge of business and management principles involved in strategic planning, resource allocation, human resources modeling, leadership technique, production methods, and coordination of people and resources. **English Language:** Knowledge of the structure and content of the English language, including the meaning and spelling of words, rules of composition, and grammar. **Law and Government:** Knowledge of laws, legal codes, court procedures, precedents, government regulations, executive orders, agency rules, and the democratic political process. **Personnel and Human Resources:** Knowledge of principles and procedures for personnel recruitment, selection, training, compensation and benefits, labor relations and negotiation, and personnel information systems. **Mathematics:** Knowledge of arithmetic, algebra, geometry, calculus, and statistics and their applications.

Psychiatrists

- ▲ Education/Training Required: First professional degree
- ▲ Annual Earnings: $ 118,640
- ▲ Growth: 18%
- ▲ Annual Job Openings: 27,000
- ▲ Self-Employed: 20.4%
- ▲ Part-Time: 7.2%

Diagnose, treat, and help prevent disorders of the mind. Analyzes and evaluates patient data and test or examination findings to diagnose nature and extent of mental disorder. Prescribes, directs, and administers psychotherapeutic treatments or medications to treat mental, emotional, or behavioral disorders. Examines or conducts laboratory or diagnostic tests on patient to provide infor-

mation on general physical condition and mental disorder. Reviews and evaluates treatment procedures and outcomes of other psychiatrists and medical professionals. Prepares case reports and summaries for government agencies. Teaches, conducts research, and publishes findings to increase understanding of mental, emotional, and behavioral states and disorders. Advises and informs guardians, relatives, and significant others of patient's condition and treatment. Gathers and maintains patient information and records, including social and medical history obtained from patient, relatives, and other professionals. **SKILLS—** Social Perceptiveness: Being aware of others' reactions and understanding why they react as they do. Reading Comprehension: Understanding written sentences and paragraphs in work-related documents. Judgment and Decision Making: Considering the relative costs and benefits of potential actions to choose the most appropriate one. Writing: Communicating effectively in writing as appropriate for the needs of the audience. Active Listening: Giving full attention to what other people are saying, taking time to understand the points being made, asking questions as appropriate, and not interrupting at inappropriate times. Service Orientation: Actively looking for ways to help people.

GOE INFORMATION—Interest Area: 14. Medical and Health Services. **Work Group:** 14.02. Medicine and Surgery. **Other Job Titles in This Work Group:** Anesthesiologists; Family and General Practitioners; Internists, General; Medical Assistants; Obstetricians and Gynecologists; Pediatricians, General; Pharmacists; Pharmacy Aides; Pharmacy Technicians; Physician Assistants; Physicians and Surgeons, All Other; Registered Nurses; Surgeons; Surgical Technologists. **PERSONALITY**

TYPE—Investigative. Investigative occupations frequently involve working with ideas and require an extensive amount of thinking. These occupations can involve searching for facts and figuring out problems mentally.

EDUCATION/TRAINING PROGRAM(S)— Child Psychiatry Residency; Psychiatry Residency. **RELATED KNOWLEDGE/COURSES—Psychology:** Knowledge of human behavior and performance; individual differences in ability, personality, and interests; learning and motivation; psychological research methods; and the assessment and treatment of behavioral and affective disorders. **Therapy and Counseling:** Knowledge of principles, methods, and procedures for diagnosis, treatment, and rehabilitation of physical and mental dysfunctions and for career counseling and guidance. **Medicine and Dentistry:** Knowledge of the information and techniques needed to diagnose and treat human injuries, diseases, and deformities. This includes symptoms, treatment alternatives, drug properties and interactions, and preventive health-care measures. **English Language:** Knowledge of the structure and content of the English language, including the meaning and spelling of words, rules of composition, and grammar. **Education and Training:** Knowledge of principles and methods for curriculum and training design, teaching and instruction for individuals and groups, and the measurement of training effects.

Psychology Teachers, Postsecondary

- ▲ Education/Training Required: Master's degree
- ▲ Annual Earnings: $51,640
- ▲ Growth: 24% for all Postsecondary Teachers
- ▲ Annual Job Openings: 184,000 for all Postsecondary Teachers
- ▲ Self-Employed: 0%
- ▲ Part-Time: 32.3% for all Postsecondary Teachers

Teach courses in psychology, such as child, clinical, and developmental psychology and psychological counseling. Prepares and delivers lectures to students. Stimulates class discussions. Compiles, administers, and grades examinations or assigns this work to others. Compiles bibliographies of specialized materials for outside reading assignments. Directs research of other teachers or graduate students working for advanced academic degrees. Advises students on academic and vocational curricula. Conducts research in particular field of knowledge and publishes findings in professional journals. Serves on faculty committee providing professional consulting services to government and industry. Acts as adviser to student organizations. **SKILLS**—Reading Comprehension: Understanding written sentences and paragraphs in work-related documents. Instructing: Teaching others how to do something. Speaking: Talking to others to convey information effectively. Active Learning: Understanding the implications of new information for both current and future problem-solving and decision-making. Learning Strategies: Selecting and using training/instructional methods and procedures appropriate for the situation when learning or teaching new things. Active Listening: Giving full attention to what other people are saying, taking time to understand the points being made, asking questions as appropriate, and not interrupting at inappropriate times. Writing: Communicating effectively in writing as appropriate for the needs of the audience.

GOE INFORMATION—**Interest Area:** 12. Education and Social Service. **Work Group:** 12.03. Educational Services. **Other Job Titles in This Work Group:** Adult Literacy, Remedial Education, and GED Teachers and Instructors; Agricultural Sciences Teachers, Postsecondary; Anthropology and Archeology Teachers, Postsecondary; Architecture Teachers, Postsecondary; Archivists; Area, Ethnic, and Cultural Studies Teachers, Postsecondary; Art, Drama, and Music Teachers, Postsecondary; Atmospheric, Earth, Marine, and Space Sciences Teachers, Postsecondary; Audio-Visual Collections Specialists; Biological Science Teachers, Postsecondary; Business Teachers, Postsecondary; Chemistry Teachers, Postsecondary; Child Care Workers; Communications Teachers, Postsecondary; Computer Science Teachers, Postsecondary; Criminal Justice and Law Enforcement Teachers, Postsecondary; Curators; Economics Teachers, Postsecondary; Education Teachers, Postsecondary; Educational Psychologists; Educational, Vocational, and School Counselors; Elementary School Teachers, Except Special Education; Engineering Teachers, Postsecondary; English Language and Literature Teachers, Postsecondary; Environmental Science Teachers, Postsecondary; Farm and Home Management Advisors; Foreign Language and Literature Teachers, Postsecondary; Forestry and Conservation Science Teachers, Postsecondary; Geography Teachers, Postsecondary; Graduate Teaching Assistants; Health Specialties Teachers, Postsecondary; History Teachers, Postsecondary; Home Economics Teachers, Postsecondary; Kindergarten Teachers, Except Special Education; Law Teachers, Postsecondary; Librarians; Library Assistants, Clerical; others. **PERSONALITY TYPE**—Social. Social occupations frequently involve working with, communicating with, and teaching people. These occupations often involve helping or providing service to others.

EDUCATION/TRAINING PROGRAM(S)— Clinical Psychology; Cognitive Psychology and Psycholinguistics; Community Psychology; Counseling Psychology; Developmental and Child Psychology; Experimental Psychology; Industrial and Organizational Psychology; Physiological Psychology/Psychobiology; Psychology, General; Psychology, Other; School Psychology; Social Psychology; Social Science Teacher Education. **RELATED KNOWLEDGE/COURSES**—**Education and Training:** Knowledge of principles and methods for curriculum and training design, teaching and instruction for individuals and groups, and the measurement of training effects. **Sociology and Anthropology:** Knowledge of group behavior and dynamics, societal trends and influences, human migrations, ethnicity, cultures, and their history and origins. **History and Archeology:** Knowledge of historical events and their causes, indicators, and effects on civilizations and cultures. **English Language:** Knowledge of the structure and content of the English language, including the meaning and spelling of words, rules of composition, and grammar. **Psychology:** Knowledge of human behavior and performance; individual differences in ability, personality, and interests; learning and motivation; psychological research methods; and the assessment and treatment of behavioral and affective disorders.

Public Relations Managers

- ▲ Education/Training Required: Work experience, plus degree
- ▲ Annual Earnings: $54,540
- ▲ Growth: 36%
- ▲ Annual Job Openings: 7,000
- ▲ Self-Employed: 2.4%
- ▲ Part-Time: 2.6%

Plan and direct public relations programs designed to create and maintain a favorable public image for employer or client, or if engaged in fundraising, plan and direct activities to solicit and maintain funds for special projects and non-profit organizations. SKILLS—No data available.

GOE INFORMATION—Interest Area: 13. General Management and Support. Work Group: 13.01. General Management Work and Management of Support Functions. Other Job Titles in This Work Group: Chief Executives; Compensation and Benefits Managers; Farm, Ranch, and Other Agricultural Managers; Financial Managers; Financial Managers, Branch or Department; Funeral Directors; General and Operations Managers; Government Service Executives; Human Resources Managers; Human Resources Managers, All Other; Legislators; Managers, All Other; Postmasters and Mail Superintendents; Private Sector Executives; Property, Real Estate, and Community Association Managers; Purchasing Managers; Storage and Distribution Managers; Training and Development Managers; Transportation, Storage, and Distribution Managers; Treasurers, Controllers, and Chief Financial Officers. PERSONALITY TYPE—No data available.

EDUCATION/TRAINING PROGRAM(S)—Public Relations and Organizational Communications. RELATED KNOWLEDGE/COURSES—No data available.

Public Relations Specialists

- ▲ Education/Training Required: Bachelor's degree
- ▲ Annual Earnings: $39,580
- ▲ Growth: 36%
- ▲ Annual Job Openings: 19,000
- ▲ Self-Employed: 5.6%
- ▲ Part-Time: 25.3%

Engage in promoting or creating goodwill for individuals, groups, or organizations by writing or selecting favorable publicity material and releasing it through various communications media. May prepare and arrange displays and make speeches. Plans and directs development and communication of informational programs designed to keep public informed of client's products, accomplishments, or agenda. Prepares and distributes fact sheets, news releases, photographs, scripts, motion pictures, or tape recordings to media representatives and others. Promotes sales and/or creates goodwill for client's products, services, or persona by coordinating exhibits, lectures, contests, or public appearances. Prepares or edits organizational publications such as newsletters to employees or public or stockholders' reports to favorably present client's viewpoint. Consults with advertising agencies or staff to arrange promotional campaigns in all types of media for products, organizations, or

P

individuals. Arranges for and conducts public-contact programs designed to meet client's objectives. Represents client during community projects and at public, social, and business gatherings. Confers with production and support personnel to coordinate production of advertisements and promotions. Purchases advertising space and time as required to promote client's product or agenda. Counsels clients in effective ways of communicating agents with public. Conducts market and public opinion research to introduce or test specific products or measure public opinion. Studies needs, objectives, and policies of organization or individual seeking to influence public opinion or promote specific products. **SKILLS**—Speaking: Talking to others to convey information effectively. Writing: Communicating effectively in writing as appropriate for the needs of the audience. Reading Comprehension: Understanding written sentences and paragraphs in work-related documents. Persuasion: Persuading others to change their minds or behavior. Active Listening: Giving full attention to what other people are saying, taking time to understand the points being made, asking questions as appropriate, and not interrupting at inappropriate times. Critical Thinking: Using logic and reasoning to identify the strengths and weaknesses of alternative solutions, conclusions, or approaches to problems.

GOE INFORMATION—**Interest Area:** 01. Arts, Entertainment, and Media. **Work Group:** 01.03. News, Broadcasting and Public Relations. **Other Job Titles in**

This Work Group: Broadcast News Analysts; Caption Writers; Interpreters and Translators; Reporters and Correspondents. **PERSONALITY TYPE**—Enterprising. Enterprising occupations frequently involve starting up and carrying out projects. These occupations can involve leading people and making many decisions. They sometimes require risk taking and often deal with business.

EDUCATION/TRAINING PROGRAM(S)—Public Relations and Organizational Communications. **RELATED KNOWLEDGE/COURSES**—**Sales and Marketing:** Knowledge of principles and methods for showing, promoting, and selling products or services. This includes marketing strategy and tactics, product demonstration, sales techniques, and sales control systems. **Communications and Media:** Knowledge of media production, communication, and dissemination techniques and methods. This includes alternative ways to inform and entertain via written, oral, and visual media. **Mathematics:** Knowledge of arithmetic, algebra, geometry, calculus, and statistics and their applications. **Telecommunications:** Knowledge of transmission, broadcasting, switching, control, and operation of telecommunications systems. **Psychology:** Knowledge of human behavior and performance; individual differences in ability, personality, and interests; learning and motivation; psychological research methods; and the assessment and treatment of behavioral and affective disorders.

Purchasing Agents, Except Wholesale, Retail, and Farm Products

- ▲ Education/Training Required: Bachelor's degree
- ▲ Annual Earnings: $41,370
- ▲ Growth: 12%
- ▲ Annual Job Openings: 23,000
- ▲ Self-Employed: 0%
- ▲ Part-Time: 2.3%

Purchase machinery, equipment, tools, parts, supplies, or services necessary for the operation of an establishment. Purchase raw or semi-finished materials for manufacturing. Negotiates or renegotiates and administers contracts with suppliers, vendors, and other representatives. Arbitrates claims and resolves complaints generated during performance of con-

tract. Confers with personnel, users, and vendors to discuss defective or unacceptable goods or services and determines corrective action. Maintains and reviews computerized or manual records of items purchased, costs, delivery, product performance, and inventories. Evaluates and monitors contract performance to determine need for changes and to ensure compliance with contractual obligations. Locates and arranges for purchase of goods and services necessary for efficient operation of organization. Analyzes price proposals, financial reports, and other data and information to determine reasonable prices. Prepares purchase orders or bid proposals and reviews requisitions for goods and services. Directs and coordinates workers' activities involving bid proposals and procurement of goods and services. Formulates policies and procedures for bid proposals and procurement of goods and services. **SKILLS**—Judgment and Decision Making: Considering the relative costs and benefits of potential actions to choose the most appropriate one. Reading Comprehension: Understanding written sentences and paragraphs in work-related documents. Writing: Communicating effectively in writing as appropriate for the needs of the audience. Management of Financial Resources: Determining how money will be spent to get the work done and accounting for these expenditures. Mathematics: Using mathematics to solve problems. Negotiation: Bringing others together and trying to reconcile differences. Active Listening: Giving full attention to what other people are saying, taking time to understand the points being made, asking questions as appropriate, and not interrupting at inappropriate times.

GOE INFORMATION—**Interest Area:** 13. General Management and Support. **Work Group:** 13.02. Management Support. **Other Job Titles in This Work Group:** Accountants; Accountants and Auditors; Appraisers and Assessors of Real Estate; Appraisers, Real Estate; Assessors; Auditors; Budget Analysts; Claims Adjusters, Examiners, and Investigators; Claims Examiners, Property and Casualty Insurance; Compensation, Benefits, and Job Analysis Specialists; Cost Estimators; Credit Analysts; Employment Interviewers, Private or Public Employment Service; Employment, Recruitment, and Placement Specialists; Financial Analysts; Human Resources, Training, and Labor Relations Specialists, All Other; Insurance Ad-

justers, Examiners, and Investigators; Insurance Appraisers, Auto Damage; Insurance Underwriters; Loan Counselors; Loan Officers; Logisticians; Management Analysts; Market Research Analysts; Personnel Recruiters; Purchasing Agents and Buyers, Farm Products; Tax Examiners, Collectors, and Revenue Agents; Training and Development Specialists; Wholesale and Retail Buyers, Except Farm Products. **PERSONALITY TYPE**—Enterprising. Enterprising occupations frequently involve starting up and carrying out projects. These occupations can involve leading people and making many decisions. They sometimes require risk taking and often deal with business.

EDUCATION/TRAINING PROGRAM(S)—General Buying Operations. **RELATED KNOWLEDGE/COURSES**—**Administration and Management:** Knowledge of business and management principles involved in strategic planning, resource allocation, human resources modeling, leadership technique, production methods, and coordination of people and resources. **Mathematics:** Knowledge of arithmetic, algebra, geometry, calculus, and statistics and their applications. **Economics and Accounting:** Knowledge of economic and accounting principles and practices, the financial markets, banking, and the analysis and reporting of financial data. **English Language:** Knowledge of the structure and content of the English language, including the meaning and spelling of words, rules of composition, and grammar. **Computers and Electronics:** Knowledge of circuit boards, processors, chips, electronic equipment, and computer hardware and software, including applications and programming. **Clerical Studies:** Knowledge of administrative and clerical procedures and systems such as word processing, managing files and records, stenography and transcription, designing forms, and other office procedures and terminology.

Purchasing Managers

- ▲ Education/Training Required: Work experience, plus degree
- ▲ Annual Earnings: $53,030
- ▲ Growth: –6%
- ▲ Annual Job Openings: 17,000
- ▲ Self-Employed: 0.4%
- ▲ Part-Time: 2.9%

Plan, direct, or coordinate the activities of buyers, purchasing officers, and related workers involved in purchasing materials, products, and services. Directs and coordinates activities of personnel engaged in buying, selling, and distributing materials, equipment, machinery, and supplies. Prepares, reviews, and processes requisitions and purchase orders for supplies and equipment. Prepares report regarding market conditions and merchandise costs. Analyzes market and delivery systems to determine present and future material availability. Represents company in formulating policies and negotiating contracts with suppliers. Develops and implements office, operations, and systems instructions, policies, and procedures. Determines merchandise costs and formulates and coordinates merchandising policies and activities to ensure profit. Conducts inventory and directs buyers in purchase of products, materials, and supplies. **SKILLS—** Judgment and Decision Making: Considering the relative costs and benefits of potential actions to choose the most appropriate one. Writing: Communicating effectively in writing as appropriate for the needs of the audience. Management of Personnel Resources: Motivating, developing, and directing people as they work, identifying the best people for the job. Management of Material Resources: Obtaining and seeing to the appropriate use of equipment, facilities, and materials needed to do certain work. Coordination: Adjusting actions in relation to others' actions.

GOE INFORMATION—Interest Area: 13. General Management and Support. **Work Group:** 13.01. General Management Work and Management of Support Functions. **Other Job Titles in This Work Group:** Chief Executives; Compensation and Benefits Managers; Farm, Ranch, and Other Agricultural Managers; Financial Managers; Financial Managers, Branch or Department; Funeral Directors; General and Operations Managers; Government Service Executives; Human Resources Man-

agers; Human Resources Managers, All Other; Legislators; Managers, All Other; Postmasters and Mail Superintendents; Private Sector Executives; Property, Real Estate, and Community Association Managers; Public Relations Managers; Storage and Distribution Managers; Training and Development Managers; Transportation, Storage, and Distribution Managers; Treasurers, Controllers, and Chief Financial Officers. **PERSONALITY TYPE—**Enterprising. Enterprising occupations frequently involve starting up and carrying out projects. These occupations can involve leading people and making many decisions. They sometimes require risk taking and often deal with business.

EDUCATION/TRAINING PROGRAM(S)— Purchasing, Procurement and Contracts Management. **RELATED KNOWLEDGE/COURSES—Administration and Management:** Knowledge of business and management principles involved in strategic planning, resource allocation, human resources modeling, leadership technique, production methods, and coordination of people and resources. **Economics and Accounting:** Knowledge of economic and accounting principles and practices, the financial markets, banking, and the analysis and reporting of financial data. **Mathematics:** Knowledge of arithmetic, algebra, geometry, calculus, and statistics and their applications. **Sales and Marketing:** Knowledge of principles and methods for showing, promoting, and selling products or services. This includes marketing strategy and tactics, product demonstration, sales techniques, and sales control systems. **English Language:** Knowledge of the structure and content of the English language, including the meaning and spelling of words, rules of composition, and grammar. **Production and Processing:** Knowledge of raw materials, production processes, quality control, costs, and other techniques for maximizing the effective manufacture and distribution of goods.

Radiation Therapists

- ▲ Education/Training Required: Associate's degree
- ▲ Annual Earnings: $47,470
- ▲ Growth: 23%
- ▲ Annual Job Openings: 1,000
- ▲ Self-Employed: 0%
- ▲ Part-Time: 17.5%

Provide radiation therapy to patients as prescribed by a radiologist according to established practices and standards. Duties may include reviewing prescription and diagnosis; acting as liaison with physician and supportive care personnel; preparing equipment, such as immobilization, treatment, and protection devices; and maintaining records, reports, and files. May assist in dosimetry procedures and tumor localization. Reviews prescription, diagnosis, patient chart, and identification. Enters data into computer and sets controls to operate and adjust equipment and regulate dosage. Photographs treated area of patient and processes film. Observes and reassures patient during treatment and reports unusual reactions to physician. Follows principles of radiation protection for patient, self, and others. Prepares equipment, such as immobilization, treatment, and protection devices, and positions patient according to prescription. Acts as liaison with physicist and supportive care personnel. Maintains records, reports, and files as required. **SKILLS**—Reading Comprehension: Understanding written sentences and paragraphs in work-related documents. Operation and Control: Controlling operations of equipment or systems. Science: Using scientific rules and methods to solve problems. Active Listening: Giving full attention to what other people are saying, taking time to understand the points being made, asking questions as appropriate, and not interrupting at inappropriate times. Coordination: Adjusting actions in relation to others' actions. Critical Thinking: Using logic and reasoning to identify the strengths and weaknesses of alternative solutions, conclusions, or approaches to problems. Writing: Communicating effectively in writing as appropriate for the needs of the audience.

GOE INFORMATION—**Interest Area:** 14. Medical and Health Services. **Work Group:** 14.06. Medical

Therapy. **Other Job Titles in This Work Group:** Audiologists; Massage Therapists; Occupational Therapist Aides; Occupational Therapist Assistants; Occupational Therapists; Physical Therapist Aides; Physical Therapist Assistants; Physical Therapists; Recreational Therapists; Respiratory Therapists; Respiratory Therapy Technicians; Speech-Language Pathologists; Therapists, All Other. **PERSONALITY TYPE**—Social. Social occupations frequently involve working with, communicating with, and teaching people. These occupations often involve helping or providing service to others.

EDUCATION/TRAINING PROGRAM(S)— Medical Radiologic Technologist/Technician; Rehabilitation/Therapeutic Services, Other. **RELATED KNOWLEDGE/COURSES**—**Medicine and Dentistry:** Knowledge of the information and techniques needed to diagnose and treat human injuries, diseases, and deformities. This includes symptoms, treatment alternatives, drug properties and interactions, and preventive health-care measures. **Computers and Electronics:** Knowledge of circuit boards, processors, chips, electronic equipment, and computer hardware and software, including applications and programming. **English Language:** Knowledge of the structure and content of the English language, including the meaning and spelling of words, rules of composition, and grammar. **Therapy and Counseling:** Knowledge of principles, methods, and procedures for diagnosis, treatment, and rehabilitation of physical and mental dysfunctions and for career counseling and guidance. **Clerical Studies:** Knowledge of administrative and clerical procedures and systems such as word processing, managing files and records, stenography and transcription, designing forms, and other office procedures and terminology.

Radiologic Technicians

▲ Education/Training Required: Associate's degree

▲ Annual Earnings: $36,000

▲ Growth: 23%

▲ Annual Job Openings: 13,000

▲ Self-Employed: 0%

▲ Part-Time: 17.5%

Maintain and use equipment and supplies necessary to demonstrate portions of the human body on X-ray film or fluoroscopic screen for diagnostic purposes. Uses beam-restrictive devices and patient-shielding skills to minimize radiation exposure to patient and staff. Moves X-ray equipment into position and adjusts controls to set exposure factors, such as time and distance. Operates mobile X-ray equipment in operating room, in emergency room, or at patient's bedside. Explains procedures to patient to reduce anxieties and obtain patient cooperation. Positions patient on examining table and adjusts equipment to obtain optimum view of specific body area requested by physician. **SKILLS**—Reading Comprehension: Understanding written sentences and paragraphs in work-related documents. Active Listening: Giving full attention to what other people are saying, taking time to understand the points being made, asking questions as appropriate, and not interrupting at inappropriate times. Operation and Control: Controlling operations of equipment or systems. Social Perceptiveness: Being aware of others' reactions and understanding why they react as they do. Speaking: Talking to others to convey information effectively.

GOE INFORMATION—**Interest Area:** 14. Medical and Health Services. **Work Group:** 14.05. Medical Technology. **Other Job Titles in This Work Group:** Cardiovascular Technologists and Technicians; Diagnostic Medical Sonographers; Health Technologists and Technicians, All Other; Medical and Clinical Laboratory Technicians; Medical and Clinical Laboratory Technologists; Medical Equipment Preparers; Nuclear Medicine Tech-

nologists; Orthotists and Prosthetists; Radiologic Technologists; Radiologic Technologists and Technicians. **PERSONALITY TYPE**—Realistic. Realistic occupations frequently involve work activities that include practical, hands-on problems and solutions. They often deal with plants, animals, and real-world materials like wood, tools, and machinery. Many of the occupations require working outside and do not involve a lot of paperwork or working closely with others.

EDUCATION/TRAINING PROGRAM(S)— Health and Medical Diagnostic and Treatment Services, Other; Medical Radiologic Technologist/Technician. **RELATED KNOWLEDGE/COURSES**—**Medicine and Dentistry:** Knowledge of the information and techniques needed to diagnose and treat human injuries, diseases, and deformities. This includes symptoms, treatment alternatives, drug properties and interactions, and preventive health-care measures. **English Language:** Knowledge of the structure and content of the English language, including the meaning and spelling of words, rules of composition, and grammar. **Biology:** Knowledge of plant and animal organisms and their tissues, cells, functions, interdependencies, and interactions with each other and the environment. **Customer and Personal Service:** Knowledge of principles and processes for providing customer and personal services. This includes customer needs assessment, meeting quality standards for services, and evaluation of customer satisfaction. **Computers and Electronics:** Knowledge of circuit boards, processors, chips, electronic equipment, and computer hardware and software, including applications and programming.

Radiologic Technologists

▲ Education/Training Required: Associate's degree

▲ Annual Earnings: $36,000

▲ Growth: 23%

▲ Annual Job Openings: 13,000

▲ Self-Employed: 0%

▲ Part-Time: 17.5%

Take X rays and CAT scans or administer non-radioactive materials into patient's bloodstream for diagnostic purposes. Includes technologists

who specialize in other modalities, such as computed tomography, ultrasound, and magnetic resonance. Operates or oversees operation of radiologic and magnetic imaging equipment to produce photographs of the body for diagnostic purposes. Administers oral or injected contrast media to patients. Positions imaging equipment and adjusts controls to set exposure time and distance according to specification of examination. Monitors use of radiation safety measures to comply with government regulations and to ensure safety of patients and staff. Monitors video display of area being scanned and adjusts density or contrast to improve picture quality. Keys commands and data into computer to document and specify scan sequences, adjust transmitters and receivers, or photograph certain images. Operates fluoroscope to aid physician to view and guide wire or catheter through blood vessels to area of interest. Positions and immobilizes patient on examining table. Develops departmental operating budget and coordinates purchase of supplies and equipment. Assigns duties to radiologic staff to maintain patient flows and achieve production goals. Demonstrates new equipment, procedures, and techniques and provides technical assistance to staff. Explains procedures and observes patients to ensure safety and comfort during scan. Reviews and evaluates developed X rays, video tape, or computer generated information for technical quality. **SKILLS**—Reading Comprehension: Understanding written sentences and paragraphs in work-related documents. Operation and Control: Controlling operations of equipment or systems. Operation Monitoring: Watching gauges, dials, or other indicators to make sure a machine is working properly. Mathematics: Using mathematics to solve problems. Equipment Selection: Determining the kind of tools and equipment needed to do a job. Critical Thinking: Using logic and reasoning to identify the strengths and weaknesses of alternative solutions, conclusions, or approaches to problems. Active Listening: Giving full attention to what other people are saying, taking time to understand the points being made, asking questions as appropriate, and not interrupting at inappropriate times.

GOE INFORMATION—**Interest Area:** 14. Medical and Health Services. **Work Group:** 14.05. Medical

Technology. **Other Job Titles in This Work Group:** Cardiovascular Technologists and Technicians; Diagnostic Medical Sonographers; Health Technologists and Technicians, All Other; Medical and Clinical Laboratory Technicians; Medical and Clinical Laboratory Technologists; Medical Equipment Preparers; Nuclear Medicine Technologists; Orthotists and Prosthetists; Radiologic Technicians; Radiologic Technologists and Technicians. **PERSONALITY TYPE**—Realistic. Realistic occupations frequently involve work activities that include practical, hands-on problems and solutions. They often deal with plants, animals, and real-world materials like wood, tools, and machinery. Many of the occupations require working outside and do not involve a lot of paperwork or working closely with others.

EDUCATION/TRAINING PROGRAM(S)— Health and Medical Diagnostic and Treatment Services, Other; Medical Radiologic Technologist/Technician. **RELATED KNOWLEDGE/COURSES**—**Medicine and Dentistry:** Knowledge of the information and techniques needed to diagnose and treat human injuries, diseases, and deformities. This includes symptoms, treatment alternatives, drug properties and interactions, and preventive health-care measures. **Computers and Electronics:** Knowledge of circuit boards, processors, chips, electronic equipment, and computer hardware and software, including applications and programming. **Biology:** Knowledge of plant and animal organisms and their tissues, cells, functions, interdependencies, and interactions with each other and the environment. **Chemistry:** Knowledge of the chemical composition, structure, and properties of substances and of the chemical processes and transformations that they undergo. This includes uses of chemicals and their interactions, danger signs, production techniques, and disposal methods. **Public Safety and Security:** Knowledge of relevant equipment, policies, procedures, and strategies to promote effective local, state, or national security operations for the protection of people, data, property, and institutions.

Radiologic Technologists and Technicians

▲ Education/Training Required: Associate's degree

▲ Annual Earnings: $36,000

▲ Growth: 23%

▲ Annual Job Openings: 13,000

▲ Self-Employed: 0%

▲ Part-Time: 17.5%

Take X rays and CAT scans or administer non-radioactive materials into patient's bloodstream for diagnostic purposes. Includes technologists who specialize in other modalities, such as computed tomography and magnetic resonance. Includes workers whose primary duties are to demonstrate portions of the human body on X-ray film or fluoroscopic screen. SKILLS—No data available.

GOE INFORMATION—Interest Area: 14. Medical and Health Services. Work Group: 14.05. Medical Technology. Other Job Titles in This Work Group: Cardiovascular Technologists and Technicians; Diagnostic Medical Sonographers; Health Technologists and Technicians, All Other; Medical and Clinical Laboratory Technicians; Medical and Clinical Laboratory Technologists; Medical Equipment Preparers; Nuclear Medicine Technologists; Orthotists and Prosthetists; Radiologic Technicians; Radiologic Technologists. PERSONALITY TYPE—No data available.

EDUCATION/TRAINING PROGRAM(S)—Health and Medical Diagnostic and Treatment Services, Other; Medical Radiologic Technologist/Technician. RELATED KNOWLEDGE/COURSES—No data available.

Range Managers

▲ Education/Training Required: Bachelor's degree

▲ Annual Earnings: $47,140

▲ Growth: 8%

▲ Annual Job Openings: 1,000

▲ Self-Employed: 2.4%

▲ Part-Time: 6.6%

Research or study range land management practices to provide sustained production of forage, livestock, and wildlife. Studies range lands to determine best grazing seasons. Develops improved practices for range reseeding. Develops methods for protecting range from fire and rodent damage. Plans and directs construction of range improvements, such as fencing, corrals, stock-watering reservoirs, and soil-erosion control structures. Plans and directs maintenance of range improvements. Develops methods for controlling poisonous plants in range lands. Studies forage plants and their growth requirements to determine varieties best suited to particular range. Studies range lands to determine number and kind of livestock that can be most profitably grazed. SKILLS—Judgment and Decision Making: Considering the relative costs and benefits of potential actions to choose the most appropriate one. Active Learning: Understanding the implications of new information for both current and future problem-solving and decision-making. Operations Analysis: Analyzing needs and product requirements to create a design. Systems Evaluation: Identifying measures or indicators of system performance and the actions needed to improve or correct performance relative to the goals of the system. Complex Problem Solving: Identifying complex problems and reviewing related information to develop and evaluate options and implement solutions.

GOE INFORMATION—Interest Area: 02. Science, Math, and Engineering. **Work Group:** 02.03. Life Sciences. **Other Job Titles in This Work Group:** Agricultural and Food Science Technicians; Agricultural Technicians; Animal Scientists; Biochemists; Biochemists and Biophysicists; Biological Scientists, All Other; Biologists; Biophysicists; Conservation Scientists; Environmental Scientists and Specialists, Including Health; Epidemiologists; Food Science Technicians; Food Scientists and Technologists; Foresters; Life Scientists, All Other; Medical Scientists, Except Epidemiologists; Microbiologists; Plant Scientists; Soil and Plant Scientists; Soil Conservationists; Soil Scientists; Zoologists and Wildlife Biologists. **PERSONALITY TYPE**—Investigative. Investigative occupations frequently involve working with ideas and require an extensive amount of thinking. These occupations can involve searching for facts and figuring out problems mentally.

EDUCATION/TRAINING PROGRAM(S)— Conservation and Renewable Natural Resources, Other; Forest Management; Forestry and Related Sciences, Other; Forestry Sciences; Forestry, General; Natural Resources Conservation, General; Natural Resources Law Enforcement and Protective Services; Natural Resources Management and Policy; Natural Resources Management and Protective Services, Other; Wildlife and Wildlands Management. **RELATED KNOWLEDGE/ COURSES—Administration and Management:** Knowledge of business and management principles involved in strategic planning, resource allocation, human resources modeling, leadership technique, production methods, and coordination of people and resources. **Biology:** Knowledge of plant and animal organisms and their tissues, cells, functions, interdependencies, and interactions with each other and the environment. **Food Production:** Knowledge of techniques and equipment for planting, growing, and harvesting food products (both plant and animal) for consumption, including storage/handling techniques. **Mathematics:** Knowledge of arithmetic, algebra, geometry, calculus, and statistics and their applications. **Geography:** Knowledge of principles and methods for describing the features of land, sea, and air masses, including their physical characteristics, locations, interrelationships, and distribution of plant, animal, and human life. **Building and Construction:** Knowledge of materials, methods, and tools involved in the construction or repair of houses, buildings, or other structures, such as highways and roads.

Recreation and Fitness Studies Teachers, Postsecondary

▲ Education/Training Required: Master's degree

▲ Annual Earnings: $42,030

▲ Growth: 24% for all Postsecondary Teachers

▲ Annual Job Openings: 184,000 for all Postsecondary Teachers

▲ Self-Employed: 0%

▲ Part-Time: 32.3% for all Postsecondary Teachers

Teach courses pertaining to recreation, leisure, and fitness studies, including exercise physiology and facilities management. **SKILLS**—No data available.

GOE INFORMATION—Interest Area: 12. Education and Social Service. **Work Group:** 12.03. Educational Services. **Other Job Titles in This Work Group:** Adult Literacy, Remedial Education, and GED Teachers and Instructors; Agricultural Sciences Teachers, Postsecondary; Anthropology and Archeology Teachers, Postsecondary; Architecture Teachers, Postsecondary; Archivists; Area, Ethnic, and Cultural Studies Teachers,

Postsecondary; Art, Drama, and Music Teachers, Postsecondary; Atmospheric, Earth, Marine, and Space Sciences Teachers, Postsecondary; Audio-Visual Collections Specialists; Biological Science Teachers, Postsecondary; Business Teachers, Postsecondary; Chemistry Teachers, Postsecondary; Child Care Workers; Communications Teachers, Postsecondary; Computer Science Teachers, Postsecondary; Criminal Justice and Law Enforcement Teachers, Postsecondary; Curators; Economics Teachers, Postsecondary; Education Teachers, Postsecondary; Educational Psychologists; Educational, Vocational, and School Counselors; Elementary School Teachers, Except Special Education; Engineering Teachers, Postsecondary; English Language and Literature Teachers, Postsecondary; Environmental Science Teachers, Postsecondary; Farm and Home Management Advisors; Foreign Language and Literature Teachers, Postsecondary; Forestry and Conservation Science Teachers, Postsecondary; Geography Teachers, Postsecondary; Graduate Teaching Assistants; Health Specialties Teachers, Postsecondary; History Teachers, Postsecondary; Home Economics Teachers, Postsecondary; Kindergarten Teachers, Except Special Education; Law Teachers, Postsecondary; Librarians; Library Assistants, Clerical; others. **PERSONALITY TYPE**—No data available.

EDUCATION/TRAINING PROGRAM(S)— Parks, Recreation and Leisure Studies. **RELATED KNOWLEDGE/COURSES**—No data available.

Recreation Workers

- ▲ Education/Training Required: Bachelor's degree
- ▲ Annual Earnings: $17,130
- ▲ Growth: 20%
- ▲ Annual Job Openings: 32,000
- ▲ Self-Employed: 0%
- ▲ Part-Time: 14%

Conduct recreation activities with groups in public, private, or volunteer agencies or recreation facilities. Organize and promote activities, such as arts and crafts, sports, games, music, dramatics, social recreation, camping, and hobbies, taking into account the needs and interests of individual members. Organizes, leads, and promotes interest in facility activities, such as arts, crafts, sports, games, camping, and hobbies. Conducts recreational activities and instructs participants to develop skills in provided activities. Arranges for activity requirements, such as entertainment and setting up equipment and decorations. Schedules facility activities and maintains record of programs. Explains principles, techniques, and safety procedures of facility activities to participants and demonstrates use of material and equipment. Ascertains and interprets group interests, evaluates equipment and facilities, and adapts activities to meet participant needs. Meets and collaborates with agency personnel, community organizations, and other professional personnel to plan balanced recreational programs for participants. Enforces rules and regulations of facility, maintains discipline, and ensures safety. Greets and introduces new arrivals to other guests, acquaints arrivals with facilities, and encourages group participation. Tests and documents content of swimming pool water and schedules maintenance and use of facilities. Supervises and coordinates work activities of personnel, trains staff, and assigns duties. Schedules maintenance and use of facilities. Evaluates staff performance and records reflective information on performance evaluation forms. Completes and maintains time and attendance forms and inventory lists. Meets with staff to discuss rules, regulations, and work-related problems. Administers first aid, according to prescribed procedures, or notifies emergency medical personnel when necessary. Assists management to resolve complaints. **SKILLS**—Coordination: Adjusting actions in relation to others' actions. Speaking: Talking to others to convey information effectively. Service Orientation: Actively looking for ways to help people. Social Perceptiveness: Being aware of others' reactions and understanding why they react as they do. Time Management: Managing one's own time and the time of others.

GOE INFORMATION—Interest Area: 11. Recreation, Travel, and Other Personal Services. **Work Group:** 11.02. Recreational Services. **Other Job Titles in This Work Group:** Amusement and Recreation Attendants; Entertainment Attendants and Related Workers, All Other; Gaming and Sports Book Writers and Runners; Gaming Dealers; Gaming Service Workers, All Other; Motion Picture Projectionists; Slot Key Persons; Tour Guides and Escorts; Travel Guides; Ushers, Lobby Attendants, and Ticket Takers. **PERSONALITY TYPE—** Social. Social occupations frequently involve working with, communicating with, and teaching people. These occupations often involve helping or providing service to others.

EDUCATION/TRAINING PROGRAM(S)— Health and Physical Education/Fitness, Other; Parks, Recreation and Leisure Facilities Management; Parks, Recreation and Leisure Studies; Parks, Recreation, Leisure and Fitness Studies, Other; Sport and Fitness Administration/Management. **RELATED KNOWL-**

EDGE/COURSES—Customer and Personal Service: Knowledge of principles and processes for providing customer and personal services. This includes customer needs assessment, meeting quality standards for services, and evaluation of customer satisfaction. **Administration and Management:** Knowledge of business and management principles involved in strategic planning, resource allocation, human resources modeling, leadership technique, production methods, and coordination of people and resources. **Education and Training:** Knowledge of principles and methods for curriculum and training design, teaching and instruction for individuals and groups, and the measurement of training effects. **English Language:** Knowledge of the structure and content of the English language, including the meaning and spelling of words, rules of composition, and grammar. **Psychology:** Knowledge of human behavior and performance; individual differences in ability, personality, and interests; learning and motivation; psychological research methods; and the assessment and treatment of behavioral and affective disorders.

Recreational Therapists

- ▲ Education/Training Required: Bachelor's degree
- ▲ Annual Earnings: $28,650
- ▲ Growth: 9%
- ▲ Annual Job Openings: 1,000
- ▲ Self-Employed: 9.8%
- ▲ Part-Time: 20.8%

Plan, direct, or coordinate medically approved recreation programs for patients in hospitals, nursing homes, or other institutions. Activities include sports, trips, dramatics, social activities, and arts and crafts. May assess a patient condition and recommend appropriate recreational activity. Plans, organizes, and participates in treatment programs and activities to facilitate the physical, mental, or emotional rehabilitation or health of patients. Counsels and encourages patients to develop leisure activities. Conducts therapy sessions to improve patient's mental and physical well-being. Prepares and submits reports and charts to treatment team to reflect patients' reactions and evi-

dence of progress or regression. Confers with members of treatment team to determine patient's needs, capabilities, and interests and to determine objectives of therapy. Instructs patient in activities and techniques, such as sports, dance, gardening, music, or art, designed to meet their specific physical or psychological needs. Develops treatment plan to meet needs of patient, based on needs assessment and objectives of therapy. Evaluates patient's reactions to treatment experiences to assess progress or regression and effectiveness of treatment plan. Modifies content of patient's treatment program based on observation and evaluation of progress. Observes and confers with patient to assess patient's needs, capabilities, and interests and to devise treatment plan. **SKILLS**—Instructing: Teaching others how to do something. Service Orientation: Actively looking for ways to help people. Social Perceptiveness: Being aware of others' reactions and understanding why they react as they do. Monitoring: Monitoring/Assessing your performance or that of other individuals or organizations to make improvements or take corrective action. Critical Thinking: Using logic and reasoning to identify the strengths and weaknesses of alternative solutions, conclusions, or approaches to problems. Learning Strategies: Selecting and using training/instructional methods and procedures appropriate for the situation when learning or teaching new things. Active Listening: Giving full attention to what other people are saying, taking time to understand the points being made, asking questions as appropriate, and not interrupting at inappropriate times.

GOE INFORMATION—**Interest Area:** 14. Medical and Health Services. **Work Group:** 14.06. Medical Therapy. **Other Job Titles in This Work Group:** Audiologists; Massage Therapists; Occupational Therapist Aides; Occupational Therapist Assistants; Occupational Therapists; Physical Therapist Aides; Physical Therapist Assistants; Physical Therapists; Radiation Therapists; Respiratory Therapists; Respiratory Therapy Technicians; Speech-Language Pathologists; Therapists, All Other. **PERSONALITY TYPE**—Social. Social occupations fre-

quently involve working with, communicating with, and teaching people. These occupations often involve helping or providing service to others.

EDUCATION/TRAINING PROGRAM(S)— Adapted Physical Education/Therapeutic Recreation; Recreational Therapy. **RELATED KNOWLEDGE/ COURSES**—**Therapy and Counseling:** Knowledge of principles, methods, and procedures for diagnosis, treatment, and rehabilitation of physical and mental dysfunctions and for career counseling and guidance. **Psychology:** Knowledge of human behavior and performance; individual differences in ability, personality, and interests; learning and motivation; psychological research methods; and the assessment and treatment of behavioral and affective disorders. **Education and Training:** Knowledge of principles and methods for curriculum and training design, teaching and instruction for individuals and groups, and the measurement of training effects. **Medicine and Dentistry:** Knowledge of the information and techniques needed to diagnose and treat human injuries, diseases, and deformities. This includes symptoms, treatment alternatives, drug properties and interactions, and preventive health-care measures. **English Language:** Knowledge of the structure and content of the English language, including the meaning and spelling of words, rules of composition, and grammar.

Registered Nurses

> ▲ Education/Training Required: Associate's degree
> ▲ Annual Earnings: $44,840
> ▲ Growth: 26%
> ▲ Annual Job Openings: 140,000
> ▲ Self-Employed: 0.9%
> ▲ Part-Time: 26.3%

Assess patient health problems and needs, develop and implement nursing care plans, and maintain medical records. Administer nursing care to ill, injured, convalescent, or disabled patients. May advise patients on health maintenance and disease prevention or provide case management. Licensing or registration required. Includes advanced practice nurses such as nurse

practitioners, clinical nurse specialists, certified nurse midwives, and certified registered nurse anesthetists. Advanced practice nursing is practiced by RNs who have specialized formal, post-basic education and who function in highly autonomous and specialized roles. Provides health care, first aid, and immunization in facilities such as schools, hospitals, and industry. Observes patient's skin color, dilation of pupils, and computerized equipment to monitor vital signs. Administers local, inhalation, intravenous, and other anesthetics. Orders, interprets, and evaluates diagnostic tests to identify and assess patient's condition. Prescribes or recommends drugs or other forms of treatment, such as physical therapy, inhalation therapy, or related therapeutic procedures. Refers students or patients to community agencies furnishing assistance and cooperates with agencies. Delivers infants and performs postpartum examinations and treatment. Instructs on topics such as health education, disease prevention, childbirth, and home nursing and develops health improvement programs. Advises and consults with specified personnel concerning necessary precautions to be taken to prevent possible contamination or infection. Administers stipulated emergency measures and contacts obstetrician when deviations from standard are encountered during pregnancy or delivery. Informs physician of patient's condition during anesthesia. Discusses cases with physician or obstetrician. Provides prenatal and postnatal care to obstetrical patients under supervision of obstetrician. Contracts independently to render nursing care, usually to one patient, in hospital or private home. Directs and coordinates infection control program in hospital. Maintains stock of supplies. Conducts specified laboratory tests. Prepares rooms, sterile instruments, equipment, and supplies and hands items to surgeon. Prepares patients for and assists with examinations. Records patient's medical information and vital signs. **SKILLS**—Reading Comprehension: Understanding written sentences and paragraphs in work-related documents. Active Listening: Giving full attention to what other people are saying, taking time to understand the points being made, asking questions as appropriate, and not interrupting at inappropriate times. Speaking: Talking to others to convey information effectively. Service Orientation: Actively looking for ways to help people. Instructing: Teaching others how to do something.

GOE INFORMATION—**Interest Area:** 14. Medical and Health Services. **Work Group:** 14.02. Medicine and Surgery. **Other Job Titles in This Work Group:**

Anesthesiologists; Family and General Practitioners; Internists, General; Medical Assistants; Obstetricians and Gynecologists; Pediatricians, General; Pharmacists; Pharmacy Aides; Pharmacy Technicians; Physician Assistants; Physicians and Surgeons, All Other; Psychiatrists; Surgeons; Surgical Technologists. **PERSONALITY TYPE**—Social. Social occupations frequently involve working with, communicating with, and teaching people. These occupations often involve helping or providing service to others.

EDUCATION/TRAINING PROGRAM(S)—Nursing (R.N. Training); Nursing Anesthetist (Post-R.N.); Nursing Midwifery (Post-R.N.); Nursing Science (Post-R.N.); Nursing, Adult Health (Post-R.N.); Nursing, Family Practice (Post-R.N.); Nursing, Maternal/Child Health (Post-R.N.); Nursing, Other; Nursing, Pediatric (Post-R.N.); Nursing, Psychiatric/Mental Health (Post-R.N.); Nursing, Public Health (Post-R.N.); Nursing, Surgical (Post-R.N.). **RELATED KNOWLEDGE/COURSES**—**Medicine and Dentistry:** Knowledge of the information and techniques needed to diagnose and treat human injuries, diseases, and deformities. This includes symptoms, treatment alternatives, drug properties and interactions, and preventive health-care measures. **Biology:** Knowledge of plant and animal organisms and their tissues, cells, functions, interdependencies, and interactions with each other and the environment. **Customer and Personal Service:** Knowledge of principles and processes for providing customer and personal services. This includes customer needs assessment, meeting quality standards for services, and evaluation of customer satisfaction. **Chemistry:** Knowledge of the chemical composition, structure, and properties of substances and of the chemical processes and transformations that they undergo. This includes uses of chemicals and their interactions, danger signs, production techniques, and disposal methods. **Therapy and Counseling:** Knowledge of principles, methods, and procedures for diagnosis, treatment, and rehabilitation of physical and mental dysfunctions and for career counseling and guidance.

Rehabilitation Counselors

▲ Education/Training Required: Bachelor's degree
▲ Annual Earnings: $24,450
▲ Growth: 24%
▲ Annual Job Openings: 12,000
▲ Self-Employed: 3.1%
▲ Part-Time: 11.9%

Counsel individuals to maximize the independence and employability of persons coping with personal, social, and vocational difficulties that result from birth defects, illness, disease, accidents, or the stress of daily life. Coordinate activities for residents of care and treatment facilities. Assess client needs and design and implement rehabilitation programs that may include personal and vocational counseling, training, and job placement. SKILLS—No data available.

GOE INFORMATION—Interest Area: 12. Education and Social Service. Work Group: 12.02. Social Services. Other Job Titles in This Work Group: Child, Family, and School Social Workers; Clergy; Clinical Psychologists; Clinical, Counseling, and School Psychologists; Community and Social Service Specialists, All Other; Counseling Psychologists; Counselors, All Other; Directors, Religious Activities and Education; Marriage and Family Therapists; Medical and Public Health Social Workers; Mental Health and Substance Abuse Social Workers; Mental Health Counselors; Probation Officers and Correctional Treatment Specialists; Religious Workers, All Other; Residential Advisors; Social and Human Service Assistants; Social Workers, All Other; Substance Abuse and Behavioral Disorder Counselors. PERSONALITY TYPE—No data available.

EDUCATION/TRAINING PROGRAM(S)—Vocational Rehabilitation Counseling. RELATED KNOWLEDGE/COURSES—No data available.

Respiratory Therapists

▲ Education/Training Required: Associate's degree
▲ Annual Earnings: $37,680
▲ Growth: 35%
▲ Annual Job Openings: 4,000
▲ Self-Employed: 0%
▲ Part-Time: 20.8%

Assess, treat, and care for patients with breathing disorders. Assume primary responsibility for all respiratory care modalities, including the supervision of respiratory therapy technicians. Initiate and conduct therapeutic procedures; maintain patient records; and select, assemble, check, and operate equipment. Sets up and operates devices, such as mechanical ventilators, therapeutic gas administration apparatus, environmental control systems, and aerosol generators. Operates equipment to administer medicinal gases and aerosol drugs to patients following specified parameters of treatment. Reads prescription, measures arterial blood gases, and reviews patient information to assess patient condition. Monitors patient's physiological responses to therapy, such as vital signs, arterial blood gases, and blood chemistry changes. Performs pulmonary function and adjusts equipment to obtain optimum results to therapy. Inspects and tests respiratory therapy equipment to ensure equipment is functioning safely and efficiently. Determines requirements for treatment, such as type and duration of therapy and medication and dosages. Determines most suitable method of administering inhalants, precautions to be observed, and potential modifications needed, compatible with physician's orders. Performs bronchopulmonary drainage and assists patient in performing breathing exercises. Consults with physician in event of adverse reactions. Maintains patient's chart that contains pertinent identification and therapy information. Orders repairs when necessary. Demonstrates respiratory care procedures to trainees and other health care personnel. **SKILLS**—Reading Comprehension: Understanding written sentences and paragraphs in work-related documents. Service Orientation: Actively looking for ways to help people. Active Listening: Giving full attention to what other people are saying, taking time to understand the points being made, asking questions as appropriate, and not interrupting at inappropriate times. Monitoring: Monitoring/Assessing your performance or that of other individuals or organizations to make improvements or take corrective action. Critical Thinking: Using logic and reasoning to identify the strengths and weaknesses of alternative solutions, conclusions, or approaches to problems. Active Learning: Understanding the implications of new information for both current and future problem-solving and decision-making.

GOE INFORMATION—**Interest Area:** 14. Medical and Health Services. **Work Group:** 14.06. Medical Therapy. **Other Job Titles in This Work Group:** Audiologists; Massage Therapists; Occupational Therapist Aides; Occupational Therapist Assistants; Occupa-tional Therapists; Physical Therapist Aides; Physical Therapist Assistants; Physical Therapists; Radiation Therapists; Recreational Therapists; Respiratory Therapy Technicians; Speech-Language Pathologists; Therapists, All Other. **PERSONALITY TYPE**—Investigative. Investigative occupations frequently involve working with ideas and require an extensive amount of thinking. These occupations can involve searching for facts and figuring out problems mentally.

EDUCATION/TRAINING PROGRAM(S)—Respiratory Therapy Technician. **RELATED KNOWL-EDGE/COURSES**—**Medicine and Dentistry:** Knowledge of the information and techniques needed to diagnose and treat human injuries, diseases, and deformities. This includes symptoms, treatment alternatives, drug properties and interactions, and preventive health-care measures. **Biology:** Knowledge of plant and animal organisms and their tissues, cells, functions, interdependencies, and interactions with each other and the environment. **Therapy and Counseling:** Knowledge of principles, methods, and procedures for diagnosis, treatment, and rehabilitation of physical and mental dysfunctions and for career counseling and guidance. **Chemistry:** Knowledge of the chemical composition, structure, and properties of substances and of the chemical processes and transformations that they undergo. This includes uses of chemicals and their interactions, danger signs, production techniques, and disposal methods. **Psychology:** Knowledge of human behavior and performance; individual differences in ability, personality, and interests; learning and motivation; psychological research methods; and the assessment and treatment of behavioral and affective disorders.

Sales Agents, Financial Services

- ▲ Education/Training Required: Bachelor's degree
- ▲ Annual Earnings: $56,080
- ▲ Growth: 22%
- ▲ Annual Job Openings: 55,000
- ▲ Self-Employed: 22.4%
- ▲ Part-Time: 8.6%

Sell financial services such as loan, tax, and securities counseling to customers of financial in-stitutions and business establishments. Sells services and equipment, such as trust, investment, and check processing services. Develops prospects from current commercial customers, referral leads, and sales and trade meetings. Reviews business trends and advises customers regarding expected fluctuations. Makes presentations on financial services to groups to attract new clients. Determines customers' financial services needs and prepares proposals to sell services. Contacts prospective customers to present information and explain available services. Prepares forms or agreement to complete sale. Evaluates costs and revenue of agreements to determine continued profitability. **SKILLS**—Persuasion: Persuading others to change their minds or behavior. Active Learning: Understanding the implications of new information for both current and future problem-solving and decision-making. Monitoring: Monitoring/Assessing your performance or that of other individuals or organizations to make improvements or take corrective action. Systems Analysis: Determining how a system should work and how changes in conditions, operations, and the environment will affect outcomes. Critical Thinking: Using logic and reasoning to identify the strengths and weaknesses of alternative solutions, conclusions, or approaches to problems. Reading Comprehension: Understanding written sentences and paragraphs in work-related documents.

GOE INFORMATION—**Interest Area:** 10. Sales and Marketing. **Work Group:** 10.02. Sales Technology. **Other Job Titles in This Work Group:** Advertising Sales Agents; Insurance Sales Agents; Sales Agents, Securities and Commodities; Sales Representatives, Agricultural; Sales Representatives, Chemical and Pharmaceutical; Sales

Representatives, Electrical/Electronic; Sales Representatives, Instruments; Sales Representatives, Mechanical Equipment and Supplies; Sales Representatives, Medical; Sales Representatives, Services, All Other; Sales Representatives, Wholesale and Manufacturing, Technical and Scientific Products; Securities, Commodities, and Financial Services Sales Agents. **PERSONALITY TYPE**—Enterprising. Enterprising occupations frequently involve starting up and carrying out projects. These occupations can involve leading people and making many decisions. They sometimes require risk taking and often deal with business.

EDUCATION/TRAINING PROGRAM(S)—Financial Planning; Financial Services Marketing Operations; Investments and Securities. **RELATED KNOWLEDGE/COURSES**—**Economics and Accounting:** Knowledge of economic and accounting principles and practices, the financial markets, banking, and the analysis and reporting of financial data. **Sales and Marketing:** Knowledge of principles and methods for showing, promoting, and selling products or services. This includes marketing strategy and tactics, product demonstration, sales techniques, and sales control systems. **Mathematics:** Knowledge of arithmetic, algebra, geometry, calculus, and statistics and their applications. **English Language:** Knowledge of the structure and content of the English language, including the meaning and spelling of words, rules of composition, and grammar. **Law and Government:** Knowledge of laws, legal codes, court procedures, precedents, government regulations, executive orders, agency rules, and the democratic political process.

Sales Agents, Securities and Commodities

- ▲ Education/Training Required: Bachelor's degree
- ▲ Annual Earnings: $56,080
- ▲ Growth: 22%
- ▲ Annual Job Openings: 55,000
- ▲ Self-Employed: 22.4%
- ▲ Part-Time: 8.6%

Buy and sell securities in investment and trading firms and develop and implement financial plans for individuals, businesses, and organizations. Develops financial plan based on analysis of client's finan-

cial status and discusses financial options with client. Contacts exchange or brokerage firm to execute order or buys and sells securities based on market quotation and competition in market. Records transactions accurately and keeps client informed about transactions. Analyzes market conditions to determine optimum time to execute securities transactions. Reads corporate reports and calculates ratios to determine best prospects for profit on stock purchase and to monitor client account. Identifies potential clients, using advertising campaigns, mailing lists, and personal contacts, and solicits business. Prepares financial reports to monitor client or corporate finances. Informs and advises concerned parties regarding fluctuations and securities transactions affecting plan or account. Completes sales order tickets and submits for processing of client-requested transaction. Prepares documents to implement plan selected by client. Reviews all securities transactions to ensure accuracy of information and that trades conform to regulations of governing agencies. Interviews client to determine client's assets, liabilities, cash flow, insurance coverage, tax status, and financial objectives. Keeps informed about political and economic trends that influence stock prices. **SKILLS**—Management of Financial Resources: Determining how money will be spent to get the work done and accounting for these expenditures. Systems Analysis: Determining how a system should work and how changes in conditions, operations, and the environment will affect outcomes. Active Learning: Understanding the implications of new information for both current and future problem-solving and decision-making. Systems Evaluation: Identifying measures or indicators of system performance and the actions needed to improve or correct performance relative to the goals of the system. Persuasion: Persuading others to change their minds or behavior. Critical Thinking: Using logic and reasoning to identify the strengths and weaknesses of alternative solutions, conclusions, or approaches to problems. Judgment and Decision Making: Considering the relative costs and benefits of potential actions to choose the most appropriate one.

GOE INFORMATION—Interest Area: 10. Sales and Marketing. **Work Group:** 10.02. Sales Technology. **Other Job Titles in This Work Group:** Advertising Sales Agents; Insurance Sales Agents; Sales Agents, Finan-

cial Services; Sales Representatives, Agricultural; Sales Representatives, Chemical and Pharmaceutical; Sales Representatives, Electrical/Electronic; Sales Representatives, Instruments; Sales Representatives, Mechanical Equipment and Supplies; Sales Representatives, Medical; Sales Representatives, Services, All Other; Sales Representatives, Wholesale and Manufacturing, Technical and Scientific Products; Securities, Commodities, and Financial Services Sales Agents. **PERSONALITY TYPE**—Enterprising. Enterprising occupations frequently involve starting up and carrying out projects. These occupations can involve leading people and making many decisions. They sometimes require risk taking and often deal with business.

EDUCATION/TRAINING PROGRAM(S)— Financial Planning; Financial Services Marketing Operations; Investments and Securities. **RELATED KNOWLEDGE/COURSES**—**Economics and Accounting:** Knowledge of economic and accounting principles and practices, the financial markets, banking, and the analysis and reporting of financial data. **Mathematics:** Knowledge of arithmetic, algebra, geometry, calculus, and statistics and their applications. **Sales and Marketing:** Knowledge of principles and methods for showing, promoting, and selling products or services. This includes marketing strategy and tactics, product demonstration, sales techniques, and sales control systems. **English Language:** Knowledge of the structure and content of the English language, including the meaning and spelling of words, rules of composition, and grammar. **Customer and Personal Service:** Knowledge of principles and processes for providing customer and personal services. This includes customer needs assessment, meeting quality standards for services, and evaluation of customer satisfaction. **Clerical Studies:** Knowledge of administrative and clerical procedures and systems such as word processing, managing files and records, stenography and transcription, designing forms, and other office procedures and terminology.

Sales Engineers

- ▲ Education/Training Required: Bachelor's degree
- ▲ Annual Earnings: $56,520
- ▲ Growth: 18%
- ▲ Annual Job Openings: 4,000
- ▲ Self-Employed: 2.7%
- ▲ Part-Time: 4.5%

Sell business goods or services, the selling of which requires a technical background equivalent to a baccalaureate degree in engineering. Calls on management representatives at commercial, industrial, and other establishments to convince prospective client to buy products or services offered. Assists sales force in sale of company products. Demonstrates and explains product or service to customer representatives, such as engineers, architects, and other professionals. Draws up sales or service contract for products or services. Provides technical services to clients relating to use, operation, and maintenance of equipment. Arranges for trial installations of equipment. Designs and drafts variations of standard products in order to meet customer needs. Reviews customer documents to develop and prepare cost estimates or projected production increases from use of proposed equipment or services. Draws up or proposes changes in equipment, processes, materials, or services resulting in cost reduction or improvement in customer operations. Assists in development of custom-made machinery. Diagnoses problems with equipment installed. Provides technical training to employees of client. **SKILLS**—Speaking: Talking to others to convey information effectively. Operations Analysis: Analyzing needs and product requirements to create a design. Reading Comprehension: Understanding written sentences and paragraphs in work-related documents. Active Learning: Understanding the implications of new information for both current and future problem-solving and decision-making. Mathematics: Using mathematics to solve problems. Technology Design: Generating or adapting equipment and technology to serve user needs. Troubleshooting: Determining causes of operating errors and deciding what to do about them.

GOE INFORMATION—Interest Area: 02. Science, Math, and Engineering. **Work Group:** 02.07. Engineering. **Other Job Titles in This Work Group:** Aerospace Engineers; Agricultural Engineers; Architects, Except Landscape and Naval; Biomedical Engineers; Chemical Engineers; Civil Engineers; Computer Hardware Engineers; Computer Software Engineers, Applications; Computer Software Engineers, Systems Software; Electrical Engineers; Electronics Engineers, Except Computer; Engineers, All Other; Environmental Engineers; Fire-Prevention and Protection Engineers; Health and Safety Engineers, Except Mining Safety Engineers and Inspectors; Industrial Engineers; Industrial Safety and Health Engineers; Landscape Architects; Marine Architects; Marine Engineers; Marine Engineers and Naval Architects; Materials Engineers; Mechanical Engineers; Mining and Geological Engineers, Including Mining Safety Engineers; Nuclear Engineers; Petroleum Engineers; Product Safety Engineers. **PERSONALITY TYPE**—Enterprising. Enterprising occupations frequently involve starting up and carrying out projects. These occupations can involve leading people and making many decisions. They sometimes require risk taking and often deal with business.

EDUCATION/TRAINING PROGRAM(S)— General Retailing and Wholesaling Operations and Skills, Other; Systems Engineering. **RELATED KNOWLEDGE/COURSES—Sales and Marketing:** Knowledge of principles and methods for showing, promoting, and selling products or services. This includes marketing strategy and tactics, product demonstration, sales techniques, and sales control systems. **Engineering and Technology:** Knowledge of the practical application of engineering science and technology. This includes applying principles, techniques, procedures, and equipment to the design and production of various goods and services. **Design:** Knowledge of design techniques, tools, and principles involved in production of precision technical plans, blueprints, drawings, and models. **Customer and Personal Service:** Knowledge of principles and processes for providing customer and personal services. This includes customer needs assessment, meeting quality standards for

services, and evaluation of customer satisfaction. **English Language:** Knowledge of the structure and content of the English language, including the meaning and spelling of words, rules of composition, and grammar.

Sales Managers

- ▲ Education/Training Required: Work experience, plus degree
- ▲ Annual Earnings: $68,520
- ▲ Growth: 33%
- ▲ Annual Job Openings: 21,000
- ▲ Self-Employed: 2.4%
- ▲ Part-Time: 2.6%

Direct the actual distribution or movement of a product or service to the customer. Coordinate sales distribution by establishing sales territories, quotas, and goals and establish training programs for sales representatives. Analyze sales statistics gathered by staff to determine sales potential and inventory requirements and monitor the preferences of customers. Confers with potential customers regarding equipment needs and advises customers on types of equipment to purchase. Visits franchised dealers to stimulate interest in establishment or expansion of leasing programs. Advises dealers and distributors on policies and operating procedures to ensure functional effectiveness of business. Reviews operational records and reports to project sales and determine profitability. Confers or consults with department heads to plan advertising services and secure information on appliances, equipment, and customer-required specifications. Directs clerical staff to maintain export correspondence, bid requests, and credit collections and current information on tariffs, licenses, and restrictions. Resolves customer complaints regarding sales and service. Directs product research and development. Directs conversion of products from USA to foreign standards. Inspects premises of assigned stores for adequate security exits and compliance with safety codes and ordinances. Represents company at trade association meetings to promote products. **SKILLS—Coordination:** Adjusting actions in relation to others' actions. **Speaking:** Talking to others to convey information effectively. **Monitoring:** Monitoring/Assessing your performance or that of other individuals or organizations to make improvements or take

corrective action. **Time Management:** Managing one's own time and the time of others. **Active Listening:** Giving full attention to what other people are saying, taking time to understand the points being made, asking questions as appropriate, and not interrupting at inappropriate times.

GOE INFORMATION—Interest Area: 10. Sales and Marketing. **Work Group:** 10.01. Managerial Work in Sales and Marketing. **Other Job Titles in This Work Group:** Advertising and Promotions Managers; First-Line Supervisors/Managers of Non-Retail Sales Workers; First-Line Supervisors/Managers of Retail Sales Workers; Marketing Managers. **PERSONALITY TYPE—**Enterprising. Enterprising occupations frequently involve starting up and carrying out projects. These occupations can involve leading people and making many decisions. They sometimes require risk taking and often deal with business.

EDUCATION/TRAINING PROGRAM(S)—Business Administration and Management, General; Business Marketing and Marketing Management; Marketing Management and Research, Other. **RELATED KNOWLEDGE/COURSES—Administration and Management:** Knowledge of business and management principles involved in strategic planning, resource allocation, human resources modeling, leadership technique, production methods, and coordination of people and resources. **Sales and Marketing:** Knowledge of principles and methods for showing, promoting, and selling products or services. This includes marketing strategy and tactics, product demonstration, sales techniques, and sales control systems. **Customer and Personal Service:** Knowledge of principles and processes for providing customer and personal services. This includes customer needs assessment, meeting quality standards for services, and evaluation of customer satisfaction. **English Language:** Knowledge of the structure and content of the English language, including the meaning and spelling of words, rules of composition, and grammar. **Mathematics:** Knowledge of arithmetic, algebra, geometry, calculus, and statistics and their applications.

Secondary School Teachers, Except Special and Vocational Education

- ▲ Education/Training Required: Bachelor's degree
- ▲ Annual Earnings: $40,870
- ▲ Growth: 19%
- ▲ Annual Job Openings: 60,000
- ▲ Self-Employed: 0%
- ▲ Part-Time: 10.6%

Instruct students in secondary public or private schools in one or more subjects at the secondary level, such as English, mathematics, or social studies. May be designated according to subject matter specialty, such as typing instructors, commercial teachers, or English teachers. Instructs students, using various teaching methods such as lecture and demonstration. Maintains discipline in classroom. Selects, stores, orders, issues, and inventories classroom equipment, materials, and supplies. Performs advisory duties, such as sponsoring student organizations or clubs, helping students select courses, and counseling students with problems. Keeps attendance records. Participates in faculty and professional meetings, educational conferences, and teacher training workshops. Confers with students, parents, and school counselors to resolve behavioral and academic problems. Develops and administers tests. Prepares course outlines and objectives according to curriculum guidelines or state and local requirements. Evaluates, records, and reports student progress. Uses audiovisual aids and other materials to supplement presentations. Assigns lessons and corrects homework. **SKILLS—Learning Strategies:** Selecting and using training/instructional methods and procedures appropriate for the situation when learning or teaching new things. **Speaking:** Talking to others to convey information effectively. **Reading Comprehension:** Understanding written sentences and paragraphs in work-related documents. **Instructing:** Teaching others how to do something. **Mathematics:** Using mathematics to solve problems.

GOE INFORMATION—Interest Area: 12. Education and Social Service. **Work Group:** 12.03. Educational Services. **Other Job Titles in This Work Group:** Adult Literacy, Remedial Education, and GED Teachers and Instructors; Agricultural Sciences Teachers, Postsecondary; Anthropology and Archeology Teachers, Postsecondary; Architecture Teachers, Postsecondary; Archivists; Area, Ethnic, and Cultural Studies Teachers, Postsecondary; Art, Drama, and Music Teachers, Postsecondary; Atmospheric, Earth, Marine, and Space Sciences Teachers, Postsecondary; Audio-Visual Collections Specialists; Biological Science Teachers, Postsecondary; Business Teachers, Postsecondary; Chemistry Teachers, Postsecondary; Child Care Workers; Communications Teachers, Postsecondary; Computer Science Teachers, Postsecondary; Criminal Justice and Law Enforcement Teachers, Postsecondary; Curators; Economics Teachers, Postsecondary; Education Teachers, Postsecondary; Educational Psychologists; Educational, Vocational, and School Counselors; Elementary School Teachers, Except Special Education; Engineering Teachers, Postsecondary; English Language and Literature Teachers, Postsecondary; Environmental Science Teachers, Postsecondary; Farm and Home Management Advisors; Foreign Language and Literature Teachers, Postsecondary; Forestry and Conservation Science Teachers, Postsecondary; Geography Teachers, Postsecondary; Graduate Teaching Assistants; Health Specialties Teachers, Postsecondary; History Teachers, Postsecondary; Home Economics Teachers, Postsecondary; Kindergarten Teachers, Except Special Education; Law Teachers, Postsecondary; Librarians; Library Assistants, Clerical; others. **PERSONALITY TYPE**—Social. Social occupations frequently involve working with, communicating with, and teaching people. These occupations often involve helping or providing service to others.

EDUCATION/TRAINING PROGRAM(S)—Agricultural Teacher Education (Vocational); Art Teacher Education; Biology Teacher Education; Business Teacher Education (Vocational); Chemistry Teacher Education; Computer Teacher Education; Drama and Dance Teacher Education; Driver and Safety Teacher Education; English Teacher Education; Foreign Languages Teacher Education; French Language Teacher Education; German Language Teacher Education; Health Occupations Teacher Education (Vocational); Health Teacher Education; History Teacher Education; Home Economics Teacher Education (Vocational); Junior High/Intermediate/Middle School Teacher Education; Marketing Operations Teacher Education/Marketing & Distribution Teacher; Mathematics Teacher Education; Music Teacher Education; Physical Education Teaching and Coaching; Physics Teacher Education; Reading Teacher Education; Science Teacher Education, General; Secondary Teacher Education; Social Science Teacher Education; Social Studies Teacher Educa-

tion; Spanish Language Teacher Education; Speech Teacher Education; Teacher Education, Specific Academic and Vocational Programs; Technology Teacher Education/Industrial Arts Teacher Education. **RELATED KNOWL-EDGE/COURSES**—**Education and Training:** Knowledge of principles and methods for curriculum and training design, teaching and instruction for individuals and groups, and the measurement of training effects. **English Language:** Knowledge of the structure and content of the English language, including the meaning and spelling of words, rules of composition, and grammar. **Mathematics:** Knowledge of arithmetic, algebra, geometry, calculus, and statistics and their applications. **Therapy and Counseling:** Knowledge of principles, methods, and procedures for diagnosis, treatment, and rehabilitation of physical and mental dysfunctions and for career counseling and guidance. **Clerical Studies:** Knowledge of administrative and clerical procedures and systems such as word processing, managing files and records, stenography and transcription, designing forms, and other office procedures and terminology. **Psychology:** Knowledge of human behavior and performance; individual differences in ability, personality, and interests; learning and motivation; psychological research methods; and the assessment and treatment of behavioral and affective disorders.

Securities, Commodities, and Financial Services Sales Agents

- ▲ Education/Training Required: Bachelor's degree
- ▲ Annual Earnings: $56,080
- ▲ Growth: 22%
- ▲ Annual Job Openings: 55,000
- ▲ Self-Employed: 22.4%
- ▲ Part-Time: 8.6%

Buy and sell securities in investment and trading firms or call upon businesses and individuals to sell financial services. Provide financial services, such as loan, tax, and securities counseling. May advise securities customers about such things as stocks, bonds, and market conditions. **SKILLS**—No data available.

GOE INFORMATION—Interest Area: 10. Sales and Marketing. **Work Group:** 10.02. Sales Technology. **Other Job Titles in This Work Group:** Advertising Sales Agents; Insurance Sales Agents; Sales Agents, Financial Services; Sales Agents, Securities and Commodities; Sales Representatives, Agricultural; Sales Representatives, Chemical and Pharmaceutical; Sales Representatives, Electrical/Electronic; Sales Representatives, Instruments; Sales Representatives, Mechanical Equipment and Supplies; Sales Representatives, Medical; Sales Representatives, Services, All Other; Sales Representatives, Wholesale and Manufacturing, Technical and Scientific Products. **PERSONALITY TYPE**—No data available.

Semiconductor Processors

EDUCATION/TRAINING PROGRAM(S)—Financial Planning; Financial Services Marketing Operations; Investments and Securities. **RELATED KNOWLEDGE/COURSES**—No data available.

▲ Education/Training Required: Associate's degree

▲ Annual Earnings: $25,430

▲ Growth: 32%

▲ Annual Job Openings: 7,000

▲ Self-Employed: 0%

▲ Part-Time: 2.7%

Perform any or all of the following functions in the manufacture of electronic semiconductors: Load semiconductor material into furnace; saw formed ingots into segments; load individual segment into crystal growing chamber and monitor controls; locate crystal axis in ingot using X-ray equipment and saw ingots into wafers; clean, polish, and load wafers into series of special-purpose furnaces, chemical baths, and equipment used to form circuitry and change conductive properties. Measures and weighs amounts of crystal growing materials, mixes and grinds materials, and loads materials into container, following procedures. Forms seed crystal for crystal growing or locates crystal axis of ingot, using X-ray equipment, drill, and sanding machine. Aligns photo mask pattern on photoresist layer, exposes pattern to ultraviolet light, and develops pattern, using specialized equipment. Attaches ampoule to diffusion pump to remove air from ampoule and seals ampoule, using blowtorch. Places semiconductor wafers in processing containers or equipment holders, using vacuum wand or tweezers. Monitors operation and adjusts controls of processing machines and equipment to produce compositions with specific electronic properties. Manipulates valves, switches, and buttons or keys commands into control panels to start semiconductor processing cycles. Etches, laps, polishes, or grinds wafers or ingots, using etching, lapping, polishing, or grinding equipment. Operates saw to cut remelt into sections of specified size or to cut ingots into wafers. Cleans

and dries materials and equipment using solvent, etching or sandblasting equipment, and drying equipment to remove contaminants or photoresist. Studies work order, instructions, formulas, and processing charts to determine specifications and sequence of operations. Loads and unloads equipment chambers and transports finished product to storage or to area for further processing. Inspects materials, components, or products for surface defects and measures circuitry, using electronic test equipment, precision measuring instruments, and standard procedures. Counts, sorts, and weighs processed items. Stamps or etches identifying information on finished component. Maintains processing, production, and inspection information and reports. **SKILLS**—Operation Monitoring: Watching gauges, dials, or other indicators to make sure a machine is working properly. Operation and Control: Controlling operations of equipment or systems. Science: Using scientific rules and methods to solve problems. Equipment Selection: Determining the kind of tools and equipment needed to do a job. Reading Comprehension: Understanding written sentences and paragraphs in work-related documents. Mathematics: Using mathematics to solve problems. Writing: Communicating effectively in writing as appropriate for the needs of the audience.

GOE INFORMATION—**Interest Area:** 08. Industrial Production. **Work Group:** 08.03. Production Work. **Other Job Titles in This Work Group:** Bakers, Manufacturing; Bindery Machine Operators and Tenders; Brazers; Cementing and Gluing Machine Operators and Tenders; Chemical Equipment Controllers and Operators; Chemical Equipment Operators and Tenders; Chemical Equipment Tenders; Cleaning, Washing, and Metal Pickling Equipment Operators and Tenders; Coating, Painting, and Spraying Machine Operators and Tenders; Coil Winders, Tapers, and Finishers; Combination Machine Tool Operators and Tenders, Metal and Plastic; Computer-Controlled Machine Tool Operators, Metal and Plastic; Cooling and Freezing Equipment Operators and Tenders; Crushing, Grinding, and Polishing Machine Setters, Operators, and Tenders; Cutters and Trimmers, Hand; Cutting and Slicing Machine Operators and Tenders; Cutting and Slicing Machine Setters, Operators, and Tenders; Design Printing Machine Setters and Set-Up Operators; Electrolytic Plating and Coating Machine Operators and Tenders, Metal and Plastic; Electrolytic Plating and Coating Machine Setters and Set-Up Operators, Metal and Plastic; Electrotypers and Stereotypers; Embossing Machine Set-Up Operators; Engraver Set-Up Operators; Extruding and Forming Machine Operators and Tenders, Synthetic or Glass Fibers; Extruding and Forming Machine Setters, Operators, and Tenders, Synthetic and Glass Fibers; Extruding, Forming, Pressing, and Compacting Machine Operators and Tenders; Fabric and Apparel Patternmakers; Fiber Product Cutting Machine Setters and Set-Up Operators; Fiberglass Laminators and Fabricators; others. **PERSONALITY TYPE**—Realistic. Realistic occupations frequently involve work activities that include practical, hands-on problems and solutions. They often deal with plants, animals, and real-world materials like wood, tools, and machinery. Many of the occupations require working outside and do not involve a lot of paperwork or working closely with others.

EDUCATION/TRAINING PROGRAM(S)—Industrial Electronics Installer and Repairer. **RELATED KNOWLEDGE/COURSES**—**Production and Processing:** Knowledge of raw materials, production processes, quality control, costs, and other techniques for maximizing the effective manufacture and distribution of goods. **Mathematics:** Knowledge of arithmetic, algebra, geometry, calculus, and statistics and their applications. **Principles of Mechanical Devices:** Knowledge of machines and tools, including their designs, uses, repair, and maintenance. **Engineering and Technology:** Knowledge of the practical application of engineering science and technology. This includes applying principles, techniques, procedures, and equipment to the design and production of various goods and services. **Computers and Electronics:** Knowledge of circuit boards, processors, chips, electronic equipment, and computer hardware and software, including applications and programming.

Set and Exhibit Designers

- ▲ Education/Training Required: Bachelor's degree
- ▲ Annual Earnings: $31,440
- ▲ Growth: 27%
- ▲ Annual Job Openings: 2,000
- ▲ Self-Employed: 31.9%
- ▲ Part-Time: 20%

Design special exhibits and movie, television, and theater sets. May study scripts, confer with directors, and conduct research to determine appropriate architectural styles. **SKILLS**—No data available.

GOE INFORMATION—**Interest Area:** 01. Arts, Entertainment, and Media. **Work Group:** 01.04. Visual Arts. **Other Job Titles in This Work Group:** Cartoonists; Commercial and Industrial Designers; Designers, All Other; Exhibit Designers; Fashion Designers; Fine Artists, Including Painters, Sculptors, and Illustrators; Floral Designers; Graphic Designers; Interior Designers; Merchandise Displayers and Window Trimmers; Multi-Media Artists and Animators; Painters and Illustrators; Sculptors; Set Designers; Sketch Artists. **PERSONALITY TYPE**—No data available.

EDUCATION/TRAINING PROGRAM(S)—
Design and Applied Arts, Other; Design and Visual
Communications; Technical Theater/Theater Design

and Stagecraft. **RELATED KNOWLEDGE/
COURSES**—No data available.

Set Designers

▲ Education/Training Required: Bachelor's degree

▲ Annual Earnings: $31,440

▲ Growth: 27%

▲ Annual Job Openings: 2,000

▲ Self-Employed: 31.9%

▲ Part-Time: 20%

**Design sets for theatrical, motion picture, and
television productions.** Integrates requirements including script, research, budget, and available locations to develop design. Presents drawings for approval and makes
changes and corrections as directed. Selects furniture, draperies, pictures, lamps, and rugs for decorative quality and
appearance. Confers with heads of production and direction to establish budget and schedules and discuss design
ideas. Directs and coordinates set construction, erection,
or decoration activities to ensure conformance to design,
budget, and schedule requirements. Assigns staff to complete design ideas and prepare sketches, illustrations, and
detailed drawings of sets or graphics and animation. Examines dressed set to ensure props and scenery do not inter-
fere with movements of cast or view of camera. Reads
script to determine location, set, or decoration requirements. Estimates costs of design materials and construction or rental of location or props. Researches and consults
experts to determine architectural and furnishing styles to
depict given periods or locations. Designs and builds scale
models of set design or miniature sets used in filming backgrounds or special effects. Prepares rough draft and scale
working drawings of sets, including floor plans, scenery,
and properties to be constructed. **SKILLS**—Reading
Comprehension: Understanding written sentences and
paragraphs in work-related documents. Management of
Material Resources: Obtaining and seeing to the appropriate use of equipment, facilities, and materials needed to do
certain work. Active Listening: Giving full attention to
what other people are saying, taking time to understand
the points being made, asking questions as appropriate,
and not interrupting at inappropriate times. Coordina-

tion: Adjusting actions in relation to others' actions. Active Learning: Understanding the implications of new information for both current and future problem-solving and
decision-making. Management of Financial Resources:
Determining how money will be spent to get the work
done and accounting for these expenditures. Critical Thinking: Using logic and reasoning to identify the strengths and
weaknesses of alternative solutions, conclusions, or approaches to problems.

GOE INFORMATION—**Interest Area:** 01. Arts,
Entertainment, and Media. **Work Group:** 01.04. Visual
Arts. **Other Job Titles in This Work Group:** Car-
toonists; Commercial and Industrial Designers; Designers,
All Other; Exhibit Designers; Fashion Designers; Fine Art-
ists, Including Painters, Sculptors, and Illustrators; Floral
Designers; Graphic Designers; Interior Designers; Mer-
chandise Displayers and Window Trimmers; Multi-Media
Artists and Animators; Painters and Illustrators; Sculptors;
Set and Exhibit Designers; Sketch Artists. **PERSONAL-
ITY TYPE**—Artistic. Artistic occupations frequently
involve working with forms, designs, and patterns. They
often require self-expression, and the work can be done
without following a clear set of rules.

EDUCATION/TRAINING PROGRAM(S)—
Design and Applied Arts, Other; Design and Visual
Communications; Technical Theater/Theater Design
and Stagecraft. **RELATED KNOWLEDGE/
COURSES**—**Design:** Knowledge of design techniques,
tools, and principles involved in production of precision
technical plans, blueprints, drawings, and models. **Fine
Arts:** Knowledge of the theory and techniques required to

compose, produce, and perform works of music, dance, visual arts, drama, and sculpture. **Building and Construction:** Knowledge of materials, methods, and tools involved in the construction or repair of houses, buildings, or other structures, such as highways and roads. **Sociology and Anthropology:** Knowledge of group behavior and dynamics, societal trends and influences, human migrations, ethnicity, cultures, and their history and origins.

English Language: Knowledge of the structure and content of the English language, including the meaning and spelling of words, rules of composition, and grammar. **Psychology:** Knowledge of human behavior and performance; individual differences in ability, personality, and interests; learning and motivation; psychological research methods; and the assessment and treatment of behavioral and affective disorders.

Social and Community Service Managers

▲ Education/Training Required: Bachelor's degree

▲ Annual Earnings: $39,130

▲ Growth: 25%

▲ Annual Job Openings: 13,000

▲ Self-Employed: 49.4%

▲ Part-Time: 7.2%

Plan, organize, or coordinate the activities of a social service program or community outreach organization. Oversee the program or organization's budget and policies regarding participant involvement, program requirements, and benefits. Work may involve directing social workers, counselors, or probation officers. Confers and consults with individuals, groups, and committees to determine needs and plan, implement, and extend organization's programs and services. Determines organizational policies and defines scope of services offered and administration of procedures. Establishes and maintains relationships with other agencies and organizations in community to meet and not duplicate community needs and services. Assigns duties to staff or volunteers. Plans, directs, and prepares fund-raising activities and public relations materials. Researches and analyzes member or community needs as basis for community development. Participates in program activities to serve clients of agency. Prepares, distributes, and maintains records and reports, such as budgets, personnel records, or training manuals. Coordinates volunteer service programs, such as Red Cross, hospital volunteers, or vocational training for disabled individuals. Speaks to community groups to explain and interpret agency purpose, programs, and policies. Advises volunteers and volunteer leaders to ensure quality of pro-

grams and effective use of resources. Instructs and trains agency staff or volunteers in skills required to provide services. Interviews, recruits, or hires volunteers and staff. Observes workers to evaluate performance and ensure work meets established standards. **SKILLS—Speaking:** Talking to others to convey information effectively. Coordination: Adjusting actions in relation to others' actions. Reading Comprehension: Understanding written sentences and paragraphs in work-related documents. Social Perceptiveness: Being aware of others' reactions and understanding why they react as they do. Service Orientation: Actively looking for ways to help people. Instructing: Teaching others how to do something. Writing: Communicating effectively in writing as appropriate for the needs of the audience.

GOE INFORMATION—Interest Area: 12. Education and Social Service. **Work Group:** 12.01. Managerial Work in Education and Social Service. **Other Job Titles in This Work Group:** Education Administrators, All Other; Education Administrators, Elementary and Secondary School; Education Administrators, Postsecondary; Education Administrators, Preschool and Child Care Center/Program; Instructional Coordinators; Park Naturalists. **PERSONALITY TYPE—Social.** Social occupations frequently involve working with, communicating with, and teaching people. These occupations often involve helping or providing service to others.

EDUCATION/TRAINING PROGRAM(S)—Arts Management; Business Administration and Management, General; Business Administration and Management, Other; Business Management and Administrative Services, Other; Business, General; Community Organization, Resources and Services; Enterprise Management and Operation, General; Enterprise Management and Operation, Other; Entrepreneurship; Franchise Operation; Hospitality Services Management, Other; Non-Profit and Public Management; Public Administration; Travel-Tourism Management. **RELATED KNOWLEDGE/COURSES—Administration and Management:** Knowledge of business and management principles involved in strategic planning, resource allocation, human resources modeling, leadership technique, production methods, and coordination of people and resources. **Customer and Personal Service:** Knowledge of principles and processes for providing customer and personal services. This includes customer needs assessment, meeting quality standards for services, and evaluation of customer satisfaction. **Education and Training:** Knowledge of principles and methods for curriculum and training design, teaching and instruction for individuals and groups, and the measurement of training effects. **Personnel and Human Resources:** Knowledge of principles and procedures for personnel recruitment, selection, training, compensation and benefits, labor relations and negotiation, and personnel information systems. **English Language:** Knowledge of the structure and content of the English language, including the meaning and spelling of words, rules of composition, and grammar.

Social Work Teachers, Postsecondary

- ▲ Education/Training Required: Master's degree
- ▲ Annual Earnings: $48,640
- ▲ Growth: 24% for all Postsecondary Teachers
- ▲ Annual Job Openings: 184,000 for all Postsecondary Teachers
- ▲ Self-Employed: 0%
- ▲ Part-Time: 32.3% for all Postsecondary Teachers

Teach courses in social work. **SKILLS**—No data available.

GOE INFORMATION—Interest Area: 12. Education and Social Service. **Work Group:** 12.03. Educational Services. **Other Job Titles in This Work Group:** Adult Literacy, Remedial Education, and GED Teachers and Instructors; Agricultural Sciences Teachers, Postsecondary; Anthropology and Archeology Teachers, Postsecondary; Architecture Teachers, Postsecondary; Archivists; Area, Ethnic, and Cultural Studies Teachers, Postsecondary; Art, Drama, and Music Teachers, Postsecondary; Atmospheric, Earth, Marine, and Space Sciences Teachers, Postsecondary; Audio-Visual Collections Specialists; Biological Science Teachers, Postsecondary; Business Teachers, Postsecondary; Chemistry Teachers, Postsecondary; Child Care Workers; Communications Teachers, Postsecondary; Computer Science Teachers, Postsecondary; Criminal Justice and Law Enforcement Teachers, Postsecondary; Curators; Economics Teachers, Postsecondary; Education Teachers, Postsecondary; Educational Psychologists; Educational, Vocational, and School Counselors; Elementary School Teachers, Except Special Education; Engineering Teachers, Postsecondary; English Language and Literature Teachers, Postsecondary; Environmental Science Teachers, Postsecondary; Farm and Home Management Advisors; Foreign Language and Literature Teachers, Postsecondary; Forestry and Conservation Science Teachers, Postsecondary; Geography Teachers, Postsecondary; Graduate Teaching Assistants; Health Specialties Teachers, Postsecondary;

History Teachers, Postsecondary; Home Economics Teachers, Postsecondary; Kindergarten Teachers, Except Special Education; Law Teachers, Postsecondary; Librarians; Library Assistants, Clerical; others. **PERSONALITY TYPE**—No data available.

EDUCATION/TRAINING PROGRAM(S)—Clinical and Medical Social Work; Social Work; Teacher Education, Specific Academic and Vocational Programs. **RELATED KNOWLEDGE/COURSES**—No data available.

Sociology Teachers, Postsecondary

- ▲ Education/Training Required: Master's degree
- ▲ Annual Earnings: $48,010
- ▲ Growth: 24% for all Postsecondary Teachers
- ▲ Annual Job Openings: 184,000 for all Postsecondary Teachers
- ▲ Self-Employed: 0%
- ▲ Part-Time: 32.3% for all Postsecondary Teachers

Teach courses in sociology. Prepares and delivers lectures to students. Stimulates class discussions. Compiles, administers, and grades examinations or assigns this work to others. Compiles bibliographies of specialized materials for outside reading assignments. Serves on faculty committee providing professional consulting services to government and industry. Acts as adviser to student organizations. Conducts research in particular field of knowledge and publishes findings in professional journals. Directs research of other teachers or graduate students working for advanced academic degrees. Advises students on academic and vocational curricula. **SKILLS**—Reading Comprehension: Understanding written sentences and paragraphs in work-related documents. Instructing: Teaching others how to do something. Speaking: Talking to others to convey information effectively. Active Learning: Understanding the implications of new information for both current and future problem-solving and decision-making. Active Listening: Giving full attention to what other people are saying, taking time to understand the points being made, asking questions as appropriate, and not interrupting at inappropriate times. Writing: Communicating effectively in writing as appropriate for the needs of the audience. Learning Strategies: Selecting and using training/instructional methods and procedures appropriate for the situation when learning or teaching new things.

GOE INFORMATION—**Interest Area:** 12. Education and Social Service. **Work Group:** 12.03. Educational Services. **Other Job Titles in This Work Group:** Adult Literacy, Remedial Education, and GED Teachers and Instructors; Agricultural Sciences Teachers, Postsecondary; Anthropology and Archeology Teachers, Postsecondary; Architecture Teachers, Postsecondary; Archivists; Area, Ethnic, and Cultural Studies Teachers, Postsecondary; Art, Drama, and Music Teachers, Postsecondary; Atmospheric, Earth, Marine, and Space Sciences Teachers, Postsecondary; Audio-Visual Collections Specialists; Biological Science Teachers, Postsecondary; Business Teachers, Postsecondary; Chemistry Teachers, Postsecondary; Child Care Workers; Communications Teachers, Postsecondary; Computer Science Teachers, Postsecondary; Criminal Justice and Law Enforcement Teachers, Postsecondary; Curators; Economics Teachers, Postsecondary; Education Teachers, Postsecondary; Educational Psychologists; Educational, Vocational, and School Counselors; Elementary School Teachers, Except Special Education; Engineering Teachers, Postsecondary; English Language and Literature Teachers, Postsecondary; Environmental Science Teachers, Postsecondary; Farm and Home Management Advisors; Foreign Language and Literature Teachers, Postsecondary; Forestry and Conservation Science Teachers, Postsecondary; Geography Teachers, Postsecondary; Graduate Teaching

Assistants; Health Specialties Teachers, Postsecondary; History Teachers, Postsecondary; Home Economics Teachers, Postsecondary; Kindergarten Teachers, Except Special Education; Law Teachers, Postsecondary; Librarians; Library Assistants, Clerical; others. **PERSONALITY TYPE**—Social. Social occupations frequently involve working with, communicating with, and teaching people. These occupations often involve helping or providing service to others.

EDUCATION/TRAINING PROGRAM(S)— Social Science Teacher Education; Sociology. **RELATED KNOWLEDGE/COURSES—Education and Training:** Knowledge of principles and methods for curriculum and training design, teaching and instruction for individuals and groups, and the measurement of training effects. **Sociology and Anthropology:** Knowledge of group behavior and dynamics, societal trends and influences, human migrations, ethnicity, cultures, and their history and origins. **History and Archeology:** Knowledge of historical events and their causes, indicators, and effects on civilizations and cultures. **Psychology:** Knowledge of human behavior and performance; individual differences in ability, personality, and interests; learning and motivation; psychological research methods; and the assessment and treatment of behavioral and affective disorders. **English Language:** Knowledge of the structure and content of the English language, including the meaning and spelling of words, rules of composition, and grammar.

Soil Conservationists

▲ Education/Training Required: Bachelor's degree

▲ Annual Earnings: $47,140

▲ Growth: 8%

▲ Annual Job Openings: 1,000

▲ Self-Employed: 2.4%

▲ Part-Time: 6.6%

Plan and develop coordinated practices for soil erosion control, soil and water conservation, and sound land use. Plans soil management practices, such as crop rotation, reforestation, permanent vegetation, contour plowing, or terracing, to maintain soil and conserve water. Conducts surveys and investigations of various land uses, such as rural or urban, agriculture, construction, forestry, or mining. Develops or participates in environmental studies. Computes cost estimates of different conservation practices based on needs of land users, maintenance requirements, and life expectancy of practices. Discusses conservation plans, problems, and alternative solutions with land users, applying knowledge of agronomy, soil science, forestry, or agricultural sciences. Revisits land users to view implemented land use practices and plans. Surveys property to mark locations and measurements, using surveying instruments. Monitors projects during and after construction to ensure projects conform to design specifications. Computes design specification for implementation of conservation practices, using survey and field information tech-

nical guides, engineering manuals, and calculator. Analyzes results of investigations to determine measures needed to maintain or restore proper soil management. Develops plans for conservation, such as conservation cropping systems, woodlands management, pasture planning, and engineering systems. **SKILLS**—Monitoring: Monitoring/Assessing your performance or that of other individuals or organizations to make improvements or take corrective action. Mathematics: Using mathematics to solve problems. Reading Comprehension: Understanding written sentences and paragraphs in work-related documents. Judgment and Decision Making: Considering the relative costs and benefits of potential actions to choose the most appropriate one. Complex Problem Solving: Identifying complex problems and reviewing related information to develop and evaluate options and implement solutions.

GOE INFORMATION—Interest Area: 02. Science, Math, and Engineering. **Work Group:** 02.03. Life Sciences. **Other Job Titles in This Work Group:**

Agricultural and Food Science Technicians; Agricultural Technicians; Animal Scientists; Biochemists; Biochemists and Biophysicists; Biological Scientists, All Other; Biologists; Biophysicists; Conservation Scientists; Environmental Scientists and Specialists, Including Health; Epidemiologists; Food Science Technicians; Food Scientists and Technologists; Foresters; Life Scientists, All Other; Medical Scientists, Except Epidemiologists; Microbiologists; Plant Scientists; Range Managers; Soil and Plant Scientists; Soil Scientists; Zoologists and Wildlife Biologists. **PERSONALITY TYPE**—Investigative. Investigative occupations frequently involve working with ideas and require an extensive amount of thinking. These occupations can involve searching for facts and figuring out problems mentally.

EDUCATION/TRAINING PROGRAM(S)—Conservation and Renewable Natural Resources, Other; Forest Management; Forestry and Related Sciences, Other; Forestry Sciences; Forestry, General; Natural Resources Conservation, General; Natural Resources Law Enforce-

ment and Protective Services; Natural Resources Management and Policy; Natural Resources Management and Protective Services, Other; Wildlife and Wildlands Management. **RELATED KNOWLEDGE/COURSES—Biology:** Knowledge of plant and animal organisms and their tissues, cells, functions, interdependencies, and interactions with each other and the environment. **Mathematics:** Knowledge of arithmetic, algebra, geometry, calculus, and statistics and their applications. **Engineering and Technology:** Knowledge of the practical application of engineering science and technology. This includes applying principles, techniques, procedures, and equipment to the design and production of various goods and services. **Food Production:** Knowledge of techniques and equipment for planting, growing, and harvesting food products (both plant and animal) for consumption, including storage/handling techniques. **English Language:** Knowledge of the structure and content of the English language, including the meaning and spelling of words, rules of composition, and grammar.

Special Education Teachers, Middle School

- ▲ Education/Training Required: Bachelor's degree
- ▲ Annual Earnings: $38,600
- ▲ Growth: 24%
- ▲ Annual Job Openings: 6,000
- ▲ Self-Employed: 0%
- ▲ Part-Time: 12.9%

Teach middle school subjects to educationally and physically handicapped students. Includes teachers who specialize and work with audibly and visually handicapped students and those who teach basic academic and life processes skills to the mentally impaired. Teaches socially acceptable behavior, employing techniques such as behavior modification and positive reinforcement. Instructs students, using special educational strategies and techniques to improve sensory-motor and perceptual-motor development, memory, language, and cognition. Instructs students in academic subjects, utilizing various teaching techniques, such as phonetics, multisensory learning, and repetition, to reinforce learning. Instructs students in daily living skills required for independent maintenance and economic self-

sufficiency, such as hygiene, safety, and food preparation. Plans curriculum and other instructional materials to meet students' needs, considering such factors as physical, emotional, and educational abilities. Administers and interprets results of ability and achievement tests. Confers with other staff members to plan programs designed to promote educational, physical, and social development of students. Provides consistent reinforcement to learning and continuous feedback to student. Meets with parents to provide support, guidance in using community resources, and skills in dealing with students' learning impairment. Observes, evaluates, and prepares reports on progress of students. Works with students to increase motivation. Confers with parents, administrators, testing specialists, social workers, and others to develop individual educational plan for student. Selects and teaches reading material and math problems related to everyday life of individual student. **SKILLS**—Learning Strategies: Selecting and using training/instructional methods and procedures appropriate for the situation when learning or teaching new things. Social Perceptiveness: Being aware of others' reactions and understanding why they react as they do. Instructing: Teaching others how to do something. Active Listening: Giving full attention to what other people are saying, taking time to understand the points being made, asking questions as appropriate, and not interrupting at inappropriate times. Speaking: Talking to others to convey information effectively. Monitoring: Monitoring/Assessing your performance or that of other individuals or organizations to make improvements or take corrective action.

GOE INFORMATION—**Interest Area:** 12. Education and Social Service. **Work Group:** 12.03. Educational Services. **Other Job Titles in This Work Group:** Adult Literacy, Remedial Education, and GED Teachers and Instructors; Agricultural Sciences Teachers, Postsecondary; Anthropology and Archeology Teachers, Postsecondary; Architecture Teachers, Postsecondary; Archivists; Area, Ethnic, and Cultural Studies Teachers, Postsecondary; Art, Drama, and Music Teachers, Postsecondary; Atmospheric, Earth, Marine, and Space Sciences Teachers, Postsecondary; Audio-Visual Collections Specialists; Biological Science Teachers, Postsecondary; Business Teachers, Postsecondary; Chemistry Teachers, Postsecondary; Child Care Workers; Communications Teachers, Postsecondary; Computer Science Teachers, Postsecondary; Criminal Justice and Law Enforcement Teachers, Postsecondary; Curators; Economics Teachers, Postsecondary; Education Teachers, Postsecondary; Educational Psychologists; Educational, Vocational, and School Counselors; Elementary School Teachers, Except Special Education; Engineering Teachers, Postsecondary; English Language and Literature Teachers, Postsecondary; Environmental Science Teachers, Postsecondary; Farm and Home Management Advisors; Foreign Language and Literature Teachers, Postsecondary;

Forestry and Conservation Science Teachers, Postsecondary; Geography Teachers, Postsecondary; Graduate Teaching Assistants; Health Specialties Teachers, Postsecondary; History Teachers, Postsecondary; Home Economics Teachers, Postsecondary; Kindergarten Teachers, Except Special Education; Law Teachers, Postsecondary; Librarians; Library Assistants, Clerical; others. **PERSONALITY TYPE**—Social. Social occupations frequently involve working with, communicating with, and teaching people. These occupations often involve helping or providing service to others.

EDUCATION/TRAINING PROGRAM(S)—Education of the Autistic; Education of the Blind and Visually Handicapped; Education of the Deaf and Hearing Impaired; Education of the Emotionally Handicapped; Education of the Mentally Handicapped; Education of the Multiple Handicapped; Education of the Physically Handicapped; Education of the Specific Learning Disabled; Education of the Speech Impaired; Special Education, General; Special Education, Other. **RELATED KNOWLEDGE/COURSES**—Education and Training: Knowledge of principles and methods for curriculum and training design, teaching and instruction for individuals and groups, and the measurement of training effects. **Psychology:** Knowledge of human behavior and performance; individual differences in ability, personality, and interests; learning and motivation; psychological research methods; and the assessment and treatment of behavioral and affective disorders. **Therapy and Counseling:** Knowledge of principles, methods, and procedures for diagnosis, treatment, and rehabilitation of physical and mental dysfunctions and for career counseling and guidance. **English Language:** Knowledge of the structure and content of the English language, including the meaning and spelling of words, rules of composition, and grammar. **Customer and Personal Service:** Knowledge of principles and processes for providing customer and personal services. This includes customer needs assessment, meeting quality standards for services, and evaluation of customer satisfaction.

Special Education Teachers, Preschool, Kindergarten, and Elementary School

- ▲ Education/Training Required: Bachelor's degree
- ▲ Annual Earnings: $40,880
- ▲ Growth: 37%
- ▲ Annual Job Openings: 15,000
- ▲ Self-Employed: 0%
- ▲ Part-Time: 12.9%

Teach elementary and preschool school subjects to educationally and physically handicapped students. Includes teachers who specialize and work with audibly and visually handicapped students and those who teach basic academic and life processes skills to the mentally impaired. Teaches socially acceptable behavior, employing techniques such as behavior modification and positive reinforcement. Instructs students in academic subjects, utilizing various teaching techniques, such as phonetics, multisensory learning, and repetition, to reinforce learning. Instructs students, using special educational strategies and techniques to improve sensory-motor and perceptual-motor development, memory, language, and cognition. Plans curriculum and other instructional materials to meet students' needs, considering such factors as physical, emotional, and educational abilities. Administers and interprets results of ability and achievement tests. Confers with other staff members to plan programs designed to promote educational, physical, and social development of students. Provides consistent reinforcement to learning and continuous feedback to student. Meets with parents to provide support, guidance in using community resources, and skills in dealing with students' learning impairment. Observes, evaluates, and prepares reports on progress of students. Works with students to increase motivation. Confers with parents, administrators, testing specialists, social workers, and others to develop individual educational plan for student. Selects and teaches reading material and math problems related to everyday life of individual student. Instructs students in daily living skills required for independent maintenance and economic self-sufficiency, such as hygiene, safety, and food preparation. **SKILLS**—Learning Strategies: Selecting and using training/instructional methods and procedures appropriate for the situation when learning or teaching new things. Social Perceptiveness: Being aware of others' reactions and understanding why they react as they do. Instructing: Teaching others how to do something. Active Listening: Giving full attention to what other people are saying, taking time to understand the points being made, asking questions as appropriate, and not interrupting at inappropriate times. Monitoring: Monitoring/Assessing your performance or that of other individuals or organizations to make improvements or take corrective action. Speaking: Talking to others to convey information effectively.

GOE INFORMATION—Interest Area: 12. Education and Social Service. **Work Group:** 12.03. Educational Services. **Other Job Titles in This Work Group:** Adult Literacy, Remedial Education, and GED Teachers and Instructors; Agricultural Sciences Teachers, Postsecondary; Anthropology and Archeology Teachers, Postsecondary; Architecture Teachers, Postsecondary; Archivists; Area, Ethnic, and Cultural Studies Teachers, Postsecondary; Art, Drama, and Music Teachers, Postsecondary; Atmospheric, Earth, Marine, and Space Sciences Teachers, Postsecondary; Audio-Visual Collections Specialists; Biological Science Teachers, Postsecondary; Business Teachers, Postsecondary; Chemistry Teachers, Postsecondary; Child Care Workers; Communications Teachers, Postsecondary; Computer Science Teachers, Postsecondary; Criminal Justice and Law Enforcement Teachers, Postsecondary; Curators; Economics Teachers, Postsecondary; Education Teachers, Postsecondary; Educational Psychologists; Educational, Vocational, and School Counselors; Elementary School Teachers, Except Special Education; Engineering Teachers, Postsecondary; English Language and Literature Teachers, Postsecondary; Environmental Science Teachers,

Postsecondary; Farm and Home Management Advisors; Foreign Language and Literature Teachers, Postsecondary; Forestry and Conservation Science Teachers, Postsecondary; Geography Teachers, Postsecondary; Graduate Teaching Assistants; Health Specialties Teachers, Postsecondary; History Teachers, Postsecondary; Home Economics Teachers, Postsecondary; Kindergarten Teachers, Except Special Education; Law Teachers, Postsecondary; Librarians; Library Assistants, Clerical; others. **PERSONALITY TYPE**—Social. Social occupations frequently involve working with, communicating with, and teaching people. These occupations often involve helping or providing service to others.

EDUCATION/TRAINING PROGRAM(S)— Education of the Autistic; Education of the Blind and Visually Handicapped; Education of the Deaf and Hearing Impaired; Education of the Emotionally Handicapped; Education of the Mentally Handicapped; Education of the Multiple Handicapped; Education of the Physically Handicapped; Education of the Specific Learning Disabled; Education of the Speech Impaired; Special Education, General;

Special Education, Other. **RELATED KNOWLEDGE/COURSES—Education and Training:** Knowledge of principles and methods for curriculum and training design, teaching and instruction for individuals and groups, and the measurement of training effects. **Psychology:** Knowledge of human behavior and performance; individual differences in ability, personality, and interests; learning and motivation; psychological research methods; and the assessment and treatment of behavioral and affective disorders. **Therapy and Counseling:** Knowledge of principles, methods, and procedures for diagnosis, treatment, and rehabilitation of physical and mental dysfunctions and for career counseling and guidance. **English Language:** Knowledge of the structure and content of the English language, including the meaning and spelling of words, rules of composition, and grammar. **Customer and Personal Service:** Knowledge of principles and processes for providing customer and personal services. This includes customer needs assessment, meeting quality standards for services, and evaluation of customer satisfaction.

Special Education Teachers, Secondary School

▲ Education/Training Required: Bachelor's degree

▲ Annual Earnings: $41,290

▲ Growth: 25%

▲ Annual Job Openings: 8,000

▲ Self-Employed: 0%

▲ Part-Time: 12.9%

Teach secondary school subjects to educationally and physically handicapped students. Includes teachers who specialize and work with audibly and visually handicapped students and those who teach basic academic and life processes skills to the mentally impaired. Teaches socially acceptable behavior, employing techniques such as behavior modification and positive reinforcement. Confers with parents, administrators, testing specialists, social workers, and others to develop individual educational plan for student. Works with students to increase motivation. Meets with parents to provide support, guidance in using community resources,

and skills in dealing with students' learning impairment. Observes, evaluates, and prepares reports on progress of students. Provides consistent reinforcement to learning and continuous feedback to student. Confers with other staff members to plan programs designed to promote educational, physical, and social development of students. Administers and interprets results of ability and achievement tests. Instructs students in academic subjects, utilizing various teaching techniques, such as phonetics, multisensory learning, and repetition, to reinforce learning. Instructs students in daily living skills required for independent maintenance and economic self-sufficiency, such as hygiene, safety, and food preparation. Selects and teaches reading material and math problems related to everyday life of individual student. Plans curriculum and other instructional materials to meet students' needs, considering such factors as physical, emotional, and educational abilities. Instructs students, using special educational strategies and techniques to improve sensory-motor and perceptual-motor development, memory, language, and cognition. **SKILLS**—Learning Strategies: Selecting and using training/instructional methods and procedures appropriate for the situation when learning or teaching new things. Social Perceptiveness: Being aware of others' reactions and understanding why they react as they do. Instructing: Teaching others how to do something. Monitoring: Monitoring/Assessing your performance or that of other individuals or organizations to make improvements or take corrective action. Active Listening: Giving full attention to what other people are saying, taking time to understand the points being made, asking questions as appropriate, and not interrupting at inappropriate times. Speaking: Talking to others to convey information effectively.

GOE INFORMATION—**Interest Area:** 12. Education and Social Service. **Work Group:** 12.03. Educational Services. **Other Job Titles in This Work Group:** Adult Literacy, Remedial Education, and GED Teachers and Instructors; Agricultural Sciences Teachers, Postsecondary; Anthropology and Archeology Teachers, Postsecondary; Architecture Teachers, Postsecondary; Archivists; Area, Ethnic, and Cultural Studies Teachers, Postsecondary; Art, Drama, and Music Teachers, Postsecondary; Atmospheric, Earth, Marine, and Space Sciences Teachers, Postsecondary; Audio-Visual Collections Specialists; Biological Science Teachers, Postsecondary; Business Teachers, Postsecondary; Chemistry Teachers, Postsecondary; Child Care Workers; Communications Teachers, Postsecondary; Computer Science Teachers, Postsecondary; Criminal Justice and Law Enforcement Teachers, Postsecondary; Curators; Economics Teachers, Postsecondary; Education Teachers, Postsecondary; Educational Psychologists; Educational, Vocational, and School Counselors; Elementary School Teachers, Except Special Education; Engineering Teachers, Postsecondary; English Language and Literature Teach-

ers, Postsecondary; Environmental Science Teachers, Postsecondary; Farm and Home Management Advisors; Foreign Language and Literature Teachers, Postsecondary; Forestry and Conservation Science Teachers, Postsecondary; Geography Teachers, Postsecondary; Graduate Teaching Assistants; Health Specialties Teachers, Postsecondary; History Teachers, Postsecondary; Home Economics Teachers, Postsecondary; Kindergarten Teachers, Except Special Education; Law Teachers, Postsecondary; Librarians; Library Assistants, Clerical; others. **PERSONALITY TYPE**—Social. Social occupations frequently involve working with, communicating with, and teaching people. These occupations often involve helping or providing service to others.

EDUCATION/TRAINING PROGRAM(S)—Education of the Autistic; Education of the Blind and Visually Handicapped; Education of the Deaf and Hearing Impaired; Education of the Emotionally Handicapped; Education of the Mentally Handicapped; Education of the Multiple Handicapped; Education of the Physically Handicapped; Education of the Specific Learning Disabled; Education of the Speech Impaired; Special Education, General; Special Education, Other. **RELATED KNOWLEDGE/COURSES**—Education and Training: Knowledge of principles and methods for curriculum and training design, teaching and instruction for individuals and groups, and the measurement of training effects. **Therapy and Counseling:** Knowledge of principles, methods, and procedures for diagnosis, treatment, and rehabilitation of physical and mental dysfunctions and for career counseling and guidance. **Psychology:** Knowledge of human behavior and performance; individual differences in ability, personality, and interests; learning and motivation; psychological research methods; and the assessment and treatment of behavioral and affective disorders. **English Language:** Knowledge of the structure and content of the English language, including the meaning and spelling of words, rules of composition, and grammar. **Customer and Personal Service:** Knowledge of principles and processes for providing customer and personal services. This includes customer needs assessment, meeting quality standards for services, and evaluation of customer satisfaction.

Speech-Language Pathologists

- ▲ Education/Training Required: Master's degree
- ▲ Annual Earnings: $46,640
- ▲ Growth: 39%
- ▲ Annual Job Openings: 4,000
- ▲ Self-Employed: 10.5%
- ▲ Part-Time: 20.8%

Assess and treat persons with speech, language, voice, and fluency disorders. May select alternative communication systems and teach their use. May perform research related to speech and language problems. Administers hearing or speech/language evaluations, tests, or examinations to patients to collect information on type and degree of impairment. Counsels and instructs clients in techniques to improve speech or hearing impairment, including sign language or lip-reading. Refers clients to additional medical or educational services if needed. Participates in conferences or training to update or share knowledge of new hearing or speech disorder treatment methods or technology. Advises educators or other medical staff on speech or hearing topics. Records and maintains reports of speech or hearing research or treatments. Evaluates hearing and speech/language test results and medical or background information to determine hearing or speech impairment and treatment. Conducts or directs research and reports findings on speech or hearing topics to develop procedures, technology, or treatments. **SKILLS**—Writing: Communicating effectively in writing as appropriate for the needs of the audience. Reading Comprehension: Understanding written sentences and paragraphs in work-related documents. Instructing: Teaching others how to do something. Speaking: Talking to others to convey information effectively. Critical Thinking: Using logic and reasoning to identify the strengths and weaknesses of alternative solutions, conclusions, or approaches to problems. Active Learning: Understanding the implications of new information for both current and future problem-solving and decision-making. Learning Strategies: Selecting and using training/instructional methods and procedures appropriate for the situation when learning or teaching new things.

GOE INFORMATION—**Interest Area:** 14. Medical and Health Services. **Work Group:** 14.06. Medical Therapy. **Other Job Titles in This Work Group:** Audiologists; Massage Therapists; Occupational Therapist Aides; Occupational Therapist Assistants; Occupational Therapists; Physical Therapist Aides; Physical Therapist Assistants; Physical Therapists; Radiation Therapists; Recreational Therapists; Respiratory Therapists; Respiratory Therapy Technicians; Therapists, All Other. **PERSONALITY TYPE**—Social. Social occupations frequently involve working with, communicating with, and teaching people. These occupations often involve helping or providing service to others.

EDUCATION/TRAINING PROGRAM(S)—Communication Disorders Sciences and Services, Other; Communication Disorders, General; Speech-Language Pathology; Speech-Language Pathology and Audiology. **RELATED KNOWLEDGE/COURSES**—**Therapy and Counseling:** Knowledge of principles, methods, and procedures for diagnosis, treatment, and rehabilitation of physical and mental dysfunctions and for career counseling and guidance. **Medicine and Dentistry:** Knowledge of the information and techniques needed to diagnose and treat human injuries, diseases, and deformities. This includes symptoms, treatment alternatives, drug properties and interactions, and preventive healthcare measures. **English Language:** Knowledge of the structure and content of the English language, including the meaning and spelling of words, rules of composition, and grammar. **Education and Training:** Knowledge of principles and methods for curriculum and training design, teaching and instruction for individuals and groups, and the measurement of training effects. **Personnel and Human Resources:** Knowledge of principles and procedures for personnel recruitment, selection, training, compensation and benefits, labor relations and negotiation, and personnel information systems. **Administration and Management:** Knowledge of business and management principles involved in strategic planning, resource allocation, human resources modeling, leadership technique, production methods, and coordination of people and resources.

Statisticians

- ▲ Education/Training Required: Master's degree
- ▲ Annual Earnings: $51,990
- ▲ Growth: 2%
- ▲ Annual Job Openings: 2,000
- ▲ Self-Employed: 0%
- ▲ Part-Time: 5.2%

Engage in the development of mathematical theory or apply statistical theory and methods to collect, organize, interpret, and summarize numerical data to provide usable information. May specialize in fields such as bio-statistics, agricultural statistics, business statistics, economic statistics, or other fields. Applies statistical methodology to provide information for scientific research and statistical analysis. Conducts surveys utilizing sampling techniques or complete enumeration bases. Develops and tests experimental designs, sampling techniques, and analytical methods and prepares recommendations concerning their use. Describes sources of information and limitations on reliability and usability. Presents numerical information by computer readouts, graphs, charts, tables, written reports, or other methods. Examines theories, such as those of probability and inference, to discover mathematical bases for new or improved methods of obtaining and evaluating numerical data. Develops statistical methodology. Evaluates reliability of source information, adjusts and weighs raw data, and organizes results into form compatible with analysis by computers or other methods. Investigates, evaluates, and reports on applicability, efficiency, and accuracy of statistical methods used to obtain and evaluate data. Analyzes and interprets statistics to identify significant differences in relationships among sources of information. Plans methods to collect information and develops questionnaire techniques according to survey design. **SKILLS—Mathematics:** Using mathematics to solve problems. Critical Thinking: Using logic and reasoning to identify the strengths and weaknesses of alternative solutions, conclusions, or approaches to problems. Active Learning: Understanding the implications of new information for both current and future problem-solving and decision-making. Reading Comprehension: Understanding written sentences and paragraphs in work-related documents. Complex Problem Solving: Identifying complex problems and reviewing related information to develop and evaluate options and implement solutions.

GOE INFORMATION—Interest Area: 02. Science, Math, and Engineering. **Work Group:** 02.06. Mathematics and Computers. **Other Job Titles in This Work Group:** Actuaries; Computer and Information Scientists, Research; Computer Programmers; Computer Security Specialists; Computer Specialists, All Other; Computer Support Specialists; Computer Systems Analysts; Database Administrators; Mathematical Science Occupations, All Other; Mathematical Technicians; Mathematicians; Network and Computer Systems Administrators; Network Systems and Data Communications Analysts; Operations Research Analysts; Statistical Assistants. **PERSONALITY TYPE—Investigative.** Investigative occupations frequently involve working with ideas and require an extensive amount of thinking. These occupations can involve searching for facts and figuring out problems mentally.

EDUCATION/TRAINING PROGRAM(S)— Applied Mathematics, General; Business Statistics; Health and Medical Biostatistics; Mathematical Statistics;

Mathematics. **RELATED KNOWLEDGE/ COURSES—Mathematics:** Knowledge of arithmetic, algebra, geometry, calculus, and statistics and their applications. **Computers and Electronics:** Knowledge of circuit boards, processors, chips, electronic equipment, and computer hardware and software, including applications and programming. **English Language:** Knowledge of the structure and content of the English language, including the meaning and spelling of words, rules of composition, and grammar. **Economics and Accounting:** Knowledge of economic and accounting principles and practices, the financial markets, banking, and the analysis and reporting of financial data. **Administration and Management:** Knowledge of business and management principles involved in strategic planning, resource allocation, human resources modeling, leadership technique, production methods, and coordination of people and resources. **Clerical Studies:** Knowledge of administrative and clerical procedures and systems such as word processing, managing files and records, stenography and transcription, designing forms, and other office procedures and terminology.

Substance Abuse and Behavioral Disorder Counselors

- ▲ Education/Training Required: Master's degree
- ▲ Annual Earnings: $28,510
- ▲ Growth: 35%
- ▲ Annual Job Openings: 7,000
- ▲ Self-Employed: 8.4%
- ▲ Part-Time: 20.8%

Counsel and advise individuals with alcohol, tobacco, drug, or other problems, such as gambling and eating disorders. May counsel individuals, families, or groups or engage in prevention programs. Plans and conducts programs to prevent substance abuse or improve health and counseling services in community. Supervises and directs other workers providing services to client or patient. Intervenes as advocate for client or patient to resolve emergency problems in crisis situation. Counsels clients and patients, individually and in group sessions, to assist in overcoming dependencies, adjusting to life, and making changes. Counsels family members to assist in understanding, dealing with, and supporting client or patient. Interviews clients, reviews records, and confers with other professionals to evaluate mental or physical condition of client or patient. Formulates or coordinates program plan for treatment, care, and rehabilitation of client or patient, based on social work experience and knowledge. Modifies treatment plan to comply with changes in client's status. Refers patient, client, or family to community resources to assist in recovery from mental or physical illness. Monitors, evaluates, and records client progress according to measurable goals described in treatment and care plan. **SKILLS—Social Perceptiveness:** Being aware of others' reactions and understanding why they react as they do. **Reading Comprehension:** Understanding written sentences and paragraphs in work-related documents. **Critical Thinking:** Using logic and reasoning to identify the strengths and weaknesses of alternative solutions, conclusions, or approaches to problems. **Service Orientation:** Actively looking for ways to help people. **Management of Financial Resources:** Determining how money will be spent to get the work done and accounting for these expenditures. **Active Listening:** Giving full attention to what other people are saying, taking time to understand the points being made, asking questions as appropriate, and not interrupting at inappropriate times.

GOE INFORMATION—Interest Area: 12. Education and Social Service. **Work Group:** 12.02. Social Services. **Other Job Titles in This Work Group:** Child, Family, and School Social Workers; Clergy; Clinical Psychologists; Clinical, Counseling, and School Psychologists; Community and Social Service Specialists, All Other; Counseling Psychologists; Counselors, All Other; Directors, Religious Activities and Education; Marriage and Family Therapists; Medical and Public Health Social Workers; Mental Health and Substance Abuse Social Workers; Mental Health Counselors; Probation Officers and Correctional Treatment Specialists; Rehabilitation Counselors; Religious Workers, All Other; Residential Advisors; Social and Human Service Assistants; Social Workers, All Other. **PERSONALITY TYPE**—Social. Social occupations frequently involve working with, communicating with, and teaching people. These occupations often involve helping or providing service to others.

EDUCATION/TRAINING PROGRAM(S)— Alcohol/Drug Abuse Counseling; Clinical and Medical Social Work; Mental Health Services, Other. **RELATED KNOWLEDGE/COURSES**—**Therapy and Counseling:** Knowledge of principles, methods, and procedures for diagnosis, treatment, and rehabilitation of physical and mental dysfunctions and for career counseling and guidance. **Psychology:** Knowledge of human behavior and performance; individual differences in ability, personality, and interests; learning and motivation; psychological research methods; and the assessment and treatment of behavioral and affective disorders. **Customer and Personal Service:** Knowledge of principles and processes for providing customer and personal services. This includes customer needs assessment, meeting quality standards for services, and evaluation of customer satisfaction. **Education and Training:** Knowledge of principles and methods for curriculum and training design, teaching and instruction for individuals and groups, and the measurement of training effects. **English Language:** Knowledge of the structure and content of the English language, including the meaning and spelling of words, rules of composition, and grammar.

Survey Researchers

- ▲ Education/Training Required: Bachelor's degree
- ▲ Annual Earnings: $26,200
- ▲ Growth: 34%
- ▲ Annual Job Openings: 3,000
- ▲ Self-Employed: No data available
- ▲ Part-Time: No data available

Design or conduct surveys. May supervise interviewers who conduct the survey in person or over the telephone. May present survey results to client. SKILLS—No data available.

GOE INFORMATION—**Interest Area:** 02. Science, Math, and Engineering. **Work Group:** 02.04. Social Sciences. **Other Job Titles in This Work Group:** Anthropologists; Anthropologists and Archeologists; Archeologists; City Planning Aides; Economists; Historians; Industrial-Organizational Psychologists; Political Scientists; Psychologists, All Other; Social Science Research Assistants; Social Scientists and Related Workers, All Other; Sociologists; Urban and Regional Planners. **PERSONALITY TYPE**—No data available.

EDUCATION/TRAINING PROGRAM(S)— Applied and Resource Economics; Business/Managerial Economics; Economics, General. **RELATED KNOWLEDGE/COURSES**—No data available.

Surveyors

▲ Education/Training Required: Bachelor's degree
▲ Annual Earnings: $36,700
▲ Growth: 8%
▲ Annual Job Openings: 7,000
▲ Self-Employed: 7.3%
▲ Part-Time: 4.5%

Make exact measurements and determine property boundaries. Provide data relevant to the shape, contour, gravitation, location, elevation, or dimension of land or land features on or near the earth's surface for engineering, mapmaking, mining, land evaluation, construction, and other purposes. Plans ground surveys designed to establish base lines, elevations, and other geodetic measurements. Conducts research in surveying and mapping methods using knowledge of techniques of photogrammetric map compilation, electronic data processing, and flight and control planning. Computes geodetic measurements and interprets survey data to determine position, shape, and elevations of geomorphic and topographic features. Prepares charts and tables, makes precise determinations of elevations, and records other characteristics of terrain. Establishes fixed points for use in making maps, using geodetic and engineering instruments. Coordinates findings with work of engineering and architectural personnel, clients, and others concerned with project. Computes data necessary for driving and connecting underground passages, underground storage, and volume of underground deposits. Determines appropriate and economical methods and procedures for establishing survey control. Analyzes survey objectives and specifications, utilizing knowledge of survey uses. Surveys water bodies to determine navigable channels and to secure data for construction of breakwaters, piers, and other marine structures. Keeps accurate notes, records, and sketches to describe and certify work performed. Takes instrument readings of sun or stars and calculates longitude and latitude to determine specific area location. Studies weight, shape, size, and mass of earth and variations in earth's gravitational field, using astronomic observations and complex computation. Estimates cost of survey. Locates and marks sites selected for geophysical prospecting

activities, such as locating petroleum or mineral products. Determines photographic equipment to be used and altitude from which to photograph terrain and directs aerial surveys of specified geographical area. Prepares survey proposal or directs one or more phases of survey proposal preparation. Drafts or directs others to draft maps of survey data. **SKILLS**—Mathematics: Using mathematics to solve problems. Active Learning: Understanding the implications of new information for both current and future problem-solving and decision-making. Science: Using scientific rules and methods to solve problems. Reading Comprehension: Understanding written sentences and paragraphs in work-related documents. Writing: Communicating effectively in writing as appropriate for the needs of the audience.

GOE INFORMATION—Interest Area: 02. Science, Math, and Engineering. **Work Group:** 02.08. Engineering Technology. **Other Job Titles in This Work Group:** Aerospace Engineering and Operations Technicians; Architectural and Civil Drafters; Architectural Drafters; Calibration and Instrumentation Technicians; Cartographers and Photogrammetrists; Civil Drafters; Civil Engineering Technicians; Construction and Building Inspectors; Drafters, All Other; Electrical and Electronic Engineering Technicians; Electrical and Electronics Drafters; Electrical Drafters; Electrical Engineering Technicians; Electro-Mechanical Technicians; Electronic Drafters; Electronics Engineering Technicians; Engineering Technicians, Except Drafters, All Other; Environmental Engineering Technicians; Industrial Engineering Technicians; Mapping Technicians; Mechanical Drafters; Mechanical Engineering Technicians; Numerical Tool and Process Control Programmers; Pressure Vessel Inspectors; Surveying and Mapping Technicians; Surveying Technicians. **PERSONALITY TYPE**—Investigative. Investigative occupations frequently involve working with ideas and require an extensive amount of thinking. These occupations can involve searching for facts and figuring out problems mentally.

EDUCATION/TRAINING PROGRAM(S)— Surveying. **RELATED KNOWLEDGE/ COURSES—Mathematics:** Knowledge of arithmetic, algebra, geometry, calculus, and statistics and their applications. **Geography:** Knowledge of principles and methods for describing the features of land, sea, and air masses, including their physical characteristics, locations, interrelationships, and distribution of plant, animal, and human

life. **Physics:** Knowledge and prediction of physical principles and laws and their interrelationships and applications to understanding fluid, material, and atmospheric dynamics and mechanical, electrical, atomic, and sub-atomic structures and processes. **Design:** Knowledge of design techniques, tools, and principles involved in production of precision technical plans, blueprints, drawings, and models. **Administration and Management:** Knowledge of business and management principles involved in strategic planning, resource allocation, human resources modeling, leadership technique, production methods, and coordination of people and resources.

Tax Examiners, Collectors, and Revenue Agents

- ▲ Education/Training Required: Bachelor's degree
- ▲ Annual Earnings: $40,180
- ▲ Growth: 8%
- ▲ Annual Job Openings: 6,000
- ▲ Self-Employed: 0%
- ▲ Part-Time: 4.2%

Determine tax liability or collect taxes from individuals or business firms according to prescribed laws and regulations. Examines and analyzes tax assets and liabilities to determine resolution of delinquent tax problems. Examines selected tax returns to determine nature and extent of audits to be performed. Analyzes accounting books and records to determine appropriateness of accounting methods employed and compliance with statutory provisions. Directs service of legal documents, such as subpoenas, warrants, notices of assessment, and garnishments. Participates in informal appeals hearings on contested cases from other agents. Recommends criminal prosecutions and civil penalties. Serves as member of regional appeals board to reexamine unresolved issues in terms of relevant laws and regulations. Confers with taxpayer or representative to explain issues involved and applicability of pertinent tax laws and regulations. Secures taxpayer's agreement to discharge tax assessment or submits contested determination to other administrative or judicial conferees for appeals hearings. Selects appropriate remedy, such as partial-payment agreement, offer of compromise, or seizure and sale of property. Investigates legal instruments, other documents, financial transactions,

operation methods, and industry practices to assess inclusiveness of accounting records and tax returns. Conducts independent field audits and investigations of federal income tax returns to verify or amend tax liabilities. **SKILLS—Reading Comprehension:** Understanding written sentences and paragraphs in work-related documents. **Mathematics:** Using mathematics to solve problems. **Judgment and Decision Making:** Considering the relative costs and benefits of potential actions to choose the most appropriate one. **Critical Thinking:** Using logic and reasoning to identify the strengths and weaknesses of alternative solutions, conclusions, or approaches to problems. **Active Listening:** Giving full attention to what other people are saying, taking time to understand the points being made, asking questions as appropriate, and not interrupting at inappropriate times.

GOE INFORMATION—Interest Area: 13. General Management and Support. **Work Group:** 13.02. Management Support. **Other Job Titles in This Work Group:** Accountants; Accountants and Auditors; Appraisers and Assessors of Real Estate; Appraisers, Real Estate; Assessors; Auditors; Budget Analysts; Claims Adjusters,

Examiners, and Investigators; Claims Examiners, Property and Casualty Insurance; Compensation, Benefits, and Job Analysis Specialists; Cost Estimators; Credit Analysts; Employment Interviewers, Private or Public Employment Service; Employment, Recruitment, and Placement Specialists; Financial Analysts; Human Resources, Training, and Labor Relations Specialists, All Other; Insurance Adjusters, Examiners, and Investigators; Insurance Appraisers, Auto Damage; Insurance Underwriters; Loan Counselors; Loan Officers; Logisticians; Management Analysts; Market Research Analysts; Personnel Recruiters; Purchasing Agents and Buyers, Farm Products; Purchasing Agents, Except Wholesale, Retail, and Farm Products; Training and Development Specialists; Wholesale and Retail Buyers, Except Farm Products. **PERSONALITY TYPE**—Conventional. Conventional occupations frequently involve following set procedures and routines. These occupations can include working with data and details more than with ideas. Usually there is a clear line of authority to follow.

EDUCATION/TRAINING PROGRAM(S)—Accounting; Management Science; Taxation. **RELATED KNOWLEDGE/COURSES—Economics and Accounting:** Knowledge of economic and accounting principles and practices, the financial markets, banking, and the analysis and reporting of financial data. **Mathematics:** Knowledge of arithmetic, algebra, geometry, calculus, and statistics and their applications. **Law and Government:** Knowledge of laws, legal codes, court procedures, precedents, government regulations, executive orders, agency rules, and the democratic political process. **English Language:** Knowledge of the structure and content of the English language, including the meaning and spelling of words, rules of composition, and grammar. **Administration and Management:** Knowledge of business and management principles involved in strategic planning, resource allocation, human resources modeling, leadership technique, production methods, and coordination of people and resources.

Technical Writers

- ▲ Education/Training Required: Bachelor's degree
- ▲ Annual Earnings: $47,790
- ▲ Growth: 30%
- ▲ Annual Job Openings: 5,000
- ▲ Self-Employed: 31.2%
- ▲ Part-Time: 18.5%

Write technical materials, such as equipment manuals, appendices, or operating and maintenance instructions. May assist in layout work. Organizes material and completes writing assignment according to set standards regarding order, clarity, conciseness, style, and terminology. Studies drawings, specifications, mock-ups, and product samples to integrate and delineate technology, operating procedure, and production sequence and detail. Assists in laying out material for publication. Interviews production and engineering personnel and reads journals and other material to become familiar with product technologies and production methods. Reviews published materials and recommends revisions or changes in scope, format, content, and methods of

reproduction and binding. Reviews manufacturer's and trade catalogs, drawings, and other data relative to operation, maintenance, and service of equipment. Analyzes developments in specific field to determine need for revisions in previously published materials and development of new material. Selects photographs, drawings, sketches, diagrams, and charts to illustrate material. Draws sketches to illustrate specified materials or assembly sequence. Confers with customer representatives, vendors, plant executives, or publisher to establish technical specifications and to determine subject material to be developed for publication. Arranges for typing, duplication, and distribution of material. Maintains records and files of work and revisions. Observes production, developmental, and experimental activities to determine operating procedure and detail. Edits, standardizes, or makes changes to material prepared by other writers or establishment personnel. **SKILLS**— Writing: Communicating effectively in writing as appropriate for the needs of the audience. Reading Comprehension: Understanding written sentences and paragraphs in work-related documents. Active Listening: Giving full attention to what other people are saying, taking time to understand the points being made, asking questions as appropriate, and not interrupting at inappropriate times. Active Learning: Understanding the implications of new information for both current and future problem-solving and decision-making. Critical Thinking: Using logic and reasoning to identify the strengths and weaknesses of alternative solutions, conclusions, or approaches to problems.

GOE INFORMATION—Interest Area: 01. Arts, Entertainment, and Media. **Work Group:** 01.02. Writing and Editing. **Other Job Titles in This Work Group:** Copy Writers; Creative Writers; Editors; Poets and Lyricists; Writers and Authors. **PERSONALITY TYPE**—Artistic. Artistic occupations frequently involve working with forms, designs, and patterns. They often re-

quire self-expression, and the work can be done without following a clear set of rules.

EDUCATION/TRAINING PROGRAM(S)— Business Communications; Technical and Business Writing. **RELATED KNOWLEDGE/COURSES**— **English Language:** Knowledge of the structure and content of the English language, including the meaning and spelling of words, rules of composition, and grammar. **Communications and Media:** Knowledge of media production, communication, and dissemination techniques and methods. This includes alternative ways to inform and entertain via written, oral, and visual media. **Computers and Electronics:** Knowledge of circuit boards, processors, chips, electronic equipment, and computer hardware and software, including applications and programming. **Education and Training:** Knowledge of principles and methods for curriculum and training design, teaching and instruction for individuals and groups, and the measurement of training effects. **Design:** Knowledge of design techniques, tools, and principles involved in production of precision technical plans, blueprints, drawings, and models.

Training and Development Specialists

- ▲ Education/Training Required: Bachelor's degree
- ▲ Annual Earnings: $40,830
- ▲ Growth: 19%
- ▲ Annual Job Openings: 20,000
- ▲ Self-Employed: 2.6%
- ▲ Part-Time: 6.9%

Conduct training and development programs for employees. Develops and conducts orientation and training for employees or customers of industrial or commercial establishment. Confers with managers, instructors, or customer representatives of industrial or commercial establishment to determine training needs. Assigns instructors to conduct training and assists them in obtaining required training materials. Coordinates recruitment and placement of participants in skill training. Attends meetings and seminars to obtain information useful to train staff and to in-

form management of training programs and goals. Screens, hires, and assigns workers to positions based on qualifications. Refers trainees with social problems to appropriate service agency. Monitors training costs to ensure budget is not exceeded and prepares budget report to justify expenditures. Supervises instructors, monitors and evaluates instructor performance, and refers instructors to classes for skill development. Maintains records and writes reports to monitor and evaluate training activities and program effectiveness. Organizes and develops training procedure manuals and guides. Schedules classes based on availability of classrooms, equipment, and instructors. Evaluates training materials, such as outlines, text, and handouts, prepared by instructors. **SKILLS**—Learning Strategies: Selecting and using training/instructional methods and procedures appropriate for the situation when learning or teaching new things. Writing: Communicating effectively in writing as appropriate for the needs of the audience. Monitoring: Monitoring/Assessing your performance or that of other individuals or organizations to make improvements or take corrective action. Management of Financial Resources: Determining how money will be spent to get the work done and accounting for these expenditures. Speaking: Talking to others to convey information effectively. Active Listening: Giving full attention to what other people are saying, taking time to understand the points being made, asking questions as appropriate, and not interrupting at inappropriate times.

GOE INFORMATION—Interest Area: 13. General Management and Support. **Work Group:** 13.02. Management Support. **Other Job Titles in This Work Group:** Accountants; Accountants and Auditors; Appraisers and Assessors of Real Estate; Appraisers, Real Estate; Assessors; Auditors; Budget Analysts; Claims Adjusters, Examiners, and Investigators; Claims Examiners, Property and Casualty Insurance; Compensation, Benefits, and Job Analysis Specialists; Cost Estimators; Credit Analysts; Employment Interviewers, Private or Public Employment Service; Employment, Recruitment, and Placement Specialists; Financial Analysts; Human Resources, Training, and Labor Relations Specialists, All Other; Insurance Adjusters, Examiners, and Investigators; Insurance Appraisers, Auto Damage; Insurance Underwriters; Loan Counselors; Loan Officers; Logisticians; Management Analysts; Market Research Analysts; Personnel Recruiters; Purchasing Agents and Buyers, Farm Products; Purchasing Agents, Except Wholesale, Retail, and Farm Products; Tax Examiners, Collectors, and Revenue Agents; Wholesale and Retail Buyers, Except Farm Products. **PERSONALITY TYPE**—Social. Social occupations frequently involve working with, communicating with, and teaching people. These occupations often involve helping or providing service to others.

EDUCATION/TRAINING PROGRAM(S)—Human Resources Management; Human Resources Management, Other; Labor/Personnel Relations and Studies; Organizational Behavior Studies. **RELATED KNOWLEDGE/COURSES—Education and Training:** Knowledge of principles and methods for curriculum and training design, teaching and instruction for individuals and groups, and the measurement of training effects. **Personnel and Human Resources:** Knowledge of principles and procedures for personnel recruitment, selection, training, compensation and benefits, labor relations and negotiation, and personnel information systems. **Psychology:** Knowledge of human behavior and performance; individual differences in ability, personality, and interests; learning and motivation; psychological research methods; and the assessment and treatment of behavioral and affective disorders. **English Language:** Knowledge of the structure and content of the English language, including the meaning and spelling of words, rules of composition, and grammar. **Sales and Marketing:** Knowledge of principles and methods for showing, promoting, and selling products or services. This includes marketing strategy and tactics, product demonstration, sales techniques, and sales control systems. **Economics and Accounting:** Knowledge of economic and accounting principles and practices, the financial markets, banking, and the analysis and reporting of financial data. **Clerical Studies:** Knowledge of administrative and clerical procedures and systems such as word processing, managing files and records, stenography and transcription, designing forms, and other office procedures and terminology.

Treasurers, Controllers, and Chief Financial Officers

- ▲ Education/Training Required: Work experience, plus degree
- ▲ Annual Earnings: $67,020
- ▲ Growth: 18%
- ▲ Annual Job Openings: 53,000
- ▲ Self-Employed: 1.4%
- ▲ Part-Time: 2.6%

Plan, direct, and coordinate the financial activities of an organization at the highest level of management. Includes financial reserve officers. Coordinates and directs financial planning, budgeting, procurement, and investment activities of organization. Prepares reports or directs preparation of reports summarizing organization's current and forecasted financial position, business activity, and reports required by regulatory agencies. Delegates authority for receipt, disbursement, banking, protection, and custody of funds, securities, and financial instruments. Analyzes past, present, and expected operations. Advises management on economic objectives and policies, investments, and loans for short- and long-range financial plans. Evaluates need for procurement of funds and investment of surplus. Arranges audits of company accounts. Ensures that institution reserves meet legal requirements. Interprets current policies and practices and plans and implements new operating procedures to improve efficiency and reduce costs. **SKILLS**—Management of Financial Resources: Determining how money will be spent to get the work done and accounting for these expenditures. Judgment and Decision Making: Considering the relative costs and benefits of potential actions to choose the most appropriate one. Systems Analysis: Determining how a system should work and how changes in conditions, operations, and the environment will affect outcomes. Systems Evaluation: Identifying measures or indicators of system performance and the actions needed to improve or correct performance relative to the goals of the system. Mathematics: Using mathematics to solve problems. Critical Thinking: Using logic and reasoning to identify the strengths and weaknesses of alternative solutions, conclusions, or approaches to problems.

GOE INFORMATION—Interest Area: 13. General Management and Support. **Work Group:** 13.01.

General Management Work and Management of Support Functions. **Other Job Titles in This Work Group:** Chief Executives; Compensation and Benefits Managers; Farm, Ranch, and Other Agricultural Managers; Financial Managers; Financial Managers, Branch or Department; Funeral Directors; General and Operations Managers; Government Service Executives; Human Resources Managers; Human Resources Managers, All Other; Legislators; Managers, All Other; Postmasters and Mail Superintendents; Private Sector Executives; Property, Real Estate, and Community Association Managers; Public Relations Managers; Purchasing Managers; Storage and Distribution Managers; Training and Development Managers; Transportation, Storage, and Distribution Managers. **PERSONALITY TYPE**—Enterprising. Enterprising occupations frequently involve starting up and carrying out projects. These occupations can involve leading people and making many decisions. They sometimes require risk taking and often deal with business.

EDUCATION/TRAINING PROGRAM(S)—Finance, General; Financial Management and Services, Other; International Finance; Public Finance. **RELATED KNOWLEDGE/COURSES**—Economics and Accounting: Knowledge of economic and accounting principles and practices, the financial markets, banking, and the analysis and reporting of financial data. **Administration and Management:** Knowledge of business and management principles involved in strategic planning, resource allocation, human resources modeling, leadership technique, production methods, and coordination of people and resources. **Mathematics:** Knowledge of arithmetic, algebra, geometry, calculus, and statistics and their applications. **Law and Government:** Knowledge of laws, legal codes, court procedures, precedents, government regulations, executive orders, agency rules, and the democratic political process. **English Language:** Knowledge of the structure and content of the English language, including the meaning and spelling of words, rules of composition, and grammar.

Urban and Regional Planners

▲ Education/Training Required: Master's degree
▲ Annual Earnings: $46,500
▲ Growth: 16%
▲ Annual Job Openings: 3,000
▲ Self-Employed: 3.5%
▲ Part-Time: 18.1%

Develop comprehensive plans and programs for use of land and physical facilities of local jurisdictions, such as towns, cities, counties, and metropolitan areas. Develops alternative plans with recommendations for program or project. Compiles, organizes, and analyzes data on economic, social, and physical factors affecting land use, using statistical methods. Recommends governmental measures affecting land use, public utilities, community facilities, housing, and transportation. Evaluates information to determine feasibility of proposals or to identify factors requiring amendment. Reviews and evaluates environmental impact reports applying to specific private and public planning projects and programs. Discusses purpose of land use projects, such as transportation, conservation, residential, commercial, industrial, and community use, with planning officials. Determines regulatory limitations on project. Advises planning officials on feasibility, cost-effectiveness, regulatory conformance, and alternative recommendations for project. Maintains collection of socioeconomic, environmental, and regulatory data related to land use for governmental and private sectors. Conducts field investigations, economic or public opinion surveys, demographic studies, or other research to gather required information. Prepares or requisitions graphic and narrative report on land use data. **SKILLS**—Judgment and Decision Making: Considering the relative costs and benefits of potential actions to choose the most appropriate one. Complex Problem Solving: Identifying complex problems and reviewing related information to develop and evaluate options and implement solutions. Systems Analysis: Determining how a system should work and how changes in conditions, operations, and the environment will affect outcomes. Critical Think-

ing: Using logic and reasoning to identify the strengths and weaknesses of alternative solutions, conclusions, or approaches to problems. Reading Comprehension: Understanding written sentences and paragraphs in work-related documents.

GOE INFORMATION—**Interest Area:** 02. Science, Math, and Engineering. **Work Group:** 02.04. Social Sciences. **Other Job Titles in This Work Group:** Anthropologists; Anthropologists and Archeologists; Archeologists; City Planning Aides; Economists; Historians; Industrial-Organizational Psychologists; Political Scientists; Psychologists, All Other; Social Science Research Assistants; Social Scientists and Related Workers, All Other; Sociologists; Survey Researchers. **PERSONALITY TYPE**—Investigative. Investigative occupations frequently involve working with ideas and require an extensive amount of thinking. These occupations can involve searching for facts and figuring out problems mentally.

EDUCATION/TRAINING PROGRAM(S)—Architectural Urban Design and Planning; City/Urban, Community and Regional Planning. **RELATED KNOWLEDGE/COURSES**—**Mathematics:** Knowledge of arithmetic, algebra, geometry, calculus, and statistics and their applications. **Sociology and Anthropology:** Knowledge of group behavior and dynamics, societal trends and influences, human migrations, ethnicity, cultures, and their history and origins. **Law and Government:** Knowledge of laws, legal codes, court procedures, precedents, government regulations, executive orders, agency rules, and the democratic political process. **English Language:** Knowledge of the structure and content of the English language, including the meaning and spelling of words, rules of composition, and grammar. **Economics and Accounting:** Knowledge of economic and accounting principles and practices, the financial markets, banking, and the analysis and reporting of financial data. **Building and Construction:** Knowledge of materials, methods, and tools involved in the construction or repair of houses, buildings, or other structures, such as highways and roads. **Administration and Management:** Knowledge of business and management principles involved in strategic planning, resource allocation, human resources modeling, leadership technique, production methods, and coordination of people and resources.

Veterinarians

- ▲ Education/Training Required: First professional degree
- ▲ Annual Earnings: $60,910
- ▲ Growth: 32%
- ▲ Annual Job Openings: 2,000
- ▲ Self-Employed: 39.6%
- ▲ Part-Time: 10.5%

Diagnose and treat diseases and dysfunctions of animals. May engage in a particular function, such as research and development, consultation, administration, technical writing, sale or production of commercial products, or rendering of technical services to commercial firms or other organizations. Includes veterinarians who inspect livestock. Examines animal to detect and determine nature of disease or injury and treats animal surgically or medically. Inspects and tests horses, sheep, poultry flocks, and other animals for diseases and inoculates animals against various diseases, including rabies. Establishes and conducts quarantine and testing procedures to prevent spread of disease and compliance with governmental regulations. Participates in research projects, plans procedures, and selects animals for scientific research based on knowledge of species and research principles. Oversees activities concerned with feeding, care, and maintenance of animal quarters to ensure compliance with laboratory regulations. Exchanges information with zoos and aquariums concerning care, transfer, sale, or trade of animals to maintain all-species nationwide inventory. Trains personnel in handling and care of animals. Participates in planning and executing nutrition and reproduction programs for animals. Ensures compliance with regulations governing humane and ethical treatment of animals used in scientific research. Inspects housing and advises animal owners regarding sanitary measures, feeding, and general care to promote health of animals. Conducts postmortem studies and analysis results to determine cause of death. **SKILLS**—Reading Comprehension: Understanding written sentences and paragraphs in work-related documents. Active Learning: Understanding the implications of new information for both current and future problem-solving and decision-making. Science: Using scientific rules and methods to solve problems. Critical Thinking: Using logic and reasoning to identify the strengths and weaknesses of alternative solutions, conclusions, or approaches to problems. Complex Problem Solving: Identifying complex problems and reviewing related information to develop and evaluate options and implement solutions.

GOE INFORMATION—**Interest Area:** 03. Plants and Animals. **Work Group:** 03.02. Animal Care and Training. **Other Job Titles in This Work Group:** Animal Breeders; Animal Trainers; Nonfarm Animal Caretakers; Veterinary Assistants and Laboratory Animal Caretakers; Veterinary Technologists and Technicians. **PERSONALITY TYPE**—Investigative. Investigative occupations frequently involve working with ideas and require an extensive amount of thinking. These occupations can involve searching for facts and figuring out problems mentally.

EDUCATION/TRAINING PROGRAM(S)— Laboratory Animal Medicine; Theriogenology; Veterinary Anesthesiology; Veterinary Clinical Sciences (M.S., Ph.D.);

Veterinary Dentistry; Veterinary Dermatology; Veterinary Emergency and Critical Care Medicine; Veterinary Internal Medicine; Veterinary Medicine (D.V.M.); Veterinary Microbiology; Veterinary Nutrition; Veterinary Ophthalmology; Veterinary Pathology; Veterinary Practice; Veterinary Preventive Medicine; Veterinary Radiology; Veterinary Residency Programs, Other; Veterinary Surgery; Veterinary Toxicology; Zoological Medicine. **RELATED KNOWLEDGE/COURSES—Biology:** Knowledge of plant and animal organisms and their tissues, cells, functions, interdependencies, and interactions with each other and the environment. **Medicine and Dentistry:** Knowledge of the information and techniques needed to diagnose and treat human injuries, diseases, and deformities. This includes symptoms, treatment alternatives, drug properties and interactions, and preventive health-care measures. **English Language:** Knowledge of the structure and content of the English language, including the meaning and spelling of words, rules of composition, and grammar. **Chemistry:** Knowledge of the chemical composition, structure, and properties of substances and of the chemical processes and transformations that they undergo. This includes uses of chemicals and their interactions, danger signs, production techniques, and disposal methods. **Education and Training:** Knowledge of principles and methods for curriculum and training design, teaching and instruction for individuals and groups, and the measurement of training effects. **Mathematics:** Knowledge of arithmetic, algebra, geometry, calculus, and statistics and their applications.

Veterinary Technologists and Technicians

- ▲ Education/Training Required: Associate's degree
- ▲ Annual Earnings: $21,640
- ▲ Growth: 39%
- ▲ Annual Job Openings: 6,000
- ▲ Self-Employed: 0%
- ▲ Part-Time: 11.7%

Perform medical tests in a laboratory environment for use in the treatment and diagnosis of diseases in animals. Prepare vaccines and serums for prevention of diseases. Prepare tissue samples, take blood samples, and execute laboratory tests, such as urinalysis and blood counts. Clean and sterilize instruments and materials and maintain equipment and machines. **SKILLS**—No data available.

GOE INFORMATION—Interest Area: 03. Plants and Animals. **Work Group:** 03.02. Animal Care and Training. **Other Job Titles in This Work Group:** Animal Breeders; Animal Trainers; Nonfarm Animal Caretakers; Veterinarians; Veterinary Assistants and Laboratory Animal Caretakers. **PERSONALITY TYPE**—No data available.

EDUCATION/TRAINING PROGRAM(S)—Veterinarian Assistant/Animal Health Technician. **RELATED KNOWLEDGE/COURSES**—No data available.

Vocational Education Teachers, Middle School

- ▲ Education/Training Required: Bachelor's degree
- ▲ Annual Earnings: $39,330
- ▲ Growth: 13%
- ▲ Annual Job Openings: 2,000
- ▲ Self-Employed: 0%
- ▲ Part-Time: 42.5%

Teach or instruct vocational or occupational subjects at the middle school level. Instructs students, using various teaching methods such as lecture and demonstration. Evaluates, records, and reports student progress. Maintains discipline in classroom. Performs advisory duties, such as sponsoring student organizations or clubs, helping students select courses, and counseling students with problems. Keeps attendance records. Selects, stores, orders, issues, and inventories classroom equipment, materials, and supplies. Participates in faculty and professional meetings, educational conferences, and teacher training workshops. Confers with students, parents, and school counselors to resolve behavioral and academic problems. Uses audiovisual aids and other materials to supplement presentations. Assigns lessons and corrects homework. Develops and administers tests. Prepares course outlines and objectives according to curriculum guidelines or state and local requirements. **SKILLS**—Learning Strategies: Selecting and using training/instructional methods and procedures appropriate for the situation when learning or teaching new things. Speaking: Talking to others to convey information effectively. Reading Comprehension: Understanding written sentences and paragraphs in work-related documents. Instructing: Teaching others how to do something. Mathematics: Using mathematics to solve problems.

GOE INFORMATION—**Interest Area:** 12. Education and Social Service. **Work Group:** 12.03. Educational Services. **Other Job Titles in This Work Group:** Adult Literacy, Remedial Education, and GED Teachers and Instructors; Agricultural Sciences Teachers, Postsecondary; Anthropology and Archeology Teachers, Postsecondary; Architecture Teachers, Postsecondary; Archivists; Area, Ethnic, and Cultural Studies Teachers, Postsecondary; Art, Drama, and Music Teachers, Postsecondary; Atmospheric, Earth, Marine, and Space Sciences Teachers, Postsecondary; Audio-Visual Collections Specialists; Biological Science Teachers, Postsecondary; Business Teachers, Postsecondary; Chemistry Teachers, Postsecondary; Child Care Workers; Communications Teachers, Postsecondary; Computer Science Teachers, Postsecondary; Criminal Justice and Law Enforcement Teachers, Postsecondary; Curators; Economics Teachers, Postsecondary; Education Teachers, Postsecondary; Educational Psychologists; Educational, Vocational, and School Counselors; Elementary School Teachers, Except Special Education; Engineering Teachers, Postsecondary; English Language and Literature Teachers, Postsecondary; Environmental Science Teachers, Postsecondary; Farm and Home Management Advisors; Foreign Language and Literature Teachers, Postsecondary; Forestry and Conservation Science Teachers, Postsecondary; Geography Teachers, Postsecondary; Graduate Teaching Assistants; Health Specialties Teachers, Postsecondary; History Teachers, Postsecondary; Home Economics Teachers, Postsecondary; Kindergarten Teachers, Except Special Education; Law Teachers, Postsecondary; Librarians; Library Assistants, Clerical; others. **PERSONALITY TYPE**—Social. Social occupations frequently involve working with, communicating with, and teaching people. These occupations often involve helping or providing service to others.

EDUCATION/TRAINING PROGRAM(S)—Agricultural Teacher Education (Vocational); Business Teacher Education (Vocational); Health Occupations Teacher Education (Vocational); Home Economics Teacher Education (Vocational); Marketing Operations Teacher Education/Marketing & Distribution Teacher; Secondary Teacher Education; Technical Teacher Education (Vocational); Trade and Industrial Teacher Education (Vocational). **RELATED KNOWLEDGE/COURSES—Education and Training:** Knowledge of principles and methods for curriculum and training design, teaching and instruction for individuals and groups, and the measurement of training effects. **English Language:** Knowledge of the structure and content of the English language, including the meaning and spelling of words, rules of composition, and grammar. **Mathematics:** Knowledge of arithmetic, algebra, geometry, calculus, and statistics and their applications. **Therapy and Counseling:** Knowledge of principles, methods, and procedures for diagnosis, treatment, and rehabilitation of physical and mental dysfunctions and for career counseling and guidance. **Clerical Studies:** Knowledge of administrative and clerical procedures and systems such as word processing, managing files and records, stenography and transcription, designing forms, and other office procedures and terminology. **Psychology:** Knowledge of human behavior and performance; individual differences in ability, personality, and interests; learning and motivation; psychological research methods; and the assessment and treatment of behavioral and affective disorders.

Vocational Education Teachers, Secondary School

- ▲ Education/Training Required: Bachelor's degree
- ▲ Annual Earnings: $42,080
- ▲ Growth: 13%
- ▲ Annual Job Openings: 7,000
- ▲ Self-Employed: 0%
- ▲ Part-Time: 42.5%

Teach or instruct vocational or occupational subjects at the secondary school level. Instructs students, using various teaching methods such as lecture and demonstration. Assigns lessons and corrects homework. Develops and administers tests. Prepares course outlines and objectives according to curriculum guidelines or state and local requirements. Uses audiovisual aids and other materials to supplement presentations. Evaluates, records, and reports student progress. Confers with students, parents, and school counselors to resolve behavioral and academic problems. Maintains discipline in classroom. Participates in faculty and professional meetings, educational conferences, and teacher training workshops. Selects, stores, orders, issues, and inventories classroom equipment, materials, and supplies. Keeps attendance records. Performs advisory duties, such as sponsoring student organizations or clubs, helping students select courses, and counseling students with problems. **SKILLS—Learning Strategies:** Selecting and using training/instructional methods and procedures appropriate for the situation when learning or teaching new things. **Speaking:** Talking to others to convey information effectively. **Reading Comprehension:** Understanding written sentences and paragraphs in work-related documents. **Mathematics:** Using mathematics to solve problems. **Instructing:** Teaching others how to do something.

GOE INFORMATION—Interest Area: 12. Education and Social Service. **Work Group:** 12.03. Educational Services. **Other Job Titles in This Work Group:** Adult Literacy, Remedial Education, and GED Teachers and Instructors; Agricultural Sciences Teachers, Postsecondary; Anthropology and Archeology Teachers, Postsecondary; Architecture Teachers, Postsecondary; Archivists; Area, Ethnic, and Cultural Studies Teachers, Postsecondary; Art, Drama, and Music Teachers, Postsecondary; Atmospheric, Earth, Marine, and Space Sciences Teachers, Postsecondary; Audio-Visual Collections Specialists; Biological Science Teachers, Postsecondary; Business Teachers, Postsecondary; Chemistry Teachers, Postsecondary; Child Care Workers; Communications Teachers, Postsecondary; Computer Science Teachers, Postsecondary; Criminal Justice and Law Enforcement Teachers, Postsecondary; Curators; Economics Teachers, Postsecondary; Education Teachers, Postsecondary; Educational Psychologists; Educational, Vocational, and School Counselors; Elementary School Teachers, Except Special Education; Engineering Teach ers, Postsecondary; English Language and Literature Teachers, Postsecondary; Environmental Science Teachers, Postsecondary; Farm and Home Management Advisors; Foreign Language and Literature Teachers, Postsecondary; Forestry and Conservation Science Teachers, Postsecondary; Geography Teachers, Postsecondary; Graduate Teaching Assistants; Health Specialties Teachers, Postsecondary; History Teachers, Postsecondary; Home Economics Teachers, Postsecondary; Kindergarten Teachers, Except Special Education; Law Teachers, Postsecondary; Librarians; Library Assistants, Clerical; others. **PERSONALITY TYPE**—Social. Social occupations frequently involve working with, communicating with, and teaching people. These occupations often involve helping or providing service to others.

EDUCATION/TRAINING PROGRAM(S)— Agricultural Teacher Education (Vocational); Business Teacher Education (Vocational); Health Occupations Teacher Education (Vocational); Home Economics Teacher Education (Vocational); Marketing Operations Teacher Education/Marketing & Distribution Teacher; Secondary Teacher Education; Technical Teacher Education (Vocational); Trade and Industrial Teacher Education (Voca-

tional). **RELATED KNOWLEDGE/COURSES**— **Education and Training:** Knowledge of principles and methods for curriculum and training design, teaching and instruction for individuals and groups, and the measurement of training effects. **English Language:** Knowledge of the structure and content of the English language, including the meaning and spelling of words, rules of composition, and grammar. **Mathematics:** Knowledge of arithmetic, algebra, geometry, calculus, and statistics and their applications. **Therapy and Counseling:** Knowledge of principles, methods, and procedures for diagnosis, treatment, and rehabilitation of physical and mental dysfunctions and for career counseling and guidance. **Psychology:** Knowledge of human behavior and performance; individual differences in ability, personality, and interests; learning and motivation; psychological research methods; and the assessment and treatment of behavioral and affective disorders. **Clerical Studies:** Knowledge of administrative and clerical procedures and systems such as word processing, managing files and records, stenography and transcription, designing forms, and other office procedures and terminology.

Wholesale and Retail Buyers, Except Farm Products

- ▲ Education/Training Required: Bachelor's degree
- ▲ Annual Earnings: $37,200
- ▲ Growth: –9%
- ▲ Annual Job Openings: 18,000
- ▲ Self-Employed: 10.5%
- ▲ Part-Time: 16.5%

Buy merchandise or commodities, other than farm products, for resale to consumers at the wholesale or retail level, including both durable and nondurable goods. Analyze past buying trends, sales records, price, and quality of merchandise to determine value and yield. Select, order, and authorize payment for merchandise according to contractual agreements. May conduct meetings with sales personnel and introduce new products. Consults with store or merchandise managers about budget and goods to be purchased. Analyzes sales records and trends to determine current or expected demand and

minimum inventory required. Inspects, grades, or approves merchandise or products to determine value or yield. Authorizes payment of invoices or return of merchandise. Arranges for transportation of purchases. Provides clerks with information such as price, mark-ups or mark-downs, manufacturer number, season code, and style number to print on price tags. Approves advertising materials. Trains purchasing or sales personnel. Sets or recommends mark-up rates, mark-down rates, and selling prices for merchandise. Conducts staff meetings with sales personnel to introduce new merchandise. Examines, selects, orders, and purchases merchandise from suppliers or other merchants.

Confers with sales and purchasing personnel to obtain information about customer needs and preferences. **SKILLS**—Speaking: Talking to others to convey information effectively. Management of Material Resources: Obtaining and seeing to the appropriate use of equipment, facilities, and materials needed to do certain work. Active Listening: Giving full attention to what other people are saying, taking time to understand the points being made, asking questions as appropriate, and not interrupting at inappropriate times. Reading Comprehension: Understanding written sentences and paragraphs in work-related documents. Critical Thinking: Using logic and reasoning to identify the strengths and weaknesses of alternative solutions, conclusions, or approaches to problems. Active Learning: Understanding the implications of new information for both current and future problem-solving and decision-making.

GOE INFORMATION—**Interest Area:** 13. General Management and Support. **Work Group:** 13.02. Management Support. **Other Job Titles in This Work Group:** Accountants; Accountants and Auditors; Appraisers and Assessors of Real Estate; Appraisers, Real Estate; Assessors; Auditors; Budget Analysts; Claims Adjusters, Examiners, and Investigators; Claims Examiners, Property and Casualty Insurance; Compensation, Benefits, and Job Analysis Specialists; Cost Estimators; Credit Analysts; Employment Interviewers, Private or Public Employment Service; Employment, Recruitment, and Placement Specialists; Financial Analysts; Human Resources, Training, and Labor Relations Specialists, All Other; Insurance Adjusters, Examiners, and Investigators; Insurance Appraisers, Auto Damage; Insurance Underwriters; Loan Counselors; Loan Officers; Logisticians; Management Analysts; Market Research Analysts; Personnel Recruiters; Purchasing Agents and Buyers, Farm Products; Purchasing Agents, Except Wholesale, Retail, and Farm Products; Tax Examiners, Collectors, and Revenue Agents; Training and Development Specialists. **PERSONALITY TYPE**—Enterprising. Enterprising occupations frequently involve starting up and carrying out projects. These occupations can involve leading people and making many decisions. They sometimes require risk taking and often deal with business.

EDUCATION/TRAINING PROGRAM(S)—Fashion Merchandising; General Buying Operations. **RELATED KNOWLEDGE/COURSES**—**Sales and Marketing:** Knowledge of principles and methods for showing, promoting, and selling products or services. This includes marketing strategy and tactics, product demonstration, sales techniques, and sales control systems. **Mathematics:** Knowledge of arithmetic, algebra, geometry, calculus, and statistics and their applications. **Administration and Management:** Knowledge of business and management principles involved in strategic planning, resource allocation, human resources modeling, leadership technique, production methods, and coordination of people and resources. **Customer and Personal Service:** Knowledge of principles and processes for providing customer and personal services. This includes customer needs assessment, meeting quality standards for services, and evaluation of customer satisfaction. **Economics and Accounting:** Knowledge of economic and accounting principles and practices, the financial markets, banking, and the analysis and reporting of financial data. **Transportation:** Knowledge of principles and methods for moving people or goods by air, rail, sea, or road, including the relative costs and benefits. **English Language:** Knowledge of the structure and content of the English language, including the meaning and spelling of words, rules of composition, and grammar.

Writers and Authors

▲ Education/Training Required: Bachelor's degree

▲ Annual Earnings: $42,270

▲ Growth: 28%

▲ Annual Job Openings: 18,000

▲ Self-Employed: 31.2%

▲ Part-Time: 18.5%

Originate and prepare written material, such as scripts, stories, advertisements, and other material. **SKILLS**—No data available.

GOE INFORMATION—**Interest Area:** 01. Arts, Entertainment, and Media. **Work Group:** 01.02. Writing and Editing. **Other Job Titles in This Work Group:** Copy Writers; Creative Writers; Editors; Poets and Lyricists; Technical Writers. **PERSONALITY TYPE**—No data available.

Zoologists and Wildlife Biologists

EDUCATION/TRAINING PROGRAM(S)—Broadcast Journalism; Business Communications; Communications, Other; English Creative Writing; Journalism; Mass Communications; Playwriting and Screenwriting; Technical and Business Writing. **RELATED KNOWLEDGE/COURSES**—No data available.

- ▲ Education/Training Required: Doctoral degree
- ▲ Annual Earnings: $43,980
- ▲ Growth: 21%
- ▲ Annual Job Openings: 5,000
- ▲ Self-Employed: 4.9%
- ▲ Part-Time: 6.6%

Study the origins, behavior, diseases, genetics, and life processes of animals and wildlife. May specialize in wildlife research and management, including the collection and analysis of biological data to determine the environmental effects of present and potential use of land and water areas. Studies origin, interrelationships, classification, life histories and diseases, development, genetics, and distribution of animals. Studies animals in their natural habitats and assesses effects of environment on animals. Analyzes characteristics of animals to identify and classify animals. Collects and dissects animal specimens and examines specimens under microscope. Conducts experimental studies, using chemicals and various types of scientific equipment. Raises specimens for study and observation or for use in experiments. Prepares collections of preserved specimens or microscopic slides for species identification and study of species development or animal disease. **SKILLS**—Science: Using scientific rules and methods to solve problems. Reading Comprehension: Understanding written sentences and paragraphs in work-related documents. Active Learning: Understanding the implications of new information for both current and future problem-solving and decision-making. Writing: Communicating effectively in writing as appropriate for the needs of the audience. Critical Think-

ing: Using logic and reasoning to identify the strengths and weaknesses of alternative solutions, conclusions, or approaches to problems.

GOE INFORMATION—**Interest Area:** 02. Science, Math, and Engineering. **Work Group:** 02.03. Life Sciences. **Other Job Titles in This Work Group:** Agricultural and Food Science Technicians; Agricultural Technicians; Animal Scientists; Biochemists; Biochemists and Biophysicists; Biological Scientists, All Other; Biologists; Biophysicists; Conservation Scientists; Environmental Scientists and Specialists, Including Health; Epidemiologists; Food Science Technicians; Food Scientists and Technologists; Foresters; Life Scientists, All Other; Medical Scientists, Except Epidemiologists; Microbiologists; Plant Scientists; Range Managers; Soil and Plant Scientists; Soil Conservationists; Soil Scientists. **PERSONALITY TYPE**—Investigative. Investigative occupations frequently involve working with ideas and require an extensive amount of thinking. These occupations can involve searching for facts and figuring out problems mentally.

EDUCATION/TRAINING PROGRAM(S)—Cell and Molecular Biology, Other; Ecology; Entomology; Pathology, Human and Animal; Pharmacology, Human and Animal; Physiology, Human and Animal; Zoology, General; Zoology, Other. **RELATED KNOWLEDGE/COURSES—Biology:** Knowledge of plant and animal organisms and their tissues, cells, functions, interdependencies, and interactions with each other and the environment. **Mathematics:** Knowledge of arithmetic, algebra, geometry, calculus, and statistics and their applications. **Chemistry:** Knowledge of the chemical composition, structure, and properties of substances and of the chemical processes and transformations that they undergo. This includes uses of chemicals and their interactions, danger signs, production techniques, and disposal methods. **Clerical Studies:** Knowledge of administrative and clerical procedures and systems such as word processing, managing files and records, stenography and transcription, designing forms, and other office procedures and terminology. **English Language:** Knowledge of the structure and content of the English language, including the meaning and spelling of words, rules of composition, and grammar.

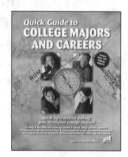

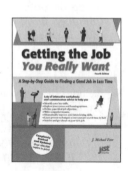